AMERICA'S BLACK PAST

AMERICA'S BLACK PAST

America's Black Past

A Reader in Afro-American History

Edited by ERIC FONER

HARPER & ROW, PUBLISHERS

NEW YORK, EVANSTON, AND LONDON

LIBRARY OF CONGRESS CATALOG CARD NUMBER: 70–96804

For my parents

Contents

Your country? How came it yours? Before the Pilgrims landed we were here. Here we have brought our three gifts and mingled them with yours: a gift of story and song—soft, stirring melody in an ill-harmonized and unmelodious land; the gift of sweat and brawn to beat back the wilderness, conquer the soil and lay the foundations of this vast economic empire . . . [and] a gift of the Spirit. Around us the history of the land has centered for thrice a hundred years. . . . Actively we have woven ourselves with the very warp and woof of this nation—we fought their battles, shared their sorrow, mingled our blood with theirs, and generation after generation have pleaded with a headstrong, careless people to despise not Justice, Mercy, and Truth, lest the nation be smitten with a curse. . . . Would America have been America without her Negro people?

—W. E. B. Du Bois

Introduction

Although the role of black men and women in contemporary America is evident to anyone who reads today's newspapers, many Americans still believe that blacks are a people without a past. In recent years, however, there has been a renaissance of interest in black history. Today's black movement has turned to history for a "usable past"—a definition of the identity of the black man in America. And whites are coming to realize that they know far too little of the lives of their black fellow citizens. As a result, schools and colleges across the country have rushed to institute courses and programs in the field; newspapers, magazines and television stations have produced expensive series on black history, and publishers have reproduced long-out-of-print monographs. The contemporary crisis in race relations, moreover, has made Americans more aware than ever of the ethnic dimension of their history, and interest in the black past has gone hand in hand with a desire to study the history of immigrants, American Indians, and other ethnic groups.

Despite the fact that black and white historians have been writing black history for many years, the field is in many ways still in its infancy. This is partially because almost every phase of the black past has been shrouded in myths and misconceptions, one of the most pervasive and pernicious of which is the picture of blacks as inactive agents in history. The historian Ulrich B. Phillips, for example, wrote of blacks in the era of the American Revolution: "In actuality . . . they were a passive element whose fate was affected only so far as the master race determined." As a result of this kind of attitude, we have many studies of whites' attitudes and actions toward blacks, but little historical record of the independent ideas and activities of the black community.

The development of white racial attitudes and mechanisms of racial control is, of course, a vitally important subject, and I have included a number of selections in this area. In general, however, I have attempted to focus on the black community, its leaders, institutions, and ideologies. In choosing selections on slavery, for example, I have avoided works on the planter regime, the economics of the institution, and the slave codes, and have focused instead on the effects of slavery upon the masses of the slaves, the extent to which they were able to develop an autonomous community, and their means of resistance. I have also tried to resist the temptation to present black history as a series of biographies of black leaders, although a number of selections emphasize the outlooks and achievements of such men as Booker T. Washington, W. E. B. Du Bois, Marcus Garvey, and Martin Luther King, Jr. But to focus exclusively on "black achievers" or "black leaders" is to ignore the changing structure, institutions, and values of the black community as a whole.

I would like to express my gratitude to several scholars who assisted me in putting this book together. Professors Gilbert Osofsky, of the University of Illinois, Chicago Circle, and Eugene D. Genovese, of the University of Rochester, looked over the list of selections and made several helpful suggestions. Professor James P. Shenton of Columbia University and my father, Professor Jack D. Foner of Colby College read the introductions to the selections, and gave me useful advice and criticism. I would also like to thank Mr. Alfred Prettyman of Harper & Row for his advice and encouragement. Finally, thanks are due to all the scholars who graciously allowed their work to be reprinted here. Some of the selections are complete chapters from books or complete essays; others, unavoidably, are abridged. It goes without saying that in abridging some of the selections I have done my best not to alter the meaning or interpretation of any writer.

For convenience, footnotes have been gathered at the end of the book, and their numbering has been made consistent. Chapter numbers from the selections have been deleted.

ERIC FONER

AMERICA'S BLACK PAST

1. The African Heritage

"What is Africa to me?" the black poet Countee Cullen asks at the beginning of his poem "Heritage." At many points in American history, blacks have turned spiritually and intellectually to the land of their fathers in their effort to assess their identity in this country. Yet it was not long ago that historians were writing that Africa had no history before the arrival of the Europeans, and even today a survey of American high-school students has revealed a portrait of Africa as a primitive land whose inhabitants still hunt with spears and have never shown themselves capable of economic or political advancement. Even the geography of the African continent is often misconceived. Although Africa is usually associated with deserts and tropical jungle, it also has wide stretches of savannah grassland, ideal for settled agricultural existence.

Over fifty years ago two black scholars, W. E. B. Du Bois and Carter G. Woodson, and a white scholar, Melville J. Herskovits, began the work of demolishing these myths. But only with the decline of European colonialism and the emergence of independent black states in Africa in the past twenty years has interest in African history become widespread in this country. Utilizing such neglected sources as the reports of Arab travelers in the Middle Ages, and uncovering new kinds of historical evidence in oral tradition and folklore, historians have been reconstructing and reevaluating the political, economic, and social history of pre-European Africa. Among their findings is that ancient Egypt, long considered a white civilization, was in reality a melting pot of races in which blacks played an important role. Historians have begun to trace the influence which the black kingdom of Kush, located further up the Nile, had on Egypt, and have traced the skill of ironmaking as it was carried deeper into Africa from ancient Kush.

The best-known African empires whose stories have been reconstructed were Ghana (which lay about a thousand miles north of the present state of Ghana), Mali, and Songhai, which flourished successively in the western part of the Sudan—the broad belt of grassland just south of the Sahara Desert. All three of these states owed their existence to international commerce, for they stood astride trade routes which linked gold-producing areas to the south with Saharan salt-mining towns and the North African coast. Ghana, known to the Arabs as the land of gold, had its origins in about the fourth century and existed until conquered by the Almoravids, a fanatical Islamic sect, in 1076. It was succeeded by Mali, which became widely known outside Africa when the emperor Mansa Musa conducted his pilgrimage to Mecca in 1324, accompanied by an entourage of 60,000 persons and, more startling, 24,000 pounds of gold. After Mali's decline Songhai, the greatest of the Sudanic states, was established, embracing a territory equal in area to the continental United States. Songhai was conquered at the end of the seventeenth century by a Moroccan army equipped with firearms.

These Sudanic states had a complex political structure. Each was ruled by a divine monarch who governed with the aid of an elaborate bureaucracy, taxation system, and army. Askia the Great, a ruler of Songhai, had judges stationed throughout his empire, a regular standing army, and a fleet of canoes patrolling the Niger River, the main thoroughfare of the empire. The emperors of Mali and

Songhai were Moslems and their empires formed part of the Islamic civilization, which reached from Spain through North Africa and the Middle East. Their mosques and schools attracted Arab scholars from far and wide, and the universities of Timbuktu and Jenne were world-renowned for their learning. Leo Africanus, an African captured by slave traders who eventually made his way to Rome, reported that the rulers of Songhai paid great respect to men of learning and that more profit was made from the trade in books than from any other business.

Ghana, Mali, and Songhai were the most famous African states, but by no means the only ones. Further east there were the Hausa states, famed for their skilled craftsmen, and to the south lay Oyo and Benin, where a flowering of art in the fourteenth and fifteenth centuries produced brass sculptures whose beauty is still enthralling. All these states had economies with elaborate divisions of labor and specialization and all were heavily engaged in international trade. Agriculture was the basis of the African economy, but sufficient agricultural surpluses were produced to support the cities which existed in every state.

The political history of the great African empires, however, does not give us sufficient understanding of the life of the average African. For these state structures were superimposed on a pattern of local loyalties and customs which remained relatively unchanged as central authorities rose and fell. There were many social ties and institutions more important to the African than state loyalty; among these, the family, the basic unit of African society, was preeminent. The real wielders of authority in African life were local patriarchs—heads of families and leaders of clans (groupings of families who worshiped the same ancestor). Land was owned collectively by the family or clan, administered by the family patriarch, and often worked by cooperative teams. Because family ancestors were worshiped as the mediating links between living men and gods, the family also played a vital role in religion, which permeated every aspect of African life. Despite the conversion of the rulers of Mali and Songhai to Islam, traditional religious practices in the villages remained unchanged for centuries, and the court religion did not begin to seep down to the masses of Africans until the nineteenth century.

The social and religious life of Africa is obviously a more difficult subject to investigate than the history of rulers and kingdoms, but it is vitally important for a full understanding of African life before the coming of the Europeans. Melville J. Herskovits, late Professor of Anthropology at Northwestern University, was one of the pioneers in this kind of history, and in the selection that follows, from a chapter in *The Myth of the Negro Past,* he summarized two decades of research, much of it field work in Africa. Herskovits' book was frankly written to challenge many of the misconceptions of African history and it played a crucial role in undermining the myth of a savage and backward continent with no history. He begins by criticizing some of the errors and stereotypes of previous historians and then proceeds with a survey of the economic and social structure, religious beliefs and artistic achievements of West Africa.

The African Heritage
MELVILLE J. HERSKOVITS

1

Judged by references in the literature, the writers who in the United States have most influenced concepts of the Negro's African heritage are Tillinghast,[1]* Dowd[2] and Weatherford.[3] But since

FROM Melville J. Herskovits, *The Myth of the Negro Past.* Copyright 1941 by Melville J. Herskovits. Reprinted by permission of Harper & Row, Publishers, Inc.

* Superior figures refer to a section of notes starting on page 579.

all these went to the same sources for their African materials, where they did not draw on the works of each other, and none had firsthand contact with any of the native peoples he mentions, their substantial agreement in describing and, what is more significant, in evaluating the civilizations of Guinea is not surprising. The unanimity of their findings is important for the support it has afforded the concepts of aboriginal cultural endowment of the Negro presented by any one of them.

It is of some interest to outline briefly the materials which they employed. Most frequent are references to what were but secondary sources even when they were first made available. Especially useful to them were the several compendia that were written to give ready access to the various forms of primitive civilizations known at the time they were written, a feat impossible today, with the development of scientific ethnology and its rich and numerous field studies. Citations to such works as A. H. Keane's *Man: Past and Present,* Ratzel's *History of Mankind,* Waitz' *Anthropologie der Naturvölker,* D. G. Brinton's *Races and Peoples,* and Elisée Reclus' *Universal Geography,* appear again and again. Even granting the contemporary usefulness of these works, it is questionable whether there ever was justification for the student of the Negro in the United States, concerned with the problem of African background, to base his analysis of the aboriginal cultures on "sources" such as these. Yet the tradition lingers on, and the failure of more recent scholars to employ the modern data and the critical tools at their disposal is lamentable. If the plea is entered that these recent scientific analyses of West African cultures are difficult to use, this is but a confession of an inadequacy which speaks for itself when conclusions are evaluated. . . .

While in the case of Tillinghast, at least, most of the available sources of his time were drawn on, no attempt was made by him to test his conclusions by reference to the textual consistency of the data themselves. An acquaintance with the writings which he and others like him cite need not be extensive to show that the estimates of African culture found in these books by no means always flow from the facts as presented. Using him as an example, then, his assertions may be sampled to determine whether his descriptions of West African culture are valid in the light of modern findings. We are told that the West African:

. . . lives under conditions adverse to the growth of industrial efficiency; . . . so abundant is nature's provision for food and other
wants, that with little effort they obtain what is needed. . . . In the
case of cultivated produce, the fertility of the soil and the climatic
advantages are such that very large returns are yielded to slight labor.[4]

Actually, the climate of West Africa is like all tropical climates at
low altitudes. It permits a rich yield if crops are undisturbed, but
crops are so rarely undisturbed that the hazards of agriculture are
far greater than in the temperate zone. The conception of the
native as one pampered by nature is thus entirely fallacious. The
African's ability for sustained toil, his need to work and work hard
if he is to extract a living from the soil, have been remarked by all
those who have made serious firsthand studies of the labor required to maintain life in the region. Should precise testimony be
desired awaiting the appearance of Harris' analyses of the actual
number of hours spent in work by the Ibo,[5] reference may be
made to the study by Forde,[6] wherein the effort and planning
involved in carrying on agriculture among the Yakö of the region
which lies at the bend of the west coast are made plain.

Again, Tillinghast informs us:

Previous to the appearance of Europeans, the extreme west coast of
Africa was completely isolated from the outside world; its inhabitants
lived in scattered villages buried in the forest, and remained in dense
ignorance of any other desirable objects than the necessities of their
own savage life. Among the forces which have helped to civilize other
peoples has been the stimulus to effort arising from newly conceived
wants, quickened into being at the discovery of commodities, first
brought by strangers. The appearance of Europeans with new and attractive commodities, produced a great effect. To get them in exchange
for native products, thousands of negroes were moved to unwonted
exertions, while foreigners taught them new and better methods of
production. All this, however, has been comparatively recent, and for
ages the negroes were without such incitements to industry.[7]

Once more, misstatements are found in almost every line. The
philosophy underlying most of the assertions, a kind of naïve
laissez-faire economics which holds progress to be in some way
related to a constant accretion in the range of wants, is immediately apparent. That isolation in terms of lack of contact by sea

might be replaced with land-borne commerce across the Sahara never seems to have occurred to this writer, as it seldom occurs to others who speak of the "isolation" of Africa. Yet from the earliest times the Ashanti, for example, acquired silk cloths from Tunis and Morocco, which they unraveled, redyed and rewove into great chiefs' silk cloths. The "isolated villages" spoken of are in many cases population centers of considerable size—Ibadan, Nigeria, has some 325,000 inhabitants—while the dense forests are in many parts nonexistent, since the land is required to support this population.

"Division of labor has proceeded but a very little way,"[8] we are told—this perhaps being written with Adam Smith's statement regarding the importance of this factor in making for economic advancement in mind.

The number of handicraftsmen in any given tribe is small, and their special skill is jealously withheld from the common herd. . . . These simple folk exist somehow on an incredibly meagre supply of implements and weapons. Even in the manual arts women are compelled to do all the drudgery of collecting raw material, etc. All these facts reveal how the great mass of male population escapes distasteful toil.[9]

Here also we are confronted with assertions that are directly contravened by the facts. As will be seen, the large number of specialized crafts are indicative of a corresponding degree of division of labor. The popular assumption of the savage male as lazy, allowing his women to carry on the work necessary for subsistence, is far removed from the actuality of the sex division of labor, which invades all fields. That the women do agricultural labor[10] is but an expression of the forms of sex division of labor universal in human societies, literate or not; in Africa the arrangement makes the men responsible for the really heavy work of preparing the fields, and leaves to the women the lighter tasks of caring for the growing plants, harvesting the crops, and preparing food. As a matter of fact, the economic position of women in West Africa is high. It is based on the fact that the women are traders quite as much as agricultural workers, and on recognition that what they earn is their own. They do none of the ironworking or wood carving or house-building or weaving or carrying of burdens or other heavy labor. This is reserved for the men. They unquestionably contribute their share to the support of the household and the community; but they are not the exploited creatures undisciplined fancy would have them.

It is not possible here to detail all the misconceptions which characterize Tillinghast's descriptions of West African life, among them statements expounding a presumed inadequacy of West African technology, simplicity of the system of trade, and absence of social morality in the religious concepts of the people—a fact refuted by the widely spread incidence of belief that the gods punish antisocial behavior, which, needless to say, is an important moral sanction. It could be shown how Tillinghast agrees that wives are "bought" and that cannibalism was "once practised universally."[11] Political development is indicated as being "on a par with the low stage attained in all other directions"[12]—specific reference being made to the Ashanti and to Dahomey, where "vanquished tribes are extinguished by slaughter or held as slaves." Or we learn of "customs regulating property and personal relations after a crude fashion,"[13] another error the more glaring in the light of general recognition of the African's "legal genius." All these misconceptions are evaluated with a wealth of adjectival embroidery which makes it impossible for the reader to conceive of the civilizations of the region as anything but outstanding examples of a low state of savagery—a savagery that, as the author surmises, is the source of the Negro's assumed insufficiency in mastering white culture in the United States.

Similarly, it is not possible, even were it necessary, to cite from the works of those others who have perpetuated these misinterpretations of African culture. Excerpts from the writings of Dowd, or Weatherford, or others would be repetitious, but to illustrate the tenaciousness of the point of view, quotations from two volumes will be given. The first of these books, by Mecklin, was published in 1914, and, like the others, is found in most bibliographies of books and articles dealing with the Negro in the United States:

The most striking feature of the African negro is the low forms of social organization, the lack of industrial and political cooperation, and consequently the almost entire absence of social and national self-consciousness. This rather than intellectual inferiority explains the lack

of social sympathy, the presence of such barbarous institutions as cannibalism and slavery, the low position of woman, inefficiency in the industrial and mechanical arts, the low type of group morals, rudimentary
art-sense, lack of race pride and self-assertiveness, and an intellectual
and religious life largely synonymous with fetishism and sorcery.[14]

It is scarcely necessary to point out once more that almost every
assertion in this statement is incorrect; indeed, it is rare, even in
works on the Negro, to come upon a paragraph with such a high
concentration of error as this. The most glaring of these misconceptions, viewed from the perspective of the last three decades of
art history, is the statement concerning the "rudimentary art-
sense" of the Africans. For an outstanding development of modern
art has been the steady growth of interest in African—West African—wood carving and other art forms, and the influence of these
forms on many of the painters of the present day.

Reuter, whose textbook . . . [is] an example of the manner in
which this approach and point of view still lives in standard works
dealing with the Negro population of the United States, will give
our series its most recent instance. The excerpt is from the second
edition, which, appearing in 1938, can be taken to represent the
present position of its author. Social life in West Africa is dismissed
in this edition (the earlier one[15] went into some detail concerning
African family life in terms typical of what has been cited in the
way of misconception), with the statement that, "The family institution [was] never highly developed among the West African
tribes." No qualification is given this statement, as the author
proceeds to explain how such a weak institution could not but give
way under slavery in the United States, when it encountered the
presumably stronger European type of family. . . .

2

Today, as in the days of the great traffic in slaves, the tribes
living in the heart of the slaving area are the Akan-Ashanti folk of
the Gold Coast, the Dahomeans, the Yoruba of western Nigeria,
and the Bini of eastern Nigeria. Composites of many smaller
groups, welded through a long process of conquest into more or
less homogeneous kingdoms, they share many traits in common.

Their numbers are large as primitive societies go, and consequently many problems of economic, social, and political organization must be met if smooth functioning is to be achieved. It follows that complex institutions in those fields are the rule. The ensuing discussion will touch upon those aspects of the cultures of these kingdoms which, germane to their functioning, have been impinged upon but little by the circumstances of European political domination.

The economic life, adapted to the support of large populations, is far more intricate than is customarily expected or, indeed, found among nonliterate folk. Essentially agricultural, all these societies manifest a considerable degree of specialization, from which are derived the arrangements for the exchange of goods that take the form principally of stated markets, wherein operations are carried on with the aid of a monetary system which, in pre-European days, was based on the cowry shell to facilitate the expression of values. The economic system permits the production of a substantial surplus over the needs of subsistence, and the support of rulers, priests, and their subordinates. As a result, a class structure has been erected on this economic base that has tended to encourage that disciplined behavior which marks every phase of life. In the field of production, this discipline takes the form of a pattern of cooperative labor under responsible direction, and such mutual self-help is found not only in agricultural work, but in the craft guilds, characteristically organized on the basis of kinship. This genius for organization also manifests itself in the distributive processes. Here the women play an important part. Women, who are for the most part the sellers in the market, retain their gains for themselves, often becoming independently wealthy. With their high economic status, they have likewise perfected disciplined organizations to protect their interests in the markets. These organizations comprise one of the primary price-fixing agencies, prices being set on the basis of supply and demand, with due consideration for the cost of transporting goods to market.

Slavery has long existed in the entire region, and in at least one of its kingdoms, Dahomey, a kind of plantation system was found under which an absentee ownership, with the ruler as principal, demanded the utmost return from the estates, and thus created conditions of labor resembling the regime the slaves were to encounter in the New World. Whether this system was the exception rather than the rule cannot be said, for this aspect of the economic order, as the first suppressed under European rule, is not easy to document satisfactorily. On the whole, slaveholding was of the household variety, with large numbers of slaves the property of the chief, and important either as export goods (to enable the rulers to obtain guns, gunpowder, European cloths, and other commodities) or as ritual goods (for the sacrifices, required almost exclusively of royalty, in the worship of their powerful ancestors).

The economic base of the social structure is most apparent when the role of the relationship group in the production and distribution of wealth is considered. Essentially, this structure comprises as its principal elements the polygynous family; legal recognition of kinship through one line, with the nonrelated side of varying importance—ranging from the noninstitutionalized sentimental relationship with the mother's family in patrilineal Dahomey and among the Yoruba to the Ashanti system wherein an individual inherits his position in society on the maternal side and his spiritual affiliations from the father; the "extended family," a well-recognized institution which affords a more restricted relationship grouping than the sib (clan); and finally the sib itself, comprising large numbers of persons whose face-to-face contact with each other may be intimate or casual or nonexistent. Guild organization tends, in the majority of cases, to follow the lines of these kinship groupings. Since the principal occupation is agriculture, landholdings are conceived in terms of family rather than individual rights; and while, as in all primitive societies, a man has the exclusive ownership of the produce of whatever land he works, the land itself is not his. As a member of a relationship group of considerable size, however, he has an assurance of support in time of need. This has contributed largely to the stability of these societies, since the economic aspect reinforces the social one in a peculiarly intimate manner, and causes the relationship group to hold added significance for its members.

The fundamental sanction of the kinship system is the ancestral cult, which, in turn, is a closely knit component of the prevailing world view. The power of a man does not end with death, for the dead are so integral a part of life that differences in power of the living are carried on into the next world. Just as among the living individuals of royal or chiefly blood are the most powerful, so the royal or chiefly ancestors are conceived as the most potent of all the dead. The dead in Dahomey and among the Yoruba, at least, are deified; among the Ashanti, this remains to be studied. The relationship between the ancestors and the gods is close, but the origin of this collaboration is obscure and extremely difficult to establish. Evidence adduced by Bascom[16] indicates that at least in the Nigerian city of Ife, the spiritual center of Yoruba religious life, the beings conceived elsewhere as gods are there regarded as ancestors. The sib mythologies collected in Dahomey would also seem to indicate something of a similar order, certain sibs being considered as descended from various gods, though there is no sib without its "oldest ancestor," who figures importantly in the daily life of each member of the group.

The elaborateness of funeral rites in the area is cast in terms of the role of the ancestors in the lives of their descendants, and because it is important to have the assurance of the ancestral good will, the dead are honored with extended and costly rituals. In all this region, in fact, the funeral is the true climax of life, and no belief drives deeper into the traditions of West African thought. For the problem of New World survivals this is of paramount importance, for whatever else has been lost of aboriginal custom, the attitudes toward the dead as manifested in meticulous rituals cast in the mold of West African patterns have survived.

As in most primitive societies, the sib functions in regulating marriage, since mating between sib mates or other relatives of legally established affiliation and, among the Ashanti, on the side of "spiritual" affiliation, is forbidden as incestuous. This is not as much a handicap in finding a mate as in smaller groups having similar prohibitions, since with dense populations such as are found in West Africa there is no lack of eligible mates outside the sib. The major problem, where a marriage is contemplated, thus merely involves the tracing of descent lines to ensure that no common affiliation stands in the way. Far more important, as a matter of fact, is the assurance that the suitor has resources and substantial family support to make of him a responsible husband,

and that the young woman has had the training to make a competent wife.

Qualifications are carefully scrutinized by both families, for, as in so many primitive societies, marriage is a matter of family alliance. This is not to be construed that the common dictum, that affection does not enter, is valid. In contradiction to this may be cited the frequency of runaway marriages—recognized by the Dahomeans as one of the principal forms of marriage—as an expedient of the young people to circumvent unwelcome matings arranged by those of their social group who have legal control over their behavior. In all this region the obligations of the man to the parents of his bride are paramount, not only before but after marriage. Yet the characterization of African marriage as "bride purchase" is no more valid here than elsewhere. As a matter of fact, in this region what the husband gives his parents-in-law is regarded essentially as a form of collateral for good behavior, though the social worth to a man's sib of prospective issue does figure psychologically.

The widespread character of polygyny gives rise to a number of important research problems. In so far as New World Negro life is concerned, the deep-seated nature of the pattern of plural marriage aids greatly in accounting for some of the aberrant types of family organization to be found. Of outstanding significance in this connection is the relationship between father and children as against mother and children. For where a man has plural wives, the offspring of any one woman must share their father with those of other women, while they share their mother with none but other children by her. This psychological fact is reinforced by the physical setting of family life in this area, as well as by the principles of inheritance of wealth, which obtain at least among the Yoruba and in Dahomey. The family is typically housed in a compound, which is a group of structures surrounded by a wall or a hedge, to give the total complex a physical unity. The head of the household, the eldest male, and all other adult males, married or unmarried (for in some parts of the area, young married sons, or younger married brothers and their children, may live in a father's or elder brother's compound), have individual huts of their own, to which their wives come in turn to live with them and, for a stated period, to care for their needs. Each wife has her own dwelling, however, where she lives with her children. Once she conceives, she drops out of the routine of visits—a factor in restricting the number of children a woman may bear, and well recognized in Dahomey, at least, as a hygienic measure—to resume it only when she has weaned her child. Naturally, not every household is polygynous, though the degree to which even those not among upper-class groups have more than one wife gives rise to a problem, as yet unsolved, of a possible differential in sex ratio.

Among the Yoruba and Dahomeans, a chosen son succeeds to the wealth of his father, and here again, as in matters of personal jealousies, conflict among wives in terms of jockeying for position to obtain advantageous consideration for a son makes for closeness of relationship between mother and children as against father and children. Among the Ashanti, wealth, like position, is inherited from a maternal uncle, hence this particular economic factor does not obtain in attitudes toward the father, but takes form in rivalries for the uncle's favor. But even where questions of succession do not enter, the very nature of the life in any polygynous household is such that it gives the psychological generalization validity. In Dahomey the explicit recognition of the difference is emphatic. Phrased in terms of inheritance, while there is always bitter dispute over the apportionment of the wealth of a father, such quarreling, it is asserted, is unthinkable even when the property of a wealthy woman is to be distributed. "They are children of the same mother," would seem for these people, as for various New World Negro folk, to be an explanation that needs no clarification.

The political organization of the tribes of our region has two distinct aspects, historically of great importance. It is simplest to think of each of the three aggregates we are describing as political entities, since in each we find the kings, courts, and subchiefs that mark them as units. Yet once we probe more deeply, it becomes apparent that for the people themselves the unit is smaller. Where, as among the Ashanti, in Dahomey, in Benin, and among the Oyo of Nigeria, powerful states were in existence during the time of the slave traffic, and until European conquest, they were actually but glosses on an underlying pattern of local autonomy and local loyalties. One of the most confusing aspects of the study of New World Negro origins based on the documents is a semantic one, which arises out of the difference between the conception held by the early writers of a king and a kingdom, and the ethnological reality of African concept. To this day, in a small village, one may be introduced to its "king" by a loyal follower of this petty, powerless potentate; and the village will likewise be designated a "kingdom." It is this, as much as anything else, that has misled students in attempting to understand the importance of the political units named in the slavers' accounts. If we take, for example, the oft-mentioned kingdom of Pawpaw—the Popo of present-day Togoland—we find it to be a village whose ruler commanded a "kingdom" of perhaps not more than 250 square miles at its greatest! Yet the identity of this "kingdom" has persisted under the French as it persisted in the face of Dahomean conquest. In exactly the same way we encounter the local loyalties of the inhabitants of Kumawo as against Mampong among the Ashanti of the Gold Coast, of Allada as against Abomey in the interior of Dahomey, of Ife as against Oyo among the Yoruba. These reflect identifications which, earlier, were to independent states whose inhabitants, after their absorption, never attained complete identification with the larger kingdom. From this it follows that the realms found in our area had to exercise control over the local chiefs; while, in addition, in the interstices between their fluid boundaries local communities could, and did, persist without giving up their autonomies.

The larger aggregates were no less significant political realities, nor did they function any the less efficiently because of these local loyalties, for their organization was remarkable in the light of conceptions generally held of the simple nature of the primitive political institutions. Given cultures without writing, and with local traditions as strong as those existing in West Africa, the rulers accomplished their ends with an expeditiousness that can only be realized by studying the writings of firsthand observers who visited the courts of the Ashanti, Dahomean, and Yoruban potentates. It is thus particularly ironical that, in this field, the simplicity and crudity of primitive life attributed to the African should have been permitted to loom as so important a trait of African culture. Stable dynasties were the rule, not the exception. Courts and related institutions ensured the operation of orderly processes of law, while specialists in warfare saw to it that the territory of the ruler was not only defended in case of attack, but that he could extend his dominion as opportunity offered.

In outlining the ordering of life in this area, there is no intention of picturing the West African as a kind of natural man living in a golden age. For if rulers were efficient, they were also exacting and ruthless; if they ensured orderly processes of law in the courts, they were also given to pecuniary persuasion that helped to dim the identity of law with justice. In terms of native standards, their way of life was lavish, and they did not scruple to tax heavily in order to maintain their status. In war, all males were liable to service, and any member of an enemy people who came within reach of their armies was fair game; men, women, and children were taken captive, and the category of noncombatant was unknown. The institution of polygyny reached fantastic proportions, for any woman who took the fancy of the ruler was liable to be claimed for his harem. In Dahomey, also, where centralization of authority and the despotic exercise of power were most developed, battalions of women warriors were kept as nominal wives of the ruler, and hence unapproachable by another man. Many women were thus not permitted normal life, which from the point of view of population policy prevented the kingdom from reproducing the numbers needed to support the expense, in human life and wealth, of its expansionist policy, and eventually contributed to its downfall.

Yet within these despotisms, life went on with a degree of regularity and security rarely envisaged when African polity is thought of. Authority was divided and redivided in terms of a precept under which the delegation of power was accompanied by sharply defined responsibility. The head of the family group, for example, was responsible to the village chief or, in the more populous centers, to the head of his "ward" or "quarter." The local chief was responsible to a district chief, and he to the head of a larger area, who in turn had to account for the administration of his "province" to the king himself or to one of the highest ministers of state. These chiefs sat with their elders and passed judgment when disputes arose among their people. Various devices were employed in the courts. In some cases testimony was taken, in others an ordeal was administered; on occasion a chief might point the way to informal amicable compromise of a dispute. Appeals to a higher court might be taken by plaintiff or defendant. Such crimes as theft were rare, but when the culprit was apprehended his punishment was severe.

The cost of these central governments was met by the taxes levied on the population at large. As reported for the Ashanti and for Dahomey, tax programs were administered so as to exact from the people the greatest possible return. Taxes in Ashanti took two principal forms, death dues and levies on goods in transit. The Ashanti traded with the tribes to the north and with coastal folk to the south, and caravans going in either direction were liable for imposts according to the nature of the goods they carried. Commodities which were seasonal might not be traded in by commoners until royalty had had the opportunity to profit by the high prices for the early crop. Ashanti death dues were indirect but heavy. A proportion of each estate became the property of the local ruler, to go to the next higher officer on the death of this official, until it finally reached the royal treasury.

In Dahomey, indirection was the rule. Everything, including the population, was counted, and all commodities were taxed; but the people were not told when they were being counted, and taxable goods were often enumerated by subterfuge. In some of the methods the priests collaborated; in others, it was merely a matter of subtracting a balance on hand from an observed rate of production. As an indication of the ingeniousness of some of these indirections, the case of pepper, a prized commodity, may be indicated. To prohibit its general cultivation would have made for discontent, hence each man was permitted to raise enough plants to give him a small bag for his own use. But this was far from sufficient, and he had to buy the rest in the market, which was supplied by plantations in remote parts of the country. Even then, no direct tax was levied on the sale of pepper, but since all roads had tollgates at which porters' taxes were collected, and since all the pepper sold had to be brought from these plantations far removed from centers of population, the tolls paid by those who brought this commodity to market came to a substantial sum which was, in effect, a tax on pepper. Death dues in Dahomey were more directly assessed than among the Ashanti. The movable goods of the dead were brought to the local administrative center; what was returned to the heir was given as a gracious gift of the king. That the portion of the estate returned never equaled what had gone into the royal enclosure was no excuse for the recipient to fail in a show of gratitude.

One point must be emphasized concerning the political, social, and economic institutions of this part of West Africa, which, it may again be recalled, was the heart of the slaving belt, and from which came the people who have left the most definite traces of their culture in the New World. Despite wars that were at times of some magnitude and the serious inroads on population made by the slave trade, so well integrated were the cultures that little or no demoralization seems to have resulted. Today, in all this area, despite the fact of European control, which has changed the role of the native ruler where it has not obliterated him; which, in the economic sphere, has been responsible for the introduction of stable currency and the raising of cash crops that make the native dependent on the vagaries of the world market; and which, in the realm of social institutions has subjected such a deep-lying pattern as that of the polygynous family to the impact of Christian conceptions of morality, these cultures continue with all vitality. Even in the field of technology, European influence has had but relatively slight effect.

In coastal cities, it is true, certain indications of deculturation are to be perceived, especially in those centers where Africans from all parts of the coast have been indiscriminately thrown together. But once away from these seaports, the aboriginal culture is found functioning much as it must have functioned during the days before European control and even in the coastal cities, far more of aboriginal pattern persists than is apparent on first sight. This resilience, when manifested in those aspects of culture most susceptible to outside influence, argues a high degree of tenaciousness for the cultures of this part of West Africa, and, if this is true, is a significant point for New World Negro studies.

3

The religion of West Africa, as described by most of those who have written of it, is customarily encompassed in the word "fetish."

Without defining the term, it is broadly held to refer to magical practices of some sort or other, which characteristically are represented as so preoccupying the minds of the people that they live in a state of abject fear. How loosely the word has been used has been demononstrated by Rattray, who, in one passage, indicts the practice as something "the indiscriminate use of which, I believe, has done infinite harm." In the specific case of the Ashanti, after showing how it is applicable only to charms of various sorts from any "category of non-human spirits," he continues:

The native pastor and the European missionary alike found a word already in universal use, i.e., "fetish." They were possibly quite ready to welcome a designation which obviated any necessity for using a term which, even when written with a small initial letter, they considered much too good to apply to these "false gods" about whom we really still know so little. Thus West Africa became "the Land of Fetish" and its religion "Fetishism." It would be as logical to speak in these terms of the religion of ancient Greece and Rome, pulling down from their high places the Olympian Deities and . . . Daemons—(those which were the souls of men who lived in the Golden Age, and those which were never incarnate in human form, but were gods created by the Supreme God), and branding all indiscriminately as "fetishes," and the great thinkers of old, e.g., Plato and Socrates, as fetish worshippers. "I owe a cock to Aesculapius," said the latter almost with his last breath, and this pious injunction to his friend would be understood by every old Ashanti today.[17]

In so far as the complex concepts that mark the world view of the Ashanti, the Dahomeans, and the Yoruba are given systematic expression, their religion may be analyzed into several major subdivisions. As has been said, the ancestral cult sanctions and stabilizes kinship groupings, and there is reason to believe that in some cases these sanctions are to be traced even back to the major deities. For the Ashanti, Rattray was convinced that the ultimate force of the universe is lodged in the Great God Nyame, as befits another widespread conception of the African world view, in terms of which the universe, created by an all-powerful deity, has been so left to itself by the creator that he need not be worshiped. This is not the place to discuss whether this is in fact a valid concept of the African's belief; it may be indicated, however, that on the basis of field studies, of comparative analyses, and of the internal evidence in Rattray's own works there is reason to believe that this hypothesis will ultimately be revised. In Dahomey and among the Yoruba, in any event, the Great Gods are envisaged as a series of family groupings, who represent the forces of nature and function as agencies for the enforcement of right living as conceived in terms of conformity to the patterns of morality and probity. That is, the gods, in Dahomey fully, and in a manner not entirely clear among the Yoruba, are grouped in pantheons, which follow the organization of the social units among men, each member having specific names, titles, functions, and worshipers. The cult groups are organized in honor of these deities, and the outstanding religious festivals are held for them.

Closely associated with the gods, yet not included in the pantheons, are certain other deities or forces. The cult of Fate, with its specialized divining technique, is particularly important in Dahomey and among the Yoruba. Here divination is principally based on a complex system of combinations and permutations arrived at by throwing a set number of seeds, and ties in with a whole body of mythology, interpreted by the diviner in the light of the particular situation involved, and the relation to this body of lore of the particular tale that is called for by a given throw. This means that the training which the diviner must have is quite comparable to that of specialists in our own culture; the very period of study required to become a diviner, between five and ten years, suggests an analogy with the doctorate of philosophy or medicine among ourselves. In the Gold Coast, where, as has been indicated, divination is less formal, training of this kind has not been recorded.

In Dahomey, and among the Yoruba, the philosophical implications of the divining system are impressive. Though the universe is held to be ruled by Fate and the destiny of each man worked out according to a predetermined scheme, there are ways of escape through invoking the good will of the god, the youngest child of the principal deity, who speaks the differing languages of the various divine "families," and as intepreter carries to them the messages which ensure that a man experience whatever is in store for him. For this divinity, the trickster among the gods, can be induced to change the orders he carries, and does so on occasion; so that if an unpleasant fate is in store for an assiduous worshiper, it is believed a simple matter for him to aid such a person by substituting a good for an evil destiny. Yet as a philosophical conception, this deification of Accident in a universe where predetermination is the rule is evidence of the sophistication of the prevailing world concept. For our special problem, it has a further significance. For it gives insight into deep-rooted patterns of thought under which a man refuses to accept any situation as inescapable, and thus reflects the diplomacy of the New World Negro in approaching human situations that is quite comparable to the manner in which the decrees of Fate itself are in West Africa not accepted as final.

Thus far we have seen that the West African's world view comprehends Great Gods (who may be remote deified ancestors), other deities and forces, such as Fate and the divine trickster, and the ancestors who, in the other world, look after the concerns of their descendants moving on the plane of the living. Other phases of African religion will be considered shortly, but one aspect of this polytheistic system which likewise concerns the flexibility of Negro thought patterns must be discussed at this point. This has to do with the lack of interest the Africans manifest in proselytizing; which, in obverse, means that they have no zeal for their own gods so great as to exclude the acceptance of new deities. In this area they themselves recognize this fact, and will readily give an affirmative answer to direct questions concerning the tradition of accepting new gods or, more convincingly, will of their own volition designate certain gods as theirs and indicate other deities they worship as adopted from outside the tribe.

This tendency to adopt new gods is to be referred to the conception of the deities as forces which function intimately in the daily life of the people. For a supernatural power, if he is to be accepted, must justify his existence (and merit the offerings of his worshipers) by accomplishing what his devotees ask of him. He need not be completely effective, for errors in cult practice can always be referred to in explaining why on occasion the prayers of worshipers are not fulfilled. But the gods must as a minimum care for the well-being of their people, and protect them not only from the forces of nature but also from human enemies. If one tribe is conquered by another, it therefore follows that the gods of the conquerors are more powerful than those of the conquered, and all considerations dictate that the deities of this folk be added to the less powerful gods already worshiped. Yet this is not the entire story, for an autochthonous god, if not propitiated, may still turn his considerable powers against the conquerors and do them harm. Therefore, political ferment in West Africa was something correlated with religious ferment, and brought about an interchange of deities which tended to give to the tribes in this part of Africa the gods of their neighbors.

The relevance of this for the situation to be met with in New World Negro cultures is apparent, for it sanctions a conception of the relationship between comparative power of gods and the strength of those who worship them. In these terms, the importance of the European's God to people enslaved by those who worshiped Him must have been self-evident. That this was actually the case is to be seen in those parts of the New World where opportunities have presented themselves to retain African gods despite contact with Europeans; it will be seen how in such countries, especially where Catholicism prevails, the resulting syncretisms furnish one of the most arresting aspects of Negro religious life. In Protestant countries, especially the United States, where retention of the African gods was made difficult if not impossible, this attitude likewise goes far toward explaining the readiness of the Negroes to take over the conceptions of the universe held by the white man; and this points the way, also, to an understanding how, though forms of worship may have been accepted, not all of African world view or ritual practice was lost.

Magic is extremely important in all our area; as has been seen, the ubiquity of the magic charm is such that the term "fetishism" has come to be applied to all West African religion, with its other resources ignored in favor of this most immediate—and most apparent—technique of coping with the supernatural. Magic is easy to understand; it is not foreign to European belief, and, in its African form, is so specific in its operation that it can be readily explained by the native to an untrained inquirer. That its underlying philosophy is not so simple, and its relationship to the other forces of the universe still more obscure, is another matter. Its outward manifestations, to be encountered everywhere, are the charms people wear on arm or leg or about the neck, or that they suspend from their houses or insert in carved figurines or in the very shrines of their gods. The principle of "like to like" operates here as elsewhere, and the knowledge of how to manipulate the specific powers that reside in specific charms is widespread. There are, of course, specialists who deal in charms, but many laymen also know enough about these matters to make charms that are entirely adequate for a given purpose.

As has been indicated, the outstanding trait of the charm is its specific reference. Characteristically, a charm has certain taboos which its owner or wearer must observe lest it lose its power, while its ownership entails certain definite prescribed actions which must be carried out if it is to retain its force. Charms help in meeting every situation in life and magic has its place even in the worship of the gods themselves. It is customary to classify magic as good and bad, but whatever dichotomy obtains is not the kind ordinarily thought of, for good and bad are conceived as but the two sides of a single shield. A charm, that is, which protects its owner can bring harm to an attacker; thus a charm to cure smallpox turned out to be a virulent instrument of black magic which could kill—by giving a man the same disease.

From this fact we gain further insight into African patterns of thought, for here we encounter a refinement of concept in terms of a hardheaded realism that is as far removed as can be from that simplicity held to mark the mentality of "savages." For it is realistic, not naïve, to refuse to evaluate life in those terms of good and bad, white and black, desirable and undesirable that the European is so prone to employ in responding to an equally deep-seated pattern of his own manner of thinking. The African, rather, recognizes the fact that in reality there is no absolute good and no absolute evil, but that nothing can exert an influence for good without at the very least causing inconvenience elsewhere; that nothing is so evil that it cannot be found to have worked benefit to someone. The concepts of good and bad thus become relative, not absolute, and in understanding the magic of West Africa from which New World Negro magic has derived, we can the better understand why, of all Africanisms, this element of belief has most persisted in the mores of Negro life everywhere in the New World.

What of the fear so often indicated as the outstanding aspect of the Negro's reaction to the universe—especially his fear of the magic forces he must constantly contend against? Such an assertion runs quite contrary to the findings of students who have succeeded in peering beneath the surface of West African life. Religion is close to the everyday experience of the West African. Supernatural forces are potentially dangerous, it is true, but so are wild animals or illness. An analogy can be drawn in terms of our own reaction to electricity and automobiles. For those who work with either or benefit from the use of either, the potential dangers —of shock or of accident—are considerable. Yet, if we are normal, we do not set up phobias which preoccupy our waking moments and torment our sleep with nightmares concerning electricity and automobiles. For, if these are dangerous, they are also helpful; if they can harm us when not handled properly, their proper use is beneficial. So with the West African's gods, and so with his magic. What can potentially harm, if not handled properly, can also be of the greatest aid; and just as we have specialists who see to it that our electrical devices are properly insulated and our automobiles are in proper working order, so in West Africa priests and diviners and dealers in magic charms are likewise on hand to exercise the proper controls.

Religion, in short, is important in the life of West Africa because it is an intimate part of that life. If it is difficult for us to comprehend such a point of view, this merely means that the institution in our culture which we label by the term "religion" does not, in the case of vast numbers of our people, enter into considerations of everyday living. It thus follows that what we designate by the term is not the same reality as what is similarly designated in the case of these folk. Just because the supernatural does function intimately in the daily life of West Africa, because the powers of the universe are of passionate interest to these West Africans, it does not follow that they have no time for other thoughts or that their emotional life is centered about fear of a universe which is held by outsiders to be far more hostile to them than they themselves regard it.

As might be expected among people whose world view is so complex, a rich mythology is encountered. These myths, however, are only one part of the literary repertory of the folk living in this core of the slaving belt, since "historical" tales, stories for children, and other types are likewise of great number. The popularity of the Uncle Remus stories in this country, and the circulation of Joel Chandler Harris's volumes of Negro tales[18] over the entire world, have caused these American Negro stories to be regarded as the characteristic form of African folk tales. In Africa, however, even where animal tales are told, they are neither naïve nor necessarily for children. Many elements of the Uncle Remus stories are encountered in the sacred myths, and these elements, even where the animal personnel has been retained, are handled in a subtle and sophisticated manner. They often exhibit a *double-entendre* that permits them to be employed as moralizing tales for children or as stories enjoyed by adults for their obscenity. In addition to the tales are numerous proverbs and riddles, the former in particular being used at every possible opportunity to make a point in an argument, or to document an assertion, or to drive home an admonition. Poetry is likewise not lacking, though poetic quality derives principally from a rich imagery; the association of poetry with song, moreover, is so intimate that it is not found as an independent form.

Aesthetic expression is profuse in other fields. The outstanding musical form of these folk is the song, though musical instruments are found—the ubiquitous drum in its many forms, the gong, rattles, and types of zithers and flutes. The musical bow, the sanza, or "African piano," and other instruments that have a distribution elsewhere on the continent are absent from the part of the west coast with which we are at present concerned. Though only one collection of songs of any size has been made in this region,[19] the four hundred and more recordings not only indicate that many different kinds of songs are to be encountered, but that an equally wide range of singing styles exists. If it does nothing else, indeed, this collection shows the impossibility of comprehending "African" music under a single rubric or even of considering the songs of one tribal group as constituting a single describable type. The significance of this fact for the problem of New World Negro music will be probed later in our discussion; here it is sufficient to indicate the complexity of West African musical forms with respect to scale, rhythm, and general organization, and to mention the many varieties of songs—ranging from lullabies through work songs, and songs of derision, and social dance songs, to sacred melodies as varied as are the individual deities to whom they are directed—that are found not alone in this region as a whole, but in the musical resources of any one of its tribal units.

Nor is it possible here to do more than make mention of the dance, also a fundamental element in aesthetic expression everywhere in Africa. Dancing takes multitudinous forms, and all who have had firsthand contact with the area of our special interest speak of the many varieties of dances found there. These may be ritual or recreational, religious or secular, fixed or improvised, and the dance itself has in characteristic form carried over into the New World to a greater degree than almost any other trait of African culture. To attempt verbal descriptions of dance types requires a technique as yet scarcely developed, since analysis must also await the utilization of motion pictures as an aid to the study of these special aspects of motor behavior, we can here but record the fact of its prominence in the culture, and its pervasiveness in the life of the people.

Great competence in a variety of media characterizes the graphic and plastic arts. Wood carving is the best known of African arts, though among the Ashanti other techniques take prior rank. These people are supremely competent weavers (as is to be seen in the discussion of their silk and cotton cloth designs by Rattray[20]), and they are also famous for the metal gold weights they cast from bronze, accurate to the fraction of an ounce and fashioned in a wide range of representative and geometric figures. In Dahomey, the high degree of economic specialization permits art to find expression in numerous forms. Wood carving, not as well known as it deserves among devotees of what, in art circles, is called "African sculpture," reaches a high degree of perfection. Stylistically, these carvings are especially interesting because of strength of line and balanced proportions which characterize the statuettes found in shrines of the gods or otherwise employed in the cult life of these people. Brass castings are made by a family guild which is differentiated from other metalworkers. These figurines, resembling our own art objects in that they have nonutilitarian value after a fashion not often encountered among primitive peoples, are prized essentially for the aesthetic pleasure they give and as a mark of leisure-class status, since only the wealthy can today afford them and since, in the days of Dahomean autonomy, to own them was a prerogative of royalty. Clothworkers make distinctive appliquéd hangings which, in the manner of the brass figures, are valued for their beauty alone.

The wood carvings of the Yoruba are known much more widely, and the Yoruban area has long been recognized as one of the principal centers of this form. Not only does one encounter single three-dimensional figures of considerable size, but also "masks," as the representations of human and other heads worn atop the heads of dancers are termed, bas-relief carving on doors, houseposts with human and animal forms superimposed one on the other, objects used in the Fate cult, and the like. In addition, however, these people, like the Dahomeans, do ironwork of distinction, weave cloth of cotton and raffia, and produce minor art forms in basketry, pottery, and other media.

2. The Slave Trade

The arrival of Europeans in West Africa and America in the fifteenth century ushered in a new era of world and African history. Beginning in the early 1400's, Prince Henry the Navigator of Portugal sponsored a series of voyages down the African coast in hope of finding an all-water commercial route to India, and Christopher Columbus's journey westward in 1492 had the same motivation. By the late fifteenth and early sixteenth centuries the Portuguese had already established trading stations in West Africa, and the flow of slaves both to the Iberian peninsula and the New World had begun. The Europeans, however, did not introduce slavery to Africa. Criminals, debtors, and war captives had known bondage there for hundreds of years and the Sudanic empires had exported slaves to the Middle East. But African slavery was a far cry from the institution introduced into the New World. African slaves were usually considered part of the family for which they worked. They had the right to own property, purchase their freedom, and marry freemen. Slaves were more often engaged in household work than field labor, and slavery was peripheral to the economies of most African states.

Slavery had also existed throughout the Middle Ages in the Mediterranean world, and Italian merchants had sold Bulgarians, Serbs, and Armenians into slavery in Italy,

Spain, and Portugal. This prior acquaintance with slavery helps explain why the Portuguese began shipping African slaves to Europe and why Spain and Portugal turned first to Indian slavery and then to African to supply the labor necessary to work the mines and plantations of the New World. The attempt to enslave the Indian inhabitants of the Caribbean and Central and South America was a disastrous failure. In many areas the indigenous economy was so backward that the Indians lacked the basic skills and discipline necessary for slave labor. It is one of the tragic ironies of Afro-American history that Africans were imported to the New World because their level of culture and economic skill made them better slave laborers than the Indians. In fact, African slaves introduced techniques of tropical farming and mining which were adopted by the Europeans. Moreover, Africans were more resistant to the diseases like malaria, smallpox, and yellow fever which they and the Europeans introduced to America and which annihilated the Indian population in many areas. In Central Mexico, for example, it is estimated that a population of twenty-five million in 1519 was reduced to one million by 1600, partly by overwork in the Mexican mines, but primarily by epidemic.

This was the background, then, for the development of the transatlantic slave trade. European powers established trading stations or "factories" along the African coast and it is estimated that they transported anywhere from ten to twenty million persons to slavery in the New World from the sixteenth through the nineteenth centuries. On the African side, most of the trade was in black hands. Coastal rulers refused to let Europeans venture inland to capture slaves, and the factors had to wait for African merchants to bring coffles of chained captives down from the interior. Most of the slaves were captured in raids or wars, and came from the densely populated forest area near the coast. Great slave-trading African kingdoms like Dahomey and Ashanti arose on the basis of the trade, their military power resting on the guns supplied by the

Europeans. For some rulers and merchants, the slave trade brought wealth and power, but for the average West African it meant unrelieved misery—a life of constant fear of capture and sale into slavery. And for West African society the slave trade meant ruinous social dislocation and economic stagnation, the collapse of crafts and skills which did not serve the interests of the trade, and the perversion of both legal and economic life to serve the traffic in human flesh.

The stimulus for the expansion and continuation of the slave trade in the New World was the rise of the plantation system in the seventeenth and eighteenth centuries. As the large-scale production of sugar for the European market came to dominate the economies of the Caribbean islands and parts of North and South America, the demand for a regular supply of cheap labor steadily increased. More and more slaves were exported from Africa, crowded in the holds of the slave ships where disease regularly killed anywhere from 10 to 40 per cent of the human cargo before the Atlantic was crossed. The economies of islands like Barbados, Jamaica, and Martinique were totally dominated by sugar, and since the expansion of the plantation system forced most of the independent white farmers off the islands, blacks came to outnumber whites in the population by as much as ten to one. The life span of the slaves on these plantations was extremely short, since it was cheaper to work slaves to death and import new ones than to develop a self-sustaining black population.

The transatlantic slave trade is one of the darkest chapters in the history of human injustice. Yet it is one of the major points of the selection which follows, from Eric Williams' controversial and pioneering work *Capitalism and Slavery,* that the slave trade and the plantation formed the economic basis of the first British Empire. Williams shows how all elements of English society, including church, state, and aristocracy, encouraged the trade and grew rich by it, and how the profits of the slave trade and West Indian sugar production helped accumulate wealth for ports like Bristol and Liverpool. The trade stimulated such economic activities as shipbuilding, insurance, and banking, and the capital accumulated in it helped finance the industrial revolution in eighteenth-century England. The West Indian islands were the jewels of the British Empire, far more important and profitable than the North American colonies. The involuntary labor of millions of black slaves not only built the New World, but also made possible the rise of modern industry and capitalism.

From *Capitalism and Slavery*

ERIC WILLIAMS

The Development of the Negro Slave Trade

The Negro slaves were "the strength and sinews of this western world."[1] Negro slavery demanded the Negro slave trade. Therefore the preservation and improvement of the trade to Africa was "a matter of very high importance to this kingdom and the plantations thereunto belonging."[2] And thus it remained, up to 1783, a cardinal object of British foreign policy.

The first English slave-trading expedition was that of Sir John Hawkins in 1562. Like so many Elizabethan ventures, it was a buccaneering expedition, encroaching on the papal arbitration of 1493 which made Africa a Portuguese monopoly. The slaves obtained were sold to the Spaniards in the West Indies. The English slave trade remained desultory and perfunctory in character until the establishment of British colonies in the Caribbean and the

FROM Eric Williams, *Capitalism and Slavery*. Copyright 1944 by University of North Carolina Press. Reprinted by permission of University of North Carolina Press.

introduction of the sugar industry. When by 1660 the political and social upheavals of the Civil War period came to an end, England was ready to embark wholeheartedly on a branch of commerce whose importance to her sugar and her tobacco colonies in the New World was beginning to be fully appreciated.

In accordance with the economic policies of the Stuart monarchy, the slave trade was entrusted to a monopolistic company, the Company of Royal Adventurers trading to Africa, incorporated in 1663 for a period of one thousand years. The Earl of Clarendon voiced the enthusiasm current at the time, that the company would "be found a model equally to advance the trade of England with that of any other company, even that of the East Indies."[3] The optimistic prediction was not realized, largely as a result of losses and dislocations caused by war with the Dutch, and in 1672 a new company, the Royal African Company, was created.

The policy of monopoly however remained unchanged and provoked determined resistance in two quarters—the merchants in the outports, struggling to break down the monopoly of the capital; and the planters in the colonies, demanding free trade in blacks as vociferously and with as much gusto as one hundred and fifty years later they opposed free trade in sugar. The mercantilist intelligentsia were divided on the question. Postlethwayt, most prolific of the mercantilist writers, wanted the company, the whole company and nothing but the company.[4] Joshua Gee emphasized the frugality and good management of the private trader.[5] Davenant, one of the ablest economists and financial experts of his day, at first opposed the monopoly,[6] and then later changed his mind, arguing that other nations found organized companies necessary, and that the company would "stand in place of an academy, for training an indefinite number of people in the regular knowledge of all matters relating to the several branches of the African trade."[7]

The case against monopoly was succinctly stated by the free traders—or interlopers as they were then called—to the Board of Trade in 1711. The monopoly meant that the purchase of British manufactures for sale on the coast of Africa, control of ships employed in the slave trade, sale of Negroes to the plantations, importation of plantation produce—"this great circle of trade and navigation," on which the livelihood, direct and indirect, of many thousands depended, would be under the control of a single company.[8] The planters in their turn complained of the quality, prices, and irregular deliveries, and refused to pay their debts to the company.[9]

There was nothing unique in this opposition to the monopoly of the slave trade. Monopoly was an ugly word, which conjured up memories of the political tyranny of Charles I, though no "free trader" of the time could have had the slightest idea of the still uglier visions the word would conjure up one hundred and fifty years later when it was associated with the economic tyranny of the West Indian sugar planter. But in the last decade of the seventeenth century the economic current was flowing definitely against monopoly. In 1672 the Baltic trade was thrown open and the monopoly of the Eastland Company overthrown. One of the most important consequences of the Glorious Revolution of 1688 and the expulsion of the Stuarts was the impetus it gave to the principle of free trade. In 1698 the Royal African Company lost its monopoly and the right of a free trade in slaves was recognized as a fundamental and natural right of Englishmen. In the same year the Merchant Adventurers of London were deprived of their monopoly of the export trade in cloth, and a year later the monopoly of the Muscovy Company was abrogated and trade to Russia made free. Only in one particular did the freedom accorded in the slave trade differ from the freedom accorded in other trades—the commodity involved was man.

The Royal African Company was powerless against the competition of the free traders. It soon went bankrupt and had to depend on parliamentary subsidy. In 1731 it abandoned the slave trade and confined itself to the trade in ivory and gold dust. In 1750 a new organization was established, called the Company of Merchants trading to Africa, with a board of nine directors, three each from London, Bristol and Liverpool. Of the slave traders listed in 1755, 237 belonged to Bristol, 147 to London, and 89 to Liverpool.[10]

With free trade and the increasing demands of the sugar plantations, the volume of the British slave trade rose enormously. The

Royal African Company, between 1680 and 1686, transported an annual average of 5,000 slaves.[11] In the first nine years of free trade Bristol alone shipped 160,950 Negroes to the sugar plantations.[12] In 1760, 146 ships sailed from British ports for Africa, with a capacity for 36,000 slaves;[13] in 1771, the number of ships had increased to 190 and the number of slaves to 47,000.[14] The importation into Jamaica from 1700 to 1786 was 610,000, and it has been estimated that the total import of slaves into all the British colonies between 1680 and 1786 was over two million.[15]

But the slave trade was more than a means to an end, it was also an end in itself. The British slave traders provided the necessary laborers not only for their own plantations but for those of their rivals. The encouragement thereby given to foreigners was contrary not only to common sense but to strict mercantilism, but, in so far as this foreign slave trade meant the Spanish colonies, there was some defence for it. Spain was always, up to the nineteenth century, dependent on foreigners for her slaves, either because she adhered to the papal arbitration which excluded her from Africa, or because of a lack of capital and the necessary goods for the slave trade. The privilege of supplying these slaves to the Spanish colonies, called the Asiento, became one of the most highly coveted and bitterly contested plums of international diplomacy. British mercantilists defended the trade, legal or illegal, with the Spanish colonies, in Negroes and manufactured goods, as of distinct value in that the Spaniards paid in coin, and thus the supply of bullion in England was increased. The supply of slaves to the French colonies could plead no such justification. Here it was clearly a clash of interest between the British slave trader and the British sugar planter, as the trade in the export of British machinery after 1825 led to a clash of interests between British shippers and British producers.

The sugar planter was right and the slave trader wrong. But in the first half of the eighteenth century this was noticed only by the very discerning. Postlethwayt condemned the Asiento of 1713 as scandalous and ruinous, an exchange of the substance for the shadow: "a treaty could scarce have been contrived of so little benefit to the nation."[16] During the nine months of British occupation of Cuba in the Seven Years' War, 10,700 slaves were introduced, over one-sixth of the importations from 1512 to 1763, over one-third of the importations from 1763 to 1789.[17] Forty thousand Negroes were introduced into Guadeloupe by the British in three years during the same war.[18] The Privy Council Committee of 1788 paid special attention to the fact that of the annual British export of slaves from Africa two-thirds were disposed of to foreigners.[19] During the whole of the eighteenth century, according to Bryan Edwards, British slave traders furnished the sugar planters of France and Spain with half a million Negroes, justifying his doubts of "the wisdom and policy of this branch of the African commerce."[20] Britain was not only the foremost slave trading country in the world; she had become, in Ramsay's phrase, the "honourable slave carriers" of her rivals.[21]

The story of this increase in the slave trade is mainly the story of the rise of Liverpool. Liverpool's first slave trader, a modest vessel of thirty tons, sailed for Africa in 1709. This was the first step on a road which, by the end of the century, gained Liverpool the distinction of being the greatest slave trading port in the Old World. Progress at first was slow. The town was more interested in the smuggling trade to the Spanish colonies and the tobacco trade. But, according to a historian of the town, it soon forged ahead by its policy of cutting down expenses to a minimum, which enabled it to undersell its English and continental rivals. In 1730 it had fifteen ships in the slave trade; in 1771 seven times as many. The proportion of slave ships to the total shipping owned by the port was slightly over one in a hundred in 1709; in 1730 it was one-eleventh; in 1763, one-fourth; in 1771, one-third.[22] In 1795 Liverpool had five-eighths of the British slave trade and three-sevenths of the whole European slave trade.[23]

The "horrors" of the Middle Passage have been exaggerated. For this the British abolitionists are in large part responsible. There is something that smacks of ignorance or hypocrisy or both in the invectives heaped by these men upon a traffic which had in their day become less profitable and less vital to England. A West Indian planter once reminded Parliament that it ill became the elected representative of a country which had pocketed the gains from the slave trade to stigmatize it as a crime.[24] The age which had seen the mortality among indentured servants saw no reason for squeamishness about the mortality among slaves, nor did the exploitation of the slaves on the plantations differ fundamentally from the exploitation of the feudal peasant or the treatment of the poor in European cities.

Mutinies and suicides were obviously far more common on slave ships than on other vessels, and the brutal treatment and greater restrictions on the movements of the slaves would doubt-less have tended to increase their mortality. But the fundamental causes of this high mortality on the slave ships, as on ships carrying indentured servants and even free passengers, must be found firstly in epidemics, the inevitable result of the long voyages and the difficulty of preserving food and water, and secondly in the practice of overcrowding the vessels. The sole aim of the slave merchants was to have their decks "well covered with black ones."[25] It is not uncommon to read of a vessel of 90 tons carrying 390 slaves or one of 100 tons carrying 414.[26] Clarkson's investigations in Bristol revealed a sloop of twenty-five tons des-tined for seventy human beings, and another of a mere eleven tons for thirty slaves.[27] The space allotted to each slave on the Atlantic crossing measured five and a half feet in length by sixteen inches in breadth. Packed like "rows of books on shelves," as Clarkson said, chained two by two, right leg and left leg, right hand and left hand, each slave had less room than a man in a coffin. It was like the transportation of black cattle, and where sufficient Negroes were not available cattle were taken on.[28] The slave trader's aim was profit and not the comfort of his victims, and a modest measure in 1788 to regulate the transportation of the slaves in accordance with the capacity of the vessel evoked a loud howl from the slave traders. "If the alteration takes place," wrote one to his agent, "it will hurt the trade, so hope you will make hay while the sun shines."[29]

The journal of one slave dealer during his residence in Africa admits that he had "found no place in all these several countrys of England, Ireland, America, Portugall, the Caribes, the Cape de Verd, the Azores or all the places I have been in . . . where I can inlarge my fortune so soon as where I now live." Money made the man. The prodigal who returned home empty-handed would have to be content with the common name of "the Mallato just came from Guinea." If, however, he returned with his pockets well stuffed with gold, "that very perticular hides all other infirmities, then you have hapes of frinds of all kinds thronging and wateing for your commands. Then your known by the name of 'the African gentleman' at every great man's house, and your discource is set down as perticular as Cristopher Culumbus's expedition in America."[30]

About 1730 in Bristol it was estimated that on a fortunate voyage the profit on a cargo of about 270 slaves reached £7,000 or £8,000, exclusive of the returns from ivory. In the same year the net return from an "indifferent" cargo which arrived in poor condition was over £5,700.[31] Profits of 100 per cent were not uncommon in Liverpool, and one voyage netted a clear profit of at least 300 per cent. The *Lively,* fitted out in 1737 with a cargo worth £1,307, returned to Liverpool with colonial produce and bills of exchange totalling £3,080, in addition to cotton and sugar remitted later. The *Ann,* another Liverpool ship, sailed in 1751 with an outfit and a cargo costing £1,604; altogether the voyage produced £3,287 net. A second voyage in 1753 produced £8,000 on a cargo and outfit amounting to £3,153.[32]

An eighteenth century writer has estimated the sterling value of the 303,737 slaves carried in 878 Liverpool ships between 1783 and 1793 at over fifteen million pounds. Deducting commissions and other charges and the cost of the outfit of the ships and maintenance of the slaves, he concluded that the average annual profit was over 30 per cent.[33] Modern scholarship has tended to reproach contemporary observers with undue exaggeration. But even taking the reduced estimates of Professor Dumbell, the net profit of the *Enterprise* in 1803, estimated on cost of outfit and cost of cargo, was 38 per cent, while that of the *Fortune* in 1803, for a cargo of poor slaves, was over 16 per cent. Again with these reduced estimates the profit of the *Lottery* in 1802 was thirty-six pounds per slave, the *Enterprise* sixteen pounds, and the *Fortune* five.[34] The slave trade on the whole was estimated to bring Liverpool alone in the eighties a clear profit of £300,000 a year; and it was a common saying in the town of the far less profitable West Indian trade that if one ship in three came in a man was no loser, while if two came in he was a good gainer. On an average only one ship in five miscarried. . . .[35]

The "attractive African meteor,"[36] as a contemporary Liverpool historian called it, therefore became immensely popular. Though a large part of the Liverpool slave traffic was monopolized by about ten large firms, many of the small vessels in the trade were fitted out by attorneys, drapers, grocers, barbers and tailors. The shares in the ventures were subdivided, one having one-eighth, another one-fifteenth, a third one-thirty-second part of a share and so on. "Almost every man in Liverpool is a merchant, and he who cannot send a bale will send a band-box . . . almost every order of people is interested in a Guinea cargo, it is to this influenza that (there are) so many small ships."[37]

The purchase of slaves called for a business sense and shrewd discrimination. An Angolan Negro was a proverb for worthlessness; Coromantines (Ashantis), from the Gold Coast, were good workers but too rebellious; Mandingoes (Senegal) were too prone to theft; the Eboes (Nigeria) were timid and despondent; the Pawpaws or Whydahs (Dahomey) were the most docile and best-disposed.[38] The slaves were required for arduous field work, hence women and children were less valuable than robust males, the former because they were liable to interruptions from work through pregnancies, the latter because they required some attention until able to care for themselves. One Liverpool merchant cautioned his agents against buying ruptured slaves, idiots or any "old spider leged quality."[39] A West Indian poet advised the slave trader to see that the slave's tongue was red, his chest broad and his belly not prominent.[40] Buy them young, counselled one overseer from Nevis; "them full grown fellers think it hard to work never being brought up to it they take it to heart and dye or is never good for any thing. . . ."[41]

But the slave trade was always a risky business. "The African Commerce," it was written in 1795, "holds forward one constant train of uncertainty, the time of slaving is precarious, the length of the middle passage uncertain, a vessel may be in part, or wholly cut off, mortalities may be great, and various other incidents may arise impossible to be foreseen."[42] Sugar cultivation, moreover, was a lottery. The debts of the planters, their bankruptcies and demand for long credits gave the merchants many worries. "As you know," wrote one of them, "quick dispatch is the life of trade, I have had many anxious hours this year, I wou'd not wish the same again for double the profits I may get if any."[43] From 1763 to 1778 the London merchants avoided all connection with the Liverpool slave traders, on the conviction that the slave trade was being conducted at a loss; between 1772 and 1778 the Liverpool merchants were alleged to have lost £700,000.[44] Of thirty leading houses which dominated the slave trade from 1773, twelve had by 1788 gone bankrupt, while many others had sustained considerable losses.[45] The American Revolution seriously interrupted the trade. "Our once extensive trade to Africa is at a stand," lamented a Liverpool paper in 1775. Her "gallant ships laid up and useless," Liverpool's slave traders turned to privateering,[46] anxiously awaiting the return of peace, with never a thought that they were witnessing the death rattles of an old epoch and the birth pangs of a new.

Prior to 1783, however, all classes in English society presented a united front with regard to the slave trade. The monarchy, the government, the church, public opinion in general, supported the slave trade. There were few protests, and those were ineffective. . . .

The British government, prior to 1783, was uniformly consistent in its encouragement of the slave trade. The first great rivals were the Dutch, who monopolized the carrying trade of the British colonies. The bitter commercial warfare of the second half of the seventeenth century between England and Holland represented an effort on the part of England to break the commercial net the Dutch had woven about England and her colonies. "What we want," said Monk with military bluntness, "is more of the trade the Dutch now have."[47] Whether it was nominal peace or actual war, a sort of private war was maintained, for thirty years, between the Dutch West India Company and the Royal African Company.

England's victory over Holland left her face to face with France. Anglo-French warfare, colonial and commercial, is the dominant theme in the history of the eighteenth century. It was a conflict of rival mercantilisms. The struggle was fought out in the Caribbean, Africa, India, Canada and on the banks of the Mississippi, for the privilege of looting India and for the control of certain vital and strategic commodities—Negroes; sugar and tobacco; fish; furs and naval stores.[48] Of these areas the most important were the Caribbean and Africa; of these commodities the most important were Negroes and sugar. The outstanding single issue was the control of the Asiento. This privilege was conceded to England by the Treaty of Utrecht in 1713 as one result of her victory in the War of the Spanish Succession, and produced popular rejoicings in the country. It was the proud boast of Chatham that his war with France had given England almost the entire control of the African coast and of the slave trade.

Colonial assemblies frequently impeded the slave traders by imposing high duties on imported slaves, partly to raise revenue, partly out of their fear of the growing slave population. All such laws were frustrated by the home government, on the insistence of British merchants, who opposed taxes on British trade. The Board of Trade ruled in 1708 that it was "absolutely necessary that a trade so beneficial to the kingdom should be carried on to the greatest advantage. The well supplying of the plantations and colonies with a sufficient number of negroes at reasonable prices is in our opinion the chief point to be considered."[49] In 1773 the Jamaica Assembly, for the purpose of raising revenue and to reduce the fear of slave rebellions, imposed a duty on every Negro imported. The merchants of London, Liverpool and Bristol protested, and the Board of Trade condemned the law as unjustifiable, improper and prejudicial to British commerce. The governor was sharply reprimanded for his failure to stop efforts made to "check and discourage a traffic so beneficial to the nation."[50] As counsel for the sugar planters later argued: "in every variation of our administration of public affairs, in every variation of parties, the policy, in respect to that trade, has been the same. . . . In every period of our history, in almost every variation of our politics, each side and description of party men have, in terms, approved this very trade, voted its encouragement, and considered it as beneficial to the nation."[51]

Parliament appreciated the importance of slavery and the slave trade to Britain and her plantations. In 1750 Horace Walpole wrote scornfully of "the British Senate, that temple of liberty, and bulwark of Protestant Christianity . . . pondering methods to make more effectual that horrid traffic of selling negroes."[52] Parliament heard many debates in its stately halls over abolition and emancipation, and its records show the doughty defenders the slave traders and slave owners possessed. Among them was Edmund Burke. The champion of conciliation of America was an accessory to the crucifixion of Africa. In 1772 a bill came before the House of Commons to prohibit the control of the African Committee by outsiders who were not engaged in the slave trade. Burke protested, not against the slave trade, however, but against depriving of the right to vote those who had legally purchased that right. Only a few, he argued, were so accused. "Ought we not rather to imitate the pattern set us in sacred writ, and if we find ten just persons among them, to spare the whole? . . . Let us not then counteract the wisdom of our ancestors, who considered and reconsidered this subject, nor place upon the footing of a monopoly what was intended for a free trade."[53] Bristol could well afford to share in the general admiration of the great Liberal.

The Church also supported the slave trade. The Spaniards saw in it an opportunity of converting the heathen, and the Jesuits, Dominicans and Franciscans were heavily involved in sugar cultivation which meant slave-holding. The story is told of an old elder of the Church in Newport who would invariably, the Sunday following the arrival of a slaver from the coast, thank God that "another cargo of benighted beings had been brought to a land where they could have the benefit of a gospel dispensation."[54] But in general the British planters opposed Christianity for their slaves. It made them more perverse and intractable and therefore less valuable. It meant also instruction in the English language, which allowed diverse tribes to get together and plot sedition.[55] There were more material reasons for this opposition. The governor of Barbados in 1695 attributed it to the planters' refusal to give the slaves Sundays and feast days off,[56] and as late as 1823 British public opinion was shocked by the planters' rejection of a proposal to give the Negroes one day in the week in order to permit the abolition of the Negro Sunday market.[57] The Church obediently toed the line. The Society for the Propagation of the Gospel prohibited Christian instruction to its slaves in Barbados,[58] and branded "Society" on its new slaves to distinguish them from those of the laity;[59] the original slaves were the legacy of Christopher Codrington.[60] Sherlock, later Bishop of London, assured the planters that "Christianity and the embracing of the Gospel does not make the least difference in civil property."[61] Neither did it impose any barriers to clerical activity; for his labors with regard to the Asiento, which he helped to draw up as a British plenipotentiary at Utrecht, Bishop Robinson of Bristol was promoted to the see of London.[62] The bells of the Bristol churches pealed merrily on the news of the rejection by Parliament of Wilberforce's bill for the abolition of the slave trade.[63] The slave trader John Newton gave thanks in the Liverpool churches for the success of his last venture before his conversion and implored God's blessing on his next. He established public worship twice every day on his slaver, officiating himself, and kept a day of fasting and prayer, not for the slaves but for the crew. "I never knew," he confessed, "sweeter or more frequent hours of divine communion than in the last two voyages to Guinea."[64] The famous Cardinal Manning of the nineteenth century was the son of a rich West Indian merchant dealing in slave-grown produce.[65] Many missionaries found it profitable to drive out Beelzebub by Beelzebub. According to the most recent English writer on the slave trade, they "considered that the best way in which to remedy abuse of negro slaves was to set the plantation owners a good example by keeping slaves and estates themselves, accomplishing in this practical manner the salvation of the planters and the advancement of their foundations."[66] The Moravian missionaries in the islands held slaves without hesitation; the Baptists, one historian writes with charming delicacy, would not allow their earlier missionaries to deprecate ownership of slaves.[67] To the very end the Bishop of Exeter retained his 655 slaves, for whom he received over £12,700 compensation in 1833. . . .[68]

Slavery existed under the very eyes of eighteenth century Englishmen. An English coin, the guinea, rare though it was and is, had its origin in the trade to Africa.[69] A Westminster goldsmith

made silver padlocks for blacks and dogs.[70] Busts of blackamoors
and elephants, emblematical of the slave trade, adorned the Liverpool Town Hall. The insignia and equipment of the slave traders
were boldly exhibited for sale in the shops and advertised in the
press. Slaves were sold openly at auction.[71] Slaves being valuable
property, with title recognized by law, the postmaster was the
agent employed on occasions to recapture runaway slaves and
advertisements were published in the official organ of the government.[72] Negro servants were common. Little black boys were the
appendages of slave captains, fashionable ladies or women of easy
virtue. Hogarth's heroine, in *The Harlot's Progress,* is attended by
a Negro boy, and Marguerite Steen's Orabella Burmester typifies
eighteenth century English opinion in her desire for a little black
boy whom she could love as her long-haired kitten.[73] Freed
Negroes were conspicuous among London beggars and were
known as St. Giles blackbirds. So numerous were they that a
parliamentary committee was set up in 1786 for relieving the black
poor. . . .[74]

The prosecution of the slave trade was not the work of the dregs
of English society. The daughter of a slave trader has assured us
that her father, though a slave captain and privateer, was a kind
and just man, a good father, husband, and friend.[75] This was
probably true. The men most active in this traffic were worthy
men, fathers of families and excellent citizens. The abolitionist
Ramsay acknowledged this with real sorrow, but pleaded that
"they had never examined the nature of this commerce and went
into it, and acted as others had done before them in it, as a thing
of course, for which no account was to be given in this world or
the next."[76] The apology is unnecessary. The slave trade was a
branch of trade and a very important branch. An officer in the
trade once said that "one real view, one minute absolutely spent in
the slave rooms on the middle passage would do more for the
cause of humanity than the pen of a Robertson, or the whole
collective eloquence of the British senate."[77] This is dubious. As
it was argued later about the Cuban and Brazilian slave trade, it
was no use saying it was an unholy or unchristian occupation. It
was a lucrative trade, and that was enough.[78] The slave trade has

even been justified as a great education. "Think of the effect, the result of a slave voyage on a youngster starting in his teens. . . . What an education was such a voyage for the farmer lad. What an enlargement of experience for a country boy. If he returned to the farm his whole outlook on life would be changed. He went out a boy; he returned a man."[79]

The slave traders were among the leading humanitarians of their age. John Cary, advocate of the slave trade, was conspicuous for his integrity and humanity and was the founder of a society known as the "Incorporation of the Poor."[80] The Bristol slaver "Southwell" was named after a Bristol parliamentarian, whose monument depicts him as true to king and country and steady to what he thought right.[81] Bryan Blundell of Liverpool, one of Liverpool's most prosperous merchants, engaged in both the slave and West Indian trades, was for many years trustee, treasurer, chief patron and most active supporter of a charity school, the Blue Coat Hospital, founded in 1709.[82] To this charity another Liverpool slave trader, Foster Cunliffe, contributed largely. He was a pioneer in the slave trade. He and his two sons are listed as members of the Liverpool Committee of Merchants trading to Africa in 1752. Together they had four ships capable of holding 1,120 slaves, the profits from which were sufficient to stock twelve vessels on the homeward journey with sugar and rum. An inscription to Foster Cunliffe in St. Peter's Church describes him thus: "a Christian devout and exemplary in the exercise of every private and publick duty, friend to mercy, patron to distress, an enemy only to vice and sloth, he lived esteemed by all who knew him . . . and died lamented by the wise and good. . . ."[83] Thomas Leyland, one of the largest slave traders of the same port, had, as mayor, no mercy for the engrosser, the forestaller, the regrater, and was a terror to evil doers.[84] The Heywoods were slave traders and the first to import the slave-grown cotton of the United States. Arthur Heywood was treasurer of the Manchester Academy where his sons were educated. One son, Benjamin, was elected member of the Literary and Philosophical Society of Manchester, and was admitted to the Billiard Club, the most *recherché* club Manchester has ever possessed, which admitted only the very best men as regards manners, position and attainments. To be admitted to the charmed circle of the Forty meant unimpeachable recognition as a gentleman. Later Benjamin Heywood organized the first of the Manchester exhibitions of works of art and industry.[85]

The slave traders held high office in England. The Royal Adventurers trading to Africa in 1667, a list headed by royalty, included two aldermen, three dukes, eight earls, seven lords, one countess, and twenty-seven knights.[86] The signatures of the mayors of Liverpool and Bristol appear on a petition of the slave traders in 1739.[87] The Bristol Committee set up in 1789 to oppose abolition of the slave trade included five aldermen, one an ex-captain of a slaver.[88] Many a slave trader held Liverpool's highest municipal dignity.[89] The slave traders were firmly established in both houses of Parliament. Ellis Cunliffe represented Liverpool in Parliament from 1755 to 1767.[90] The Tarleton family, prominent in the slave trade, voiced Liverpool's opposition to abolition in Parliament.[91] The House of Lords, traditionally conservative, was confirmed in its instinctive opposition to abolition by the presence of many ennobled slave traders. It gave sympathetic hearing to the Earl of Westmoreland's statement that many of them owed their seats in the Upper House to the slave trade,[92] and that abolition was Jacobinism.[93] No wonder Wilberforce feared the Upper Chamber.[94] Not without confidence did the Assembly of Jamaica state categorically in 1792 that "the safety of the West Indies not only depends on the slave trade not being abolished, but on a speedy declaration of the House of Lords that they will not suffer the trade to be abolished.". . .[95]

The Triangular Trade

According to Adam Smith, the discovery of America and the Cape route to India are "the two greatest and most important events recorded in the history of mankind." The importance of the discovery of America lay not in the precious metals it provided but in the new and inexhaustible market it afforded for European commodities. One of its principal effects was to "raise the mercantile system to a degree of splendour and glory which it could never otherwise have attained to."[96] It gave rise to an enormous increase in world trade. The seventeenth and eighteenth centuries were the centuries of trade, as the nineteenth century was the century of production. For Britain that trade was primarily the triangular trade. In 1718 William Wood said that the slave trade was "the spring and parent whence the others flow."[97] A few years later Postlethwayt described the slave trade as "the first principle and foundation of all the rest, the mainspring of the machine which sets every wheel in motion."[98]

In this triangular trade England—France and Colonial America equally—supplied the exports and the ships; Africa the human merchandise; the plantations the colonial raw materials. The slave ship sailed from the home country with a cargo of manufactured goods. These were exchanged at a profit on the coast of Africa for Negroes, who were traded on the plantations, at another profit, in exchange for a cargo of colonial produce to be taken back to the home country. As the volume of trade increased, the triangular trade was supplemented, but never supplanted, by a direct trade between home country and the West Indies, exchanging home manufactures directly for colonial produce.

The triangular trade thereby gave a triple stimulus to British industry. The Negroes were purchased with British manufactures; transported to the plantations, they produced sugar, cotton, indigo, molasses and other tropical products, the processing of which created new industries in England; while the maintenance of the Negroes and their owners on the plantations provided another market for British industry, New England agriculture and the Newfoundland fisheries. By 1750 there was hardly a trading or a manufacturing town in England which was not in some way connected with the triangular or direct colonial trade.[99] The profits obtained provided one of the main streams of that accumulation of capital in England which financed the Industrial Revolution.

The West Indian islands became the hub of the British Empire, of immense importance to the grandeur and prosperity of England. It was the Negro slaves who made these sugar colonies the most precious colonies ever recorded in the whole annals of imperialism. To Postlethwayt they were "the fundamental prop and support" of the colonies, "valuable people" whose labor supplied Britain with all plantation produce. The British Empire was "a magnificent superstructure of American commerce and naval power on an African foundation."[100]

Sir Josiah Child estimated that every Englishman in the West Indies, "with the ten blacks that work with him, accounting what they eat, use and wear, would make employment for four men in England."[101] By Davenant's computation one person in the islands, white or Negro, was as profitable as seven in England.[102] Another writer considered that every family in the West Indies gave employment to five seamen and many more artificers, manufacturers and tradesmen, and that every white person in the islands brought in ten pounds annually clear profit to England, twenty times as much as a similar person in the home country.[103] William Wood reckoned that a profit of seven shillings per head per annum was sufficient to enrich a country; each white man in the colonies brought a profit of over seven pounds.[104] Sir Dalby Thomas went further—every person employed on the sugar plantations was 130 times more valuable to England than one at home.[105] Professor Pitman has estimated that in 1775 British West Indian plantations represented a valuation of fifty millions sterling,[106] and the sugar planters themselves put the figure at seventy millions in 1788.[107] In 1798 Pitt assessed the annual income from West Indian plantations at four million pounds as compared with one million from the rest of the world.[108] As Adam Smith wrote: "The profits of a sugar plantation in any of our West Indian colonies are generally much greater than those of any other cultivation that is known either in Europe or America."[109]

According to Davenant, Britain's total trade at the end of the seventeenth century brought in a profit of £2,000,000. The plantation trade accounted for £600,000; re-export of plantation goods £120,000; European, African and Levant trade £600,000; East India trade £500,000; re-export of East India goods £180,000.[110]

Sir Charles Whitworth, in 1776, made a complete compilation, from official records, of the import and export trade of Great Britain for the years 1697–1773. His book is invaluable for an appreciation of the relative importance of the Caribbean and mainland colonies in the British Empire of the eighteenth century. For the year 1697 the West Indian colonies supplied nine per cent of British imports, the mainland colonies eight per cent; four per cent of British exports went to the West Indies, slightly under four per cent to the mainland; the West Indies accounted for seven per cent of Britain's total trade, the mainland for six per cent. In 1773 the West Indies still maintained their lead, though as an export market they had become inferior to the mainland colonies with their larger white population. In that year nearly one-quarter of British imports came from all Caribbean areas, one-eighth from the entire mainland; the Caribbean consumed somewhat over eight per cent of British exports, the mainland sixteen per cent; fifteen per cent of Britain's total trade was with the West Indies, fourteen per cent with the mainland. Taking the totals for the years 1714–1773, and including in those totals trade with new acquisitions, foreign colonies temporarily occupied by British forces during the war, or foreign colonies in general, we get the following picture: One-fifth of British imports came from the Caribbean, one-ninth from the mainland; six per cent of British exports went to the Caribbean, nine per cent to the mainland; twelve per cent of Britain's total foreign commerce was accounted for by the Caribbean, ten per cent by the mainland. During these same years one-half per cent of British imports came from Africa, two per cent of British exports went to Africa, while African trade represented nearly one and a half per cent of total British trade. Leaving out of account, therefore, the plantation colonies on the mainland, Virginia, Maryland, Carolina, Georgia, the triangular and West Indian trades represented nearly one-seventh of total British trade during the years 1714–1773.

The amazing value of these West Indian colonies can more graphically be presented by comparing individual West Indian islands with individual mainland colonies. In 1697 British imports from Barbados were five times the combined imports from the bread colonies; the exports to Barbados were slightly larger. Little Barbados, with its 166 square miles, was worth more to British capitalism than New England, New York and Pennsylvania combined. In 1773 British imports from Jamaica were more than five times the combined imports from the bread colonies; British exports to Jamaica were nearly one-third larger than those to New England and only slightly less than those to New York and Pennsylvania combined. For the years 1714–1773 British imports from

Montserrat were three times the imports from Pennsylvania, imports from Nevis were almost double those from New York, imports from Antigua were over three times those from New England. Imports from Barbados were more than twice as large as those from the bread colonies, imports from Jamaica nearly six times as large. For the same years Jamaica as an export market was as valuable as New England; Barbados and Antigua combined meant as much to British exporters as New York; Montserrat and Nevis combined were a better market than Pennsylvania. British exports to Africa during these years were only one-tenth less than those to New England, British imports from Africa one-quarter more than those from New York and more than double those from Pennsylvania.[111]

Mercantilists were enthusiastic. The triangular trade, and the associated trade with the sugar islands, because of the navigation they encouraged, were more valuable to England than her mines of tin or coal.[112] These were ideal colonies. But for them Britain would have no gold or silver, except what she received from illicit commerce with the Spanish colonies, and an unfavorable balance of trade.[113] Their tropical products, unlike those of the northern part of the mainland, did not compete with those of the home country. They showed little sign of that industrial development which was the constant fear where the mainland was concerned. Their large black population was an effective guarantee against aspirations to independence.[114] It all combined to spell one word, sugar. "The pleasure, glory and grandeur of England," wrote Sir Dalby Thomas, "has been advanced more by sugar than by any other commodity, wool not excepted."[115]

3. The Development of Slavery in the United States

In 1619, a year before the landing of the *Mayflower* at Plymouth Rock, the Virginia planter John Rolfe recorded in his journal that "twenty Negars" had arrived in Virginia. Historians are agreed that this piece of evidence marks the earliest presence of blacks in the English colonies which were to become the United States. But they have long differed as to the exact legal status of the arrivals. One group has argued that blacks were held as slaves from the beginning, but this view was challenged in 1950 by Oscar and Mary Handlin in their influential article "Origins of the Southern Labor System." At first, the Handlins insisted, blacks in Virginia had the same legal position as white indentured servants—after a number of years at labor they were entitled to freedom. Gradually, however, Virginia began to differentiate between white and black servants, making the length of service for whites shorter and defining more clearly their legal rights, in order to attract white settlers. There was no reason to improve the condition of blacks, since they did not come voluntarily, and compared with that of whites, the position of black servants became increasingly debased. But it was not until the 1670's that the status of black slavery for life was fully defined.

Nine years after the Handlins' article appeared, Carl Degler published a critique of their argument, entitled "Slavery and the Genesis of American Race Prejudice." The Handlins' line of reasoning strongly implied that racial prejudice against blacks had not existed in Virginia at the outset, and only developed later as an outgrowth of slavery. Degler insisted that prejudice preceded slavery and that the status of blacks was worked out within a context of belief in white supremacy. The legal status of blacks, he admitted, was indeterminate for a number of years, but from the outset they were regarded as inferior and slavery became relatively fixed by the 1640's. Each of these historical interpretations had important implications for contemporary race relations. For if, as the Handlins argued, blacks and whites had once been treated equally, it might be possible to eradicate racial prejudice in the modern world. On the other hand, if prejudice preceded slavery, it should be expected to persist even after all legal discriminations between the races are erased from the statute books.

The most recent, and apparently the definitive, contribution to this historiographical controversy is in Winthrop Jordan's prize-winning study of American racial attitudes to 1812, *White Over Black*. As for the question of when slavery actually became formalized, Jordan gives the frustrating but accurate response that the historical evidence is simply too scanty to permit an answer. But his interpretation is certainly in the Degler tradition. He emphasizes that even before their encounter with Africans Englishmen had an image of blackness as dirty and evil, and in trying to account for the color of Africans they resorted to explanations which associated a black skin with heathenness, savagery, and lack of sexual restraint. Most of all, Englishmen were from the first impressed with the difference between themselves and black men. This sense of blacks as a group apart was the key to their debasement into slaves not only in Virginia, where some form of forced labor was an economic necessity for many years, but also in the New England colonies, where there was no real economic necessity for black slavery. Blacks were viewed as uniquely enslavable, for no white man or woman ever served as a hereditary slave for life in the English colonies.

In the selection which follows, Jordan explains Englishmen's initial impressions of blacks in Africa, and the gradual "unthinking decision" by which they were enslaved in Virginia. Utilizing evidence from court records and wills, Jordan shows that slavery existed in Virginia for some blacks many years before laws were enacted recognizing and enforcing bondage. The first evidence of slavery appeared in the 1640's, at a time when the black population of the colony was still extremely small. It was only when the number of blacks began to increase (reaching about two thousand in 1671) that their status became sufficiently important to cause community problems and responsibilities and thus be the subject of legal enactments. Between 1670 and 1700, Virginia's economy was increasingly dominated by the tobacco plantation. Repeating processes which had occurred in the West Indies, large planters engrossed the best land and pushed out many small white farmers. During these years there was a marked increase in slavery legislation in order to clarify uncertain legal points and improve police regulation of . slaves. Finally in 1705, soon after the British ended the Royal Africa Company's monopoly on the slave trade, which greatly increased the importation of slaves to the English colonies, the disjointed acts previously adopted were codified in a comprehensive slave code.

The evolution of slavery differed from colony to colony, but in most cases the institution existed before being specifically authorized or protected by law. In the Carolinas slavery was recognized in the Fundamental Constitutions drafted by John Locke, but it was only after the introduction of rice and the rise of the plantation system that the first comprehensive slave code was adopted, in the 1690's. The proprietors of Georgia, which was established in the 1730's, at first barred slavery from the colony, not from any humanitarian impulse (the chief proprietor, James Oglethorpe, was a member of the slave-trading Royal Africa Company), but because of the fear that in the event of military conflict with Indians or the nearby Spanish colonies slaves might side with the enemy. But by 1750 the white settlers had demanded and won the right to own slaves. The northern colonies also allowed slavery, although in a much milder form than in the South. Northern slaves tended to be held in small units and so the need for rigid police regulations was less pronounced than where slaves were concentrated on large plantations and composed half or even more of the total population of the colony. By the time of the American Revolution, slavery existed in every colony and race prejudice was already deeply engraved in the American mind.

From *White Over Black*

WINTHROP JORDAN

First Impressions
Initial English Confrontation with Africans

When the Atlantic nations of Europe began expanding overseas in the sixteenth century, Portugal led the way in Africa and to the east while Spain founded a great empire in America. It was not until the reign of Elizabeth that Englishmen came to realize that overseas exploration and plantations could bring home wealth, power, glory, and fascinating information. By the early years of

FROM Winthrop Jordan, *White Over Black*. Copyright © 1968 by University of North Carolina Press. Reprinted by permission of University of North Carolina Press (Published for the Institute of Early American History and Culture).

the seventeenth century Englishmen had developed a taste for empire and for tales of adventure and discovery. More than is usual in human affairs, one man, the great chronicler Richard Hakluyt, had roused enthusiasm for western planting and had stirred the nation with his monumental compilation, *The Principal Navigations, Voyages, Traffiques and Discoveries of the English Nation*. Here was a work to widen a people's horizons. Its exhilarating accounts of voyages to all quarters of the globe (some by foreigners, in translation) constituted a national hymn, a sermon, an adventure story, and a scientific treatise. It was these accounts, together with ones added during the first quarter of the seventeenth century by Hakluyt's successor Samuel Purchas, which first acquainted Englishmen at home with the newly discovered lands of Africa.

English voyagers did not touch upon the shores of West Africa until after 1550, nearly a century after Prince Henry the Navigator had mounted the sustained Portuguese thrust southward for a water passage to the Orient. Usually Englishmen came to Africa to trade goods *with* the natives; the principal hazards of these ventures proved to be climate, disease, and the jealous opposition of the "Portingals" who had long since entrenched themselves in forts along the coast. The earliest English descriptions of West Africa were written by adventurous traders, men who had no special interest in converting the natives or, except for the famous Hawkins voyages, in otherwise laying hands on them. Extensive English participation in the slave trade did not develop until well into the seventeenth century. The first permanent English settlement on the African coast was at Kormantin in 1631, and the Royal African Company was not chartered for another forty years.[1] Initially, therefore, English contact with Africans did not take place primarily in a context which prejudged the Negro as a slave, at least not as a slave of Englishmen. Rather, Englishmen met Negroes merely as another sort of men.

Englishmen found the natives of Africa very different from themselves. Negroes looked different; their religion was un-Christian; their manner of living was anything but English; they seemed to be a particularly libidinous sort of people. All these clusters of perceptions were related to each other, though they may be spread apart for inspection, and they were related also to circumstances of contact in Africa, to previously accumulated traditions concerning that strange and distant continent, and to certain special qualities of English society on the eve of its expansion into the New World.

The Blackness Without

The most arresting characteristic of the newly discovered African was his color. Travelers rarely failed to comment upon it; indeed when describing Negroes they frequently began with complexion and then moved on to dress (or rather lack of it) and manners. At Cape Verde, "These people are all blacke, and are called Negros, without any apparell, saving before their privities."[2] Robert Baker's narrative poem recounting his two voyages to the West African coast in 1562 and 1563 first introduced the natives with these engaging lines:

> And entering in [a river], we see
> a number of blacke soules,
> Whose likelinesse seem'd men to be,
> but all as blacke as coles.
> Their Captaine comes to me
> as naked as my naile,
> Not having witte or honestie
> to cover once his taile.[3]

Even more sympathetic observers seemed to find blackness a most salient quality in Negroes: "although the people were blacke and naked, yet they were civill."[4]

Englishmen actually described Negroes as *black*—an exaggerated term which in itself suggests that the Negro's complexion had powerful impact upon their perceptions. Even the peoples of northern Africa seemed so dark that Englishmen tended to call them "black" and let further refinements go by the board. Blackness became so generally associated with Africa that every African seemed a black man. In Shakespeare's day, the Moors, including Othello, were commonly portrayed as pitchy black and the terms *Moor* and *Negro* used almost interchangeably.[5] With curious inconsistency, however, Englishmen recognized that Africans

south of the Sahara were not at all the same people as the much
more familiar Moors.[6] Sometimes they referred to Negroes as
"black Moors" to distinguish them from the peoples of North
Africa. During the seventeenth century the distinction became
more firmly established and indeed writers came to stress the
difference in color, partly because they delighted in correcting their
predecessors and partly because Negroes were being taken up as
slaves and Moors, increasingly, were not. In the more detailed and
accurate reports about West Africa of the seventeenth century,
moreover, Negroes in different regions were described as varying
considerably in complexion. In England, however, the initial impression of Negroes was not appreciably modified: the firmest fact
about the Negro was that he was "black."

The powerful impact which the Negro's color made upon Englishmen must have been partly owing to suddenness of contact.
Though the Bible as well as the arts and literature of antiquity and
the Middle Ages offered some slight introduction to the "Ethiope,"
England's immediate acquaintance with black-skinned peoples
came with relative rapidity. While the virtual monopoly held by
Venetian ships in England's foreign trade prior to the sixteenth
century meant that people much darker than Englishmen were not
entirely unfamiliar, really black men were virtually unknown
except as vaguely referred to in the hazy literature about the sub-
Sahara which had filtered down from antiquity. Native West
Africans probably first appeared in London in 1554; in that year
five "Negroes," as the legitimate trader William Towrson reported,
were taken to England, "kept till they could speake the language,"
and then brought back again "to be a helpe to Englishmen" who
were engaged in trade with Negroes on the coast. Hakluyt's later
discussion of these Negroes, who he said "could wel agree with our
meates and drinkes" though "the colde and moyst aire doth
somewhat offend them," suggests that these "blacke Moores" were
a novelty to Englishmen.[7] In this respect the English experience
was markedly different from that of the Spanish and Portuguese,
who for centuries had been in close contact with North Africa and
had actually been invaded and subjected by people both darker
and more highly civilized than themselves. The impact of the
Negro's color was the more powerful upon Englishmen, moreover,

because England's principal contact with Africans came in West Africa and the Congo, where men were not merely dark but almost literally black: one of the fairest-skinned nations suddenly came face to face with one of the darkest peoples on earth.

Viewed from one standpoint, Englishmen were merely participating in Europe's discovery that the strange men who stood revealed by European expansion overseas came in an astounding variety of colors. A Spanish chronicle translated into English in 1555 was filled with wonder at this diversity: "One of the marveylous thynges that god useth in the composition of man, is coloure: whiche doubtlesse can not bee consydered withowte great admiration in beholding one to be white and an other blacke, beinge coloures utterlye contrary. Sum lykewyse to be yelowe whiche is betwene blacke and white: and other of other colours as it were of dyvers liveres."[8] As this passage suggests, the juxtaposition of black and white was the most striking marvel of all. And for Englishmen this juxtaposition was more than a curiosity.

In England perhaps more than in southern Europe, the concept of blackness was loaded with intense meaning. Long before they found that some men were black, Englishmen found in the idea of blackness a way of expressing some of their most ingrained values. No other color except white conveyed so much emotional impact. As described by the *Oxford English Dictionary,* the meaning of *black* before the sixteenth century included, "Deeply stained with dirt; soiled, dirty, foul. . . . Having dark or deadly purposes, malignant; pertaining to or involving death, deadly; baneful, disastrous, sinister. . . . Foul, iniquitous, atrocious, horrible, wicked. . . . Indicating disgrace, censure, liability to punishment, etc." Black was an emotionally partisan color, the handmaid and symbol of baseness and evil, a sign of danger and repulsion.

Embedded in the concept of blackness was its direct opposite—whiteness. No other colors so clearly implied opposition, "beinge coloures utterlye contrary"; no others were so frequently used to denote polarization:

> Everye white will have its blacke,
> And everye sweete its sowre.[9]

White and black connoted purity and filthiness, virginity and sin,
virtue and baseness, beauty and ugliness, beneficence and evil,
God and the devil.[10]

Whiteness, moreover, carried a special significance for Elizabethan Englishmen: it was, particularly when complemented by
red, the color of perfect human beauty, especially *female* beauty.
This ideal was already centuries old in Elizabeth's time,[11] and
their fair Queen was its very embodiment: her cheeks were "roses
in a bed of lillies." (Elizabeth was naturally pale but like many
ladies then and since she freshened her "lillies" at the cosmetic
table.)[12] An adoring nation knew precisely what a beautiful
Queen looked like.

> Her cheeke, her chinne, her neck, her nose,
> This was a lillye, that was a rose;
> Her hande so white as whales bone,
> Her finger tipt with Cassidone;
> Her bosome, sleeke as Paris plaster,
> Held upp twoo bowles of Alabaster.[13]

Shakespeare himself found the lily and the rose a compelling
natural coalition.

> 'Tis beauty truly blent, whose red and white
> Nature's own sweet and cunning hand laid on.[14]

By contrast, the Negro was ugly, by reason of his color and also
his "horrid Curles" and "disfigured" lips and nose.[15] As Shakespeare wrote apologetically of his black mistress,

> My mistress' eyes are nothing like the sun;
> Coral is far more red than her lips' red:
> If snow be white, why then her breasts are dun;
> If hairs be wires, black wires grow on her head.
> I have seen roses damask'd, red and white,
> But no such roses see I in her cheeks.[16]

Some Elizabethans found blackness an ugly mask, superficial but
always demanding attention.

> Is *Byrrha* browne? Who doth the question aske?
> Her face is pure as Ebonie jeat blacke,
> It's hard to know her face from her faire maske,

> Beautie in her seemes beautie still to lacke.
> Nay, she's snow-white, but for that russet skin,
> Which like a vaile doth keep her whitenes in.[17]

A century later blackness still required apology and mitigation: one of the earliest attempts to delineate the West African Negro as a heroic character, Aphra Behn's popular story *Oroonoko* (1688), presented Negroes as capable of blushing and turning pale.[18] It was important, if incalculably so, that English discovery of black Africans came at a time when the accepted standard of ideal beauty was a fair complexion of rose and white. Negroes not only failed to fit this ideal but seemed the very picture of perverse negation.[19]

From the first, however, many English observers displayed a certain sophistication about the Negro's color. Despite an ethnocentric tendency to find blackness repulsive, many writers were fully aware that Negroes themselves might have different tastes. As early as 1621 one writer told of the "Jetty coloured" Negroes, "Who in their native beauty most delight,/And in contempt doe paint the Divell white"; this assertion became almost a commonplace and even turned up a hundred and fifty years later in Newport, Rhode Island.[20] Many accounts of Africa reported explicitly that the Negro's perference in colors was inverse to the European's.[21] Even the Negro's features were conceded to be appealing to Negroes. By the late seventeenth century, in a changing social atmosphere, some observers decided that the Negro's jet blackness was more handsome than the lighter tawny hues; this budding appreciativeness was usually coupled, though, with expressions of distaste for "Large Breasts, thick Lips, and broad Nostrils" which many Negroes "reckon'd the Beauties of the Country."[22] As one traveler admiringly described an African queen, "She was indifferently tall and well shap'd, of a perfect black; had not big Lips nor was she flat Nos'd as most of the Natives are, but well featur'd and very comely."[23] By this time, the development of the slave trade to America was beginning to transform the Negro's color from a marvel into an issue. In what was surely a remarkable complaint for the master of a slaving vessel, Captain Thomas Phillips wrote in 1694 that he could not "imagine why they should be despis'd for their colour, being what they cannot help, and the effect of the climate it has pleas'd God to appoint them. I can't think there is any intrinsick value in one colour more than another, nor that white is better than black, only we think it so because we are so, and are prone to judge favourably in our own case, as well as the blacks, who in odium of the colour, say, the devil is white, and so paint him."[24] During the eighteenth century the Negro's color was to come into service as an argument for "diversitarian" theories of beauty;[25] Europe's discovery of "blacks" and "tawnies" overseas helped nurture a novel relativism. More important so far as the Negro was concerned, his color was to remain for centuries what it had been from the first, a standing problem for natural philosophers. . . .

Unthinking Decision

The Necessities of a New World

When Englishmen crossed the Atlantic to settle in America, they were immediately subject to novel strains. In some settlements, notably Jamestown and Plymouth, the survival of the community was in question. An appalling proportion of people were dead within a year, from malnutrition, starvation, unconquerable diseases, bitter cold, oppressive heat, Indian attacks, murder, and suicide. The survivors were isolated from the world as they had known it, cut off from friends and family and the familiar sights and sounds and smells which have always told men who and where they are. A similar sense of isolation and disorientation was inevitable even in the settlements that did not suffer through a starving time. English settlers were surrounded by savages. They had to perform a round of daily tasks to which most were unaccustomed. They had undergone the shock of detachment from home in order to set forth upon a dangerous voyage of from ten to thirteen weeks that ranged from unpleasant to fatal and that seared into every passenger's memory the ceaselessly tossing distance that separated him from his old way of life.[1]

Life in America put great pressure upon the traditional social and economic controls that Englishmen assumed were to be exercised by civil and often ecclesiastical authority. Somehow the empty woods seemed to lead much more toward license than restraint. At the same time, by reaction, this unfettering resulted in an almost pathetic social conservatism, a yearning for the forms and symbols of the old familiar social order. When in 1618, for example, the Virginia Company wangled a knighthood for a newly appointed governor of the colony the objection from the settlers was not that this artificial elevation was inappropriate to wilderness conditions but that it did not go far enough to meet them; several planters petitioned that a governor of higher rank be sent, since some settlers had "only Reverence of the Comanders Eminence, or Nobillitye (whereunto by Nature everye man subordinate is ready to yeild a willing submission without contempt, or repyning)."[2] English social forms were transplanted to America not simply because they were nice to have around but because without them the new settlements would have fallen apart and English settlers would have become men of the forest, savage men devoid of civilization.

For the same reason, the communal goals that animated the settlement of the colonies acquired great functional importance in the wilderness; they served as antidotes to social and individual disintegration. The physical hardships of settlement could never have been surmounted without the stiffened nerve and will engendered by commonly recognized if sometimes unarticulated purposes. In New England lack of articulation was no problem. The Puritans knew precisely who they were (the chosen of God, many of them) and that they were seeking to erect a Godly community. Though that community (eventually) eluded them, they retained their conviction that they manned a significant outpost of English civilization. As Cotton Mather grandly told the Massachusetts governor and General Court in 1700, "It is no Little Blessing of God, that we are a part of the *English nation*."[3] A similar deep sense of self-transplantation buttressed the settlements in Virginia and Maryland. While there was less talk than in New England about God's special endorsement, virtually every settler knew that Englishmen were serving His greater glory by removing to Virginia and by making a prosperous success of the project. They recognized also that their efforts at western planting aggrandized English wealth and power and the cause of reformed

Christianity. As Richard Hakluyt summarized these purposes, "This enterprise may staye the spanishe kinge ["the supporter of the greate Antechriste of Rome"] from flowinge over all the face of that waste firme of America, yf wee seate and plante there in time."[4] For Englishmen planting in America, then, it was of the utmost importance to know that they were Englishmen, which was to say that they were educated (to a degree suitable to their station), Christian (of an appropriate Protestant variety), civilized, and (again to an appropriate degree) free men.

It was with personal freedom, of course, that wilderness conditions most suddenly reshaped English laws, assumptions, and practices. In America land was plentiful, labor scarce, and, as in all new colonies, a cash crop desperately needed. These economic conditions were to remain important for centuries; in general they tended to encourage greater geographical mobility, less specialization, higher rewards, and fewer restraints on the processes and products of labor. Supporting traditional assumptions and practices, however, was the need to retain them simply because they were familiar and because they served the vital function of maintaining and advancing orderly settlement. Throughout the seventeenth century there were pressures on traditional practices which similarly told in opposite directions.

In general men who invested capital in agriculture in America came under fewer customary and legal restraints than in England concerning what they did with their land and with the people who worked on it. On the other hand their activities were constrained by the economic necessity of producing cash crops for export, which narrowed their choice of how they could treat it. Men without capital could obtain land relatively easily: hence the shortage of labor and the notably blurred line between men who had capital and men who did not. Men and women in England faced a different situation. A significant amount of capital was required in order to get to America, and the greatest barrier to material advancement in America was the Atlantic Ocean.

Three major systems of labor emerged amid the interplay of these social and economic conditions in America. One, which was present from the beginning, was free wage labor, in which contractual arrangements rested upon a monetary nexus. Another, which was the last to appear, was chattel slavery, in which there were no contractual arrangements (except among owners). The third, which virtually coincided with first settlement in America, was temporary servitude, in which complex contractual arrangements gave shape to the entire system. It was this third system, indentured servitude, which permitted so many English settlers to cross the Atlantic barrier. Indentured servitude was linked to the development of chattel slavery in America, and its operation deserves closer examination.

A very sizable proportion of settlers in the English colonies came as indentured servants bound by contract to serve a master for a specified number of years, usually from four to seven or until age twenty-one, as repayment for their ocean passage. The time of service to which the servant bound himself was negotiable property, and he might be sold or conveyed from one master to another at any time up to the expiration of his indenture, at which point he became a free man. (Actually it was his *labor* which was owned and sold, not his *person,* though this distinction was neither important nor obvious at the time.) Custom and statute law regulated the relationship between servant and master. Obligation was reciprocal: the master undertook to feed and clothe and sometimes to educate his servant and to refrain from abusing him, while the servant was obliged to perform such work as his master set him and to obey his master in all things. This typical pattern, with a multitude of variations, was firmly established by mid-seventeenth century. In Virginia and Maryland, both the legal and actual conditions of servants seem to have improved considerably from the early years when servants had often been outrageously abused and sometimes forced to serve long terms. Beginning about 1640 the legislative assemblies of the two colonies passed numerous acts prescribing maximum terms of service and requiring masters to pay the customary "freedom dues" (clothing, provisions, and so forth) at the end of the servant's time.[5] This legislation may have been actuated partly by the need to attract more immigrants with guarantees of good treatment, in which case underpopulation in relation to level of technology and to natural resources in the English colonies may be said to have made for greater personal freedom. On the other hand, it may also have been a matter of protecting traditional freedoms threatened by this same fact of underpopulation which generated so powerful a need for labor which would not be transient and temporary. In this instance, very clearly, the imperatives enjoined by settlement in the wilderness interacted with previously acquired ideas concerning personal freedom. Indeed without some inquiry into Elizabethan thinking on that subject, it will remain impossible to comprehend why Englishmen became servants in the plantations, and Negroes slaves. . . .

Enslavement: Virginia and Maryland

In Virginia and Maryland . . . geographic conditions and the intentions of the settlers quickly combined to produce a successful agricultural staple. The deep tidal rivers, the long growing season, the fertile soil, and the absence of strong communal spirit among the settlers opened the way. Ten years after settlers first landed at Jamestown they were on the way to proving, in the face of assertions to the contrary, that it was possible "to found an empire upon smoke." More than the miscellaneous productions of New England, tobacco required labor which was cheap but not temporary, mobile but not independent, and tireless rather than skilled. In the Chesapeake area more than anywhere to the northward, the shortage of labor and the abundance of land—the "frontier"— placed a premium on involuntary labor.

This need for labor played more directly upon these settlers' ideas about freedom and bondage than it did either in the West Indies or in New England. Perhaps it would be more accurate to say that settlers in Virginia (and in Maryland after settlement in 1634) made their decisions concerning Negroes while relatively virginal, relatively free from external influences and from firm preconceptions. Of all the important early English settlements, Virginia had the least contact with the Spanish, Portuguese, Dutch, and other English colonies. At the same time, the settlers of Virginia did not possess either the legal or Scriptural learning of the New England Puritans, whose conception of the just war had opened the way to the enslavement of Indians. Slavery in the tobacco colonies did not begin as an adjunct of captivity; in marked contrast to the Puritan response to the Pequot War the settlers of Virginia did *not* generally react to the Indian massacre of 1622 with propositions for taking captives and selling them as "slaves." It was perhaps a correct measure of the conceptual atmosphere in Virginia that there was only one such proposition after the 1622 disaster and that one was defective in precision as to how exactly one treated captive Indians.[6]

In the absence, then, of these influences which obtained in other English colonies, slavery as it developed in Virginia and Maryland assumes a special interest and importance over and above the fact that Negro slavery was to become a vitally important institution there and, later, to the southwards. In the tobacco colonies it is possible to watch Negro slavery *develop,* not pop up full-grown overnight, and it is therefore possible to trace, very imperfectly, the development of the shadowy, unexamined rationale which supported it. The concept of Negro slavery there was neither borrowed from foreigners, nor extracted from books, nor invented out of whole cloth, nor extrapolated from servitude, nor generated by English reaction to Negroes as such, nor necessitated by the exigencies of the New World. Not any one of these made the Negro a slave, but all.

In rough outline, slavery's development in the tobacco colonies seems to have undergone three stages. Negroes first arrived in 1619, only a few days late for the meeting of the first representative assembly in America. John Rolfe described the event with the utmost unconcern: "About the last of August came in a dutch man of warre that sold us twenty Negars."[7] Negroes continued to trickle in slowly for the next half century; one report in 1649 estimated that there were three hundred among Virginia's population of fifteen thousand—about 2 per cent.[8] Long before there were more appreciable numbers, the development of slavery had, so far as we can tell, shifted gears. Prior to about 1640, there is very little evidence to show how Negroes were treated—though we will need to return to those first twenty years in a moment. After 1640 there is mounting evidence that some Negroes were in fact being treated as slaves, at least that they were being held in hereditary lifetime service. This is to say that the twin essences of slavery— the two kinds of perpetuity—first become evident during the twenty years prior to the beginning of legal formulation. After 1660 slavery was written into statute law. Negroes began to flood into the two colonies at the end of the seventeenth century. In 1705 Virginia produced a codification of laws applying to slaves.

Concerning the first of these stages, there is only one major historical certainty, and unfortunately it is the sort which historians find hardest to bear. There simply is not enough evidence to indicate with any certainty whether Negroes were treated like white servants or not. At least we can be confident, therefore, that the two most common assertions about the first Negroes—that they were slaves and that they were servants—are *unfounded,* though not necessarily incorrect. And what of the positive evidence?

Some of the first group bore Spanish names and presumably had been baptized, which would mean they were at least nominally Christian, though of the Papist sort. They had been "sold" to the English; so had other Englishmen but not by the Dutch. Certainly these Negroes were not fully free, but many Englishmen were not. It can be said, though, that from the first in Virginia Negroes were set apart from white men by the word *Negroes.* The earliest Virginia census reports plainly distinguished Negroes from white men, often giving Negroes no personal name; in 1629 every commander of the several plantations was ordered to "take a generall muster of all the inhabitants men woemen and Children as well *Englishe* as Negroes."[9] A distinct name is not attached to a group unless it is regarded as distinct. It seems logical to suppose that this perception of the Negro as being distinct from the Englishman must have operated to debase his status rather than to raise it, for in the absence of countervailing social factors, the need for labor in the colonies usually told in the direction of nonfreedom. There were few countervailing factors present, surely, in such instances as in 1629 when a group of Negroes were brought to Virginia freshly captured from a Portuguese vessel which had snatched them from Angola a few weeks earlier.[10] Given the context of English thought and experience sketched in this chapter, it seems probable that the Negro's status was not ever the same as that accorded the white servant. But we do not know for sure.

When the first fragmentary evidence appears about 1640 it becomes clear that *some* Negroes in both Virginia and Maryland were serving for life and some Negro children inheriting the same obligation.[11] Not all Negroes, certainly, for Nathaniel Littleton had released a Negro named Anthony Longoe from all service whatsoever in 1635, and after the mid-1640's the court records show that other Negroes were incontestably free and were accumulating property of their own. At least one Negro freeman, Anthony Johnson, himself owned a Negro. Some Negroes served only terms of usual length, but others were held for terms far longer than custom and statute permitted with white servants.[12] The first fairly clear indication that slavery was practiced in the tobacco colonies appears in 1639, when a Maryland statute declared that "all the Inhabitants of this Province being Christians (Slaves excepted) Shall have and enjoy all such rights liberties immunities priviledges and free customs within this Province as any naturall born subject of England." Another Maryland law passed the same year provided that "all persons being Christians (Slaves excepted)" over eighteen who were imported without indentures would serve for four years.[13] These laws make very little sense unless the term *slaves* meant Negroes and perhaps Indians.

The next year, 1640, the first definite indication of outright enslavement appears in Virginia. The General Court pronounced sentence on three servants who had been retaken after absconding to Maryland. Two of them, a Dutchman and a Scot, were ordered to serve their masters for one additional year and then the colony for three more, but "the third being a negro named John Punch shall serve his said master or his assigns for the time of his natural life here or else where." No white servant in any English colony, so far as is known, ever received a like sentence. Later the same month a Negro (possibly the same enterprising fellow) was again singled out from a group of recaptured runaways; six of the seven culprits were assigned additional time while the Negro was given none, presumably because he was already serving for life.[14]

After 1640, when surviving Virginia county court records began to mention Negroes, sales for life, often including any future progeny, were recorded in unmistakable language. In 1646 Francis Pott sold a Negro woman and boy to Stephen Charlton "to the use of him . . . forever." Similarly, six years later William Whittington sold to John Pott "one Negro girle named Jowan; aged about Ten yeares and with her Issue and produce duringe her (or either

of them) for their Life tyme. And their Successors forever"; and a
Maryland man in 1649 deeded two Negro men and a woman "and
all their issue both male and Female." The executors of a York
County estate in 1647 disposed of eight Negroes—four men, two
women, and two children—to Captain John Chisman "to have
hold occupy posesse and injoy and every one of the afforemen-
tioned Negroes forever."[15] The will of Rowland Burnham of
"Rapahanocke," made in 1657, dispensed his considerable number of Negroes and white servants in language which clearly
differentiated between the two by specifying that the whites were to
serve for their "full terme of tyme" and the Negroes "for ever."[16]
Nothing in the will indicated that this distinction was exceptional
or novel.

Further evidence that some Negroes were serving for life in this
period lies in the prices paid for them. In many instances the
valuations placed on Negroes (in estate inventories and bills of
sale) were far higher than for white servants, even those servants
with full terms yet to serve. Higher prices must have meant that
Negroes were more highly valued because of their greater length of
service. Negro women may have been especially prized, moreover,
because their progeny could also be held perpetually. In 1643, for
example, William Burdett's inventory listed eight servants, with the
time each had still to serve, at valuations ranging from 400 to
1,100 pounds of tobacco, while a "very anntient" Negro was
valued at 3,000 and an eight-year-old Negro girl at 2,000 pounds,
with no time remaining indicated for either. In the late 1650's an
inventory of Thomas Ludlow's estate evaluated a white servant
with six years to serve at less than an elderly Negro man and only
one half of a Negro woman.[17] Similarly, the labor owned by
James Stone in 1648 was evaluated as follows:

	lb tobo
Thomas Groves, 4 yeares to serve	1300
Francis Bomley for 6 yeares	1500
John Thackstone for 3 yeares	1300
Susan Davis for 3 yeares	1000
Emaniell a Negro man	2000
Roger Stone 3 yeares	1300
Mingo a Negro man	2000[18]

The 1655 inventory of Argoll Yeardley's estate provides clear evidence of a distinction between perpetual and limited service for Negroes. Under the heading "Servants" were listed "Towe Negro men, towe Negro women (their wifes) one Negro girle aged 15 yeares, Item One Negro girle aged about teen yeares and one Negro child aged about sixe moneths," valued at 12,000 pounds, and under the heading "Corne" were "Servants, towe men their tyme three months," valued at 300 pounds, and "one Negro boye ["about three yeares old"] (which by witness of his godfather) is to bee free att twenty foure yeares of age and then to have towe cowes given him," valued at 600 pounds.[19] Besides setting a higher value on Negroes, these inventories failed to indicate the number of years they had still to serve, presumably because their service was for an unlimited time.

Where Negro women were involved, higher valuations probably reflected the facts that their issue were valuable and that they could be used for field work while white women generally were not. This latter discrimination between Negro and white women did not necessarily involve perpetual service, but it meant that Negroes were set apart in a way clearly not to their advantage. This was not the only instance in which Negroes were subjected to degrading distinctions not immediately and necessarily attached to the concept of slavery. Negroes were singled out for special treatment in several ways which suggest a generalized debasement of Negroes as a group. Significantly, the first indications of this debasement appeared at about the same time as the first indications of actual enslavement.

The distinction concerning field work is a case in point. It first appears on the written record in 1643, when Virginia almost pointedly endorsed it in a tax law. Previously, in 1629, tithable persons had been defined as "all those that worke in the ground of what qualitie or condition soever." The new law provided that *all* adult men were tithable and, in addition, *Negro* women. The same distinction was made twice again before 1660. Maryland adopted a similar policy beginning in 1654.[20] This official discrimination between Negro and other women was made by men who were accustomed to thinking of field work as being ordinarily the work of men rather than women. As John Hammond wrote in a 1656 tract defending the tobacco colonies, servant women were not put to work in the fields but in domestic employments, "yet som wenches that are nasty, and beastly and not fit to be so employed are put into the ground."[21] The essentially racial character of this discrimination stood out clearly in a law passed in 1668 at the time slavery was taking shape in the statute books:

Whereas some doubts, have arisen whether negro women set free were still to be accompted tithable according to a former act, *It is declared by this grand assembly* that negro women, though permitted to enjoy their Freedome yet ought not in all respects to be admitted to a full fruition of the exemptions and impunities of the English, and are still lyable to payment of taxes.[22]

Virginia law set Negroes apart from all other groups in a second way by denying them the important right and obligation to bear arms. Few restraints could indicate more clearly the denial to Negroes of membership in the white community. This first foreshadowing of the slave codes came in 1640, at just the time when other indications first appeared that Negroes were subject to special treatment.[23]

Finally, an even more compelling sense of the separateness of Negroes was revealed in early reactions to sexual union between the races. Prior to 1660 the evidence concerning these reactions is equivocal, and it is not possible to tell whether repugnance for intermixture preceded legislative enactment of slavery. In 1630 an angry Virginia court sentenced "Hugh Davis to be soundly whipped, before an assembly of Negroes and others for abusing himself to the dishonor of God and shame of Christians, by defiling his body in lying with a negro," but it is possible that the "negro" may not have been female. With other instances of punishment for interracial union in the ensuing years, fornication rather than miscegenation may well have been the primary offense, though in 1651 a Maryland man sued someone who he claimed had said "that he had a black bastard in Virginia." (The court recognized the legitimacy of his complaint, but thought his claim for £20,000 sterling somewhat overvalued his reputation and awarded him 1500 pounds "of Tobacco and Cask.")[24] There may have been no racial feeling involved when in 1640 Robert Sweet, a gentleman, was compelled "to do penance in church according to laws of

England, for getting a negroe woman with child and the woman whipt."[25] About 1650 a white man and a Negro woman were required to stand clad in white sheets before a congregation in lower Norfolk County for having had relations, but this punishment was sometimes used in cases of fornication between two whites.[26] A quarter century later in 1676, however, the emergence of distaste for racial intermixture was unmistakable. A contemporary account of Bacon's Rebellion caustically described one of the ringleaders, Richard Lawrence, as a person who had eclipsed his learning and abilties "in the darke imbraces of a Blackamoore, his slave: And that in so fond a Maner, . . . to the noe meane Scandle and affrunt of all the Vottrisses in or about towne."[27]

Such condemnation was not confined to polemics. In the early 1660's when slavery was gaining statutory recognition, the assemblies acted with full-throated indignation against miscegenation. These acts aimed at more than merely avoiding confusion of status. In 1662 Virginia declared that "if any christian shall commit Fornication with a negro man or woman, hee or shee soe offending" should pay double the usual fine. (The next year Bermuda prohibited all sexual relations between whites and Negroes.) Two years later Maryland banned interracial marriages: "forasmuch as divers freeborne English women forgettfull of their free Condicion and to the disgrace of our Nation doe intermarry with Negro Slaves by which alsoe divers suites may arise touching the Issue of such woemen and a great damage doth befall the Masters of such Negros for prevention whereof for deterring such freeborne women from such shamefull Matches," strong language indeed if "divers suites" had been the only problem. A Maryland act of 1681 described marriages of white women with Negroes as, among other things, "always to the Satisfaccion of theire Lascivious and Lustfull desires, and to the disgrace not only of the English butt allso of many other Christian Nations." When Virginia finally prohibited all interracial liaisons in 1691, the Assembly vigorously denounced miscegenation and its fruits as "that abominable mixture and spurious issue."[28]

From the surviving evidence, it appears that outright enslavement and these other forms of debasement appeared at about the same time in Maryland and Virginia. Indications of perpetual service, the very nub of slavery, coincided with indications that English settlers discriminated against Negro women, withheld arms from Negroes, and—though the timing is far less certain—reacted unfavorably to interracial sexual union. The coincidence suggests a mutual relationship between slavery and unfavorable assessment of Negroes. Rather than slavery causing "prejudice," or vice versa, they seem rather to have generated each other. Both were, after all, twin aspects of a general debasement of the Negro. Slavery and "prejudice" may have been equally cause and effect, continuously reacting upon each other, dynamically joining hands to hustle the Negro down the road to complete degradation. Much more than with the other English colonies, where the enslavement of Negroes was to some extent a borrowed practice, the available evidence for Maryland and Virginia points to less borrowing and to this kind of process: a mutually interactive growth of slavery and unfavorable assessment, with no cause for either which did not cause the other as well. If slavery caused prejudice, then invidious distinctions concerning working the fields, bearing arms, and sexual union should have appeared *after* slavery's firm establishment. If prejudice caused slavery, then one would expect to find these lesser discriminations preceding the greater discrimination of outright enslavement. Taken as a whole, the evidence reveals a process of debasement of which hereditary lifetime service was an important but not the only part.

White servants did not suffer this debasement. Rather, their position improved, partly for the reason that they were not Negroes. By the early 1660's white men were loudly protesting against being made "slaves" in terms which strongly suggest that they considered slavery not as wrong but as inapplicable to themselves. The father of a Maryland apprentice petitioned in 1663 that "he Craves that his daughter may not be made a Slave a tearme soe Scandalous that if admitted to be the Condicon or tytle of the Apprentices in this Province will be soe distructive as noe free borne Christians will ever be induced to come over servants."[29] An Irish youth complained to a Maryland court in 1661 that he had been kidnapped and forced to sign for fifteen years, that he had already served six and a half years and was now twenty-one, and that eight and a half more years of service was "contrary to the lawes of God and man that a Christian Subject should be made a Slave." (The jury blandly compromised the dispute by deciding that he should serve only until age twenty-one, but that he was now only nineteen.) Free Negro servants were generally increasingly less able to defend themselves against this insidious kind of encroachment.[30] Increasingly, white men were more clearly free because Negroes had become so clearly slave.

Certainly it was the case in Maryland and Virginia that the legal enactment of Negro slavery followed social practice, rather than vice versa, and also that the assemblies were slower than in other English colonies to declare how Negroes could or should be treated. These two patterns in themselves suggest that slavery was less a matter of previous conception or external example in Maryland and Virginia than elsewhere.

The Virginia Assembly first showed itself incontrovertibly aware that Negroes were not serving in the same manner as English servants in 1660 when it declared "that for the future no servant comeing into the country without indentures, of what christian nation soever, shall serve longer then those of our own country, of the like age." In 1661 the Assembly indirectly provided statutory recognition that some Negroes served for life: "That in case any English servant shall run away in company with any negroes who are incapable of makeing satisfaction by addition of time," he must serve for the Negroes' lost time as well as his own. Maryland enacted a closely similar law in 1663 (possibly modeled on Virginia's) and in the following year, on the initiative of the lower house, came out with the categorical declaration that Negroes were to serve "Durante Vita."[31] During the next twenty-odd years a succession of acts in both colonies defined with increasing precision what sorts of persons might be treated as slaves.[32] Other acts dealt with the growing problem of slave control, and especially after 1690 slavery began to assume its now familiar character as a complete deprivation of all rights.[33] As early as 1669 the Virginia Assembly unabashedly enacted a brutal law which showed where the logic of perpetual servitude was inevitably tending. Unruly servants could be chastened by sentences to additional terms, but "WHEREAS the only law in force for the punishment of refractory servants resisting their master, mistris or overseer cannot be inflicted upon negroes, nor the obstinacy of many of them by other then violent meanes supprest," if a slave "by the extremity of the correction should chance to die" his master was not to be adjudged guilty of felony "since it cannot be presumed that prepensed malice (which alone makes murther Felony) should induce any man to destroy his owne estate."[34] Virginia planters felt they acted out of mounting necessity: there were disturbances among slaves in several areas in the early 1670's.[35]

By about 1700 the slave ships began spilling forth their black cargoes in greater and greater numbers. By that time, racial slavery and the necessary police powers had been written into law. By that time, too, slavery had lost all resemblance to a perpetual and hereditary version of English servitude, though service for life still seemed to contemporaries its most essential feature.[36] In the last quarter of the seventeenth century the trend was to treat Negroes more like property and less like men, to send them to the fields at younger ages, to deny them automatic existence as inherent members of the community, to tighten the bonds on their personal and civil freedom, and correspondingly to loosen the traditional restraints on the master's freedom to deal with his human property as he saw fit.[37] In 1705 Virginia gathered up the random statutes of a whole generation and baled them into a "slave code" which would not have been out of place in the nineteenth century.[38]

4. Two Views of Slave Culture

For the approximately half-million blacks in this country in 1776, the promise of the American Revolution was only partially fulfilled. For the first time in American history, slavery became the subject of intense public scrutiny, and Americans of all sections of the nation freely acknowledged the contradiction between their rhetoric of liberty and equality, and the black man's bondage. Between 1777 and 1804 every northern state provided for the abolition of slavery, either by court decision or gradual emancipation laws. But while Jefferson, Washington, Henry, and many other southern statesmen spoke out on the iniquities of slavery, no southern state came close to abolishing the institution. Nor did the Constitutional Convention act, for the founders were too reluctant to disturb rights of property, too uncertain that the races could live in harmony if the blacks were freed, and too concerned with avoiding divisive issues which might imperil the unity of the new nation. The bloody revolution in Haiti in the 1790's stimulated fears about the conduct of freed blacks, and when Virginia in 1806 decreed that all manumitted slaves must leave the state within one year, it symbolized the end of the revolutionary impulse so far as blacks were concerned.

Slavery thus survived the American Revolution, but the institution underwent profound changes in the first part of the nineteenth century. Foremost among these was the westward expansion of the slave system and the rise of the cotton kingdom. With the acceleration of the industrial revolution in England the textile industry felt the full impact of steam power and factory production. As a result British textile mills demanded an ever-increasing supply of cotton. Eli Whitney's invention in 1793 of the cotton gin—a device for separating the cotton seed from the plant's fiber—made possible a tremendous expansion of cotton production and inaugurated a revolution in the slave system. Slaveholders and their slaves poured into the virgin territories of the Southwest, particularly the fertile land known as the Black Belt. The Southwest supplanted the older eastern states as the center of the plantation system, and states like Virginia increasingly became supply areas, shipping slaves to the Lower South. By the 1850's southerners seemed to have every justification for claiming that cotton was king. Three-fourths of the world's cotton supply came from the United States, mostly from the large-scale plantations of the Deep South, and cotton supplied the nation with the bulk of the foreign capital necessary for internal improvements and industrial development. Statistically the planters comprised but a small portion of the southern white population, the majority of whom owned no slaves at all. Yet, as Frederick Douglass wrote, the plantation was "a little nation by itself, having its own language, its own rules, regulations and customs." He might have added that these rules and customs set the style of life and value system for all of southern society.

Slavery began as a system of labor, and labor was the activity which occupied most of the time of the slaves. The plantation was a diversified community, and slaves performed all kinds of work. Among the 125 slaves on one typical plantation, for instance, were a butler, two waitresses, a nurse, a dairymaid, a gardener, two carpenters and two shoemakers. Slaves also worked in southern industry, especially ironworks and tobacco factories in the

Upper South, and in southern cities they were often employed as skilled craftsmen and artisans. For most slaves, however, labor meant work in the fields. On the typical rice, sugar, or cotton plantation working hours stretched from sun-up to dusk. Slaves were usually worked in either the gang system, in which a white overseer and one or two black drivers supervised a large group of laborers, or the task system, in which each hand was given a specific amount of work for the day and could retire when his job was completed. Overseers had a reputation, which was probably overdrawn, for treating slaves harshly, because their salary and reputation often depended upon the size of the crops produced and, unlike the planters, they had no economic stake in the well-being of the slaves. "The requisite qualifications for an overseer," wrote Solomon Northrup, a New York free black who was kidnaped and held in slavery in Louisiana for twelve years, "are utter heartlessness, brutality, and cruelty. It is his business to produce large crops, no matter what amount of suffering it may have cost."

Before the law, slaves were property. They had few legal rights, and could be sold or leased by their owners at will. Slave marriages had no legal standing, and one of the commonest scenes in the reminiscences of fugitive slaves is the auction at which grieving mothers are separated from their children. On the other hand, the slave codes do not give a full picture of plantation life, for many planters were quite lax in enforcing the law. Despite legal prohibitions, slaves sometimes learned to read and write, left their plantations without permission, and were allowed to cultivate small gardens and sell the produce, keeping the money for themselves. Legally, masters could punish slaves at will, but most historians agree that severe whippings were the exception rather than the rule. On the other hand, hardly any slave could expect to go through his life without gaining an acquaintance with the lash. Yet such punishment was only one of many means of controlling the slave population. Masters encouraged and exploited divisions among the slaves themselves, particularly animosities between privileged house servants and the field hands, and they skillfully used incentives like extra payments for good work, added time off, or petty privileges, to encourage loyalty.

The plantation system, the attitudes and conduct of the slaveholders, and legal and extralegal mechanisms of control have all been the subject of investigation by historians for many years. The life and culture of the slaves, however, is far more elusive. Because of the absence of traditional historical evidence like letters, speeches, and newspaper accounts, some historians have concluded that the life of the slaves is an "unrecorded experience." The records historians have traditionally utilized—plantation journals, reports by travelers, census returns, and the like—have yielded interesting facts about slave life, but all were written from the masters' point of view. Yet recently historians have shown that it is possible to use new kinds of evidence to gain insight into the effect of slavery on the life and culture of the slaves. In 1959, Stanley Elkins published his highly influential book, *Slavery,* which marked a turning point in the historiography of the subject. Elkins broke from the controversies which had engaged previous historians, such as whether masters were kind or cruel, and how well slaves were treated, and attempted to evaluate the effect of slavery on slave personality. He began by defining slavery in the United States as a system of "absolute power." In Latin America, he argued, the Church, royal officials, and feudal laws had limited the power of the slaveholder over his slave, and given the slave a set of authorities to whom he could appeal to protect certain basic rights. In the United States, on the other hand, the master's control of the slave was absolute. In perhaps the most controversial portion of his book, Elkins turned to the experiences of the German concentration camps during the Second World War to assess the adjustment of men to conditions of absolute power. He discovered that in situations where men are totally dependent on a single authority, they react not by rebellion but by identifying with this authority. In the concentration camps the result was an almost complete submissiveness on the part of the inmates; in American slavery, the slave became a Sambo, an irresponsible, docile child who accepted the value system and culture of his masters.

Elkins' book opened a new era in slavery interpretation, but his opinions have hardly gone unchallenged. Many critics have argued that Elkins greatly overstated the differences between Latin American and United States slavery and that he exaggerated the absolute character of the masters' power in this country. Others insist that the slaves may have acted the role of Sambo because they knew this was expected of them, but that their outward mask did not reveal their inner feelings. One of Elkins' recent critics is Sterling Stuckey, author of the article "Through the Prism of Folklore: The Black Ethos in Slavery." Stuckey insists that the slaves were able to fashion an autonomous culture and community with its own life style and set of values, and that this prevented the total infantilization which Elkins describes. Like Elkins, Stuckey makes use of new kinds of evidence, particularly folklore and slave songs and spirituals, which show that many slaves were quite conscious of exploitation and oppression and were hardly content with their lot. One of his most revealing insights concerns the dual nature of slave religion. Masters taught their slaves Christianity in order to inculcate obedience, but spirituals like "Oh, Mary," "Go Down, Moses," and others indicate that some slaves identified with those Biblical heroes who had challenged slavery in ancient times. The fugitive slave Charles Ball wrote after his escape that "the idea of a revolution in the conditions of the whites and the blacks" was "the cornerstone" of black religion.

Slave culture is one of the areas of black history which cries out for new treatment. We need to know more, for example, not only about cohesion in the slave community, but also about divisions between field hands and house servants. We are still uncertain whether the slave driver was primarily an agent of the master or an intermediary who could stand up for the rights of the slaves. And we need to know to what degree the slave family, an institution which was apparently severely damaged by slavery, managed to survive at all, and to what extent the concept of family took on different dimensions under slavery.

Slavery and Personality

STANLEY ELKINS

Personality Types and Stereotypes

An examination of American slavery, checked at certain critical points against a very different slave system, that of Latin America, reveals that a major key to many of the contrasts between them was an institutional key: The presence or absence of other powerful institutions in society made an immense difference in the character of slavery itself. In Latin America, the very tension and balance among three kinds of organizational concerns—church, crown, and plantation agriculture—prevented slavery from being carried by the planting class to its ultimate logic. For the slave, in terms of the space thus allowed for the development of men and women as moral beings, the result was an "open system": a system of contacts with free society through which ultimate absorption into that society could and did occur with great frequency. The rights of personality implicit in the ancient traditions of slavery and in the church's most venerable assumptions on the nature of the human soul were thus in a vital sense conserved, whereas to a staggering extent the very opposite was true in North American slavery. The latter system had developed virtually unchecked by

FROM *Slavery* by Stanley Elkins. Copyright © 1968 by Stanley Elkins. Reprinted by permission of the University of Chicago Press.

institutions having anything like the power of their Latin counterparts; the legal structure which supported it, shaped only by the demands of a staple-raising capitalism, had defined with such nicety the slave's character as chattel that his character as a moral individual was left in the vaguest of legal obscurity. In this sense American slavery operated as a "closed" system—one in which, for the generality of slaves in their nature as men and women, *sub specie aeternitatis,* contacts with free society could occur only on the most narrowly circumscribed of terms. The next question is whether living within such a "closed system" might not have produced noticeable effects upon the slave's very personality.

The name "Sambo" has come to be synonymous with "race stereotype." Here is an automatic danger signal, warning that the analytical difficulties of asking questions about slave personality may not be nearly so great as the moral difficulties. The one inhibits the other; the morality of the matter has had a clogging effect on its theoretical development that may not be to the best interests of either. And yet theory on group personality is still in a stage rudimentary enough that this particular body of material—potentially illuminating—ought not to remain morally impounded any longer.

Is it possible to deal with "Sambo" as a type? The characteristics that have been claimed for the type come principally from Southern lore. Sambo, the typical plantation slave, was docile but irresponsible, loyal but lazy, humble but chronically given to lying and stealing; his behavior was full of infantile silliness and his talk inflated with childish exaggeration. His relationship with his master was one of utter dependence and childlike attachment: it was indeed this childlike quality that was the very key to his being. Although the merest hint of Sambo's "manhood" might fill the Southern breast with scorn, the child, "in his place," could be both exasperating and lovable.

Was he real or unreal? What order of existence, what rank of legitimacy, should be accorded him? Is there a "scientific" way to talk about this problem? For most Southerners in 1860 it went without saying not only that Sambo was real—that he was a dominant plantation type—but also that his characteristics were the clear product of racial inheritance. That was one way to deal

with Sambo, a way that persisted a good many years after 1860.
But, in recent times, the discrediting, as unscientific, of racial
explanations for any feature of plantation slavery has tended in the
case of Sambo to discredit not simply the explanation itself but
also the thing it was supposed to explain. Sambo is a mere stereotype—"stereotype" is itself a bad word, insinuating racial inferiority and invidious discrimination.[1] This modern approach to
Sambo had a strong counterpart in the way Northern reformers
thought about slavery in ante-bellum times: they thought that
nothing could actually be said about the Negro's "true" nature
because that nature was veiled by the institution of slavery. It
could only be revealed by tearing away the veil.[2] In short, no
order of reality could be given to assertions about slave character,
because those assertions were illegitimately grounded on race,
whereas their only basis was a corrupt and "unreal" institution.
"To be sure," a recent writer concedes, "there were plenty of
opportunists among the Negroes who played the role assigned to
them, acted the clown, and curried the favor of their masters in
order to win the maximum rewards within the system. . . ."[3] To
impeach Sambo's legitimacy in this way is the next thing to talking
him out of existence.

There ought, however, to be still a third way of dealing with the
Sambo picture, some formula for taking it seriously. The picture
has far too many circumstantial details, its hues have been stroked
in by too many different brushes, for it to be denounced as
counterfeit. Too much folk-knowledge, too much plantation literature, too much of the Negro's own lore, have gone into its making
to entitle one in good conscience to condemn it as "conspiracy."
One searches in vain through the literature of the Latin-American
slave systems for the "Sambo" of our tradition—the perpetual
child incapable of maturity. How is this to be explained?[4] If
Sambo is not a product of race (that "explanation" can be con-
signed to oblivion) and not simply a product of "slavery" in the
abstract (other societies have had slavery),[5] then he must be
related to our own peculiar variety of it. And if Sambo is uniquely
an American product, then his existence, and the reasons for his
character, must be recognized in order to appreciate the very scope
of our slave problem and its aftermath. The absoluteness with

which such a personality ("real" or "unreal") had been stamped upon the plantation slave does much to make plausible the ante-bellum Southerner's difficulty in imagining that blacks anywhere could be anything but a degraded race—and it goes far to explain his failure to see any sense at all in abolitionism. It even casts light on the peculiar quality of abolitionism itself; it was so all-enveloping a problem in human personality that our abolitionists could literally not afford to recognize it. Virtually without exception, they met this dilemma either by sidetracking it altogether (they explicitly refused to advance plans for solving it, arguing that this would rob their message of its moral force) or by countering it with theories of infinite human perfectibility. The question of personality, therefore, becomes a crucial phase of the entire problem of slavery in the United States, having conceivably something to do with the difference—already alluded to—between an "open" and a "closed" system of slavery. . . .

Let the above, then, be a preface to the argument of the present essay. It will be assumed that there were elements in the very structure of the plantation system—its "closed" character—that could sustain infantilism as a normal feature of behavior. These elements, having less to do with "cruelty" per se than simply with the sanctions of authority, were effective and pervasive enough to require that such infantilism be characterized as something much more basic than mere "accommodation." It will be assumed that the sanctions of the system were in themselves sufficient to produce a recognizable personality type.[6]

It should be understood that to identify a social type in this sense is still to generalize on a fairly crude level—and to insist for a limited purpose on the legitimacy of such generalizing is by no means to deny that, on more refined levels, a great profusion of individual types might have been observed in slave society. Nor need it be claimed that the "Sambo" type, even in the relatively crude sense employed here, was a universal type. It was, however, a plantation type, and a plantation existence embraced well over half the slave population.[7] Two kinds of material will be used in the effort to picture the mechanisms whereby this adjustment to absolute power—an adjustment whose end product included infantile features of behavior—may have been effected. One is drawn from the theoretical knowledge presently available in social psychology, and the other, in the form of an analogy, is derived from some of the data that have come out of the German concentration camps. It is recognized in most theory that social behavior is regulated in some general way by adjustment to symbols of authority—however diversely "authority" may be defined either in theory or in culture itself—and that such adjustment is closely related to the very formation of personality. A corollary would be, of course, that the more diverse those symbols of authority may be, the greater is the permissible variety of adjustment to them—and the wider the margin of individuality, consequently, in the development of the self. The question here has to do with the wideness or narrowness of that margin on the ante-bellum plantation.

The other body of material, involving an experience undergone by several million men and women in the concentration camps of our own time, contains certain items of relevance to the problem here being considered. the experience was analogous to that of slavery and was one in which wide-scale instances of infantilization were observed. The material is sufficiently detailed, and sufficiently documented by men who not only took part in the experience itself but who were versed in the use of psychological theory for analyzing it, that the advantages of drawing upon such data for purposes of analogy seem to outweigh the possible risks.

The introduction of this second body of material must to a certain extent govern the theoretical strategy itself. It has been recognized both implicitly and explicitly that the psychic impact and effects of the concentration-camp experience were not anticipated in existing theory and that consequently such theory would require some major supplementation. It might be added, parenthetically, that almost any published discussion of this modern Inferno, no matter how learned, demonstrates how "theory," operating at such a level of shared human experience, tends to shed much of its technical trappings and to take on an almost literary quality. The experience showed, in any event, that infantile personality features could be induced in a relatively short time among large numbers of adult human beings coming from very diverse backgrounds. . . .

These cues, accordingly, will guide the argument on Negro slavery. Several million people were detached with a peculiar effectiveness from a great variety of cultural backgrounds in Africa—a detachment operating with infinitely more effectiveness upon those brought to North America than upon those who came to Latin America. It was achieved partly by the shock experience inherent in the very mode of procurement but more specifically by the type of authority-system to which they were introduced and to which they had to adjust for physical and psychic survival. The new adjustment, to absolute power in a closed system, involved infantilization, and the detachment was so complete that little trace of prior (and thus alternative) cultural sanctions for behavior and personality remained for the descendants of the first generation. For them, adjustment to clear and omnipresent authority could be more or less automatic—as much so, or as little, as it is for anyone whose adjustment to a social system begins at birth and to whom that system represents normality. We do not know how generally a full adjustment was made by the first generation of fresh slaves from Africa. But we do know—from a modern experience—that such an adjustment is possible, not only within the same generation but within two or three years. This proved possible for people in a full state of complex civilization, for men and women who were not black and not savages. . . .

Adjustment to Absolute Power in the Concentration Camp

A certain amount of the mellowness in Ulrich Phillips' picture of ante-bellum plantation life has of necessity been discredited by recent efforts not only to refocus attention upon the brutalities of the slave system but also to dispose once and for all of Phillips' assumptions about the slave as a racially inferior being. And yet it is important—particularly in view of the analogy about to be presented—to keep in mind that for all the system's cruelties there were still clear standards of patriarchal benevolence inherent in its human side, and that such standards were recognized as those of the best Southern families. This aspect, despite the most drastic changes of emphasis, should continue to guarantee for Phillips' view more than just a modicum of legitimacy; the patriarchal quality, whatever measure of benevolence or lack of it one wants to impute to the regime, still holds a major key to its nature as a social system.

Introducing, therefore, certain elements of the German concentration-camp experience involves the risky business of trying to balance two necessities—emphasizing both the vast dissimilarities of the two regimes and the essentially limited purpose for which they are being brought together, and at the same time justifying the use of the analogy in the first place. The point is perhaps best made by insisting on an order of classification. The American plantation was not even in the metaphorical sense a "concentration camp"; nor was it even "like" a concentration camp, to the extent that any standards comparable to those governing the camps might be imputed to any sector of American society, at any time; but it should at least be permissible to turn the thing around—to speak of the concentration camp as a special and highly perverted instance of human slavery. Doing so, moreover, should actually be of some assistance in the strategy, now universally sanctioned, of demonstrating how little the products and consequences of slavery ever had to do with race. The only mass experience that Western people have had within recorded history comparable in any way with Negro slavery was undergone in the nether world of Nazism. The concentration camp was not only a perverted slave system; it was also—what is less obvious but even more to the point—a perverted patriarchy.

The system of the concentration camps was expressly devised in the 1930's by high officials of the German government to function as an instrument of terror. The first groups detained in the camps consisted of prominent enemies of the Nazi regime; later, when these had mostly been eliminated, it was still felt necessary that the system be institutionalized and made into a standing weapon of intimidation—which required a continuing flow of incoming prisoners. The categories of eligible persons were greatly widened to include all real, fancied, or "potential" opposition to the state. They were often selected on capricious and random grounds, and together they formed a cross-section of society which was virtually complete: criminals, workers, businessmen, professional people, middle-class Jews, even members of the aristocracy. The teeming camps thus held all kinds—not only the scum of the underworld but also countless men and women of culture and refinement. During the war a specialized objective was added, that of exterminating the Jewish populations of subject countries, which required special mass-production methods of which the gas chambers and crematories of Auschwitz-Birkenau were outstanding examples. Yet the basic technique was everywhere and at all times the same: the deliberate infliction of various forms of torture upon the incoming prisoners in such a way as to break their resistance and make way for their degradation as individuals. These brutalities were not merely "permitted" or "encouraged"; they were prescribed. Duty in the camps was a mandatory phase in the training of SS guards, and it was here that particular efforts were made to overcome their scruples and to develop in them a capacity for relishing spectacles of pain and anguish.

The concentration camps and everything that took place in them were veiled in the utmost isolation and secrecy. Of course complete secrecy was impossible, and a continuing stream of rumors circulated among the population. At the same time so repellent was the nature of these stories that in their enormity they transcended the experience of nearly everyone who heard them; in self-protection it was somehow necessary to persuade oneself that they could not really be true. The results, therefore, contained elements of the diabolical; the undenied existence of the camps cast a shadow of nameless dread over the entire population; on the other hand the *individual* who actually became a prisoner in one of them was in most cases devastated with fright and utterly demoralized to discover that what was happening to *him* was not less, but rather far more terrible than anything he had imagined. The shock sequence of "procurement," therefore, together with the initial phases of the prisoner's introduction to camp life, is not without significance in assessing some of the psychic effects upon those who survived as long-term inmates.

The arrest was typically made at night, preferably late; this was standing Gestapo policy, designed to heighten the element of shock, terror, and unreality surrounding the arrest. After a day or so in the police jail came the next major shock, that of being transported to the camp itself. "This transportation into the camp, and the 'initiation' into it," writes Bruno Bettelheim (an ex-inmate of Dachau and Buchenwald), "is often the first torture which the prisoner has ever experienced and is, as a rule, physically and psychologically the worst torture to which he will ever be exposed."[8] It involved a planned series of brutalities inflicted by guards making repeated rounds through the train over a twelve- to thirty-six-hour period during which the prisoner was prevented from resting. If transported in cattle cars instead of passenger cars, the prisoners were sealed in, under conditions not dissimilar to those of the Middle Passage.[9] Upon their arrival—if the camp was one in which mass exterminations were carried out—there might be sham ceremonies designed to reassure temporarily the exhausted prisoners, which meant that the fresh terrors in the offing would then strike them with redoubled impact. An SS officer might deliver an address, or a band might be playing popular tunes, and it would be in such a setting that the initial "selection" was made. The newcomers would file past an SS doctor who indicated, with a motion of the forefinger, whether they were to go to the left or to the right. To one side went those considered capable of heavy labor; to the other would go wide categories of "undesirables"; those in the latter group were being condemned to the gas chambers.[10] Those who remained would undergo the formalities of "registration," full of indignities, which culminated in the marking of each prisoner with a number.[11]

There were certain physical and psychological strains of camp life, especially debilitating in the early stages, which should be classed with the introductory shock sequence. There was a state of chronic hunger whose pressures were unusually effective in detaching prior scruples of all kinds; even the sexual instincts no longer functioned in the face of the drive for food.[12] The man who at his pleasure could bestow or withhold food thus wielded, for that reason alone, abnormal power. Another strain at first was the demand for absolute obedience, the slightest deviation from which brought savage punishments.[13] The prisoner had to ask permission—by no means granted as a matter of course—even to defecate.[14] The power of the SS guard, as the prisoner was hourly reminded, was that of life and death over his body. A more exquisite form of pressure lay in the fact that the prisoner had never a moment of solitude: he no longer had a private existence; it was no longer possible, in any imaginable sense, for him to be an "individual."[15]

Another factor having deep disintegrative effects upon the prisoner was the prospect of a limitless future in the camp. In the immediate sense this meant that he could no longer make plans for the future. But there would eventually be a subtler meaning: it made the break with the outside world a *real* break; in time the "real" life would become the life of the camp, the outside world an abstraction. Had it been a limited detention, whose end could be calculated, one's outside relationships—one's roles, one's very "personality"—might temporarily have been laid aside, to be reclaimed more or less intact at the end of the term. Here, however, the prisoner was faced with the apparent impossibility of his old roles or even his old personality ever having any future at all; it became more and more difficult to imagine himself resuming them.[16] It was this that underlay the "egalitarianism" of the camps; old statuses had lost their meaning.[17] A final strain, which must have been particularly acute for the newcomer, was the omnipresent threat of death and the very unpredictable suddenness with which death might strike. Quite aside from the periodic gas-chamber selections, the guards in their sports and caprices were at liberty to kill any prisoner any time.[18]

In the face of all this, one might suppose that the very notion of an "adjustment" would be grotesque. The majority of those who entered the camps never came out again, but our concern here has to be with those who survived—an estimated 700,000 out of nearly eight million.[19] For them, the regime must be considered not as a system of death but as a way of life. These survivors did make an adjustment of some sort to the system; it is they themselves who report it. After the initial shocks, what was the nature of the "normality" that emerged? . . .

"If you survive the first three months you will survive the next three years." Such was the formula transmitted from the old prisoners to the new ones,[20] and its meaning lay in the fact that the first three months would generally determine a prisoner's capacity for survival and adaptation. "Be inconspicuous": this was the golden rule.[21] The prisoner who called attention to himself, even in such trivial matters as the wearing of glasses, risked doom. Any show of bravado, any heroics, any kind of resistance condemned a man instantly. There were no rewards for martyrdom: not only did the martyr himself suffer, but mass punishments were wreaked upon his fellow inmates. To "be inconspicuous" required a special kind of alertness—almost an animal instinct[22]—against the apathy which tended to follow the initial shocks.[23] To give up the struggle for survival was to commit "passive suicide"; a careless mistake meant death. There were those, however, who did come through this phase and who managed an adjustment to the life of the camp. It was the striking contrasts between this group of two- and three-year veterans and the perpetual stream of newcomers which made it possible for men like Bettelheim and Cohen to speak of the "old prisoner" as a specific type.

The most immediate aspect of the old inmates' behavior which struck these observers was its *childlike* quality. "The prisoners developed types of behavior which are characteristic of infancy or early youth. Some of these behaviors developed slowly, others were immediately imposed on the prisoners and developed only in intensity as time went on."[24] Such infantile behavior took innumerable forms. The inmates' sexual impotence brought about a disappearance of sexuality in their talk;[25] instead, excretory functions occupied them endlessly. They lost many of the customary inhibitions as to soiling their beds and their persons.[26] Their humor was shot with silliness and they giggled like children when one of them would expel wind. Their relationships were highly unstable. "Prisoners would, like early adolescents, fight one another tooth and nail . . . only to become close friends within a few minutes."[27] Dishonesty became chronic. "Now they suddenly appeared to be pathological liars, to be unable to restrain themselves, to be unable to make objective evaluation, etc."[28] "In hundreds of ways," writes Colaço Belmonte, "the soldier, and to an even greater extent the prisoner of war, is given to understand that he is a child. . . . Then dishonesty, mendacity, egotistic actions in order to obtain more food or to get out of scrapes reach full development, and theft becomes a veritable affliction of camp life."[29] This was all true, according to Elie Cohen, in the concentration camp as well.[30] Benedikt Kautsky observed such things in his own behavior: "I myself can declare that often I saw myself as I used to be in my school days, when by sly dodges and clever pretexts we avoided being found out, or could 'organize' something."[31] Bruno Bettelheim remarks on the extravagance of the stories told by the prisoners to one another. "They were boastful, telling tales about what they had accomplished in their former lives, or how they succeeded in cheating foremen or guards, and how they sabotaged the work. Like children they felt not at all set back or ashamed when it became known that they had lied about their prowess."[32]

This development of childlike behavior in the old inmates was the counterpart of something even more striking that was happening to them: *"Only very few of the prisoners escaped a more or less intensive identification with the SS."*[33] As Mr. Bettelheim puts it: "A prisoner had reached the final stage of adjustment to the camp situation when he had changed his personality so as to accept as his own the values of the Gestapo."[34] The Bettelheim study furnishes a catalogue of examples. The old prisoners came to share the attitude of the SS toward the "unfit" prisoners; newcomers who behaved badly in the labor groups or who could not withstand the strain became a liability for the others, who were often instrumental in getting rid of them. Many old prisoners actually imitated the SS; they would sew and mend their uniforms in such a way as to make them look more like those of the SS—even though they risked punishment for it. "When asked why they did it, they admitted that they loved to look like . . . the guards." Some took great enjoyment in the fact that during roll call "they really had stood well at attention." There were cases of nonsensical rules, made by the guards, which the older prisoners would continue to observe and try to force on the others long after the SS had forgotten them.[35] Even the most abstract ideals of the SS, such as their intense German nationalism and anti-Semitism, were often absorbed by the old inmates—a phenomenon observed among the politically well-educated and even among the Jews themselves.[36] The final quintessence of all this was seen in the "Kapo"—the prisoner who had been placed in a supervisory position over his fellow inmates. These creatures, many of them professional criminals, not only behaved with slavish servility to the SS, but the way in which they often outdid the SS in sheer brutality became one of the most durable features of the concentration-camp legend.

To all these men, reduced to complete and childish dependence upon their masters, the SS had actually become a father-symbol. "The SS man was all-powerful in the camp, he was the lord and master of the prisoner's life. As a cruel father he could, without fear of punishment, even kill the prisoner and as a gentle father he could scatter largesse and afford the prisoner his protection."[37] The result, admits Dr. Cohen, was that "for all of us the SS was a father image. . . ."[38] The closed system, in short, had become a kind of grotesque patriarchy.

The literature provides us with three remarkable tests of the profundity of the experience which these prisoners had undergone and the thoroughness of the changes which had been brought about in them. One is the fact that few cases of real resistance were ever recorded, even among prisoners going to their death.

With a few altogether insignificant exceptions, the prisoners, no matter in what form they were led to execution, whether singly, in groups, or in masses, never fought back! . . . there were thousands who had by no means relapsed into fatal apathy. Nevertheless, in mass liquidations they went to their death with open eyes, without assaulting the enemy in a final paroxysm, without a sign of fight. Is this not in conflict with human nature, as we know it?[39]

Even upon liberation, when revenge against their tormentors at last became possible, mass uprisings very rarely occurred. "Even when the whole system was overthrown by the Allies," says David Rousset writing of Buchenwald, "nothing happened. . . . The American officer appointed to command of the camp was never called upon to cope with any inclination toward a popular move-ment. No such disposition existed."[40]

A second test of the system's effectiveness was the relative scarcity of suicides in the camps.[41] Though there were suicides, they tended to occur during the first days of internment, and only one mass suicide is known; it took place among a group of Jews at Mauthausen who leaped into a rock pit three days after their arrival.[42] For the majority of prisoners the simplicity of the urge to survive made suicide, a complex matter of personal initiative and decision, out of the question. Yet they could, when commanded by their masters, go to their death without resistance.

The third test lies in the very absence, among the prisoners, of hatred toward the SS. This is probably the hardest of all to understand. Yet the burning spirit of rebellion which many of their liberators expected to find would have had to be supported by fierce and smoldering emotions; such emotions were not there. "It is remarkable," one observer notes, "how little hatred of their wardens is revealed in their stories."[43] . . .

Daily life in the camp, with its fear and tensions, taught over and over the lesson of absolute power. It prepared the personality for a drastic shift in standards. It crushed whatever anxieties might have been drawn from prior standards; such standards had become meaningless. It focused the prisoner's attention constantly on the moods, attitudes, and standards of the only man who mattered. A truly childlike situation was thus created: utter and abject dependency on one, or on a rigidly limited few, significant others. All the conditions which in normal life would give the individual leeway— which allowed him to defend himself against a new and hostile significant other, no matter how powerful—were absent in the camp. No competition of significant others was possible; the prisoner's comrades for practical purposes were helpless to assist him. He had no degree of independence, no lines to the outside, in any matter. Everything, every vital concern, focused on the SS: food, warmth, security, freedom from pain, all depended on the omnipotent significant other, all had to be worked out within the closed system. Nowhere was there a shred of privacy; everything one did was subject to SS supervision. The pressure was never absent. It is thus no wonder that the prisoners should become "as children." It is no wonder that their obedience became unquestioning, that they did not revolt, that they could not "hate" their masters. Their masters' attitudes had become *internalized* as a part of their very selves; those attitudes and standards now dominated all others that they had. They had, indeed been "changed.". . .

It is hoped that the very hideousness of a special example of slavery has not disqualified it as a test for certain features of a far milder and more benevolent form of slavery. But it should still be possible to say, with regard to the individuals who lived as slaves within the respective systems, that just as on one level there is every difference between a wretched childhood and a carefree one, there are, for other purposes, limited features which the one may be said to have shared with the other.

Both were closed systems from which all standards based on prior connections had been effectively detached. A working adjustment to either system required a childlike conformity, a limited choice of "significant others." Cruelty per se cannot be considered the primary key to this; of far greater importance was the simple "closedness" of the system, in which all lines of authority descended from the master and in which alternative social bases that might have supported alternative standards were systematically suppressed.[44] The individual, consequently, for his very psychic security, had to picture his master in some way as the "good father,"[45] even when, as in the concentration camp, it made no sense at all.[46] But why should it not have made sense for many a simple plantation Negro whose master did exhibit, in all the ways that could be expected, the features of the good father who was really "good"? If the concentration camp could produce in two or three years the results that it did, one wonders how much more pervasive must have been those attitudes, expectations, and values which had, certainly, their benevolent side and which were accepted and transmitted over generations.

For the Negro child, in particular, the plantation offered no really satisfactory father-image other than the master. The "real" father was virtually without authority over his child, since discipline, parental responsibility, and control of rewards and punishments all rested in other hands; the slave father could not even protect the mother of his children except by appealing directly to the master. Indeed, the mother's own role loomed far larger for the slave child than did that of the father. She controlled those few activities—household care, preparation of food, and rearing of children—that were left to the slave family. For that matter, the very etiquette of plantation life removed even the honorific attributes of fatherhood from the Negro male, who was addressed as "boy"—until, when the vigorous years of his prime were past, he was allowed to assume the title of "uncle."

From the master's viewpoint, slaves had been defined in law as property, and the master's power over his property must be absolute. But then this property was still human property. These slaves might never be quite as human as *he* was, but still there were certain standards that could be laid down for their behavior: obedience, fidelity, humility, docility, cheerfulness, and so on. Industry and diligence would of course be demanded, but a final element in the master's situation would undoubtedly qualify that expectation. Absolute power for him meant absolute dependency for the slave—the dependency not of the developing child but of the perpetual child. For the master, the role most aptly fitting such a relationship would naturally be that of the father. As a father he could be either harsh or kind, as he chose, but as a *wise* father he would have, we may suspect, a sense of the limits of his situation. He must be ready to cope with *all* the qualities of the child, exasperating as well as ingratiating. He might conceivably have to expect in this child—besides his loyalty, docility, humility, cheerfulness, and (under supervision) his diligence—such additional qualities as irresponsibility, playfulness, silliness, laziness, and (quite possibly) tendencies to lying and stealing. Should the entire prediction prove accurate, the result would be something resembling "Sambo."

The social and psychological sanctions of role-playing may in the last analysis prove to be the most satisfactory of the several approaches to Sambo, for, without doubt, of all the roles in American life that of Sambo was by far the most pervasive. The outlines of the role might be sketched in by crude necessity, but what of the finer shades? The sanctions against overstepping it were bleak enough,[47] but the rewards—the sweet applause, as it were, for performing it with sincerity and feeling—were something to be appreciated on quite another level. The law, untuned to the deeper harmonies, could command the player to be present for the occasion, and the whip might even warn against his missing the grosser cues, but could those things really insure the performance that melted all hearts? Yet there was many and many a performance, and the audiences (whose standards were high) appear to have been for the most part well pleased. They were actually viewing their own masterpiece. Much labor had been lavished upon this chef d'oeuvre, the most genial resources of Southern society had been available for the work; touch after touch had been applied throughout the years, and the result—embodied not in the unfeeling law but in the richest layers of Southern lore—had been the product of an exquisitely rounded collective creativity. And indeed, in a sense that somehow transcended the merely ironic, it was a labor of love. "I love the simple and unadulterated slave, with his geniality, his mirth, his swagger, and his nonsense," wrote Edward Pollard. "I love to look upon his countenance shining with content and grease; I love to study his affectionate heart; I love to mark that peculiarity in him, which beneath all his buffoonery exhibits him as a creature of the tenderest sensibilities, mingling his joys and his sorrows with those of his master's home.[48] Love, even on those terms, was surely no inconsequential reward.

But what were the terms? The Negro was to be a child forever. "The Negro . . . in his true nature, is always a boy, let him be ever so old. . . ."[49] "He is . . . a dependent upon the white race; dependent for guidance and direction even to the procurement of his most indispensable necessaries. Apart from this protection he has the helplessness of a child—without foresight, without faculty of contrivance, without thrift of any kind."[50] Not only was he a child; he was a happy child. Few Southern writers failed to describe with obvious fondness the bubbling gaiety of a plantation holiday or the perpetual good humor that seemed to mark the Negro character, the good humor of an everlasting childhood.

The role, of course, must have been rather harder for the earliest generations of slaves to learn. "Accommodation," according to John Dollard, "involves the renunciation of protest or aggression against undesirable conditions of life and the organization of the character so that protest does not appear, but acceptance does. It may come to pass in the end that the unwelcome force is idealized, that one identifies with it and takes it into the personality; it sometimes even happens that what is at first resented and feared is finally loved."[51]

Might the process, on the other hand, be reversed? It is hard to imagine its being reversed overnight. The same role might still be played in the years after slavery—we are told that it was[52]—and yet it was played to more vulgar audiences with cruder standards, who paid much less for what they saw. The lines might be repeated more and more mechanically, with less and less conviction; the incentives to perfection could become hazy and blurred, and the excellent old piece could degenerate over time into low farce. There could come a point, conceivably, with the old zest gone, that it was no longer worth the candle. The day might come at last when it dawned on a man's full waking consciousness that he had really grown up, that he was, after all, only playing a part.

Through the Prism of Folklore:
The Black Ethos in Slavery

STERLING STUCKEY

I

It is not excessive to advance the view that some historians, because they have been so preoccupied with demonstrating the absence of significant slave revolts, conspiracies, and "day to day" resistance among slaves, have presented information on slave behavior and thought which is incomplete indeed. They have, in short, devoted very little attention to trying to get "inside" slaves to discover what bondsmen thought about their condition. Small wonder we have been saddled with so many stereotypical treatments of slave thought and behavior.[1]

Though we do not know enough about the institution of slavery or the slave experience to state with great precision how slaves felt about their condition, it is reasonably clear that slavery, however draconic and well supervised, was not the hermetically sealed

FROM Sterling Stuckey, "The Black Ethos in Slavery," *The Massachusetts Review,* 1968. Copyright © 1968 by The Massachusetts Review Inc. Reprinted by permission of The Massachusetts Review Inc.

monolith—destructive to the majority of slave personalities—that some historians would have us believe. The works of Herbert Aptheker, Kenneth Stampp, Richard Wade, and the Bauers, allowing for differences in approach and purpose, indicate that slavery, despite its brutality, was not so "closed" that it robbed most of the slaves of their humanity.[2]

It should, nevertheless, be asserted at the outset that blacks could not have survived the grim experience of slavery unscathed. Those historians who, for example, point to the dependency complex which slavery engendered in many Afro-Americans, offer us an important insight into one of the most harmful effects of that institution upon its victims. That slavery caused not a few bondsmen to question their worth as human beings—this much, I believe, we can posit with certitude. We can also safely assume that such self-doubt would rend one's sense of humanity, establishing an uneasy balance between affirming and negating aspects of one's being. What is at issue is not whether American slavery was harmful to slaves but whether, in their struggle to control self-lacerating tendencies, the scales were tipped toward a despair so consuming that most slaves, in time, became reduced to the level of "Sambos."[3]

My thesis, which rests on an examination of folk songs and tales, is that slaves were able to fashion a life style and set of values—an ethos—which prevented them from being imprisoned altogether by the definitions which the larger society sought to impose. This ethos was an amalgam of Africanisms and New World elements which helped slaves, in Guy Johnson's words, "feel their way along the course of American slavery, enabling them to endure. . . ."[4] As Sterling Brown, that wise student of Afro-American culture, has remarked, the values expressed in folklore acted as a "wellspring to which slaves" trapped in the wasteland of American slavery "could return in times of doubt to be refreshed."[5] In short, I shall contend that the process of dehumanization was not nearly as pervasive as Stanley Elkins would have us believe; that a very large number of slaves, guided by this ethos, were able to maintain their essential humanity. I make this contention because folklore, in its natural setting, is of, by and for those who create and respond to it, depending for its

survival upon the accuracy with which it speaks to needs and
reflects sentiments. I therefore consider it safe to assume that the
attitudes of a very large number of slaves are represented by the
themes of folklore.[6]

II

Frederick Douglass, commenting on slave songs, remarked his
utter astonishment, on coming to the North, "to find persons who
could speak of the singing among slaves as evidence of their
contentment and happiness."[7] The young Du Bois, among the first
knowledgeable critics of the spirituals, found white Americans as
late as 1903 still telling Afro-Americans that "life was joyous to
the black slave, careless and happy." "I can easily believe this of
some," he wrote, "of many. But not all the past South, though it
rose from the dead, can gainsay the heart-touching witness of these
songs."

They are the music of an unhappy people, of the children of disappointment; they tell of death and suffering and unvoiced longing toward
a truer world, of misty wanderings and hidden ways.[8]

Though few historians have been interested in such wanderings
and ways, Frederick Douglass, probably referring to the spirituals,
said the songs of slaves represented the sorrows of the slave's
heart, serving to relieve the slave "only as an aching heart is
relieved by its tears." "I have often sung," he continued, "to
drown my sorrow, but seldom to express my happiness. Crying for
joy, and singing for joy, were alike uncommon to me while in the
jaws of slavery."[9]

Sterling Brown, who has much to tell us about the poetry and
meaning of these songs, has observed: "As the best expression of
the slave's deepest thoughts and yearnings, they (the spirituals)
speak with convincing finality against the legend of contented
slavery."[10] Rejecting the formulation that the spirituals are mainly
otherworldly, Brown states that though the creators of the spirituals looked toward heaven and "found their triumphs there, they
did not blink their eyes to trouble here." The spirituals, in his

view, "never tell of joy in the 'good old days.' . . . The only joy in the spirituals is in dreams of escape."[11]

Rather than being essentially otherworldly, these songs, in Brown's opinion, "tell of this life, of 'rollin' through an unfriendly world!" To substantiate this view, he points to numerous lines from spirituals: "Oh, bye and bye, bye and bye, I'm going to lay down this heavy load"; "My way is cloudy"; "Oh, stand the storm, it won't be long, we'll anchor by and by"; "Lord help me from sinking down"; and "Don't know what my mother wants to stay here fuh, Dis ole world ain't been no friend to huh."[12] To those scholars who "would have us believe that when the Negro sang of freedom, he meant only what the whites meant, namely freedom from sin," Brown rejoins:

Free individualistic whites on the make in a prospering civilization, nursing the American dream, could well have felt their only bondage to be that of sin, and freedom to be religious salvation. But with the drudgery, the hardships, the auction block, the slave-mart, the shackles, and the lash so literally present in the Negro's experience, it is hard to imagine why for the Negro they would remain figurative. The scholars certainly did not make this clear, but rather take refuge in such dicta as: "the slave never contemplated his low condition."[13]

"Are we to believe," asks Brown, "that the slave singing 'I been rebuked, I been scorned, done had a hard time sho's you bawn,' referred to his being outside the true religion?" A reading of additional spirituals indicates that they contained distinctions in meaning which placed them outside the confines of the "true religion." Sometimes, in these songs, we hear slaves relating to divinities on terms more West African than American. The easy intimacy and argumentation, which come out of a West African frame of reference, can be heard in "Hold the Wind."[14]

When I get to heaven, gwine be at ease,
Me and my God *gonna do as we please*.

Gonna chatter with the Father, argue with the Son,
Tell um 'bout the world I just come from.[15] (Italics added.)

If there is a tie with heaven in those lines from "Hold the Wind," there is also a clear indication of dislike for the restrictions imposed by slavery. And at least one high heavenly authority might have a few questions to answer. *"Tell um 'bout the world I just come from"* makes it abundantly clear that some slaves—even when released from the burdens of the world—would keep alive painful memories of their oppression.

If slaves could argue with the son of God, then surely, when on their knees in prayer, they would not hesitate to speak to God of the treatment being received at the hands of their oppressors.

> Talk about me much as you please, (2)
> Chillun, talk about me much as you please,
> Gonna talk about you when I get on my knees.[16]

That slaves could spend time complaining about treatment received from other slaves is conceivable, but that this was their only complaint, or even the principal one, is hardly conceivable. To be sure, there is a certain ambiguity in the use of the word "chillun" in this context. The reference appears to apply to slaveholders.

The spiritual "Samson," as Vincent Harding has pointed out, probably contained much more (for some slaves) than mere biblical implications. Some who sang these lines from "Samson," Harding suggests, might well have meant tearing down the edifice of slavery. If so, it was the ante-bellum equivalent of today's "burn, baby, burn."

> He said, "An' if I had-'n my way,"
> He said, "An' if I had-'n my way,"
> He said, "An' if I had-'n my way,"
> I'd tear the build-in' down!"
>
> He said, "And now I got my way, (3)
> And I'll tear this buildin' down."[17]

Both Harriet Tubman and Frederick Douglass have reported that some of the spirituals carried double meanings. Whether most of the slaves who sang those spirituals could decode them is another matter. Harold Courlander has made a persuasive case against widespread understanding of any given "loaded" song,[18] but it seems to me that he fails to recognize sufficiently a further aspect of the subject: slaves, as their folktales make eminently clear, used irony repeatedly, especially with animal stories. Their symbolic world was rich. Indeed, the various masks which many put on were not unrelated to this symbolic process. It seems logical to infer that it would occur to more than a few to seize upon some songs, even though created originally for religious purposes, assign another meaning to certain words, and use these songs for a variety of purposes and situations.

At times slave bards created great poetry as well as great music. One genius among the slaves couched his (and their) desire for freedom in a magnificent line of verse. After God's powerful voice had "Rung through Heaven and down in Hell," he sang, "My dungeon shook and my chains, they fell."[19]

In some spirituals, Alan Lomax has written, Afro-Americans turned sharp irony and "healing laughter" toward heaven, again like their West African ancestors, relating on terms of intimacy with God. In one, the slaves have God engaged in a dialogue with Adam:

> "Stole my apples, I believe."
> "No, marse Lord, I spec it was Eve."
> Of this tale there is no mo'
> Eve et the apple and Adam de co'.[20]

Douglass informs us that slaves also sang ironic seculars about the institution of slavery. He reports having heard them sing: "We raise de wheat, dey gib us de corn;/We sift de meal, dey gib us de huss;/We peel de meat, dey gib us de skin;/An dat's de way dey take us in."[21] Slaves would often stand back and see the tragi-comic aspects of their situation, sometimes admiring the swiftness of blacks:

> Run, nigger, run, de patrollers will ketch you,
> Run, nigger, run, it's almost day.
> Dat nigger run, dat nigger flew;
> Dat nigger tore his shirt in two.[22]

And there is:

> My ole mistiss promise me
> W'en she died, she'd set me free,
> She lived so long dat 'er head got bal'
> An' she give out'n de notion a-dyin' at all.[23]

In the ante-bellum days, work songs were of crucial import to slaves. As they cleared and cultivated land, piled levees along rivers, piled loads on steamboats, screwed cotton bales into the holds of ships, and cut roads and railroads through forest, mountain and flat, slaves sang while the white man, armed and standing in the shade, shouted his orders.[24] Through the sense of timing and coordination which characterized work songs well sung, especially by the leaders, slaves sometimes quite literally created works of art. These songs not only militated against injuries but enabled the bondsmen to get difficult jobs done more easily by not having to concentrate on the dead level of their work. "In a very real sense the chants of Negro labor," writes Alan Lomax, "may be considered the most profoundly American of all our folk songs, for they were created by our people as they tore at American rock and earth and reshaped it with their bare hands, while rivers of sweat ran down and darkened the dust."

> Long summer day makes a white man lazy,
>   Long summer day.
> Long summer day makes a nigger run away, sir,
>   Long summer day.[25]

Other slaves sang lines indicating their distaste for slave labor:

> Ol' massa an' ol' missis,
> Sittin' in the parlour,
> Jus' fig'in' an' a-plannin'
> How to work a nigger harder.[26]

And there are these bitter lines, the meaning of which is clear:

> Missus in the big house,
> Mammy in the yard,
> Missus holdin' her white hands,
> Mammy workin' hard (3)
> Missus holdin' her white hands,
> Mammy workin' hard.
>
> Old Marse ridin' all time,
> Niggers workin' round,
> Marse sleepin' day time,
> Niggers diggin' in the ground, (3)
> Marse sleepin' day time,
> Niggers diggin' in the ground.[27]

Courlander tells us that the substance of the work songs "ranges from the humorous to the sad, from the gentle to the biting, and from the tolerant to the unforgiving." The statement in a given song can be metaphoric, tangent or direct, the meaning personal or impersonal. "As throughout Negro singing generally, there is an incidence of social criticism, ridicule, gossip, and protest."[28] Pride in their strength rang with the downward thrust of axe—

> When I was young and in my prime, (hah!)
> Sunk my axe deep every time. (hah!)

Blacks later found their greatest symbol of manhood in John Henry, descendant of Trickster John of slave folk tales:

> A man ain't nothing but a man,
> But before I'll let that steam driver beat me down
> I'll die with my hammer in my hand.[29]

Though Frances Kemble, an appreciative and sensitive listener to work songs, felt that "one or two barbaric chants would make the fortune of an opera," she was on one occasion "displeased not a little" by a self-deprecating song, one which "embodied the opinion that 'twenty-six black girls not make mulatto yellow girl,' and as I told them I did not like it, they have since omitted it."[30] What is pivotal here is not the presence of self-laceration in folklore, but its extent and meaning. While folklore contained some self-hatred, on balance it gives no indication whatever that blacks, as a group, liked or were indifferent to slavery, which is the issue.[31]

To be sure, only the most fugitive of songs sung by slaves contained direct attacks upon the system. Two of these were associated with slave rebellions. The first, possibly written by ex-slave Denmark Vesey himself, was sung by slaves on at least one island off the coast of Charleston, S.C., and at meetings convened by Vesey in Charleston. Though obviously not a folksong, it was sung by the folk.

> Hail! all hail! ye Afric clan,
> Hail! ye oppressed, ye Afric band,
> Who toil and sweat in slavery bound
> And when your health and strength are gone

Are left to hunger and to mourn,
Let independence be your aim,
Ever mindful what 'tis worth.
Pledge your bodies for the prize,
Pile them even to the skies![32]

The second, a popular song derived from a concrete reality, bears the marks of a conscious authority:

You mought be rich as cream
And drive you coach and four-horse team,
But you can't keep de world from moverin' round
Nor Nat Turner from gainin' ground.

And your name it mought be Caesar sure,
And got you cannon can shoot a mile or more,
But you can't keep de world from moverin' round
Nor Nat Turner from gainin' ground.[33]

The introduction of Denmark Vesey, class leader in the A.M.E. Church, and Nat Turner, slave preacher, serves to remind us that some slaves and ex-slaves were violent as well as humble, impatient as well as patient.

It is also well to recall that the religious David Walker, who had lived close to slavery in North Carolina, and Henry Highland Garnet, ex-slave and Presbyterian minister, produced two of the most inflammatory, vitriolic and doom-bespeaking polemics America has yet seen.[34] There was theological tension here, loudly proclaimed, a tension which emanated from and was perpetuated by American slavery and race prejudice. This dimension of ambiguity must be kept in mind, if for no other reason than to place in bolder relief the possibility that a great many slaves and free Afro-Americans could have interpreted Christianity in a way quite different from white Christians.

Even those songs which seemed most otherworldly, those which expressed profound weariness of spirit and even faith in death, through their unmistakable sadness, were accusatory, and God was not their object. If one accepts as a given that some of these appear to be almost wholly escapist, the indictment is no less real. Thomas Wentworth Higginson came across one—". . . a flower of poetry in that dark soil," he called it.[35]

> I'll walk in de graveyard, I'll walk through de graveyard,
>   To lay dis body down.
> I'll lie in de grave and stretch out my arms,
>   Lay dis body down.

Reflecting on "I'll lie in de grave and stretch out my arms," Higginson said that "Never, it seems to me, since man first lived and suffered, was his infinite longing for peace uttered more plaintively than in that line."[36]

There seems to be small doubt that Christianity contributed in large measure to a spirit of patience which militated against open rebellion among the bondsmen. Yet to overemphasize this point leads one to obscure a no less important reality: Christianity, after being reinterpreted and recast by slave bards, also contributed to that spirit of endurance which powered generations of bondsmen, bringing them to that decisive moment when for the first time a real choice was available to scores of thousands of them.

When that moment came, some slaves who were in a position to decide for themselves did so. W. E. B. Du Bois re-created their mood and the atmosphere in which they lived.

> There came the slow looming of emancipation.
> Crowds and armies of the unknown, inscrutable,
> unfathomable Yankees; cruelty behind and before;
> rumors of a new slave trade, but slowly,
> continuously, the wild truth, the bitter truth,
> the magic truth, came surging through. There
> was to be a new freedom! And a black nation
> went tramping after the armies no matter what
> it suffered; no matter how it was treated, no
> matter how it died.[37]

The gifted bards, by creating songs with an unmistakable freedom ring, songs which would have been met with swift, brutal repression in the ante-bellum days, probably voiced the sentiments of all but the most degraded and dehumanized. Perhaps not even the incredulous slavemaster could deny the intent of the new lyrics. "In the wake of the Union Army and in the contraband camps," remarked Sterling Brown, "spirituals of freedom sprang up suddenly. . . . Some celebrated the days of Jubilo: 'O Freedom; O

Freedom!' and 'Before I'll be a slave, I'll be buried in my grave!,' and 'Go home to my lord and be free.' " And there was: " 'No more driver's lash for me. . . . Many thousand go.' "[38]

Du Bois brought together the insights of the poet and historian to get inside the slaves:

There was joy in the South. It rose like perfume—like a prayer. Men stood quivering. Slim dark girls, wild and beautiful with wrinkled hair, wept silently; young women, black, tawny, white and golden, lifted shivering hands, and old and broken mothers, black and gray, raised great voices and shouted to God across the fields, and up to the rocks and the mountains.[39]

Some sang:

Slavery chain done broke at last, broke at last, broke at last,
Slavery chain done broke at last,
Going to praise God till I die.

I did tell him how I suffer,
In de dungeon and de chain,
And de days I went with head bowed down,
And my broken flesh and pain,
Slavery chain done broke at last, broke at last, broke at last.[40]

Whatever the nature of the shocks generated by the war, among those vibrations felt were some that had come from Afro-American singing ever since the first Africans were forcibly brought to these shores. Du Bois was correct when he said that the new freedom song had not come from Africa, but that "the dark throb and beat of that Ancient of Days was in and through it."[41] Thus, the psyches of those who gave rise to and provided widespread support for folk songs had not been reduced to *tabulae rasae* on which a slave-holding society could at pleasure sketch out its wish fulfillment fantasies.

We have already seen the acute degree to which some slaves realized they were being exploited. Their sense of the injustice of slavery made it so much easier for them to act out their aggression against whites (by engaging in various forms of "day to day" resistance) without being overcome by a sense of guilt, or a feeling of being ill-mannered. To call this nihilistic thrashing about would be as erroneous as to refer to their use of folklore as esthetic thrashing about.[42] For if they did not regard themselves as the equals of whites in many ways, their folklore indicates that the generality of slaves must have at least felt superior to whites morally. And that, in the context of oppression, could make the difference between a viable human spirit and one crippled by the belief that the interests of the master are those of the slave.

When it is borne in mind that slaves created a large number of extraordinary songs and greatly improved a considerable proportion of the songs of others, it is not at all difficult to believe that they were conscious of the fact that they were leaders in the vital area of art—giving protagonists rather than receiving pawns. And there is some evidence that slaves were aware of the special talent which they brought to music. Higginson has described how reluctantly they sang from hymnals—"even on Sunday"—and how "gladly" they yielded "to the more potent excitement of their own 'spirituals.'"[43] It is highly unlikely that the slaves' preference for their own music went unremarked among them, or that this preference did not affect their estimate of themselves. "They soon found," commented Alan Lomax, "that when they sang, the whites recognized their superiority as singers, and listened with respect."[44] He might have added that those ante-bellum whites who listened probably seldom understood.

What is of pivotal import, however, is that the esthetic realm was the one area in which slaves knew they were not inferior to whites. Small wonder that they borrowed many songs from the larger community, then quickly invested them with their own economy of statement and power of imagery rather than yield to the temptation of merely repeating what they had heard. Since they were essentially group rather than solo performances, the values inherent in and given affirmation by the music served to strengthen bondsmen in a way that solo music could not have done.[45] In a word, slave singing often provided a form of group therapy, a way in which a slave, in concert with others, could fend off some of the debilitating effects of slavery.

The field of inquiry would hardly be complete without some mention of slave tales. Rich in quantity and often subtle in conception, these tales further illuminate the inner world of the bondsmen, disclosing moods and interests almost as various as those found in folksongs. That folk tales, like the songs, indicate an African presence, should not astonish; for the telling of tales, closely related to the African griot's vocation of providing oral histories of families and dynasties, was deeply rooted in West African tradition. Hughes and Bontemps have written that the slaves brought to America the "habit of storytelling as pastime, together with a rich bestiary." Moreover, they point out that the folk tales of slaves "were actually projections of personal experiences and hopes and defeats, in terms of symbols," and that this important dimension of the tales "appears to have gone unnoticed."[46]

Possessing a repertoire which ranged over a great many areas, perhaps the most memorable tales are those of Brer Rabbit and John.[47] Brer Rabbit, now trickster, ladies' man and braggart, now wit, joker and glutton, possessed the resourcefulness, despite his size and lack of strength, to outsmart stronger, larger animals. "To the slave in his condition," according to Hughes and Bontemps, "the theme of weakness overcoming strength through cunning proved endlessly fascinating."[48] John, characterized by a spiritual resilience born of an ironic sense of life, was a secular high priest of mischief and guile who delighted in matching wits with Ole Marster, and "patterollers," Ole Missy, and the devil himself. He was clever enough to sense the absurdity of his predicament and that of white people, smart enough to know the limits of his powers and the boundaries of those of the master class. While not always victorious, even on the spacious plane of the imagination, he could hardly be described as a slave with an inferiority complex. And in this regard it is important to note that his varieties of triumphs, though they sometimes included winning freedom, often realistically cluster about ways of coping with everyday negatives of the system.[49]

Slaves were adept in the art of storytelling, as at home in this area as they were in the field of music. But further discussion of the scope of folklore would be uneconomical, for we have already seen a depth and variety of thought among bondsmen which embarrasses stereotypical theories of slave personality. Moreover, it should be clear by now that there are no secure grounds on which to erect the old, painfully constricted "Sambo" structure.[50] For the personalities which lay beneath the plastic exteriors which slaves turned on and off for white people were too manifold to be contained by cheerful, childlike images. When it is argued, then, that "too much of the Negro's own lore" has gone into the making of the Sambo picture "to entitle one in good conscience to condemn it as 'conspiracy,' "[51] one must rejoin: Only if you strip the masks from black faces while refusing to read the irony and ambiguity and cunning which called the masks into existence. Slave folklore, on balance, decisively repudiates the thesis that Negroes *as a group* had internalized "Sambo" traits, committing them, as it were, to psychological marriage.

III

It is one of the curiosities of American historiography that a people who were as productive esthetically as American slaves could be studied as if they had moved in a cultural cyclotron, continually bombarded by devastating, atomizing forces which denuded them of meaningful Africanisms while destroying any and all impulses toward creativity. One historian, for example, has been tempted to wonder how it was ever possible that *"all* this (West African) native resourcefulness and vitality have been brought to such a point of *utter* stultification in America."[52] (Italics added.) This sadly misguided view is, of course, not grounded in any recognition or understanding of the Afro-American dimension of American culture. In any event, there is a great need for students of American slavery to attempt what Gilberto Freyre tried to do for Brazilian civilization—an effort at discovering the contributions of slaves toward the shaping of the Brazilian national character.[53] When such a study has been made of the American slave we shall probably discover that, though he did not rival his Brazilian brother in staging bloody revolutions, the quality and place of art in his life compared favorably. Now this suggests that the humanity of people can be asserted through means other than open and widespread rebellion, a consideration that has not been appreciated in violence-prone America. We would do well to recall the words of F. S. C. Northrop who has observed:

During the pre-Civil War period shipowners and southern landowners brought to the United States a considerable body of people with a color of skin and cultural values different from those of its other inhabitants. . . . Their values are more emotive, esthetic and intuitive . . . (These) characteristics can become an asset for our culture. For these are values with respect to which Anglo-American culture is weak.[54]

These values were expressed on the highest level in the folklore of slaves. Through their folklore black slaves affirmed their humanity and left a lasting imprint on American culture. No study of the institutional aspects of American slavery can be complete, nor can the larger dimensions of slave personality and style be adequately explored, as long as historians continue to avoid that realm in which, as Du Bois has said, "the soul of the black slave spoke to man."[55]

In its nearly two and one half centuries of existence, the grim system of American slavery doubtless broke the spirits of uncounted numbers of slaves. Nevertheless, if we look through the prism of folklore, we can see others transcending their plight, appreciating the tragic irony of their condition, then seizing upon and putting to use those aspects of their experience which sustain in the present and renew in the future. We can see them opposing their own angle of vision to that of their oppressor, fashioning their own techniques of defense and aggression in accordance with their own reading of reality and doing those things well enough to avoid having their sense of humanity destroyed.

Slave folklore, then, affirms the existence of a large number of vital, tough-minded human beings who, though severely limited and abused by slavery, had found a way both to endure and preserve their humanity in the face of insuperable odds. What they learned about handling misfortune was not only a major factor in their survival as a people, but many of the lessons learned and esthetic standards established would be used by future generations of Afro-Americans in coping with a hostile world. What a splendid affirmation of the hopes and dreams of their slave ancestors that some of the songs being sung in ante-bellum days are the ones Afro-Americans are singing in the freedom movement today: "Michael, row the boat ashore"; "Just like a tree planted by the water, I shall not be moved."

5. Resistance to Slavery

The subject of the slaves' resistance to bondage is one of the thorniest and most troublesome in Afro-American history. In his controversial book *American Negro Slave Revolts,* Herbert Aptheker claims that over two hundred rebellions took place between the seventeenth and nineteenth centuries. On the other hand, writers like Stanley Elkins insist that slave revolts were few and far between in the United States, and that "compared with the countless uprisings of the Brazilian Negroes, the slave revolts in our own country appear rather desperate and futile." There is no question that, as Elkins says, revolts occurred on a far more extensive scale in Latin America and the West Indies than in the United States. In seventeenth-century Brazil, escaped slaves established Palmares, a state fashioned after African political and religious customs, which grew to a population of over twenty thousand by the 1690's, and was only conquered when the Portuguese army leveled the main town with artillery. The island of Jamaica witnessed several rebellions in the seventeenth and eighteenth centuries, most notably the uprising of 1831, which involved twenty thousand slaves and resulted in the burning of several plantations and property damage of over a million pounds. The greatest of all slave rebellions took place in Haiti, and lasted for over a decade. Toussaint L'Ouverture, the man the black historian

Lerone Bennett considers "the greatest Negro produced in the Western Hemisphere," welded the rebellious blacks into an army capable of defeating expeditionary forces of the two greatest European powers, France and Great Britian.

Compared with those in Brazil, Jamaica, and Haiti, United States slave revolts do have a rather limited appearance. Those who deny their existence altogether are certainly mistaken, but most (though not all) American uprisings involved only a few dozen slaves at most. Such was the case in New York colony in 1712, when a group of twenty-five slaves gathered in an orchard, set fire to a house, and killed the first nine whites who arrived on the scene. But the slaves were soon overwhelmed and eighteen were executed. In 1739 a group of slaves in South Carolina took up arms and attempted to march to the Spanish colony of Florida, but they were overtaken and defeated by the militia. Forty-four blacks and twenty-one whites were killed in this episode. Two years later fear of a slave conspiracy swept New York City, and in the hysteria and accusations which followed, thirty-one slaves and four whites were hanged. But some historians have concluded that, as was the case in the Salem witch trials, the conspiracy existed only in the inflamed imaginations of the accusers.

The three greatest slave revolts in the United States occurred within the space of thirty-one years in the nineteenth century. The first, in 1800, was led by a twenty-four-year-old Virginia slave, Gabriel, who devised a plan for three columns of armed slaves to attack Richmond, seize the arsenal, and kill all the whites, except Quakers, Methodists, and Frenchmen. (The two religious groups were thought to be antislavery, and the United States was in an undeclared war with France in 1800, so the slaves may have expected assistance from France.) How many slaves Gabriel organized is impossible to tell, for on the night when his men were to gather a storm washed out the road to Richmond and disbanded the blacks who did arrive at the meeting place. Some historians say the plot involved a thousand slaves or more, but the most recent study has reduced this number to fewer than fifty. At any rate, before Gabriel could regroup, the militia had been alerted and he and twenty-five other conspirators were executed.

In the year of Gabriel's plot, Denmark Vesey, a slave carpenter in Charleston, won enough money in a lottery to buy his freedom. Vesey was a remarkable man, deeply religious and sensitive to the wrongs of his people. He was given to rebuking blacks who stepped off Charleston sidewalks to let whites pass, and he lectured at a black church on the Bible and the Declaration of Independence. In 1822, Vesey began organizing for an armed insurrection among slaves in Charleston and the surrounding countryside. Perhaps the most remarkable of his lieutenants was Gullah Jack, an Angolese witch doctor, whose wild gestures and secret potions guaranteeing immortality alternately terrorized and emboldened Vesey's recruits. Vesey's plot was betrayed by a privileged slave, and information about it is so scarce that one writer has suggested that the plot never existed at all. But most historians would rank Vesey with Gabriel and Nat Turner as the leading slave rebels of American history.

Nat Turner's rebellion, which occurred nine years after Vesey was executed, is the best known of all American revolts, not only because Turner is the subject of a controversial novel, but because his was the last major revolt which got beyond the planning stage. Yet in some ways Turner was less successful a revolutionary leader than Gabriel and Vesey. These men had systematic plans and military organizations. Turner had no plan to speak of, and started out with only a handful of followers. Turner's uprising has many affinities to European peasant revolts of the Middle Ages, which tended to be rural-oriented, and were often led by messianic leaders who believed they had been chosen by God for a mission of rebellion. Turner's life revolved around religion. He conducted religious services among slaves in Southampton County, Virginia, and between 1828 and 1830 he saw

visions and spirits, which he interpreted as divine instructions to lead a slave revolt. When he acted, in August,
1831, he began with only six followers, although they
were soon joined by others. Turner and his men killed
about sixty whites before being killed or captured. When
asked in person whether he regretted what he had done,
Turner replied, "Was not Christ crucified?"

Despite Gabriel, Vesey, and Turner, there is no question
that slaves in the United States were not as rebellious as
those elsewhere in the Western Hemisphere. But this does
not necessarily mean that they were more contented with
their lot. Many factors influenced the occurrence of slave
revolts, and in many ways the United States was the least
favorable area for such uprisings. In the West Indies, for
example, blacks far outnumbered whites in the population,
but the reverse was true in the United States. Because the
slave trade was cut off to the United States in 1808, this
country developed a predominantly native-born slave
population, while continuous imports of African slaves in
other countries added a highly volatile element to the slave
population. The sugar plantations of Brazil and the West
Indies were far larger than plantations in the southern
states, and consequently the slave community had more
autonomy and strength. And the whites in the United
States maintained a remarkable degree of political unity,
while in Haiti, for example, divisions within the white
community caused by the French Revolution meant that
the response to slave revolt was weakened.

Because of these and other conditions, slaves in the
United States had to choose less dramatic ways of expressing their grievances. The various types of "day to day
resistance to slavery" are the subject of the following
section from Kenneth Stampp's *The Peculiar Institution*.
Such tactics as malingering, doing poor work, feigning
illness, and petty theft were a source of irritation to almost
all slaveholders. Sometimes resistance took on an organized quality, particularly when slaves tested the resolve of
a new overseer. Although Stampp sometimes has a tendency to equate every piece of bad work by a slave, and

every broken tool, with conscious resistance, he does demonstrate the variety of ways in which slaves could express discontent. In addition, he describes a more active expression of resistance, running away, which was the most frequent slave "crime" in southern court records. Although the runaway is usually associated with the underground railroad and flight to the North, Stampp rightly points out that most fugitives remained in the general vicinity of the plantation, and either returned voluntarily or were captured within a short period of time.

Robert Toplin's article "Peter Still Versus the Peculiar Institution" documents still other ways in which slaves expressed their opposition to bondage. This remarkable individual worked to buy his freedom, attempted to assist slaves to escape to the North, and raised money to purchase his family's freedom. Still's experience points up what the historian Larry Gara found in his investigation of the underground railroad: that this renowned organized system of aiding fugitives has been greatly exaggerated, that most fugitives who reached the North did so because of their own efforts, and that they were far more likely to be assisted by slaves and free blacks than by philanthropic whites.

A Troublesome Property

KENNETH STAMPP

I

The masses of slaves, for whom freedom could have been little more than an idle dream, found countless ways to exasperate their masters—and thus saw to it that bondage as a labor system had its

FROM Kenneth Stampp, *The Peculiar Institution*. Copyright © 1956 by Kenneth Stampp. Reprinted by permission of Alfred A. Knopf, Inc.

limitations as well as its advantages. Many slaves were doubtless pulled by conflicting impulses: a desire for the personal satisfaction gained from doing a piece of work well, as against a desire to resist or outwit the master by doing it badly or not at all. Which impulse dominated a given slave at a given time depended upon many things, but the latter one was bound to control him at least part of the time. Whether the master was humane or cruel, whether he owned a small farm or a large plantation, did not seem to be crucial considerations, for almost all slaveholders had trouble in managing this kind of labor.

Not that every malingering or intractable bondsman was pursuing a course calculated to lead toward freedom for his people, or at least for himself. He was not always even making a conscious protest against bondage. Some of his "misdeeds" were merely unconscious reflections of the character that slavery had given him—evidence, as one planter explained, that slavery tended to render him "callous to the ideas of honor and even honesty" (as the master class understood those terms). "Come day, go day, God send Sunday," eloquently expressed the indifference of the "heedless, thoughtless," slave.[1]

But the element of conscious resistance was often present too; whether or not it was the predominant one the master usually had no way of knowing. In any case, he was likely to be distressed by his inability to persuade his slaves to "assimilate" their interest with his. "We all know," complained one slaveholder, that the slave's feeling of obligation to his master "is of so flimsy a character that none of us rely upon it."[2]

Slaveholders disagreed as to whether "smart" Negroes or "stupid" ones caused them the greater trouble. A Mississippian told Olmsted that the "smart" ones were "rascally" and constantly "getting into scrapes," and a Louisianan confessed that his slave Lucy was "the greatest rascal" and the "smartest negro of her age" he had ever known.[3] On the other hand, many masters were annoyed by the seeming stupidity of some of their slaves, by their unwillingness to "think for themselves." A Negro recently imported from Africa was said to be especially prone to this kind of stubborn obtuseness: "let a hundred men shew him how to hoe, or drive a wheelbarrow, he'll still take the one by the Bottom and the other by the Wheel."[4]

According to a former slave, the bondsmen had good reason for encouraging their master to underrate their intelligence. Ignorance was "a high virtue in a human chattel," he suggested, and since it was the master's purpose to keep his bondsmen in this state, they were shrewd enough to make him think he succeeded.[5] A Virginia planter concluded from his own long experience that many slaveholders were victimized by the "sagacity" of Negroes whom they mistakenly thought they understood so well. He was convinced that the slaves, "under the cloak of great stupidity," made "dupes" of their masters: "The most general defect in the character of the negro, is hypocrisy; and this hypocrisy frequently makes him pretend to more ignorance than he possesses; and if his master treats him as a fool, he will be sure to act the fool's part. This is a very convenient trait, as it frequently serves as an apology for awkwardness and neglect of duty."[6]

Slaveowners generally took it as a matter of course that a laborer would shirk when he could and perform no more work than he had to. They knew that, in most cases, the only way to keep him "in the straight path of duty" was to watch him "with an eye that never slumbers."[7] They frequently used such terms as "slow," "lazy," "wants pushing," "an eye servant," and "a trifling negro" when they made private appraisals of their slaves. "Hands won't work unless I am in sight," a small Virginia planter once wrote angrily in his diary. "I left the Field at 12 [with] all going on well, but very little done after [that]."[8] Olmsted, watching an overseer riding among the slaves on a South Carolina plantation, observed that he was "constantly directing and encouraging them, but . . . as often as he visited one end of the line of operations, the hands at the other end would discontinue their labor, until he turned to ride towards them again." Other visitors in the South also noticed "the furtive cessation from toil that invariably took place, as the overseer's eye was turned from them."[9]

Slaves sought to limit the quantity of their services in many different ways. At cotton picking time they carried cotton from the gin house to the field in the morning to be weighed with the day's picking at night. They concealed dirt or rocks in their cotton baskets to escape punishment for loafing. They fixed their own work quotas, and masters had to adopt stern measures to persuade them that they had been unduly presumptuous. Where the task system was used, they stubbornly resisted any attempt to increase the size of the daily tasks fixed by custom.[10] Athletic and muscular slaves, as Frederick Douglass recalled, were inclined to be proud of their capacity for labor, and the master often sought to promote rivalry among them; but they knew that this "was not likely to pay," for "if, by extraordinary exertion, a large quantity of work was done in one day, the fact, becoming known to the master, might lead him to require the same amount every day." Some refused to become skilled craftsmen, for, as one of them explained, he would gain nothing by learning a craft.[11] Few seemed to feel any personal shame when dubbed "eye servants."

Slaves retaliated as best they could against those who treated them severely, and sometimes their reprisals were at least partly successful. Experience taught many slaveholders "that every attempt to force a slave beyond the limit that he fixes himself as a sufficient amount of labor to render his master, instead of extorting more work, only tends to make him unprofitable, unmanageable, a vexation and a curse. If you protract his regular hours of labor, his movements become proportionally slower." The use of force might cause him to work still more slowly until he fell "into a state of impassivity" in which he became "insensible and indifferent to punishment, or even to life."[12] After a slave was punished in the Richmond tobacco factories, the other hands "gave neither song nor careless shout for days, while the bosses fretted at slackened production."[13]

Besides slowing down, many slaves bedeviled the master by doing careless work and by damaging property. They did much of this out of sheer irresponsibility, but they did at least part of it deliberately, as more than one master suspected. A Louisiana doctor, Samuel W. Cartwright, attributed their work habits to a disease, peculiar to Negroes, which he called *Dysaethesia Æthiopica* and which overseers "erroneously" called "rascality." An African who suffered from this exotic affliction was "apt to do much mischief" which appeared "as if intentional." He destroyed or wasted everything he touched, abused the livestock, and injured the crops. When he was driven to his labor he performed his tasks "in a headlong, careless manner, treading down with his feet or cutting with his hoe the plants" he was supposed to cultivate, breaking his tools, and "spoiling everything." This, wrote the doctor soberly, was entirely due to "the stupidity of mind and insensibility of the nerves induced by the disease."[14]

But slaveowners ignored this clinical analysis and persisted in diagnosing the disease as nothing but "rascality." To overcome it, they had to supervise the work closely. They searched for methods to prevent slaves from abusing horses and mules, plowing and hoeing "badly," damaging tools, killing young plants, and picking "trashy cotton." James H. Hammond noted in his diary: "I find [hoe-hands] chopping up cotton dreadfully and begin to think that my stand has every year been ruined in this way." A Louisiana sugar planter advised his son to turn to cotton production, because it was "trouble enough to have to manage negroes in the simplest way, without having to overlook them in the manufacture of sugar and management of Machinery."[15] "Rascality" was also a major problem for those who employed slaves in factories.

Olmsted found slaveholders fretting about this problem everywhere in the South. In Texas an angry mistress complained that her domestics constantly tracked mud through the house: "What do they care? They'd just as lief clean the mud after themselves as [do] anything else—*their time isn't any value to themselves.*" A Virginia planter said that he grew only the coarser and cheaper tobaccos, because the finer varieties "required more pains-taking and discretion than it was possible to make a large gang of negroes use." Another Virginian complained that slaves were "excessively careless and wasteful, and, in various ways . . . subject us to very annoying losses." Some masters used only crude, clumsy tools, because they were afraid to give their hands better ones.[16] One slaveholder felt aggrieved when he saw that the small patches which his Negroes cultivated for themselves were better cared for and more productive than his own fields.[17]

Masters were also troubled by the slave who idled in the quarters because of an alleged illness or disability. They often suspected that they were being victimized, for feigning illness was a favorite method of avoiding labor. Olmsted found one or more bondsmen "complaining" on almost every plantation he visited, and the proprietor frequently expressed "his suspicion that the invalid was really as well able to work as anyone else." Some masters and overseers believed that they could tell when a slave was deceiving them, but others were afraid to risk permanent injury to their human property. According to one overseer, trying to detect those who were "shamming illness" was "the most disagreeable duty he had to perform. Negroes were famous for it."[18]

Slave women had great success with this stratagem. The overseer on Pierce Butler's Georgia plantation reported that they were constantly *"shamming* themselves into the family way in order to obtain a diminution of their labor." One female enjoyed a "protracted pseudo-pregnancy" during which she "continued to reap increased rations as the reward of her expectation, till she finally had to disappoint and receive a flogging."[19] A Virginian asserted that a slave woman was a less profitable worker after reaching the "breeding age," because she so often pretended to be suffering from what were delicately called "female complaints." "You have to take her word for it . . . and you dare not set her to work; and so she will lay up till she feels like taking the air again, and plays the lady at your expense."[20]

Almost every slaveholder discovered at one time or another that a bondsman had outwitted him by "playing possum" or by some ingenious subterfuge. One Negro spread powdered mustard on his tongue to give it a foul appearance before he was examined by a doctor. Another convinced his owner that he was totally disabled by rheumatism, until one day he was discovered vigorously rowing a boat. A master found two of his slaves "grunting" (a common term), one affecting a partial paralysis and the other declaring that he could not walk; but he soon learned that they "used their limbs very well when they chose to do so." For many years a slave on a Mississippi plantation escaped work by persuading his master that he was nearly blind. After the Civil War, however, he produced "no less than eighteen good crops for himself" and became one of "the best farmers in the country."[21]

In these and other ways a seemingly docile gang of slaves drove an inefficient manager well nigh to distraction. They probed for his weaknesses, matched their wits against his, and constantly contrived to disrupt the work routine. An efficient manager took cognizance of the fact that many of his bondsmen were "shrewd and cunning," ever ready to "disregard all reasonable restraints," and eager "to practice upon the old maxim, of 'give an inch and take an ell.' "[22] This was the reason why the owner of a small cotton plantation rejoiced when at last he could afford to employ an overseer: "I feel greatly relieved at the idea of getting a lazy trifling set of negroes off my hands. . . . They have wearied out all the patience I had with them."[23]

Whenever a new master assumed control of a gang of slaves, there was a period of tension; the outcome of this crucial period might determine the success or failure of his enterprise. The bondsmen seemed to think that if the work burden were to be reduced, or the discipline relaxed, it would have to be accomplished at a time such as this. If during this crisis the master had the advantage of superior authority, the slaves at least had the advantage of superior numbers. They could share the results of their experiments as they put him to the test; and, therefore, they probably knew him sooner than he knew them. (Doubtless slaves *always* knew their master better than he knew them.) Shortly after James H. Hammond took over Silver Bluff Plantation on the Savannah River, he wrote in his diary: "All confusion here yet. Just getting things in order and negroes trying me at every step."[24]

In these contests the bondsmen were sometimes able to celebrate a victory over their unhappy master, frustrated in his efforts to make profitable use of their labor. Once they found an incompetent owner, they pressed their advantage to the point where normal discipline was completely destroyed. Cases can be found of slaves who established a dominating influence over their master, or who, "for want of a better control, would not make crops adequate to the[ir] support." The slaves of a small South Carolina planter were so "unmanageable" and so "unproductive as to render it necessary for him to borrow money."[25] This kind of situation was almost certain to culminate in a sale of the slaves to a new owner. And this in turn marked the beginning of another contest of wills.

A similar period of crisis developed each time a new overseer took command of a plantation labor force. The chances were that discipline had been lax and affairs generally in an unfavorable state during the last weeks of the previous overseer's regime. The first problem, therefore, was to restore order and to re-establish discipline, while the slaves tried every trick they knew to spread and perpetuate chaos.

Though the early weeks of an overseer's administration were the most critical ones, his problems were never permanently solved. His interests and those of the workers under his control clashed at almost every point, and so a feud between them continuously smoldered and occasionally, perhaps, flared up. Let an overseer slacken his control momentarily, let him permit some plantation rule to be violated with impunity, let him tolerate some slipshod work, and the slaves lost no time in putting him to a thorough test. In an essay entitled "Overseers and Their Enjoyments" a Louisiana overseer described graphically what it was like to be "bedeviled with 40 niggers." He concluded bitterly: "Oh, what a fine time of it a manager of a large Louisiana plantation does have."[26]

Plantation records amply illustrate the ways that slaves capitalized upon the weaknesses of an overseer. In Arkansas, an overseer "made himself so familiar with the hands, that they do [with] him as they please." Another, on a Georgia plantation, "elated by a strong and very false religious feeling," placed himself "on a par with the Negroes, by even joining with them at their prayer meetings, breaking down long established discipline, which in every Case is so *difficult* to preserve."[27] Still another, employed on the North Carolina plantation of Ebenezer Pettigrew, found the slaves more than he could handle when the owner was away. They even "had a great feast" to which they invited the slaves on a neighboring plantation. By the end of a year, as he confessed, they had bothered him "near a bout to death."[28]

When a severe overseer assumed control of one of the Florida plantations of George Noble Jones, the slaves resorted to nearly every conceivable method of active and passive resistance. Eventually they attempted a deliberate slowdown at cotton picking time. "I regret to say," the overseer reported to Jones, "that I never have had as hard work to git cotton picked and that don in good order befor. It seames that those people was determine to not pick cotton."[29]

If an overseer emerged the victor in such a struggle, as he usually did, the slaves might try one last stratagem. They might attempt to cause trouble between the overseer and his employer.

An Arkansas planter warned slaveholders that Negroes were "unprincipled creatures" who would "frequently evince a great deal of shrewdness in fixing up a 'tale' on an overseer they do not like." It was his policy, therefore, to whip any slave who made complaints against the overseer. "The impropriety and absurdity of listening to what negroes have to say about their overseer, is perfectly evident to any who will reflect a minute on the subject."[30]

But frequent complaints nevertheless might weaken a master's confidence in his overseer and lead to his dismissal. Anyhow, an overseer was likely to be more circumspect in his treatment of a slave who had the courage to approach the master. Some planters permitted their slaves to bring in their grievances and prohibited overseers from punishing them for it. Overseers always deplored this practice as a sure way to undermine their authority. "Your Negroes behave badly behind my back and then Run to you and you appear to beleave what they say," one complained to his employer as he tendered his resignation. On another plantation a slave managed to produce a long controversy between owner and overseer until his responsibility was finally discovered.[31] Occasionally the slaves had the pleasure of watching a hated overseer depart in a futile rage. An Alabama planter was troubled with a recently discharged overseer who threatened "to shoot and whip sundries of the Negroes" for "telling tales on him." He behaved "like a madman."[32]

For the most part the slaves who thus provoked masters and overseers were the meek, smiling ones whom many thought were contented though irresponsible. They were not reckless rebels who risked their lives for freedom; if the thought of rebellion crossed their minds, the odds against success seemed too overwhelming to attempt it. But the inevitability of their bondage made it none the more attractive. And so, when they could, they protested by shirking their duties, injuring the crops, feigning illness, and disrupting the routine. These acts were, in part, an unspectacular kind of "day to day resistance to slavery."[33]

II

According to Dr. Cartwright, there was a second disease peculiar to Negroes which he called *Drapetomania:* "the disease causing negroes to run away." Cartwright believed that it was a "disease of the mind" and that with "proper medical advice" it could be cured. The first symptom was a "sulky and dissatisfied" attitude. To forestall the full onset of the disease, the cause of discontent must be determined and removed. If there were no ascertainable cause, then "whipping the devil out of them" was the proper "preventive measure against absconding."[34]

Though Cartwright's dissertations on Negro diseases are mere curiosities of medical history, the problem he dealt with was a real and urgent one to nearly every slaveholder. Olmsted met few planters, large or small, who were not more or less troubled by runaways. A Mississippian realized that his record was most unusual when he wrote in his diary: "Harry ran away; *the first* negro that ever ran from me." Another slaveholder betrayed his concern when he avowed that he would "rather a negro would do anything Else than runaway."[35]

The number of runaways was not large enough to threaten the survival of the peculiar institution, because slaveholders took precautions to prevent the problem from growing to such proportions. But their measures were never entirely successful, as the advertisements for fugitives in southern newspapers made abundantly clear. Actually, the problem was much greater than these newspapers suggested, because many owners did not advertise for their absconding property. (When an owner did advertise, he usually waited until his slave had been missing for several weeks.) In any case, fugitive slaves were numbered in the thousands every year. It was an important form of protest against bondage.

Who were the runaways? They were generally young slaves, most of them under thirty, but occasionally masters searched for fugitives who were more than sixty years old. The majority of them were males, though female runaways were by no means uncommon. It is not true that most of them were mulattoes or of predominantly white ancestry. While this group was well represented among the fugitives, they were outnumbered by slaves who were described as "black" or of seemingly "pure" African ancestry. Domestics and skilled artisans—the ones who supposedly had the most intimate ties with the master class—ran away as well as common field-hands.

Some bondsmen tried running away only once, or on very rare

occasions. Others tried it repeatedly and somehow managed to escape in spite of their owners' best efforts to stop them. Such slaves were frequently identified as "habitual" or "notorious" runaways. While a few of them were, according to their masters, "unruly scoundrels" or "incorrigible scamps," most of them seemed to be "humble," "inoffensive," or "cheerful" slaves. Thus an advertisement for a Maryland fugitive stated: he "always appears to be in a good humor, laughs a good deal, and runs on with a good deal of foolishness." A Louisiana master gave the following description of three slaves who escaped from him: the first was "very industrious" and always answered "with a smile" when spoken to; the second, a "well-disposed and industrious boy," was "very timid" and spoke to white men "very humbly, with his hand to his hat"; and the third addressed whites "humbly and respectfully with a smile."[36] Slaves such as these apparently concealed their feelings and behaved as they were expected to—until one day they suddenly made off.

Runaways usually went singly or in small groups of two or three. But some escaped in groups of a dozen or more, and in a few instances in groups of more than fifty. They ran off during the warm summer months more often than during the winter when sleeping out of doors was less feasible and when frost-bitten feet might put an end to flight.

Many fugitives bore the marks of cruelty on their bodies, but humane treatment did not necessarily prevent attempts to escape. More than a few masters shared the bewilderment of a Marylander who advertised for his slave Jacob: "He has no particular marks, and his appearance proves the fact of the kind treatment he has always received." Slaveholders told Olmsted that slaves who were treated well, fed properly, and worked moderately ran away even when they knew that it would cause them hardship and, eventually, severe punishment. "This is often mentioned to illustrate the ingratitude and especial depravity of the African race."[37]

In advertising for a runaway, owners frequently insisted that he had absconded for no cause, or for none that they could understand. A Virginia slave ran off without the excuse "either of whipping, or threat, or angry word"; the slaves Moses and Peter left an Alabama plantation "without provocation." A small Virginia planter recorded in his diary that he had punished a slave woman for running away, because there was "no cause" for it but "badness."[38] "Poor ignorant devils, for what do they run away?" asked a puzzled master. "They are well clothed, work easy and have all kinds of plantation produce."[39] Some masters, it appears, were betrayed by their own pessimistic assumptions about human nature, especially about the nature of Negroes!

When slaves protested against bondage (or some specific aspect of it) by flight, however, they normally had a clear personal grievance or an obvious objective. One of their most common grievances was being arbitrarily separated from families and friends. Hired slaves often became fugitives as they attempted to get back to their homes. Many of the runaways had recently been carried from an eastern state to the Southwest; torn by loneliness they tried frantically to find their ways back to Virginia or to one of the Carolinas. Sometimes a timid slave had never before attempted escape until he was uprooted by sale to a trader or to another master.

The advertisements for runaways were filled with personal tragedies such as the following: "I think it quite probable that this fellow has succeeded in getting to his wife, who was carried away last Spring out of my neighborhood." Lawrence, aged fourteen, was trying to make his way from Florida to Atlanta where "his mother is supposed to be." Mary "is no doubt lurking about in the vicinity of Goose Creek, where she has children." Will, aged fifty, "has recently been owned in Savannah, where he has a wife and children."[40] Items such as these appeared regularly in the southern press.

Occasionally running away enabled a slave to defeat an attempt to move him against his will. A North Carolina slave fled to the woods when his master tried to take him to Tennessee, and a Georgia slave escaped to his old home after being taken to Alabama. In both cases the owners decided to sell them to owners in the neighborhoods where they wished to remain, rather than be troubled with potential "habitual runaways."[41]

Flight was also a means by which slaves resisted attempts to work them too severely. The heavier labor burdens as well as the more favorable climatic conditions accounted for the higher incidence of runaways in summer. Cotton growers found the number increasing at picking time, sugar growers during the grinding season. Planters who used the task system faced the danger of "a general stampede to the 'swamp' " when they attempted to increase the standardized tasks. The overseer on a Florida plantation, dissatisfied with the rate at which the hands were picking cotton, tried "pushing them up a Little," whereupon some of them retaliated by absconding. Sometimes these escapes resembled strikes, and master or overseer had to negotiate terms upon which the slaves would agree to return. A small slaveholder in Louisiana once wrote in his diary: "I arose this morning as usual to proceed to the day's work, but there were none to do it, with the exception of Sib and Jess." The rest had run off in protest against his work regimen.[42]

Slaves ran away to avoid punishment for misdeeds or to get revenge for punishments already received. Most masters knew that it was folly to threaten slaves with "correction," for this usually caused them to disappear. An overseer reported the escape of a slave to his employer: "I went to give him a Floging for not coming to work in due time and he told me that he would not take it and run off."[43] Olmsted learned that slaves "often ran away after they had been whipped, or something else had happened to make them angry." Those who advertised for fugitives confirmed this fact; they frequently stated that a bondsman "was well paddled before he left," or that "on examination he will be found to have been severely whipped." Slaveholders discovered that some of their human chattels would not tolerate being "dealt harshly with—otherwise they will run off—and if once the habit of absconding is fixed, it is difficult to conquer it."[44]

In other cases escape was simply the result of a longing for at least temporary relief from the restraints and discipline of slavery. "John's running off," explained an overseer, "was for no other cause, than that he did not feel disposed to be governed, by the same rules and regulations that the other negroes . . . are governed by."[45] This seemed to be the most common motive, and in spite of severe punishment some ran away time after time. The most talented fugitives reduced the technique to a science. For example, Remus and his wife Patty escaped from James Battle's

Alabama plantation; were caught and jailed in Montgomery; escaped again; were caught and jailed in Columbus, Georgia; escaped again; and were then still at large. Battle urged the next jailer to "secure Remus well."[46]

Slaves like Remus set "evil" examples for others. A small slaveholder in South Carolina was distressed by his "runaway fellow" Team: "this is the 2^d or 3^d time he has ranaway, and lost together nearly a years work, I cannot afford to keep him at this rate, he will spoil the rest of my people by his bad example." Moreover, the skilled, "habitual" runaway often persuaded friends or relatives to decamp with him. A Mississippian advertised for his slave Jim, "a dangerous old scoundrel to be running at large, as he has the tact of exercising great influence with other negroes to induce them to run away."[47] No punishment could break the spirit of such a slave, and he remained an "incorrigible scamp" as long as he lived.

In most cases the runaways were at large for only a short time—a few days or, at most, a few weeks—before they were caught or decided to return voluntarily. But some of them, though remaining in the South, eluded their pursuers with amazing success. It took a South Carolinian a year to catch a slave woman who was over fifty years old. A Florida master advertised for a slave who had been a fugitive for three years. In 1832, a Virginia master was still searching for two slaves who had escaped fifteen years earlier. And a jailer in Jones County, North Carolina, gave notice that he had captured a bondsman who had been a runaway for twenty-five years.[48]

The success of runaway expeditions depended upon the willingness of other slaves to give the fugitives aid. Some of them were helped by literate bondsmen who provided them with passes. One slave carpenter made a business of writing passes for his friends; when he was finally detected he ran away himself.[49] Slaveholders knew that their bondsmen fed and concealed runaways, but they were unable to stop them. In Louisiana a fugitive was found to have been "lurking" about his master's premises for nearly a year while sympathetic bondsmen "harbored" him.[50]

A few slaves betrayed runaways, but usually it was futile for a master to expect their help in catching his property. Even domestics often refused to be informers. One house servant was whipped for not reporting that she had heard a runaway "talking in the yard." James H. Hammond demoted two domestics to field labor for aiding runaways and cut off the meat allowance of all his slaves until they would help him bring them in. A Mississippi planter wrote angrily that his slave woman Nancy, who had been treated "with the greatest indulgence," was "taken in the very act" of carrying food to some runaways. "There is no gratitude among them," he concluded, "and there is nothing more true, than that they will not bear indulgence."[51]

Bands of fugitives sometimes fled into the fastness of a forest or swamp where they established camps and lived in rude huts. Occasionally they tried to grow their own food, but more often they obtained it by raiding nearby farms. One such camp in South Carolina was in a "clearing in a very dense thicket" from which the runaways "killed the hogs and sheep and robbed the fields of the neighbors." A party hunting fugitives in the same state found another camp which was "well provided with meal, cooking utensils, blankets, etc.," and near which "corn, squashes, and peas were growing." Slaves rarely betrayed the locations of these camps. A Louisiana planter, searching for runaways, "very foolish[ly]" tried to force a captured slave woman to lead him to their camp and thus "fooled the day off to no purpose."[52]

Some bold fugitives, because of the lightness of their complexions or because they possessed forged "free papers," made no attempt to conceal themselves. An Alabama master sounded a warning that appeared frequently in fugitive-slave advertisements: Daniel would "no doubt change his name and have a free pass, or pass to hire his time as he has done before."[53] This Negro was, in effect, trying to work and live as a free man while remaining in the South. A fugitive blacksmith repeatedly wrote passes for himself authorizing him to travel about and work at his trade; another managed to find employment in the turpentine industry for nearly two years.[54] Still others, pretending to be "free persons of color," were eventually caught working in the fisheries, on the wharves, or on river boats. They could scarcely have given stronger evidence of their longing for freedom and of their ability to take care of themselves.

Peter Still Versus The Peculiar Institution

ROBERT BRENT TOPLIN

One would have to search carefully among the accounts of slaves who found their way to freedom in the ante-bellum period to find a reference to Peter Still. His activities never produced the political impact or excited public attention as did those of Frederick Douglass, Dred Scott and other historic figures of slave background. Yet, Still's experiences are significant, for they encompassed a variety of approaches utilized to free a fortunate minority of slaves from bondage. Manumission, escape, philanthropy—all were involved in his efforts to secure liberty for himself and his family. And the list of individuals who aided Still in his endeavors reads like an honor roll of the leading antislavery figures of the 1850's.

An incomplete biography of Peter Still appeared in 1856 as *Peter Still: The Kidnapped and the Ransomed*. Written by Kate E. R. Pickard of Syracuse, New York, the book was presented primarily as an antislavery polemic. However, the market became flooded with similar works in the 1850's, and the Pickard book never received the attention it deserved.[1]

The experiences that Peter Still encountered during his forty-nine years in slavery are revealing enough of the peculiar institution to deserve special attention. A full account of this aspect of Still's life can be found in the Pickard biography. Only a brief sketch is presented here as background to his activities as a freedman.

FROM Robert B. Toplin, "Peter Still versus the Peculiar Institution," *Civil War History*, John T. Hubbell, Editor. Copyright © December 1967 by Kent State University. Reprinted by permission of Kent State University.

The efforts of Still's parents to break away from slavery resembled, in some ways, his own quest for freedom. His mother and father were slaves in Maryland when Peter was born in 1801. A few years later, his father purchased his own freedom and settled near Greenwich, New Jersey, to await his family's preplanned escape. Their first attempt was abortive. After a sojourn in Greenwich, the mother and four children were discovered by slave hunters and taken back to Maryland. In the second escape, Still's mother managed to take only her two daughters. After a second reunion, the family settled near Burlington, New Jersey, changing their name from Steel to Still to avoid detection.

The two boys were left in bondage. Shortly after their separation from their mother, Peter and his brother Levin, ages six and eight respectively, were sold in Kentucky. After thirteen years in that state, they were transported to Alabama. There, in 1831, Levin died. His death was a cruel blow to Peter. The brothers had been very close through their years in slavery, and Levin apparently had been responsible for keeping alive the hope for reunion with their parents, even though the memory of their family became fainter each year.

During his years in Alabama, Peter Still lived near the towns of Florence and Tuscumbia, in the northwestern part of the state, not far from Muscle Shoals. Changes in the estate of his owners led to his being "hired out" for a variety of assignments. At times he worked on plantations where he was often appointed household servant or slave foreman—positions usually reserved for the most capable slaves. Sometimes he was hired to merchants in the neighboring towns.

When Still was twenty-five years old, he married a househol slave from a nearby plantation. They each remained the property of their original owners during their years in Alabama, although Still visited his wife frequently.

He became popular with the white townspeople in the area, and they respected him for his abilities. Many years later, a woman who had known him in the South recalled that he was regarded as "faithful and industrious" and "strictly truthful, one upon whose word you may rely upon implicitly."[2] Still became friendly with many of the businessmen in Tuscumbia and Florence, and the good will he earned there was to help him in later years.

A few times he entertained thoughts of escape. Only once did this idea seem to have even a slight chance of materializing. In 1844 he was hired as a cook for the Whig Party Convention at Nashville. During the evening, he walked down to the river searching for a boat which might provide a hiding place for a trip north. Finding none, he was forced to temporarily abandon his hopes for freedom.

In 1846 Still's fortunes began to change and he began working in a different direction to achieve his goal of liberation. He was hired to a bookseller in Tuscumbia who arranged an equitable working relationship. Explaining that he had little for him to do, the merchant proposed that Still hire his own time after meeting his responsibilities. He could keep everything he earned above the basic hiring cost that the merchant had to pay for his services. As this arrangement, though practiced in some of the states in the Upper South, was illegal in Alabama, the merchant led others to believe that he was receiving all of his slave's earnings.[3]

The new opportunity proved fruitful for Still. After a year of maintenance work, servantry, and other odd jobs, he managed to save about $75.00. This encouraged him to continue saving secretly with the ultimate goal of purchasing his freedom. As he did not yet trust any person outside his family enough to reveal his long-range purposes, he told his temporary manager that he spent all his earnings.

During his year of extra work, he became acquainted with Joseph Friedman, an immigrant merchant.[4] Friedman never made a direct statement about his opinions concerning Still's status, but his occasional remarks gave the impression that he was strongly opposed to the principle of slavery. Therefore, at the termination of his work contract, Still requested that his master transfer him to Friedman. The master consented, and Still entered into a new private agreement. When he finally became confident that he could reveal his plans, he found the merchant interested and sympathetic. Together they agreed that Friedman should offer the master $500.00 to buy Still. Then Still would continue working in order to reimburse his new owner and purchase his own freedom.

Friedman immediately tried to consummate the purchase, but for two years the master refused to consider selling Still. He had long been a valuable family servant and the owner intended to keep him as long as he lived. The direct approach failing, Still began to feign a cough and suggested that his master sell him, for the good of all concerned. Perhaps Friedman would be able to cure the ailment through intensive treatment.

But the owner continued to believe that Still was worth much more than $500.00. Friedman's attempts found little reception until 1849 when a number of "choice" young slaves were auctioned in Tuscumbia from the property of a recently deceased owner. Still's anxious master now agreed to complete the sale of his older slave in order to accumulate cash to purchase two healthy boys.

Joseph Friedman was out of town at the time, but his brother Isaac, who was familiar with the secret agreement, paid the $500.00. The quietly jubilant slave gave his new master about $200.00 that he had saved and was, henceforth, permitted to work entirely for his own benefit. After paying the remaining $300.00, he was given a receipt, together with a handwritten certificate of freedom.[5]

Shortly after, Isaac Friedman prepared to travel to Cincinnati and Still decided to go with him, ostensibly as his servant. He bade farewell to his wife and three children and then joined Friedman for the journey up the Tennessee and Ohio rivers. Between Cincinnati and Pittsburgh, he was accosted by several individuals who suspected he was a fugitive slave. With characteristic caution, Still managed to evade their inquiries and finally arrived safely in Philadelphia.[6]

He now set out to find his parents, only aware that he should look for a "Levin" and a "Cidney" who had settled somewhere near Philadelphia after leaving two sons more than forty years before. He especially feared revealing his purpose to an unfriendly party; in the South Still had been warned, as strange as it may sound, that abolitionists were ever ready to entrap free Negroes and sell them back into slavery!

Still soon encountered a helpful Negro who referred him to a clergyman's boarding house. There he was advised to go to the Philadelphia Anti-Slavery Office to search for records of his parents. He was introduced to a Negro clerk in the office, and as Still related the story of his background and purposes, the young man became intensely interested. Then, the clerk revealed his own identity—that his name was William Still, that his parents' names were Levin and Cidney and, indeed, they had lost two sons more than forty years before.[7] The father had been dead for many years, but the mother lived in Burlington, New Jersey, and seven other children resided between Philadelphia and Brooklyn. It was not until Peter Still personally met almost all of these people that he fully believed he had found his own family.

Still now commenced a five-year effort to take his wife and children from slavery. After a short stay in New Jersey, he traveled to Cincinnati to see Isaac Friedman. He obtained a new freedom certificate from Friedman, this one officially registered in the state of Ohio. Then he returned to Alabama, again posing as Friedman's slave. He took odd jobs as he had done before and managed to inform his family about his experiences in the North. He told them he would work to purchase their freedom, but that they should also be prepared to leave if they were approached by a stranger, as there had been some talk of an escape. He then returned north to find a way to earn money.

Still was reluctant to consent to the escape scheme. But since raising enough money to purchase his entire family seemed almost impossible, he finally allowed the dangerous adventure to be carried through. The self-appointed abductor was Seth Concklin. Little was known about him except that he had previously approached the Philadelphia Anti-Slavery Society to offer to help slaves escape from the District of Columbia. Concklin had seen a copy of the *Pennsylvania Freeman* containing a short story about Still's achievements and volunteered to go to Alabama and bring the wife and children north for only the cost of his expenses.

A daring enterprise followed. Concklin was able to lead the fugitives to escape in a small skiff on which they slowly made their way down the Tennessee River. Whenever they encountered inquisitive citizens, Concklin posed as the family's master. In the free states they received some assistance from "friends" due to the prearranged planning of the Quaker, Levi Coffin, one of the principal organizers of the underground railroad. Just when their efforts seemed close to success they were discovered by some suspicious individuals in Vincennes, Indiana. The wife and children were returned to their owner, who had offered a reward for their capture. Concklin was placed on a boat for transportation to Alabama, where he was to be tried. The events that followed are not completely clear. Levi Coffin and N. R. Johnston, who relayed the reports to William Still, believed that Concklin tried to escape. His body was found in a river with his hands and feet in chains and his skull fractured.[8]

Still was sickened by the news of failure and the death of Concklin. He now tried to find a way to purchase his family. A friend wrote to the owner of Still's family to ask his price. In his reply, the master, B. McKiernan, reasoned:

I recovered & Brought Back said 4 negroes or as You would say coulard people under the Belief that Peter the Husband was acsessery to the offence thereby putting me to much Expense & Truble to the amt $1000 which if he gets them he or his Friends must refund These 4 negroes here are worth in the market about for tha are Extraordenary fine & likely & but for the fact of Elopement I would not take 8000 Dollars for them but as the thing now stands you can say to Peter & his new discovered relations in Philadelphi I will take 5000 for the 4 culerd people. . . .[9]

William Still replied to McKiernan, asking if the price for the family could be reduced, as it seemed impossible for Peter Still or his relatives to raise the money. Parenthetically, he asked: "If the entire family cannot be purchased or freed, what can Vina and her daughter be purchased for?"[10] McKiernan gave a clearly negative answer. His price remained at $5,000, and he would not separate the family.[11]

Despite this setback, Still was undaunted. He decided to seek financial aid from friends in the North, but first he attempted to obtain certificates of character in order to make his case more effective. With the help of the Philadelphia Anti-Slavery Society, he searched for two women who had taught in the Tuscumbia Seminary in 1847 and had befriended him when he was a maintenance worker in the school. A communication with Reverend Samuel J. May in Syracuse proved helpful. May was an influential Unitarian abolitionist whose home was a station in the underground railroad.[12] He referred the case to Mrs. Kate E. R. Pickard, one of the women for whom Still had been searching.

May and Mrs. Pickard soon became deeply interested in Still's progress and counseled him in his efforts. Mrs. Pickard later wrote Still's biography, while May penned the introduction.

In 1852 Still prepared to begin his journeys in search of financial support. His brother William was sympathetic to his hopes, "But what can your Brothers do!" he asked. William was skeptical about the possibility of Peter obtaining $5,000 to purchase his own family when so many others, equally deserving, were living under similar conditions of slavery.[13] Shortly after Peter left on his tour to solicit aid, his brother wrote: "I must confess to you, that I am some times led almost to despair, in reference to your accomplishing the object sought. But you must not be discouraged. persevere. hope on. and the difficulties may yet be overcome."[14]

Even Mrs. Pickard, who probably encouraged him more than anyone else to seek assistance, at first felt his chances of success were slight. In March, 1853, she told Still that a physician in Tuscumbia had informed her that there seemed very little hope that the purchase could be accomplished. "(I) ought not to flatter you with unreasonable hopes" she cautioned Still, reminding him of "poor Uncle Tom."[15]

For two years (from November, 1852 to October, 1854) Peter Still was engaged in a traveling appeal for financial assistance. He began his journey with letters of recommendation from J. Miller McKim, Secretary of the Philadelphia Anti-Slavery Office, and some of the principal citizens of Burlington, New Jersey.[16] In Syracuse he met May and renewed his old friendship with Mrs. Pickard. Then he moved on to Auburn, New York, where he addressed a church group for the first time. As Mrs. Pickard describes Still's reaction in the biography: "I was mighty skeered when Mr. Millard took me with him into the pulpit, and told me I must stand up myself, and tell my story to the people. 'Peared like I couldn't stand no how, but I said a few words, and Mr. Millard, he helped me out; so I got along mighty well."[17]

His journeys now took him to meet some of the leading antislavery spokesmen in the country. In Andover, Massachusetts, Still was received by Harriet Beecher Stowe, who gave him a letter which enhanced his appeal considerably:

Having examined the claims of this unfortunate man, I am satisfied that his is a case that calls for compassion and aid.

Though the sum demanded is so large as to look hopeless, yet if every man who is so happy as to be free, and have his own wife and children for his own, would give even a small amount, the sum might soon be raised.

As ye would that men should do for you—do ye even so for them.[18]

Then he moved on to Boston where he presented his papers to William Lloyd Garrison, Theodore Parker and others. Garrison, the most influential figure among the radical abolitionists, temporarily held some of the money Still collected in the Boston area. Garrison was especially interested in the exploits of Seth Concklin. A short narrative of Concklin's life, which formed the appendix of *Peter Still: The Kidnapped and the Ransomed,* was sent to him before its publication.[19]

Still then continued traveling through the Northeast. In New York he met Horace Greeley, the eccentric editor of the *Tribune,* and in Albany, Thurlow Weed, the New York Whig party leader, made a contribution and gave him a letter of recommendation.[20] He stayed at the home of Gerrit Smith, the wealthy citizen of Peterboro, New York, who worked closely with Reverend May in the underground railroad.[21] In New Haven he was received by Leonard Bacon, an influential Congregationalist minister who, though previously opposed to antislavery agitation, was becoming increasingly abolitionist in sentiment at this time.[22]

By October, 1854, Still reached his goal of collecting $5,000. Before returning home, he visited Toronto because, as he explained to a minister in that city:

his only object in visiting Canada was not for the purpose of asking aid or to make an effort to raise money from among friends here, but for the pleasure of treading upon the "free soil of this part of her Majesty's minions" of which he had heard so much; and to see how his breathren (the fugitives from slavery) prospered. He is highly gratified with what he saw and heard. . . .[23]

During the two years that Still was soliciting aid, several of his friends were attempting to arrange the purchase of the family. At times their efforts seemed almost hopeless. After the Concklin incident, McKiernan was extremely angry with Still. Once he even told an inquirer that the family could not be bought on any terms.[24]

Besides William Still and Reverend May, three individuals were especially active in guiding the efforts to purchase the family. They were Joseph Parish, a respected physician in Burlington, New Jersey; Hamilton Willis, a Boston businessman; and Morris Hollowell, a wealthy Philadelphia merchant.

They had to exercise caution in approaching McKiernan. If he became aware of the number of people involved in the effort to purchase the family's freedom, he might raise his price. Still, himself, had to take cognizance of this possibility. Consequently, he did not try to advertise his travels. A few notices appeared in the local newspapers, but usually he relied on letters of introduction that were passed on from one minister or antislavery leader to another.[25]

Still's friends tried to find ways to buy the family through independent agents in order to free them at a lower price. They believed that a person passing as a slave merchant and not showing any connection with Still might be able to acquire them for $3,000 to $4,000, an amount which they estimated to be closer to their market value. One of these attempts involved D. B. Birney, son of James Birney, the political abolitionist and twice presidential candidate of the Liberty party. The younger Birney, who was working in the South as an agent for a Philadelphia mercantile company, was asked to approach McKiernan to bargain for the family. But it appears that Birney gave very little effort to the project, and William Still noted that the money to be used for the purchase was carefully watched, to Birney's apparent consternation.[26]

The sale was finally negotiated late in 1854. The preliminary arrangements were made by John Simpson, a Florence, Alabama, businessman and long-time friend of Still. An agent of Hollowell's company completed the sale and escorted the family north. However, there was not sufficient money available to purchase a recently-born grandson. Still had not prepared for this contingency and the agent had no choice but to leave the child in Alabama.

Still's joyous reunion with his family brought new pressure from his friends to plan his future. What was he to do with his success story? Mrs. Pickard believed that Still and his family could become a model for the antislavery crusade. She wanted his children to "show the world that freedom is better than slavery."[27] "Everybody is watching them," she explained, "to see if it pays to buy people out of slavery."[28] She was also optimistic about the potential political and moral impact of the biography of Still that she was writing. She suggested that he meet with her in Syracuse to plan their use of the money from the book sales.

Still was apparently reluctant to participate in Mrs. Pickard's projects. He did not go to Syracuse despite her continued requests, and his brother William was uncooperative in sending information about the family to her—facts which would have facilitated completion of the book.[29] The most important reason for this attitude was the Still family's fear for their safety. When Peter Still made his appeals in the North, he continually told a minor lie. He described his separation from his mother as due to kidnapping. He portrayed his mother as a free woman, not a slave, as she technically was. The true history of his mother's background could not be revealed until after the Civil War. As the children's status would be determined by the previous condition of the mother, Still's mother and his relations in the North could still be legally considered slaves. Consequently, the biography that Mrs. Pickard published in 1856 told the same story that Still had doctored during his travels.[30]

Peter Still: The Kidnapped and the Ransomed never became as popular as Mrs. Pickard had imagined it would be. Soon after the first edition was completed, the publisher closed his business. The book, a moral appeal as well as a biography, faced a market glutted with an abundance of polemical works on slavery.[31]

Still lived his remaining years in relative obscurity. He purchased a ten-acre truck-farm near Burlington, New Jersey, and died there in 1868 after seeing the destruction of the institution against which he had so long held a personal grievance.[32]

It required nine years of labor for Still to take himself and his family out of slavery. To overcome the extremely difficult barriers to his success he had to employ a variety of subtle, informal and sometimes illegal methods. He could share the secret of his effort to purchase himself with only a few others. From the position of his own freedom, the purchase of his entire family at first seemed impossible. Reluctantly, he consented to an extreme measure and the escape attempt ended tragically with the return of the fugitives and the violent death of the organizer. Then Still endeavored to solicit financial support for his cause. This approach, too, had to be carried out quietly to succeed. A public campaign would only have jeopardized his efforts to purchase his family's freedom.

At a time when the peculiar institution was becoming increasingly inflexible, the achievements of Peter Still were truly extraordinary.

6.   Free Blacks in the Ante-Bellum North

Racial prejudice, as we have seen, was part of the cultural heritage which English colonists brought to the New World, and white supremacy has been a feature of American society from the very beginning. But it was not until the nineteenth century that racism emerged as a full-blown ideology, a comprehensive view of the world which holds that a person's race is the determinant of all his other capacities and qualities, and that the subordination of "inferior" races by "superior" ones is necessary for the preservation of social order. The ideology of racism was bulwarked by the investigations of anthropologists and other scientists, who debated whether blacks had been created separately from other men and constituted a distinct species. Craniologists reported that their measurements of human skulls revealed that blacks were deficient in intellectual capacity, and historians like Parkman and Prescott attributed America's democratic institutions to the special genius of the Anglo-Saxon race. One of the most striking manifestations of the racism which pervaded American society, North and South, before the Civil War, was the immense popularity of minstrel shows. Minstrels, whites performing in blackface, reinforced commonly accepted racial stereotypes by their portrayals of musical, lazy, childlike blacks. The phrase "Jim Crow" originated as the name of a character depicted by one of the best-known minstrels, Thomas Rice.

When he visited the United States in the 1830's, Alexis de Tocqueville observed that "race prejudice seems stronger in those states that have abolished slavery than in those where it still exists, and nowhere is it more intolerant than in those states where slavery was never known." The 220,000 blacks who resided in the "free" states on the eve of the Civil War were subjected to legal and extra-legal discrimination in every phase of their lives. The federal government denied their citizenship, refused to issue them passports, and barred them from benefiting from homestead laws. In 1857, Chief Justice Taney declared in the Dred Scott decision that blacks could not be citizens of the United States, formed no part of "the people" referred to in the Declaration of Independence and Constitution, and had "no rights which white men are bound to respect." In most northern states, blacks were barred from marrying whites and serving on juries, and in the new states of the Northwest they were often excluded from public schools, forced to post bonds for good behavior, and were legally prohibited from entering the states of Indiana, Illinois, and Oregon. Throughout the North, public accommodations and transportation facilities commonly were segregated or reserved for whites only. As for voting rights, at the beginning of the nineteenth century blacks were not legally disfranchised in any northern state, although in practice they were often kept away from the polls. But the western states, beginning with Ohio in 1802, restricted the suffrage to whites, and in the older states black suffrage underwent a process of steady decline. The key state constitutional convention as far as blacks were concerned was New York's in 1821, for at the same time that the delegates all but eliminated property qualifications for white male voters, they imposed a prohibitive requirement that blacks own $250 in property to vote. It is one of the ironies of this period that the democratic impulse associated with the age of Jackson contained so strong an element of racism. By 1860, free blacks were only allowed to vote in five states, all in New England, where they formed only a minuscule percentage of the population.

Even more serious for the mass of free blacks was the economic repression which relegated them to the most menial, unskilled jobs in northern cities. In slavery, northern blacks had been engaged in all sorts of skilled crafts, but after emancipation they were excluded from one craft after another. Southern free blacks, although subject to even more stringent legal restrictions than their northern counterparts, were often better off economically. In 1850, for example, New Orleans, with about the same free black population as New York, had 355 black carpenters to 12 in New York, and 15 black blacksmiths to only one in New York. Many northern employers simply refused to hire blacks in skilled positions, and when they did white workmen often refused to work alongside them. And labor unions usually limited membership to whites.

In the following selection from *North of Slavery,* the standard work on the ante-bellum northern free black, Leon Litwack discusses this economic discrimination, and also examines the housing segregation which relegated blacks to the poorest areas of northern cities. These sections differed from modern ghettos because they were not wholly black, but they did experience many of the sanitation, housing, and crime problems which characterize urban slums today. And from time to time they were the objects of violent attacks by whites, particularly during the Philadelphia riot of 1838 and the New York City draft riots of July, 1863.

Yet, despite this pattern of segregation and discrimination, a small black middle class did emerge, composed of ministers, doctors, and skilled entrepreneurs like caterers, who serviced both the black and white communities. Litwack indicates that the social attitudes of the black middle class were similar to the outlook of the black bourgeoisie of our own time, which have been described by the sociologist E. Franklin Frazier. This tiny middle class aped the customs of white society and accepted white values, even to the extent of respecting lightness of skin and straight hair. On the other hand, the black community also produced an indigenous leadership concerned with the problems of the mass of free blacks. The focus of the black community was the church, whose origins and varied functions as a social center, political forum, and educational institution, Litwack discusses. Throughout American history, the church has been the best-organized institution in the black community and has provided the widest arena for the growth of a black leadership class. Before the Civil War, as today, the minister was one of the most influential figures in the black community.

From *North of Slavery*

LEON F. LITWACK

The Economics of Repression

In an era of expanding opportunities and social mobility, northern Negroes faced economic discrimination and exploitation. For the greater portion of the black labor force, racial prejudice meant much more than restrictions at the polls, in the theaters, or on public conveyances; it manifested itself in the daily struggle for existence, in the problems of subsistence living, employment in the lowest-paid unskilled jobs, hostile native and immigrant white workers, exclusionist trade unions, and deplorable housing in the "Negro section" of town. This was the Negro's "place" in a white-dominated society. Economic necessity demanded acquiescence, but it could neither motivate Negro youths nor make them optimistic about the future. "Why should I strive hard and acquire all the constituents of a man," the valedictorian of a Negro school asked in 1819, "if the prevailing genius of the land admit me not

FROM Leon F. Litwack, *North of Slavery*. Copyright © 1961 by University of Chicago Press. Reprinted by permission of University of Chicago Press and Leon F. Litwack.

as such, or but in an inferior degree! Pardon me if I feel insignificant and weak. . . . What are my prospects? To what shall I turn my hand? Shall I be a mechanic? No one will employ me; white boys won't work with me. Shall I be a merchant? No one will have me in his office; white clerks won't associate with me. Drudgery and servitude, then, are my prospective portion. Can you be surprised at my discouragement?"[1]

Although they had been recently employed under slavery in a variety of skilled as well as unskilled occupations, emancipated Negroes found their economic opportunities limited largely to jobs as servants, seamen, or common laborers.[2] "Some of the men follow Mechanick trades," the Pennsylvania Abolition Society reported in 1795, "and a number of them are mariners, but the greatest part are employed as Day labourers. The Women generally, both married and single, wash clothes for a livelihood." Were such employments, the Society asked five years later, conducive to the Negro's "regularity and industry" or to his "natural propensity to thoughtlessness and amusements"?[3] In 1788, a French traveler noted that most northern free Negroes worked as servants, kept small shops, cultivated land, or found jobs on the coasting vessels. This seemed to constitute the extent of their economic opportunity. "The reason is obvious," he concluded. "The Whites, though they treat them with humanity, like not to give them credit to enable them to undertake any extensive commerce, nor even to give them the means of a common education, by receiving them into their counting-houses. If, then, the Blacks are confined to the retails of trade, let us not accuse their capacity, but the prejudices of the Whites, which lay obstacles in their way."[4]

The situation had not changed materially by 1860. Although some Negroes could be found in the skilled trades and professions, most of them continued to labor in the service and menial occupations. In New York, Philadelphia, and Boston, the men worked largely as laborers, mariners, servants, waiters, barbers, coachmen, bootblacks, porters, second-hand-clothing dealers, and hod carriers, while the women worked as washerwomen, dressmakers, seamstresses, and cooks. Only a few Negroes managed to obtain the financial and educational prerequisites for entrance into business or the professions. As late as 1855, some 87 per cent of the gainfully employed Negroes of New York City worked in menial or unskilled jobs, and this appears to represent their economic condition in other northern cities.[5]

The absence of Negroes from the skilled and professional occupations allegedly confirmed their inferiority. "We see them engaged in no business that requires even ordinary capacity," a Pennsylvanian observed, "in no enterprizes requiring talents to conduct them. The mass are improvident, and seek the lowest avocations, and most menial stations."[6] Fortified with an elaborate set of racial beliefs, whites argued that this situation indicated racial adjustment rather than economic exploitation. The Negro was simply unfit—physically and mentally—to perform skilled labor or enter the professions; he was naturally shifty and lazy, childlike and immature, untrustworthy, irresponsible, unable to handle complicated machines or run business establishments, and seriously lacking in initiative and ingenuity. Recognizing these qualities, a New York merchant insisted that Negro laborers must be treated as children requiring adult white guardianship.[7] Under these circumstances, how could Negroes qualify for anything but simple, unskilled labor? Such a lowly economic status, however, allegedly imposed no real hardships on the Negro, for he possessed little motivation for economic advancement and demanded only the satisfaction of immediate needs and desires. "He can supply all his physical wants without industry," the Connecticut Colonization Society contended, "and beyond the supply of his immediate physical wants, he has little inducement to look."[8] Such racial stereotypes as these reinforced the determination to keep Negro labor in its proper place; they both explained and justified the economic plight of northern Negroes.

In filling the menial occupations, Negroes not only acted "naturally" but performed, at the same time, a valuable economic and psychological service for white society. "They submit themselves to do menial service, and we get the profit," a Pennsylvanian declared. "If they would not do this, we ourselves would be compelled to do it." For this very reason, the Senate Foreign Relations Committee, in 1828, objected to the colonization of the American Negro in Africa. Since the blacks performed "various necessary menial duties," the Committee concluded, colonization would create a vacuum in the seaboard cities, increase the price of labor, and attract rural Negroes and fugitive slaves to the urban centers.[9] Just as slavery allegedly freed southern whites for the leisurely pursuit of culture, so did the free Negro worker enable northern whites to engage in more vital activities. In the event Negroes were colonized, a New England journal warned, "white men must hew our wood, draw our water, and perform our menial offices. They supply the place of so many whites, who may be spared for higher purposes."[10] Finally, Negroes performed a psychological service in that their work allowed the whites to assume aristocratic airs on occasion. In New York, for example, an English traveler observed that whites preferred Negro hackney coachmen "because they had no fear that they would assume any thing like equality,—because they could order them about in the tone of masters,—and still more, because it might be thought they were riding in their own carriages—like our cockneys, who put a livery-servant at the back of a glass-coach, and then pass it off as their own." In this way, the Englishman concluded, Negroes were able to improve their economic position "by the means employed to degrade it."[11]

Prevailing racial stereotypes, white vanity, and the widely held conviction that God had made the black man to perform disagreeable tasks combined to fix the Negro's economic status and bar him from most "respectable" jobs. White workers refused to accept the Negro as an apprentice; businessmen rejected his application for credit; and educational restrictions severely hampered his training for the professions. When Frederick Douglass, a skilled caulker, escaped to the North and sought work in the New Bedford shipyards, he was told that his employment would drive every white man away. For the next three years, Douglass worked as a common laborer, a coachman, and a waiter, earning an average of a dollar a day. In 1853, he remarked that it would be easier to find employment for his son in a lawyer's office than in a blacksmith's shop.[12] But even those few Negroes who managed to train themselves for professional careers found obstacles in their way. In Pennsylvania, for example, a committee of the bar refused to examine a qualified Negro applicant, and the district court upheld the decision on grounds that the state did not recognize Negro citizenship.[13] Moreover, trained Negro teachers labored in inferior school buildings at substandard wages.

White labor feared not only the competition of Negroes in the skilled trades but also the loss of social status which resulted from associating with them. White mechanics thus refused to work with Negroes in the same shops, and white servants considered it degrading to eat with them. One English traveler concluded that most white men "would rather starve than accept a menial office under a black."[14] Where the two races worked together, such as in the service occupations, whites insisted on different titles in order to preserve the sanctity of their color. Such distinctions confounded many a foreign observer. "As is well known," one Englishman commented, "a domestic servant of American birth, and without negro blood in his or her veins, who condescends to help the mistress or master of a household in making the beds, milking the cows, cooking the dinner, grooming the horse, or driving the carriage, is not a servant, but a 'help.' 'Help wanted,' is the common heading of advertisements in the North, where servants are required. . . . Let negroes be servants, and if not negroes, let Irishmen fill their place; but for an American, an Englishman, or a Scotsman to be a servant or a waiter is derogatory." This same traveler noted that even the recently arrived Irishman soon began to assert the supremacy of his white blood "and to come out of what he considers the degrading ranks of 'service.' "[15]

Where Negroes competed with whites for the same jobs or threatened to do so, violence often resulted. Such clashes were bound to be more severe during times of economic depression. Unemployed white workers swelled the Philadelphia mobs of 1842 in protest against the hiring of Negroes. In nearby Columbia, "a town meeting of the working men" warned the populace that Negroes were taking jobs formerly reserved for whites and that this might soon lead them into every branch of skilled trade, where "their known disposition to work for almost any price may well excite our fears."[16] The prejudices of white labor and the fear of violence caused New York City authorities to refuse licenses to Negro carmen and porters. If such licenses were granted, authorities warned, "it would bring them [Negro carmen and porters] into collision with white men of the same calling, and they would get their horses and carts 'dumped' into the dock, and themselves abused and beaten." While New York maintained its restriction, Negroes in Philadelphia endured some initial hostility long enough to obtain positions as carmen.[17]

Organized labor reinforced working-class antipathy toward Negro labor competition. Although trade-unions exerted a minor influence on ante-bellum workers, they occasionally voiced labor's principal demands, aspirations, and prejudices. Such was the case when they rejected racial unity as a way of achieving higher economic standards, insisted on all-white unions, and vigorously opposed abolitionism. Indeed, anti-slavery advocates, who were themselves often oblivious to the plight of northern industrial labor, found few friends in trade-union ranks. After all, emancipation posed the serious threat of thousands of former slaves pouring into the North to undermine wages and worsen working conditions. Rather than prepare for such an eventuality by organizing Negro workers, trade-unions decided on exclusion. The Industrial Congress—a short-lived national organization of reformers and workingmen—admitted Negro delegates to an 1851 convention, but this had no apparent effect on other labor societies.[18] When New York Negro and white barbers agreed to organize to secure higher prices for their labor, the whites insisted on separate organizations. Carrying these sentiments to an extreme, a Cincinnati "mechanical association" publicly tried its president for teaching a trade to a Negro youth.[19]

Against this background of exclusion and hostility, Negro workers could hardly be expected to rally to the side of organized labor when it sought to press its demands through strike action. Instead, in several cases the Negro laborer willingly acted as a strikebreaker. When New York longshoremen struck in 1855 against wage cuts and an employer attack on their union, Negroes took their jobs on the water front and precipitated some violent clashes. Commenting on the strike, *Frederick Douglass' Paper* expressed little sympathy with the demands of the white longshoremen and pointed out that thousands of idle whites and Negroes would gladly work at half the price. "Of course," the newspaper continued, "colored men can feel under no obligation to hold out in a 'strike' with the whites, as the latter have never recognized them." Despite the violent opposition of the strikers, "the sympathies of the employers, the public, and the law, are on the side of the blacks; consequently, the white laborers have been restrained from any overt acts, though, at times, very threatening."[20] Such was the price paid by organized labor in both the ante-bellum and post–Civil War years for the maintenance of white supremacy and exclusionism.

In addition to creating anxiety among white workers, the Negro labor force, increasingly augmented by emancipated and fugitive slaves, also aroused the concern of white citizens' groups and several northern legislatures and constitutional conventions. "The white man cannot labor upon equal terms with the negro," a group of Connecticut petitioners declared in 1834. "Those who have just emerged from a state of barbarism or slavery have few artificial wants. Regardless of the decencies of life, and improvident of the future, the black can afford his services at a lower price than the white man." Unless the legislature adopted appropriate entry restrictions, the petitioners warned, the sons of Connecticut would soon be driven from the state by the great influx of "black porters, black truckmen, black sawyers, black mechanics, and black laborers of every description." Agreeing that exclusion constituted the only remedy, delegates to California's constitutional convention warned that local capitalists planned to import Negroes to work in the mines and predicted the outbreak of "fearful collisions." In virtually every ante-bellum northern legislature and constitutional convention, similar fears were expressed concerning the entrance of Negroes into occupations which had been dominated by native whites.[21]

By the 1830's, the rapid increase of the nation's population, urbanization, and competition among whites threatened the Negro's hold on even the lowly employments. The Pennsylvania Abolition Society protested that "prejudice and pride" excluded blacks from turnpikes, canals, coal mines, brick-making, street-paving, and street-cleaning, and a Philadelphia Negro complained of extensive discrimination among local common laborers. While thousands of persons worked to clean gutters and level drifts during a snowstorm, he found no Negroes so employed, but "hundreds of them . . . going about the streets with shovels in their hands, looking for work and finding none."[22] Although Negroes continued to work in menial jobs, one observer concluded in 1837 that "the time may come when they will not be able to make a living by such means; and then they will be obliged to resort to something still more humble. In this manner the whites will chase and harass them from post to post, until misery will complete their destruction."[23] In addition to the impact of the Panic of 1837 and the ensuing depression, Negro workers faced a new and serious challenge to their already weakened economic position—the Irish immigrant. . . .

Economic exploitation and segregation produced the Negro ghetto. In Boston, Negroes congregated on "Nigger Hill" and along the wharves in "New Guinea"; in Cincinnati, they crowded into wooden shacks and shanties in "Little Africa"; in New York, they concentrated in a few wards and mixed with poor whites in the notorious "Five Points," described by one visitor as "but a step into Hades" and "the worst hell of America"; and in Philadelphia, they settled in gloomy cellars and squalid houses located along narrow courts and alleys.[24] Although some observers also pointed to the remarkable number of fine houses owned by Negroes in attractive neighborhoods, few could turn their eyes from the squalor of the Negro slums or deny their existence. To southern visitors in the North, such conditions demonstrated the folly of emancipation. "Thar they was," one southerner wrote, "covered with rags and dirt, livin in houses and cellars, without hardly any furniture; and sum of 'em without dores or winders. . . . This, thinks I, is nigger freedom; this is the condition to which the filanthropists of the North wants to bring the happy black people of the South!"[25]

Such surroundings obviously had their impact on the general health of the Negro residents. In New York City, tuberculosis proved fatal to twice as many blacks as whites, a reflection of adverse living conditions.[26] Philadelphia's coroner attributed the high mortality rate in Negro districts to intemperance, exposure, and malnutrition. After conducting an inspection in 1848, he reported that many Negroes had been "found dead in cold and exposed rooms and garrets, board shanties five and six feet high, and as many feet square, erected and rented for lodging purposes, mostly without any comforts, save the bare floor, with the cold penetrating between the boards, and through the holes and crevices on all sides." Some bodies had been recovered "in cold, wet, and damp cellars," while still others had been found lying in back yards and alleys. Most of these Negroes had sold rags and bones for a living. Not too far away, however, middle- and upper-class Negroes maintained some respectable living quarters.[27]

The vigorous exclusion of Negroes from white residential neighborhoods made escape from the ghetto virtually impossible. The fear of depreciated property values overrode virtually every other consideration. As early as 1793, the attempt to locate "a Negro hut" in Salem, Massachusetts, prompted a white minister to protest that such buildings depreciated property, drove out decent residents, and generally injured the welfare of the neighborhood. Some years later, New Haven petitioners complained that the movement of Negroes into previously white neighborhoods deteriorated real estate values from 20 to 50 per cent; an Indianan asserted that the proposed establishment of a Negro tract would reduce the value of nearby white-owned lots by at least 50 per cent.[28] Obviously, then, the Negro had to be contained in his own area. Thus when a Boston Negro schoolmistress considered moving to a better neighborhood, the inhabitants of the block where she proposed to settle resolved either to eject her or to destroy the house. By 1847, the residents of South Boston could boast that "not a single colored family" lived among them—only immigrants "of the better class who will not live in cellars."[29]

Although whites frequently deprecated the Negro slums, some profited from them. In Cincinnati's Little Africa, for example, whites owned most of the wooden shacks and shanties and protested the attempt of municipal authorities to bar further construction of wooden buildings in the center of town. "Heaven preserve the shanties," a Cincinnati editor sarcastically remarked, "and supply the proprietors with tenants from whom the rent can be screwed, without respect to color or character."[30] While white critics continued to deplore Negro housing conditions, white landlords made few, if any, improvements. Both conveniently concluded that Negroes naturally lived that way. . . . .

Wealth, occupation, family, nativity, color, and education largely determined a Negro's position in the social order. By 1860, inroads into business and the professions provided the basis for an increasing accumulation of propertied and liquid wealth.[31] Social segregation afforded a growing number of opportunities and insured an important position in the Negro class structure for doctors, lawyers, shopkeepers, ministers, and undertakers. Within the narrowly circumscribed economic world of the Negro, the upper and middle classes included professionals, successful businessmen, large-scale farmers, carpenters, skilled mechanics, barbers, and high-placed waiters, servants, and coachmen, while the lower class consisted of common laborers and comprised the bulk of the population. Rather than admit a permanent working-class status, however, many lower-class Negroes attempted to improve their position by obtaining regular employment and an education, virtual prerequisites for any successful escape from slum neighborhoods and for admission into the middle class. But the segregated Negro community provided a limited number of opportunities for a Negro bourgeoisie and sharply curtailed the amount of social mobility.

Successful Negro entrepreneurs often extended their services beyond their own communities. In several cities, for example, Negro restaurateurs, caterers, bootmakers, tailors, and barbers acquired a fashionable white clientele. Of course the maintenance of a good reputation among whites required Negro businessmen to show proper respect and not to tamper with deep rooted prejudices. In the restaurant and barbering businesses, for example, Negroes frequently, if not generally, had to bar members of their own race. A New York restaurateur called a friend from the dining-room and offered to serve him behind a screen or in the kitchen, explaining that "his customers *now* were not as those in William Street, where he formerly kept."[32] After witnessing the ouster of a prospective Negro customer from a New York barber-shop, an astonished English visitor requested an explanation from the Negro barber. "Ay, I guessed you were not raised here," the barber replied. "Now I reckon you do not know that my boss [also a Negro] would not have a single . . . gentleman come to his store, if he cut coloured men; now my boss, I guess, ordered me to turn out every coloured man from the store right away, and if I did not, he would send me off slick." That evening, the English visitor related the incident to three American "gentlemen . . . of education and of liberal opinions." "Ay right, perfectly right," one exclaimed, "I would never go to a barber's where a coloured man was cut!"[33] Such practices finally prompted an Ohio Negro convention to condemn any "colored man who refuses to shave a colored man because he is colored" as "much worse than a white man who refuses to eat, drink, ride, walk, or be educated with a colored man . . . for the former is a party *de facto* to riveting chains around his own neck and the necks of his much injured race." Inasmuch as the same convention called upon Negroes to equal the "Saxon" in wealth and enterprise, this must have presented somewhat of a dilemma to many successful Negro entrepreneurs.[34]

Nativity proved less important to status than occupation in the Negro class structure. A recently arrived southern-born immigrant who obtained a good economic position would find little to bar him from acceptance in the Negro upper or middle classes, but the fact that so many of the newcomers had neither education nor skill and comprised "the most numerous in those crowded streets and alleys where the destruction and wretchedness is most intense and infectious" resulted in some hostility between the northern-born free Negro and the escaped or emancipated southern slave.[35] Upper- and middle-class northern Negroes often held aloof from the new immigrants and complained that they threatened to besmirch the reputation of the community. In Philadelphia, for example, Joseph W. Wilson attributed much of the disaffection within the Negro upper class to "real or pretended sectional preferences," such as those between "the natives and the southern families." Although he concluded that the natives generally respected their southern brethren, he also found that some of them "can't bear the southerners!"[36] Among the lower classes, there existed more substantial grounds for antagonism because native Negro workers resented additional competition. When an English traveler arrived in Philadelphia in 1846, two Negro porters greeted him and offered to carry his baggage. While one claimed he was "in de cheap line," the other retorted: "Cheap!—neber mind him, Sa; he's only a nigga from Baltimore, just come to Philadelphy. I'se born her, Sa, and know de town like a book. Dat ere negga not seen good society yet—knows nuffin—habn't got de polish on."[37]

Equally significant in determining a Negro's place in the social order was the relative darkness of his skin. By 1850, mulattoes comprised some 25 per cent of the northern Negroes.[38] Although a light color did not automatically secure a Negro's place in the hierarchy, it often afforded him greater economic opportunities, which, in turn, assured him of a high rank in Negro society. In many cases, whites simply preferred to hire mulattoes, feeling that their closer proximity to Caucasian features also made them more intelligent and physically attractive. Such preference invariably had its effect on some mulattoes and made them feel socially superior to the blacks. Nevertheless, a mulatto was still not welcome in white society and had to share the legal disabilities of the blacks. In most cases, then, he took his place in the Negro community and, in fact, produced much of its militant leadership, including such men as Frederick Douglass, James Forten, Robert Purvis, Charles L. Remond, James McCune Smith, William Still, John Mercer Langston, William Wells Brown, and David Walker.

Although whites understandably associated a lighter skin with a superior type of Negro, the surprising fact is that so many Negroes consciously or unconsciously accepted this color valuation. The mulatto's high social position thus resulted in large measure from the strong tendency among Negroes, particularly those in the upper and middle classes, to envy a light complexion, accept white standards of beauty, and do everything possible to alter their own appearances accordingly. In too many cases, one Negro protested, parents taught their children "that he or she is pretty, just in proportion as the features approximate to the Anglo-Saxon standard." To conform to these standards, "flat noses must be pinched up. Kinky hair must be subjected to a straightening process— oiled, and pulled, twisted up, tied down, sleeked over and pressed under, or cut off so short that it can't curl, sometimes the natural hair is shaved off, and its place supplied by a straight wig, thus presenting the ludicrous anomaly of Indian hair over negro features. Thick lips are puckered up. . . . Beautiful black and brown faces by the application of rouge and lily white are made to assume unnatural tints, like the livid hue of painted corpses." Such attempts to alter nature, he concluded, illustrated the power of public sentiment and required that parents cultivate in their children a respect for their race and color and refrain from characterizing straight hair as "good hair" or Anglo-Saxon features as "good features."[39] Ironically, the persistence of such practices, as well as the force of social segregation, formed the basis for some important Negro economic enterprises.

As more schools for Negro youths opened, education became increasingly important and necessary for social status, especially if it led to professional employment. It also tended to solidify class lines. Economic comfort and security enabled upper- and middle-class parents to insure the regular attendance of their children at public or private schools, while lower-class children frequently had to start work at an early age. Among the upper classes, education served important social and economic functions. In Philadelphia, for example, Joseph W. Wilson found that upper-class Negroes often pursued an education "more for its own sake—the adornment which it gives them—than from any relative or collateral advantages," and they did not necessarily utilize it to learn a specific trade. Actually, the relative merits of a classical or vocational education would long be a subject of dispute among Negroes. Moreover, Wilson found that the educated Negro was by no means "the happiest man." Qualified for a useful and honorable place in life, he still found it difficult to secure a good position and thus felt more acutely than others the effects of racial prejudice.[40] Partly for this reason, professional and educated men furnished the most numerous and aggressive portion of Negro leadership.

In social intercourse, upper- and middle-class Negroes sought to achieve much of the decorum and display of white society. Observing Philadelphia's Negro society, Wilson found social exchanges conducted on a very respectable and dignified level, a remarkable degree of refinement and cultivation, ease and grace of manner, and "a strict observance of all the nicer etiquettes, proprieties and observances that are characteristic of the well bred."[41]

Although both races indulged in ostentatious displays of their real or pretended wealth, foreign travelers particularly noted such excesses among Negroes. "Many of the blacks carry walking-canes," an Englishman wrote, "and parade the streets arm in arm, bowing most affectedly to the negresses, who are often dressed in a style so costly, that it is difficult to conceive how they can procure such finery." In Philadelphia, another visitor noted that the "most extravagant funeral" he had seen "was that of a black; the coaches were very numerous, as well as the pedestrians, who were all well dressed, and behaving with the utmost decorum."[42] Such ostentation, contrasting sharply with the general economic status of the Negro, disgusted many white and Negro abolitionists. The Pennsylvania Abolition Society, for example, accused Negroes of aping "those silly white people who pride themselves in their outward adorning to the neglect of their minds," and a Negro leader berated his brethren for spending thousands of dollars each year "for an hour's display of utter emptiness."[43] But protests such as these largely ignored the fact that middle- and upper-class Negroes, having been segregated from white society and in most public places, had few other opportunities to demonstrate their social success and position. . . .

The Church and the Negro

Seeking an escape from the drudgery and disabilities of everyday existence, many Negroes found spiritual comfort and opportunities for social expression in the church. Indeed, the minister was unquestionably the most important and influential figure in the ante-bellum Negro community. While exercising a powerful political, social, and moral influence, he contributed some of the most militant leadership to the Negro's struggle for equal rights, a fact well demonstrated by such men as Theodore S. Wright, Henry Highland Garnet, Samuel R. Ward, Charles B. Ray, J. W. C. Pennington, Amos G. Beman, and Daniel A. Payne. Both a politician and a spiritual leader, the Negro minister frequently used his position and prestige to arouse his congregations on issues affecting their civil rights as well as their morals; he not only condemned colonization, segregation, and disfranchisement, but persistently attacked "licentious literature," the immoral and corrupting influence of the theater, infidelity, and atheism.[1]

Encompassing virtually every aspect of Negro life, the church provided innumerable services. In addition to being a center of religious devotion and ceremony, it was a school, a political meeting hall, a community recreation and social center, and, not too infrequently, a haven for fugitive slaves. Amos G. Beman, pastor of New Haven's African Congregational Church, effectively illustrated the pivotal importance of the ante bellum Negro religious leader and the church as a center of community life. Under his direction, New Haven Negroes organized a benevolent association, a library club, "Circles of Improvement," and forums; at the same time, they helped to organize a four-state temperance society which not only condemned alcoholic beverages but also discussed slavery, education, national organization, employment officers, and the merits of mechanical arts and agriculture. In addition to using the church for these various activities, Negro children displayed their school work in the basement and received regular Sunday School instruction. As an antislavery leader, Beman welcomed fugitive slaves, convened abolitionist meetings in his church, helped to organize state and national Negro conventions, campaigned for Negro suffrage, published a newspaper, and contributed to the various abolitionist journals. In short, Beman effectively combined the roles of Sunday orator, politician, and social leader. . . .[2]

In November, 1787, an incident in Philadelphia helped to launch the independent Negro church movement in the North. Two prominent Negro leaders—Richard Allen and Absalom Jones —and several of their friends entered the St. George Methodist Episcopal Church for a regular Sunday service. Large numbers of Negroes had been drawn to this church and had been permitted to occupy comfortable seats on the main floor, but the increasing popularity of St. George's finally prompted church officials to announce that henceforth Negroes would be expected to sit in the gallery. Aware of this new seating arrangement, Allen, Jones, and other Negroes took seats in the front of the gallery, overlooking the places which they had previously occupied. But the church authorities had actually reserved an even less conspicuous place for their Negro worshipers in the rear of the gallery, and they soon made this quite apparent. "We had not been long upon our knees," Allen later recalled, "before I heard considerable scuffling and low talking. I raised my head up and saw one of the trustees . . . having hold of the Reverend Absalom Jones, pulling him up off of his knees, and saying, 'You must get up—you must not kneel here.' " Jones thereupon requested that the officials wait until the prayers had been completed. When the trustees persisted, however, and threatened forcible removal, "we all went out of the Church in a body, and they were no more plagued with us." In fact, "we were filled with fresh vigor to get a house erected to worship God in."[3]

Several other factors, including personal ambitions and growing race consciousness, contributed to the final separation, but the Philadelphia incident dramatically illustrated the plight of the Negro in the white man's church. Actually, Allen had previously favored separate facilities to accommodate the large number of Negro worshipers; however, opposition from both races had compelled him to abandon the idea. Even after the secession from St. George's, religious differences prevented any immediate organization of a new church. Instead, a group of Philadelphia Negroes, led by Allen and Jones and representing "the scattered appendages of most of the churches in the city," met on April 12, 1787, and organized the Free African Society, a mutual-aid association "without regard to religious tenets, provided the persons lived an orderly and sober life." Strict, Quaker-like practices and discipline governed the conduct of the members, and the society provided benefits for the sick and for widows and orphans, communicated with free Negroes in other cities, applied for a plot in Philadelphia's potter's field as a burial place for its members, and offered its assistance to the Pennsylvania Abolition Society for a proposed study of the free Negro population.[4]

As the movement for an independent Negro church gained momentum, the Free African Society organized a campaign to raise funds for the purchase of a church site and enlisted the assistance of several prominent whites, including Benjamin Rush, Benjamin Franklin, George Washington, and Thomas Jefferson. Local white churches, particularly the Episcopalian and Quaker, expressed grave doubts over the wisdom of the Negro move. The

Episcopal bishop of Pennsylvania frankly asserted that the project "originated in pride," although, in fact, white pride bore the greater responsibility for the break. Nevertheless, such opposition undoubtedly made it more difficult to secure white support and funds. Most of the contributions, Benjamin Rush remarked, would probably have to come from Deists, "swearing captains of vessels," and Philadelphia brokers. "The old and established societies look shy at them [the Negroes], each having lost some of its members by the new associations. To feel or to exercise the true Spirit of the Gospel nowadays seems to require a total separation from all sects, for they seem more devoted to their forms or opinions than to the doctrines and precepts of Jesus Christ." Two years after they had launched their fund-raising campaign, Philadelphia Negroes held a dinner to celebrate the raising of the church roof. "About 100 white persons, chiefly carpenters, dined at one table," Rush recorded, "who were waited upon by Africans. Afterward about 50 black people sat down at the same table, who were waited upon by white people. Never did I see people more happy." Contributing a toast to the occasion, Rush proposed: "May African Churches everywhere soon succeed African bondage." The assembled throng cheered him enthusiastically.[5]

Although Philadelphia Negroes united to erect a church building, they could not agree on the issue of religious affiliation. Recalling the treatment accorded them by St. George Methodist Episcopal Church, most of the members of the Free African Society voted to affiliate with the Episcopalians. In accordance with this decision, Absalom Jones parted company with Richard Allen to head the first independent northern Negro church—the St. Thomas Protestant Episcopal Church of Philadelphia. Refusing to abandon his old sect, Allen then took steps to form a Methodist church, contending that its "plain and simple gospel" best answered the spiritual needs of the Negro people. "All other denominations," Allen asserted, "preached so high flown that we were not able to comprehend their doctrine. Sure I am that reading sermons will never prove as beneficial to the colored people as spiritual or extempore preaching." Before the end of 1794, Bishop Frances Asbury had dedicated the Bethel African Methodist Episcopal Church. Justifying their separation from the whites, the

Bethelites recalled that racial mixing in public assemblies, particularly churches, had caused considerable grief. An independent church, however, made such mixing unnecessary, provided a convenient assembling place for Negroes, and might protect "our weak-minded brethren . . . from the crafty wiles of the enemy." Although admitting only descendants of the African race to membership, the new church denied any schismatic intentions and welcomed reciprocal meetings with whites, such as "bands, classes, and love feasts." In 1799, Bishop Asbury ordained Allen a deacon, and the following year, the General Conference of the Methodist Episcopal church officially indorsed the separation and agreed to the ordination of Negro ministers.[6]

Although they were still affiliated with their white counterparts, several Negro churches moved quickly to affirm their vital independence in local matters. Bishop Asbury of Philadelphia noted, for example, that local Negro worshipers desired full control of temporal matters and had asked for even greater rights and privileges than any white trustees had ever demanded. By 1816, the Bethelites won most of their demands for local autonomy and established a pattern followed by other Negro denominations. In that year, Negro Methodists from various cities gathered in Philadelphia, established the national African Methodist Episcopal church, and elected Richard Allen as its first bishop. Eight years later, their membership reached 9,888, including 14 elders, 26 deacons, and 101 itinerant and local licentiates, and the rapid organization of Methodists in Ohio necessitated the formation of a western conference.[7]

While Negro Methodists and Episcopalians laid the foundation for an independent northern Negro church, the Baptists took steps to effect a similar separation. On May 14, 1809, thirteen Philadelphians formed the first African Baptist church, and in that same year, the Reverend Thomas Paul organized independent Baptist churches in Boston and New York. Already active in the South, the independent Negro Baptist church attracted a large northern following and soon vied with the Methodists as the most important and powerful Negro denomination. The formation of separate groups within the other religious affiliations was much less extensive.[8]

By 1830, the Negro church movement reflected much of the chaos and multiplicity of sects that prevailed among the whites. Although the Methodists and Baptists exerted the greatest influence, Negroes could be found in almost all of the organized religions. In New York, many Negroes attended the newly established and fashionable St. Philip's Episcopal Church or the African Methodist Episcopal Zion Church, while in New Haven, middle- and upper-class Negroes crowded into Beman's prosperous and active Temple Street Congregational Church. Within those denominations which had already broken away from the whites, further splits occurred and new Negro sects emerged. Having hoped that Negroes might forego religious differences, many "friends of the colored people" soon lamented the fact that "the same causes which produced sects and dissonant creeds throughout Christendom, operated to divide and subdivide the colored people."[9] Nevertheless, the Negro church had become a reality in the North. Although it further separated the two races, it proved to be the most dynamic social institution in the Negro community, affording its members an all too rare opportunity to assemble freely, vote for officers, and express themselves spiritually, socially, and politically. . . .

7. Black Abolitionism

Among the neglected aspects of black history has been the role blacks played in the antislavery crusade. Historians have rightly stressed the contributions of white abolitionists like William Lloyd Garrison and Theodore Weld in the antislavery movement, but until the appearance of Benjamin Quarles' recent book *Black Abolitionists,* there was no comprehensive treatment of the role of blacks. Yet the first black newspaper, *Freedom's Journal,* was established in 1827, four years before Garrison's *Liberator,* and the fiery denunciation of slavery and racial prejudice by the Boston free black David Walker also preceded the emergence of Garrison. And it is too often forgotten that, from the beginning, Garrison's newspaper and his antislavery organizations were founded upon black support. Four hundred of the first four hundred fifty subscribers to the *Liberator* were black and the New England Anti-Slavery Society was founded at a meeting in an African Baptist Church in Boston. The wealthy free black sailmaker of Philadelphia, James Forten, gathered subscriptions for Garrison and helped finance antislavery activities in the 1830's.

Black abolitionists—many of whom have slipped into an undeserved historical oblivion—performed a wide variety of activities in the antislavery movement. Reverend Samuel R. Ward taught in black schools and helped

organize the Liberty and Free Soil parties in New York
State. David Ruggles opened a book shop in New York
City where he sold antislavery literature, and helped organize the New York vigilance committee, which assisted
fugitive slaves and kept a watch for slave catchers. Samuel
Cornish and Charles B. Ray edited two short-lived newspapers, *The Rights of All* and the *Colored American,* which
denounced slavery and racial discrimination, and insisted
that blacks must play an independent role in the antislavery
crusade. The towering figure among black abolitionists
was the self-educated former slave, Frederick Douglass,
whose eloquent addresses in the North and in Great Britain
gave him an international reputation. Douglass always insisted that racial prejudice was as much the black man's
enemy as slavery, and that these two closely related evils
must be combatted together. He resisted the pessimism
which characterized other black leaders in the 1850's, and
never abandoned his conviction that the nation would one
day live up to its ideals and establish a truly just interracial
society.

Douglass' rise to prominence in the 1840's and 1850's
reflected in part the increasing importance of fugitive
slaves in the abolitionist movement. "The public have
itching ears to hear a colored man speak, and particularly
a *slave,*" the abolitionist organizer John Collins reported
in 1842, and ex-slaves like Douglass, Henry Bibb, William
and Ellen Craft and Henry Highland Garnet gave northern
audiences a first-hand account of slavery which whites, or
even northern-born blacks, could not hope to equal. The
fugitives also took the lead in a growing militancy and
race consciousness which marked black abolitionism in
the 1840's and 1850's. Garnet, for example, told the 1843
National Negro Convention that the slaves should strike
for their liberties by armed rebellion if necessary. "Brethren, arise, arise," he exclaimed. ". . . Rather die freemen than live to be slaves. . . . Let your motto be
resistance, resistance, resistance." The passage of the
Fugitive Slave Act in 1850 led many blacks to advocate

forcible resistance to the law, and several rescues of captured fugitive slaves were organized and carried out by blacks.

The 1850's also witnessed the rise of emigrationist sentiments among a substantial portion of black abolitionist leaders, who despaired of ever achieving emancipation and equal rights in this country. A nation emigration convention was held in 1854 and throughout the decade black leaders like Martin Delany, Garnet, and James T. Holly debated whether Haiti, Africa, or Latin America would be the best place to establish a black nation. The emigrationist impulse reflected a growing racial consciousness and pride among free blacks, and went along with the insistence that blacks constituted "a nation within a nation," who had to create a separate national identity and power base of their own. The leading critic of emigration was, predictably, Frederick Douglass, who argued that the scheme was wildly impractical, that despite prejudice blacks had greater opportunities for advancement in the United States than in underdeveloped areas like Africa or Latin America, and that the emigration of skilled and educated black leaders would be an abandonment of the slaves to permanent bondage.

Many of these trends in black abolitionist thought are discussed by Leon Litwack in the essay below. Litwack also touches on the complex problem of racial prejudice among white abolitionists. There is no question that, whatever their limitations, white abolitionists were far in advance of their time in their racial outlook, and that many were sincerely committed to equal rights for free blacks. It is equally true that some whites had the tendency to downgrade the equal-rights aspect of the anti-slavery struggle and that many were hesitant about social relations with their black co-workers. Most serious, many black abolitionists found from bitter experience that they were acceptable in leadership positions only if they followed the ideological line set down by whites. The fierce reaction of some whites to Garnet's militant speech of 1843 showed this, as did the bitter denunciations of

Frederick Douglass after he announced that he had abandoned Garrison's line of constitutional interpretation. "They talk down there," Douglass wrote of the Boston Garrisonians, "as if the Anti Slavery Cause belonged to them." The ironic title of Litwack's essay, "The Emancipation of the Negro Abolitionist," points to the growing conviction among blacks that they could not merely follow the lead of whites but must find a special and independent role in the antislavery crusade.

The Emancipation of the Negro Abolitionist

Leon F. Litwack

When William Lloyd Garrison launched his antislavery offensive, Negro abolitionists responded with warm enthusiasm. It "has roused up a Spirit in our Young People," one Negro leader wrote, "that had been slumbering for years."[1] Encouraged by this emergence of antislavery militancy among whites, Negroes helped to sustain *The Liberator,* joined the newly formed abolition societies, and cheered the announced intention of white abolitionists to establish a Negro industrial college. It appeared to be an auspicious beginning of effective interracial cooperation for mutual goals. But the attempted coalition, though not unproductive, was to reveal to the abolitionists—white and black—fundamental differences in assumptions, goals, and emphasis. "Thus, was the cause espoused," Negro leader Martin R. Delany wrote in 1852, "and thus did we expect much. But in all this, we were doomed to disappointment, sad, sad disappointment. Instead of realizing what we had hoped for, we find ourselves occupying the very same

FROM Leon F. Litwack, "The Emancipation of the Negro Abolitionist," originally published in *The Anti-Slavery Vanguard: New Essays on the Abolitionists,* edited by Martin Duberman. Copyright © 1965 by Princeton University Press. Reprinted by permission of Princeton University Press.

position in relation to our Anti-Slavery friends, as we do in relation to the proslavery part of the community—a mere secondary,
underling position." The time had come, he insisted, for Negroes
to break the chains of this bondage.[2]

The Negro's initial enthusiasm was readily understandable.
Several years of independent Negro agitation had produced few
results. And now, in the wake of the Nat Turner insurrection, new
racial tensions gripped large sections of the country, for not only
the South but the North, too, was forced to consider the possible
consequences of a disgruntled racial minority in its midst. Both
sections embraced the prevailing image of the Negro as an inferior
race, incapable of assuming any of the responsibilities of citizenship, but in the North the Negro could at least challenge this
assumption and strive to improve his position. Thus Garrison's
antislavery debut had come at an opportune moment. Subjected to
incessant harassment and racist propaganda, the Negro found encouragement in the advent of a movement which forcefully challenged the colonizationists, the doctrine of racial inferiority, and
any antislavery which did not include as an objective the elevation
of the free Negro—politically, socially, and economically. The
publication of *The Liberator,* Garrison declared, had "operated
like a trumpet-call" on the Northern Negro community. "They
have risen in their hopes and feelings to the perfect stature of men:
in this city, every one of them is as tall as a giant."[3]

Notwithstanding some opposition or misgivings, most of the
white abolition societies admitted Negroes, and some elevated
them to positions on the executive committee. The Negro's most
important function, however, was that of an antislavery lecturer,
for "eloquent" Negro speakers were able to draw "in most places
far larger" audiences than their white counterparts. "The public
have itching ears to hear a colored man speak," one abolitionist
wrote to Garrison, "and particularly *a slave*. Multitudes will flock
to hear one of this class speak."[4] Such was the response to
Frederick Douglass, for example, that he soon became a leading
abolitionist orator. The Negro who committed himself to the
abolitionist cause incurred obvious risks. If the average white man
expected anything of the Negro, it was that he acquiesce in the
racial status quo and act the clownish, childish, carefree, irrespon-

sible Uncle Tom that whites had long presumed him to be. But the Negro abolitionist betrayed the white man's trust and confidence; more than that, he confounded by his very example the white man's rationale for a benevolent guardianship over an inferior and helpless race. Rare, indeed, was the Negro abolitionist who did not have to face a hostile mob at some point in his antislavery career; it was the price he paid for having committed the most unpardonable sin of all—impudence.

In a society racked by racial tensions, misunderstanding and suspicion were almost bound to precipitate divisions between white and black abolitionists. Such questions as Negro membership in abolition societies and race mixing at antislavery functions, for example, provoked considerable debate among white abolitionists.[5] Many feared that a bold defiance of prevailing customs might endanger the eventual success of the antislavery cause. Outside of official gatherings, such intercourse also posed challenges to well-meaning white abolitionists. Sarah Forten, a Philadelphia Negro, recalled a white friend who told her that when walking with a Negro "the darker the night, the better Abolitionist was I." Nevertheless, she was willing to forgive such conduct on the ground that abolitionists were often forced to make "great sacrifices to public sentiment." Still, it was disconcerting. "Many, very many anxious to take up the cross," she lamented, "but how few are strong enough to bear it."[6] Less forgiving was the Rev. Theodore S. Wright, who entreated white abolitionists to "annihilate in their own bosoms the cord of caste. We must be consistent—recognize the colored man in every respect as a man and brother." And this must be applied, he said, to "the church, the stage, the steamboat, the public house, in all places."[7]

Equally annoying to Negroes was the patronizing attitude of some white abolitionists and the application of a double standard which strongly suggested the Negro's inherent inferiority. After exiling himself to England, along with his white wife, Negro abolitionist William G. Allen wrote to Garrison that the English had treated him warmly, in contrast to the "patronizing (and, of course, insulting) spirit, even of hundreds of the American abolitionists," who had always seemed so overly conscious of color differences.[8] More pointedly, however, some Negroes complained that white abolitionists tended to establish different standards by which to judge the respective abilities of the two races. Thus whites expected less of Negro students in the classroom, spoke exultantly of the academic work of Negroes which would have been barely passable if performed by whites, and willingly tolerated Negro ministers and teachers who fell far short of the qualifications of whites for the same positions. "Our white friends," commented a Negro newspaper, "are deceived when they imagine they are free from prejudice against color, and yet are content with a lower standard of attainments for colored youth, and inferior exhibitions of talent on the part of colored men. This is, in our view, the worst feature of abolitionism—the one which grieves us most. It is the highest rock of danger; the only one on which we fear a shipwreck of our high and holy cause."9

But that was not all. Of what use, asked Negroes, was the right to vote, attend school, and enter the homes of abolitionists if it was still impossible to gain access to any but the most menial employment. The economic condition of the Negro was at best deplorable, and the new waves of immigrants, competing for many positions which Negroes had long monopolized, only made matters worse. Although some white abolitionists had agitated vigorously in the areas of civil rights and educational opportunities, little had been done in the way of economic assistance, except to call upon Negroes to improve themselves. Perhaps this simply reflected the dominant middle-class ideology of self-help which affected abolitionists, like other whites, but Negroes found little encouragement in such a doctrine and appealed to the antislavery movement to meet this true test of its stated determination to elevate the free Negro.

That the Negro should have placed considerable emphasis on the economic question is understandable. To many Negroes, in fact, this was a key point if they were ever to achieve the respect of white society. The abolitionist, then, was called upon to render practical assistance. But when the *Colored American* reviewed the economic plight of the Negro in the wake of the Panic of 1837, it noted that not one local abolitionist had placed a Negro in any conspicuous position in his business establishment; in fact, it could not even find a Negro in the offices of the New York Anti-Slavery

Society. The newspaper beseeched abolitionists to correct this grievous situation, and preferably not by passing a resolution at their next convention.[10] In the absence of any measurable progress along these lines, Negro delegates to an abolition convention in 1852 charged that the antislavery movement had failed in its responsibility. Proposals had been made to leading abolitionists to employ Negroes in their commercial establishments but the appeal had been largely in vain. True, one delegate conceded, Negroes had found employment in Arthur Tappan's department store, but, he added, only in a menial capacity. "Wherever the colored man is connected with the houses of these gentlemen, it is as the lowest drudges."[11]

In demanding economic assistance, the Negro denied any desire for preferential treatment; he simply wanted an equal opportunity to compete for respectable employment. And since many white abolitionists were in a position to make this possible, they were asked to give practical implementation to their antislavery professions. After all, one Negro leader argued, the struggle for equal rights cannot be won on "the bare ground of abstract principles"; abolitionists must strive not only to abolish chattel slavery but "that other kind of slavery" which doomed the free Negro to economic dependence and pauperism; indeed, he deplored the preoccupation of abolitionists with such reforms as capital punishment, temperance, and women's rights, while they refused in their own establishments to afford equal economic opportunities to depressed Negroes.[12] But such strictures yielded few concrete results, thus prompting a Negro convention delegate to charge that some of those who professed to be "the strongest abolitionists" have refused to grant Negroes anything but sympathy; they have persistently evaded a more practical application of their principles. True, some "might employ a colored boy as a porter or packer," but most abolitionists "would as soon put a hod-carrier to the clerk's desk as a colored boy, ever so well educated though he be."[13] It was left to Frederick Douglass to issue a more direct challenge to the abolitionists: "What boss anti-slavery mechanic will take a black boy into his wheelwright's shop, his blacksmith's shop, his joiner's shop, his cabinet shop? Here is something *practical;* where are the whites and where are the blacks that will respond to it?"[14] The response was difficult to discern. This "is not the song that anti-slavery sung," wrote the disillusioned Delany, "in the first love of the new faith, proclaimed by its disciples."[15]

Perhaps the Negro had been unrealistic in his expectations. By the late 1830's, at any rate, Negro leaders began to reassess their role in the antislavery movement; increasing factional quarrels among the whites made such a reappraisal all the more necessary. Although some Negro abolitionists, such as Robert Purvis and Charles Remond, remained loyal Garrisonians, a growing restlessness within the Negro abolitionist camp manifested itself in more frequent demands for ideological and political independence; moreover, as Negroes became more articulate themselves, they tended increasingly to voice their own aspirations and to question the white abolitionist's prerogative to speak for them. "As long as we let them think and act for us," the *Colored American* warned in 1839, "as long as we will bow to their opinions, and acknowledge that their word is counsel, and their will is law; so long they will outwardly treat us as men, while in their hearts they still hold us as slaves."[16]

Under the editorial supervision of Charles B. Ray and Philip A. Bell, the *Colored American* was the most prominent voice of this quest for independent expression. Published in New York, the newspaper first took to task the recently formed American Moral Reform Society, dominated largely by pro-Garrison Philadelphia Negroes, for its criticism of separate Negro conventions and the term "colored people," both of which allegedly implied degradation. To the *Colored American,* such positions not only were preposterous but they ignored the primary problems facing the Negro in a hostile society. "[W]hile these sages are frightened half to death, at the idea of being called colored, their FRIENDS and their FOES, in the convention, in the Assembly and in the Senate; through the pulpit and the press, call them nothing else but NE-GROES, NEGROES, THE NEGROES OF PENNSYLVANIA."[17]

But the *Colored American* found even more distasteful the destructive factional warfare among abolitionists, for it threatened to undermine the antislavery effort. "The controversy," the newspaper asserted, "has . . . engrossed all their powers, and been prosecuted with a spirit wholly unworthy the character of the brethren engaged in it. . . . There is nothing to be gained by brother contending with brother."[18] That was heresy enough, in the eyes of some Garrisonians, but what followed must have confirmed their suspicions. Accepting political action as a legitimate antislavery weapon, the *Colored American* urged qualified Negroes to vote. When the Garrisonians then attacked the newspaper for abandoning the true faith (which deprecated political action), the editors affirmed their right to take an independent position. Notwithstanding the noble motives of most abolitionists, the *Colored American* insisted that they had no right to dictate antislavery doctrine to the Negro. "Sooner than abate one jot or tittle of our right to think, speak and act like men, we will suffer our enterprise to perish, and the *Colored American* will be numbered with the things that were."[19]

When the Garrisonian press claimed that separate Negro conventions perpetuated the idea of segregation, the *Colored American* and its supporters reaffirmed their defense of independent action. The multiplicity of wrongs inflicted on the Negro, Samuel Ward argued, made frequent meetings and independent organization indispensable; his white friends, he thought, would appreciate this need if they had "worn a colored skin from October '17 to June '40, as I have, in this pseudo-republic." Although conceding some valuable service by the white antislavery men, Ward was still dissatisfied, especially with those "abolitionists in *profession*" who had yet to conquer prejudice within themselves. "Too many," he regretted, ". . . best love the colored man at a distance."[20]

If there remained any doubts as to the determination of Negroes to voice their opinions, regardless of prevailing antislavery creeds, Henry Highland Garnet quickly dispelled them in 1843 when he told a national Negro convention that slaves would be justified in using violent means to win their freedom.[21] The convention refused by a single vote to endorse the address; nevertheless, the issue had been permanently raised and the narrow vote suggested a growing impatience among Negroes with the traditional reliance on moral force to conquer slavery. But the aftermath of this debate was in many ways even more revealing. Condemned by *The Liberator* for his militant appeal to the slaves and for his endorsement of the Liberty party, Garnet accepted the challenge. "If it has come to this," he replied, "that I must think and act as you do, because you are an abolitionist, or be exterminated by your thunder, then I do not hesitate to say that your abolitionism is abject slavery."[22] Six years later, an Ohio Negro convention ordered the "gratuitous" circulation of Garnet's convention address;[23] and by this time Frederick Douglass, who had opposed Garnet at the convention, was on the verge of breaking with the Garrisonians and adding his considerable force and prestige to the cause of independent Negro expression and agitation.

The Douglass heresy, made public at the American Anti-Slavery Society convention of 1851, struck particular dismay into the Garrisonian camp, for he had been their principal Negro spokesman. The estrangement stemmed from Douglass' revised position on the dissolution of the Union, political action, nonresistance, and the nature of the Constitution. In each case, he broke with prevailing Garrisonian ideology. To seek the dissolution of the Union, he now argued, was to violate his duty as an abolitionist, for it left the slave helpless; to abstain from voting was to ignore "a legitimate and powerful means for abolishing slavery"; and to hold that the Constitution was a proslavery document was to distort both its letter and spirit.[24] The Garrisonians, Douglass charged, had abandoned the original purposes of the antislavery movement. "It started to free the slave," he contended. "It ends by leaving the slave to free himself. It started with the purpose to imbue the heart of the nation with sentiments favorable to the abolition of slavery, and ends by seeking to free the North from all responsibility of slavery." To Douglass, this was not practical antislavery; his alleged apostasy, he insisted, was not from "the Anti-Slavery Cause, for all know that I am as faithful to that cause as I ever was," but from "Garrisonism."[25]

Even before these ideological differences, there had been indications that Douglass was growing restive in the Garrisonian camp. When he first began to lecture, his white friends told him to confine his remarks to his experiences as a slave, for that was what the audiences wanted to hear. "Give us the facts," an abolitionist remarked to Douglass, "we will take care of the philosophy."[26] But Douglass soon found it impossible to confine himself in this way; indeed, his rapid intellectual development had already created some concern among his friends. "People won't believe you ever were a slave, Frederick, if you keep on this way," one abolitionist exclaimed, and another added, "Be yourself and tell your story. Better have a little of the plantation speech than not; it is not best that you seem too learned."[27]

When Douglass went to England in 1846 on a lecture tour, a Boston abolitionist, Mrs. Maria W. Chapman, expressed her concern to an English friend that Douglass might not be able to withstand the pressure of the anti-Garrison faction. Hearing of this letter, Douglass wrote Mrs. Chapman that "if you wish to drive me from the Anti-Slavery Society, put me under overseership and the work is done."[28] Three years earlier, Douglass had objected to abolitionist John Collins' injection of utopian socialism into antislavery meetings, for it imposed "an additional burden of unpopularity on our cause"; reprimanded by Mrs. Chapman for his remarks, Douglass later recalled that this "first offense against our anti-slavery Israel" had been "a strange and distressing revelation to me, and one of which I was not soon relieved."[29]

When the still restive Douglass decided to establish a newspaper in Rochester, despite the contrary advice of his Garrisonian friends, the subsequent break was almost assured, for he now had an independent means of expression. The newspaper project, Douglass contended, was no reflection on the quality of existing antislavery journals; the time had come, however, for Negroes to demonstrate their own capabilities, to produce their own authors, editors, and journals, and to be their "own representatives and advocates, not exclusively, but peculiarly—not distinct from, but in connection with our white friends."[30] But since independence also involved divergence in antislavery creed, it was insufferable to the Garrisonians. Before long, Garrison and Douglass were engaged in a vituperative editorial war, while other abolitionists looked on in dismay. To Douglass, it was ironic that the proved champions of human freedom—the Garrisonians—should presume to suppress dissent within their own movement. Apparently the only true faith was that proclaimed in Boston. "They talk down there," he wrote to Gerrit Smith, "just as if the Anti-Slavery Cause belonged to them—and as if all Anti-Slavery ideas originated with them and that no man has a right to 'peep or mutter' on the subject, who does not hold letters patent from them."[31] Such subordination was more than an ex-slave could accept.

Whatever the merits of the conflicting abolition doctrines, Douglass' actions, when combined with those of various state and national Negro conventions, dramatized the increasing demand of Negro abolitionists for a greater voice in the tactics, strategy, and creed of the movement. And this reflected not only conflict over doctrine but considerable dissatisfaction with the pace of the equal rights struggle in the North. Some Negroes questioned whether or not racial equality had been relegated to a position of secondary importance in the abolition crusade. "I have seen constitutions of abolition societies," one Negro leader charged, "where nothing was said about the improvement of the man of color! They have overlooked the great sin of prejudice. They have passed by this foul monster, which is at once the parent and offspring of slavery."[32] Pursuing this subject, the *Colored American* charged that the American Anti-Slavery Society had made "secondary and collateral what ought to have been the primary object of all their efforts. In their strong zeal and fiery indignation against slavery in the South, they half overlooked slavery in the North." Indeed, more is known of slavery in the Carolinas "than of the deep and damning thralldom which grinds to the dust, the colored inhabitants of New York."[33] On the eve of the election of 1860, Douglass noted with regret that the equal suffrage movement in New York was almost exclusively in the hands of Negroes, for neither abolitionists nor Republicans "seem to care much for it."[34] But these differences in emphasis were perhaps inevitable and never effectively reconciled; the black abolitionist was generally moved by compelling personal need, his white cohort acted more from the abstractions of conscience; for one, the primary problem was the Negro; for the other, the slave. Each sought, in his own way, to enlarge the area of freedom.

During the crucial decade of the 1850's, the Negro abolitionist grew ever more restive and impatient. The Fugitive Slave Act, the resurgence of the American Colonization Society, the unsuccessful attempts to win equal suffrage, and, finally, the Dred Scott decision, impressed many Negroes with the increasing helplessness of their position in the face of the white man's apparent determination to maintain racial supremacy. Despite two decades of militant antislavery, the Negro's position seemed little improved. Moreover, the emergence of the Republican party made the very term "antislavery" difficult to define with any precision. If the Republican party was "antislavery," why did it refuse to move against racial oppression in the free states? and why in some areas did it proclaim principles of white supremacy? If the Kansas free staters were, indeed, "antislavery," how does one account for their determined efforts to keep all Negroes out of the territory? The answer was obvious: it was possible to be both "antislavery" and anti-Negro, to proclaim both free soil and white supremacy. "Opposing slavery and hating its victims," Douglass observed, "has come to be a very common form of abolitionism."[35] Disillusioned with Republican pronouncements, an Illinois Negro leader was moved to declare that he cared "nothing about that anti-slavery which wants to make the Territories free, while it is unwilling to extend to me, as a man, in the free States, all the rights of a man."[36] Of course, many white abolitionists had come to an identical conclusion about the "cowardly and contemptible" antislavery of the Republican party. When Stephen S. Foster accordingly called for a convention to reorganize the abolitionist movement, Douglass enthusiastically endorsed the proposal. Reviewing the history of the antislavery struggle, the Negro leader contrasted the heroic beginnings of militant abolitionism with the "Sentimental Abolitionism" of the Republican party, the "fratricidal conduct" of the American Anti-Slavery Society, and the political impotency of the Liberty party. If the "noble objects" of Foster's convention were put into effect, abolitionists—white and black—might once again unite into "one solid abolition organization" which would agitate for the exercise of Federal and State power to abolish the institution of slavery. Thus might the confusion between Republican antislavery and true abolitionism be ended.[37]

But in the absence of any such unified movement, the Negro abolitionist continued to advance an increasingly independent position. Tired of exhortations to be patient and await that "impartial and just God" who would inevitably rid the nation of slavery, Negroes began to talk of organized insubordination, slave insurrections, the use of physical force to resist the newly passed Fugitive Slave Act, the organization of state leagues to combat repressive legislation, and, in view of the Dred Scott decision, some even argued that Negroes no longer had any obligation to the United States and should welcome the overthrow of the government if necessary to exterminate slavery.[38] The vindication of the Negro's rights now seemed to demand a position more advanced than that of moral suasion. "Every slavehunter who meets a bloody death in his infernal business," Douglass wrote, "is an argument in favor of the manhood of our race."[39] Had not John Brown demonstrated, a Boston Negro leader asserted, that physical force might prove more effective than the "gradual diffusion of anti-slavery gospel." Although he hoped that slavery might be abolished peaceably, "if, as appears to be the case, there is no use in crying peace, then let us not shrink from the responsibility. My motto has always been, 'Better die freemen than live to be slaves.' "[40]

The espousal of increasingly radical measures mirrored the Negro's deepening sense of alienation from American society. The antislavery crusade had not altered the image of the Negro in the eyes of white America, nor measurably improved his position. "We are slaves in the midst of freedom," Delany wrote, "waiting patiently, and unconcernedly—indifferently, and stupidly, for masters to come and lay claim to us, trusting to their generosity, whether or not they will own us and carry us into endless bondage. . . . I must admit, that I have no hopes in this country—no confidence in the American people."[41] The movement which Delany advocated in the 1850's, that of emigration, began to attract more Negroes; it enunciated a vigorous race nationalism, rejected the democratic pretensions of white Americans, questioned the motives and effectiveness of white abolitionists, and urged the establishment of an independent Negro state. To remain any longer in the United States was to remain "the dupes of, and deluded by the whites, even our most professed anti-slavery friends." The Negro must find his own identity, apart from that of the whites. "The truth is," an emigration convention declared, "we are not identical with the Anglo-Saxon or any other race of the Caucasian or pure white type of the human family, and the sooner we know and acknowledge this truth, the better for ourselves and posterity."[42] Although most Negroes rejected emigration, they did so uneasily, for the logic of the argument seemed difficult to refute.

The emigrationists had challenged the assumption of most white and Negro abolitionists that racial equality was a realizable goal in the United States and that some day Negroes would attain the level of the white man's civilization. But some Negroes chose to question that level. Were white standards of success worthy models for the Negro? Did success in war and material gain, for example, truly constitute "the great ends of human existence"? Was there any other standard of excellence than that "which revolves around the almighty dollar"? In raising these questions, *The Anglo-African Magazine* regretted the fact that most Negroes wanted only to reach the level of the white man; the apparent ideal is "comfortable subsistence; with many, a comfortable room and bedroom, on the same floor, in a front building; with many, in addition, a handsome carpet, a few mahogany chairs, a sofa, and a piano." Most Negro men, it found, would be well satisfied with a "Morphy cap, one well-fitting suit of clothes, patent-leather boots of the latest fashion, an ingot or two of gold in the form of a chain hanging over their breast, a long nine and a sherry cobbler at the St. Charles." And the ideal for Negro women "reaches no higher than the polka and redowa, and agreeable flirting at a picnic." Such goals, the magazine argued, were unoriginal, "imitative and artificial." The Negro must seek a higher goal; despite his present degradation, he must "look up, above, and beyond the whites, and determine to whip, to beat, to excel them. . . . Once bent upon beating this Yankee Nation, who are beating all creation, and there will come upon us an inspiration, a power, hitherto unknown— hitherto unfelt by any other men, or race of men." The nature of this higher ideal was not indicated, except to suggest that it would not be money; economic changes, the magazine concluded, were already anticipating a day when "wealth will cease to be God of the American heart" and give way to some "nobler idolatry."[43]

On the eve of the Civil War, most Negroes aspired no higher than the goal of incorporation into white American society. Nevertheless, a strong undercurrent of race pride and consciousness, made explicit in the emigration movement, was clearly present, and white reformers would henceforth have to contend with its implications. Although the "wealth, the intellect, the Legislation (State and Federal), the pulpit, and the science of America" still tended to dismiss the Negro "as something less than a man," one Negro journal prophesied in 1859 that such arguments would become increasingly insupportable and that "this great black sluggard" may yet "shake the pillars of the commonweal."[44] In the meantime, the Negro had begun to produce his own spokesmen and media of expression; he had achieved increased recognition within the antislavery movement, and though he continued to express his appreciation of the efforts and sacrifices of white abolitionists, he made it clear that they were no longer to dominate the cause or confine its limits. The entire question of racial equality was at issue, not merely the elimination of chattel slavery. "The time is come," a Negro conference announced in 1854, "when our people must assume the rank of a first-rate power in the battle against caste and Slavery; it is emphatically our battle; no one else can fight it for us, and with God's help we must fight it ourselves.— Our relations to the Anti-Slavery movement must be and are changed. Instead of depending upon it we must lead it."[45]

8. Blacks and the Civil War

The American Civil War began as an attempt to prevent armed secession and preserve the Union; it ended as a revolutionary crusade for the emancipation of the slaves. In this transformation, blacks played a crucial role. From the beginning of the conflict, black and white abolitionists and radical Republicans pressured the Lincoln administration to inaugurate an emancipation policy. In August, 1861, General John C. Frémont proclaimed emancipation as a measure of military necessity in Missouri, but his order was modified by the President. The same reception was accorded an order of Major General David Hunter, who in March, 1862, declared slaves free in the military department under his command. Yet President Lincoln was moving slowly but steadily toward emancipation. In the spring of 1862 he signed bills abolishing slavery in the territories, and proclaiming emancipation, with compensation for the slaveholders, in the District of Columbia. But he continued to grope for a policy which would not alienate the Border slave states, whose loyalties were crucial to Union success, and not aggravate northern fears that emancipation would result in a flood of freedmen coming to the North to challenge white men for jobs and social status. Lincoln's plan was compensated emancipation, coupled with voluntary colonization of the freedmen in Haiti or Central America. But as 1862 wore on, the

Border States evinced no interest in emancipation even with compensation, and black spokesmen made it plain they disapproved of emigration. Lincoln decided that emancipation was the only measure which could bolster the sagging spirit of the Union army, provide a fresh pool of manpower for the armed forces, and convince world opinion that the Union cause was something more than an attempt to suppress the South's desire for independence. In July, 1862, he resolved upon emancipation, and in September issued a preliminary proclamation. On January 1, 1863, all slaves in areas not under the control of the Union army were declared forever free, and blacks were welcomed to enlist in the Union army.

The Emancipation Proclamation, many historians have observed, was a flawed document. It is by now customary to point out that where Lincoln had the power to free the slaves—in areas under Union control—he chose not to do so, and that he proclaimed emancipation only where he did not have the power to enforce it. Yet this argument overlooks the revolutionary change the Proclamation wrought in the war. From January 1, 1863, forward, the Union army became an agent of emancipation; wherever that army went, emancipation automatically followed. It was a recognition of this fundamental fact which led blacks throughout the nation to gather in their churches on New Year's Eve, singing hymns and celebrating the arrival of "the Year of Jubilee." For the same reason, Jefferson Davis, president of the Confederacy, condemned the Proclamation as "the most execrable measure recorded in the history of guilty man."

The Emancipation Proclamation thus ushered in a new period of black and American history. Yet there was still a war to be fought and blacks played a crucial role in winning it. From the very outset, free blacks had volunteered their services to the Union army, only to be turned away. In 1862, some commanders did begin organizing small units of blacks and in November of that year the War Department authorized the creation of an all-black regi-

ment, the First South Carolina Volunteers, with the
Boston abolitionist, Thomas Wentworth Higginson in
command. Higginson's record of his experiences, *Army
Life in a Black Regiment,* provides one of the most
insightful and passionate descriptions of the performance
of blacks as fighting men. It was only in 1863 that the
enlistment of black troops began in earnest, and by the
end of the war about 200,000 blacks—free Negroes from
the North and escaped or freed slaves from the South—
had served in the Union army and navy. Naval vessels
were integrated, but in the army blacks served in segregated units, and at first received a reduced rate of pay. One
of the most famous of these all-black regiments was the
54th Massachusetts Volunteers, organized by Governor
John Andrew early in 1863. A committee of black leaders,
including Martin Delany, Henry Highland Garnet, and
Frederick Douglass, traveled throughout the North urging
blacks to enlist in the 54th. In its first engagement, the
54th was ordered to attack an entrenched Confederate
position and suffered severe losses,—247 killed or
wounded of 600 men engaged, and the death of its
commander, Boston aristocrat Robert Gould Shaw. But
the 54th had proved beyond the shadow of a doubt that
blacks could become good fighting men.

The contribution of the mass of southern blacks to the
Union cause is a more difficult subject to investigate than
the service of blacks to the Union army. One controversial
interpretation is the following section from W. E. B. Du
Bois' classic *Black Reconstruction,* a book which helped
alter historians' perceptions of the postwar years, but also
contains much information on the war itself. Some historians, pointing out that there were no major slave rebellions during the Civil War despite the drain on southern
white manpower, had concluded that southern blacks were
relatively passive and even loyal to their masters. That
many—particularly house servants—were loyal is beyond
question; yet Du Bois points out that, as the war pro-
gressed, whenever a Union army entered southern terri-

tory, slaves simply abandoned their plantations and flocked to the military camps. Some blacks came over to the Union side through spectacular acts of individual heroism, including Robert Smalls, the pilot on a vessel in the Confederate navy, who brought his ship out of Charleston harbor and over to the Union navy. The "contrabands" as these blacks who abandoned slavery were called, provided invaluable military information for the Union forces, and many served as laborers, spies, and soldiers. Others, Du Bois points out, were put to work as free laborers on abandoned or confiscated plantations. Whether or not one agrees with Du Bois that this flight from slavery was sufficiently organized to be termed a "general strike," it is difficult to resist the conclusion that through their contribution to the Union's victory both in and out of the army, blacks in a real sense freed themselves during the Civil War.

The General Strike

W. E. B. Du Bois

How the Civil War meant emancipation and how the black worker won the war by a general strike which transferred his labor from the Confederate planter to the Northern invader, in whose army lines workers began to be organized as a new labor force

When Edwin Ruffin, white-haired and mad, fired the first gun at Fort Sumter, he freed the slaves. It was the last thing he meant to do but that was because he was so typically a Southern oligarch. He did not know the real world about him. He was pro-

FROM W. E. B. DuBois, *Black Reconstruction*. Copyright © 1962 by Meridian. Reprinted by permission of Jaffe, Shaw & Rosenberg.

vincial and lived apart on his plantation with his servants, his books and his thoughts. Outside of agriculture, he jumped at conclusions instead of testing them by careful research. He knew, for instance, that the North would not fight. He knew that Negroes would never revolt.

And so war came. War is murder, force, anarchy and debt. Its end is evil, despite all incidental good. Neither North nor South had before 1861 the slightest intention of going to war. The thought was in many respects ridiculous. They were not prepared for war. The national army was small, poorly equipped and without experience. There was no file from which someone might draw plans of subjugation.

When Northern armies entered the South they became armies of emancipation. It was the last thing they planned to be. The North did not propose to attack property. It did not propose to free slaves. This was to be a white man's war to preserve the Union, and the Union must be preserved. . . .

Thus the Negro himself was not seriously considered by the majority of men, North or South. And yet from the very beginning, the Negro occupied the center of the stage because of very simple physical reasons: the war was in the South and in the South were 3,953,740 black slaves and 261,918 free Negroes. What was to be the relation of this mass of workers to the war? What did the war mean to the Negroes, and what did the Negroes mean to the war? There are two theories, both rather over-elaborated: the one that the Negro did nothing but faithfully serve his master until emancipation was thrust upon him; the other that the Negro immediately, just as quickly as the presence of Northern soldiers made it possible, left serfdom and took his stand with the army of freedom.

It must be borne in mind that nine-tenths of the four million black slaves could neither read nor write, and that the overwhelming majority of them were isolated on country plantations. Any mass movement under such circumstances must materialize slowly and painfully. What the Negro did was to wait, look and listen and try to see where his interest lay. There was no use in seeking refuge in an army which was not an army of freedom; and there was no sense in revolting against armed masters who were conquering the world. As soon, however, as it became clear that the Union armies

would not or could not return fugitive slaves, and that the masters
with all their fume and fury were uncertain of victory, the slave
entered upon a general strike against slavery by the same methods
that he had used during the period of the fugitive slave. He ran
away to the first place of safety and offered his services to the
Federal Army. So that in this way it was really true that he served
his former master and served the emancipating army; and it was
also true that this withdrawal and bestowal of his labor decided the
war.

The South counted on Negroes as laborers to raise food and
money crops for civilians and for the army, and even in a crisis, to
be used for military purposes. Slave revolt was an ever-present
risk, but there was no reason to think that a short war with the
North would greatly increase this danger. Publicly, the South
repudiated the thought of its slaves even wanting to be rescued.
The New Orleans *Crescent* showed "the absurdity of the assertion
of a general stampede of our Negroes." The London *Dispatch* was
convinced that Negroes did not want to be free. "As for the slaves
themselves, crushed with the wrongs of Dred Scott and Uncle
Tom—most provoking—they cannot be brought to 'burn with
revenge.' They are spies for their masters. They obstinately refuse
to run away to liberty, outrage and starvation. They work in the
fields as usual when the planter and overseer are away and only
the white women are left at home."

Early in the war, the South had made careful calculation of the
military value of slaves. The Alabama *Advertiser* in 1861 discussed the slaves as a "Military Element in the South." It said that
"The total white population of the eleven states now comprising the
Confederacy is 5,000,000, and, therefore, to fill up the ranks of
the proposed army, 600,000, about ten per cent of the entire white
population, will be required. In any other country than our own
such a draft could not be met, but the Southern states can furnish
that number of men, and still not leave the material interest of the
country in a suffering condition."

The editor, with fatuous faith, did not for a moment contemplate any mass movement against this program on the part of the
slaves. "Those who are incapacitated for bearing arms can oversee
the plantations, and the Negroes can go on undisturbed in their

usual labors. In the North, the case is different; the men who join the army of subjugation are the laborers, the producers and the factory operatives. Nearly every man from that section, especially those from the rural districts, leaves some branch of industry to suffer during his absence. The institution of slavery in the South alone enables her to place in the field a force much larger in proportion to her white population than the North, or indeed any country which is dependent entirely on free labor. The institution is a tower of strength to the South, particularly at the present crisis, and our enemies will be likely to find that the 'Moral Cancer' about which their orators are so fond of prating, is really one of the most effective weapons employed against the Union by the South."[1]

Soon the South of necessity was moving out beyond this plan. It was no longer simply a question of using the Negroes at home on the plantation to raise food. They could be of even more immediate use, as military labor, to throw up breastworks, transport and prepare food and act as servants in camp. In the Charleston *Courier* of November 22, able-bodied hands were asked to be sent by their masters to work upon the defenses. "They would be fed and properly cared for."

In 1862, in Charleston, after a proclamation of martial law, the governor and counsel authorized the procuring of Negro slaves either by the planter's consent or by impressment "to work on the fortifications and defenses of Charleston harbor."

In Mississippi in 1862, permission was granted the Governor to impress slaves to work in New Iberia for salt, which was becoming the Confederacy's most pressing necessity. In Texas, a thousand Negroes were offered by planters for work on the public defenses.

By 1864, the matter had passed beyond the demand for slaves as military laborers and had come to the place where the South was seriously considering and openly demanding the use of Negroes as soldiers. Distinctly and inevitably, the rigor of the slave system in the South softened as war proceeded. Slavery showed in many if not all respects its best side. The harshness and the cruelty, in part, had to disappear, since there were left on the plantations mainly women and children, with only a few men, and there was a certain feeling and apprehension in the air on the part

of the whites which led them to capitalize all the friendship and
kindness which had existed between them and the slaves. No race
could have responded to this so quickly and thoroughly as the
Negroes. They felt pity and responsibility and also a certain new
undercurrent of independence. Negroes were still being sold rather
ostentatiously in Charleston and New Orleans, but the long lines of
Virginia Negroes were not marching to the Southwest. In a certain
sense, after the first few months everybody knew that slavery was
done with; that no matter who won, the conditions of the slave
could never be the same after this disaster of war. And it was,
perhaps, these considerations, more than anything else, that held
the poised arm of the black man; for no one knew better than the
South what a Negro crazed with cruelty and oppression and beaten
back to the last stand could do to his oppressor.

The Southerners, therefore, were careful. Those who had been
kind to their slaves assured them of the bad character of the
Yankee and of their own good intentions.

Thus while the Negroes knew there were Abolitionists in the
North, they did not know their growth, their power or their intentions and they did hear on every side that the South was overwhelmingly victorious on the battlefield. On the other hand, some
of the Negroes sensed what was beginning to happen. The Negroes
of the cities, the Negroes who were being hired out, the Negroes of
intelligence who could read and write, all began carefully to watch
the unfolding of the situation. At the first gun of Sumter, the black
mass began not to move but to heave with nervous tension and
watchful waiting. Even before war was declared, a movement
began across the border. Just before the war large numbers of
fugitive slaves and free Negroes rushed into the North. It was
estimated that two thousand left North Carolina alone because of
rumors of war.

When W. T. Sherman occupied Port Royal in October, 1861, he
had no idea that he was beginning emancipation at one of its
strategic points. On the contrary, he was very polite and said that
he had no idea of interfering with slaves. In the same way, Major
General Dix, on entering two counties of Virginia, was careful to
order that slavery was not to be interfered with or slaves to be
received into the line. Burnside went further, and as he brought his

Rhode Island regiment through Baltimore in June, he courteously returned two Negroes who tried to run away with him. They were "supposed to be slaves," although they may have been free Negroes. On the 4th of July, Colonel Pryor of Ohio delivered an address to the people of Virginia in which he repudiated the accusation that the Northern army were Abolitionists.

"I desire to assure you that the relation of master and servant as recognized in your state shall be respected. Your authority over that species of property shall not in the least be interfered with. To this end, I assure you that those under my command have peremptory orders to take up and hold any Negroes found running about the camp without passes from their masters."[2]

Halleck in Missouri in 1862 refused to let fugitive slaves enter his lines. Burnside, Buell, Hooker, Thomas Williams and McClellan himself, all warned their soldiers against receiving slaves and most of them permitted masters to come and remove slaves found within the lines.

The constant charge of Southern newspapers, Southern politicians and their Northern sympathizers, that the war was an abolition war, met with constant and indignant denial. Loyal newspapers, orators and preachers, with few exceptions, while advocating stringent measures for putting down the Rebellion, carefully disclaimed any intention of disturbing the "peculiar institution" of the South. The Secretary of State informed foreign governments, through our ministers abroad, that this was not our purpose. President Lincoln, in his earlier messages, substantially reiterated the statement. Leading generals, on entering Southern territory, issued proclamations to the same effect. One even promised to put down any slave insurrection "with an iron hand," while others took vigorous measures to send back the fugitives who sought refuge within their lines.

"In the early years of the war, if accounts do not err, during the entire period McClellan commanded the Army of the Potomac, 'John Brown's Body' was a forbidden air among the regimental bands. The Hutchinsons were driven from Union camps for singing abolition songs, and in so far as the Northern army interested itself at all in the slavery question, it was by the use of force to return to their Southern masters fugitives seeking shelter in the Union lines. While the information they possessed, especially respecting the roads and means of communication, should have been of inestimable service to the Federals, they were not to be employed as laborers or armed as soldiers. The North avoided the appearance of a desire to raise the Negroes from the plane of chattels to the rank of human beings."[3]

Here was no bid for the coöperation of either slaves or free Negroes. In the North, Negroes were not allowed to enlist and often refused with indignation. "Thus the weakness of the South temporarily became her strength. Her servile population, repulsed by Northern pro-slavery sentiment, remained at home engaged in agriculture, thus releasing her entire white population for active service in the field; while, on the other hand, the military resources of the North were necessarily diminished by the demands of labor."[4]

It was as Frederick Douglass said in Boston in 1865, that the Civil War was begun "in the interests of slavery on both sides. The South was fighting to take slavery out of the Union, and the North fighting to keep it in the Union; the South fighting to get it beyond the limits of the United States Constitution, and the North fighting for the old guarantees;—both despising the Negro, both insulting the Negro."

It was, therefore, at first by no means clear to most of the four million Negroes in slavery what this war might mean to them. They crouched consciously and moved silently, listening, hoping and hesitating. The watchfulness of the South was redoubled. They spread propaganda: the Yankees were not only not thinking of setting them free, but if they did anything, they would sell them into worse slavery in the West Indies. They would drive them from even the scant comfort of the plantations into the highways and purlieus. Moreover, if they tried to emancipate the slaves, they would fail because they could not do this without conquest of the South. The South was unconquerable.

The South was not slow to spread propaganda and point to the wretched condition of fugitive Negroes in order to keep the loyalty of its indispensable labor force. The Charleston *Daily Courier* said February 18, 1863: "A company of volunteers having left Fayette County for the field of action, Mr. Nance sent two Negro boys along to aid the company. Their imaginations became dazzled with the visions of Elysian fields in Yankeedom and they went to find them. But Paradise was nowhere there, and they again sighed for home. The Yanks, however, detained them and cut off their ears close to their heads. These Negroes finally made their escape and are now at home with Mr. Nance in Pickens. They are violent haters of Yankees and their adventures and experiences are a terror to Negroes of the region, who learned a lesson from their brethren whose ears are left in Lincolndom!"

The Charleston *Mercury,* May 8, 1862, said: "The Yankees are fortifying Fernandina (Florida) and have a large number of Negroes engaged on their works. Whenever the Negroes have an opportunity, they escape from their oppressors. They report that they are worked hard, get little rest and food and no pay."

The Savannah *Daily News* reports in 1862 that many stolen Negroes had been recaptured: "The Yankees had married a number of the women and were taking them home with them. I have seen some who refused to go and others who had been forced off at other times who had returned."

It was a lovely dress parade of Alphonse and Gaston until the Negro spoiled it and in a perfectly logical way. So long as the Union stood still and talked, the Negro kept quiet and worked. The moment the Union army moved into slave territory, the Negro joined it. Despite all argument and calculation and in the face of refusals and commands, wherever the Union armies marched, appeared the fugitive slaves. It made no difference what the obstacles were, or the attitudes of the commanders. It was "like thrusting a walking stick into an anthill," says one writer. And yet the army chiefs at first tried to regard it as an exceptional and temporary matter, a thing which they could control, when as a matter of fact it was the meat and kernel of the war.

Thus as the war went on and the invading armies came on, the way suddenly cleared for the onlooking Negro, for his spokesmen in the North, and for his silent listeners in the South. Each step, thereafter, came with curious, logical and inevitable fate. First there were the fugitive slaves. Slaves had always been running away to the North, and when the North grew hostile, on to Canada. It was the safety valve that kept down the chance of insurrection in the South to the lowest point. Suddenly, now, the chance to run away not only increased, but after preliminary repulse and hesitation, there was actual encouragement.

Not that the government planned or foresaw this eventuality; on the contrary, having repeatedly declared the object of the war as the preservation of the Union and that it did not propose to fight for slaves or touch slavery, it faced a stampede of fugitive slaves.

Every step the Northern armies took then meant fugitive slaves. They crossed the Potomac, and the slaves of northern Virginia began to pour into the army and into Washington. They captured Fortress Monroe, and slaves from Virginia and even North Carolina poured into the army. They captured Port Royal, and the masters ran away, leaving droves of black fugitives in the hands of the Northern army. They moved down the Mississippi Valley, and if the slaves did not rush to the army, the army marched to the slaves. They captured New Orleans, and captured a great black city and a state full of slaves.

What was to be done? They tried to send the slaves back, and even used the soldiers for recapturing them. This was all well enough as long as the war was a dress parade. But when it became real war, and slaves were captured or received, they could be used as much-needed laborers and servants by the Northern army.

This but emphasized and made clearer a truth which ought to have been recognized from the very beginning: The Southern worker, black and white, held the key to the war; and of the two groups, the black worker raising food and raw materials held an even more strategic place than the white. This was so clear a fact that both sides should have known it. Frémont in Missouri took the logical action of freeing slaves of the enemy round about him by proclamation, and President Lincoln just as promptly repudiated what he had done. Even before that, General Butler in Virginia, commander of the Union forces at Fortress Monroe, met three slaves walking into his camp from the Confederate fortifications where they had been at work. Butler immediately declared these men "contraband of war" and put them to work in his own camp. More slaves followed, accompanied by their wives and children. The situation here was not quite so logical. Nevertheless, Butler kept the fugitives and freed them and let them do what work they could; and his action was approved by the Secretary of War.

"On May twenty-sixth, only two days after the one slave appeared before Butler, eight Negroes appeared; on the next day, forty-seven, of all ages and both sexes. Each day they continued to come by twenties, thirties and forties until by July 30th the number had reached nine hundred. In a very short while the number ran up into the thousands. The renowned Fortress took the name of the 'freedom fort' to which the blacks came by means of a 'mysterious spiritual telegraph.' "[5]

In December, 1861, the Secretary of War, Simon Cameron, had written, printed and put into the mails his first report as Secretary of War without consultation with the President. Possibly he knew that his recommendations would not be approved, but "he recommended the general arming of Negroes, declaring that the Federals had as clear a right to employ slaves taken from the enemy as to use captured gunpowder." This report was recalled by the President by telegraph and the statements of the Secretary were modified. The incident aroused some unpleasantness in the cabinet.

The published report finally said:

"Persons held by rebels, under such laws, to service as slaves, may, however, be justly liberated from their constraint, and made more valuable in various employments, through voluntary and compensated service, than if confiscated as subjects of property."

Transforming itself suddenly from a problem of abandoned plantations and slaves captured while being used by the enemy for military purposes, the movement became a general strike against the slave system on the part of all who could find opportunity. The trickling streams of fugitives swelled to a flood. Once begun, the general strike of black and white went madly and relentlessly on like some great saga.

"Imagine, if you will, a slave population, springing from antecedent barbarism, rising up and leaving its ancient bondage, forsaking its local traditions and all the associations and attractions of the old plantation life, coming garbed in rags or in silks, with feet shod or bleeding, individually or in families and larger groups, —an army of slaves and fugitives, pushing its way irresistibly toward an army of fighting men, perpetually on the defensive and perpetually ready to attack. The arrival among us of these hordes was like the oncoming of cities. There was no plan in this exodus, no Moses to lead it. Unlettered reason or the mere inarticulate decision of instinct brought them to us. Often the slaves met prejudices against their color more bitter than any they had left behind. But their own interests were identical, they felt, with the objects of our armies; a blind terror stung them, an equally blind hope allured them, and to us they come."[6]

"Even before the close of 1862, many thousands of blacks of all ages, ragged, with no possessions, except the bundles which they carried, had assembled at Norfolk, Hampton, Alexandria and Washington. Others, landless, homeless, helpless, in families and in multitudes, including a considerable number of wretched white people, flocked North from Tennessee, Kentucky, Arkansas and Missouri. All these were relieved in part by army rations, irregularly issued, and by volunteer societies of the North, which gained their money from churches and individuals in this country and abroad. In the spring of 1863, there were swarming crowds of Negroes and white refugees along the line of defense made between the armies of the North and South and reaching from Maryland to Virginia, along the coast from Norfolk to New Orleans. Soldiers and missionaries told of their virtues and vices, their joy and extreme suffering. The North was moved to an extraordinary degree, and endless bodies of workers and missionaries were organized and collected funds for materials.

"Rude barracks were erected at different points for the temporary shelter of the freedmen; but as soon as possible the colonies thus formed were broken up and the people encouraged to make individual contracts for labor upon neighboring plantations. In connection with the colonies, farms were cultivated which aided to meet the expenses. Hospitals were established at various points for the sick, of whom there were great numbers. The separation of families by the war, and illegitimate birth in consequence of slavery, left a great number of children practically in a state of orphanage."[7]

This was the beginning of the swarming of the slaves, of the quiet but unswerving determination of increasing numbers no longer to work on Confederate plantations, and to seek the freedom of the Northern armies. Wherever the army marched and in spite of all obstacles came the rising tide of slaves seeking freedom. For a long time, their treatment was left largely to the discretion of the department managers; some welcomed them, some drove them away, some organized them for work. Gradually, the fugitives became organized and formed a great labor force for the army. Several thousand were employed as laborers, servants, and spies.

A special war correspondent of the New York *Tribune* writes: " 'God bless the Negroes,' say I, with earnest lips. During our entire captivity, and after our escape, they were ever our firm, brave, unflinching friends. We never made an appeal to them they did not answer. They never hesitated to do us a service at the risk even of life, and under the most trying circumstances revealed a devotion and a spirit of self-sacrifice that was heroic. The magic word 'Yankee' opened all their hearts, and elicited the loftiest virtues. They were ignorant, oppressed, enslaved; but they always cherished a simple and a beautiful faith in the cause of the Union and its ultimate triumph, and never abandoned or turned aside from a man who sought food or shelter on his way to Freedom."[8]

This whole move was not dramatic or hysterical, rather it was like the great unbroken swell of the ocean before it dashes on the reefs. The Negroes showed no disposition to strike the one terrible blow which brought black men freedom in Haiti and which in all history has been used by all slaves and justified. There were some plans for insurrection made by Union officers:

"The plan is to induce the blacks to make a simultaneous movement of rising, on the night of the 1st of August next, over the entire States in rebellion, to arm themselves with any and every kind of weapon that may come to hand, and commence operations by burning all the railroad and country bridges, and tear up railroad tracks, and to destroy telegraph lines, etc., and then take to the woods, swamps, or the mountains, where they may emerge as occasion may offer for provisions and for further depredations. No blood is to be shed except in self-defense. The corn will be ripe about the 1st of August and with this and hogs running in the woods, and by foraging upon the plantations by night, they can subsist. This is the plan in substance, and if we can obtain a concerted movement at the time named it will doubtless be successful."[9]

Such plans came to naught for the simple reason that there was an easier way involving freedom with less risk.

The South preened itself on the absence of slave violence. Governor Walker of Florida said in his inaugural in 1865: "Where, in all the records of the past, does history present such an instance of steadfast devotion, unwavering attachment and constancy as was exhibited by the slaves of the South throughout the fearful contest that has just ended? The country invaded, homes desolated, the master absent in the army or forced to seek safety in flight and leave the mistress and her helpless infants unprotected, with every incitement to insubordination and instigation, to rapine and murder, no instance of insurrection, and scarcely one of voluntary desertion has been recorded."

The changes upon this theme have been rung by Southern orators many times since. The statement, of course, is not quite true. Hundreds of thousands of slaves were very evidently leaving their masters' homes and plantations. They did not wreak vengeance on unprotected women. They found an easier, more effective and more decent way to freedom. Men go wild and fight for freedom with bestial ferocity when they must—where there is no other way; but human nature does not deliberately choose blood— at least not black human nature. On the other hand, for every slave that escaped to the Union army, there were ten left on the untouched and inaccessible plantations.

Another step was logical and inevitable. The men who handled a spade for the Northern armies, the men who fed them, and as spies brought in information, could also handle a gun and shoot. Without legal authority and in spite of it, suddenly the Negro became a soldier. Later his services as soldier were not only permitted but were demanded to replace the tired and rebellious white men of the North. But as a soldier, the Negro must be free.

The North started out with the idea of fighting the war without touching slavery. They faced the fact, after severe fighting, that Negroes seemed a valuable asset as laborers, and they therefore declared them "contraband of war." It was but a step from that to attract and induce Negro labor to help the Northern armies. Slaves were urged and invited into the Northern armies; they became military laborers and spies; not simply military laborers, but laborers on the plantations, where the crops went to help the Federal army or were sold North. Thus wherever Northern armies appeared, Negro laborers came, and the North found itself actually freeing slaves before it had the slightest intention of doing so, indeed when it had every intention not to.

The experience of the army with the refugees and the rise of the departments of Negro affairs were a most interesting, but unfortunately little studied, phase of Reconstruction. Yet it contained in a sense the key to the understanding of the whole situation. At first, the rush of the Negroes from the plantations came as a surprise and was variously interpreted. The easiest thing to say was that Negroes were tired of work and wanted to live at the expense of the government; wanted to travel and see things and places. But in contradiction to this was the extent of the movement and the terrible suffering of the refugees. If they were seeking peace and quiet, they were much better off on the plantations than trailing in the footsteps of the army or squatting miserably in the camps. They were mistreated by the soldiers; ridiculed; driven away, and yet they came. They increased with every campaign, and as a final gesture, they marched with Sherman from Atlanta to the sea, and met the refugees and abandoned human property on the Sea Islands and the Carolina Coast.

This was not merely the desire to stop work. It was a strike on a wide basis against the conditions of work. It was a general strike that involved directly in the end perhaps a half million people. They wanted to stop the economy of the plantation system, and to do that they left the plantations. At first, the commanders were disposed to drive them away, or to give them quasi-freedom and let them do as they pleased with the nothing that they possessed. This did not work. Then the commanders organized relief and afterward, work. This came to the attention of the country first in Pierce's "Ten Thousand Clients." Pierce of Boston had worked with the refugees in Virginia under Butler, provided them with food and places to live, and given them jobs and land to cultivate. He was successful. He came from there, and, in conjunction with the Treasury Department, began the work on a vaster scale at Port Royal. Here he found the key to the situation. The Negroes were willing to work and did work, but they wanted land to work, and they wanted to see and own the results of their toil. It was here and in the West and the South that a new vista opened. Here was a chance to establish an agrarian democracy in the South: peasant holders of small properties, eager to work and raise crops, amenable to suggestion and general direction. All they needed was honesty in treatment, and education. Wherever these conditions were fulfilled, the result was little less than phenomenal. This was testified to by Pierce in the Carolinas, by Butler's agents in North Carolina, by the experiment of the Sea Islands, by Grant's department of Negro affairs under Eaton, and by Banks' direction of Negro labor in Louisiana. It is astonishing how this army of striking labor furnished in time 200,000 Federal soldiers whose evident ability to fight decided the war.

General Butler went from Virginia to New Orleans to take charge of the city newly captured in April, 1862. Here was a whole city half-filled with blacks and mulattoes, some of them wealthy free Negroes and soldiers who came over from the Confederate side and joined the Federals.

Perhaps the greatest and most systematic organizing of fugitives took place in New Orleans. At first, Butler had issued orders that no slaves would be received in New Orleans. Many planters were unable to make slaves work or to support them, and sent them back of the Federal lines, planning to reclaim them after the war was over. Butler emancipated these slaves in spite of the fact that he knew this was against Lincoln's policy. As the flood kept coming, he seized abandoned sugar plantations and began to work them with Negro labor for the benefit of the government.

By permission of the War Department, and under the authority of the Confiscation Act, Butler organized colonies of fugitives, and regulated employment. His brother, Colonel Butler, and others worked plantations, hiring the Negro labor. The Negroes stood at Butler's right hand during the trying time of his administration, and particularly the well-to-do free Negro group were his strongest allies. He was entertained at their tables and brought down on himself the wrath and contempt, not simply of the South, but even of the North. He received the black regiment, and kept their black officers, who never forgot him. Whatever else he might have been before the war, or proved to be afterwards, "the colored people of Louisiana under the proper sense of the good you have done to the African race in the United States, beg leave to express to you their gratitude."

From 1862 to 1865, many different systems of caring for the escaped slaves and their families in this area were tried. Butler and his successor, Banks, each sought to provide for the thousands of destitute freedmen with medicine, rations and clothing. When General Banks took command, there was suffering, disease and death among the 150,000 Negroes. On January 30, 1863, he issued a general order making labor on public works and elsewhere compulsory for Negroes who had no means of support.

Just as soon, however, as Banks tried to drive the freedmen back to the plantations and have them work under a half-military slave régime, the plan failed. It failed, not because the Negroes did not want to work, but because they were striking against these particular conditions of work. When, because of wide protest, he began to look into the matter, he saw a clear way. He selected Negroes to go out and look into conditions and to report on what was needed, and they made a faithful survey. He set up a little state with its department of education, with its landholding and organized work, and after experiment it ran itself. More and more here and up the Mississippi Valley, under other commanders and agents, experiments extended and were successful.

Further up the Mississippi, a different system was begun under General Grant. Grant's army in the West occupied Grand Junction, Mississippi, by November, 1862. The usual irregular host of slaves then swarmed in from the surrounding country. They begged for protection against recapture, and they, of course, needed food, clothing and shelter. They could not now be reënslaved through army aid, yet no provision had been made by anybody for their sustenance. A few were employed as teamsters, servants, cooks and scouts, yet it seemed as though the vast majority must be left to freeze and starve, for when the storms came with the winter months, the weather was of great severity.

Grant determined that Negroes should perform many of the camp duties ordinarily done by soldiers; that they should serve as fatigue men in the departments of the surgeon general, quartermaster, and commissary, and that they should help in building roads and earthworks. The women worked in the camp kitchens and as nurses in the hospitals. Grant said, "It was at this point where the first idea of the Freedmen's Bureau took its origin."

Grant selected as head of his Department of Negro Affairs, John Eaton, chaplain of the Twenty-Seventh Ohio Volunteers, who was soon promoted to the colonelcy of a colored regiment, and later for many years was a Commissioner of the United States Bureau of Education. He was then constituted Chief of Negro Affairs for the entire district under Grant's jurisdiction.

"I hope I may never be called on again to witness the horrible scenes I saw in those first days of the history of the freedmen in the Mississippi Valley. Assistants were hard to get, especially the kind that would do any good in our camps. A detailed soldier in each camp of a thousand people was the best that could be done. His duties were so onerous that he ended by doing nothing. . . . In reviewing the condition of the people at that time, I am not surprised at the marvelous stories told by visitors who caught an occasional glimpse of the misery and wretchedness in these camps. . . . Our efforts to do anything for these people, as they herded together in masses, when founded on any expectation that they would help themselves, often failed; they had become so completely broken down in spirit, through suffering, that it was almost impossible to arouse them.

"Their condition was appalling. There were men, women and children in every stage of disease or decrepitude, often nearly naked, with flesh torn by the terrible experiences of their escapes. Sometimes they were intelligent and eager to help themselves; often they were bewildered or stupid or possessed by the wildest notions of what liberty might mean—expecting to exchange labor, and obedience to the will of another, for idleness and freedom from restraint. Such ignorance and perverted notions produced a veritable moral chaos. Cringing deceit, theft, licentiousness—all the vices which slavery inevitably fosters—were hideous companions of nakedness, famine, and disease. A few had profited by the misfortunes of the master and were jubilant in their unwonted ease and luxury, but these stood in lurid contrast to the grimmer aspects of the tragedy—the women in travail, the helplessness of childhood and of old age, the horrors of sickness and of frequent death. Small wonder that men paused in bewilderment and panic, foreseeing the demoralization and infection of the Union soldier and the downfall of the Union cause."[10]

There were new and strange problems of social contact. The white soldiers, for the most part, were opposed to serving Negroes in any manner, and were even unwilling to guard the camps where they were segregated or protect them against violence. "To undertake any form of work for the contrabands, at that time, was to be forsaken by one's friends and to pass under a cloud."[11]

There was, however, a clear economic basis upon which the whole work of relief and order and subsistence could be placed. All around Grand Junction were large crops of ungathered corn and cotton. These were harvested and sold North and the receipts were placed to the credit of the government. The army of fugitives were soon willing to go to work; men, women and children. Wood was needed by the river steamers and woodcutters were set at work. Eaton fixed the wages for this industry and kept accounts with the workers. He saw to it that all of them had sufficient food and clothing, and rough shelter was built for them. Citizens round about who had not abandoned their plantations were allowed to hire labor on the same terms as the government was using it. Very soon the freedmen became self-sustaining and gave little trouble. They began to build themselves comfortable cabins, and the government constructed hospitals for the sick. In the case of the sick and dependent, a tax was laid on the wages of workers. At first it was thought the laborers would object, but, on the contrary, they were perfectly willing and the imposition of the tax compelled the government to see that wages were promptly paid. The freedmen freely acknowledged that they ought to assist in helping bear the burden of the poor, and were flattered by having the government ask their help. It was the reaction of a new labor group, who, for the first time in their lives, were receiving money in payment for their work. Five thousand dollars was raised by this tax for hospitals, and with this money tools and property were bought. By wholesale purchase, clothes, household goods and other articles were secured by the freedmen at a cost of one-third of what they might have paid the stores. There was a rigid system of accounts and monthly reports through army officials.

In 1864, July 5, Eaton reports: "These freedmen are now disposed of as follows: In military service as soldiers, laundresses, cooks, officers' servants, and laborers in the various staff departments, 41,150; in cities, on plantations and in freedmen's villages and cared for, 72,500. Of these 62,300 are entirely self-supporting—the same as any industrial class anywhere else—as planters, mechanics, barbers, hackmen, draymen, etc., conducting enterprises on their own responsibility or working as hired laborers. The remaining 10,200 receive subsistence from the government. 3,000 of them are members of families whose heads are carrying on plantations and have under cultivation 4,000 acres of cotton. They are to pay the government for their sustenance from the first income of the crop. The other 7,200 include the paupers—that is to say, all Negroes over and under the self-supporting age, the crippled and sick in hospital, of the 113,650 and those engaged in their care. Instead of being unproductive, this class has now under cultivation 500 acres of corn, 790 acres of vegetables and 1,500 acres of cotton, besides working at wood-chopping and other industries. There are reported in the aggregate over 100,000 acres of cotton under cultivation. Of these about 7,000 acres are leased and cultivated by blacks. Some Negroes are managing as high as 300 or 400 acres."

The experiment at Davis Bend, Mississippi, was of especial interest. The place was occupied in November and December, 1864, and private interests were displaced and an interesting socialistic effort made with all the property under the control of the government. The Bend was divided into districts with Negro sheriffs and judges who were allowed to exercise authority under the general control of the military officers. Petty theft and idleness were soon reduced to a minimum and "the community distinctly demonstrated the capacity of the Negro to take care of himself and exercise under honest and competent direction the functions of self-government. . . ."[12]

Confusion and lack of system were the natural result of the general strike. Yet, the Negroes had accomplished their first aim in those parts of the South dominated by the Federal army. They had largely escaped from the plantation discipline, were receiving wages as free laborers, and had protection from violence and justice in some sort of court.

About 20,000 of them were in the District of Columbia;

100,000 in Virginia; 50,000 in North Carolina; and as many more each in Georgia and Louisiana. The Valley of the Mississippi was filled with settlers under the Treasury Department and the army. Here were nearly 500,000 former slaves. But there were 3,500,-000 more. These Negroes needed only the assurance that they would be freed and the opportunity of joining the Northern army. In larger and larger numbers, they filtered into the armies of the North. And in just the proportion that the Northern armies became in earnest, and proposed actually to force the South to stay in the Union, and not to make simply a demonstration, in just such proportion the Negroes became valuable as laborers, and doubly valuable as withdrawing labor from the South. After the first foolish year when the South woke up to the fact that there was going to be a real, long war, and the North realized just what war meant in blood and money, the whole relation of the North to the Negro and the Negro to the North changed.

The position of the Negro was strategic. His was the only appeal which would bring sympathy from Europe, despite strong economic bonds with the South, and prevent recognition of a Southern nation built on slavery. The free Negroes in the North, together with the Abolitionists, were clamoring. To them a war against the South simply had to be a war against slavery. Gradually, Abolitionists no longer need fear the mob. Disgruntled leaders of church and state began to talk of freedom. Slowly but surely an economic dispute and a political test of strength took on the aspects of a great moral crusade.

The Negro became in the first year contraband of war; that is, property belonging to the enemy and valuable to the invader. And in addition to that, he became, as the South quickly saw, the key to Southern resistance. Either these four million laborers remained quietly at work to raise food for the fighters, or the fighter starved. Simultaneously, when the dream of the North for man-power produced riots, the only additional troops that the North could depend on were 200,000 Negroes, for without them, as Lincoln said, the North could not have won the war.

But this slow, stubborn mutiny of the Negro slave was not merely a matter of 200,000 black soldiers and perhaps 300,000 other black laborers, servants, spies and helpers. Back of this half

million stood 3½ million more. Without their labor the South
would starve. With arms in their hands, Negroes would form a
fighting force which could replace every single Northern white
soldier fighting listlessly and against his will with a black man
fighting for freedom. . . .

Meantime, with perplexed and laggard steps, the United States
Government followed the footsteps of the black slave. It made no
difference how much Abraham Lincoln might protest that this was
not a war against slavery, or ask General McDowell "if it would
not be well to allow the armies to bring back those fugitive slaves
which have crossed the Potomac with our troops" (a communication which was marked "secret"). It was in vain that Lincoln
rushed entreaties and then commands to Frémont in Missouri, not
to emancipate the slaves of rebels, and then had to hasten similar
orders to Hunter in South Carolina. The slave, despite every effort,
was becoming the center of war. Lincoln, with his uncanny insight,
began to see it. He began to talk about compensation for emancipated slaves, and Congress, following almost too quickly, passed
the Confiscation Act in August, 1861, freeing slaves which were
actually used in war by the enemy. Lincoln then suggested that
provision be made for colonization of such slaves. He simply could
not envisage free Negroes in the United States. What would become of them? What would they do? Meantime, the slave kept
looming. New Orleans was captured and the whole black population of Louisiana began streaming toward it. When Vicksburg fell,
the center of perhaps the vastest Negro population in North
America was tapped. They rushed into the Union lines. Still Lincoln held off and watched symptoms. Greeley's "Prayer of Twenty
Millions" received the curt answer, less than a year before Emancipation, that the war was not to abolish slavery, and if Lincoln
could hold the country together and keep slavery, he would do it.

But he could not, and he had no sooner said this than he began to
realize that he could not. In June, 1862, slavery was abolished in
the territories. Compensation with possible colonization was
planned for the District of Columbia. Representatives and Senators from the Border States were brought together to talk about
extending this plan to their states, but they hesitated.

In August, Lincoln faced the truth, front forward; and that truth was not simply that Negroes ought to be free; it was that thousands of them were already free, and that either the power which slaves put into the hands of the South was to be taken from it, or the North could not win the war. Either the Negro was to be allowed to fight, or the draft itself would not bring enough white men into the army to keep up the war.

More than that, unless the North faced the world with the moral strength of declaring openly that they were fighting for the emancipation of slaves, they would probably find that the world would recognize the South as a separate nation; that ports would be opened; that trade would begin, and that despite all the military advantage of the North, the war would be lost.

In August, 1862, Lincoln discussed Emancipation as a military measure; in September, he issued his preliminary proclamation; on January 1, 1863, he declared that the slaves of all persons in rebellion were "henceforward and forever free."

The guns at Sumter, the marching armies, the fugitive slaves, the fugitives as "contrabands," spies, servants and laborers; the Negro as soldier, as citizen, as voter—these steps came from 1861 to 1868 with regular beat that was almost rhythmic. It was the price of the disaster of war, and it was a price that few Americans at first dreamed of paying or wanted to pay. The North was not Abolitionist. It was overwhelmingly in favor of Negro slavery, so long as this did not interfere with Northern moneymaking. But, on the other hand, there was a minority of the North who hated slavery with perfect hatred; who wanted no union with slaveholders; who fought for freedom and treated Negroes as men. As the Abolition-democracy gained in prestige and in power, they appeared as prophets, and led by statesmen, they began to guide the nation out of the morass into which it had fallen. They and their black friends and the new freedmen became gradually the leaders of a Reconstruction of Democracy in the United States, while marching millions sang the noblest war-song of the ages to the tune of "John Brown's Body":

Mine eyes have seen the glory of the coming of the Lord,
He is trampling out the vintage where the grapes of wrath are stored,
He hath loosed the fateful lightning of his terrible swift sword,
His Truth is marching on!

9. Black Reconstruction

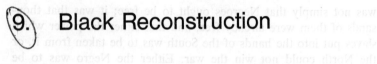

No area of black history has been so thoroughly reexamined in recent years as Reconstruction. As a result most historians have abandoned the older view, in which a virtuous President Andrew Johnson was pitted against corrupt carpetbaggers, scalawags, and blacks, and in which the radical state governments of the postwar period were condemned as corrupt, vindictive, and lacking in achievement. Historians today are more likely to view Johnson as an inept politician whose out-of-date political and social outlook made him incapable of coping with the revolutionary situation created by the Civil War. They are less inclined to stress economic interest or the desire for revenge as motivations of radical Republicans and are more willing to credit the radicals' idealism and commitment to civil rights. The image of a South struggling under "Negro rule" has been undermined by the cold statistical facts that only in South Carolina did blacks constitute a majority of a constitutional convention, or control even one house of a state legislature, and that no black was elected governor of a southern state during Reconstruction. Most important, historians are today emphasizing what Du Bois pointed out as long ago as 1910—that the achievements of the Reconstruction governments far outweighed their failures. For the first time, real democracy came to the South, and all citizens, black and white, were assured legal and political equality. The archaic legal and taxation codes of the South were modernized and several states enacted legislation prohibiting racial discrimination in public accommodations. Perhaps most important, a system of universal public education was established for the first time.

Vernon Lane Wharton's *The Negro in Mississippi* was one of the early and influential revisionist studies of Reconstruction. In his chapter on black politicians, Wharton dispels many of the myths concerning the post-war years in Mississippi. The radical government which came to power after the Reconstruction acts of 1867 established black suffrage in the South was by no means controlled by blacks, despite the fact that former slaves formed a majority of Mississippi's population. In fact, Wharton shows, blacks were underrepresented at almost every level of government. Nonetheless, a group of talented black politicians did emerge, including the first two blacks to sit in the United States Senate, Hiram Revels and Blanche K. Bruce. Wharton's sketches of these men indicate that they were probably better educated than most of the white politicians of the South, a situation paralleled in other states. Francis L. Cardozo, secretary of state and treasurer of South Carolina during Reconstruction, was educated at the University of Glasgow; Jonathan Gibbs, superintendent of education in Florida, was a graduate of Dartmouth; and Robert Elliot, Congressman from South Carolina, studied at Eton in England. Even more striking than the achievements of these distinguished leaders, however, was what Wharton calls "the amazingly rapid development of efficient local leaders among the Negroes." This flowering of local political talent, most of whom must have been ex-slaves, was cut short by the end of Reconstruction, yet it proved beyond doubt the capacity and interest of the black population in democratic processes.

Wharton's judgment on the black leadership of Reconstruction Mississippi is by no means wholly favorable. He finds that for the most part blacks played a subordinate role in the Republican party and that black voters lacked the group consciousness to insist on an equitable racial distribution of state and local offices or to press for legislation which would specifically benefit their race. The black experience in Mississippi should be contrasted with that of South Carolina, another state in which a majority of the population was black. As Joel Williamson shows in his recent study of South Carolina Reconstruction, blacks in that state were a highly organized political force. They consciously pursued political policies which would further their group interests, and black voters demonstrated a striking tendency to prefer black to white candidates in caucuses and elections. The greater political sophistication of South Carolina's black voters and leaders is no doubt related to the fact that before the Civil War Charleston had had a prosperous free black community, and that many South Carolina blacks served as soldiers in the Union army. Early in Reconstruction, moreover, a group of talented northern blacks entered the state as teachers, church missionaries, and agents of the Freedmen's Bureau. These black carpetbaggers played a leading role in organizing the Republican party in the state and many, including associate justice of the state supreme court Jonathan J. Wright, Congressmen Robert Elliot and R. H. Cain, and Martin Delany, who had been a leading abolitionist and emigrationist before the Civil War, became powerful political leaders.

In the end, of course, Reconstruction failed, and many historians are inclined to blame its demise on the failure of land reform in the South. The freed slaves, like any peasantry newly awakened to political consciousness, wanted land above all else. During the Civil War many thousands of acres were confiscated by the federal government, and in a few areas an effort was made to settle former slaves on these lands. But, soon after President Lincoln's assassination, Johnson began restoring lands to their former owners, exempting only property which had been sold outright by the government. Since most of the blacks had leased their land, they were now dispossessed and soon fell into the status of either agricultural laborers or sharecroppers. Only on the South Carolina Sea Islands, where a substantial number of ex-slaves had been able to purchase land from the government, did a black yeomanry emerge. Nor did the radical Republicans follow the advice of Thaddeus Stevens and grant forty acres to every former slave, when they seized control of Reconstruction in 1867. Basically middle-class in orientation, the radicals were willing to assure blacks civil and political equality, but they would not undermine the right of property by a policy of land confiscation and redistribution. In a sense, there- fore, Reconstruction was doomed from the start, for without economic independence the black population's new political rights proved extremely fragile. Although cowed for a time by black votes and the threat of federal intervention, southern whites were able to organize politi- cally and extra-legally in state after state. The violence of the Ku Klux Klan was only the most extreme example of the widespread use of physical and economic coercion. And there was no need to fear outside intervention, for the northern public had grown weary of the long years of controversy over the "Negro problem." For the first and last time since the American Revolution, duly elected state governments were overthrown by violence, and the South's only experiment in democracy came to an end.

The Negro and Politics, 1870–1875

VERNON LANE WHARTON

Negro Leaders

The Republican party which took control of the politics of the state in 1869 included in its membership at least ninety per cent of the more than one hundred thousand registered Negro voters. It also included at times from fifteen to twenty thousand of the seventy to eighty thousand white voters.[1] In the beginning, these white Republicans were largely a poverty-stricken element who had been Unionists during the war. There was also an element of planters and businessmen which increased rapidly in numbers until 1874. Many of these men had been Whigs before the war, and they regarded the Democratic party as the organ of their enemies, the small farmers.

The Republican leadership in Mississippi contained an unusually large number of prominent white men who were old residents of the state. The names of J. L. Alcorn, H. F. Simrall, J. L. Wofford, J. F. H. Claiborne, Joshua Morris, R. W. Flournoy, Jason Niles, and R. W. Millsaps will serve as examples. The motives which caused these men to enter the party were many and varied. Colonel R. W. Flournoy, who before the war was the largest slaveholder in northeastern Mississippi, was essentially a humanitarian. For him, the protection and elevation of the Negro was a project that sprang out of deep Christian convictions.[2] To a certain extent, this was also true of Major Millsaps, but he represented especially the rising commercial and financial element that saw the Republican party as the promoter of its interests both in

FROM Vernon Lane Wharton, *The Negro in Mississippi*. Copyright 1947 by University of North Carolina Press. Reprinted by permission of University of North Carolina Press.

the nation and in the state. Judge W. W. Chisholm of Kemper County was an example of a fairly large group who carried personal feuds into politics. The mortal enemies of his clan, the Gullys and the Balls, were Democrats. Where they went, Chisholm and his friends and relatives could not go. Even less respectable were those native whites, a relatively small group, who became Republicans entirely for the sake of personal advantage. The prominent Dr. William M. Compton of Marshall County furnished an excellent example. A leader of the irreconcilable anti-radicals in the convention of 1868, a "nigger-hater" of high degree, and an organizer of Ku-Klux Klans, he later entered the Alcorn faction, and became superintendent of the state insane asylum.[3]

Among the "carpet-baggers" there was the same variety of types. Adelbert Ames, absolutely honest, and to a large extent unselfish, had become more and more impressed with the needs and possibilities of the Negroes. Almost forty years later, as a cynical old man, he said: "My explanation may seem ludicrous now, but then, it seemed to me that I had a mission with a large M."[4] His constant refusal to sell out the interests of the freedmen made him their idol; one terrified Negro in 1875 addressed him as "Gov. Ames Dar Father of the State."[5] There were other able and honest Republican leaders from the North who had little sympathy for the Negroes, and regarded their presence in the party as a necessary evil. Among such men were H. R. Pease, R. C. Powers, and George C. McKeel. Finally, there were some unscrupulous "carpet-baggers" who sought only personal advantage and profit, and held to no principle. The white leader of the corrupt Negro-Republican Vicksburg ring, for example, neatly leaped the divide in 1875 and remained a prominent figure in the equally corrupt Democratic machine in that city.

Whatever the motives or character of these white Republicans might be, to the Democratic press and to the growing mass of white-liners, they were all scoundrels, carpet-baggers, and scalawags. Thus Jason Niles, described by Charles Nordhoff as "a man of singular purity of character, a quiet scholar, and an old resident of the State," was the subject of constant abuse.[6] Colonel Flournoy was so bitterly attacked that J. W. Garner has spoken of him as "the most extreme and obnoxious radical in the state." Yet the

Democratic historian of his home county, of which he was the wealthiest and most distinguished old citizen, wrote that he was "highly respected and beloved." He took an active part in church affairs, and gave freely to all charities. "The ideas he advocated [among them complete equality for Negroes] were the mistakes of his life."[7] On the other hand, almost no "carpet-bagger" was too vile to shift to the Democratic party and become a "respectable citizen." Thus C. E. Furlong, a Northern white who took heavy profits from the Vicksburg ring, received high state offices after changing parties, and in 1877 was suggested for the governorship by one of the leading Democratic papers.[8]

Mississippi was extremely fortunate in the character of her more important Negro Republican leaders. In the words of Alexander K. McClure:

Mississippi is exceptionable also in the reputable character of her most prominent colored leaders. In all the other southern States the negro leaders have rivaled the white adventurers in reckless and bewildering robbery, but they have not done so in Mississippi. Three black men have here reached national fame as leaders of their race, and they are all esteemed as honest men.

. . . .

These three men . . . have maintained the manhood that should be the pride of every race, and, much as Mississippi has suffered from the carpet-bag and colored rule, there has not been a tithe of the demoralization and waste here that has dishonored the reign of the black man in the Carolinas and the Gulf States. That much of this comparatively good record of a bad domination is due to Revels, Bruce, and Lynch, who successfully breasted the wave of corruption, is a fact that should be confessed and justly appreciated.[9]

Hiram Rhodes Revels, the least important of the three named by McClure, was the first Negro to serve in the United States Senate, in which body he completed the unexpired term of Jefferson Davis. Born of free parents in Fayetteville, North Carolina, September 27, 1827, he received his early education in a school taught by a Negro woman. The desire to continue his studies caused him to leave North Carolina and go to Indiana, where he attended a Quaker seminary. After further work at a Negro seminary in Ohio, he completed his training at Knox College, in

Galesburg, Illinois. After his ordination as an African Methodist Episcopal preacher, Revels taught, lectured, and preached in Indiana, Illinois, Ohio, Missouri, and Maryland. During the war, after assisting in the organization of Negro regiments in Maryland and Missouri, he went to Mississippi, where he organized churches, lectured, and attempted to organize schools. An interlude of two years in Kansas and Missouri was followed by his return to Mississippi, where he settled in Natchez as presiding elder of the Methodist Episcopal Church. Immediately, and almost entirely against his will, he was drawn into politics.[10]

After a term of service on the city council of Natchez, Revels was persuaded by John R. Lynch to enter the race for the state senate. His election to that body opened the way for his advancement to a much higher office. It had been agreed that the short term available in the United States Senate should go to a Negro. So impressive was the prayer with which Revels opened the proceedings of the upper house that he immediately became the candidate of the Negro legislators.

In Washington, Revels naturally attracted a great deal of attention. Tall, portly, dignified, and an excellent speaker, he delighted those who had worked for the elevation of his race, and to some extent eased the misgivings of those who had opposed it. His actual accomplishments as a new man in the short session of the Senate were few. None of the bills introduced by him was passed. He did, however, speak effectively on several occasions, and in his speaking and voting he showed intelligence and moderation. His support of a bill for the general removal of the political disabilities of Southern whites was especially effective. In his work outside the Senate, he succeeded in obtaining the admission of Negro mechanics to work in the United States Navy Yard.[11]

Upon his return to Mississippi, Revels was appointed to the presidency of Alcorn University, the new state college for Negroes. His work there was complicated by unruly elements in the faculty and student body, but in his appearances outside the college he gained the approval of most of the leading whites. After one of his speeches, the editor of a Democratic paper wrote: "As everywhere and on other occasions he impressed those who saw and heard him as a good man, honestly intent upon doing his people real good and quieting so far as he is able the bitterness between the races. In this work he will have the sympathy and encouragement of the white people."[12] So thoroughly did Revels gain the "sympathy and encouragement of the white people" that he soon lost the confidence of the masses of his own race. Essentially a timid man, more of a scholar than a leader, and anxiously desirous of peace, he came more and more to be dominated by white Democrats. After a brief term as acting secretary of state, he returned to the presidency of Alcorn, only to be ousted from the office by Governor Ames. He worked with the Democrats in the election of 1875, and once more received the presidency of the university from Governor J. M. Stone. After his retirement from that office on account of poor health, he continued to be active in church work until his death at a Methodist Episcopal conference in 1901.[13] In spite of his extreme caution and timidity, Revels throughout his career was a credit to his race. Had there been more like him, both white and black, some compromise would have brought peace in Mississippi.

A much more prominent figure than Revels was Blanche Kelso Bruce, the only Negro ever to serve a full term in the United States Senate, and the man described by Benjamin Brawley as "probably the most astute political leader the Negro ever had."[14] A light mulatto, born in Prince Edward County, Virginia, March 1, 1841, of a mother who was the slave of a wealthy planter, Bruce knew few of the burdens of slavery. He received his early education from a private tutor. Nominally a slave, he was carried before the war to Missouri, where he studied the printing trade, and later dealt in books and papers. Soon after the opening of the war, he went to Hannibal, Missouri, where he organized the first Negro school in the state. In 1868, after two years at Oberlin College, Bruce moved to Mississippi, and almost immediately began his political career. After brief experience as election commissioner and as sergeant-at-arms of the state senate, he became assessor, and then sheriff and tax collector of the rich Delta county of Bolivar. His experience also included service as county superintendent of schools and as levee commissioner. During this time he was gaining wealth as a planter. By 1874, after a long campaign in his favor by the Floreyville *Star,* Bruce was ready to make his bid for election to the Senate. In this, with the backing of Governor Ames and of the Negro leader James Hill, he obtained an easy victory.[15]

Upon his entrance to the Senate in March, 1875, Bruce immediately made a favorable impression. A man of magnificent physique and handsome countenance, he was described by a contemporary Mississippi Democrat as possessing "almost the manners of a Chesterfield."[16] Through the influence of Roscoe Conkling, he obtained good committee appointments, and after his first session he became active on the floor. His chief interests lay in the improvement of the Mississippi River, the establishment of a more enlightened policy toward the Indians, the development of interracial harmony, and the clearing up of the affairs of the Freedmen's Bank. On the floor of the Senate, he was often surrounded by a circle of friends similar to those which centered around Blaine, Edmunds, Bayard, and Lamar; while in his home, he and his cultured wife entertained a distinguished group which included the wives of Supreme Court justices and other officials. With the Democrats of the Mississippi delegation, Bruce maintained surprisingly pleasant relations, being especially close to his colleague L. Q. C. Lamar.[17]

After the close of his senatorial term, Bruce was suggested for a place in Garfield's cabinet, receiving the unqualified endorsement of such Mississippi Democrats as Senator Lamar and Congressmen Chalmers, Money, Muldrow, and Singleton.[18] Instead, however, he received an appointment as register of the treasury. Under Harrison, he served as recorder of deeds for the District of Columbia, and with the election of McKinley he once more became register of the treasury. While holding this office he died, March 17, 1898. To the end of his distinguished career, Bruce was always the gentleman, graceful, polished, self-assured, and never humble. He scorned the use of the phrase "colored man," often declaring "I am a negro, and proud of my race."[19]

Equally remarkable was the career of John R. Lynch. The son of a slave mother and a wealthy white planter, Lynch was born near Vidalia, Louisiana, September 10, 1847. After the death of the father, both mother and son were sold, and were taken to Natchez, where the boy became the favored body-servant of one of the leading citizens. Upon the occupation of the city by Federal troops, Lynch began to attend night school. Later he continued his studies through wide reading and work with tutors. After a brief term as a justice of the peace, he resigned to become, at the age of twenty-two, a member of the state legislature.[20] There he made a remarkable impression. In spite of his youth, and in spite of the fact that there were only thirty-two Negroes in the House, he was elected speaker in 1872. Democrats and Republicans alike praised his ability and impartiality.[21] In November, 1872, he was elected to Congress, and in December, 1873, he entered that body as its youngest member.

On the floor, Lynch showed himself to be perfectly at ease, making his first formal speech within eight days of the opening of the session. Of a distinctly aristocratic appearance, slender and active, with a very light complexion and regular features, he spoke fluently, tersely, and correctly.[22] Franklin A. Montgomery wrote that he had few, if any, superiors as a stump speaker. His effective delivery and ready wit appealed to blacks and whites alike. Montgomery advised Democratic speakers to avoid clashing with him in debate.[23] Serving in the Forty-Third, Forty-Fourth, and Forty-Seventh Congresses, he probably possessed as much influence at the White House as any Negro has ever had, being frequently called for consultation by Grant and Garfield. Throughout his public career, no scandal ever touched him, and by 1880 the Jackson *Clarion* was calling him "the ablest man of his race in the South."[24]

Refusing offers from Lamar and Cleveland of appointments based on his retirement from politics, Lynch remained in the Republican party, serving as the temporary chairman of its national convention in 1884, and as fourth auditor of the treasury under Harrison. After studying and practicing law, he entered the army in 1898, and served until 1911, when he retired with the rank of major.[25] He then opened law offices in Chicago, and became a power in the Republican organization in that city. In the meantime, he wrote three books on Reconstruction and his political experiences. Two of these, along with a number of articles, have been published. Shortly before his death in November, 1939, at the age of ninety-three, he reported that he was "taking life quite easily."[26] In view of the few advantages he had in his youth, and of the distinguished career which he achieved in the face of difficulties, he must be judged worthy of the honors and comforts that came to him in his declining years.

To McClure's list of the outstanding Negro leaders in Mississippi one more must be added. James Hill, a light mulatto, was born July 25, 1846, on the plantation of one J. Hill, near Holly Springs. He received his early education from two daughters of his master, and continued it while working as a youth in the railroad shops at Holly Springs. He received no formal training, although he recognized its value and sent his younger brother Frank to Oberlin. For James Hill himself, study and work were serious businesses. He had no time for any diversions.[27] He possessed none of the brilliance or oratorical ability of Bruce or Lynch, but for the larger part of the period he was probably a more influential factor in the politics of the state than either of his much more famous colleagues.

After a year as sergeant-at-arms of the house of representatives, Hill entered that body as a member in 1871. By the latter part of 1872, he was powerful enough to promise Bruce that he would be elected senator in 1874.[28] For himself, Hill chose the office of secretary of state, which he filled quietly and efficiently for three years after the overthrow of 1875. Against him there was never any charge of dishonesty.[29] After the close of his term, he was postmaster at Vicksburg for a time, and then collector of internal revenue. In 1882, he waged a hopeless campaign for a place in Congress. After that year, he centered his attention on business, and acquired a modest fortune as a successful land agent for the Louisville, New Orleans & Texas Railroad. He closed his career as receiver for the Federal Land Office in Jackson, as an active leader in the African Methodist Church, and as sponsor of other projects looking toward the advancement of his race. His career was at times mysterious and hard to explain. He stood very high in the favor of all of the Republican administrations at Washington. With the exception of the brief periods of his apparently useless campaigns for Congress, the white Democrats of the state seem almost never to have attacked him, and indeed to have worked with him as a colleague. He engaged in large business enterprises, and in projects for the aid of Negroes, almost as quietly and obscurely as he aided the family of the white man who had formerly been his master. The Democratic historian of Marshall County wrote, "He was extremely well thought of by the citizens, and is remembered as a good negro."[30] He was also "extremely well thought of" by the Negroes, who have named their largest public school in Jackson for "Jim Hill."

Mississippi was not so fortunate in the two other Negroes, A. K. Davis and T. W. Cardozo, who held high offices in the state. Both these men were obscure local politicians, and little can be learned of their background. Davis, who served as lieutenant-governor from 1874 until his impeachment in 1875, was weak, treacherous, and apparently dishonest, although he was cleared in a criminal court of the charge of bribery on which he was convicted by the legislature. He had practically no influence outside his home district of Noxubee County.

Cardozo, superintendent of education from 1874 until his resignation under threat of impeachment in 1876, was an educated mulatto from New York. Nominated as a result of pressure from the Vicksburg machine, he was almost unknown outside Warren County before his election. Although both Ames and Lynch testify as to his intellectual and educational qualifications, neither of them defends his character.[31] He was undoubtedly involved in the corruption at Vicksburg, and was shown to have embezzled more than two thousand dollars of the funds of Tougaloo University.[32] After this episode, he returned to the obscurity from which he came.

Local Leaders and the Loyal Leagues

Even more remarkable than the rise of Bruce, Lynch, and others to prominent positions in the state and nation was the amazingly rapid development of efficient local leaders among the Negroes. There is something fascinating about the suddenness with which, all over the state, they emerged from the anonymity of slavery to become directors and counselors for their race. In general, it can be said that they were not Negroes who had held positions of leadership under the old regime; the characteristics which made a man a slave driver or foreman were not those which

would allow him to organize a Loyal League. Almost none of them
came from the small group who had been free before the war. Such
men, as barbers, artisans, or small farmers, had depended too long
on the favor of the whites for the maintenance of their existence.
Servility had become a part of them. Most of this group became
Democrats, although a number of the younger element in the
comparatively liberal region around Natchez gained prominence in
the Republican organization.

A large portion of the minor Negro leaders were preachers,
lawyers, or teachers from the free states or from Canada. Their
education and their independent attitude gained for them immediate favor and leadership. Of the natives who became their rivals,
the majority had been urban slaves, blacksmiths, carpenters, clerks,
or waiters in hotels and boarding houses; a few of them had
been favored body-servants of affluent whites. Most of them were
more intelligent than the mass of their fellows, and had picked up
some smattering of education, at least to the point of being able to
read and write. There was a general tendency for them to combine
preaching with their politics; as Sir George Campbell has said, they
were rather preachers because they were leaders than leaders
because they were preachers. The death rate of these local organizers, both during and immediately after Reconstruction, was
alarmingly high.[33]

The organ through which the local leaders worked was the
"Loyal League." This body, an outgrowth of a Northern patriotic
organization established during the war, continued to maintain a
very vague national connection. The state set-up was equally
sketchy. The local groups, of which there was at least one in
almost every black-belt community, were extremely active, especially during periods immediately preceding elections. Given a
start by whites and Negroes from the North, they made an
immediate appeal to the freedmen, and quickly came to rival the
churches as centers of social activities. With their elaborate rituals,
their multiplicity of officers, and their sashes and badges, they
performed a function which later was taken over by the Negro
lodges. The general practice in Mississippi was for the Leagues to
hold a social gathering twice each month. At these meetings, the
Negroes danced and played games, and discussed local affairs,

their churches, and their schools. As a rule, the gatherings took place in church or school buildings except in times of violence, when the members collected secretly in secluded spots in the woods.[34]

The clubs also had a political significance, which at times of elections became preëminent. The oath taken by the initiate generally included a section similar to that in the ritual of Tarbell Council no. 4, at Morton: "Furthermore, that I will do all in my power to elect true and reliable Union men and supporters to the Government and none others, to all offices of profit or trust, from the lowest to the highest in Ward, Town, County, State and General Government. And should I ever be called to fill any office, I will faithfully carry out the objects and principles of this L. [sic]"[35] Local or visiting speakers urged the Negroes to protect their freedom and their rights by voting for Republican nominees, and in some of the Leagues a majority vote bound all of the members to vote for the candidates chosen.[36] It was also in the Leagues that preparations were made for gathering the Negroes in large groups early on the morning of election days. With their courage thus bolstered, they monopolized the polls during the early hours, and left them to the white Democrats in the afternoon.[37]

These clubs also provided political banquets and barbecues, and arranged political processions that were most attractive to the freedmen and annoying to the white Democrats. These activities involved the wearing of sashes and badges, the building of floats, and the loud beating of drums. At a night parade in Holly Springs, the Negroes wore red oilcloth caps with red feathers, red sashes, and enormous red and blue badges. Torches and transparencies completed the equipment.[38] At a barbecue in Lawrence County, the members of the League formed into a large procession and marched in double file around the courthouse and under a cross of blue cloth, bowing as they passed beneath it.[39]

These activities, and especially the pompous processions, aroused the wrath of the white Democrats.[40] Conditions in Oktibbeha County were typical:

In the early seventies the Democratic political organizations made it a point to intimidate and if necessary to whip the leaders of the negro drum companies and break up the meetings of these organizations. If possible the drums were always secured and destroyed and threats made of more drastic treatment if any further meeting, marching or drumming was attempted. These measures of expediency were not always carried through without bloodshed.[41]

This development of a symbolic significance for the use of drums by the Negroes gave an excuse for violent attacks by white Democratic organizations. In 1876, Negroes in De Soto County published an announcement that in order to avoid further trouble they would entirely abandon the use of drums and fifes. This move, although largely ineffective, became a general policy throughout the state.[42]

Democratic efforts to break up the Leagues also involved the use of white "detectives" and Negro spies to learn the meeting places of the groups, and especially to identify their leaders.[43] With this information, "the Ku Klux Klan lost no time in getting rid of the chief offenders and leaders."[44] After the successful revolution of 1875, the Leagues rapidly disappeared, and lodges and benevolent societies gradually took their places.

Negro Officials in County and Municipal Governments

By a provision of the new constitution of the state, the terms of all local officials expired with the readmission of Mississippi to the Union. Appointments to local offices were then to be made by the Governor with the advice and consent of the senate. Thus there were no municipal or county elections in the state until the fall of 1871. The Governor, J. L. Alcorn, as an old and relatively conservative citizen of the state, made appointments that at least were up to the usual standard for such officials. In some cases, the entire county lists were made up of Democrats or old Whigs.[45] Alcorn's selections for the judiciary were made up almost entirely of leading members of the state bar.[46] Altogether, the total of his appointments included 247 Republicans, 217 Democrats, and seventy-two members of other opposition groups.[47] So far as possible, Alcorn avoided the appointment of Negroes.[48] It appears that no member of that race except Robert H. Wood of Natchez was made mayor of any town.[49] With the possible exception of Coffeeville and

Greenville, no town had a Negro majority on its board of aldermen.

Even after the election of 1871, a Negro majority in a municipal government seems to have been unknown.[50] The city of Jackson, with a powerful Republican machine that maintained its control for thirteen years after the overthrow of the party in the state, only once had more than one Negro on its city council of six members. The one exception followed the election of 1874, when two Negroes became aldermen.[51] In Natchez, where the Negroes held an enormous majority, they placed only three members on a council of seven.[52] Efforts of the Negro majority to gain control of the board in Vicksburg in 1874 lost the support of the white members of their party, and with it the election.[53]

The chief complaint against the participation of the freedmen in the government of the towns grew out of their appointment as policemen. The presence of such officials helped to bring on the Meridian riot in 1871,[54] and furnished the central theme of the attack on the Republican government in Jackson.[55] The general attitude of the whites, as expressed by Ethelbert Barksdale, was that "negroes ought not to be put in a position to discharge constabulary functions which it is proper for white men to exercise." Law enforcement implied domination, and as Barksdale said, the white race was "not in the habit of being dominated by the colored race."[56]

In general the few towns which had Republican governments as late as 1874 overthrew them before the state government fell in the fall of 1875. The Democrats took Vicksburg in August, 1874, and Columbus in December. Yazoo City was captured in April, 1875, and Okolona in August. The methods generally used in this process, combining persuasion, intimidation, economic pressure, and violence, were similar to those used later in the state campaign. For towns which had Negro majorities, the legislature assured the continuation of Democratic control by excluding from the corporate limits large portions of the Negro residential sections.[57] The one important exception to the overthrow of Republican municipal governments in the years 1874 and 1875 was the city of Jackson, where a peculiar situation and a large number of white votes maintained that party in power until 1888.

Very little information is available as to the participation of the Negroes in the various county governments. More than half of the counties held white majorities, and most of these naturally eliminated in the elections of 1871 the few Negro officials appointed by Alcorn in 1870. In the elections of 1873, the Democrats carried thirty-nine of the seventy-four counties, and in 1875 sixty-two of the seventy-four. Of course, in several of the predominantly white counties, black beats at times elected one or two supervisors or justices of the peace. Yalobusha, Scott, and Lawrence counties, as examples, generally had one Negro supervisor on the board of five.[58] Such Negroes were almost entirely without influence, and generally found it to their advantage to be "very quiet, good negroes," to use the description given of those in Lawrence.[59]

Even in the minority of the counties which had Negro and Republican majorities, the freedmen seldom obtained many of the offices. By 1873, however, they became assertive enough to take control of a number of counties in which the white population was small. In Marshall County, for example, three of the five supervisors were Negroes who could barely read and write.[60] The three on the board in Yazoo County, the three in Warren, four of the five in Madison, and all five in Issaquena were described as "illiterate."[61] In these counties, there were also varying numbers of Negro justices of the peace, few of whom were capable of carrying out properly even the simple duties of their office. There were also a small number of Negro chancery and circuit clerks varying in ability from an "illiterate" in Yazoo to the highly cultured L. J. Winston, who remained as circuit clerk in Adams County, under white Democratic control, until his appointment as collector of the port of Vicksburg in 1897. According to John R. Lynch, "Out of seventy-two counties in the State at that time, electing on an average twenty-eight officers to a county, it is safe to assert that not over five out of one hundred of such officers were colored men."[62] This statement seems to be approximately correct.

The most important office in the counties, both in responsibilities and in financial returns, was that of sheriff. According to Lynch, not more than twelve Negroes in Mississippi ever held this office.[63] Available material supplies the names Blanche K. Bruce of Bolivar, J. J. Evans of De Soto, John Brown of Coahoma,

Winslow of Washington, Sumner of Holmes, Merrimon Howard of Jefferson, Peter Crosby of Warren, William McCary and Robert H. Wood of Adams, W. H. Harney of Hinds, Scott of Issaquena, and Joe Spencer Watkins of Monroe. In regard to Sumner and Watkins, there is almost no information. Of Blanche K. Bruce, it is sufficient to say that his handling of the office of sheriff fully merited the confidence of the white planters who supplied his bond of $120,000. The offices of Evans and Winslow seem to have been managed very largely by the whites who supplied their bonds.[64] Charges of embezzlement against Evans,[65] an ex-slave who was described as a good, sound Negro, seem to have been entirely unjustified.[66] Scott, judged by his testimony before the Boutwell Committee, was a man of intelligence and ability who, although he was elected by the votes of the Negroes, was completely under the control of white Democrats. Almost exactly the same description applies to Merrimon Howard of Jefferson, although he at times showed a bit more independence than Scott.[67] John Brown, run out of Coahoma County after a "race riot" during the campaign of 1875, six years later was declared to have embezzled a large sum for which his sureties were liable.[68] Peter Crosby, whose violent expulsion by white leaguers led to the Vicksburg riots in 1874, was a member of the infamous ring of that city. Yet, strangely enough, subsequent examination of his accounts disclosed them to be entirely in order.[69] Nordhoff's statement that he was illiterate is incorrect.[70] W. H. Harney of Hinds County was a Canadian Negro of some education and ability. He was popular with whites and blacks alike until the development of the bitter campaign of 1875. Charges that he was from twelve to twenty-one thousand dollars short in his accounts occupied the courts for five years. Newspaper reports of the settlement are confusing and contradictory.[71] William McCary and Robert Wood were intelligent members of families who had been free and respected residents of Natchez for several generations.[72] Their conduct seems to have given general satisfaction.

In regard to the quality and activity of county governments between 1870 and 1875, a few generalizations may be drawn. As compared with the period before the war, this was one of greatly increased activity. Bridges, roads, and public buildings destroyed or allowed to go to pieces during the war had to be reconstructed. In addition, the greatly increased business of country stores, the rapid growth of small towns, and expanded social and political activities called for the building of new roads. Under the new system of public education, there were schools to be built and a great number of teachers to be employed. The admission of the freedmen to the courts more than doubled their business. Then too, there was a great burst of enthusiasm for the building of railroads. County after county and town after town made contributions for this purpose after overwhelmingly favorable votes by whites and blacks, and Democrats and Republicans alike. All of this implied an enormous increase in county expenditures, and a proportional increase in taxation. Furthermore, the burden of this increase fell directly on the owners of real estate. The large revenue from the head-tax on slaves was no longer available, and the Republican party, made up largely of propertyless Negroes and of business and professional men, quickly lightened the heavy levies that formerly had been made on artisans, professional men, and commercial enterprisers.

Interestingly enough, there seems to be no correlation at all between the rate of taxation and the political or racial character of the counties. In 1874, at the height of Negro-Republican control, the average rate for the thirty-nine Democratic counties was 12 7/13 mills. That for the thirty-four Republican counties was 13 7/17—a difference of less than one mill. The county tax in the Democratic units ranged from 6.2 mills in Pontotoc to 20.3 in Chickasaw. In the Republican counties, the range was from 5.3 in De Soto to 23.2 in Colfax. Negro influence was probably greatest in Madison, Issaquena, Amite, Washington, Warren, Yazoo, Wilkinson, and Hinds. As compared with a state average of 13, the rates in these counties were, respectively, 11, 16, 11, 13½, 14, 10, 19, and 11.4 mills.[73] Warrants in counties with heavy Negro populations were running at from forty to seventy-five cents on the dollar.[74] On the other hand, those in Lee County, where no Negro or Republican of any kind ever held office, fell to thirty cents.[75] The conclusion must be drawn that everywhere in the state a large part of the increase in expenditures was unavoidable. Then too, the wave of extravagance which was sweeping the nation did not

fail to touch Mississippi. To a certain extent, the situation probably reflects the new feeling of self-importance and the new influence that had come to the poor whites.

The question of how much fraud existed in the various counties
is difficult to answer. Charges, in general terms, were frequently
made in the Democratic press. The leading Republican paper
assembled the available evidence, and attempted to show that a
great deal more dishonesty had been uncovered in Democratic
than in Republican counties.[76] With the exception of J. H. Jones,
who charges graft in Wilkinson,[77] it is the general conclusion of
the few students who have investigated individual counties that
while there was some extravagance, there is no evidence of open
fraud.[78] Their conclusions are hard to reconcile with the many
charges which were prevalent at the time.

There can be little doubt that there was a rotten situation in
Vicksburg, a city which seldom knew an honest government before
the war, and has almost never had one since. City expenditures
were enormous. Most of them went for improvement of streets and
wharves, and other projects which were really necessary for a town
that was rapidly becoming a city, but if half of the charges of
extravagance and graft were true, the city was getting little for its
money. In this exploitation, Democrats and Republicans shared
alike. It is also true that the enormous grants to railroads met
almost no opposition at the polls.[79] It is therefore difficult to say
just how much of the extravagance and corruption was real, or
how much of it should be charged to Negroes and white Republicans.

The Vicksburg ring also controlled the government of Warren
County, and there can be little doubt, in spite of the curious fact
that Sheriff Crosby's accounts were found to be in order, that
several of the county officials, Negroes and whites, were engaged
in extensive embezzlement through such methods as the forgery of
warrants.[80] Unfortunately, it must be recorded that the thrifty
black and white tax-payers who joined the violent white "Modocs"
in overthrowing the Republican city government in 1874, and the
county government in the following year, saw control pass into the
hands of the least desirable element of the whites. The result was
that conditions in city and county became worse rather than
better.[81]

In conclusion it may be stated that although Negroes formed a majority of the population in thirty counties in Mississippi, they almost never took advantage of their opportunity to place any large number of their race in local offices. Of those who did hold offices, the twelve sheriffs were moderately satisfactory; most of them were at least capable of exercising the functions of their office. No Negro in the state ever held any higher judicial office than that of justice of the peace, and those who held that office seem generally to have been incompetent. Among the small number of chancery and circuit clerks there was a wide range of ability; most of them were not suitable men for their positions. Negroes who gained election to the boards of supervisors of the various counties, even in those cases where they formed a majority, generally were dominated by white Republicans either natives or Northerners. Although many of the Negro supervisors were ignorant and incompetent, little difference can be discovered in the administration of their counties and that of counties under Democratic control.

Negroes and State Government

The first legislature under the new constitution assembled in Jackson in January, 1870. Of the 107 men in the house of representatives, twenty-five were Democrats and eighty-two were Republicans. The number of Negro representatives, originally thirty-one, was immediately reduced to thirty by the death of C. A. Yancey of Panola County. Thus, in a state which held a large Negro majority, members of that race made up less than two-sevenths of the total membership of the house, and less than three-eighths of the Republican majority. Their representation in the senate was even smaller. In the total membership of thirty-three, and in a Republican group of twenty-eight, only five were Negroes.[82]

Of the thirty Negroes in the house, eight had served in the constitutional convention. A dozen or more of the group, either by education or unusual native ability, were entirely capable of meeting their obligations as legislators. Among these were H. P. Jacobs, Henry Mayson, J. F. Boulden, M. T. Newsome, Merrimon Howard, John R. Lynch, J. Aaron Moore, H. M. Foley, J. J. Spelman, and J. H. Piles. All of these men made distinguished records in fields other than politics. Almost as capable were Albert Johnson, Nathan McNeese, A. K. Davis, Doctor Stites, Emanuel Handy, Richard Griggs, and W. H. Foote. The other fourteen members were inclined to be self-effacing, and took little part in the formation of policy.

Of the five members of the senate, three, Charles Caldwell, Hiram Revels, and T. W. Stringer, have already been discussed. Robert Gleed, of Columbus, was a man of fair education, good character, and some financial ability, although he had been a slave until the close of the war.[83] An excellent speaker, he was employed by the Democratic administration after the overthrow of the Republican regime to lecture to the Negroes of the state on educational and agricultural matters. The fifth senator, William Gray of Greenville, was a young Baptist preacher of some education and much natural cleverness. A leader in the demands for civil rights for Negroes, he was lacking in tact, and was probably at times guilty of double-dealing both in politics and in religious affairs.

The election of a new house of representatives in 1871, for the term of 1872 and 1873, brought a heavy reduction of the Republican majority. Of the 115 members, the Republicans claimed sixty-six. Actually, however, several of the white members of their group, calling themselves independents, generally voted with the Democrats and against the administration. Negro membership rose to thirty-eight, but R. R. Applewhite of Copiah was completely under Democratic control, and later announced himself a member of that party. The Negroes now had a theoretical control of the Republican caucus in the lower house, but actually any attempt to press their advantage was generally blocked by the desertion of a number of their white colleagues. It was only after Alcorn urged it as a political necessity that John R. Lynch received enough white Republican votes to gain the speakership.

It may therefore be said that during the first four years of Republican control the dominant group in both houses of the legislature was a combination of native and Northern white Republicans, who were influenced by the desires of their Negro constituents, but were also attentive to the large white element in their party, an element whose numbers they earnestly desired to increase. Their leader until late in 1871 was Governor Alcorn, an old Whig with Hamiltonian sentiments and a dream of bringing into the Republican party of the state men in the Democratic and Conservative groups who shared his beliefs. When Alcorn resigned in November, 1871, to take his place in the United States Senate, he was succeeded by R. C. Powers, a man of the same sentiments.[84] Both of these men wished to carry out a program which they considered to be for the best interest of whites and blacks alike. Both of them, like many of the white Republicans in the legislature, avoided social contacts with the Negroes as much as possible, and were absolutely opposed to any real control of their party by the Negroes.

In this situation, the Negro minority in the legislature generally followed the lead of the white Republicans, with whom, in matters of routine legislation, they were usually naturally in accord. In such routine business, the more able Negroes, including Stringer, Boulden, Jacobs, Spelman, and Lynch, were about as prominent as any of the white leaders. In fact, when the proportion of their numbers is kept in mind, a survey of the *Journals* reveals little difference between the whites and Negroes in attendance, in service on committees, or in activity on the floor. Negro members almost never suggested legislation to obtain special privileges for their race. The more able Negroes either recognized the weakness of their position or had no desire to gain undue advantage. The few who would have gone further received no encouragement or support.

In his inaugural address, in January, 1870, Governor Alcorn outlined clearly the two basic problems faced by the Republicans. "The obligations resting on us under the new order of things," he said, "extend very greatly the breadth of duty of the State Government. The 'patriarchal' groupings of our society in the days of slavery confined the work of our political organizations, to a very great extent, to the heads of what we called 'families.'" Under the new regime, every individual had become a distinct entity. In addition to the great increase in the number of individuals concerned, a large increase in the *amount* of government was contemplated. The costs of the new administration must be much greater than those of the old. He would therefore urge the legislature to take advantage of every opportunity for economy. In regard to the state's new citizens, he said: "In the face of memories that might have separated them from me as the wronged from the wronger, they have offered me their confidence. . . . In response to that touching reliance, the most profound anxiety with which I enter my office . . . is that of making the colored man the equal, before the law, of any other man. . . ."[85] Thus, in the beginning, Alcorn presented the problems that doomed the Republican regime. There were many whites who were alienated by the extension of the powers of the state, and even more by the increase in costs and taxes. A larger group, including, to a certain extent, Alcorn himself, absolutely refused to accept the implications of Negro equality before the law. Such revolutions, unless maintained by overwhelming force, cannot be accomplished in a decade.

With a treasury balance of about fifty dollars in cash and five hundred dollars in negotiable paper, the Republicans entered upon the program that was to reconstruct the state. During the next four years, they set up, organized, and maintained at state expense a bi-racial system of common school education which, although it did not approach the national average in facilities or expense, was an amazing advance beyond anything the state had known before. They gave state support to normal schools at Holly Springs and Tougaloo, and established Alcorn as a Negro counterpart to the state university. They completely reorganized, coordinated, and centralized the state judiciary, and gave to it a new code of laws. Old public buildings were renovated and enlarged and new ones were constructed. State hospitals were set up and supported at Natchez and Vicksburg, and the facilities of the state asylums for the blind, deaf and dumb, and insane were greatly expanded. All racial discrimination was eliminated from the laws of the state. Finally, after much disagreement, the legislature granted to the Negroes in 1873 a civil rights bill, which in theory guaranteed to them equal access to all places of public entertainment.

Although much of this legislation was expensive, and almost all of it was controversial, a partial acceptance of the program and a loss of faith in the Democratic party produced a sweeping victory

in 1872, and the election of Republicans to five of the six congressional seats. By the summer of 1873, the Republican party had
reached the height of its power in the state. In this very strength,
however, there was a great weakness. The breakdown of Democratic opposition, in the state as in the nation, opened the way for
a struggle among the discordant elements in the dominant party.
Between 1867 and 1872, it had appeared that this struggle, when
it came, would involve a choice by the Negroes between Northern
and native whites as their leaders.[86] In spite of efforts of the
Democrats to aggravate differences on this basis, it had greatly
declined in importance by 1873. The great line of division had
come to be the question of the extent to which Negroes were to be
allowed to hold offices and to dominate the councils of the party.

This became apparent in the state and county conventions in the
summer of 1873. The Negroes, after six years of domination of the
party by whites, now declared that they must have a larger share of
the offices. Although, in general, their demands were not yet
proportional to their party membership, the Negroes overestimated
their ability to supply suitable candidates. This became evident
when, after Bruce's refusal to accept the lieutenant-governorship,
that office went to the weak A. K. Davis. Matters became worse
when the Vicksburg ring, threatening violence and secession,
secured the post of superintendent of education for Cardozo. This
left James Hill, candidate for the office of secretary of state, as the
only really acceptable candidate offered by the Negroes for the
three state positions which they demanded. Similar weaknesses
were to be found in many of the men whom they chose for places
in the legislature and in the county governments. The most important point at issue, however, was the fact that it was now clear that
actual domination of the party by the mass of its Negro membership would probably come in the near future. By thousands of
white members of the party, and by a majority of its white leaders,
such a development could not be accepted.

J. L. Alcorn, already repudiated by the Negroes, undertook to
lead the opposition, and announced his candidacy for the governorship in opposition to Adelbert Ames. With him went most of
the Republican leaders who were native whites, and a number of
those from the North. To this group, calling itself the "Republican

Party of Mississippi," the Democrat-Conservative organization immediately threw its support.[87]

In an election in which the color line was rather sharply drawn, Ames defeated Alcorn by a vote of 69,870 to 50,490. Seventy-seven of the 115 members of the lower house were Republicans of either the Alcorn or the Ames faction. Fifty-five were Negroes, but one or two of these were Democrats. In a senate of thirty-seven members, twenty-five were Republicans, including nine Negroes. All of the seven state officers were regular Ames Republicans, and three of them, the lieutenant-governor, the secretary of state, and the superintendent of education, were Negroes. Furthermore, a Negro from Warren County, I. D. Shadd, soon became the none-too-competent speaker of the house.

In his inaugural address, Governor Ames made a good impression. After pledging himself to work for economy and reform, he turned to the race problem, analyzed the causes of conflict, and called for tolerance and a mutual recognition of rights and interests.[88] Thus, as Alcorn had done four years before, Ames recognized the two great problems which neither of them could solve. The elevation of the Negro involved a rapid expansion of state services which were inconsistent with the old ideas of economy. The readjustment of the relationship between the races was a matter beyond the power of the governor or the legislature.

The heavy increase in the number of Negroes in the government of the state did not greatly decrease its efficiency or change its character. The secretary of state was both competent and honest, and the superintendent of education at least was competent. The Negro legislators, as a group, were fairly capable of handling their duties, and probably represented their race more worthily than did the Negroes in any other Southern legislature. Visiting the state in 1874, Edward King wrote:

. . . [Negroes] lounge everywhere, and there are large numbers of smartly dressed mulattoes, or sometimes full blacks, who flit here and there with the conscious air which distinguishes the freedman. I wish here to avow, however, that those of the negroes in office, with whom I came in contact in Mississippi, impressed me much more powerfully as worthy, intelligent, and likely to progress, than many whom I saw elsewhere in the South. There are some who are exceedingly capable, and none of those immediately attached to the government at Jackson are incapable. In the Legislature there are now and then negroes who are ignorant; but of late both branches have been freer of this curse than have those of Louisiana or South Carolina.

A visit to the Capitol showed me that the negroes, who form considerably more than half the population of Mississippi, had certainly secured a fair share of the offices. Colored men act as officials or assistants in the offices of the Auditor, the Secretary of State, the Public Library, the Commissioner of Emigration [sic], and the Superintendent of Public Instruction. The Secretary of State [James Hill], who has some negro blood in his veins, is the natural son of a well-known Mississippian of the old regime, formerly engaged in the politics of his State; and the Speaker of the House of Representatives at the last session was a black man. The blacks who went and came from the Governor's office seemed very intelligent, and some of them entered into general conversation in an interesting manner.[89]

In spite of Ames' evidently sincere interest in economy, he and his legislature found it very difficult to make any substantial reduction in the expenses of the state government. Under the Republican administration, expenses had grown to what the Democrats declared were fantastic proportions. As a matter of fact, when the abnormal years of the war are omitted, the figures of the state auditors do give the impression that the Republican administrations were extravagant:

Year	Democratic Administrations	Year	Republican Administrations
1856 through		1870	$1,061,249.90
1860—average	$ 767,438.78	1871	1,729,046.34
1865	1,410,250.13	1872	1,596,828.64
1866	1,860,809.89	1873	1,450,632.80
1867	625,817.80	1874	1,319,281.60
1868	525,678.80	1875	1,430,192.83
1869	463,219.71		
1876	518,709.03		
1877	697,018.86		
1878	707,022.46		
1879	553,326.81		
1880	803,191.31		

Thus the average yearly cost of the state government under the six years of Republican control was $1,431,205.35, or almost twice the normal expenditure of the years immediately preceding the war. Even more spectacular, however, had been the increase in taxation of real estate. For many years, real property had been practically exempt from taxation in Mississippi. In 1869, the last year of Democratic control, the rate on this class of property was only one mill, or a tax of only twenty dollars a year on a plantation assessed by its owner at twenty thousand dollars and worth perhaps fifty thousand. The great sources of revenue were a tax of a dollar a bale on cotton, and privilege and license taxes which seem to have been inordinately high. The Republican regime reversed this system; after abolishing the tax on cotton and almost entirely eliminating the privilege taxes, the Republicans placed almost the entire burden of the support of the state on real and personal property. The result was a rate that rose from five mills in 1871 to fourteen in 1874. However pleasing such a system might be to the advocate of the single tax, there can be no doubt that it brought wrath to the landowners in a period of agricultural depression.

So strong had the protest of the landowners become by the spring of 1875 that the legislature could no longer afford to overlook it. Governor Ames insisted that changes were necessary, and the representatives undertook the problem. The reductions for which they provided, like those made later by the Democrats, were more apparent than real. For a centralized government in a state of more than a million people, it was a simple fact that a cost of $1,400,000 per year was not extravagant. To meet the situation, the legislature put back on the counties the cost of jury, witness, and inquest fees that had been assumed by the state. Thus, at one blow, an item of two hundred thousand dollars a year was chopped from the cost of the government of the state, but it was added to that of the counties. In addition, the legislature presented to the people a constitutional amendment to provide for a great reduction in the number of the circuit judges. It also reduced printing costs by cutting down the number of the legislative journals, and by eliminating the publication of departmental reports. Then, against the opposition of about half of the Negro members, it reduced the salaries of the governor and other state officials, and provided for biennial rather than annual sessions of the legislature. Appropriations to the state universities were reduced, and scholarships were abolished. Another amendment to the constitution provided for the distribution of income from state lands, fines, and liquor licenses rather than their incorporation in the permanent school endowment fund. The ratification of this amendment was to allow a heavy reduction in the state school tax. Finally, turning to the system of taxation, the legislature reduced the *ad volerem* levy to nine and one-fourth mills, placed a tax on railroads, and made a partial return to the use of privilege taxes.[90] Ironically enough, the effect of most of these reforms could not become apparent until the following year, at which time their benefits were easily claimed by the triumphant Democrats. Their adoption went almost unnoticed in the midst of the tumultuous movement toward the revolution of 1875.

Unlike the Republican administrations in most of the other Southern states, those in Mississippi financed their enterprises almost entirely through taxation. When the party assumed control in January, 1871, the state had an empty treasury and a debt of $1,178,175.33.[91] When the Democrats returned to power in January, 1876, they found $524,388.68 in the treasury and a debt of $3,341,162.89.[92] With the deduction in each case of permanent funds which the state owed to itself, and consideration of the treasury balance, the payable debt in 1876, as in 1871, was approximately half a million dollars, a negligible amount.

Furthermore, the Republican state regime left a remarkable record of honesty. The conclusion of J. W. Garner seems to be approximately correct:

So far as the conduct of state officials who were entrusted with the custody of public funds is concerned, it may be said that there were no great embezzlements or other cases of misappropriation during the period of Republican rule. . . . The treasurer of the Natchez hospital seems to have been the only defaulting state official during the administration of Governor Ames. He was a carpet-bagger, and the amount of the shortage was $7,251.81. The colored state librarian during Alcorn's administration was charged with stealing books from the library. The only large case of embezzlement during the post-bellum period was that of the Democratic treasurer in 1866. The amount of the shortage was $61,962.[93]

It may be added that the next embezzlement of any importance was that of the Democratic "redemption" treasurer who was elected in 1875. His shortage was $315,612.19.[94]

Altogether, as governments go, that supplied by the Negro and white Republicans in Mississippi between 1870 and 1876 was not a bad government. Never, in state, counties, or towns, did the Negroes hold office in proportion of their numbers, although their demands in this direction were undeniably increasing. The Negroes who held county offices were often ignorant, but under the control of white Democrats or Republicans they supplied a form of government which differed little from that in counties where they held no offices. The three who represented the state in the national Congress were above reproach. Those in the legislature sought no special advantages for their race, and in one of their very first acts they petitioned Congress to remove all political disabilities from the whites. With their white Republican colleagues, they gave to the state a government of greatly expanded functions at a cost that was low in comparison with that of almost any other state. The legislature of 1875 reduced that cost to some extent, and opened the way for further reductions by the passage of constitutional amendments. It also removed some of the apparent injustices in the system of taxation. But one situation it did not alter. The Republican party had come to be branded as a party of Negroes, and it was apparent that the Negroes were more and more determined to assert their right to control that party. It is also true that many of the Negroes, probably a majority, favored a further expansion of the functions of the state, entirely at the expense, according to the whites, of white tax-payers. The way was open for the formation of a "white-line" party.

10. Blacks in the "New South"

With the end of Reconstruction, southern whites reclaimed political control of the South. The new leaders—
the "Redeemers"—were representatives of the southern
business class, men concerned with developing the industry, transportation, and commerce of their region. Yet it is
sometimes forgotten that black participation in politics did
not end in 1877. The business class had little reason to
share the poor whites' fierce antagonism to the black,
based on economic competition, and it inherited the paternalistic racial ethos of the old South. Men like Wade
Hampton of South Carolina, Lucius Quintus Lamar of
Mississippi, and Joe Brown of Georgia, though believers
in white supremacy, pledged to respect the Negro's newly-
won legal and political rights. As governor of South
Carolina, Hampton gave many local offices to blacks, and
did not attempt to suppress the black vote. The civil-rights
legislation of Reconstruction days remained on the statute
books, and the new state constitutions remained in force.
Blacks continued to win election to state legislatures in the
late 1870's and 1880's, and a few continued to serve in
Congress. The last southern black Congressman, George
White of North Carolina, did not leave office until 1901.

At the same time, however, southern blacks were sinking deeper and deeper into the economic dependence
which would make it difficult for them to defend their

237

political and legal rights if the white majority was determined to repeal them. The failure of land reform during Reconstruction meant that the bulk of southern blacks had to earn their living from land owned by whites. Increasing numbers slipped into sharecropping, the system in which the owner of the land furnished the farmer with land, seed, fertilizer, and equipment, and in return took a fixed proportion of the cotton crop. Sharecropping was quickly linked with the lien system, by which the cropper could obtain credit by pledging future crops as security. This pernicious system made the cropper a virtual peon of local merchants, the major suppliers of credit in the rural South. These merchants charged exorbitant interest rates and utilized dishonest bookkeeping practices, with the result that it was common for the cropper to have to surrender his entire crop at the end of the year and still continue in debt, pledging future crops. Sharecropping was an interracial phenomenon—there were always more white sharecroppers in the South than black. Yet it became the major economic relation for the black farmer, and condemned him to an irrevocable cycle of poverty and despair. As it turned out, emancipation had not really altered the economic condition of the mass of blacks in the South.

In the following excerpt from *Origins of the New South,* one of the landmarks in the writing of southern history, C. Vann Woodward discusses some of the forms of economic oppression of blacks in the "New South," including sharecropping and the convict lease system. He then outlines the process by which the black voter was legally disfranchised between 1890 and 1910. The background for this disfranchisement was the rise of southern Populism, and with it the emergence of the poor white as a political force. In some states, the Populists initially adopted the policy of interracial cooperation, in recognition of the fact that black and white farmers shared many of the same economic and social grievances. But the Populists soon found that such a policy was politically suicidal. Many poor whites were alarmed by the Democrats' charges of "Negro rule," and voted their race prejudices instead of their class interests. Equally important, in the heavily Negro Black Belt counties of the South, Democratic politicians controlled the election machinery and stuffed ballot boxes with fraudulent black votes, to defeat the Populists. By the late 1890's, many Populists had concluded that only when the black was eliminated as a factor in southern politics could whites settle their economic and political differences without distraction.

Woodward discusses below the complicated politics of disfranchisement, and the various methods adopted by southern legislatures and constitutional conventions to end black voting. These measures were extremely effective, but despite the assurances of Democratic political leaders, the new laws also barred many poor whites from the suffrage. Poor whites were often illiterate and had just as much difficulty meeting property and poll-tax requirements as did blacks. In Louisiana, the new constitution reduced a previous black voting body of 130,000 to 1,300 by 1904, but at the same time 82,000 whites were also disfranchised. The most effective method of disfranchisement was the all-white Democratic primary, since in the one-party South the Democratic primary was more important than the general election. But the primary also made possible the emergence of a new figure in southern politics—the political demagogue who combined extreme race hatred with a class appeal to poor whites. Men like James Vardaman of Mississippi were able to wrest control of the Democratic party away from the older, upper-class leadership, through the all-white primary.

Coupled with the disfranchisement of the black voter was the institution of racial segregation as the South's new system of racial control. Segregation was, of course, nothing new in turn-of-the-century America, for it had existed in the ante-bellum North and to a lesser extent in southern cities before the Civil War. And, even in Reconstruction, civil-rights legislation and laws providing for integrated education often went unenforced, as the two races voluntarily patronized separate public facilities and schools. Yet the racial situation in the South in the 1870's and 1880's was quite fluid. In many areas blacks were permitted to patronize public accommodations, and rode freely in first-class railroad cars. The legalization of segregation came only after the Supreme Court, in a series of decisions in the 1880's and 1890's, whittled away the legal protection afforded blacks by Reconstruction legislation, and finally, in *Plessy v. Ferguson* in 1896, declared that railroad segregation did not violate the equal protection of the laws, so long as facilities for blacks were "separate but equal." There followed a rash of southern legislation, providing for racial separation in all kinds of public and private institutions and facilities. Jim Crow, which had previously been confined to southern cities, now became the norm of race relations throughout the South. And, as Woodward points out, at a time when the nation was utilizing racist arguments to justify its conquest of the Philippines, it was unlikely that northerners would object to the new laws. The period 1890–1910, which witnessed not only discrimination and segregation, but the rise of lynching and the complete collapse of publicly-supported black education in the South, has been called by one historian the nadir of black life in America.

From *Origins of the New South*

C. Vann Woodward

Mudsills and Bottom Rails

If Reconstruction ever set the bottom rail on top, it was not for long and never securely. Redemption seemed to leave little doubt that the bottom rail was again on the bottom—whatever its temporary dislocation. It remained for the New South to find what Reconstruction had failed to find: the measure of the emancipated slave's freedom and a definition of free labor, both black and white; for the white worker's place in the New Order would be vitally conditioned by the place assigned the free black worker.

Much discussion about the Negro's civil rights, his political significance, his social status, and his aspirations can be shortened and simplified by a clear understanding of the economic status assigned him in the New Order. Emancipation and Reconstruction had done little to change that picture. The lives of the overwhelming majority of Negroes were still circumscribed by the farm and plantation. The same was true of the white people, but the Negroes, with few exceptions were farmers without land. Questionnaires from the census of 1880 revealed that in thirty-three counties of Georgia where Negro population was thick, "not more than one in one hundred" Negro farmers owned land; the same proportion was reported from seventeen black Mississippi counties; twelve others reported not one in twenty, and many not one in fifty. From Tennessee as a whole the report was that only "a very small part of the Negroes own land or even the houses in which they live"; also from Louisiana and Alabama came report of "very few" owners.[1]

FROM C. Vann Woodward, *Origins of the New South*. Copyright 1951 by Louisiana State University Press. Reprinted by permission of Louisiana State University Press.

More specific information is provided for one state by the report of the Comptroller General of Georgia for the year ending October 1, 1880. Of a total of some $88,000,000 in land value, the Negroes, who made up nearly half the state's population, owned around $1,500,000. Of a total of some $23,000,000 value put upon cattle and farm animals, the Negroes owned about $2,000,-000, and of some $3,200,000 in agricultural tools, the Negroes reported a little more than $163,000.[2] It is pretty clear that as a rule the Negro farmer not only worked the white man's land but worked it with a white man's plow drawn by a white man's mule. In the next two decades the race's landholdings improved slightly, but in 1900 black Georgians had taxable titles to only one twenty-fifth of the land; only 14 per cent of the Negro farmers owned their farms, and in 1910 only 13 per cent.[3] In the South as a whole, by 1900, 75.3 per cent of the Negro farmers were croppers or tenants.[4]

The landless Negro farmers, like the landless whites, worked either for wages or for shares, under any of several arrangements. When the Alabama planter furnished tools, animals, and feed, as well as the land, his share was one half of all crops; when he furnished only the land he took one fourth of the cotton and one third of the corn. There were numerous variations, including the "two-day system" on Edisto Island, where the tenant worked two days of the week for the landlord in the feudal manner.[5] The impression of uniformity in the labor system that replaced slavery would seem to have been exaggerated. As late as 1881 it was reported that in Alabama "you can hardly find any two farmers in a community who are carrying on their business alike," and frequently one planter might use several methods at once: "To one he rents, to another he gives a contract for working on shares, to another he pays wages in money, and with another he swaps work, and so *ad infinitum.*" Whatever system was used "there follows the same failure, or partial failure."[6]

The share system called forth especially severe criticism from all sides as being "ruinous to the soil" and "a disgrace to farming." A large proportion of landlords preferred and used the wage system. From Tennessee in 1880 it was reported that "advocates for shares and wages are about equally divided in number." Census reports of wages paid for labor in cotton production in 1880 make no distinction between white and black workers, and there probably was little difference. Prevalent monthly wages for a man's work "from sun to sun" were $8.00 to $14.00 in Alabama; $8.00 to $15.00 in Arkansas; $6.00 to $10.00 in Florida; $5.00 to $10.00 in Georgia ($4.00 to $6.00 per month for women); $6.00 to $15.00 in Louisiana; $8.00 to $12.00 in Mississippi, South Carolina, and Tennessee; $8.00 to $15.00 in Texas. Daily wages were usually 50 cents with board, or 75 cents without. A year's wages for a man in the central cotton belt of Georgia were $60.00 to $100.00; in Tennessee they were $100.00 to $125.00. Both yearly and monthly wages included rations.[7] In 1888 it was estimated by an authority that "the regular allowance of an ordinary hand is 12 pounds of bacon and 5 pecks of meal by the month," which "would cost him twenty-three dollars in the course of twelve months."[8]

It should be noted that the year 1880, for which the wage rates are quoted, was a relatively "good" year for cotton prices. When the price fell to half that in the nineties the wages could not have been nearly so high. If a yield of only three to six bales per hand could be expected, as estimated in Arkansas in 1880, the product of a year's labor would likely bring little more than $100.00 on the market in the middle nineties. Working on shares, the cropper at that rate received about $50.00 for his year's work. Neither he nor his landlord was likely to see or handle any cash, since both were in all probability deeply enmeshed in the toils of the crop lien. They received instead meager supplies at the prices demanded of credit customers.

The tides of Negro migration that had set in during Reconstruction, as the first and most characteristic expression of freedom, continued to move in the same general directions for some years after Redemption. These movements were of three kinds: from the country to the towns; from the poorer lands to the delta, bottom, and richer lands; and from the older states to the newer states of the Southwest. Intermittent complaint and a few laws against "enticing" labor persisted through the eighties. With one striking exception, however, the Negro migrations were largely from one part of the South to another. The great exodus northward did not begin until a half century after freedom.[9]

A census survey of the relation of land and labor in the cotton state of Alabama in 1880 revealed that the Negroes were most thickly concentrated upon the most fertile soil in the state, and the whites, upon the poorest soil; that the most fertile land, where the sharecropping system was most prevalent, yielded the least product, and was rapidly being exhausted; that poorer lands under cultivation by owners produced greater yield per capita and per acre; and that the white farmer was rapidly gaining on the black in the proportion of cotton produced.[10]

In spite of these facts, there was an almost universal preference among Black-Belt landlords for Negro tenants and workers. "White labor is totally unsuited to our methods, our manners, and our accommodations," declared an Alabama planter in 1888. "No other laborer [than the Negro] of whom I have any knowledge, would be as cheerful, or so contented on four pounds of meat and a peck of meal a week, in a little log cabin 14 x 16 feet, with cracks in it large enough to afford free passage to a large sized cat."[11] "Give me the nigger every time," echoed a Mississippi planter. "The nigger will never 'strike' as long as you give him plenty to eat and half clothe him: He will live on less and do more hard work, when properly managed, than any other class, or race of people. As Arp truthfully says 'we can boss him' and that is what we southern folks like."[12]

The writer who estimated the cash value of freedom for the Negro thirty years after emancipation at a little less than one dollar a year to the individual[13] overstated his point, though not so grossly as it might seem. At least such expensive luxuries as civil liberties and political franchises were beyond his reach. He knew very well that immediate, daily necessities came first—land, mules, plows, food, and clothes, all of which had to be got from a white man who oftener than not had too little himself.

In the working out of a new code of civil rights and social status for the freedman—in the definition of the Negro's "place"—Reconstruction had been only an interruption, the importance of which varied from state to state, but which was nowhere decisive. The transition from slavery to caste as a system of controlling race relations went forward gradually and tediously. Slavery had been vastly more than a labor system, and the gap that its removal left in manners, mores, and ritual of behavior could not be filled overnight. The so-called Black Codes were soon overthrown, as were the laws imported by the Carpetbaggers. Redemption and Hayes's policy of *laissez faire* left the code to be worked out by Southern white men. It has already been pointed out that there was no unity of opinion among them concerning the Negro's political rights. There also existed a roughly comparable division with reference to his civil rights.

Hampton, Lamar, Nicholls, and Redeemers of that type gave their solemn pledges in the Compromise of 1877 to protect the Negro in all his rights. They were probably guilty of less hypocrisy than has been charged. The class they represented had little to fear from the Negro and at the same time considerable to gain for the conservative cause by establishing themselves in a paternalistic relationship as his protector and champion against the upland and lower-class whites. This would better enable them to control his vote (against the same white element), not to mention his labor. In 1877 J. L. M. Curry listened to a debate of the Virginia Assembly in Jefferson's neoclassic capitol. "A negro member," he recorded with evident satisfaction in his diary, "said that he and his race relied for the protection of their rights & liberties, not on the 'poor white trash' but on the 'well-raised' gentlemen."[14] Black-Belt white men were casual about their daily intimacy and easy personal relations with Negroes, an attitude that made upland Southerners uncomfortable and shocked Northerners, even Radical Carpetbaggers. So long as this old leadership retained strong influence, the racial code was considerably less severe than it later became.

In the early years of freedom saloons in Mississippi usually served both whites and blacks at the same bar; many public eating places, "using separate tables, served both races in the same room"; public parks and buildings were still open to both to a great extent; and segregation in common carriers was not at all strict.[15] The most common type of discrimination on railways was the exclusion of Negroes from the first-class, or "ladies'" car. The races were accustomed to sharing the second-class coach. In 1877, however, a South Carolinian wrote that Negroes were "permitted to, and frequently do ride in first-class railway and street railway cars" in his state. This had caused trouble at first but was "now so common as hardly to provoke remark."[16] In 1885 George W. Cable, who was sensitive regarding discrimination, reported that in South Carolina Negroes "ride in the first class cars as a right" and "their presence excites no comment," while "In Virginia they may ride exactly as white people do and in the same cars."[17] Even the ante-bellum practice of using a common cemetery continued for many years. White papers occasionally "mistered" Negro politicians, if they were "good" politicians, and a Richmond paper affirmed in 1886 that "nobody here objects to sitting in political conventions with negroes. Nobody here objects to serving on juries with negroes."[18] Even the Tillman legislation of 1891 defeated a Jim Crow bill for railway cars.

From the beginning, however, concessions to the harsher code and developing phobias of the hillbillies of the white counties had to be made. There were South Carolinians in numbers who did not share the Charleston *News and Courier*'s feeling that it was "a great deal pleasanter to travel with respectable and well-behaved colored people than with unmannerly and ruffianly white men."

It is one of the paradoxes of Southern history that political democracy for the white man and racial discrimination for the black were often products of the same dynamics. As the Negroes invaded the new mining and industrial towns of the uplands in greater numbers, and the hill-country whites were driven into more frequent and closer association with them, and as the two races were brought into rivalry for subsistence wages in the cotton fields, mines, and wharves, the lower-class white man's demand for Jim Crow laws became more insistent. It took a lot of ritual and Jim Crow to bolster the creed of white supremacy in the bosom of a white man working for a black man's wages. The Negro pretty well understood these forces, and his grasp of them was one reason for his growing alliance with the most conservative and politically reactionary class of whites against the insurgent white democracy. A North Carolina Negro wrote: "The best people of the South do not demand this separate car business . . . and, when they do, it is only to cater to those of their race who, in order to get a big man's smile, will elevate them [*sic*] to place and power." He believed that "this whole thing is but a pandering to the lower instincts of the worst class of whites in the South."[19]

The barriers of racial discrimination mounted in direct ratio with the tide of political democracy among whites. In fact, an increase of Jim Crow laws upon the statute books of a state is almost an accurate index of the decline of the reactionary regimes of the Redeemers and triumph of white democratic movements. Take, for example, the law requiring separate accommodations for the races in trains, said to be "the most typical Southern law." No state[20] enacted such a law for more than twenty years after 1865. Yet in the five years beginning in 1887 one after another adopted some variation of the law: Florida in 1887, Mississippi in 1888, Texas in 1889, Louisiana in 1890, Alabama, Arkansas, Kentucky, and Georgia in 1891. These were the years when the Farmers' Alliance was first making itself felt in the legislatures of these states. Mississippi, in 1888, was the first state to adopt a law providing for the separation of the races in railway stations, and Georgia, in 1891, the first to adopt the law for streetcars.[21] These laws, though significant in themselves, were often only enactment of codes already in practice. Whether by state law or local law, or by the more pervasive coercion of sovereign white opinion, "the Negro's place" was gradually defined—in the courts, schools, and libraries, in parks, theaters, hotels, and residential districts, in hospitals, insane asylums—everywhere, including on sidewalks and in cemeteries. When complete, the new codes of White Supremacy were vastly more complex than the ante-bellum slave codes or the Black Codes of 1865–1866, and, if anything, they were stronger and more rigidly enforced.

Among the institutions of the Old Order that strained to meet the needs of the New, none proved more hopelessly inadequate than the old penitentiaries. The state was suddenly called upon to take over the plantation's penal functions at a time when crime was enormously increasing. The strain was too great. One after another of the states adopted the expedient of leasing the convicts to private corporations or individuals. In Louisiana the convict-lease system had an ante-bellum origin; in the other Southern states it was introduced by the provisional or military governments and retained by the Carpetbaggers and Redeemers.

For a number of reasons the lease system took firm roots in the New Order and grew to greater proportions. For one thing, it fitted perfectly the program of retrenchment, for under it the penitentiary not only ceased to be a heavy burden on the taxpayer but became a source of revenue to the state—sometimes a very lucrative source. The system also fitted conveniently the needs occasioned by the new criminal codes of the Redemption regimes, which piled up heavy penalties for petty offenses against property, while at the same time they weakened the protection afforded the Negro in the courts. The so-called "pig law" of Mississippi defined the theft of any property over ten dollars in value, or any cattle or swine of whatever value, as grand larceny, with a sentence up to five years. After its adoption the number of state convicts increased from 272 in 1874 to 1,072 by the end of 1877. The number in Georgia increased from 432 in 1872 to 1,441 in 1877. Additional convictions meant additional revenue instead of additional taxes. The system quickly became a large-scale and sinister business. Leases of ten, twenty, and thirty years were granted by legislatures to powerful politicians, Northern syndicates, mining corporations, and individual planters. Laws limiting hours of labor and types of work for convicts were nonexistent in some states and negligible in others, and in two states protective laws were later removed or modified. Responsibility of lessees for the health and lives of convicts was extremely loose. Some states had no inspectors and in others inspection was highly perfunctory if not corrupt. Where the law permitted, the large lessees subleased convicts in small or large gangs for short periods, thus rendering responsibility to the state even more fictitious and protection of the state's prisoners all but impossible. County prisons in many cases adopted the system and in Alabama had twice as many convicts leased as the state. The South's "penitentiaries" were great rolling cages that followed construction camps and railroad building, hastily built stockades deep in forest or swamp or mining fields, or windowless log forts in turpentine flats.[22]

The degradation and brutality produced by this system would be incredible but for the amount of evidence from official sources. A report of the inspectors of the Alabama penitentiary revealed that the prisons were packed with several times the number of convicts they could reasonably hold. "They are as filthy, as a rule, as dirt could make them, and both prisons and prisoners were infested with vermin. The bedding was totally unfit for use. . . . [It was found] that convicts were excessively and sometimes cruelly punished; that they were poorly clothed and fed; that the sick were neglected, insomuch as no hospitals had been provided, that they were confined with the well convicts."[23] A grand-jury investigation of the penitentiary hospital in Mississippi reported that inmates were "all bearing on their persons marks of the most inhuman and brutal treatments. Most of them have their backs cut in great wales, scars and blisters, some with the skin peeling off in pieces as the result of severe beatings. . . . They were lying there dying, some of them on bare boards, so poor and emaciated that their bones almost came through their skin, many complaining for want of food. . . . We actually saw live vermin crawling over their faces, and the little bedding and clothing they have is in tatters and stiff with filth."[24] In mining camps of Arkansas and Alabama convicts were worked through the winter without shoes, standing in water much of the time. In both states the task system was used, whereby a squad of three was compelled to mine a certain amount of coal per day on penalty of a severe flogging for the whole squad. Convicts in the turpentine camps of Florida, with "stride-chains" and "waist-chains" riveted on their bodies, were compelled to work at a trot. "They kept this gait up all day long, from tree to tree," reported the warden.[25] The average annual death rate among Negro convicts in Mississippi from 1880 to 1885 was almost 11 per cent, for white convicts about half that, and in 1887 the general average was 16 per cent. The death rate among the prisoners of Arkansas was reported in 1881 to be 25 per cent annually. An indication of what was called "moral conditions" is provided in a report of the Committee on the Penitentiary of the Georgia Legislature: "We find in some of the camps men and women chained together and occupying the same sleeping bunks. The result is that there are now in the Penitentiary twenty-five bastard children, ranging from three months to five years of age, and many of the women are now far advanced in pregnancy."[26] For the Southern convict-lease system a modern scholar can "find parallel only in the persecutions of the Middle Ages or in the prison camps of Nazi Germany."[27]

The lease system was under bitter attack, especially from the various independent parties, and repeated attempts were made to abolish or reform it. Julia Tutwiler of Alabama was a moving spirit in the reform movement. Almost everywhere, however, the reformers were opposed by vested interests within the Redemption party—sometimes by the foremost leaders of that party. Senator Brown of Georgia was guaranteed by his twenty-year lease "three hundred able-bodied, long-term men" to work in his Dade Coal Mines, for which he paid the state about eight cents per hand per day.[28] Senator Gordon was also a member of a firm leasing convicts. Colonel Colyar, leader of one wing of the Redemption party in Tennessee, leased that state's prisoners at $101,000 a year for the Tennessee Coal and Iron Company. Control over these Southern state "slaves" was the foundation of several large fortunes, and in one case, of a great political dynasty. Robert McKee, who was in a position to know all the workings of the system, wrote that the state warden of Alabama, John H. Bankhead, "grew rich in a few years on $2000 a year," and manipulated the legislature at will. "The 'penitentiary ring' is a power in the party," he wrote privately, "and it is a corrupt power. One of the State officers is a lessee of convicts, and has a brother who is a deputy warden."[29] Former Secretary of State Rufus K. Boyd believed that the convict-lease ring was "as unscrupulous as any radical in the days of their power. . . . Are we all thieves? What is it leading to? Who can submit to these things patiently?"[30] Yet the party continued to submit.

The convict-lease system did greater violence to the moral authority of the Redeemers than did anything else. For it was upon the tradition of paternalism that the Redeemer regimes claimed authority to settle the race problem and "deal with the Negro.". . .

The Mississippi Plan as the American Way

As late as 1879 three foremost spokesmen of the South, Lamar of Mississippi, Hampton of South Carolina, and Stephens of Georgia, agreed in a public statement that the disfranchisement of the Negro was not only impossible but undesired. Lamar declared that it was "a political impossibility under any circumstances short of revolution," and that even if it were possible the South would not permit it. Hampton, who claimed the distinction of being "the first man at the South" to advocate suffrage for the emancipated slave, remarked that the Negro "naturally allies himself with the more conservative of the whites."[1] These gentlemen obviously hoped for a good deal from this new ally of conservatism.

The century had scarcely ended, however, before the prophesies of these statesmen were overturned throughout the South. Lamar's own state, famous for her "Mississippi Plan" of 1875, again led the way in race policy with a "Second Mississippi Plan," but this time by means "short of revolution." Disfranchisement was accomplished by a constitutional convention in 1890. Mississippi was the only state that took this step before the outbreak of the Populist revolt. South Carolina was next with a convention in 1895, Louisiana in 1898, North Carolina by means of an amendment in 1900, Alabama in 1901, Virginia in 1901–1902, Georgia by amendment in 1908, and Oklahoma in 1910. Over the same years Tennessee, Florida, Arkansas, and Texas accomplished disfranchisement by means of the poll tax and other devices.

The Second Mississippi Plan stirred immediate interest throughout the South, and had the times been favorable the other states would probably have followed the example much more quickly than they did. Conservatives of neighboring states, grappling with powerful Populist opposition, eyed the results of the Mississippi Plan enviously. An Alabama journal remarked in 1892 that "we would do well to imitate the wise politicians of Mississippi."[2] Ben Tillman boasted, after putting through a successful imitation, that South Carolina and Mississippi were the only Southern states to avoid a strong challenge from the third party. There were several abortive attempts at constitutional revision in the early nineties, but no further extension of the Mississippi Plan until after the collapse of Populism.[3]

For a number of reasons disfranchisement was delayed elsewhere. In the first place, faced with a mounting tide of agrarian radicalism, "with the wildest Populist ideas so prevalent," conservatives hesitated to call conventions that might seize the opportunity to write into organic law clauses that "smacked of socialism and communism" and "Kansas ideas."[4] In the second place, once Southern whites were split into two parties both the Populists and the Democrats sought to win the Negroes to their cause. The

Populists were engaged in a crusade to unite both races upon a platform of democratic reform in behalf of the common man. The conservatives at the same time found in the Negro vote the most effective means of defeating the Populists. And finally, the Lodge force bill of 1890 indicated that a Northern conscience had been reawakened on the subject of Negro suffrage, and that it might resist or overthrow disfranchisement measures of doubtful constitutionality.

In 1898 these doubts and fears and constitutional qualms were largely laid to rest. In that year, for one thing, the United States Supreme Court, in the case of *Williams* v. *Mississippi,* passed favorably upon the new plan and adopted the views of the Mississippi court.[5] By that time, also, conservatives had little to fear from agrarian radicals and the influence they might exert on new constitutions. Reaction was in the air. Some Populists favored disfranchisement in the belief that once the Negro was removed from politics, white men could divide, one-party domination would cease, and the way would lie open for white radicalism. Other Populists blamed the Negro's defection to conservatism for their defeat. The exciting vision of 1892, picturing black and white farmer and laborer marching together toward a new era, had by 1898 become dimmed by old prejudices and suspicions. It had been a precarious and handicapped experiment from the start.

On the whole, the Wade Hampton type of alliance came easier for the Negro. Writing of the situation in Georgia, the Negro educator John Hope made the claim that "Populism was defeated by the colored voters espousing the Democratic side," and that "this fact is acknowledged and to an extent appreciated by the party now in power—to the extent at least of staving off any further disfranchisement measures thus far."[6] The gratitude of the Georgia Democrats, as it turned out, meant a respite of only three more years. A Northern investigator came to the conclusion that Kolb and the Populists were defeated by Negro votes in Alabama also, where he "found, on the testimony of negroes as well as whites, that the mass of negroes had actually voted the Democratic ticket."[7]

Booker T. Washington announced to the Southern white man in 1895 a doctrine of profound significance for the future of racial relations. The implications of the so-called "Atlanta Compromise" will be explored later, but it should be noted at this point that in so far as Washington's pronouncement constituted a renunication of active political aspirations for the Negro it had an important bearing upon the movement for disfranchisement.[8]

Southern white Republicans were divided on the question of disfranchisement. The Lily-white faction, which gained ground during the nineties, more or less openly welcomed the movement in the belief that the removal of the Negro would make the party respectable in the South and permit white men to divide. With the white Republicans indifferent, the Populists divided, and the Negro himself apathetic, resistance to disfranchisement from within the South reached a low point by 1898.

In the meantime, the North had taken up the White Man's Burden, and by 1898 was looking to Southern racial policy for national guidance in the new problems of imperialism resulting from the Spanish war. Commenting on the Supreme Court's opinion upholding disfranchisement in Mississippi, the *Nation* pronounced it "an interesting coincidence that this important decision is rendered at a time when we are considering the idea of taking in a varied assortment of inferior races in different parts of the world"—races "which, of course, could not be allowed to vote."[9] Senator Morgan of Alabama was chairman of the committee of the Hawaiian Commission that framed the voting restrictions for one "assortment of inferior races." To reject the property and literacy tests recommended for Hawaiians, reported the Senator, would be to "turn the legislature over to the masses" and "deprive the more conservative elements and property owners of effective representation."[10] Senator Morgan's advice was also sought by the white-supremacy advocates of his own state who were currently debating additional franchise restrictions for Alabama. A speech in defense of American imperialism by George F. Hoar "most amply vindicated the South," said Senator John L. McLaurin of South Carolina. He thanked the Massachusetts statesman "for his complete announcement of the divine right of the Caucasian to govern the inferior races." The Boston *Evening Transcript* reluctantly admitted that the Southern way was "now the policy of the Administration of the very party which carried the country into and through a civil war to free the slave."[11]

Events in the Philippines soon indicated that the Mississippi

Plan had become the American Way. "If the stronger and cleverer race," said an editorial in the Boston *Atlantic Monthly,* "is free to impose its will upon 'new-caught, sullen peoples' on the other side of the globe, why not in South Carolina and Mississippi? The advocates of the 'shotgun policy' are quite as sincere, and we are inclined to think quite as unselfish, as the advocates of 'benevolent assimilation.' The two phrases are, in fact, two names for the same thing."[12] Professors John W. Burgess and William A. Dunning of Columbia University brought academic authority to the support of Southern policy. Burgess thought "that the Republican party, in its work of imposing the sovereignty of the United States upon eight millions of Asiatics, has changed its view in regard to the political relations of races and has at last virtually accepted the ideas of the South upon that subject." He assured the South that the leaders of the party of emancipation would never "again give themselves over to the vain imagination of the political equality of man."[13] Dunning deprecated "the trite generalities of the Rights of Man," and declared "The enfranchisement of the freedmen [to be] as reckless a species of statecraft, as that which marked 'the blind hysterics of the Celt' in 1789–95."[14]

The implications of the new American imperialism for Southern race policy were not lost upon the leaders of the disfranchisement movement. Sympathetic views from the North were quoted in the constitutional conventions and the press, and campaign orators drew the lessons of imperialism for the people. "Mr. President, this is not a sectional issue, the race problem is no longer confined to the States of the South," said a delegate to the Alabama disfranchisement convention. It was the same problem from Cuba and Alabama to Hawaii and the Philippines, and "we have the sympathy instead of the hostility of the North."[15] With the sections in rapport, the work of writing the white man's law for Asiatic and Afro-American went forward simultaneously.

Repugnance for corrupt elections was put forward everywhere as the primary reason for disfranchisement. Popular disgust with fraudulent elections was sincere and widespread. It probably reached its peak during the repression of the third party, although it was given as an important motive of the disfranchisement convention of Mississippi in 1890. The president of the convention said that fraud had become "chronic," that it was "used even as between the whites themselves," and that "Fourteen years of fraud excited nausea."[16]

Of the 183 cases of contested elections in the United States House of Representatives between 1875 and 1901, 107 came from twelve Southern states, the great majority of them involving charges of fraud.[17] And these were states from a presumably "solid" section.

"I told them to go to it, boys, count them out," admitted former Governor Oates to the constitutional convention of Alabama, recounting the methods of the conservatives in that state. "But we have gone on from bad to worse until it has become a great evil," he added. "White men have gotten to cheating each other until we don't have any honest elections."[18] It was this point of whites cheating whites that became sorest during the Populist struggle. "It is true that we win these elections," explained the leading conservative paper of Louisiana, "but at a heavy cost, and by the use of methods repugnant to our idea of political honesty and which must, in time, demoralize the people of Louisiana."[19] A "prominent Democrat" of Virginia shared this fear. "Cheating at elections is demoralizing our whole people," he said. "We are deteriorating as a people, and the principal cause of our deterioration is this idiotic nonsense about 'preserving white civilization' by cheating."[20] Others feared that corruption in political life would contaminate business and social relations.

The remedy, declared the reformers, was the disfranchisement of the Negro. A white Republican of Virginia found the argument paradoxical. "The remedy suggested here is to punish the man who has been injured," he said. The Negroes were to be disfranchised "to prevent the Democratic election officials from stealing their votes."[21] To a Democrat of Alabama, it was not a matter of ethics but of economy. "Now we are not begging for 'ballot reform' or anything of that sort," he said, "but we want to be relieved of purchasing the Negroes to carry elections. I want cheaper votes."[22]

Behind the "White Supremacy" slogans and the front of racial solidarity there raged a struggle between Southern white men that is usually overlooked. It is essential to examine this before the disfranchisement movement can be understood. The parties to the struggle were variously described as the Black Belt and the Hill Country, or the Lowlands and the Uplands, but lines of cleavage usually separated the counties predominantly black from those mainly white in population. It was not a new struggle. When the Negro was a slave, the white counties sought to tax him as property and prevent his owners from counting him as a basis for Black-Belt representation in state legislatures and party conventions. Opposing these measures, the slaveowners often fought to retain property qualifications for office holding and prevent upland counties from increasing their quota of representatives.

By 1860, but for a few exceptions, property qualifications had been removed, universal white manhood suffrage prevailed, and representation was generally apportioned according to white population. Thus the slaveowner was partly deprived of the advantage of counting the slaves. Reconstruction and the Carpetbag constitutions upset the ante-bellum arrangement and restored the Black Belt to power. The white minority in the black counties, heirs to the Carpetbag system, often defended the Radical constitutions. Vetoing a bill calling for a new constitution, Governor Robert Lowry of Mississippi said, of the Carpetbag document: "True it is that it was prepared and submitted to us in large part by aliens, but 'good can come out of Nazareth,' as was long ago proved."[23] Attacking that veto, a hillbilly paper declared that "the carpetbaggers so framed our present constitution . . . as to give a preponderance of representation to the negro counties" and that the Black-Belt whites "hypocritically raised the howl of white supremacy while debauching the ballot-boxes and through this infamous means made themselves potent factors in our State and county governments."[24]

Each side to the dispute was beset by fears and suspicions of its opponent and maneuvered for advantage. "I ask you gentlemen of the black belt," exclaimed a white-county Virginia delegate, "How do you happen to be here if the Negroes control down there?"[25] "What are we here for?" asked an Alabama delegate. "Not to preserve white supremacy. White supremacy is secure in Alabama."[26] The real question was *which whites* should be supreme. The vote for the conventions of Virginia and Alabama were decidedly sectional, with the white counties and the remnants of the Populist party largely in opposition and the black counties in support—a circumstance that led skeptics to comment upon the eagerness of the Negroes for their own disfranchisement.[27]

In the case of the first two disfranchising conventions the Black Belt was the more reluctant section, and leaders of the white farmers took the initiative. It was not Negro domination but white domination from the Black Belt that the white counties of Mississippi sought to overthrow in 1890. The two jealous factions worked together only by means of elaborate compromise. "You gentlemen of the black counties must sacrifice power, and you of the white must give up principle," declared Judge Wiley P. Harris. The "power" was the advantage enjoyed by the Black-Belt whites as a result of the voteless Negroes, and the "principle" was that of universal white manhood suffrage. The black-county delegation yielded to the creation of thirteen new seats of the state legislature, all of which were expected to be assigned to white counties, while the latter accepted the poll tax and the literacy test as limits upon suffrage.[28] A similar compromise was effected in the Alabama convention which gave the white counties of that state five additional representatives and two additional senators. The western counties of Virginia were "very much more interested in economic questions" than in "questions of suffrage," in "railroad domination" than in "Negro domination," said their delegates,[29] and as the price of their support of disfranchisement demanded and got a corporations commission.

As important as were these compromises, the storm center of the great debate was always disfranchisement. Some delegates were troubled with the uneasy awareness that they had assembled to reverse the tendency of half a century of democratic history and deprive from half to two thirds of their fellow citizens of the ballot. The sharp conflict between deep-rooted convictions and the work at hand gave rise to much searching of soul and explaining of votes. Views were often stated with revealing frankness. Delegate J. Thomas Heflin, whose conscience was emphatically not troubled by the work at hand, nevertheless opposed the publication of full records of debates. "We will say things down here in our Southern way, and in the great old commonwealth of Alabama," he suggested, "that we do not want read and criticised day after day as we deliberate in this body."[30] The records of these debates, more than any comparable documents, disclose the tortured conscience of the South.

In the campaigning stage of the movement, disfranchisement leaders in all states—for example, Charles B. Aycock of North Carolina, Ben Tillman of South Carolina, and Hoke Smith of Georgia—gave repeated assurances that no white man would be disfranchised. Once deliberations began, however, it became apparent that powerful elements of the movement saw in it an opportunity to establish in power "the intelligence and wealth of the South," which would, of course, "govern in the interest of all classes."[31] Oates, who had fought the Populists, informed his Alabama colleagues that he favored eliminating "all those who are unfit and unqualified, and if the rule strikes a white man as well as a negro, let him go. There are some white men who have no more right and no more business to vote than a negro and not as much as some of them."[32] A delegate from a Tidewater county told the Virginia convention that it was "not the negro vote which works the harm," but "the depraved and incompetent men of our own race."[33]

The conservative press urged the conventions to forget their pledges and eliminate the undesirable white voters. According to Edgar Gardner Murphy, the Alabama convention, "largely at the suggestion of the Press Association of Alabama, practically ignored any literal interpretation of the unfortunate pledge, and the completed instrument did, in effect, result in the disfranchisement of a large number of white voters."[34] "The *Times-Democrat* has all along strenuously contended that what is sauce for the goose must be made sauce for the gander," wrote the editor of the New Orleans paper, who believed that all tests "must be applied with equal rigor in the case of poor or illiterate whites and in the case of poor or illiterate Negroes."[35] Likewise the *Picayune* of the same city was "just as desirous to shut out every unworthy white man" as it was to exclude "every unworthy negro."[36] The Charlotte *Observer* described the movement as "the struggle of the white people of North Carolina to rid themselves of the dangers of the rule of negroes and the lower class of whites."[37] John B. Knox, president of the Alabama constitutional convention, denied that the Negro was the exclusive concern in his state. "The true philosophy of the movement," he later wrote, "was to establish restricted suffrage, and to place the power of government in the hands of the intelligent and virtuous."[38] The background of Populist agitation against which certain of these conventions were held suggests comparison with the Shaysite upheaval that served as a background of the Federal convention at Philadelphia in 1787.

The two commonest barriers erected against voters of the lower class by the disfranchisers were the literacy and property qualifications. Literacy was made one means of qualifying for the franchise in eight states, and in four of these property was an alternative.[39] The standards of both literacy and property would appear at first to be low—the ability to read and write, and the possession of taxable property worth from $300 to $500. But it should be borne in mind that illiteracy and poverty were far more generally characteristic of the lower class in the South then than now. In some states the per capita wealth did not equal the property qualification, and the general practice of undervaluation for tax assessment meant that property worth several times the minimum requirement would not be assessed high enough to qualify a voter.[40] Of the 231 counties in the United States in which 20 per cent or more of the whites of voting age were illiterate, 204 were in the South.

Advocates of property and literacy tests for the franchise first attempted to appeal to the patriotism of the poorer whites on somewhat the same basis that the slaveowners had appealed to them for support of the Confederacy. "Thousands of gallant sons of the South," a delegate told the Mississippi convention, "had no property in slaves or otherwise, and yet they offered their lives to protect their neighbor's property, and the same noble spirit is now ready for any concession or sacrifice that will secure and perpetuate white supremacy in Mississippi. (Great and long continued applause.)"[41]

The yeomanry, some of them graduates of the Populist school, seemed less eager for self-sacrifice in the nineties than they had been in the sixties. Their spokesmen would have no part in this type of patriotism. Delegate Monroe McClurg declared that Mississippi had "tried property qualifications in three different forms," but that "in the Constitution of 1832 the State returned to the American principle of [white] manhood suffrage" and did not intend to retreat.[42] Frank Burkitt of Chickasaw County, with other Alliancemen, fought and defeated the property qualification. Thomas L. Long of an Alabama white county where many crops were made "by white women and oxen" declared that in his part of the country "not one in ten" would ever own enough to qualify under the $300 property test.[43] In the western and mountain districts of Virginia and North Carolina suspicion and resentment flamed up fiercely against property and literacy tests. . . .

While their remedy somewhat suggests throwing out the baby with the bath, the disfranchisers could claim with a degree of truth that after their work was done Southern elections were more decorous. Disgraceful scenes of ballot-box stealing, bribery, and intimidation were much rarer after disfranchisement. One effective means of stopping the stealing of ballots, of course, is to stop the people from casting them. Elections are also likely to be more decorous when the electorate of the opposition parties has been disfranchised or decimated and the election becomes a formality in a one-party system. Opponents of the new system held that it perpetuated old evils in a legalized form. "Elections under it would turn," said one critic, "not primarily upon the will of the people but upon the partisan or factional allegiance of the registrars."[44] The debates of the conventions indicate what the registration officials were expected to do, whether they did it or not. "At best it is an enamelled lie," wrote John Spencer Bassett of the North Carolina law. To him it was "one more step in the educating of our people that it is right to lie, to steal, & to defy all honesty in order to keep a certain party in power."[45] The majority of Southerners, however, were taught to regard disfranchisement as reform.

As for the promise that disfranchisement would enable white men to divide freely on fundamental issues, it simply failed to materialize. The spirit of intolerance and proscription aroused by the white-supremacy campaigns did not stop at the bounds of race. North Carolina Red Shirts pulled white Populists from platforms, beat them up, and ran them out of town. Furnifold M. Simmons, Democratic state chairman and later United States Senator, boasted that he sent "some of our boys" to terrorize the Populist Senator Marion Butler, that they "scared him almost to death," and that the Republican governor of the state "was so badly frightened that he slipped away from Raleigh immediately after the election."[46] Dissident whites were watched shrewdly for their reaction to white-supremacy propaganda. Josephus Daniels observed with obvious satisfaction the presence of "quite a number of white Populists and white Republicans" in a Red-Shirt parade of 1,000 in 1898.[47] When three Populist members of the legislature cast their votes for the disfranchisement amendment the following year, Daniels reported that "the applause was long and deafening, shouts and yells being added to the hand clapping."[48] The next year he remarked that while "in 1892–94 and '96 the Populist convention was like a mighty torrent pouring down the mountain side; in 1900 it is like an old mill-pond after the water has been turned off."[49]

White supremacy enjoyed a success second only to that of the silver panacea as a discourager of political independence and a uniter of the Solid South.

11. Booker T. Washington and His Times

The unquestioned leader of the black race in America at the dawn of the twentieth century was Booker T. Washington. By the time of his death, Washington had exerted an influence in national affairs seldom equaled by a black man in American history. His achievements were all the more remarkable when his humble beginnings are considered. Washington was born in Virginia in 1856, the slave son of a white father and slave mother. During Reconstruction he studied at Hampton Institute, one of the educational institutions for blacks newly established by philanthropic northerners. The leading spirit of Hampton was General Samuel Armstrong, who believed that he could train an economically successful black elite which, by example, would inspire the mass of blacks to seek to better their conditions. His emphasis on the virtues of a practical, utilitarian education had a strong impact on the young Washington, and when he himself became director of an educational institution, Tuskegee Institute, Washington followed the lines laid down by Armstrong. At Tuskegee in the 1880's and 1890's, blacks were trained in such diverse skills as farming, brick making, blacksmithing and printing, and in personal habits of thrift, cleanliness and industriousness.

The occasion of Washington's emergence as a national figure was his speech in 1895 at the Atlanta Cotton States and International Exposition, before a racially mixed audience which included many prominent northern and southern whites. Washington planned his speech carefully, making doubly certain not to give offense to his white listeners. He declared that blacks for the time being would abandon their struggle for equal social and political rights, and concentrate on economic advancement. Washington reminded southern whites of the "fidelity and love" blacks had shown them, and asked in return only the assurance that they continue to employ blacks as the major labor force of the South, and that the economic progress of skilled and dedicated blacks not be impeded. The Atlanta speech won immediate acclaim throughout the nation. Frederick Douglass had died in the same year, and it appeared that the Tuskegeean had replaced Douglass as the national spokesman for the black race.

Washington's educational, social, and political philosophies were intimately related. His reading of black history convinced him that slavery and Reconstruction had not prepared blacks for freedom, because they had never been trained in the attitudes essential for economic achievement—belief in the dignity of labor and habits of thrift and hard work. At Tuskegee, therefore, he stressed character building and the inculcation of middle-class values. Industrial education, one historian has observed, meant for Washington "training in industriousness." Washington accepted the common nineteenth-century attitude that through self-help one could rise from poverty to riches; indeed his autobiography, *Up from Slavery,* was a black Horatio Alger tale. This outlook helps explain Washington's willingness to postpone political equality for blacks. The real need of the black community, he insisted, was economic power, not political participation, which could never be more than illusory so long as blacks were economically dependent on whites.

In one sense, Washington was a black leader created by whites. Ironically for an advocate of racial self-help, he was financed by the wealthiest whites in America. Contributors to Tuskegee included such multi-millionaires as J. P. Morgan, John D. Rockefeller, and Collis P. Huntington. Equally ironic is the fact that this man who urged a suspension of political activity by blacks was himself a confidant of Presidents Theodore Roosevelt and Taft and their patronage arbiter in black affairs. And Washington's influence over black affairs was further enhanced by his secret financing and manipulation of a number of black newspapers.

Washington's close relations with powerful whites goes far toward explaining his undoubted predominance in black affairs from 1895 to the founding of the NAACP in 1911. Yet it is by no means the entire story. For his outlook strongly appealed to important elements in the black community as well. For one thing, Washington's philosophy represented what might be called the politics of survival. His program of economic progress was quite possibly the only feasible one under the severe circumstances which faced southern blacks at the turn of the century. Another source of Washington's strength is indicated by August Meier, in the article "Negro Class Structure and Ideology in the Age of Booker T. Washington." Meier points out that Washington drew support from a rising black middle class, which had experienced economic success at first hand, and which almost exclusively served a black clientele. Unlike the older black leadership, which had extensive social and economic contacts with white society, this new class was more interested in business and race solidarity than political affairs. Allan Spear's study of the Chicago ghetto in the early twentieth century confirms Meier's conclusion that businessmen were wholehearted supporters of Washington's outlook. Washington spoke their language—he was devoted to middle-class capitalist values, and violently opposed to labor unions. Indeed, he often promised southern whites that they could rely on black workers not to organize or strike.

Washington's outlook was an attempt to meet the problem of a people ill-equipped by slavery for either political leadership or economic progress. He taught his people that to be accepted by white society they must absorb the middle-class values of that society and prove themselves in the terms in which white Americans judged one another— by economic success. Yet, as C. Vann Woodward has pointed out, Washington's economic outlook was fast becoming obsolete at the turn of the century. There was nothing wrong with training blacks for jobs, but the jobs Washington chose—skilled crafts and independent farming—were increasingly threatened by industrialization and mechanized agriculture. For the black population, economic opportunity lay in the city and factory, but Washington urged his people to remain in the South and on the farm.

It would be unfair to criticize Washington for abandoning political rights altogether, for he secretly fought for nondiscriminatory suffrage provisions in southern constitutions, arguing that property and literacy tests should be applied equally to both races, and he always insisted that whites would be forced to share political power with blacks once the latter had achieved economic independence. To a large extent, he was a creature of his times. As his contemporary Kelly Miller noted in comparing him with Frederick Douglass: "Douglass lived in the day of moral giants; Washington lives in the era of merchant princes. The contemporaries of Douglass emphasized the rights of man; those of Washington, his productive capacity. . . . Douglass was a moralist, insisting upon the application of righteousness to public affairs; Washington is a practical opportunist, accepting the best terms which he thinks it possible to secure."

Negro Class Structure and Ideology in the Age of Booker T. Washington[1]

AUGUST MEIER

During the period of Booker T. Washington's prominence, from the 1890's until his death in 1915, probably the leading ideological orientation of American Negroes centered on the development of Negro business enterprise through a combination of thrift, industry and racial solidarity, or Negro support of Negro business. While this ideology was a major component of Washington's philosophy—and his doctrine of industrial education was of course simply a part of this program for racial uplift through economic advancement—its formulation actually antedated Washington's fame by a number of years. It had enjoyed a considerable vogue during the 1850's, and again since the end of Reconstruction had been experiencing increasing popularity among articulate Negroes. Generally its advocates held that in the face of increasing discrimination—in the face of disfranchisement, jim crow laws and other forms of oppression—Negroes must turn from a direct attack on the American race system to an indirect program. Negroes, it was held, must first develop economically—and in view of white attitudes this must be done by Negroes within their own community. Once Negroes had proven their ability to help themselves, to acquire wealth and respectability, it was believed, prejudice and discrimination would wither away. Admittedly as Abram Harris, Ralph Bunche and Franklin Frazier have pointed out,[2] the doctrine of Negro support for Negro business could be employed as a rationalization for the Negro working classes to support Negro entrepreneurs who were basically interested in themselves rather

FROM August Meier, "Negro Class Structure and Ideology in the Age of Booker T. Washington," *Phylon*, 1962. Copyright © 1962 by Phylon. Reprinted by permission of Atlanta University.

than in the welfare of the masses of the race. Ideologically, however, this doctrine was framed in terms of improving the economic
standing of the Negro community as a whole and of indirectly
obtaining citizenship rights by demonstrating the ability of Negroes
to meet American petty-bourgeois standards of respectability and
success. In the South this doctrine, by emphasizing economics
rather than politics and civil rights, by stressing the Negro's duty to
help himself rather than placing the blame where it belonged,
proved to be an effective mechanism of accommodation—as is
exemplified in the position of Booker T. Washington. On the other
hand, this philosophy has also been associated with militant
protest doctrines and activities, as can be seen from its espousal by
Frederick Douglass in the 1840's and 1850's, by Du Bois in many
periods of his life, and by its popularity during the militant period
of the New Negro in the 1920's.

My purpose in this paper is to investigate the relationship
between the popularity of this ideology and the changing Negro
class structure during the period between the 1880's and the Great
Migration. And since occupation is such an important criterion of
social class position in our society—in fact the most important
single criterion, though I do not mean to rule out the significance
of other factors such as education and ancestry—it will be helpful
first to summarize the changes that were taking place in the economic base of the Negro bourgeoisie in that period.

Down to the close of the nineteenth century the entrepreneurial
class in the Negro community depended in considerable part upon
the support of white customers. Though the range of occupations
varied from city to city, this group was composed primarily of
blacksmiths, tailors, barbers and other skilled artisans, hackmen
and draymen, grocers, and less frequently meat dealers, hotel
owners, caterers, real estate dealers and contractors. Along with
civil servants, teachers, pullman porters of good family background, domestic servants in the most elite white families, the
more eminent and better educated ministers, a few doctors and an
occasional lawyer, the more successful among these entrepreneurs
formed the upper stratum in the Negro community during the
nineteenth century.[3]

By about 1900, however, significant economic and social

changes were well under way. A growing antipathy on the part of whites toward trading with Negro businessmen and changes in technology and business organization forced many of these small entrepreneurs out of business. At the same time the increasing urbanization of Negroes supplied a base for professional and businessmen dependent on the Negro market. Such businesses included banks (the first two founded in 1888), cemetery and realty associations, insurance enterprises, and numerous retail and service establishments. It is notable that most of the banks and insurance enterprises were outgrowths of the enterprises of mutual benefit and fraternal orders, which themselves exemplified the philosophy of mutual self-help and solidarity along social and economic lines. Of course certain businesses—such as newspapers, undertakers and some barbers and retail merchants—had previously depended on the Negro market, and this group now increased in size. At the same time there appeared larger numbers of physicians and lawyers who also served a segregated community. This shift in the economic basis of the Negro bourgeoisie proceeded at an uneven rate, earlier and more rapidly in some cities than in others. Moreover, the process was relatively gradual, extending from the 1890's through the 1920's, by which time the newer enterprises were dominant. This whole movement was effectively symbolized by the different sources of two of the largest fortunes created in these years—that of R. R. Church, based on Memphis real estate and created during the late nineteenth century, and that of Madame C. J. Walker, created during the first part of the twentieth century.[4]

There was in fact a real burgeoning of Negro enterprise after 1890 and especially after 1900, based chiefly on the Negro market. According to the National Negro Business League, which propagandized enthusiastically for racial chauvinism in business, business enterprises had doubled in total number from 20,000 in 1900 to 40,000 in 1914. In that period banks had risen from 4 to 51; undertakers from 450 to 1,000; drug stores from 250 to 695; retail merchants from 10,000 to 25,000.[5]

It is my thesis that, with certain significant exceptions, it was a newer rising group of men that formed the backbone of the entrepreneurial and professional group that depended on the Negro market, and that they in time—usually in the 1920's—came to constitute not only the economic elite, but the social elite of the Negro community. Moreover, it is my thesis that as a result of this fact, it is among what we should call this upward mobile middle class that the philosophy of racial progress through economic solidarity, or the formation of what Du Bois called a group economy, and the philosophy of Booker T. Washington found their greatest support.

Let us examine the developments in the social class system in a few illustrative Northern and Southern cities.[6]

New Orleans had a large ante-bellum group of free people of color, and the Negro Creoles continued to dominate the building and other trades for many years. However, the insurance and other substantial enterprises serving the Negro community were established not by the downtown native New Orleans Creole group (who lived north of Canal Street), but by ambitious members of the uptown group that resided south of Canal Street. The uptown group consisted of Negro Creoles who had come to New Orleans from other parts of the state and of the Protestant house servants of the wealthy, who—unlike most of the Catholic Creoles—sent their children to the Methodist, Congregationalist and Baptist colleges—New Orleans, Straight and Leland Universities—and thus were the chief source of the professional Negro elite in the city. New Orleans in effect had at that time two parallel social hierarchies—Creole and non-Creole; and it was from among the latter, who prior to the Civil War had been largely house-slaves, that the new business and professional elite first appeared.

In Charleston, which was out of the mainstream of the New South's economic development, an upper class of artisans, contractors, barbers, postal employes, butchers and professional people, with ante-bellum free antecedents, for many years enjoyed their upper class status undisturbed. Not until the 1920's did Charleston Negroes enter into the "cooperative" businesses dependent on the Negro market and not until after the Second World War did the dispersal of the better educated descendants of the old families pave the way for the rise to upper class status of those descendants of the old house-slave class who now moved into the professional and business positions that accorded them high social status.

In Nashville at the turn of the century, a light-skinned elite of barbers, contractors and merchants in the city market was gradually giving way to a darker-skinned group that consisted chiefly of physicians and dentists associated with Meharry Medical College, along with some businessmen and professors. The more important business enterprises included two banks and two publishing boards —the Baptist and the A.M.E. Sunday School Union. Some members of the old elite made the transition, like J. C. Napier, the son of an ante-bellum drayman, who became a banker, lawyer and federal office holder, while his brother maintained a fashionable livery stable.

In cities of the New South, especially Durham and Atlanta, there was developing a substantial entrepreneurial class on the basis of what Du Bois called the group economy, though enterprises like the Fitzgerald brickyards in Durham and certain contractors and real estate dealers in Atlanta continued to depend on the white market. But John Merrick of Durham and A. F. Herndon, the wealthiest Negro in Atlanta, both of whom shifted from barbering for prominent whites to founding insurance companies for Negroes, illustrated in a single career the change from the older service occupations catering to whites to the newer type of so-called cooperative enterprise catering to Negroes. Durham was so new a city that it had no older upper class; in addition to a blacksmith and the brickyard owner, the elite of the early twentieth century consisted principally of Merrick and his associates, a handful of professional men, and one or two others successful in business enterprise dependent on the Negro market. In Atlanta the late nineteenth-century elite was composed primarily (as was the Durham group) of ex-slaves of mixed ancestry and their descendants—a contractor, two real estate dealers, some of the barbers, grocers and draymen, several politicians, one or two undertakers, a lawyer, a few doctors, at least one minister, sometimes—depending upon his background—the resident bishop of the A.M.E. Church, several college professors, and postmen and teachers. Success in business and family and educational background were important criteria of upper-class status; not all of the artisan-entrepreneurs, therefore, were considered upper class. Of this group the undertaker, lawyer, doctors, clerics, professors, and some of the grocers derived their livelihood from the Negro community. Two insurance companies (the Atlanta Life and the Standard Life) were the most conspicuous examples of the shift toward cooperative enterprise; and ultimately it was through them and related enterprises that after the First World War a group of men, most of whom were not born into upper-class Atlanta families, became the core of the newer upper class, in many cases marrying descendants of the older elite.

In Washington the situation was unique owing to the large number of government workers and politicians. For many years upper-class society consisted not only of the more prominent ministers and the few successful businessmen and—after the Civil War—politicians and civil servants, but also of headwaiters, butlers, barbers and pullman porters, along with an emerging class of educators and professional men. Most prominent were the office-holders who, like the teachers and other professional people, maintained their social status, while the servant class declined socially. Though some of the leading citizens were connected as early as the 1880's with the Capital Savings Bank, a survey of thirty-five well-to-do Washington Negroes in 1898 revealed that the chief source of wealth of these professional and business men and government workers was real estate. Only twelve had any investments in colored business, though all invested in white business. Not one had grown rich off the patronage of Negroes.[7] In fact, there were complaints that for the most part the upper classes failed to patronize race enterprises, and it appears that the real triumph of the entrepreneurial class based on the Negro market did not come until after the First World War.

In Philadelphia, where coachmen, barbers and headwaiters held high status into the twentieth century, successful caterers and their families remained at the pinnacle of the social pyramid even when their economic base began to crumble. Du Bois in 1898 reported that the highest class of Philadelphia Negroes was Philadelphia-born, lived in well-appointed homes with hired servants and held themselves aloof from the Negro masses. During the next ten years there was a rapid development of a business and professional class whose economic base was in the stream of migrants coming from the South; many of this class, probably chiefly of middle-class status before the First World War, later achieved upper-class status, though, here as elsewhere, a doctor, no matter what his origins, was always considered upper class. A survey of the business development of Philadelphia Negroes in the early twentieth century will serve to establish this point. Thus in 1898 there were three building and loan associations (the first having appeared in 1886); in 1914 there were eight. In 1898 there were seven newspapers and magazines; in 1907 there were twenty. Ten insurance companies were formed between 1900 and 1914. In 1899 Du Bois was predicting the demise not only of the colored caterers (which occurred), but also of colored barbers, most of whom were serving whites; in 1907 he found barbers more numerous than ever, but now catering to Negroes—their numbers swelled by migration from the South.[8]

Chicago was to be a conspicuous example of the philosophy of self-help and racial solidarity during the 1920's and even before the War was one of two Northern cities with a Negro bank. Previous to 1900, however, the Negro market (serviced by the less lucrative restaurants, barber shops and small stores in Negro enclaves) was relatively unimportant in comparison with the white market, which Negroes served as tailors, liverymen, draymen, barbers, hairdressers and caterers. And even during the next fifteen years, while Negroes were losing many of their white customers (barber shops, for example, the largest category of business, came to serve an entirely Negro clientele), men like the lawyer E. H. Morris and the physician Daniel Hale Williams continued to have professional relationships with whites. Down to the Great Migration, the upper class in Chicago, according to Drake and Cayton, consisted of the house servants of the wealthy, pullman porters, successful politicians and a few business and professional men. It was, they observe, "the Negro market created by the Great Migration [that] resulted in the expansion of the business and professional classes who gradually displaced the Old Settlers as 'the cream of colored society.' "[9]

In Boston lingering abolitionist and egalitarian traditions created a situation where an older upper class, consisting of professional and businessmen catering largely to whites, to a considerable extent identified itself with the white community and provided the leadership of the anti-Washington protest movement. John Daniels, in a sociological study published in 1914, said that above the rank and file who formed 80 per cent of the city's Negro population came a middle-class group of widely varying occupations ranging from waiters, pullman porters, janitors and artisans, who by thrift and industry were making a modest, steady living, up to well salaried white collar workers and some of the leading business and professional people. In education and manner much closer to the masses than to the upper-class Negroes, they maintained a strong feeling of group solidarity. On the other hand, about 2 per cent of the population, mostly of Northern birth or long Northern residence, and with considerably more white ancestry than the other classes, formed the "real upper class of lawyers, physicians, salaried employees, business proprietors, literary and musical people, who are distinguished by superior education and refinement." In their work they often came in contact with whites more than they did with Negroes and many were members of white organizations and churches, lived in white neighborhoods and had many white friends. They therefore had little contact, and failed to identify themselves, with the masses and tended to criticize separate racial organizations. While they acted as race spokesmen in demanding full citizenship rights, and while they were in the forefront of the opposition to Booker T. Washington, many who were socially beneath them often accused them of lacking race pride.[10]

Thus the Boston upper class, dependent on white customers, opposed the doctrines of racial solidarity and segregated institutions espoused by the middle class. And this middle class and the respectable majority of the lower classes were the chief supporters of Negro churches, lodges, businesses and welfare organizations. In other cities some of this middle class rose into upper-class status after 1900; and with the increasing discrimination from whites, the decline of certain businesses hitherto patronized by whites and the prominence and power of Booker T. Washington, even some of the older upper class in Boston and elsewhere was forced to revise its philosophy.

There is evidence to support the thesis that elsewhere in the North there tended to be a correlation between membership in the older upper class and opposition to Booker T. Washington, though the correlation is far from complete. In Chicago the anti-Bookerite leadership centered in this class. In Cleveland the lawyer Charles W. Chesnutt and H. C. Smith, editor of the *Gazette,* enunciated a philosophy practically identical with that of the Boston "radicals" (though Chesnutt did remain on friendly terms with Washington). Such opposition as there was to Washington among the ministers seems to have been concentrated chiefly among the ministers of certain Northern and border-state upper-class churches. The Presbyterian cleric, Francis J. Grimké of Washington, and the Episcopal divine, George Freeman Bragg of Baltimore, are outstanding examples. It is clear from an examination of the ideologies of Northern lawyers that despite the bait of political office which Washington held out to many of them, there was a considerable relationship between old upper-class membership and opposition to the Tuskegeean.

Even in the South this may have been true to some degree, though undoubtedly most of the entrepreneurs with white customers supported Washington and agreed with the side of his philosophy which asserted that Negroes could get along with Southern whites and that a competent Negro businessman would have plenty of economic opportunity among them. And of course Southern upper-class Negroes dependent on the Negro market, like Napier and Merrick, were supporters of Washington and enunciated his program of economic progress and racial solidarity. However, there was at least one significant situation which suggests that to some extent at least the alignments between class and ideology that characterized the North may have had something of a counterpart in the South. In Augusta, Georgia, from the 1880's on, members of the older elite, which was descended from prominent whites—men like Judson W. Lyons, Register of the Treasury, 1897–1905, and the Reverend W. J. White, editor of the *Georgia Baptist*—were prominently associated with protest movements and were numbered among the anti-Bookerites. On the other hand, members of the rising group of dark-skinned ex-slaves—men like the Baptist minister C. T. Walker and R. R. Wright (who in 1889 became president of the state industrial school near Savannah)— were rivals of the group led by White and fostered the ideals of race solidarity and self-help. Though Wright's biographer claims that he and Washington did not get along with each other, the two men enunciated almost identical philosophies; and Wright's good friend, that Reverend Mr. Walker, was closely connected with the Tuskegeean.[11]

All in all, then, it would appear that between about 1890 and the 1920's, the process occurring at different rates and times in different cities and more markedly in those cities where the most substantial in-migration was taking place, the forces of segregation and discrimination were instrumental in creating a petit bourgeoisie of professional and business men who depended upon the Negro masses for their livelihood; and that the more successful among this group were gradually assuming upper-class status—either merging with or replacing in social class position that older upper class whose leading members were often business and professional men serving the white community. By and large it was the older pre-1900 entrepreneurial and professional upper class that, especially in the North, tended to be indifferent toward or opposed to the philosophy of racial solidarity, even though members of this group came to favor it to the extent that they were forced, or found it desirable and possible, to turn to the Negro market. As Ray Stannard Baker said of the Northern members of this group, "Their daily associations in business are largely with white people and they cling passionately to the fuller life."[12] On the other hand, the new upward mobile middle class, composed for the most part of self-made men whose economic roots were in the newly urbanized masses, naturally found the philosophy of self-help and racial solidarity—and consequently the philosophy of Booker T. Washington—congenial to its experience and interests; and its members easily appropriated the symbols of American individualism and social Darwinism to explain and rationalize their social role. It was this group that was especially instrumental in the burgeoning of the philosophy of racial solidarity, self-help and the group economy, the rationalization of the economic advantages of the disadvantages to be found in segregation and discrimination—to use a phrase commonly employed in those days. Washington's National Negro Business League was the platform on which this group expressed its point of view.

12. W. E. B. Du Bois and the New Century

At the turn of the twentieth century, the ascendancy of Booker T. Washington as a black leader appeared unchallengeable. Yet, within a few years, a substantial assault had been launched on Washington's educational, political and social outlook, and by the time of his death in 1915 he had already been supplanted in the minds of young, socially aware blacks by new leaders and philosophies. No single individual was more responsible for this transformation than W. E. B. Du Bois. The life of this remarkable man, whom many historians consider the greatest black ever produced in the United States, spanned almost ten decades and his quest for a solution to the problems of blacks in America and throughout the world led him to embrace such outlooks as militant integrationism, pan-Africanism, a separate black economy, and finally, revolutionary socialism.

W. E. B. Du Bois was born in 1868 in the sleepy rural town of Great Barrington, Massachusetts. A mulatto whose ancestors included blacks, French Huguenots, and Dutch, Du Bois was one of only fifty blacks in a population of about five thousand and in his autobiographies (three of which were written at various stages of his life), he indicates that while he experienced racial prejudice as a child, there was little overt discrimination. His sense of racial consciousness was not awakened until he journeyed to Nashville, Tennessee, to attend Fisk University. "It was to me a new experience," he later recalled. "I was thrilled for the first time to be among so many people of my own color." After Fisk, Du Bois studied at Harvard, where he was awarded a doctorate for a pioneering study on the slave trade to the United States and its suppression, and then studied and traveled for two years in Europe. He returned to the United States with the then current academic idea that the exposure of social problems was the key to their cure; that prejudice was the result primarily of ignorance. In 1899 he published an intensive sociological study of Philadelphia's black community, detailing the inadequate housing, health, and educational facilities and indicting both white prejudices and the isolation and lack of social consciousness of the city's black leadership. He then moved to Atlanta University, where he directed a series of conferences and publications dealing with such subjects as education, economic achievement, and self-help institutions among the black population. Although his grandiose scheme for a century-long study of black problems never materialized, the Atlanta studies did provide the first intensive statistical studies of the blacks of the United States.

By this time, even before his widely-publicized break with Washington, Du Bois had already emerged as an exponent of what the historian Vincent Harding calls "black messianism." Du Bois defined racial groups, not nations or individuals, as the most important elements in world history. Like other races, blacks had a unique contribution to make to world progress. By the assertion of fundamental human values, they could help redeem western civilization from the materialism and decadence into which it had fallen. This was the "spiritual message" of the black race, and in order to achieve this destiny blacks must "maintain their race identity until this mission of the Negro people is accomplished, and the ideal of human brotherhood has become a practical possibility." Du Bois' image of American society was thus similar to the modern concept of cultural pluralism—while he insisted that each ethnic group should enjoy equality of rights and opportunities, he also believed that each should maintain its special identity and gifts and not be homogenized in the "melting pot."

Du Bois' "black messianism" helps explain another fundamental aspect of his outlook—his belief that educated blacks, the "talented tenth," must provide racial leadership. Unless this occurred, he believed, blacks would have to accept white leadership, and thus lose part of their racial identity. For this reason, Du Bois rejected Washington's emphasis on industrial education for the black population. The function of education was to train people for social leadership, and therefore it must embrace all branches of knowledge, not merely technical training—it had to teach people to think, not merely to earn a living. This basic difference in educational philosophy was one of the reasons for Du Bois' break with Washington, but by no means the only one. Du Bois objected strenuously to what he called the "Tuskegee machine," and the control Washington exerted over black politics, newspapers, and educational institutions. Perhaps most important, he rejected Washington's belief that blacks should postpone political and social rights to concentrate on economic activity. In perhaps his most influential book, *The Souls of Black Folk,* published in 1903, Du Bois devoted a chapter to a criticism of Washington. He insisted that it was impossible for men to make effective economic progress if they were denied the vote and subjected to degrading discrimination, and argued that Washington's attempt at character building and racial self-respect would be doomed from the start if it was coupled with unprotesting acquiescence in dehumanizing social distinctions. Blacks, Du Bois declared, must insist upon all the rights of American citizens, particularly the right to vote, to full civic equality, and to equal educational opportunities.

The Souls of Black Folk was not the first attack on Washington from within the black community. Monroe

Trotter, the radical Boston editor, had been criticizing the Tuskegeean for several years before 1903. But the book had so great an impact that it propelled Du Bois to the forefront of Washington's critics. "With its publication," the black writer Saunders Redding has declared, "Negroes of training and intelligence, who had hitherto pretended to regard the race problem as of strictly personal concern and who sought individual salvation in a creed of detachment and silence, found a bond in their common grievances and a language through which to express them." The book also forecast the political program Du Bois would follow, for he insisted that only by unceasing agitation could blacks regain their lost rights. In 1905, Du Bois organized a meeting of black intellectuals at Niagara Falls and launched the Niagara movement, a direct challenge to Washington's policies and leadership. "We talked some of the plainest English that has been given voice to by black men in America," Du Bois later wrote, and the platforms of the movement unequivocally demanded "every single right that belongs to a freeborn American." In 1909 a group of white progressives and intellectuals joined with Du Bois in a meeting that resulted in the formation of the National Association for the Advancement of Colored People, and Du Bois became the editor of the association's magazine, *The Crisis.*

In "The Paradox of W. E. B. Du Bois," a chapter from his influential study of black social thought between 1880 and 1915, August Meier traces the early development of Du Bois' ideas and examines in detail his differences with Booker T. Washington. Du Bois' intellectual development did not end with the founding of the NAACP; indeed it had hardly begun. But throughout the ensuing decades, until his death in 1963 in Accra, Ghana, he continued to wrestle with this paradox—how to achieve equality in American society without abandoning the distinctive identity and qualities of the black race.

The Paradox of W. E. B. Du Bois[1]

AUGUST MEIER

If, of the great trio of Negro leaders, Frederick Douglass best expressed the aspirations toward full citizenship and assimilation, and Booker T. Washington the interest in economic advancement, it was Du Bois who most explicitly revealed the impact of oppression and of the American creed in creating ambivalent loyalties toward race and nation in the minds of American Negroes. As Du Bois said in 1897:

One feels his two-ness—an American, a Negro, two souls, two thoughts, two unreconciled strivings, two warring ideals in one dark body. . . .

The history of the American Negro is the history of this strife,—this longing to attain self-conscious manhood, to merge his double self into a better and truer self. . . . He would not Africanize America for America has too much to teach the world and Africa. He would not bleach the Negro soul in a flood of white Americanism, for he knows that Negro blood has a message for the world. He simply wishes to make it possible for a man to be both a Negro and an American, without being cursed and spit upon. . . .

More than any other figure Du Bois made explicit this ambivalence —an ambivalence that is perhaps the central motif in his ideological biography. Even Du Bois has described himself as integrally a part of European civilization, and "yet, more significant, one of its rejected parts; one who expressed in life and action and made vocal to many, a single whirlpool of social entanglement and inner psychological paradox."[2]

A proud and sensitive youth reared in a western Massachusetts

FROM August Meier, *Negro Thought in America.* Copyright © 1963 by University of Michigan Press. Reprinted by permission of University of Michigan Press.

town, Du Bois had occasion to know the sting of prejudice and early realized that "I was different from others; or like, mayhap in heart and life and longing, but shut out from their world by a vast veil." Subsequently he therefore found the segregated community of Fisk University, which he attended from 1885 to 1888, an enriching experience. Though he yearned for the full recognition of his American citizenship, he was also, he later recollected, "thrilled and moved to tears," and recognized "something inherently and deeply my own" as a result of his association there with a "closed racial group with rites and loyalties, with a history and a corporate future, with an art and a philosophy." By the time he received his A.B. from Fisk and entered Harvard as a Junior in 1888, "the theory of race separation was quite in my blood," and the lack of social acceptance he experienced at Harvard, he recalled later, did not disturb him. Yet it certainly was his sensitivity to discrimination that led him at this time to view Negroes as a "nation"—Americans, but rejected in the land of their birth.[3]

Meanwhile, Du Bois had been expressing himself on other subjects. As a correspondent for Fortune's New York *Globe* during the early 1880's and as editor of the Fisk *Herald,* he displayed an interest in industriousness and ambition. Furthermore, as a student at Fisk and at Harvard—where he received his Ph.D. in 1895—and as a professor at Wilberforce University (1894–96), Du Bois proved more than willing to meet Southern whites half way. He told both Fisk students and his white associates in the Tennessee prohibitionist movement that the interests of the two races were essentially the same. To his Fisk audience he proposed the admittedly unorthodox idea that Negroes should divide their vote in order not to exacerbate race relations. He assured Southern whites that they could depend on the friendship of Negroes if only the whites would grant them citizenship rights and adequate educational facilities. Since the Negro's condition was such as to encourage prejudice, for their part Negroes must stress duties as well as rights, and work for their own advancement. At both Harvard and Wilberforce he could, in a single speech, lash out at America's immoral and un-American treatment of Negroes (and at Harvard suggest that Negroes would revolt if other means failed) and at the same time adopt a conciliatory position. Since Negroes had not yet achieved what it took the Anglo-Saxons a millennium to do, they were not yet equipped to vote. What he objected to was not the disfranchisement of the Negro masses, but of intelligent, law-abiding Negroes; and what he advocated was a franchise limitation fairly applied to both races along with adequate educational opportunities for all. In 1891 it was even reported in the *Age* that Du Bois had asserted that the whole idea underlying the Lodge Elections Bill was wrong, for it was proposed on the assumption that

law can accomplish anything. . . . We must ever keep before us the fact that the South has some excuse for its present attitude. We must remember that a good many of our people . . . are not fit for the responsibility of republican government. When you have the right sort of black voters you will need no election laws. The battle of my people must be a moral one, not a legal or physical one.[4]

It was no wonder then that after Washington's [Atlanta] address Du Bois wrote the *Age* suggesting "that here might be the basis of a real settlement between whites and blacks."[5]

Meanwhile, Du Bois was formulating his notion of leadership by a college-educated elite, which he regarded as necessary for the advancement of any group. In 1891 he deplored the South's effort to make common and industrial schools rather than colleges the basis of its educational system. For only a liberally educated white leadership could perceive that, despite the justification for over-throwing the Reconstruction governments, to permanently dis-franchise the working class of a society in the process of rapid industrialization would, as socialists from Lassalle to Hindman had said, result in economic ruin. And only a liberal higher educa-tion could create an intelligent Negro leadership. Thus, while still a student at Harvard, Du Bois had suggested his theory of the talented tenth, foreshadowed his later concern with the working class, and adumbrated the thesis he later stressed so much—that without political rights Negroes, primarily a working group, could not secure economic opportunity. Furthermore, it should be noted that his educational views were not unrelated to his ethnocentric feelings. As he said at Wilberforce, the educated elite had a glorious opportunity to guide the race by reshaping its own ideals in order to provide the masses with appropriate goals and lift them to civilization.[6]

After two years at Wilberforce, Du Bois accepted a one-year research appointment at the University of Pennsylvania. Then in 1897 he became professor of sociology at Atlanta University, where he remained until 1910, teaching and editing the annual Atlanta University Studies on the American Negro.

At no time in his life did Du Bois place greater and more consistent stress upon self-help and racial solidarity than during the last four years of the century. Like many of his contemporaries he fused this emphasis with one on economic advancement; and like a few of them he synthesized it with his educational program for the talented tenth. To Du Bois in fact, the race prejudice which isolated the Negro group and threw upon it "the responsibility of evolving its own methods and organs of civilization" made the stimulation of group co-operation "the central serious problem."[7]

It was his appointment to the University of Pennsylvania that provided Du Bois with his first opportunity to begin a scientific study of the race problem. He had long awaited such an opportunity because he believed that presentation of the facts derived from scientific investigation would go a long way toward solving the race problem. The resulting monograph, *The Philadelphia Negro,* leaned toward the blame-the-Negro, self-help point of view. Yet Du Bois did describe what it meant to be snubbed in employment and in social intercourse, and he judged that the Negro's participation in politics had been, in net effect, beneficial to the city and to the Negro himself. Above all, he felt that Negroes must uplift themselves, and by racial co-operation open enterprises that would provide employment and training in trades and commerce. Whites had their duty to help but society had too many problems "for it lightly to shoulder all the burdens of a less advanced people." Negroes ought to constantly register strong protests against prejudice and injustice, but they should do so because these things hindered them in their own attempt to elevate the race. And this attempt, Du Bois held, must be marked by vigorous and persistent efforts directed toward lessening crime and toward inculcating self-respect, the dignity of labor, and the virtues of truth, honesty, and charity.[8]

Like Washington, then, Du Bois combined an enthusiasm for racial solidarity with one for economic development and the middle-class virtues. In fact, he regarded a college education as "one of the best preparations for a broad business life" and for the making of "captains of industry." Likening Negroes to other nationalities, he chided them for being ashamed of themselves, and held that such success as had been achieved by other nations no larger in population than the American Negroes could be accomplished only through a badly needed co-operation and unity. In view of the poverty of the Negro and the economic spirit of the age, it was most important to achieve success in business. Because of race prejudice the major opportunity for such achievement lay in commercial activity based on Negroes pooling their earnings and pushing forward as a group. Though their collective capital be small, thrift and industry could succeed even under the handicaps of prejudice. Under the circumstances a penny savings bank would be more helpful than the vote. Negroes should patronize and invest their money in Negro-owned enterprises, even at a personal sacrifice. For "we must cooperate or we are lost. Ten million people who join in intelligent self-help can never be long ignored or mistreated."[9]

It should be noted, of course, that Du Bois did not, during the *fin de siècle* years, give up all interest in political rights, though like the majority of articulate Southern Negroes of the day he was willing to compromise on the matter. He was among those who in 1899 petitioned the Georgia legislature not to pass the Hardwick disfranchisement bill, though like Booker T. Washington he was willing to accept an educational and/or property qualification as long as free school facilities were open to all.[10]

During this period Du Bois was more emphatic than at any other time about the value of racial integrity. Speaking on "The Conservation of Races" in 1897 he asserted that there existed subtle psychic differences, which had definitely divided men into races. Like his racist contemporaries, he was certain of the universality of "the race spirit," which he regarded as "the greatest invention of human progress." Each race had a special ideal—the English individualism, the German philosophy and science, and so forth. Therefore, "only Negroes bound and welded together, Negroes inspired by one vast ideal, can work out in its fullness the great message we have for humanity." To those who argued that their only hope lay in amalgamating with the rest of the American population, he admitted that Negroes faced a "puzzling dilemma." Every thoughtful Negro had at some time asked himself whether he was an American, or a Negro, or if he could be both; whether by striving as a Negro he was not perpetuating the very gulf that divided the two races, or whether Negroes "have in America a distinct mission as a race." Du Bois' answer was what is now called cultural pluralism. Negroes were American by birth, in language, in political ideas, and in religion. But any further than this, their Americanism did not go. Since they had given America its only native music and folk stories, "its only touch of pathos and humor amid its mad money-getting plutocracy," it was the Negroes' duty to maintain "our physical power, our intellectual endowment, our spiritual ideas; as a race, we must strive by race organizations, by race solidarity, by race unity to the realization of the broader humanity which freely recognizes differences in men, but sternly deprecates inequalities in their opportunity of development." To this end, separate racial educational, business, and cultural institutions were necessary. Despised and oppressed, the Negroes' only means of advancement was a belief in their own great destiny. No people that wished to be something other than itself "ever wrote its name in history; it must be inspired with the Divine faith of our black mothers, that out of the blood and dust of battles will march a victorious host, a mighty nation, a peculiar people, to speak to the nations of the earth a Divine truth that should make them free." Washington, it should be pointed out, while advocating race pride and race integrity, did not glory so much in the idea of a distinctive Negro culture (though he was always proud of the spirituals or "plantation melodies"). Nor did he exhibit Du Bois' sense of identification with Africans, evident in Du Bois' advocacy of "pan-Negroism" in this same address.[11]

During the last years of the century Du Bois developed his educational theories at considerable length, attempting to construct "A Rational System of Negro Education" by reconciling the two widely diverging tendencies of the day—training for making a living and training for living a broad life. All agreed, he said, on the necessity of universal common school training, and on the contribution Hampton, Tuskegee, and the Slater Fund had made in stressing the building of an economic foundation, the freedmen's primary concern. But unfortunately only three or four schools made broad culture their chief aim. Du Bois criticized the talk of rosewood pianos in dingy cabins, of ignorant farmers, of college graduates without employment, though he agreed that more stress had been placed on college training than the economic condition of the race warranted. But the vogue for industrial education had become so great that the colleges were hard-pressed for funds. This was particularly deplorable because the isolation of the Negro community demanded the creation of an indigenous leadership of college-trained captains of industry and scholars, who would advance the masses economically and culturally, and who could view the race problem from a broad perspective.[12]

There were remarkable similarities between Du Bois and Washington during the late 1890's—a period when more Negro leaders than at any other time adopted a conciliatory tactic. Both tended to blame Negroes largely for their condition, and both placed more emphasis on self-help and duties than on rights. Both placed economic advancement before universal manhood suffrage, and both were willing to accept franchise restrictions based not on race but on education and/or property qualifications equitably applied. Both stressed racial solidarity and economic co-operation. Du Bois was, however, more outspoken about injustices, and he differed sharply with Washington in his espousal of the cause of higher education.

The years from 1901 to 1903 were years of transition in Du Bois' philosophy, years in which he grew more critical of industrial education and more alarmed over disfranchisement. Writing in 1901 he engaged in sharp protest against the Southern race system, even while recognizing that Negroes must adjust to it. He denied that the "many delicate differences in race psychology" excused oppression. He complained of the economic discrimination that retarded the development of a substantial landowning and artisan class. He bemoaned the lack of contact between the races that increased prejudice by preventing the best classes of both races from knowing each other. Yet he felt that, since Negroes must accept segregation, the road to uplift and economic improvement lay in the development of college-educated leaders: "Black captains of industry and missionaries of culture" who with their knowledge of modern civilization could uplift Negro communities "by forms of precept and example, deep sympathy and the inspiration of common kindred and ideals." But while Negroes would have to temporarily acquiesce in segregation, they could not acquiesce in disfranchisement. Du Bois did not object to "legitimate efforts to purge the ballot of ignorance, pauperism and crime," and he conceded that it was "sometimes best that a partially developed people should be ruled by the best of their stronger and better neighbors for their own good," until they were ready to stand on their own feet. But since the dominant opinion of the South openly asserted that the purpose of the disfranchisement laws was the complete exclusion of Negroes from politics, the ballot was absolutely necessary for the Negro's safety and welfare. Moreover, as European experience had demonstrated, workers under modern industrial conditions needed the vote in order to protect themselves; Negroes, laboring under racial discrimination, needed it even more.[13]

Du Bois developed further his educational views and the theme of the talented tenth. He agreed that it was most important to train Negroes to work, and he conceded that industrial schools would play an important role in achieving this end. He also approved of the compromise function of industrial education, which had brought together races and sections; and although industrial education would not solve the problem he asserted that "it does mean that its settlement can be auspiciously begun." Yet he had come to criticize the overinsistence of industrial schools upon the practical, the unfortunate opposition of their advocates toward colleges, the fact that industrial schools were preparing their students in obsolete crafts, and the fact that they produced few actual artisans. Du Bois defended Negro colleges from charges that they had erred in training school teachers and professional men before turning to industrial training. He pointed out that historically the European university had preceded the common school, and that out of the liberal arts institutions came the backbone of the teaching force of the Negro common schools and of industrial schools like Tuskegee, where almost half of the executive council and a majority of the heads of departments were college graduates. All races, he held, had been civilized by their exceptional men; "the problem of education, then, among Negroes, must first of all deal with the Talented Tenth."[14]

It is evident that Washington and Du Bois had come to disagree not only in their educational philosophy, but also on the fundamental question of the immediate importance of the ballot. By 1903 Du Bois was not only pleading for higher education, but had begun to criticize the work of the industrial schools. Both men spoke of captains of industry, but where the Tuskegeean emphasized economic skills, the Atlanta educator stressed a high grade of culture. And unlike Washington, Du Bois had come to believe that educational and property qualifications for voting would not be equitably applied. True, Du Bois never gave up his belief that, in the face of white prejudice and discrimination group solidarity was necessary, especially in economic matters. But all that really remained to make the two men irreconcilable ideological opponents was for Du Bois to advocate the importance of protest rather than accommodation. This he did in his opening attack on Washington in 1903.

During the 1890's Washington and Du Bois had been cordial in their relationships. Upon returning to the United States from Germany in 1894 Du Bois accepted a position at Wilberforce, having had to turn down a somewhat later offer from Tuskegee. Again in 1896, 1899, and as late as 1902 Du Bois seriously considered invitations to Tuskegee.[15] In his correspondence with Washington, through his articles and speeches, and by attending the Hampton and Tuskegee Conferences he exhibited his sympathetic interest in Washington's work. He had, it is true, mildly criticized the Tuskegeean in an article in 1901. In it he said that some of the most prominent men of the race regarded the Hampton-Tuskegee approach as only a partial approach to the race problem, in that they stressed the highest aspirations of the race, advocated college education, and believed that Negroes should enjoy suffrage equally with whites. But as late as July 1902 the *Guardian* denounced Du Bois for siding with Washington at the St. Paul meeting of the Afro-American Council. "Like all the

others who are trying to get into the bandwagon of the Tuskegeean, he is no longer to be relied upon," declared the editor,
Monroe Trotter.[16]

Kelly Miller has asserted that Trotter wove a "subtle net"
around Du Bois and captured him for the radical cause. It would
be difficult to test the truth of this statement. Certain it is, however, that by January 1903 Trotter was praising Du Bois as a
brilliant leader who, despite temptations, "has never in public
utterance or in written article, betrayed his race in its contest for
equal opportunity and equal rights." Du Bois himself has recalled
that he was gradually growing more disturbed after 1900—less by
the ideological difference between him and Washington (which he
remembered as mainly one of emphasis) than by the immense
power over political appointments, over philanthropic largess, and
over the press wielded by what Du Bois has labeled the "Tuskegee
Machine." Du Bois found Washington's influence over the press
especially deplorable, in view of the Tuskegeean's soft-pedaling of
agitation on segregation and disfranchisement.[17] Yet whatever his
actual motivation for criticizing Washington, his first public statement on the matter was confined to ideological issues.

This statement was Du Bois' famous essay, "Of Booker T.
Washington and Others," in *Souls of Black Folk,* published in the
spring of 1903. "Easily the most striking thing," began Du Bois,
"in the history of the American Negro since 1876 is the ascendancy of Mr. Booker T. Washington." Others had failed in establishing a compromise between the North, the South, and the
Negroes. But Washington, coming with a simple though not entirely original program of industrial education, conciliation of the
South, and acceptance of disfranchisement and segregation, had
succeeded. For with "singular insight" he had grasped the spirit of
the age—"the spirit and thought of triumphant commercialism."

Du Bois went on to criticize the Tuskegeean because his policy
"practically accepted the alleged inferiority of the Negro," allowed
economic concerns to dominate over the higher aims of life, and
preached a "submission to prejudice." Although Washington had
made some statements about lynching and the franchise, generally
his speeches purveyed the "dangerous half-truths" that the Negro's
lowly condition justified the South's attitude and that the Negro's

elevation must depend chiefly on his own efforts. Du Bois perceived paradoxes in Washington's attempt to make Negro workers businessmen and property owners when it was impossible for workers to defend themselves without the ballot; in his preaching self-respect while counseling accommodation to discrimination and in his advocacy of industrial and common schools while depreciating the colleges that supplied their teachers. Furthermore, Washington's propaganda had undoubtedly hastened the disfranchisement, the increased segregation, and the decreased philanthropic concern for higher education that accompanied his ascendancy.

Washington's popularity with whites, Du Bois held, had led Negroes to accept his leadership, and criticism of the Tuskegeean had disappeared. The time was ripe therefore for thinking Negroes to undertake their responsibility to the masses by speaking out. In addition to the few who dared to openly oppose Washington, Du Bois thought that men like Archibald and Francis J. Grimké, Kelly Miller, and J. W. E. Bowen could not remain silent much longer. Such men honored Washington for his conciliatory attitude, and they realized that the condition of the masses of the race was responsible for much of the discrimination against it. But they also knew that prejudice was more often a cause than a result of the Negro's degradation; that justice could not be achieved through "indiscriminate flattery"; that Negroes could not gain their rights by voluntarily throwing them away, or obtain respect by constantly belittling themselves; and that, on the contrary, Negroes must speak out constantly against oppression and discrimination.

Du Bois had indeed moved away from his conciliatory ideology of the 1890's. Yet attempts at co-operation between him and Washington were not quite at an end. In the summer of 1903 Du Bois spoke at Tuskegee. The two men also continued their collaboration—begun in 1902—in an effort to prevent the exclusion of Negroes from Pullman cars. Nevertheless, after the "Boston Riot" Du Bois was—with reservations—lining up with Trotter. He did not, he said, agree with Trotter's intemperate tactics, but he admired his integrity and purpose, which were especially needed in view of Washington's backward steps.[18] The Carnegie Hall Meeting of January 1904 and Du Bois' appointment to the Committee of Twelve temporarily restored an uneasy working relationship between him and Washington, but he soon resigned from the Committee and in 1905 was chiefly responsible for inaugurating the Niagara Movement. Meanwhile, he has recollected, he found it increasingly difficult to obtain funds for his work at Atlanta, experienced criticism in the Negro press, and in other ways "felt the implacability of the Tuskegee Machine."[19] He was one of the most active members of the Conference on the Negro in 1909, and when the N.A.A.C.P. was organized in 1910 he became director of publicity and research and editor of the *Crisis*.

Thus by 1905 Du Bois had definitely come to the parting of the ways with Washington. And it is in the Niagara Movement manifestoes and in the pages of the *Horizon* and *Crisis* that one can best observe Du Bois as the consistent agitator, the ardent and brilliant fighter for integration and citizenship rights. For example, he insisted that disfranchisement retarded the economic development of the Negro because the voteless could not protect their property rights. He cited cases of persecution of prosperous Negroes as evidence that Washington's program would not obtain the respect of the white man and the rights of citizenship.[20] In a typical editorial he pointed out that in spite of Washington's conciliatory policy conditions had grown worse. True, as Washington said, Negroes had continued to accumulate property and education, but how Washington could assert that discrimination and prejudice were decreasing was incomprehensible to Du Bois. Horrible as race prejudice was, it could be fought if faced frankly. But "if we continually dodge and cloud the issue, and say the half truth because the whole stings and shames . . . we invite catastrophe." Elsewhere he insisted that opportunism was a dangerous policy that gave moral support to the race's enemies, and he denounced the stress on sycophancy, selfishness, mediocrity, and servility at the expense of the best education, the highest ideals, and self-respect.[21] Naturally he criticized industrial schools. On one occasion he attacked Hampton for its opposition to the work of the Negro colleges, and described it as "a center of that underground and silent intrigue which is determined to perpetuate the American Negro as a docile peasant," lacking political rights and social status. Du Bois was unequivocal in his stand on segregation. He scathingly denounced the separate-but-equal doctrine: "Separate schools for Whites and Blacks, and separate cars for Whites and Blacks are not equal, can not be made equal, and . . . are not intended to be equal." He charged that what the South wanted was not mere separation but subordination, and insisted that no "square deal" was possible as long as segregation existed. And unlike Washington he opposed a colored Episcopal bishop to work only among Negroes, even though this would have elevated a Negro to a high church office.[22]

It is evident from a reading of Du Bois' less publicized scholarly and nonpolemical statements that throughout these years he still maintained his interest in racial solidarity and self-help, in the group economy, and in the American Negro's ties to Africa. On occasion he was most explicit about his concept of economic nationalism. Just as a country can by tariffs build up its separate economy to the point where it can compete in international trade, so the Negro should create a group economy that would "so break the force of race prejudice that his right and ability to enter the national economy are assured." His enthusiasm for the group economy was indeed at times interpreted as implying a favorable attitude toward segregation, and in an exchange of letters on the subject with the editor of the Boston *Transcript,* Du Bois was finally prompted to declare that while opposed to physical separation he was prepared to accept for some time to come a "spiritual" separation in economic life that would involve Negroes trading only among themselves. True, he shifted his support from the creation of captains of industry who would exploit the Negro proletariat to the building up of a consumers' and producers' cooperative movement among Negroes. But inevitably he had to reconcile his espousal of a group economy with his demands for full integration. In 1913, replying to a communication which claimed it was hard to meet the argument that segregation forced Negroes to develop themselves, Du Bois agreed that undoubtedly thousands of Negro businesses, including the *Crisis,* had developed because of discrimination, capitalizing, in a sense, on race prejudice. But this did not make discrimination a "veiled blessing." While Negro enterprises had done creditable work under the circumstances, and although Negroes must make the best of segregation, turning even its disadvantages to their advantage, they "must never forget that none of its possible advantages can offset its miserable evils, or replace the opportunity . . . of free men in a free world."[23]

A similar paradox was involved in Du Bois' stand on intermarriage. Writing in the *Independent* in 1910 he held that a person had the right to choose his spouse, that the prohibition of intermarriage was not justified when it arbitrarily limited friendships, and that where satisfactory conditions prevailed, race mixture had often produced gifted and desirable stocks and individuals, such as the Egyptians, and Hamilton, Pushkin, Douglass, and Dumas. He believed, however, that for the present widespread intermarriage would be "a social calamity by reason of the wide cultural, ethical and traditional differences" between the races, and predicted that if Negroes were accorded their rights and thus encouraged to build up their racial self-respect, the two races would continue to exist as distinct entities, perhaps forever, and this not "at the behest of any one race which recently arrogantly assumed the heritage of the earth, but for the highest upbuilding of all peoples in their great ideal of human brotherhood."[24]

Nor was Du Bois consistent in his views on race differences. Earlier, while never accepting any idea of Negro inferiority, he had referred to Negroes as a backward, childlike, undeveloped race, and he had accepted the idea of inherent racial differences. But in March 1908 he attacked the "glib" Darwinist interpretations about undeveloped races and the survival of the fittest. After the Universal Races Congress in London in 1911 Du Bois enthusiastically reported its conclusion that there was no proven connection between race and mental or cultural characteristics. Yet in 1913 he harked back to the idea of inherent racial differences and described the Negro as primarily an artist, possessing a "sensuous nature . . . the only race which has held at bay the life destroying forces of the tropics," gaining thereby an unusual aesthetic sensitivity. This quality explained the artistic achievements of the Egyptians and the Ommiads, the literature of Pushkin, the bronze work of Benin, and the "only real American music."[25]

As a matter of fact Du Bois maintained his strong feeling of identification with other colored peoples, especially Africans. At one time he was secretary of a company which aimed to participate in the economic advancement of East Africa. Years before Melville J. Herskovits cited anthropological evidence for African origins of the culture of American Negroes, Du Bois held that their religious life and institutions, family life, burial and beneficial societies, the roots of economic co-operation, and the skill of Negro artisans all had their origins in Africa. Finally, *The Negro,* published in 1915, dealt with Negro history from ancient Egypt to the United States and was especially notable for its discussion of the history and culture of West Africa. In it he also adopted the Italian anthropologist Giuseppe Sergi's thesis that an ancient rather dark-skinned race spawned all of the ancient Mediterranean civilizations. Moreover, he predicted the emergence of a pan-African movement, uniting Negroes everywhere, and a growing unity of the darker races against the intolerable treatment accorded them by the white man. Since the colored races were in a majority, the future world would probably be what colored men make it, and "in the character of the Negro race is the best and greatest hope. For in its normal condition it is at once the strongest and gentlest of the races of men."[26]

A new theme in the pages of the *Horizon* and *Crisis* was Du Bois' interest in the labor movement and in socialism. At one time he had viewed the white working class as the Negro's "bitterest opponent." By 1904 he had come to believe that economic discrimination was in large part the cause of the race problem, and to feel sympathetic toward the socialist movement. Three years later, he was writing favorably of the socialists in the *Horizon.* Elsewhere he advised the socialists that their movement could not succeed unless it included the Negro workers, and wrote that it was simply a matter of time before white and black workers would see their common economic cause against the exploiting capitalists. Though in 1908 Du Bois did not vote for the socialists because they had no chance of winning, in 1911 he joined the party. In a Marxist exegesis in the concluding pages of *The Negro,* Du Bois viewed both American Negroes and Africans, both the white workers and the colored races, as exploited by white capital which employed the notion of race differences as a rationalization of exploitation, segregation, and subordination. And he predicted that the exploited of all races would unite and overthrow white capital, their common oppressor.[27]

Du Bois' espousal of the cause of labor was so deep-seated that he had the *Crisis* printed by members of a union that did not admit Negroes, and in its pages he welcomed the rare signs that white and Negro workers might be getting together. In this regard he was certainly ahead of his time, and even he finally expressed discouragement after the 1917 East St. Louis riot in which white unionists played such a striking role.[28] Thus Du Bois' attempts to woo union labor had succeeded no better than his related attempt to woo the Democratic party. . . . But Du Bois never gave up his vision of a union of white and black workers creating a society of economic and racial justice. He had in fact shifted from pinning his faith on the intellectuals or talented tenth of professional and business men to pinning it on the actions of the black working classes, though quite likely they were to be led, as has been suggested, by a talented-tenth intelligentsia.[29]

In W. E. B. Du Bois then, the most distinguished Negro intellectual in the age of Booker T. Washington, we find explicitly stated most of the threads of Negro thought at that time. On the one hand he had a mystic sense of race and of the mission of the Negro, which made him sympathetic toward ideas of racial pride and solidarity as sentiments useful for racial uplift. On the other hand he held explicitly and constantly, especially after 1901, to the ideal of waging a struggle for full acceptance in American society. While at times he seemed to view segregated institutions as good in themselves, actually he regarded them as second-best instruments in the struggle for advancement and citizenship rights. He envisaged not amalgamation but cultural pluralism as the goal. He was inconsistent on the question of innate race differences, but he never admitted that Negroes were inferior. Above all he insisted that Negroes wanted to be both Negroes and Americans, maintaining their racial integrity while associating on the freest terms with all American citizens, participating in American culture in its broadest sense, and contributing to it in fullest freedom.

It is notable that though Du Bois expressed the views held by most of the articulate Negroes of the age of Booker T. Washington, both in his stress on racial solidarity and economic co-operation and in his demand for full citizenship rights, nevertheless he frequently found himself in the minority. Few articulate Negroes exhibited the same extent of political independence; not many

Northern Negroes agreed with his accommodating tactic of the late nineteenth century; relatively few championed the cause of liberal education as enthusiastically as he did; few either dared or cared to follow him in the extent to which he championed the protest movement during the first years of the twentieth century; and few embraced socialism or the cause of the black workers and inter-racial working-class solidarity. It is important to note, however, that many times people, who at heart agreed with his point of view, were not courageous enough to flout the power structure both within and outside of the Negro community as he did.

Of the great trio of Negro leaders, Douglass was the orator, Du Bois the polished writer, and Washington the practical man of affairs. Like Douglass, Du Bois has been known primarily as a protest leader, though he was not as consistent in this role as Douglass. Like Douglass, too, he exhibited a marked oscillation in his ideologies—in fact his was more marked than that of Douglass. Like Douglass he clearly stated the ultimate goals which Washington obscured. Yet Du Bois displayed more of a sense of racial solidarity than Douglass usually did. Nor did he envisage the degree of amalgamation and the loss of racial consciousness that Douglass regarded as the *summum bonum*. On the contrary he, like Washington, emphasized race pride and solidarity and economic chauvinism, though after 1905 he no longer championed support of the individualist entrepreneur but favored instead a co-operative economy. Where Washington wanted to make Negroes entrepreneurs and captains of industry in accordance with the American economic dream (a dream shared with less emphasis by Douglass), Du Bois stressed the role of the college-educated elite and later developed a vision of a world largely dominated by the colored races which would combine with the white workers in overthrowing the domination of white capital and thus secure social justice under socialism. All three emphasized the moral values in American culture and the necessity of justice for the Negro if the promise of American life were to be fulfilled. But of the three men it was Douglass who was pre-eminently the moralist, while Washington and Du Bois expressed sharply divergent economic interpretations. Where Douglass and Washington were primarily petit-bourgeois in their outlook, Du Bois played the role of the Marxist intelligentsia. Where the interest of Douglass and Washington in Africa was largely perfunctory, Du Bois exhibited a deep sense of racial identity with Africans. Above all, though only Douglass favored amalgamation, all three had as their goal the integration of Negroes into American society.

Scholar and prophet; mystic and materialist; ardent agitator for political rights and propagandist for economic co-operation; one who espoused an economic interpretation of politics and yet emphasized the necessity of political rights for economic advancement; one who denounced segregation and called for integration into American society in accordance with the principles of human brotherhood and the ideals of democracy, and at the same time one who favored the maintenance of racial solidarity and integrity and a feeling of identity with Negroes elsewhere in the world; an egalitarian who apparently believed in innate racial differences; a Marxist who was fundamentally a middle-class intellectual, Du Bois becomes the epitome of the paradoxes in American Negro thought. In fact, despite his early tendencies toward an accommodating viewpoint, and despite his strong sense of race solidarity and integrity, Du Bois expressed more effectively than any of his contemporaries the protest tendency in Negro thought, and the desire for citizenship rights and integration into American society.

13. Blacks and the Labor Movement: a Case Study

American labor movements have always been faced with a difficult dilemma in their relationship with black workers. On the one hand, employers have often been able to manipulate racial prejudices within the working class to weaken unions and defeat strikes. But, on the other, with blacks constituting so large a segment of the labor force, many unions cannot hope to succeed without including black workers in their organizations. This problem has existed throughout American history, but only became acute when blacks joined the free labor force after emancipation. The first major labor group organized after the Civil War, the National Labor Union, attempted to break with the pre-war tradition of restricting union membership to whites, but the skilled white workers who made up the membership of the National Union's local affiliates objected. Black unionists did organize Colored Labor Conventions for a few years, but race prejudice and the fact that white workers tended to support the Democratic party while blacks were devoted Republicans kept black and white labor organizations from cooperating. The next major labor organization, the Knights of Labor, adopted a consciously egalitarian policy, dictated by its desire to organize all laborers, skilled and unskilled, into a single union. The Knights employed black organizers in the South and had many interracial locals, particularly the cigar makers, brick makers, carpenters, and dock workers. At the Knights' General Assembly of 1886, held in Richmond, Virginia, the union leader Terence Powderly was introduced by a black delegate, Frank Ferrell. When Ferrell was denied a seat in a local theater because of his race, several white delegates accompanying him walked out in protest, and Powderly wrote to the local newspapers that while Richmond was free to adopt the social customs it pleased, the Knights would continue to solicit black support. "The Negro is free, he is here, and he is here to stay," Powderly declared. ". . . His labor and that of the white man will be thrown upon the market side by side, and no human eye can detect a difference between the article manufactured by the white mechanic and that manufactured by the black mechanic."

The Knights were succeeded in the 1880's and 1890's by the American Federation of Labor, which at first adopted the same egalitarian racial policy, but soon began to retreat from it. Because the AFL sought to organize only skilled workers it automatically excluded the bulk of black laborers, who were confined to unskilled jobs. Yet, in the 1880's, several local unions were denied the right to affiliate with the AFL because of discriminatory clauses in their constitutions. By the mid-90's, however, President Samuel Gompers began to alter the union's policies. He agreed to admit unions whose ritual or initiation rites excluded blacks, so long as there were no offending clauses in their constitutions. Rather than insist on integrated locals, the AFL inaugurated the policy of organizing separate all-black unions in crafts where there were sizable numbers of black workers. These segregated unions, however, were usually controlled by the parallel white groups, which spoke and bargained for them. The use of blacks as strikebreakers in a number of instances around the turn of the century hardened Gompers' attitudes, and the AFL increasingly gave voice to blatantly racist attitudes. In 1904, Gompers referred to black strikebreakers in Chicago as "hordes of ignorant blacks . . . possessing but few of those attributes we have learned to revere and love . . . huge strappling fellows, ignorant and vicious, whose predominating trait was animalism." The union also participated in the drive to restrict immigration so as to protect American laborers from competition, and gave vocal support to America's imperialist ventures in the Pacific, often expounding anti-Asiatic sentiments as well as anti-black. It is hardly surprising that many black leaders shared Booker T. Washington's antipathy to labor organizations. Ministers, editors, and social leaders often urged black workers to ignore picket lines and to identify their interests with business, not labor.

The AFL's discriminatory policies continued well into the twentieth century, and were an important reason why skilled blacks were forced into the unskilled labor force and unskilled black laborers were denied the opportunity to improve their economic status. The first real break-through for blacks in the labor movement came with the organization of the Congress of Industrial Organizations in the 1930's. Committed to the organization of skilled and unskilled workers in mass-production industries on an industrywide basis, not on the basis of individual crafts, the CIO took an avowedly egalitarian position toward blacks. At the same time, A. Philip Randolph, who had organized the Brotherhood of Sleeping Car Porters in the 1920's fought against racial discrimination within the AFL. But AFL national conventions always defeated Randolph's demands for an end to segregated unions and they were not abolished until after the Second World War. As late as 1961, Randolph was censured by the AFL-CIO Congress for his assaults upon union racial policies, and today many black leaders consider union discrimination one of the major obstacles to the betterment of the lives of black workers.

There have, however, been some exceptions to this overall picture. One of these has been the policy of the United Mine Workers toward black workers. As Herbert Gutman makes clear in the following selection from his essay, "The Negro and the United Mine Workers of America," the UMW from the beginning was an inter-racial organization. In the 1890's it not only had about twenty thousand black members, but men like Richard Davis held important national offices and did extensive local organizing work. The experiences of Davis and other black unionists indicate that historians of the labor move-ment have devoted too much attention to the official policies of national organizations toward black workers, and not enough to interracial conflict and cooperation on the local level. White workers in the UMW were hardly free from prejudice, and they especially objected to the use of blacks as strikebreakers. Yet the union always sought to impress on its members the identity of interests between black and white miners and the necessity for overcoming racial prejudices. Nor was the UMW unique, for at the turn of the century a number of other unions had exten-sive black memberships, even in the South. Gutman's findings clearly demonstrate that, to answer important questions about the lives of both black and white workers, historians must devote less time to the history of labor organizations and leaders, and more to the "local world" in which the average workingman lived.

The Negro and the United Mine Workers of America[1]
The Career and Letters of Richard L. Davis and Something of Their Meaning: 1890–1900

HERBERT G. GUTMAN

I

In April 1877, fifteen hundred Braidwood, Illinois, coal miners struck against the Chicago, Wilmington & Vermillion Coal Company to protest a third wage cut in less than a year and a resulting 33 per cent drop in wages. Two months later the company imported Kentucky and West Virginia Negroes to replace the stubborn strikers, and its superintendent contentedly reported the Negroes as saying they had "found the Land of Promise." But in July the strikers chased four hundred Negroes and their families from Braidwood, and only a couple of Illinois militia regiments brought them back. When winter approached, the defeated strikers returned to work. The violence accompanying the great 1877 railroad strikes drew national attention away from Braidwood, but in that small town only the coming of the Negroes mattered, not the faraway riots in Pittsburgh and other railroad centers. John Mitchell, then a seven-year-old orphan, lived in Braidwood and witnessed these events.[2] No record exists of young Mitchell's feelings at that time, but twenty-two years later an older Mitchell, now the newly elected President of the nine-year-old United Mine Workers of America, gave testimony before the Industrial Commission (set up by Congress in 1898) that might suggest to the

FROM Herbert G. Gutman, "The Negro and the United Mine Workers of America," originally published in *The Negro and the American Labor Movement*, edited by Julius Jacobson. Copyright 1968 by Herbert G. Gutman. Reprinted by permission of Herbert G. Gutman.

innocent only that history repeats itself. Relations between Negroes and whites in the coal-mining industry troubled Mitchell and other UMW leaders. In 1898 and 1899 violence and death had followed the coming of Negro strikebreakers and armed white police to the Illinois towns of Pana, Virden, and Carterville. "I might say, gentlemen," Mitchell advised the Commission in 1899, "that the colored laborers have probably been used more to decrease the earnings in the mines . . . than in any other industry." To this fact Mitchell attributed much unrest. "I know of no element," he continued, "that is doing more to create disturbances than is the system of importing colored labor to take white men's places and to take colored men's places."[3]

Mitchell and the other UMW witnesses before the Commission did not draw the conclusion that such Negro strikebreaking justified the exclusion of Negroes from trade unions. They said the opposite and took pride in their interracial union. Although Mitchell personally believed that the Negro "standard of morality" was "not as high as that of white people," he nevertheless berated only those operators who used Negroes against the union and, insisting that the UMW constitution did not bar Negroes from membership, told the Commission: "Our obligation provides that we must not discriminate against any man on account of creed, color, or nationality."[4] Even more explicit than Mitchell, UMW Secretary-Treasurer W. C. Pearce insisted before the Commission:

As far as we are concerned as miners, the colored men are with us in the mines. They work side by side with us. They are members of our organization; [and] can receive as much consideration from the officials of the organization as any other members, no matter what color. We treat them that way. They are in the mines, many of them good men.

Pearce objected to Negroes only when they became strikebreakers, but he blamed this condition on "their ignorance of the labor movement and the labor world" and on the frequent deceptions practiced against Negroes by operators. "When they get to a certain place," he said of these Negroes, "why, they are there, and some of them, I know, many times are sorry for it."[5]

These pages consider certain aspects of the early contact between the United Mine Workers and Negro miners. Too little is yet known for that story to be told fully, much less clearly understood. By 1900, when the UMW was only ten years old, Mitchell and Pearce estimated that between 10 and 15 per cent of the nation's four hundred thousand coal miners were Negroes.[6] They almost all worked as bituminous miners, and their number varied between regions. Few labored in western Pennsylvania, and many concentrated in the Border South (West Virginia, Kentucky, and Tennessee) and Alabama. The older bituminous areas of the Middle West all had smaller numbers of Negro miners than the South—and Negro miners spread through other states, too.[7] Some first came as strikebreakers, but most Negroes became miners in a more normal fashion—seeking work as unskilled or semiskilled laborers in a rapidly expanding industry. At the same time as the mining population increased in the 1890s, its ethnic composition changed radically. Traditional dominance of native whites and British and Irish immigrants began to decline as East and South European Catholic immigrants and American Negroes settled into the industry. So heterogeneous a population posed vexatious problems for early UMW leaders. "With all of these differences," existing in industries like the mining industry, the Industrial Commission concluded in 1901, "it is an easy matter for employers and foremen to play race, religion, and faction one against the other." Even where employers made no such efforts, nationality and ethnic differences separated men in a common predicament. But although early UMW bituminous locals were based on nationalities, by 1900 they had given way to mostly "mixed" locals. In many mining districts the union "mixed" recent immigrants with "old" immigrants and native miners—and Negroes with whites.[8] Negro support explained part of the union's early successes among bituminous miners. By 1900, Negroes had contributed significantly to the building of that union, and twenty thousand Negroes belonged to it. Here we give attention mainly to the role and the ideas of one early UMW Negro leader.

I I

The most important of these Negro miners, Richard L. Davis, twice won election to the National Executive Board of the United Mine Workers, in 1896 and 1897, but it is the way his entire

career challenges traditional explanations of the relationships between Negro workers and organized labor in the 1890s and not
alone his high office that forces attention on him. Biographical
material so essential to fully knowing Davis and other Negro
UMW officers is scant, and in Davis' case comes mainly from his
printed letters and scattered references to him in the *United Mine
Workers' Journal.* Such limited information allows only the piecing
together of the barest outlines of his life. Much must be inferred
and much is unknown, even his status at birth. Davis was born in
Roanoke, Virginia, in 1864, the day before Christmas and only a
few months before the Civil War ended, but there is not even a
hint that he came of either slave or free Negro parents. The
Journal called him "a full-blooded colored man" but said nothing
else about his forebears. For several years Davis attended the
Roanoke schools during the winter months. At eight, he took
employment at a local tobacco factory and remained with that job
for nine years when, "disgusted with the very low wage rate and
other unfavorable conditions of a Southern tobacco factory," he
started work as a coal miner in West Virginia's Kanawha and New
River regions. In 1882 Davis moved to Rendville, Ohio, a mining
village in the Hocking Valley region and southeast of Columbus. He
married, supported a family of unknown size, and lived and
labored there the rest of his brief life. Apparently only union duties
took him away from Rendville and then but for brief periods.
Davis died there in 1900. Of his life other than his work as a
miner and his union career, nothing else is known.[9]

Life as a miner allowed Davis few amenities. Unsteady work
made him, like other miners, complain frequently of recurrent
unemployment. The depression in the mid–1890s hit Ohio miners
hard. "Times in our little village remain the same . . .—no work
and much destitution with no visible signs of anything better,"
Davis reported in February 1895.[10] More than a year later he
wrote again: "Work here is a thing of the past. I don't know what
we are going to do. We can't earn a living, and if we steal it we
will be prosecuted."[11] The year 1897 proved little better. One
week Davis' mine worked only half a day.[12]

His commitment to trade unionism added difficulties ordinary
miners did not face. In August 1896, after certain Negro miners
blamed Davis and another miner for organizing a strike to restore

a wage scale, Davis went without work. "Just how they could stoop so low I am unable to tell," an angered Davis wrote of these Negroes, "and some of them, if not all, call themselves Christians or children of the most High God, but in reality they are children of his satanic majesty." Some Negro coworkers he called "as true as can be found anywhere" but his betrayers were "as mean men as ever breathed."[13] The *Journal* defended Davis and reminded Ohio readers he deserved their "respect and moral support" because of "his devotion to the cause of unionism."[14] But nearly four months later Davis, still without work, feelingly complained: "Others can get all the work they want; but I, who have never harmed anyone to my knowledge, must take chances with winter and its chilly blasts without the privilege of a job so as to earn a morsel of bread for my wife and little ones."[15] Two years afterward, in 1898, and for reasons unknown, Davis lived in a pitiful condition—this time, black-listed. A letter dated May 16, 1898 poured forth a pained despair:

I have as yet never boasted of what I have done in the interest of organized labor, but will venture to say that I have done all I could and am proud that I am alive today, for I think I have had the unpleasant privilege of going into the most dangerous places in this country to organize, or in other words, to do the almost impossible. I have been threatened; I have been sandbagged; I have been stoned, and last of all, deprived of the right to earn a livelihood for myself and family.

I do not care so much for myself, but it is my innocent children that I care for most, and heaven knows that it makes me almost crazy to think of it. I have spent time and money in the labor movement during the past sixteen years, and to-day I am worse off than ever, for I have no money, nor no work. I will not beg, and I am not inclined to steal, nor will I unless compelled through dire necessity, which I hope the good God of the universe will spare me. . . . I can not think of my present circumstances and write [more], for I fear I might say too much. Wishing success to the miners of this country, I remain, as ever, a lover of labor's cause.[16]

In December of that year Davis still sought work. "I am still a miner," he remarked, "but cannot secure work as a miner. Yet I love the old principles I have always advocated. Even though a negro, I feel that which is good for the white man is good for me, provided, however, it is administered in the right way. I want to see the negro have an equal show with the white man, and especially when he deserves it. I want it in the local, in the district, and in the national."[17] Little time remained for the fulfillment of Davis' wishes. Thirteen months later, one month after his thirty-fifth birthday and while the UMW met in convention in another city, Davis died of "lung fever."[18]

Learning of his death, the UMW convention delegates paused to pay special tribute to their deceased Negro brother. Davis deserved their attention. Enduring many difficulties, he had been one of the founders and pioneer organizers of the United Mine Workers during the 1890s, its first and perhaps most difficult decade. The delegates called attention to the "many years of his life . . . devoted to advancing the interests of his craft" and lamented that the union had "lost a staunch advocate of the rights of those who toil, and his race a loyal friend and advocate."[19] The particular experiences that drew Davis toward organized labor are unknown, and only scant evidence links him to the Ohio miners' unions that preceeded the UMW in the 1880s and to the Knights of Labor. But there is no doubt of his importance to the UMW after 1890. The evidence is overwhelming. Many of his letters appeared in the weekly *Journal* and related quite fully his role in the Ohio unions, his career as a local and national organizer, and his feelings and ideas about the Negro, organized labor, and the changing structure of American industrial society.

Davis' formal role in the UMW can be described simply. In 1890 he attended its founding convention as delegate and also won election to Ohio's District 6 Executive Board. Another year he spurned efforts to nominate him for the vice-presidency of District 6. But until 1895, when he ran for the National Executive Board and lost by only a small vote, Davis won annual re-election to the District 6 office. His close defeat for national office in 1895 proved[20] "very clearly" to him that the "question of color in our miners' organization will soon be a thing of the past," and he predicted that "the next time some good man of my race will be successful."[21] The year 1896 found Davis right. He and fourteen others stood for the National Executive Board at the annual UMW convention and Davis got the highest vote, 166. The next largest

vote, 149, went to a white Illinois miner, James O'Connor.[22] A
year later, Davis won re-election and ranked second among those
vying for that high office.[23] The *Journal* celebrated Davis' first
election in its customary fashion by printing brief biographical
sketches of all new officers. It called Davis ("Dick") a man of
"very fair" education, "a good reader," and the author of a "very
good letter." It boasted that he gained election because UMW
members found him "a good representative of his race and because
the miners believe the colored men of the country should be recognized and given a representative on the [executive] board." The
Journal made much of the fact that he was Negro:

He will in a special way be able to appear before our colored miners
and preach the gospel of trade unions and at the same time will be able
to prove to our white craftsmen how much progress may be made with
very limited opportunities. . . . If it be a good principle to recognize
races or nationalities on the board in preference to individuals, per se,
the convention has done well to elect Dick, for he has certainly merited
this recognition. In fact, he has merited it from either standpoint, for
as a man, and more especially as a union man, he has deserved well
of the miners of the country.[24]

The weekly wished Davis "success," and Davis took his charge
with great seriousness, enthused over "this manifestation of kindness in recognizing my people." He felt his election to be of great
importance to all Negro miners:

Not only am I proud but my people also. I know that a great deal has
not been said publicly, but I do know that our people are very sensitive,
and upon many occasions I have heard them make vigorous kicks
against taxation without representation. Now, then, they cannot kick
this year, for although the representative himself may be a poor one,
it is representation just the same.

He promised to "try to so act that those who elected me shall not
be made to feel ashamed."[25] . . .

III

All through the difficult 1890s, as a member first of the Ohio
Executive Board and then of the National Executive Board, Davis

worked as a roving UMW organizer and helped establish new locals, strengthen existing ones, and counsel miners engaged in bitter industrial disputes. Although most of his organizing was done in Ohio, special assignments and particularly severe crises brought him to western Pennsylvania, Virginia, West Virginia, and Alabama. On certain occasions he went only because an organizer was needed, but at times he was sent to an area where the national officers felt a Negro could best appeal to nonunion Negro miners. Organizing nonunion miners was not easy in the 1890s. Employer opposition and miner apathy, fear, or ethnic division hampered Davis and his associates. In the summer of 1897, for example, Davis and other UMW organizers aided by national union leaders such as Samuel Gompers and Eugene V. Debs poured into West Virginia to urge unsuccessfully that its miners join the nationwide bituminous strike.[26] Some West Virginia miners quit work. But the overwhelming majority did not, and of them Davis wrote: "To call them slaves is putting it mildly." Injunctions limited Debs and others. Davis faced other problems. "It was like taking one's life in his hands at times," he wrote afterward. "While we never had any injunctions issued against us, we had men and Winchesters against us which were in most cases just as effective."[27]

That Davis was Negro added to his difficulties as an organizer. In May and June 1892 he worked through the southern West Virginia New River region, an area almost entirely hostile to labor organization. His color exposed him to severe hardship. Davis detailed his trip:

. . . A word about the traveling accommodations in this part of the country for one of my race. . . . Had it not been for Brother E. E. Page, traveling salesman of the West Virginia Cut and Dry Tobacco Co., of Wheeling, and Brother Moran [a UMW organizer] this boy could have seen a hard time of it. . . . We . . . arrived at Peterstown at about six o'clock, in time for supper. After washing and getting ready for eating as I thought, the colored man who worked there came to me and told me that he would show me my room. . . . Well, I went with him, and where do you suppose he took me? Away, away from the main building, out in the wood yard, to an old dilapidated log cabin. I looked in and saw the bed. I turned to the man and asked him if it was intended that I should sleep there. He said yes, that he slept there.

I told him that he might sleep there but I wouldn't, that I would walk to Lowell, 30 miles away, that night first.

Page, a white, intervened and convinced the proprietor to give Davis "the best bed in the house." "I would not be afraid to bet that I am the first negro to eat at a table in that man's dining room," Davis remarked. The next day Davis and the others stopped at a Red Sulphur Springs eating place where Davis encountered more personal insults:

I was told that I could not eat in that house. My dinner was prepared outside. I lost my appetite. . . . I didn't want anything to eat. We started from there a little after two o'clock and arrived at Lowell at about 8 o'clock. Brother Moran asked the proprietor, could I get supper there, and his answer was, oh, yes, but, lo, when the bell rang and I was to enter the dining room he caught me by the shoulder and told me to wait awhile. Brother Page turned around to him and told him I was with them. He looked as though he was thunderstruck and of course I got my supper.

Davis applauded Moran and Page. "Had it not been for those two white brothers," he believed, "I don't know but that I would have been by this time behind bars."[28]

On another occasion Davis actually feared for his life. In 1894, recent immigrants replaced disaffected native white and Negro miners in Pocahontas, Virginia. Davis went to bolster the Negroes and secretly organized them into "a good little local." But "spy" reports exposed these Negroes, and the operators fired and evicted them. Davis' role became known, too, and made his situation precarious:

I . . . [was] sitting or standing at different places when maybe two or three strange fellows would come along accompanied by one of the sucks ["spies"?]. . . . When they would get to where I was I would hear one say, there he is, or there is the s——— b———. Not only that, but I have heard myself spoken of in the same way by business men when walking along the streets; besides I have heard threats made as to what they would do to me if I did not leave.

Union adversaries also talked of "doing up" George Harris, a white union organizer, and Davis hastily left Pocahontas, explaining to his critics:

Boys, I am not yet ready to become a martyr to the cause, and I am confident that had I remained there much longer that would have been the result. . . . Now, you might say, oh, he left because he was scared, but boys, let me say to you that I was then south of Mason's and Dixon's line, and there is but little justice for the black man anywhere, and none at all down there, and for safety I thought it would be best for me to leave and even in doing this I had to be escorted to the station . . . the threats being openly made about doing me up. . . .

The gestures against Harris made Davis even more fearful. "Now, I was born in the State of Virginia, and I know that when they threaten a white man it is an absolute certainty about the negro and he had better make himself scarce, that is, if he values his life any."[29]

Physical discomfort and personal danger were not the only troubles Davis encountered. Other obstacles frustrated or made more difficult his organizing efforts. In March 1892, for example, two local Negro leaders, one a church deacon and the other a Republican Party stalwart, stymied his attempt to convert non-union McDonnell, Pennsylvania, Negro miners. They condemned interracial organizations, and the deacon explained:

. . . While I speak bear in mind that I am speaking in defense of my people. Join that thing and you will rue the day you ever thought of it. Don't you know that if you join that thing you can't get nothing out of the store. I tell you you will starve, you and your little children. I tell you I know just how you people are fixed; you are just like me. I 'aint got but one pitiful dollar and you 'aint got that. Some of you are a long way from home, in a strange land, away from North Carolina. . . . I know what I am talking about. If you don't want to sup sorrow, don't join this 'ere organization.[30]

That same year, racial mistrust blocked Davis' work in West Virginia's New River region ("the whites say they are afraid of the colored men and the colored men say they are afraid of the whites"). But in West Virginia employer hostility, the apathy of the miners toward the union, and their fear of the operators hampered him even more. Davis got permission from the Claremont school trustees to hold an organizing meeting in a schoolhouse, but local operators convinced the trustees to "shut the house up." Unable to buoy the spirit of the men ("they were that badly scared that I could get them to do nothing"), Davis left town. Although the school superintendent in nearby Alaska closed his building to him, Davis planned an open-air meeting. His description of what followed is almost a classic account of the difficulties union organizers faced when confronted with hostile employers and apathetic or frightened workers:

I notified every man on the place and . . . had them at the meeting. In fact it seemed to be my brightest meeting that I had ever gotten up in the district. We were about to open the meeting and were trying to select a chairman. Nobody would serve. Some of the men were upon box cars and some were upon the ice house. I heard some fellow in the crowd say, "Here comes a chairman; Brown will serve." I didn't know what he was talking about, but I soon learned that he was one of the head pushers of the place. Well, he came right up in the crowd and ordered the men to get down off the ice house. They didn't move fast enough and he picked up a stone and pretended that he was going to throw it and I tell you they rolled off, all except one colored boy, who remained perfectly still and who had the manhood to tell him that he had better not strike him. After this he went away, so we resumed our efforts in trying to get a chairman and seeing they were afraid, I opened the meeting, starting my talk with [the] boys.

Everything was going lovely. I suppose I had talked about twenty minutes or a half hour when that gentleman returned. I had noticed some of the men shying away, but thought nothing of it; well, he walked right up in front of me with stone in hand, and addressed me thus: "Say, look here, you —— —— black scamp, I want you to get off of these premises right away, move along or I'll knock —— out of you in a minute." I had not very far to go; I just stepped down on the railroad track and told the boys to come on with me, and we would have our meeting anyhow. That wasn't enough, he came again and says: "—— —— your black soul, I want you to move either up or down this track and —— quick." I then gave him to understand that I was not his property, and would not go any further. I tried to get the boys to follow me, but to no avail. They were afraid, and so when I left there I left for home, and that night too.

"Flowery speeches and enthusiasm" would not bring the UMW to West Virginia. Davis argued after this trip that only a permanent resident organizer together with "time and money" might assure some success.[31]

Birmingham, Alabama, tested Davis even more than his work in the Northern bituminous fields and in West Virginia. Alabama coal mining boomed in the 1890s. At the start of the decade, the state counted 8000 miners of whom 3600 were Negroes. When the new century began, the total had increased to nearly 18,000, including 9700 Negroes. Early efforts to build successful Alabama miners' unions had failed, and in 1894 the United Mine Workers of Alabama, an interracial statewide union, had fallen to pieces after a bitter four-month strike against the giant Tennessee Coal, Iron, & Railroad Company and lesser operators. A pliant Bourbon governor used state militia freely against the new union and substantial numbers of Negro strikebreakers weakened and defeated the white and Negro union miners.[32] Davis visited Alabama, the "so-called Eldorado of the South," in December 1897 and January 1898, and saw little to please him. He found much sentiment for the UMW among the miners but also formidable obstacles to successful organization. "Everything is cheap here but a living," he reported. "Labor is cheap, human life is cheap, but the necessities of life are out of sight, and yet it seems that many of these people are perfectly contented." The reasons were many. The failure of earlier local unions made many miners suspicious of the UMW. Convict labor in competing coal mines nearby weakened the bargaining position of free miners. Widespread illiteracy also added difficulties. Fear among the miners was ever present. Even men Davis had known in Ohio, who now worked in Alabama and retained strong union feeling, remained silent. "All of them are in close touch with us," Davis found. "Of course they can not express themselves here as if they were in the North. Oh, no, to do this would be to discriminate against themselves, and in consequence they do not say very much."

The "race question"—many aspects of it—most hindered Davis. Although he found "a number of good men both white and colored," relations between whites and Negroes caused him to despair. "The one great drawback is the division between white and colored. I do not mean to say all are this way, but a very large number are." The reasons for such division were not simple, and their complexity did not escape him. He focused particular attention on three causes of racial mistrust and conflict. The fact that most Negroes worked as "laborers" for white miners (and some more fortunate Negroes) but not directly for an operator gave Davis a clue to the slow progress of Southern labor organization. A variant of the traditional English subcontract system, this relationship had racial overtones, dividing Negroes from whites as well as "laborers" from "miners." Davis explained it:

I have often heard the question asked, why is it that the miners of the South will not organize? To me the reasons are plain, and the answer is simply this: For the colored men there has [*sic*] been no inducements, and for the white to organize and be honest he would simply be giving away a good thing. Understand I am now speaking of the past. In the first place, the white miners, when they went into the Southern coal fields, saw an opportunity to make money by hiring colored men to work for them; these people being ignorant of course allowed themselves to become the servant of a servant, working for from 75 cents to $1 per day, and doing all the work thereby making for his servant employer fairly good wages, while he himself only earned a pittance. This custom continued to grow until today not only the whites do this, but the colored gentlemen have adopted the system and they feel proud to stand up and tell you they made say $15 or $25 this week. But ask him, if you please, did he earn it himself, and he will answer, oh, no, I have so and so many laborers. Right here let me say that he honestly does not, for a moment, realize that he has robbed the other poor devil.

Davis found this system at all the Alabama mining camps with one exception, and there the men got rid of it "only . . . recently by giving the company 2½ cents [a ton?] to do it."

Opposition to the UMW by certain Birmingham Negroes also impeded Davis' work. A Negro minister, W. M. Storrs ("one of the most intelligent young colored men we have in the South"), publicly encouraged Davis' organizing efforts, but Davis and the UMW were bitterly condemned by the *Southern Sentinel,* a Birmingham Negro newspaper, which urged Negro miners to form their own separate labor union. Davis pleaded with the *Sentinel's* editor:

. . . If you continue to follow along the lines that you are now following, then your headlines should be changed to read as follows: "Devoted to the interests of the coal and iron monopolies of the south," for you could not possibly serve them better than you are now doing. You say that you believe in "The Unity of Man," and yet you teach disintegration. I cannot understand your philosophy. Of workingmen in this country we have two races—the white and the black. Of the two the negro constitutes a very small minority. Now I want to know how he can separate himself from the white laborer and live? I am sure that you have intelligence enough to know that an employer of labor cares not what the color of a man's skin may be; he will employ the fellow who will work the cheaper.

The United Mine Workers of America seeks to better the condition of the miners, be they white or black; we seek to place all men on a common level. For heaven's sake, don't seek to further oppress the miner, but rather seek to help him elevate himself. Do this and you will be doing right.

The *Sentinel* printed Davis' criticisms but curtly dismissed them and their author. Davis found in this newspaper another example of "what we have to contend with down here." Not all opposition to interracial trade unionism came from Southern whites.

Yet it was the "color line" in Alabama—the tradition of deeply felt racial prejudice against Negroes together with the hardening of legally enforced separation—that cast an even grimmer shadow over Davis and other advocates of biracial unionism in the South of the 1890s. Exceptions to the "rule" encouraged Davis but also proved the "rule," and he explained:

In matters of this kind I think it best to be truthful. I found in the South that while white and colored miners worked in the same mines, and maybe in adjoining rooms, they will not ride even on a work-train with their dirty mining clothes on together, nor will they meet in a miners' meeting together in a hall without the whites going to one side of the hall, while the colored occupy the other side. You may even go to the post office at Pratt City, and the white man and the colored man can not get his [*sic*] mail from the same window. Oh, no, the line is drawn; the whites go to the right and the colored to the left.

Now I do not say this is encouraged by all of the whites, for I met quite a number who made it their special business to point out these things to me, and at the same time express their disgust at such a state of affairs, yet they could not help it, though the practice might be ever so distasteful.

Davis hoped for a breakthrough among the Alabama miners and predicted that "in a short while we will get the ball rolling good and strong." But the obstacles to such an advance were too real to be ignored. He ended his January 1, 1898, Birmingham letter sadly convinced of need for dramatic changes in Alabama. "As our people [the Negroes] are celebrating the emancipation proclamation, we will stop now and go out to listen awhile. But we need another proclamation of equal importance, and that one is to emancipate the wage slaves, both white and black."[33]

Davis had frequent difficulties and disappointments as an organizer, and coupled with his frustrations in finding employment, these made his life a troubled one. But the sum of these experiences added up to a deeper commitment to the UMW and to his belief in the redemptive role of biracial industrial unionism. At all times the union commanded his support. Suggestions poured forth to strengthen it. The use of East European immigrant strikebreakers in Virginia convinced him that "a Hungarian organizer . . . be sent there as soon as possible."[34] Factionalism he called "suicide."[35] Letter after letter urged readers to gather a large defense fund and to "attend your local meetings [and] pay your dues."[36] A visit to a mining camp meant an opportunity to canvass for new subscribers to the weekly *Journal*.[37] He found holidays and national crises the occasion to prod the inactive. The Spanish-American War, for example, caused Davis to exclaim: "We are all talking of going over to free Cuba. I would like to see poor Cuba freed, but would like better to free myself, the same with every other American coal miner. Boys, get a move on yourselves, for if you don't the day may soon come when it will be almost too late."[38] . . .

IV

The evidence gathered in these pages reveals much about the early history of the United Mine Workers of America and, in particular, about that union's attitudes toward Negro workers and the important role Negro miners like Richard L. Davis and George Durden played in its formative years. But the unfortunate absence of a detailed and comprehensive history of the UMW's early decades makes it perilous to claim too much beyond these facts.[39] And yet these are hard truths filled with considerable meaning.

Any authoritative history of the UMW surely will tell of the end-less and formidable difficulties and frustrations that accompanied early efforts to build this interracial industrial union. It will include grimly detailed pages about racial and ethnic quarrels and even death and violence. But it will also make much of the successful early confrontation between the UMW, its predominantly white leaders and members, and Negro workers. And it will explain why—in a decade that saw the general deterioration of the Negro's condition, North and South, and in which C. Vann Woodward argues "the Mississippi Plan" became "the American Way"—why enormous sacrifices by white and Negro miners made this union a reality.[40]

Even though the available statistics are meager and somewhat suspect, their symbolic value so far as the Negro's direct role and primary importance in building the UMW between 1890 and 1900 is crystal-clear. The essential fact is that about 20,000 Negroes belonged to the UMW in 1900.[41] In its first decade the UMW grew fitfully and mostly among bituminous miners. At its start it had almost 17,000 members and increased rapidly, but before the 1897 nationwide bituminous strike membership had fallen to less than 11,000. Rapid growth followed that strike. In 1900, just before it made its commanding advances among anthracite miners, 91,019 miners paid UMW dues, and John Mitchell embarrassingly chided Samuel Gompers, "We are seriously contemplating the absorption of the American Federation of Labor." Mitchell's amiable jest was not without meaning.[42] The UMW was far and away the largest AFL union in 1900. The Federation counted only 548,000 workers in all of its affiliated unions that year, so that no less than 16½ per cent of its members were miners. And Negroes made up an unusually large proportion of UMW membership.[43] Of its 91,019 members, the UMW included only 8893 anthracite miners and since few, if any, were Negroes, a measure of the Negro's consequence to the UMW should count only bituminous miners.[44] If 20,000 Negro bituminous miners belonged to the UMW in 1900, then 24 per cent of the union's bituminous members were Negroes. Mitchell and other union officials figured in 1899 that Negroes made up between 10 and 15 per cent of the mining population. Leaving aside again the anthracite miners, about 30 per cent of all bituminous miners were UMW members, but between 36 and 50 per cent of Negro bituminous miners belonged to the union. And not without additional interest is the fact that 3½ per cent of the AFL's members in 1900 were Negro coal miners. Further research undoubtedly will adjust these statistics but should not appreciably alter their meaning—a meaning that affects Negro history as well as labor history.

Despite formidable hindrances, particularly in Alabama and West Virginia, the UMW's efforts to organize and to hold Negro members did not end in 1900. Take Alabama as an example. Davis had been overwhelmed and depressed by the "color line" there in 1897 and 1898. But in 1899, 23 per cent of its miners belonged to the UMW, and by 1902 the union claimed 65 per cent of them, a majority being Negroes. In 1904 certain large operators repudiated the Alabama union and caused a strike that lasted two years—"the longest strike on record" to 1906. Court injunctions held back union officers but not union funds. Through its national treasury and its districts and locals, the UMW sent more than $1,000,000 to the Alabama strikers. The Illinois District (where Pana, Virden, and Carterville still remained living memories) alone gave $100,000. The strike failed, but the UMW held on until 1908 when operators refused to renew expired contracts and also cut wages. A second and larger strike then started and lasted nearly two months. Eighteen thousand miners—all except the convict coal diggers—quit work. Violence and shootings were common; hundreds of union men, Negro and white, suffered. The UMW spent an additional $407,500 to hold the men together but without success. The power of a hostile governor, himself a former lessee of convict labor who banned public meetings, a state militia that broke up interracial "tent villages" of evicted miners, and a committee of leading Alabama citizens that argued that "the people of Alabama" never would "tolerate the organization and striking of Negroes along with white men" finally ended the strike —and severely impaired the union. A year later the UMW counted 700, not 18,000, Alabama members, and effective trade unionism did not return there until the First World War and then only for a brief time. But that is another story.[45] What matters here is that despite the Alabama setback and the loss of so many Negro members, national UMW Negro membership probably did not decline precipitously between 1900 and 1910 and the union made a vigorous and costly effort to hold districts with large Negro membership.

What, finally, is the import of the successful participation by large numbers of Negroes in the early UMW so far as the general practices and attitudes of organized labor before 1910 are concerned?

Although the subject has been inadequately studied and much misunderstood, it appears that nothing about Negro workers more agitated and angered many white trade unionists between 1890 and 1910 than the frequent use of Negroes as strikebreakers and the "threat" of "Negro competition." The Pana and Virden violence, for example, "proved" to the *Locomotive Firemen's Magazine* (its union excluded Negroes) that "the entire social fabric of the Northern states may crumble before the invasion of hordes of cheap negro labor from the South."[46] In 1900, the year Richard Davis died, Samuel Gompers' annual report to the American Federation of Labor emphasized that unorganized Negroes would be "forced down in the economic scale and used against any effort made by us for our economic and social advancement." He warned that "race prejudice" would become more "bitter" to "the injury of all."[47] Confronted with complaints from Booker T. Washington and other Negro leaders that numerous affiliated unions formally or informally excluded Negroes from membership and therefore jobs, the AFL Executive Council in 1901 did not claim "perfection" for the labor movement but defended its efforts among Negro workers. It criticized Washington for his belief that "the economic, social, and moral progress and advancement of the negro is dependent upon the philanthropic and humane consideration of their [*sic*] employers" but most severely censured Negro strikebreaking as the main cause of "economic bitterness and antagonism between the races":

The real difficulty in the matter is that the colored workers have allowed themselves to be used with too frequently telling effect by their employers as to injure the cause and interests of themselves as well as of white workers. They have too often allowed themselves to be regarded as "cheap men," and all realize that "cheap men" are not only an impediment to the attainment of the worker's just rights, and the progress of civilization, but will tie themselves to the slough of despond and despair. The antipathy that we know some union workers have against the colored man is not because of his color, but because of the fact that generally he is a "cheap man." It is the constant aim of our movement to relieve all workers, white and black, from such an unprofitable and unenviable condition.[48]

Four years later Gompers harped on the same theme but with a new twist. He argued that the labor movement sought no conflict with Negroes but warned: "If the colored man continues to lend himself to the work of tearing down what the white man has built up, a race hatred far worse than any ever known will result. Caucasian civilization will serve notice that its uplifting process is not to be interfered with in any way."[49] At that moment the UMW was pouring hundreds of thousands of dollars into Alabama to preserve its early advances among Negro and white miners.

Negro strikebreaking and the existence of much racial prejudice among white workers and their leaders were hard realities, but these conditions alone were insufficient causes for the exclusion of Negroes from many organized trades between 1890 and 1910—and even earlier in certain unions. The early history of the United Mine Workers belies such an explanation. It is impossible to measure racial prejudice among white coal miners seventy years ago, but few would deny its existence. "Negro competition" constituted a recurrent threat to the status of established white miners. Negro strikebreakers probably were used with greater frequency in the bituminous mining industry than in any other between 1890 and 1910. And yet (even though Negro strikebreaking surely intensified anti-Negro feeling among white miners in the short run and may even have displaced white unionists) an all-white or racially segregated union did not result. Overwhelmingly white and many of them self-educated British and Irish immigrants, the early UMW leaders, not without formidable difficulties, welcomed Negro members and drew them actively into the union. As a result, an unknown but significant number of Negroes held local and district offices, helped organize both white and Negro miners, diminished some of the racial prejudice and mistrust between Negro and white miners, and stabilized their union in a time of repeated crisis. Rank-and-file Negroes consequently were not to be spotted occasionally throughout the union but added greatly to its strength by their sheer numbers. And after only ten years the UMW functioned as a viable, integrated trade union and quite possibly ranked as the most thoroughly integrated voluntary association in the United States of 1900. Good reason led Negro miner O. H. Underwood to insist in 1899: "I believe that the United Mine Workers has done more to erase the word white from the Constitution than the Fourteenth Amendment."[50] . . .

V

Nothing written in these final pages should be taken to suggest that Negro workers had an easy time in Northern and Southern crafts and factories between 1890 and 1910. This evidence means merely to indicate the difficulties involved in judging the "uniqueness" of the UMW experience and to hint that the full story of the confrontation between Negro workers and organized (as well as unorganized white) labor at that time has yet to be written—and that when examined it must be from "the bottom up." Surely, however, the evidence in these pages tells us that Booker T. Washington (himself a member of the Knights of Labor as a young man) exaggerated when he boasted that "the Negro is not given to 'strikes' " and that trade unionism was "that form of slavery which prevents a man from selling his labor to whom he pleases on account of his color."[51] William Hooper Councill, the Negro head of the Agricultural and Mechanical College for Negroes at Normal, Alabama, and very much a prophet of a subordinate role for Negroes in the "New South," was also wrong in arguing that Southern labor unions "will bring into the South the disorders that will exceed the disturbances of 'reconstruction days' " and that trade unionism would chase the Negro from the South so that "Communism [will] drive the white man's coach, Nihilism cook and serve his food, Agrarianism plow his fields, and the red flag of Anarchy float over every Southern industry."[52] Equally erroneous was Samuel Gompers, who in 1910 could insist that Negroes just did not "understand the philosophy of human rights."[53]

In all of this, it is the problem of perspective and the lack of detailed knowledge that plague us. Much has been written about the trade unions and their national leaders and about their petty and significant quarrels as well as their larger successes and frequent failures, but little is yet known of the quality of life and the complexity of thought and feeling of ordinary white and Negro workers in the early modern era. August Meier has explored painstakingly and well the world of Booker T. Washington and his Negro critics and defenders,[54] but the world of men like Richard Davis awaits its historian. How difficult it is therefore to grasp the response of a Negro worker to the racial sentiment of the older Gompers or to imagine the feelings of a white trade unionist confronted with the anti-labor imprecations of Washington and Councill. When the United Brotherhood of Carpenters and Joiners disturbed so many of its Southern white members by appointing a Negro organizer, the St. Louis *Advance,* a labor weekly, applauded its action and urged further organization of Negro workers:

It is useless to read homilies on thrift and morality to under-paid labor. . . . More and more the Brotherhoods are opening their doors to him [the Negro], telling him to step in. The labor leaders know that without the Negro their organizations are lop-sided and their movements necessarily failures, and the Negro can see that as a laborer he must ally himself with his brother, or remain as he is now in the South, the poorest paid laborer in the world.[55]

The *Advance* was wrong in its prediction. Although Richard Davis and the early white leaders of the United Mine Workers of America were among those to make such a connection, theirs was not the dominant influence between 1890 and 1910. Davis died in 1900. By 1910 surely only those coal miners, Negro and white workers, who had felt his presence and benefited from his experience and courageous leadership remembered his name.[56] Historians often characterize an era by a dominant personality, a figure who looms large over a period of time and leaves more than a momentary impression or in his person symbolizes significant changes. In this sense, the years between 1890 and 1910 did not belong to men like Richard Davis. This was indeed "The Age of Samuel Gompers" and "The Age of Booker T. Washington." Men like Davis were not asked to serve as presidential advisors or as members of federal commissions. *The New York Times* did not query them for their opinions on the "race" and "labor" questions. Instead, their long-range vision and concrete aspirations for democratic interracial trade unionism were stifled by the defensive strategy of organized labor and middle-class Negro leadership as well as the rising tide of racism within the labor movement and throughout the country.

The American people have journeyed far from the Age of Washington and Gompers. One measure of the distance traveled and the losses incurred is that so little is known about working-class Negroes like Richard Davis who displayed so full an awareness of their plight and that of their brothers and who retained and exemplified older traditions of pride and hope and militancy. We know a great deal about the world of Washington and Gompers. But until we know more fully the world of men like Davis, we shall not clearly comprehend the tragedy and the hope embedded in recent American history.

14. Migration and the Rise of the Ghetto

After emancipation, the great watershed in black history has been the migration of millions of blacks from southern farms to northern cities. Although this process only reached massive proportions during and after World War I, its roots lie in the 1880's and 1890's.

During Reconstruction many leaders of the northern black community migrated to the South, where a new arena for social and political advancement had opened. With the end of Reconstruction, this pattern was reversed, and many members of the South's "talented tenth," including ministers, politicians, and businessmen, turned northward and were absorbed into the black elite of northern cities. The black population of nine major northern cities increased by 36 per cent in the 1880's and 75 per cent in the 1890's. By 1910, Manhattan had a black population of 60,000 and Chicago had 44,000 black residents. Until 1900, race relations appear to have been improving in the North. Many states in the 1870's and 1880's enacted civil-rights legislation, and the rigid color line which had existed in public accommodations before the Civil War increasingly wavered.

Despite these events, and a concurrent movement of southern black farmers into the Southwest and Kansas, the black population in 1910 lived in more or less the same areas as in slavery days—it was concentrated in the black belts of the rural South. Only with the mass migration which dates from the decade 1910 to 1920 did a real shift in the black population begin. Between 1910 and 1920 the black population of Chicago rose from 44,000 to 109,000, of New York from 91,000 to 152,000 and of Philadelphia from 85,000 to 135,000. And almost every second-line industrial city of the North—places like Akron, Buffalo, Trenton, and Columbus, showed similar gains. The shift of the black population accelerated in the 1920's, leveled off during the depression of the following decade, and then resumed again between 1940 and 1970. The striking results of this migration are seen in a few statistics: in 1910, 75 per cent of the nation's blacks lived in rural areas and nine-tenths lived in the South. Today, three-quarters are in cities and half reside outside the southern states.

What were the causes of this massive population movement? Certainly the increasing racism of southern society, evidenced in lynchings, disfranchisement, and segregation, helped dispose many blacks to seek their fortunes elsewhere. And more immediate problems, such as floods on the Mississippi River and the devastating march of the boll weevil through southern cotton fields from 1914 to 1917 made it necessary for many blacks to leave their farms. But, as the black sociologist Charles S. Johnson showed in 1923, there was no correlation between areas which lost black population through migration and those where lynchings were most prevalent. Migration, Johnson argued, is best explained not as a flight from oppression but as a quest for a better life. The decade 1910–1920 witnessed a steady expansion of northern industry, at the same time as the outbreak of war in Europe drastically curtailed the immigration which had supplied much of the North's industrial labor force. Northern factories thus turned to the South for a labor supply, and offered blacks wages far in excess of their earnings on southern farms. Many firms sent labor agents into the South who promised free transportation to prospective laborers. These appeals were especially attractive to a new generation of young southern blacks who had never known slavery and who were more impatient with southern conditions than their elders.

The migration of blacks to northern cities led to changes in almost every aspect of black northern life. For one thing, it caused a reversal of the good race relations of the late nineteenth century, as northerners experienced new competition for their jobs and housing from blacks. Racial friction was especially exacerbated when blacks were imported to northern cities as strikebreakers. Between 1900 and 1920 race riots occurred in leading northern cities, including New York, Chicago, Springfield, and, the bloodiest of all, East St. Louis. They tended to occur in areas where economic competition between the races was most severe and where the black influx put strains on housing, transportation, and park facilities. Unlike the riots of the 1960's, these outbreaks consisted of whites attacking blacks and burning black housing and businesses, although in many cases blacks armed to defend themselves. Moreover, most of the violence occurred on the fringes of black ghettos, not in their center, where whites would be outnumbered, and was directed against black persons, rather than against property.

By far the most important effect of the black migration was the rise of the northern urban ghetto. The most famous ghetto, New York's Harlem, was transformed from a genteel, upper-class white community at the turn of the century to a black ghetto and slum by 1930. The transformation was made possible by a building boom in Harlem which collapsed in 1904, leaving hundreds of apartments with no prospective tenants. Black entrepreneurs like Philip Payton organized real-estate companies which leased buildings, evicted white families who had moved into the area, and encouraged blacks to move to Harlem. But the fact that whites resisted every block of the ghetto's expansion meant that the black population density steadily increased. In addition, the cycle of high rents and low salaries forced many families to take in lodgers to help meet their rent payments. The result was that the population density in Harlem was 50 per cent higher than the white density in Manhattan, a fact which helps explain the deterioration of housing which turned the ghetto into a slum.

With the northern migration, blacks for the first time entered the industrial labor force of the nation. Before 1915, northern black workers had been concentrated in menial, domestic, and unskilled jobs, and even these positions were threatened by the increasing influx of immigrants. But during World War I blacks were drawn into the lowest levels of the industrial labor market—the unskilled and semiskilled positions. But they were faced with what sociologists St. Clair Drake and Horace Cayton have termed "the job ceiling." It was, and still is, extremely difficult for blacks to cross the line separating unskilled and semiskilled industrial labor from the better-paying skilled and professional jobs. Three-quarters of the black male laborers in Chicago in 1930, and 90 per cent of the women, were below the job ceiling.

The selection which follows, from Allan Spear's *Black Chicago,* discusses in detail the causes of the black migration, the struggle for housing and jobs in the northern ghetto, and some of the institutional changes which the migration wrought in northern black life. The church, always the center of black social life, underwent profound transformation. Many migrants rejected the more formalized and impersonal services of the larger, middle-class-dominated black churches, and flocked to the storefront churches, where the emotional, fire-and-brimstone preaching of the southern rural church was reproduced. These new institutions were one response to the more general problem of how a rural peasantry adjusts to urban life. Men used to labor regulated by the rhythms of nature had to adjust to the factory bell; men familiar with the easy-going society of rural areas had to accept the fast pace of urban life; and men accustomed to the sense of community in rural areas were now faced with alienation and anomie in the city. These complex problems of adjustment have not been studied in depth by historians of Afro-Americans, and perhaps in the future historians would do well to compare the rural black's adjustment to the city with the experiences of migrants in other nations and continents, and of white newcomers to American urban centers. For the migration of blacks in this country was one phase of a worldwide phenomenon—the movement of masses of people from the countryside to the city.

From *Black Chicago*

ALLAN H. SPEAR

From the South to the South Side

The World War I era is usually viewed as the major turning point in the history of Negroes in the North. Between 1915 and 1920, the great migration destroyed the notion that the Negro problem would remain a southern problem and that northerners could simply allow southern whites to handle "their Negroes" as they saw fit. The migration of Negroes from the rural South to the urban North became, after 1915, a mass movement. The gradual prewar influx from the border states gave way to a sudden, large-scale migration of poorly educated, unskilled Negroes from the most backward areas of the Deep South. While the earlier movement had been little noted outside of the Negro community, the new migration was charted and graphed, analyzed and evaluated, deplored and defended in the newspapers, on public platforms, and in legislative committees. It became one of the major social issues

FROM Allan H. Spear, *Black Chicago*. Copyright © 1967 by University of Chicago Press. Reprinted by permission of University of Chicago Press and Allan Spear.

of the day. In the summer of 1917 and again in the summer of 1919, the northern Negro problem moved from the forums to the streets. A series of race riots in a score of northern and border cities gave violent notice that urban white northerners could no longer ignore the Negroes who lived in their midst.

Chicago was a focal point of the great migration and of the racial violence that came in its wake. The growing stockyards, steel mills, and foundries of Chicago, deprived of immigrant labor by the outbreak of war in Europe, provided new and unprecedented industrial opportunities for southern Negroes. As the terminus of the Illinois Central Railroad, Chicago was the most accessible northern city for Negroes in Mississippi, Louisiana, and Arkansas. Moreover many southern Negroes who had barely heard of Cleveland or Detroit knew of Chicago; they read about in the most popular Negro newspaper in the country—the flamboyant and racially militant *Defender;* they addressed their mail to it when they ordered goods from the great national mail-order houses— Sears Roebuck and Montgomery Ward; and they heard tales of it from the Pullman porters and dining-car waiters who worked the rails throughout the South. So, between 1916 and 1919, they came—some 50,000 of them—to crowd into the burgeoning black belt, to make new demands upon the institutional structure of the South Side, and to arouse the hostility of the Negro community's white neighbors. For three years, journalists, ministers, Negro and white civic leaders pointed with mounting concern to the inadequacy of Negro housing and the increasingly frequent outbreaks of racial violence as the black belt expanded. But neither the political nor the economic leaders of Chicago could be stirred into action. The climax was inevitable: for four tragic days in the summer of 1919, Chicago experienced one of the worst race riots in American history. Race relations had become Chicago's most serious municipal problem.

The events of 1916–19 made white Chicagoans far more aware of the city's Negro community, but did not basically alter the pattern of Negro life in Chicago. The ghetto was already well-formed by the eve of World War I; the migration and the riot merely strengthened both the external and internal forces that had created it. The new wave of white hostility and racial friction made separate community life seem ever more necessary. At the same time, the enlarged black belt required expanded services, facilities, and institutions to meet the needs of the recent migrants. Thus the events of the war years contributed to the pattern of white discrimination and Negro self-help that had been developing since the 1890's. The period between 1915 and 1920 was more a time of continuity than of change. The black enclave that had formed during the prewar years was strengthened by population growth and racial conflict and emerged in 1920 a fully-developed Negro ghetto.

A variety of circumstances combined to produce the World War I Negro migration. Many Negroes chose to leave the rural South for the same reasons that induced thousands of white farmers to move to the city: diminishing returns in agriculture, the ebbing of opportunity on the farm compared with the city, and discontent with rural life and institutions. But other circumstances peculiar to the situation of the southern Negro contributed to the exodus. The system of share tenancy and crop liens often prevented Negro farmers from making a profit, and unscrupulous planters and merchants systematically exploited the ignorant tenants. Despite increasing industrialization, economic opportunity in the South did not keep pace with the growth of population, and the Negro, excluded from the new industries, did not share in the opportunities that developed. The caste system had begun to harden in the 1880's: Jim Crow legislation, inferior schools, legal injustice, and lynchings were ever present factors in southern Negro life. Both economic and social conditions, therefore, contributed to what Gunnar Myrdal has called "accumulated migration potentialities."[1]

Although southern Negroes had ample reason to emigrate before World War I, relatively few did. The ties of home and family exercised a natural restraining influence. But, more important, Negroes had few opportunities outside the South before 1915. Northern industry found an ample labor supply in the hundreds of thousands of European immigrants who annually made their way across the Atlantic, and except during strikes, industrialists adhered to a rigid color line in their hiring practices. Throughout the North, a pattern similar to that found in Chicago prevailed: only in domestic employment and in the service trades could Negroes find positions.

During World War I, however, the North became more attractive and the South more intolerable; new conditions transformed migration potentialities into a mass exodus. With the outbreak of the European war, immigration fell from an all-time high of 1,218,480 in 1914 to 326,700 in 1915; in 1918, only 110,618 immigrants entered the country.[2] At the same time, the war precipitated an expansion of American industry necessitating a larger labor supply. Employers were forced to turn to the home labor market in order to fill vacancies, and the color bar quickly fell.[3]

Just as opportunities were opening in the North, cotton culture experienced a crisis that uprooted thousands of Negroes in the black belts of the South. The Mexican boll weevil had crossed the Rio Grande in 1892. Steadily spreading its destruction north and eastward, it had, by 1915, ruined thousands of acres of crops in the cotton-producing areas of Mississippi and Alabama and had just begun to ravage southwestern Georgia. The weevil did not destroy southern agriculture, but it made necessary a major reorganization: planters reduced their cotton acreage, altered their methods of planting and cultivating cotton, and put greater emphasis on food crops and livestock. Mixed farming required fewer laborers, and Negro croppers and laborers were, in any case, untrained for the new agriculture. As a result, landowners reduced the number of tenants and workers on their land, forcing many of them to seek work elsewhere.[4]

The plight of the southern tenant and farm worker was further aggravated by the low price of cotton in 1913 and 1914 and by a series of disastrous floods in 1915 and 1916. In many cases, the floods provided a climax to the chain of misfortunes that had beset planters and tenants alike for years. A case recorded by a Labor Department investigator illustrates the operation of the various disruptive factors in southern agriculture and its final result—emigration:

A prominent citizen of Selma [Alabama] owns 7000 acres of land in Dallas County. Before the boll weevil reached the state he was accustomed to plant the whole of this in cotton, and ran 2500 plows annually. For the past three or four successive years he has realized no profits, but has constantly suffered a loss on the capital invested. When the floods of July, 1916, virtually wiped out the crops of his tenants, he decided that as a matter of sound business he could not afford to make additional outlay in the advancement of provisions to them, the result being that the great majority were obliged to move elsewhere.[5]

Northern fever swept through the South in 1915 and 1916 much as America fever had infected much of Europe throughout the nineteenth century. First, southern Negroes heard only vague rumors of a better life in the North. Soon, however, they were confronted with concrete alternatives to their present plight. Labor agents, sent south first by the railroads and later by the steel companies, met Negroes on street corners, at churches, in barber shops, and in pool rooms. They offered free transportation plus the prospect of high wages to any laborer who agreed to migrate.[6]

Once it had begun, the migration generated its own momentum. Although southern whites, fearful of losing their work force, passed a series of stringent ordinances that effectively crippled the agents, this did not halt the migration.[7] The arrival of each migrant in the North created a new contact with potential migrants, and personal communication made the agents superfluous. "I am well and thankful to say I am doing well," wrote a Negro woman, recently arrived in Chicago, to a friend in the South. "I work in Swifts packing Co., in the sausage department. . . . We get $1.50 a day. . . . Tell your husband work is plentiful here and he wont have to loaf if he want to work."[8] A man in East Chicago wrote to a friend in Alabama:

Now it is true that the (col.) men are making good. Never pay less than $3.00 per day for (10) hours—this is not promise. I do not see how they pay such wages the way they work labors. they do not hurry or drive you. . . . I wish many time that you could see our People up here as they are entirely in a different light.[9]

Personal letters brought news of the excitement of city life, of decent treatment by whites, and of high wages. They provided assurance that the North was not just a chimera, and they must have influenced thousands of Negroes who might otherwise have indefinitely postponed their decision. When a letter from a departed member of the family contained money, it offered even more concrete evidence of success in the North. And occasionally a migrant returned home in person, flushed with prosperity, and took back with him friends and relatives who aspired to similar affluence.[10]

Along with the letters from the North came "The World's Greatest Weekly"—Robert Abbott's lively, hard-hitting *Chicago Defender*. The *Defender* publicized and encouraged the migration and, in the process, became the leading Negro journal in the country. The migration appealed to both sides of Abbott's racial ideology—to his belief in Negro protest and his commitment to racial solidarity and self-help. On the one hand, by leaving the South, Negroes were effectively protesting against oppression and injustice; on the other hand, by coming to the North, they were swelling the urban black belts and strengthening Negro economic, political, and institutional life.

In encouraging the migration, the *Defender* played upon every emotion. It portrayed stark contrasts between northern freedom and southern tyranny. The North, the *Defender* asserted, offered not only economic opportunity but a chance for human dignity:

Every black man for the sake of his wife and daughter should leave even at a financial sacrifice every spot in the south where his worth is not appreciated enough to give him the standing of a man and a citizen in the community. We know full well that this would almost mean a depopulation of that section and if it were possible we would glory in its accomplishment.[11]

Every act of violence in the South hammered home the lesson. After a particularly brutal lynching in Memphis, the *Defender* asked: "Do you wonder at the thousands leaving the land where every foot of ground marks a tragedy, leaving the graves of their fathers and all that is dear, to seek their fortunes in the North?"[12] When southern whites told Negroes that they would freeze to death in the North, the *Defender* compiled a list of Negroes who had frozen to death in the South, and asked: "If you can freeze to death in the north and be free, why freeze to death in the south and be a slave?"[13]

In the spring of 1917, the *Defender* set a date—May 15—for the "Great Northern Drive."[14] It supplemented its polemic with photographs, cartoons, and even poems: "Some are coming on the passenger,/ Some are coming on the freight,/ Others will be found walking,/ For none have time to wait."[15] Even more persuasive were the notices of job opportunities in the North. "More positions open than men for them," read a *Defender* headline. In northern Illinois and southern Wisconsin, "there is a dire shortage of molders" and "employers will give men a chance to learn the trade at $2.25 a day."[16] These items were substantiated by advertisements for help in the *Defender*'s classified columns.[17]

The *Defender* was widely read in the South. Its local news columns indicated that its largest readership outside of Chicago was in Kentucky, Tennessee, and the Gulf States. Prospective migrants deluged the *Defender*'s office with praises for the paper's message and requests for job information. "Permitt me to inform you," wrote a correspondent from Texas, "that I have had the pleasure of reading the Defender for the first time in my life and I never dreamed that there was such a race paper published and I must say that its *some* paper."[18] White southerners attempted to control the distribution of the *Defender* as they had curbed the labor agents. A daily newspaper in Athens, Georgia, called the Chicago weekly "the greatest disturbing element that has yet entered Georgia," and elsewhere in the South city authorities seized copies of the newspaper.[19] But they could not effectively halt the *Defender*'s circulation nor minimize its influence. Emmett Scott summed up the paper's impact on southern Negroes: "In it they could read the things they wanted to hear most, expressed in a manner in which they would not dare express it. It voiced the unexpressed thoughts of many and made accusations for which they themselves would have been severely handled."[20]

The offer of an agent, an encouraging letter from a friend in the North, or the appeal of the militant Negro press, coming after years of smoldering discontent, sparked the final decision to migrate. Through these media, tenant farmers and sharecroppers, displaced by agricultural reorganization or disastrous floods, or merely weary of their marginal economic status and the proscriptions of the southern caste system, learned of the opportunities that awaited them in Chicago, Detroit, and Cleveland. Each southern Negro who chose to migrate made a highly personal decision, but he was frequently influenced by the power of mass suggestion. Wherever Negroes gathered, particularly in the country towns of the South, the North became the principal topic of conversation. Jeremiah Taylor of Bobo, Mississippi, for instance, was resigned to his farm until one day his son came back from town with the report that folks were leaving "like Judgment day." Taylor went to town, skeptical, and came back determined to move north.[21] As friends departed, many persons went along just because "it seemed like everybody was heading that way." A woman in Macon wrote to her friend in Chicago: "May you dont no how much I mis you. . . . it is lonesome her it fills my heart with sadness to write to my friends that gone. . . . May now is the time to leave here . . . if I stay here I will go crazy."[22]

The early migrants had only vague notions of what they might expect at their destinations, and they often headed north with visions of fantastic wages and unbounded liberty.[23] Moreover as the image of the North filtered south through the promises of agents, the glowing letters of friends, and the appeal of the Negro press, it took on a mythical quality that gave to the migration an almost religious significance. The rhetoric of the migration was highly charged with biblical imagery: the Flight out of Egypt; Bound for the Promised Land; Going into Canaan; Beulah Land. A party of migrants on their way from Mississippi to Chicago held solemn ceremonies when their train crossed the Ohio River; they stopped their watches, knelt down to pray, and sang the gospel hymn, "I Done Come Out of the Land of Egypt With the Good News."[24]

The lure of the Promised Land was particularly compelling for the younger generation. Their fathers had been reared in the immediate aftermath of slavery, when the plantation tradition was still strong and Negroes were loyal to those "Southern gentlemen of the old school" who took a paternalistic interest in them. But the sons came into friendly contact with whites less frequently and found it difficult to live with whites on the terms accepted by their fathers. A Negro preacher in Mississippi told a Labor Department investigator:

My father was born and brought up as a slave. He never knew anything else until after I was born. He was taught his place and was content to keep it. But when he brought me up he let some of the old customs slip by. But I know there are certain things that I must do and I do them, and it doesn't worry me; yet in bringing up my own son, I let some more of the old customs slip by. He has been through the eighth grade; he reads easily. For a year I have been keeping him from going to Chicago; but he tells me this is his last crop; that in the fall he's going. He says, "When a young white man talks rough to me, I can't talk rough to him. You can stand that; I can't. I have some education, and inside I has the feelings of a white man. I'm going."[25]

The emotions engendered by the exodus were closely linked to a growing Negro race consciousness. Despite the wide variety of individual motives, the migration developed a certain coherence; it grew out of the Negro people's common historical experiences and common grievances. Prior to 1915, southern Negroes had no means of expressing their discontent because no alternative was open to them. But with the broadening of opportunities in the North, they were able to act positively and independently to improve their status. As Ray Stannard Baker observed, Negroes were "acting for themselves, self consciously . . . they are moving of their own accord."[26] A Labor Department investigator reported that "the Negroes just quietly moved away without taking their recognized leaders into their confidence any more than they do the white people about them."[27] Here then was a self-conscious, independent racial movement. The migrants saw themselves not merely as men in search of better jobs, but also as Negroes seeking a greater degree of freedom. The initial impetus was primarily economic, but as the movement took form, as the vision of Canaan put into sharper focus the tyranny of Egypt, the exodus became, in E. Franklin Frazier's words, "one of the most crucial mass movements in the history of the Negro in the United States."[28] . . .

The Struggle for Homes and Jobs

Chicago was strange and forbidding to the Negro migrant who had lived all of his life on a Mississippi plantation or in a small Alabama town. Men in worn, outmoded suits carrying battered luggage, and women clutching ragged, barefooted children crowded into the Illinois Central station on Twelfth Street looking hopefully for a familiar face. Park Row—the little drive running from Michigan Avenue to the station—was solidly packed with people. There the migrants mingled with local Negroes who came down every Sunday to meet a friend or a relative or just to see who had arrived. If there was no one to meet them, the newcomers seldom knew where to go. They might ask a Red Cap to direct them to the home of a friend—unaware that without an address the porter could be of little help in a city as large as Chicago. Or they might employ one of the professional guides who, for a fee, would help them find lodging. Some of the guides were honest, others were little more than confidence men. Travelers Aid and the railroad police tried to help the migrants and prevent exploitation; but for the newcomer without friends or relatives, the first few days were often a terrifying experience.[1]

Somehow or other, most of the migrants made their way to the South Side black belt. There they found the constricted, increasingly self-contained Negro community that had developed in the prewar years. Housing was scarce, but not impossible to find. Although there was no new construction during the war, many of the old wooden houses west of State Street stood empty, vacated by Negroes who had moved into the more desirable homes to the east.[2] The old core of the black belt, between State and Wentworth, for many years a festering slum, deteriorated further during the migration years. Two-story frame houses, devoid of paint, stood close together in drab, dingy rows, surrounded by litters of garbage and ashes. Ordinary conveniences were often nonexistent: toilets were broken or leaked; electricity was rare; heating and hot water facilities failed to function.[3] A 1911 study of several blocks along Federal Street had shown that almost 25 per cent of the houses were in bad repair, about 50 per cent in fair repair, and another 25 per cent in good repair.[4] In a study of a comparable area in 1923, an investigator found that over 41 per cent of the residential buildings were in bad repair, 40 per cent in fair repair and only about 14 per cent in good repair.[5] Landlords had nothing to gain by improving these old houses; they merely allowed them to decay and collected whatever rent they could from Negroes who were unable to find—or to afford—better housing.

The more affluent of the migrants, who had sold their property in the South and come to Chicago with ready funds, sought homes in the more desirable neighborhood east of State Street. There the quality of housing varied widely. On the broad avenues—Wabash, Michigan, South Park, Grand Boulevard—stood homes that a generation before had been the finest in the city. Though somewhat faded now, many were still comfortable, well-equipped, and commodious. On the side streets and the lesser avenues, rows of connected flat buildings, usually of stone or brick, provided less attractive, although often adequate, accommodations.[6] But the neighborhood had declined since Negroes first entered it around 1900. Many of the old homes had begun to deteriorate and frequently were in need of repair or lacked necessary sanitary facilities.[7] The homes east of State were still far better than the rickety shacks on Wentworth and Federal; but they were no longer the choice property that they had once been.

Despite the low quality of most black belt housing, overcrowding was not yet a major problem during the migration period. To the contrary, families often found that all available housing was too large for their needs. Even the ramshackle houses in the Federal Street slum were relatively roomy. Most of the apartments there occupied an entire floor and usually housed no more than one person per room.[8] On the basis of a 1917 study, the Race Relations Commission concluded that "Negroes have more space in their living quarters than do other Chicago people housed in similar grades of dwellings."[9]

The large size of the apartments often forced families to fill vacant rooms with lodgers in order to raise money for the rent. In the 1911 study of living conditions on Federal Street, 31 per cent of the persons queried had been lodgers; 35 per cent of the postwar sampling were lodgers.[10] Lodging became a regular way of life in the black belt; "the people are rushing here by the thousands," wrote a Chicago woman to a friend in the South, "and I know if you come and rent a big house you can get all the roomers you want."[11] Many families, however, took lodgers for other than financial reasons. The survey of the Race Relations Commission indicated that "lodgers were often found in families where the income from that source did not appear to be needed."[12] During the migration, many of the older settlers took in relatives and friends, newly arrived from the South, until the newcomers could find permanent quarters of their own. There were few hotels and guest houses in the black belt, and migrants frequently depended upon their old friends for temporary housing.[13]

To meet the need for smaller apartments, some landlords began to divide up large houses into little "kitchenette" units—usually two or three rooms with cooking facilities. An owner of a spacious house east of State could increase his income substantially by renting "kitchenettes" to six or seven families rather than leasing flats to two families. In the 1920's and 1930's, when overcrowded conditions became prevalent on the South Side, the kitchenette arrangement was viewed as an evil. But at its inception it represented an advance; it allowed small families to secure housing without renting more space than they needed.[14]

The migrants did not often come into direct competition with whites for housing. Few of them could afford apartments or homes in the predominantly white districts east of the black belt, and they had no reason to seek homes among the hostile Irish and Poles in the overcrowded neighborhood west of Wentworth Avenue. But the influx of the migrants precipitated a crisis in housing by pushing the older settlers across the boundaries of the Negro ghetto. Middle- and upper-class Negroes were no longer able to find satisfactory homes on the avenues just east of State Street. Wabash and Indiana Avenues had begun to deteriorate by 1910, and with the migration, Prairie, Calumet, and even stately South Park Avenue, though still racially mixed, were becoming predominantly working-class neighborhoods. So, as Negro families had tried to escape the slum fifteen years before by moving east of State Street, many now moved beyond Cottage Grove Avenue into Kenwood and Hyde Park and south of Fifty-fifth Street into Woodlawn. The hostility they met went far beyond the sporadic resistance of the prewar years and led directly to the racial violence that terrorized Chicago in 1919.[15]

The job market for Negroes, unlike the housing market, vastly expanded during the migration years. This expansion had been a major factor in bringing the migrants to Chicago in the first place. The migrants of the prewar years had taken jobs as janitors, porters, and personal servants. The World War I migrants were hired as laborers at Swift, Armour, Pullman, and International Harvester, in jobs previously restricted to white workers.

The shift in the occupational position of Negroes in Chicago during the migration decade was striking. In 1910, over 51 per cent of the male Negro labor force was engaged in domestic and personal service trades; this figure dropped to 28 per cent in 1920. The proportion of Negroes engaged in manufacturing, on the other hand, more than doubled, and the proportion occupied in trade tripled. Factory work, rather than domestic and personal service, was the most important source of employment for Negroes by 1920. Negroes barely held their own in the various domestic services despite the sharp population increase. In manufacturing, on the other hand, the percentage of Negroes among unskilled laborers increased fivefold and the percentage among semiskilled workers tenfold. Negroes now constituted 4 per cent of the labor force in manufacturing—close to the percentage their numbers would warrant.

The change among women was less dramatic. A smaller proportion of Negro women were in domestic trades and a larger proportion were in manufacturing, but domestic service continued to be the largest source of employment. Almost 64 per cent of the Negro women were engaged in this type of work—over 30 per cent as household servants and almost 14 per cent as laundresses. Yet for the first time, a sizable minority of Negro women worked in factories. In 1910, almost all of the Negro women classified under the manufacturing trades were dressmakers, seamstresses, and milliners working in their own homes. But in 1920, over three thousand Negro women—15 per cent of the female Negro labor force—were unskilled and semiskilled factory operatives. Negro women also broke into commercial laundry work during this decade: in 1910 they had constituted only 4 per cent of the labor force in commercial laundries; by 1920, this figure had climbed to 36 per cent.

Despite this important shift in the employment pattern, Negroes remained at the bottom of the occupational ladder. Over half of the Negro men engaged in manufacturing were listed as laborers— a classification used for the unskilled.[16] Most of the Negro transportation workers were either laborers or chauffeurs; positions as engineers, motormen, switchmen, and conductors were still completely closed to them.[17] The sharp increase in the number of Negroes engaged in trade was the result of the massive influx of Negro workers into the stockyards, where they generally worked in unskilled jobs.

For Negro women, the job market remained highly constricted. Clerical occupations were still almost closed to Negroes, and the women employed by industrial and commercial firms were almost always unskilled workers—kitchen helpers, chambermaids, ironers in laundries, or common laborers in garment and lampshade factories. Women with high school—and even college—educations still had no real alternative to domestic service.[18] The two large mail order houses, Sears Roebuck and Montgomery Ward, hired Negro women as temporary help, but the downtown stores and the Chicago Telephone Company—major employers of female labor —refused to even experiment with Negro help.[19]

The migration gave birth to a black proletariat in Chicago. Before the war, Negroes had been outside the mainstream of the city's economic life. As domestic workers, porters, and waiters, they had been engaged in peculiarly Negro occupations—out of touch with white workers of similar status, isolated from the labor movement, nearly deprived of any opportunity to advance. It remained to be seen whether the Negro's new occupational position would permanently change this situation and whether Negroes would be able to maintain their foothold in industry. And it was not yet certain whether the Negroes' concentration in unskilled work would remain a permanent feature of Negro economic life or whether it would disappear as Negroes acquired skills.

The occupational adjustment of the southern migrants was frequently difficult. Most of the newcomers found themselves in work vastly different from their previous occupations. Of 225 migrants interviewed by the Race Relations Commission, only ninety-one utilized previous experience and training after moving to Chicago.[20] The majority had been farmers in the South. Others, who had worked in skilled trades at home, found that they were unable to pursue their vocation in Chicago: northern employers often imposed higher standards of competence and many craft unions maintained rigid color bars. Even professional people frequently took unskilled and personal service jobs: women who had taught in southern Negro schools, for instance, could rarely qualify to teach in Chicago and were often forced into domestic work.[21]

Many migrants from the rural South were unprepared for the

long, regular hours required in the mills, factories, and stockyards
of Chicago. As farmers, handymen, and personal servants at
home, their work schedules had often been informal and flexible.
The rigid, six-day week demanded by Chicago industries necessitated a change in the newcomers' way of life. A. L. Jackson of the
Wabash Avenue YMCA told of the migrant who had come to him
complaining that he had lost his job. Had he gone to work every
day? Jackson asked. "Goodness no," the man replied. "I just had
to have some days of the week off for pleasure."[22] The superintendent of a company employing a large number of Negroes
commented: "The southern Negroes have not yet become reconciled to working six days a week. Down South they are accustomed
to taking off Saturdays, and they are quite frequently absent on
Saturday."[23] But gradually, the migrants adjusted. "The man who
comes here," A. L. Jackson predicted, "will want to keep pace
with his brothers in the north in living and recreation and will find
it necessary to work every day in order to keep up. His manner of
living, the pleasures he affords himself . . . will be added to a
changed condition of life."[24]

The migrants were compensated for what they sacrificed in
leisure and informality. They earned more money than they ever
had before. Wages for unskilled labor in the leading Chicago industries ranged from a minimum of 42.5 cents an hour in the
packing houses to 61 cents an hour at Argo Corn Products and
International Harvester. The average was nearly 50 cents an hour.
In the building trades, an unskilled laborer could earn up to $1.00
an hour. Most companies worked from forty-eight to sixty hours a
week, so $25.00 was not an unusual week's wages.[25] For a man
who had been earning 75 cents a day as a farm laborer in the
South, this was an enormous salary. Women generally averaged
from $12.00 to $18.00 a week for factory work in Chicago and
could earn that much, plus room and board, in domestic service.[26]
Negroes received the same wages as white workers for comparable
work, although in a few instances Negroes were assigned to certain
kinds of piecework that yielded smaller earnings.[27]

A less tangible but perhaps even more important compensation
was the independence that industrial work offered. In the rural
South, Negroes were personally dependent upon white landowners

in an almost feudal sense. Personal supervision and personal responsibility permeated almost every aspect of life. In prewar Chicago, the service trades, in which Negroes were concentrated, also placed a high premium on personal loyalty and servility; domestic workers, for example, who lived in the homes of their white employers, had little time for their private lives. In the factories and yards, on the other hand, the relationship with the "boss" was formal and impersonal, and supervision was limited to working hours. Between 1918 and 1920, employers had difficulty in finding domestic help even when they offered higher wages than competing factories.[28] "I can save more when I'm in service," admitted a maid who had quit to work in a mail-order house, "but the other things you have to take—no place to entertain your friends but the kitchen, and going in and out the back doors. I hated all that. . . . They almost make you a slave." A migrant who had left domestic work in Georgia for a job in a Chicago box factory was even more vehement: "I'll never work in nobody's kitchen but my own any more. No indeed! That's the one thing that makes me stick to this job. You do have some time to call your own."[29]

In addition to higher wages and independence, there was hope that the breakthrough in industry would provide opportunity for advancement that Negroes had not previously enjoyed. Negroes, to be sure, were entering at the bottom—in the unskilled occupations—but so had the Poles and Czechs back in the 1880's, and many of them had moved into supervisory and even managerial positions. Yet, there were already indications that the Negroes' ladder of advancement in industry would have slippery rungs. In the stockyards, for instance, Negroes were systematically passed over when new foremen were named; a Negro might be appointed subforeman over an all-Negro gang, but he was never allowed to supervise a mixed group of workers.[30]

Even more portentous was the massive layoff of Negro workers during the recession of 1919–20. In the spring of 1919, the packing houses laid off 15,000 workers—a large proportion of them Negroes. One company spokesman insisted that "no discrimination is being shown in the reducing of our forces." But he admitted that many Negroes were among the first to be released.

"It is a case of the survival of the fittest, the best man staying on the job. It is a fact that the southern Negro cannot compete."[31] The Negro women who had entered industry and trade during the war found it particularly difficult to maintain their gains. The mail-order houses hired Negroes to meet a temporary rush, but they never integrated them into their regular work force and released them as soon as business leveled off. One employer told the Department of Labor that he had hired Negro girls "solely on account of the shortage of labor" and "as soon as the situation clears itself no more colored help will be employed."[32] The recession was of short duration and by 1921 jobs were plentiful again. But the experience of 1919–20 indicated that Negro industrial gains were tenuous and depended—far more than white jobs—upon continuing business prosperity. . . .

Migration and Negro Community Life

Of all aspects of community life, religious activities were most profoundly changed by the migration. Before the war, the large, middle-class Baptist and Methodist churches had dominated Negro religious life in Chicago. Although they had not completely discarded the emotionalism of traditional Negro religion, these churches had moved toward a more decorous order of worship and a program of broad social concern. The migration, however, brought into the city thousands of Negroes accustomed to the informal, demonstrative, preacher-oriented churches of the rural South. Alienated by the formality of the middle-class churches, many of the newcomers organized small congregations that met in stores and houses and that maintained the old-time shouting religion. Often affiliated with the more exotic fringe sects, Holiness or Spiritualist, these storefront churches became a permanent force in the Chicago Negro community and secured a powerful hold on thousands of working-class Negroes.

The Holiness or Pentecostal churches were the most conspicuous of the new storefront congregations. Although a few churches of this type had existed before the war, they became numerous and prominent only with the migration. By 1920, there were twenty Holiness churches in Chicago, all meeting in storefronts or houses.[1]

Most were concentrated west of State Street, among the poorest of the recent migrants. All were small, usually with no more than fifty members, and their organization was highly personal. The preacher, or presiding elder, was commonly an uneducated migrant from the South, who had founded the church while working at another job. He held his congregation together through personal loyalty, and if he died or moved away, the church rarely survived. Doctrinally, the Holiness churches were fundamentalist. Their highly emotional services were marked by rolling, shouting, or "speaking in tongues." Often too the preachers claimed the power to heal. Members of these congregations spent most of their free time in religious activities: some churches held nightly services, and all of them, in addition to Sunday worship, conducted two or three mid-week prayer meetings and periodic revivals and healing campaigns.[2]

Elder Lucy Smith was perhaps the most successful of the Holiness preachers: her All Nations Pentecostal Church became a landmark on the South Side in the 1930's. But despite her unusual success, she probably typified in background and motivation those who founded storefront churches during the migration years. A large, heavy-set woman with almost no formal education, Lucy Smith was born on a Georgia plantation in 1875, moved to Atlanta in 1909, and a year later migrated to Chicago. A Baptist by birth, she joined Olivet Church upon her arrival in Chicago. Soon dissatisfied with the formality of the large congregation, she began to attend the smaller Ebenezer Baptist Church, but here too she was unable to find the traditional kind of religion she sought. She then turned to the Stone Church, a predominantly white Pentecostal congregation. The Stone Church provided her with the inspiration she needed to begin her own religious career. "In 1914," she recalled, "I received my baptism and came into the works of the Lord. I continued going to the Stone Church until I received my calling, which is divine healing." Lucy Smith's calling coincided neatly with the arrival of the first wave of World War I migrants, who were receptive to her spiritual message. In 1916, she organized a one-room prayer meeting in her house; ten years later, after numerous moves and changes, she started to erect her own church building. Lucy Smith, according to one observer, was "a simple, ignorant, untrained woman with deep human sympathies, who believed absolutely in her own power to help and heal other people. Calm and serene in that faith, she has drawn together a following from the back streets of Chicago."[3]

Not all of the little storefront churches that sprang up during the migration years were Pentecostal. Many called themselves Baptist, although they often closely resembled the Holiness churches in their uninhibited form of worship.[4] Others were Spiritualist, a vague term used to identify those religious groups that believed in "communication of the spirit" and that attempted to relay messages to the spirits through mediums. Many Spiritualist churches were merely commercial enterprises that charged fees for readings and advice. But several true Spiritualist churches were organized between 1915 and 1920. These congregations combined the emotional worship service of the Pentecostal and Baptist storefronts with séances and spiritual readings.[5]

A dearth of material makes it difficult to assess the social significance of storefront churches in Chicago. In all probability, they were primarily migrant churches; as the newcomers became acculturated to city ways, they moved to the more established churches, leaving the storefronts to the still more recent arrivals. One observer described the members of Lucy Smith's congregation, for instance, as "new arrivals from the South and those Negroes who have not [been] and probably never will be urbanized."[6] In any case, the emergence of the storefronts was symptomatic of increasing differentiation within the Negro class structure. For the storefronts were decidedly lower-class churches. As some sophisticated upper-class Negroes had broken with the old-line churches to form Episcopalian and Presbyterian congregations, so now the southern-oriented lower class sought religious fulfillment in churches that more closely approximated their values and ideals. While the upper-class churches followed formal, decorous orders of worship and emphasized ethics and social concern, the storefronts allowed the widest range of personal expression and uninhibited emotionalism, and offered a salvation-centered religion that ignored and provided an escape from the problems of everyday life.

Despite the rise of the storefronts, the old-line Baptist and

Methodist churches grew rapidly during the migration years. Olivet Baptist Church, for example, already the largest Negro church in the city, grew from an estimated membership of four thousand in 1915 to almost nine thousand in 1920. During this period it moved into a new and larger building and vastly expanded its already sizable social and recreational program. Lacey Kirk Williams, who became pastor of the church in 1915, tried to make Olivet a community center. By 1920, a full-time professional staff of sixteen operated a program that included a labor bureau, kindergarten, nursery, and welfare department, in addition to the usual club and athletic activities. For Olivet, as for many other northern churches that tried to provide facilities for the newcomers, this expansion resulted in heavy financial debt. The migrants were unable to contribute an amount commensurate with new financial burdens they created.[7] Quinn Chapel, the Methodist counterpart of Olivet, did not grow as rapidly. More sedate and formal than Olivet, Quinn Chapel soon gained a reputation as a "swank" church, not for the "common herd." The A.M.E. denomination in Chicago claimed a total membership increase of about five thousand during the migration years; this figure was matched by Olivet alone.[8]

The Baptist churches, in general, outpaced the Methodist during this period and secured a preeminent position in Chicago, which they never lost. In 1916, Chicago had thirty-six Baptist churches and twenty-two Methodist. By 1920, the number of Methodist churches had increased to only thirty-four, while there were now eighty-six Baptist churches in the city.[9] Many of the new Baptist congregations were ephemeral little storefronts, but others, although beginning in stores or private homes, grew into large and substantial congregations. Pilgrim, Progressive, Provident, Liberty, and Monumental Baptist Churches, all founded between 1916 and 1919, began as prayer meetings in the homes of migrants recently arrived from the South. Within a decade, all of these congregations had acquired their own buildings and boasted memberships of over five hundred. Primarily migrant churches, they provided a middle ground between the formal, old-line northern congregations and the emotional, uninhibited storefronts.[10]

The churches affiliated with white denominations were least

affected by the migration. Most of these were upper-class urbanized churches with little to offer the recent arrivals. But there was one exception. St. Monica's Roman Catholic Church had always drawn its membership chiefly from Negroes who had been Catholics in the South; the large migration from Louisiana swelled its ranks between 1915 and 1920. The growth in the Negro Catholic population in Chicago came at a time when anti-Negro sentiment among the white Catholic groups in the city was mounting rapidly. In deference to this feeling, Archbishop Mundelein formulated a policy that resulted in almost complete racial segregation within the Archdiocese of Chicago. In 1917, Mundelein announced that while "until now practically anyone who so desired could affiliate himself with St. Monica's," he now desired "St. Monica's to be reserved entirely for the colored Catholics of Chicago . . .; all other Catholics of whatever race or color are to be requested not to intrude." The Archbishop said that he took this action so that his "colored children shall not feel uncomfortable in the Catholic Church," and he quickly added that he had "no intention of excluding colored Catholics from any of the other churches in the district."[11] In practice, however, the Archbishop's order provided white parishes with an excuse for excluding Negroes. Many white priests refused to marry or bury Negroes and, in some cases, would not even hear their confessions. Instead they ordered them to go to their own church, which the Archbishop had set aside for them.[12]

15. Marcus Garvey and His Movement

Black nationalism has a long history in the United States. In the nineteenth century, it often found expression in emigrationist movements, such as those led by Paul Cuffe early in the century, Martin Delany in the 1850's, and Bishop Henry M. Turner in the post-Reconstruction years. These leaders believed that blacks should preserve their racial identity and not seek absorption into white society and insisted that their race needed a national existence, preferably in the homeland of Africa, as a source of racial pride and power. Nationalists have always insisted that the goal of integration was too illusory and impractical to be an immediate concern for black organizations, and, in general, nationalist movements have had their widest appeal to the black community precisely when the hope of integration has seemed most remote.

In the following selection, from an introduction to a collection of Marcus Garvey's works, the Nigerian scholar E. U. Essien-Udom traces the life and ideas of this most remarkable of black nationalist leaders in America. He points out that the broken promises of World War I (the war to "make the world safe for democracy"), the series of race riots which swept the nation in 1919, and the realization that the North was not proving a "promised land" for the black migrant, all combined to produce a disillusionment among the black urban masses which made them ripe for the racial nationalism espoused by Garvey. Between his arrival in the United States from his native West Indies in 1915 and his deportation in 1927, Garvey succeeded in reaching and mobilizing the urban blacks, and in creating what Harold Cruse has called "the greatest mass movement yet achieved in American Negro history."

At the heart of Garvey's ideology lay his view of Africa; the liberation of Africa from foreign white domination was the consuming desire of his life. "If Europe is for the Europeans," he declared, "then Africa shall be for the black peoples of the world. . . . The other races have countries of their own and it is time for the 400,000,000 Negroes to claim Africa for themselves." Because of this emphasis, and his belief that American blacks should take the lead in the struggle to redeem Africa, Garveyism is often characterized as a back-to-Africa movement. Yet his widow, Amy Jacques-Garvey, has insisted that Garvey never advocated mass black migration to Africa, and that Garvey's enemies in the United States originated the emigrationist label in order to discredit him. Garvey did believe that skilled and educated American blacks had a duty to assist in the development and liberation of Africa, but his image of the African homeland was far more complex than his critics claimed. He explicitly stated that "the fight for African redemption does not mean that we must give up our domestic fights for political justice and industrial rights," and he argued that an independent black Africa would constitute a source of political power which would benefit blacks throughout the world. "The white man," he declared, "will only respect your rights constitutionally as a citizen of this country . . . when you have some government behind you."

Africa for Garvey also symbolized the past and future greatness of the black race, and his emphasis on the African homeland was part of his larger stress on pride in blackness. A black skin, he told his audiences, should be viewed with pride, not shame. Garvey established a provisional government-in-exile for Africa, with himself at the head, with a black cabinet, black generals, black flyers, a Black Cross contingent of nurses, and even a religion, the African Orthodox Church, with a black God. He "awakened a race-consciousness that made Harlem felt around the world," said the Harlem minister Adam Clayton Powell, Sr. And Powell added, "He is the only man who ever made Negroes who are not black ashamed of their color." For Garvey insisted on race purity and disdained mulattoes. He opposed intermarriage and social equality, on the grounds that "amalgamation" was tantamount to race suicide. Garvey went so far as to hold a widely-publicized meeting with a Ku Klux Klan leader, after which he announced that the Klan and he agreed on the necessity of keeping the races pure.

Garvey's interest in Africa was one expression of a rising tide of pan-Africanism in the 1920's. These were the years when Du Bois was organizing a series of pan-Africanist conferences in Europe. Yet there were far more differences than similarities between these two leaders, and the 1920's were marked by bitter conflict between them. Du Bois considered Garvey a dangerous demagogue, who lacked any substantive program and merely inflamed racial hatred. For his part, Garvey denounced Du Bois as a traitor to the race because of his integrationist goals and his cooperation with whites in the NAACP. Moreover, Du Bois had expanded his critique of American society into an espousal of socialism for both Africa and America, while Garvey, always a follower of Booker T. Washington in economic matters, had a pro-capitalist outlook. His Black Star shipping line and Negro Factories Corporation were attempts to put into practice Washington's philosophy that through economic self-help blacks could better their own conditions.

The success of Garvey in mobilizing the disillusioned black masses in the urban ghetto raises important questions about the nature of black leadership. Garvey differed from Du Bois and other "established" black leaders in neither asking for nor receiving white support. When a reporter asked why he didn't seek financial assistance from whites, Garvey replied, "We don't want their money, this is a black man's movement." Yet he demonstrated that a doctrine of race pride and nationalism can have a tremendous appeal to lower-class blacks. The ghetto's response to black nationalism, Essien-Udom has written in another work, reveals "the desperate character of the social situation of the lower-class Negroes in the large northern cities. . . . Their life is devoid of meaning. . . . They are estranged from the larger society which they seek to enter, but which rejects them." Nationalist movements like Garvey's succeed because they give these blacks a sense of meaning in their lives and an identification with a power center which is proudly nonwhite and openly challenges white domination.

Garvey and Garveyism

E. U. Essien-Udom

The phenomenon generally described as "black nationalism" among Negroes in the New World was given the clearest and loudest expression by Marcus Mosiah Garvey, who has been described by his biographer, Edmund D. Cronon,[1] as a "largely self-educated but supremely confident black man." Marcus Mosiah Garvey was born on August 17, 1887, to Marcus and Sarah Garvey in the little town of Saint Ann's Bay, Saint Ann, Jamaica, West Indies.

Garvey's father is said to have been a descendant of the

FROM E. U. Essien-Udom, Introduction to *Philosophy and Opinions of Marcus Garvey.* Copyright © 1967 by Frank Cass & Company Ltd. Reprinted by permission of Humanities Press, Inc. and Frank Cass Ltd.

Maroons—these were Africans who, having fled to the hills to establish free communities after the English had captured Jamaica from the Spaniards in 1655, successfully repulsed several British military assaults, and in 1739 gained local autonomy from the white rulers of Jamaica. He was a master mason and was well read. A stern and reticent man, he appears to have been self-centered, and often given to brooding. However, a contemporary has remarked that he stood shoulder-high above the inhabitants of Saint Ann's Bay. Sarah Garvey has been described as the opposite of her husband in every way. A Jewish woman who knew both Sarah and Marcus reports that "she was one of the most beautiful black women" she had seen: ". . . her skin was black and soft as velvet; her eyes jet black, large, liquid and sad. Her voice was gentle and caressing, her figure well shaped and erect. She was a regular Church-goer at the Wesleyan Methodist Church. Mr. Garvey only attended funerals, which were not often. . . ."[2]

The Garveys had eleven children; all but two, Marcus Mosiah and his sister, Indiana, died in childhood. It is said that Sarah Garvey wanted to name her youngest and only surviving son Moses, hoping that he would "be like Moses, and lead his people." His father who believed in astromancy, insisted on naming him Marcus. Said he, "any boy born under the planet Leo—the Lion—when the Sun is in the ascendancy is bound to be a leader in his line." A compromise was struck, Sarah added Mosiah as a middle name; and truly the young man named Marcus Mosiah Garvey later became the "Black Moses" for millions of his race.

The Garveys were not wealthy. Unlike the big plantation owners who sent their children to secondary schools and colleges in England, they might have been able to send their only son to Kingston (the Capital) for higher education. Marcus Mosiah indeed had hoped that he would attend school in Kingston but because of his father's involvement in unnecessary court actions, owing to his "stubbornness," he lost his properties including all his lands except the plot where his house stood. Consequently, Marcus Mosiah received his entire formal education at a local elementary school. At 14, he was forced to leave school and was apprenticed to learn printing with his godfather, Mr. Burrowes. Here, Garvey took advantage of a substantial library owned by Mr. Burrowes, who allowed him free access to it. Three years later (1904), he left Saint Ann's Bay to seek work as a printer at Kingston.

In Kingston, Garvey found employment at one of Jamaica's largest printing firms, the P. A. Benjamin Company. There, he made rapid advancements so that at 20, Garvey had become a master-printer and foreman. In 1907, he was involved in a strike called by the Printers' Union, the first labor organization to be established in Jamaica. The printers had demanded wage increases and better working conditions. When their demands were not met, they went on strike. Although the management promised an increase in Garvey's pay, the foreman went on strike with the workers. For this, he was blacklisted by his employer. Because his activities as the strike leader had prejudiced private employers against him, Garvey left the Company to work at the Government Printing Office.

His experiences had led Garvey to believe that only organized action could improve the position of the black worker. In 1910, this young man who was increasingly becoming restless started a periodical, the *Garvey's Watchman,* which proved an unsuccessful venture. He then helped to establish the National Club, a political organization which published *Our Own,* a fortnightly publication. At this time, Garvey associated with one Dr. Love, who was born in the Bahamas and educated in England. Dr. Love, publisher of the *Advocate,* spent the best years of his life in Jamaica, where he invested time and money for the uplift of the black masses. His example and support were of considerable importance for Garvey. By now, Garvey had realized that effective cultural and political activities would require full time commitment as well as money. Eventually, he left his job at the Government Printing Office and decided to go to one of his maternal uncles in Costa Rica, where he hoped to earn enough money to return and continue his work in Jamaica.

In Costa Rica, his uncle helped him to get a job as a time-keeper with the United Fruit Company. There, Garvey was terribly disturbed by the plight of the black workers in the United Fruit Company's plantations. He was now more determined than ever before to work for the improvement of the lot of the masses of his race wherever they may be. He gave up his job at the plantation to go to Port Limón (the Capital) where he protested to the British Consul about the treatment of Jamaican Negroes working on the plantations. His protest fell on deaf ears. Garvey was both disappointed and convinced that no white man would ever "regard the life of a black man equal to that of a white man." At Limón, he started another paper called *La Nacionale* but he could not sustain it owing to lack of support from the apathetic Negro peasants. His uncle helped him to go to Bocas del Toro, Republic of Panama, where he experienced the same abuse and exploitation of the black worker. He worked there for some months, then went to Colón and started another paper called *La Prensa*. Garvey continued his travels in South America. He visited Ecuador, Nicaragua, Spanish Honduras, Colombia, and Venezuela. His experience was the same everywhere: exploitation and abuse of black workers, especially West Indians. Failing to secure the co-operation of British officials in these countries for the protection of British West Indian workers, Garvey returned to Jamaica in 1911, hoping that he could enlist the Jamaican government's sympathy and action for the protection of West Indian black workers in South America. He also hoped to acquaint the Jamaicans at home with the true working conditions in South America. Apparently, Garvey found the British officials at Kingston equally as indifferent to the plight of the Negroes as those officials he had approached in South America.

In 1912, Garvey went to London to learn what he could about the condition of Negroes in other parts of the British Empire. There, he met Duse Mohammed, publisher of the *African Times and Orient Review* (London) and later the *Comet* (Lagos, Nigeria). Through this association with an ardent pan-African nationalist, and contacts with African and West Indian nationalists, students and seamen, Garvey became deeply agitated by the colonial question, especially as it affected his African "fatherland." In addition, he read extensively on Africa.

In London, Garvey had also developed a keen interest in the racial problems in the United States of America. Influenced by Booker T. Washington's autobiography, *Up from Slavery,* Garvey was traumatically struck by the deteriorated position of the Negro people throughout the world. Almost ecstatically Garvey asked himself: "Where is the black man's Government? Where is his King and kingdom? Where is his President, his country, and his ambassador, his army, his navy, his men of big affairs? I could not find them, and then I declared, I will help to make them." This fantastic reaction and resolution are best understood if it is remembered that by the end of the last century practically the whole of Africa, excepting Egypt, Ethiopia and Liberia, were firmly under foreign domination. Similarly, in the New World the optimism which followed the emancipation of African slaves during the 19th century had waned. In the United States especially this ill-founded optimism was totally shattered with the introduction of the "Black Codes" in the South, and the collapse of the Reconstruction. Attempt was made in all but name to re-enslave the Negro masses, and everywhere in the Southern United States they were denied elementary rights of citizenship, were terrorized by physical violence, and, for all practical purposes, "lynched" economically. In Northern United States, Negroes constituted the most depressed bottom of the urban proletariat.

Garvey left England in the summer of 1914 inspired with the idea of "uniting all the Negro peoples of the world into one great body to establish a country and government absolutely their own." He envisaged the coming of "a new world of black men, not peons, serfs, dogs and slaves, but of a nation of sturdy men making their impress upon civilization and causing a new light to dawn upon the human race." Five days after his arrival in Jamaica, he established the Universal Negro Improvement Association and African Communities League (U.N.I.A.) and invited all the Negro people or "persons of Negro or African parentage" to join him in the crusade for rehabilitation of the race. Garvey became the President and Travelling Commissioner of the new organization. He was to be assisted by Thomas Smikle as Vice-President, Eva Aldred as President of the Ladies' Division, and T. A. McCormack as General Secretary; and Amy Ashwood, who later became Garvey's first wife, as Associate Secretary. Between 1914 and March 1916, Garvey laboured to unite the Negro masses in Jamaica, and to educate the "black bourgeoisie" to appreciate their responsibility towards the proletarians among their race. His efforts were largely unsuccessful, partly because of the hostility of the mulattoes to the

U.N.I.A. and partly because of the apathy of the under-privileged Negro masses.

Meanwhile, Garvey had learned about Booker T. Washington and the help the latter was receiving from influential whites in the United States. He was particularly interested in Washington's program at Tuskegee Institute, Alabama, which emphasized industrial and technical education of the Negroes. Garvey believed that the establishment of trade colleges along the same lines would help in improving the skills of Jamaican Negroes. The U.N.I.A.'s campaign to establish trade colleges received support from the white Mayor of Kingston, the Governor of the Island, and a Roman Catholic Bishop, but the scheme was vigorously opposed by "some of these coloured men of the island who did not want to be classified as Negroes but as whites."

In 1915, Garvey wrote to Booker T. Washington, who encouraged him to visit Tuskegee. However, he did not visit the United States until March 23, 1916, when he arrived in Harlem, New York. Washington was dead by this time. Garvey's arrival in the United States was timely. With the death of the Sage of Tuskegee, the leadership contest which for nearly twenty years had raged between Washington and Dr. W. E. B. Du Bois, who had repudiated the former's philosophy, was far from resolved. In a sense, Garvey was to fill the vacuum left by Washington and, inevitably, he was even more savagely assailed by Du Bois and the Negro intelligentsia generally. Thus he inherited all the prejudices of the assimilationist Negro leadership against Washington but none of the support or prestige which the Sage of Tuskegee had enjoyed among Negroes and influential white leaders.

Washington's philosophy enunciated in his celebrated "Atlanta Compromise" address of 1895 has been summed up thusly: "Do not antagonize the white majority. Do not ask for the right to vote. Do not fight for civil liberties or against segregation. Go to school. Work hard. Save money. Buy property. Some day, the other things may come." These were the ideas openly challenged by Du Bois, who believed that the Negroes' retreat from demanding full social and political equality would leave them in a state of permanent subordination. To mobilize militant Negro opinion in support of full social and political equality (and certainly against Washington's conservatism), Du Bois organized the Niagara Movement in 1905. The movement comprised mainly one faction of the Negro elite, but did not directly involve the masses. Its influence on both black and white opinion was probably very limited. However, in 1909, the National Association for the Advancement of Colored People (N.A.A.C.P.), comprised of several prominent Negroes (including Du Bois) and liberal whites, was founded. The N.A.A.C.P., known for its program of integrating Negroes in the United States and for being largely responsible for destroying the legal basis of Negro subordination, was arrayed against Garvey. At any rate, intense leadership rivalry developed between spokesmen of the Negro elite and Garvey.

Garvey's arrival in the United States in 1916 was timely in another sense. The existence of large concentrations of an urbanized and disillusioned Negro proletariat in the ghettos of Northern United States provided material for his militant nationalism. Their disillusionment was keener at the end of the First World War in which many Negroes had laid down their lives in defense of democracy abroad. They had hoped that the principles for which they had fought would be extended to them at home. Nearly 400,000 Negroes had served in the armed forces during the War, and Negro civilians at home had patriotically purchased more than $250,000,000 worth of bonds and stamps in the five major Liberty Loan drives.

In spite of their sacrifice, there was little improvement in the status of Negroes. Perhaps the only real change was in the Negro mood itself. The rights of citizenship had not been extended to the vast majority. Everywhere the tempo of violence against Negroes had been intensified during and after the War. In September 1917, Negro soldiers clashed with civilians in Houston (Texas); thirteen of them were speedily and summarily tried and executed; and forty-one others were sentenced to imprisonment for life, but were later pardoned and reinstated. In the same year, East St. Louis was the scene of a violent race riot in which at least forty Negroes lost their lives. In 1919, there were a total of twenty-six race riots in a number of cities throughout the country. The Ku Klux Klan reared its ugly head again in 1915 and spread its diabolical influence in twenty-seven states, including three Midwest states, New York and parts of New England. The number of Negroes lynched annually had also increased during the War years. This was partially the state of affairs during the first few years of Garvey's arrival in the United States.

Garvey established a branch of the Universal Negro Improvement Association (U.N.I.A.) in Harlem in 1917. In two months, he built up a new organization of about 1,500 members. Five years later, the membership had increased to "several" million Negroes in the United States, the West Indies, Latin America, and Africa. Although reliable figures on total membership of the U.N.I.A. are not available, one million represents the most conservative estimate; Garvey himself suggested six million.

Garvey was a pan-African nationalist. Undoubtedly, his basic commitment and dedication were the total liberation of Africa from alien rule, and the eventual establishment of a united, virile and powerful African state. He was aware that "all of us may not live to see the higher accomplishment of an African empire—so strong and powerful as to compel respect of mankind, but we in our life time can so work and act as to make the dream a possibility within another generation." Every other activity of Garvey was either secondary or instrumental to this basic goal: the acquisition of political power in Africa by "Africans abroad and at home." He tended to analogize, and not without some justification, the problem of New World Negroes with colonialism. After all, the Negroes in diaspora as well as those in Africa were subjected to comparable economic exploitation and social discrimination by white rulers and capitalists. He believed firmly that until Africa was liberated, there was no real hope for black people anywhere.

Consistent with his pan-African objectives, Garvey tended to regard the New World Negroes as a vanguard for Africa's liberation from alien rule. His strategy may be said to have been "selected colonization" of parts of Africa by pioneering members of his organization, technicians, educators, doctors, and others equipped with the means to help in African reconstruction. His opponents generally seized on this aspect of his program and maliciously charged him with proposing a mass exodus of New World Negroes "back-to-Africa." Mrs. Amy Jacques-Garvey has appropriately summed up seven important principles of his strategy:

"(i) Awakening and uniting Negroes the world over;

(ii) Changing the thinking of the aroused to a realization of manhood potential abilities;

(iii) Channelling the newly released emotional energies and resentment into constructive individual and racial interests;

(iv) Mass sacrificial work and struggle to reach embryonic nationhood—the interim stage;

(v) Through legislation and otherwise to stress mass education along scientific and industrial lines, also character building which are the sinews of any nation in peace or war;

(vi) The preparation of nationalists for the grave responsibilities of leading and directing young nations, whose people have been denied the principles and advantages of early preparation;

(vii) The final efforts to unite and keep together the young nations not only in (sic) their own protection, but as leaders of those still suffering under Colonial and Protectorate rule."

Given these objectives, it is needless to remark that the *Philosophy and Opinions of Marcus Garvey* is, in the nature of doctrine and propaganda, meant to arouse and to induce a particular type of action. It is also a record of the reactions and yearnings of the oppressed masses of Negroes in the New World. Unswerving commitment and dedication to the cause of the "fatherland" or the race, discipline, sacrifice, and the quality of self-reliance were required of all members of the U.N.I.A.

Garvey was keenly interested in building up an economic base as an indispensable unit of racial emancipation, for, said he: "The reliance of our race upon the progress and achievements of others for a consideration in sympathy, justice and rights is like a dependence upon a broken stick, resting upon which will eventually consign you to the ground. . . ." Through effective economic organization he hoped to establish world-wide co-operation among the Negro people.

Garvey's economic program included the establishment of the Black Star Steamship Company (which consisted of four ill-fated ships) and the Negro Factory Corporation. He sent to the Republic of Liberia a commercial and industrial mission of technicians who were to establish a settlement there. However, his effort to find a foothold for the U.N.I.A. in this African Republic was foiled, partly by British, French and American pressures on the Liberian President to repudiate the agreements between his government and the U.N.I.A. The U.N.I.A.'s commercial enterprises were complete failures partly because of sheer incompetence, which is often emphasized, but also because of sabotage from within and without.

The movement had other auxiliaries: the African Orthodox Church whose influence spread beyond the United States, the Universal African Legion, a semi-military organization, the Universal Black Cross Nurses, the Universal African Motor Corps, the Juvenile and the Black Flying Eagles, all equipped with officers and uniforms. In 1924, the Negro Political Union was established "to consolidate the political union of the Negro through which the race would express its political opinion." This was Garvey's first effort to participate directly in the domestic politics of the United States. He supported Calvin Coolidge, the Republican Presidential nominee. By this time, however, Garvey had become entangled with the United States Government over the business activities of the U.N.I.A. A weekly newspaper, the *Negro World,* edited by Garvey, was the main propaganda organ of the movement.

Apart from reaching his followers, through the *Negro World,* or other publications, Garvey brought together delegates from local branches at an annual convention. The first Convention was held in New York on August 1, 1920. It was attended by delegates from 25 countries—including countries in the West Indies, Central and South America, and Africa. An estimated 25,000 Negroes including delegates assembled at the Madison Square Garden on August 2, to hear Garvey deliver the keynote address to the Convention. The ceremony opened with the Universal Ethiopian Anthem spiritedly sung by the delegates.

Addressing the Convention, Garvey told his audience, "We are the descendants of a suffering people; we are the descendants of a people determined to suffer no longer. We shall organize the 400,000,000 Negroes of the world into a vast organization to plant the banner of freedom on the great continent of Africa. . . . If Europe is for the Europeans, then Africa shall be for the black people of the world. We say it, we mean it. . . ." The Convention was a spectacular success. Harlemites were in festive mood and thousands were thrilled by the parade of the U.N.I.A.'s African Legion, the Black Cross Nurses (200 strong and smartly attired in white), and children, organized into a special auxiliary, marched along with them. The Convention adopted the "Declaration of Rights of the Negro Peoples of the World" and unanimously elected 33-year-old Garvey the Provisional President of Africa and President-General and Administrator of the U.N.I.A. A high Executive Council consisting of 18 members was also elected. Together with Garvey, they constituted the "Provisional Government" of a United Africa. After the members of the High Executive Council had been sworn in, Garvey conferred on them peerages and knighthoods such as Duke of the Nile. Others were made Knights of the Distinguished Service Order of Ethiopia, Ashanti and Mozambique. They were all provided with robes and capes, patterned after the British orders of chivalry. The Convention was a singular achievement the like of which had not been known before by the Negro people in the United States or elsewhere. Garvey had set in motion a mass movement with wide implications. In doing so, he threatened the security and courted the dedicated opposition of the established assimilation-oriented Negro leadership. Similarly, he aroused the suspicion of officials of the United States and the outright opposition of the colonial powers.

Opposition of Negro leaders to Garvey and Garveyism was both persistent and uncompromising. They resented Garvey as a person. Some, in fact, employed the most abusive epithets for describing his physical appearance. Robert Bagnall, an official of the N.A.-A.C.P., for example, described him as "of unmixed stock . . . with protruding jaws and heavy jowls, small bright pig-like eyes and rather bull-dog face." In turn, however, Garvey regarded people like Bagnall as "bastards" who "hate the Negro blood of their mothers, and endeavour to build up a society based on colour of skin, and not on achievement and worth." Garvey's antagonists regarded him as an alien, a Jamaican. He was an upstart, and had challenged the leadership of the "sons of the soil." He ought to go back to Jamaica "to carry on his work in his own home and among his own people and to accomplish some of his ideals. Let him do it. We will be the first to applaud any success he may have." (The *Crisis* said editorially in 1928.) Because he had little formal education, he was utterly despised by American Negro intellectuals and the rising black bourgeoisie generally. He was a threat to the leadership of the Negro Church as well, and the founding of the African Orthodox Church further exacerbated the rivalry. The Negro elite had always shied away from mass movements and was repelled by the U.N.I.A. Garvey was equally opposed to them, and regarded the mulattoes among his opponents as traitors of the Negro race. Ideologically, there was no meeting ground between Garvey and his Negro opponents—churchmen, politicians, trade unionists, socialists or communists. Instead, Garvey found some affinities between his ideas and those of white segregationists in Southern United States. While his opponents considered that Garvey was leading the Negro masses into a blind alley, he regarded their quest for cultural assimilation as leading Negroes ultimately to "racial suicide." His opponents were jubilant when in early January 1922, Garvey was arrested on a charge of using the mail to defraud.

The Black Star Company was Garvey's most ambitious commercial enterprise and his doom. Lacking business acumen himself or competent and honest associates, he risked his honor and movement on a highly competitive shipping business. Garvey's conception of the Black Star Line was not narrowly commercial. It was also thought of as a means of arousing self-confidence in the potentialities of the Negro people throughout the world. He appealed to followers through the pages of the *Negro World* and by mails to buy shares in the Company. He was able to raise substantial sums with which four worthless ships were purchased for a Company managed by some associates who were more cunning than scrupulous. In February 1922, a month after his arrest, Garvey and his associates were indicted and charged with knowingly using "fraudulent representations" and "deceptive artifices" in the sale of stock through the mails, and for advertising and selling space on a mythical ship. Garvey felt that this was a plot by "enemies of the Negro race" and enemies of his movement within the race, an attempt to besmirch his character and cause disaffection among his followers. With his arrest and indictment, opposition of Negro leaders to Garvey and Garveyism was intensified. Spearheaded by Chandler Owen and A. Philip Randolph, editors of the radical *Messenger Magazine,* Garvey's opponents united in August, 1922, under the auspices of a group called the Friends of Negro Freedom. They adopted the slogan "Garvey Must Go!" and demanded the deportation of the Jamaican. While his trial was pending, on January 15, 1923, eight prominent Negroes petitioned the United States Attorney-General, Mr. Harry M. Daugherty, to use his "full influence completely to disband and extirpate" the U.N.I.A. They pleaded that "the Attorney-General should vigorously and speedily push the government's case against Marcus Garvey for using the mails to defraud." The petitioners described the U.N.I.A. as a "vicious movement" and attacked Garvey as "an unscrupulous demagogue, who . . . sought to spread among Negroes distrust and hatred of all white people." The signatories included: Harry H. Pace, John E. Nail, Julia P. Coleman, all businessmen, Robert S. Abbott, Editor and Publisher of the *Chicago Defender,* Chandler Owen, Co-Editor of the *Messenger,* George V. Harris, Editor of the *New York News,* William Pickens, Field Secretary of the N.A.A.C.P., Robert W. Bagnall, Director of Branches of the N.A.A.C.P.

The trial of Garvey and his three associates, which had been delayed for nearly a year, took place in this atmosphere of opposition by influential Negroes and official suspicion. Before the trial began in May, 1923, Garvey had petitioned for the disqualification of Circuit Judge Julian W. Mack, who had been designated the trial judge. He argued that Judge Mack was a member of the National Association for the Advancement of Colored People and that he could not be impartial. Garvey recalled the fact that most of the signatories of the "Garvey Must Go!" petition to the Attorney-General five months earlier were members of the N.A.A.C.P. He observed also the sustained campaign against him and the U.N.I.A. by the *Crisis,* the official organ of the N.A.A.C.P. Garvey concluded that Judge Mack "would be unconsciously swayed to the side of the Government" and pleaded that another judge who was likely to be impartial be named. Judge Mack denied Garvey's motion. Although he admitted that he had contributed to the N.A.A.C.P., he rejected Garvey's conclusion from this fact. Garvey did not help his case when he dismissed his attorney a day after the trial had begun. He suspected his Negro lawyer, Cornelius W. McDougald, of possible complicity with the prosecution. From thence on, Garvey, a layman who probably had read some law on his own during his first visit to England, pleaded his own case before a white jury.

The Government's case rested on the assumption that Garvey and his co-defendants had knowingly and with criminal intent used the mails to sell Black Star shares fully aware that the Company was in a terrible financial condition. There is little evidence that this was the case. Specifically, Garvey was found guilty of having caused promotional material to be sent through the mails to Benny Dancy, "who had testified with some confusion to having received such matter before he purchased his fifty-three shares of Black Star stock."[3] The verdict, concludes Cronon, who has studied the record of the trial meticulously, "was somewhat strange in that the other three Black Star co-defendants were acquitted of any complicity in the crime."[4] Nevertheless, he was sentenced to five years imprisonment. Was justice done? Mr. Armin Kohn, a white lawyer who handled Garvey's appeal, asked by newspaper reporters to comment on the case, is quoted to have said: "In my twenty-three years of practice at the New York Bar, I have never handled a case in which the defendant has been treated with such manifest unfairness and with such a palpable attempt at persecution as this one."[5] It is infinitely difficult to resist the conclusion that Garvey's conviction was political. However, in 1927, President Coolidge commuted the sentence, and in December of that year, Garvey was deported from the United States as an undesirable alien. He returned to Jamaica where he continued to work for Negro emancipation. He later went to London where he established the headquarters of the U.N.I.A. but died there on June 10, 1940.

After his deportation from the United States, Garvey tried to revive the U.N.I.A. but was unable to recapture its pre-1925 influence and vitality. Disillusioned and diminished in number, Garvey's followers in the United States were split into several factions. Nevertheless, Garveyites are still active today in Harlem, Chicago, and other cities. They are few in number and organizationally weak. In New York City, the African Nationalist Pioneer Movement is one neo-Garvey group which continues to keep his memory alive on the streets of Harlem. However, the most important off-shoot of Garveyism, modified in important respects, is the Black Muslim movement, known officially as the Nation of Islam, led by Elijah Muhammad. This movement shares Garvey's belief that the Negro problem in the United States can never be satisfactorily resolved. The Muslims assert that the only satisfactory and permanent solution to the problem of black-white relations is the separation of Negroes from the dominant white majority and the establishment of a "Negro homeland" politically controlled by a black majority. In reality, however, the Muslim movement has not developed any political program whatsoever for the realization of this goal. Its influence is limited to the United States, where its survival has been precarious in recent years.

In Retrospect

The public activities and some of Garvey's striking ideas have been stressed in this brief outline. But they do not give a complete picture of this complex man who, with utter disregard to personal safety or family security, took upon himself the incredible assignment of rescuing the Negro race from what the late Pandit Nehru once called the "horrible and infinite tragedy" of Africa in the modern world. More than any of his contemporaries, Garvey appreciated the cultural, economic, and political foundations of Negro subordination in and outside Africa. He understood and exploited the profound cultural and social alienation of the masses of Negroes in the New World, especially in the United States, and their search for identity in that environment. Because he could not conceive the liberation of New World Negroes without their affirmation and assertion of an African cultural heritage, Garvey sought to instill in his followers a sense of pride and patriotism in their African "fatherland." Although this idea was not entirely original (other West Indian and American Negroes had propagated it earlier), his movement popularized it among the masses. In Africa, the necessity to affirm the dignity of African cultural heritage had its advocates in Edward W. Blyden and the Ghanaian lawyer, Casely Hayford. Today, this need finds expression in the cultural concept of *Negritude*. President Leopold S. Senghor of Senegal is one of its major proponents. A major organ through which *Negritude* is propagated is *Présence Africaine,* a cultural journal founded in 1947 by Mr. Alioun Diop "to affirm the presence or ethos, of the black communities of the world, and to defend the originality of their way of life and the dignity of their culture."

Like the proponents of *Negritude,* Garvey was keenly aware of the need for the Negro people in and outside Africa to acquire Western education, especially science and technology. In a special sense, he wanted Africans Westernized in this narrow sense so that they could develop industries for the benefit of the Negro people. However, he believed that Westernization ought to take place within the framework of an African identity and humanism. But Westernization, as well as every other aspect of Garvey's doctrines, was instrumental to one overriding objective, namely, the acquisition of political power in Africa by the Negro people. He believed that:

Power is the only argument that satisfies man.

Except the individual, the race or nation has POWER that is exclusive, it means that that individual, race or nation will be bound by the will of the other who possesses this great qualification. . . . Hence it is advisable for the Negro to get power of every kind. POWER in education, science, industry, politics and higher government. That kind of power will stand out signally, so that other races and nations can see, if they will not see, FEEL.

Negro unity, or in contemporary terms African unity, was a necessity for the true emancipation of the Negro race; for, said Garvey: "The powers opposed to Negro progress will not be influenced in the slightest by mere verbal protests on our part. They realize only too well that protests of this kind contain nothing but the breath expended in making them." The fruitless protests of African states against *apartheid* in South Africa, the Unilateral Declaration of Independence in Southern Rhodesia, and against Portugal's African Colonies may not justify Garvey's contention but it adds considerable weight to his argument. There is a

similarity between Garvey's concern for a united and powerful
Africa and a recent call for black solidarity by Chief Remi Fani-
Kayode, former Deputy Premier in Western Nigeria. In his book,
Blackism (1965), Chief Fani-Kayode writes:

> Blackism is a call to the states of Africa to unite. A positive, aggres-
> sive, and direct force. Naked and unashamed Blackism, a force to weld
> together the states of Africa into one unified entity. Not a negative
> force activated against anyone, but a positive force for progress,
> strength and power. . . . I may as well copy the communist slogan:
> "Black men of the world unite, you have nothing to lose but your shame,
> humiliation, suffering and the contempt of the white man". . . .[6]

Because of his opposition to miscegenation and advocacy of
racial purity, Negro and white opponents accused Garvey of
racism. But this was also the belief of his white contemporaries
who, almost universally, believed that miscegenation was a bad
thing. While it is not necessary to explain away Garvey's racial pre-
dispositions, there is considerable evidence that he was not a hater
of whites because they are white. He hated the way the whites have
abused the Negro people in modern times. Reflecting on power,
Garvey abhorred the thought that the Negro people could use their
prowess to oppress the human race: "I pray God that we shall
never use our physical prowess to oppress the human race, but we
will use our strength, physically, morally and otherwise to preserve
humanity and civilization."

Garvey's influence on the Negro freedom movements in the
United States and Africa will never be fully known. Its impact in
raising the morale and instilling self-esteem and racial pride among
the Negro proletariat in the New World was considerable. Because
he was a prohibited immigrant in all the colonial possessions in
Africa and in Liberia, Garvey had never set foot on African soil.
But even there, his influence on some of the budding nationalists
was equally significant. Although opinion was divided among the
African intelligentsia of his time, the majority probably regarded
Garvey highly. In Nigeria, for example, the *Lagos Weekly Record*
in its editorial of February 7, 1920 wrote of the Garvey movement:

> The American Negro is out to secure for the black race the best
> possible conditions in the after-the-war world. What is the African

Negro prepared to do? The way has been boldly and clearly marked out for us by our brothers across the sea; all we have to do is to fall in line; follow the examples they have given us of oneness of purpose and aim. The present time is the most opportune and favourable for the initiation of any great movement for the betterment of our race. . . .

Perhaps one of the most significant testimonies of the extent of Garvey's reputation is that of the King of Swaziland, who is reported to have told Mrs. Garvey that he knew the names of only two black men in the Western world: Jack Johnson, the boxer who defeated the white man, Jim Jeffries, and Marcus Garvey. Former Ghanaian President, Kwame Nkrumah, one of Africa's most ardent pan-Africanists, acknowledged Garvey's influence as the most important during his years as a student in the United States. "I think," said Dr. Nkrumah, "that of all the literature that I studied, the book that did more than any other to fire my enthusiasm was the *Philosophy and Opinions of Marcus Garvey.* . . ."[7]

Garvey's stature, in spite of his deficiencies as a leader and his utter lack of business sense, has grown steadily since the late twenties. Writing in 1930, James Weldon Johnson of the United States said of him:

Garvey failed; yet he might have succeeded with more than moderate success. He had energy and daring and the Napoleonic personality, the personality that draws masses of followers. He stirred the imagination of the Negro masses as no Negro ever had. He raised more money in a few years than any other Negro organization had ever dreamed of. He had power and great possibilities within his grasp. But his deficiencies as a leader outweighed his abilities.[8]

In 1940, the year of Garvey's death, Du Bois, who had been one of his arch-enemies, had this to say in retrospect:

It was a grandiose and bombastic scheme, utterly impracticable as a whole, but it was sincere and had some practical features; and Garvey proved not only an astonishing popular leader, but a master of propaganda. Within a few years, news of his movement, of his promises and plans, reached Europe and Asia, and penetrated every corner of Africa.[9]

Sixteen years after his death, the Council of the City of Kingston, Jamaica, honoured Garvey by erecting a memorial bust in the

King George VI Park. This monument was unveiled in 1956 in an impressive ceremony attended by thousands of people, including his widow, Mrs. Amy Jacques-Garvey, Sir Hugh Foot, then the British Governor of the Island, members of the Jamaican Executive and Legislative Councils, representatives of the Consular Corps as well as the Chambers of Commerce, and high Church dignitaries—Roman Catholic and Protestant. Since independence, the Jamaican Government has honored Garvey in many ways: it helped to exhume his body in London for burial in Jamaica, and in 1965 the Government established the Marcus Garvey Prize for Human Rights consisting of £5,000 to be awarded in 1968 to "the person, who, in this generation, has contributed most significantly to the field of Human Rights." Recently, Dr. Martin Luther King, Jr., the Nobel Peace Prize Winner, acknowledged Garvey's contribution to the Negro's struggle for human rights in the United States. Speaking at Garvey's shrine in Kingston during his visit in June, 1965, Dr. King said that Garvey was "the first man of color in the history of the United States . . . on a mass scale and level to give millions of Negroes a sense of dignity and destiny and make the Negro feel he was somebody." In Africa, Garvey's importance as one of the forerunners of African nationalism or his place in the pan-African movement is generally acknowledged. In praise of him, Osita Egbuniwe wrote in 1948:[10]

> Nigeria, oh my Nigeria,
>
> .   .   .   .   .   .
>
> For thy redemption brave Garvey fell,
> But yet in the gang of the immortals,
> Thy sons shall fight unseen by mortals,
> And ere long regain thy pride, oh Nigeria.
>
> Nigeria, oh my Nigeria,
> Preserve and arm thy nationalists,
> Infuse in them the immortals' genius,
> For thy sons to lead and thy shores to save
> From the traitor's bows and the oppressor's sceptre.

16. The Harlem Renaissance

In the 1920's, Harlem gained an international reputation as the "capital" of black America. "This was the era," the black writer and NAACP leader James Weldon Johnson later recalled, "in which was achieved the Harlem of story and song; the era in which Harlem's fame for exotic flavor and colorful sensuousness was spread to all parts of the world; when Harlem was made known as the scene of laughter, singing, dancing, and primitive passions, and as the center of the new Negro literature and art." Johnson makes clear that what whites saw in Harlem was not the emerging slum but an image which fit their conception of black people, and of themselves. For the 1920's were a period of rebellion against puritanical and materialistic values and culture by white intellectuals, and many turned to blacks as symbols of the primitive passions and freedom from restraint which they themselves desired. These were the years of "slumming"—groups of whites visiting cabarets and dance halls in Harlem—and of Carl Van Vechten's novel *Nigger Heaven,* which portrayed life in the ghetto as a series of gambling dens and night clubs. For whites, the stereotype of the black as Sambo was replaced by the no less stereotyped image of the primitive, rhythmic African.

As the literary critic Robert Bone indicates in the following selection, the new black writers who emerged in

Harlem during the twenties were part of this wider movement in American culture. Poets and novelists like
Countee Cullen, Claude McKay, and Langston Hughes
were befriended and sponsored by white intellectuals and
published by white presses. Nonetheless, a real flowering
of culture did take place within Harlem in these years. The
black theater, for example, flourished and the opportunity
to serve all-black audiences freed black playwrights and
actors from many of the restraints which white theaters
had imposed upon them. And, during the 1920's, Broadway for the first time presented black actors in serious
dramatic roles, as well as great black singers and enter-
tainers like Florence Mills, Ethel Waters, and Bill
Robinson.

The term "New Negro," which has been used to characterize the Harlem Renaissance, had, Bone points out,
many meanings in the 1920's. In politics, it was associated
with the younger generation's increasing militancy both in
demanding equal rights and in supporting Garveyism. In
art, it meant the rejection of the established traditions and
stereotypes of black literature. "The day of Uncle Remus
as well as Uncle Tom is over," one black critic observed.
Previous black writers had tended to be spokesmen for the
black middle class, and their works had centered upon
stock situations such as the worthy black who suffers
because whites associate him with the lower classes. The
color line, such works implied, was unjust because it did
not observe class distinctions within the black community.
The most famous black writer before the Renaissance,
Paul Lawrence Dunbar, won great acclaim for his dialect
poetry, which usually gave voice to white stereotypes
regarding blacks. He portrayed slavery, for example, as a
time of joy for the slaves and friendship between the races.
Dunbar also wrote conventional poems, yet these were
ignored by his white audiences, although he personally
considered them his most important works.

The dilemma symbolized by Dunbar—the constraints
which white audiences consciously or unconsciously place

on black artists—remained a serious problem for the Renaissance writers, since they too were read mostly by whites. Yet because they existed in a vital black intellectual community, not in Dunbar's isolation, they could achieve a racial self-definition which escaped him. The writings of the Renaissance were characterized by a rejection of white values and stereotypes, and a search for black values to put in their place. This quest led to the roots of the black experience: the African past, the rural South, and the life of the lower-class urban black. Like their white friends, black writers emphasized the primitive and savage in black existence, and always drew a sharp contrast between Victorian western values and the elemental character of African and urban black life. Their writing was also marked by a strong element of protest and defiance. Claude McKay's "If We Must Die," which is often cited as the best single expression of this defiant attitude, declared that blacks would no longer allow themselves to be murdered defenselessly by whites:

> If we must die—let it not be like hogs
> Hunted and penned in an inglorious spot
>
> .   .   .   .
>
> Like men we'll face the murderous, cowardly pack,
> Pressed to the wall, dying, but fighting back!

The new black writers even rejected the God of white Christianity, identifying instead with the more primitive, pagan gods of Africa, or transforming the western Jesus into a black man. In "Heritage," Countee Cullen declared that while he went through the motions of worshiping the white Christian God, he secretly wished that "He I served were black," because only then could God fully understand the suffering that a black man had experienced.

Many middle-class black critics strongly resented the writings of the Renaissance school. When Claude McKay in *Home to Harlem* made his major character a free spirit who wandered from one scene of exotic life in Harlem to another in search of a beautiful girl he had known, one critic complained, "White people think we are buffoons, thugs and rotten anyway. Why should we waste so much energy to prove it?" And when Langston Hughes ended a poem with an elevator operator leaving his job:

> I been runnin' this
> Elevator too long
> Guess I'll quit now,

another insisted that no one should leave his job until he was sure of obtaining other employment. The critics of the Renaissance clearly still held to the view that "bad" blacks gave the race a "bad name" and inhibited the efforts of the middle class to achieve equality of rights. But they did have a point when they chided the younger writers for substituting one set of stereotypes of blacks for another. The black writer Sterling Brown summed it up when he wrote during the 1930's that, like the plantation legend, the Renaissance image of black life included everything but the servitude. Despite the fact that their pages were filled with lower-class blacks, Renaissance writers rarely concerned themselves with the dismal realities of life in Harlem. "The Harlem of the doubly handicapped black masses engaged in the grim, daily struggle for existence," James Weldon Johnson observed, was missing from their pages. "There are dramatic values in that Harlem, too; but they have hardly been touched." Not until the appearance of Richard Wright's *Native Son* in 1940 did a black writer successfully cope with the problem of portraying the full complexity of urban ghetto existence.

From *The Negro Novel in America*

ROBERT A. BONE

The Background of the Negro Renaissance

The Great Migration

Alain Locke has described the Negro Renaissance as "the mass movement of the urban immigration of Negroes, projected on the plane of an increasingly articulate elite."[1] The Great Migration to which Locke refers was the most important event in the history of the American Negro since his emancipation from slavery. In the course of this migration, centuries of historical development were traversed in a few decades. It was not merely a movement of the colored population from South to North, or from country to city; it was the sudden transplanting of a debased feudal folk from medieval to modern America.

From 1890 to 1920, while the business and professional class was fighting for the right to rise, the base of the Negro social pyramid was shifting from a peasantry to an urban proletariat. In these decades more than 2,000,000 Negroes left the farm for the factory.[2] . . .

The Great Migration brought the Negro masses into contact with the quickened pulse of the modern city. There they were faced with a mass of strange experiences which forced them to revise their traditional ways of thinking. The crowded ghetto, unlike the isolated farm, provided a basis for a vigorous group life. A rising standard of living and better educational opportunities fostered new attitudes of self-respect and independence. In a word, the Negro's urban environment lifted him to a new plane of

---

FROM Robert Bone, *The Negro Novel in America*. Copyright © 1958, 1965 by Yale University Press. Reprinted by permission of Yale University Press.

consciousness. Such a profound transformation could hardly occur among the masses without reverberations in the world of letters. The new group experience called for a new literary movement to interpret it.

It was a foregone conclusion that Harlem should become the center of the new movement. The largest Negro community in the world, Harlem was itself a product of the Great Migration. Doubling its population from 1900 to 1920, it was wrested from the whites by sheer weight of numbers. As it grew to metropolitan proportions, it gradually acquired the character of a race capital. Negroes from Africa and the West Indies, from North and South, and from all classes and backgrounds poured into the crucible of dark Manhattan. Harlem thus provided the Negro artist with an infinite variety of human subjects, as well as an opportunity to observe urban life at its maximum intensity.

Moreover, this black metropolis evolved within the womb of a city which was the literary, musical, and theatrical capital of America. Harlem meant proximity to Broadway, to the little magazines and the big publishing houses, to Greenwich Village and its white intellectuals, to avant-garde literary groups and successful, established writers. It offered a unique, cosmopolitan milieu, where artists and intellectuals of all kinds could find mutual stimulation. Under the circumstances, it is hardly surprising that Harlem became the cultural center of Negro America.

Rise of an Intelligentsia

Before any group can prosper artistically, as Arthur Koestler notes, it must produce an intelligentsia.[3] This social layer arises in bourgeois society, according to Koestler, when enough gifted individuals have broken with their middle-class background to form a community of emancipated intellectuals. Shortly after World War I just such an intellectual community began to form in Harlem. Young men and women of introspective leanings came to Harlem from every corner of the nation, drawn by the changing kaleidoscope of metropolitan life.

These young intellectuals were a different breed from the Negro writers of the prewar period. Like their contemporaries of the Lost Generation, they reached maturity in a world of crumbling values.

"I had no reason to think," wrote Claude McKay, "that the world I lived in was permanent, solid, and unshakable."[4] Lacking the comforting assurance of an integrated moral universe, they were forced to cope as best they could with what Henry Adams called 20th-century multiplicity. Unsure of their positive goals, they began by sweeping aside the moral debris of the previous era. At one stroke they cut through the taboos of the Victorian Age, demolished its shallow optimism, repudiated its value system, and entered the mainstream of contemporary intellectual life.

The significance of the Negro intelligentsia, which emerged for the first time in the 1920's, lay precisely in this realm of values. The middle-class writer, as Koestler suggests, is inclined not toward new hierarchies of values but toward climbing to the top of the existing hierarchy. The intelligentsia, more independent in outlook, debunks existing values and attempts to replace them with values of its own. Koestler's theoretical point may thus serve to sharpen the contrast between the early Negro novelist and his Renaissance successor. The early novelists were loyal members of the middle class who desired only equal rights within the status quo. The younger writers of the 1920's were the second generation of educated Negroes; they were the wayward sons of the rising middle class.[5] In psychological terms, they were rebelling against their fathers and their fathers' way of life.

This pattern of rebellion appears in the lives of many Renaissance authors. Langston Hughes, for example, observes in his autobiography, "My father was what the Mexicans call *muy americano,* a typical American. . . . He was interested only in making money."[6] Hughes' most vivid memory of his father was his constant injunction to hurry up. His father tried to hurry him through a course in bookkeeping and then through Columbia University, but Hughes left college to ship out, taking his Grand Tour on a tramp steamer. Claude McKay's rebellion carried him from Greenwich Village to the Left Bank, and from militant Negro nationalism to the early Communist party. Jean Toomer abandoned a law career for literature and the Gurdjieff Institute. Countee Cullen, whose father was a minister, has recorded his rebellion against religious formalism in his novel *One Way to Heaven.*

The rebellious mood of the emerging Negro intelligentsia is

revealed by the little magazines they founded. *The Messenger,* for example, displayed as its credo:

> I am an Iconoclast.
> I break the limbs of idols
> And smash the traditions of men.

Fire, according to one of its founders, was intended "to burn up a lot of the old, dead, conventional Negro ideas of the past." In their rebelliousness and defiance the Negro writers of the 1920's were no different from their white contemporaries, who were engaged in a similar labor of destruction in such little magazines as *Broom, transition,* and *Secession.* The younger Negro intellectuals, whose consciousness was formed during the war years, were members of an uprooted generation. Critical, skeptical, iconoclastic, they raised the banner of the New Negro against the stubborn guardians of the Victorian tradition.

The New Negro Movement

The term "New Negro" presents certain difficulties, for it has been used to describe both a racial attitude and a literary movement. The extension of the term from its original meaning was the work of Alain Locke, who in 1925 published an anthology of younger writers entitled *The New Negro.* The title struck a responsive chord, and it soon became the accepted designation of the new literary movement. From the standpoint of literary history this was unfortunate. "New Negro" is not a descriptive term in any literary sense; basically it indicates a rejection of racial conservatism on the part of those who employ it. It is nonetheless of considerable subjective importance that Renaissance writers should think of themselves as "New Negroes." To establish the primary meaning of the term may therefore cast additional light on the period.

The New Negro, with his uncompromising demand for equal rights, was the end product of a long historical process which began when the Negro middle class emerged from slavery and entered upon a new kind of social relations. As the patriarchal relations of slavery were replaced by the contractual relations of bourgeois society, a corresponding psychological transformation took place. Feudal attitudes of servility and dependence were abandoned in favor of the sturdy bourgeois virtues of initiative and self-reliance. This psychological transformation crystallized politically when Du Bois challenged the "accommodating" leadership of Booker T. Washington in the name of universal manhood suffrage. Manhood suffrage, the basic aim of Du Bois' Niagara Movement, became a symbol of the new spirit which animated the Negro middle class. This sense of manhood, greatly enhanced by the Negro's participation in World War I, was passed on to the Renaissance generation as part of its spiritual heritage.

There is a direct line from the Niagara Movement of the early 1900's to the New Negro Movement of the 1920's. The descent may be traced through Negro defense organizations such as the NAACP and the National Urban League, and more precisely through their house organs, *Crisis* and *Opportunity*. These two periodicals and their editors, Jessie Fauset and Charles S. Johnson, did yeoman's work for the Negro Renaissance. They encouraged new talent, opened their pages to young writers, and offered cash prizes for outstanding literary achievement. In this manner, as well as through overt patronage, the Negro middle class made a substantial contribution to the birth of the New Negro Movement. Whether they were prepared to acknowledge the lusty and sometimes ungrateful infant which they sired is another matter.

As the Negro Renaissance gained momentum and its break with the tradition of Chesnutt and Dunbar became apparent, the term "New Negro" began to take on an additional connotation of modernism. As a result, it became intellectually fashionable to declare oneself a member of the New Negro coterie. Yet if the New Negro slogan created something of a vogue, it also provided the literary movement of the 1920's with a unifying idea. "New Negro" literary societies sprang up in several large cities;[7] New Negro magazines were founded by avant-garde writers; and one novelist playfully christened his first-born "the New Negro"! This self-consciousness, this sense of belonging to a movement, made for a high group morale, and for an atmosphere which encouraged literary effort. Moreover, in its own way the New Negro Movement expressed that determination to ring out the old and ring in the new which was the central theme of the decade.

Cultural Collaboration in the Jazz Age

The years following World War I were marked by a sudden upsurge of interest in Negro life and culture among the white intelligentsia. Manifestations of this interest were numerous and varied. Throughout the 1920's books on the Negro by white authors appeared in ever-increasing numbers. *Survey Graphic* came out with an issue devoted entirely to Harlem, while Albert and Charles Boni offered a prize of $1,000 for the best novel written by an American Negro. Musical reviews which featured Negro performers broke downtown box-office records, and nightly throngs of white "tourists" invaded Harlem, drawn to night club and cabaret by colored celebrities of musical and theatrical fame. By the mid-1920's the Negro had become a national pastime.

What had happened to change the intellectual climate from hostility and indifference to sympathetic, if often misguided, interest? For one thing the Jazz Age, which derived its very character from the Negro's music, was in full swing. With "flaming youth" leading the way, a popular uprising was in progress against the stuffiness and artificial restraint of the Victorian era. These were the years of postwar catharsis—of Freud and the sexual revolution, of heavy drinking in defiance of authority, of a wild dance called the Charleston, and of a wilder music which made its way from the bordellos of New Orleans to the night clubs of Chicago and New York. Somewhat to his surprise and not entirely to his liking, the Negro suddenly found himself called upon to uphold a new stereotype: he became a symbol of that freedom from restraint for which the white intellectual longed so ardently.

In the sophisticated art centers of Europe and America, interest in the Negro focused around the cult of the primitive. Insofar as it idealizes simpler cultures, primitivism is a romantic retreat from the complexities of modern life. Reflecting the writings of Sigmund Freud, it exalts instinct over intellect, Id over Super-Ego, and is thus a revolt against the Puritan spirit. For such an artistic movement the Negro had obvious uses: he represented the unspoiled child of nature, the noble savage—carefree, spontaneous, and sexually uninhibited. The discovery of primitive African sculpture and the ascendancy of jazz reinforced the development of this new stereotype.

Like all previous stereotypes, that of the primitive Negro exercised a coercive effect on the Negro novelist. As in the past, the degree of accommodation was astonishing; with few exceptions the Negro intelligentsia accepted this exotic image of themselves. Perhaps they found in primitivism a useful support for the cultural dualism which they espoused during the Renaissance period. In any event, the younger Negro writers were quite carried away. Langston Hughes wrote ecstatically of jazz as "the tom-tom of revolt," while Countee Cullen discovered "elemental" religion in a Harlem revival meeting. Claude McKay glorified the instinctive Negro in all of his novels, and proudly proclaimed the "primitive sexuality" of the Negro race. Jean Toomer, perhaps the most authentic exponent of Renaissance primitivism, wrote in a sophisticated vein of "the zoo-restrictions and keeper-taboos" of modern civilization.

Whatever its excesses, primitivism provided the common ground for a fruitful period of cultural collaboration. Works like Eugene O'Neill's *The Emperor Jones* (1920) and *All God's Chillun Got Wings* (1924), Waldo Frank's *Holiday* (1923), Sherwood Anderson's *Dark Laughter* (1925), Dubose Heyward's *Porgy* (1925) and *Mamba's Daughters* (1927), and Carl Van Vechten's *Nigger Heaven* (1926), acted as a spur to Negro writers and created a sympathetic audience for the serious treatment of Negro subjects. Personal association with white authors meant an end of cultural isolation and provincialism, and an immense gain in technical maturity for the Negro writer. In economic terms alone, considerable patronage and sponsorship occurred, while publishing forts and editorial desks capitulated in the face of a growing market for novels of Negro life. In the forefront of these developments, consciously promoting this cultural exchange, was a white *littérateur* named Carl Van Vechten.

Van Vechten's role in furthering the Negro Renaissance was unique. His literary salons provided a warm atmosphere in which artists and intellectuals of both races could break down their taboos against personal association. His one-man "know the Negro" campaign was eminently successful in overcoming prejudice and awkwardness among his white contemporaries. His efforts on behalf of individual Negro writers and artists were indefatigable, and were amply rewarded in later years when many of his former protégés entrusted their literary effects to his care.[8]

A more questionable contribution, at least in the eyes of some Negro critics, was Van Vechten's *Nigger Heaven,* a novel which appeared in 1926 and quickly ran through several editions. Emphasizing the bawdy and exotic aspects of Harlem life, and heavily influenced by primitivistic conceptions, *Nigger Heaven* shattered the complacency of the Negro intelligentsia by threatening to steal their literary thunder. For most of the Negro middle class the title of the novel was enough. Bitterly attacked in some quarters as a slander against the race, *Nigger Heaven* has been ably defended by James Weldon Johnson,[9] and requires no apologia here. It is sufficient to acknowledge its role in creating an audience for the exotic novel of Harlem life, and its influence on certain members of the so-called Harlem School.

The influence of white intellectuals on the Negro Renaissance ought not to be overestimated. Some Negro critics have charged the New Negro Movement with white domination, but a sober appraisal leaves no doubt of its indigenous character. The New Negro Movement was not a "vogue" initiated by white "literary faddists,"[10] but a serious attempt by the Negro artist to interpret his own group life. There were excesses, to be sure, for which the whites must bear their share of responsibility. Insofar as the Negro novelist adopted a pose in response to the "primitive" effusions of the white intellectual, it produced a certain shallowness in his work, and a legitimate suspicion that his novels, like his cabarets, were designed to entertain the white folks. In the long run, however, the Negro novelist outgrew his primitive phase; meanwhile it helped him to discover unsuspected values in his own folk culture.

The Essence of the Negro Renaissance

There is a phase in the growth of a derivative literature which corresponds to the adolescent rebellion in an individual—a time when it must cut loose from the parent literature and establish an independent existence. This phase occurred in American literature during the flowering of New England; it was highlighted by Emerson's famous Phi Beta Kappa address, in which he protests, "We have listened too long to the courtly Muses of Europe." The Negro Renaissance represents a similar impulse toward cultural autonomy on the part of the American Negro.

The Negro Renaissance was essentially a period of self-discovery, marked by a sudden growth of interest in things Negro. The Renaissance thus reversed the assimilationist trend of the prewar period, with its conscious imitation of white norms and its deliberate suppression of "racial" elements. The motivation for this sudden reversal was not primarily literary but sociological. The Negro Renaissance, as E. Franklin Frazier has observed, reflects a pattern of adjustment common to all ethnic minorities in America: "At first the group attempts to lose itself in the majority group, disdaining its own characteristics. When this is not possible, there is a new valuation placed upon these very same characteristics, and they are glorified in the eyes of the group."[11]

The discovery of autonomous "racial" values by the Renaissance generation was prompted by a wave of Negro nationalism which swept over the colored community in the wake of World War I. As a direct result of his war experience the American Negro became bitterly disillusioned with the promises of the white majority. Discrimination in the armed forces, brutal attacks on returning veterans, and the bloody riots of the summer of 1919 convinced the Negro that his sacrifices for the nation would be acknowledged only by renewed oppression. With every avenue of assimilation apparently closed, a strongly nationalistic reflex occurred on all levels of Negro society.

Among the Negro masses this reflex took the form of recruitment to Marcus Garvey's "Back to Africa" movement. Garvey's program, in spite of its utterly Utopian content, deserves the closest scrutiny, for it stirred the imagination of the Negro masses as never before or since.[12] Garvey held that the Negro must renounce all hope of assistance or understanding from American whites, leave the country, and build a new civilization in Africa. His secessionist movement preyed upon a dissatisfaction so deep that it amounted to despair of ever achieving a full life in America. His immense popularity stands as a sober warning to all who would underestimate the nationalism of the Negro masses.

Meanwhile the logic of events forced the Negro middle class to adopt what might be called a tactical nationalism. As the fluid patterns of the post-Reconstruction period hardened into a rigid and unyielding color line, it became increasingly clear to the Talented Tenth that they could never hope to breach this caste barrier as a special class of "white" Negroes. The war years in particular convinced them that they could not succeed short of an all-out assault on Jim Crow. Abandoning their former strategy, they turned to the Negro masses for support in the coming struggle.

This *rapprochement* with the black masses could not be consummated without great psychological effort. The habit of emphatically differentiating themselves from the "lower classes" was not easily relinquished by the Talented Tenth. Race leaders perceived at once that they would have to cultivate a mild nationalism in order to achieve a decent show of racial solidarity. One of their number, Jessie Fauset, has preserved this insight for posterity in her novel *Plum Bun:*

> Those of us who have forged forward are not able as yet to go our separate ways apart from the unwashed, untutored herd. We must still look back and render service to our less fortunate, weaker brethren. And the first step toward making this a workable attitude is the acquisition not so much of a racial love as a racial pride. A pride that enables us to find our own beautiful and praiseworthy, an intense chauvinism that is content with its own types, that finds completeness within its own group, that loves its own as the French love their country.[13]

The nationalist reflex of the Negro intelligentsia consisted of a withdrawal of allegiance from the values of the dominant culture, and a search for alternative values within their own tradition. Unlike the nationalism of the masses or of the middle class, that of the intelligentsia was not based on racial considerations alone. It was motivated by factors larger than, but including, race—factors related to the universal revolt of the modern artist from bourgeois civilization. The Negro intellectual of the 1920's shared fully in the spiritual alienation of the Lost Generation. Like the white expatriate, he rejected the chromium plate of American culture. His alienation as an artist caused him in turn to alter his goals as a Negro. Instead of advocating blind assimilation into a hopelessly materialistic culture, he began to think in terms of preserving his racial individuality.

The search for a distinctive tradition led in many directions. The alienated Negro intellectual fell back predominantly on the folk culture, with its antecedents in slavery, its roots in the rural South, and its final flowering on the city pavements. Where the folk culture seemed inadequate to his needs, he turned to the cult of African origins, and to primitivism. At the same time, a new concept of the Negro's manifest destiny arose, to replace the old faith in race progress. Along with a sophisticated critique of (white) European civilization, the thesis was advanced that certain enduring qualities in the racial temperament would redeem the decadent and enervated West. The sum and substance of these explorations was an unequivocal cultural dualism—a conscious attempt to endow Negro literature with a life of its own, apart from the dominant literary tradition.

The frank espousal of cultural dualism by the Negro intelligentsia was viewed with great alarm by the Negro middle class, whose long-range strategy called for eradicating cultural differences. Even at the peak of Renaissance nationalism the middle-class writer could never muster more than token enthusiasm for a distinctive Negro culture. The issues posed by cultural dualism therefore divided the novelists of the period into two schools. The Harlem School, pursuing the nationalist impulse to its logical conclusion, turned to the black masses for literary material. The Old Guard, still intent upon portraying "respectable" Negroes, remained prisoners of the Genteel Tradition.

The Harlem School

Those Negro writers of the 1920's who did not shrink from the implications of cultural dualism found that it altered their art in several important respects. To begin with, whatever is distinctively Negro is likely to be of folk, if not of slave, origin. The Harlem School therefore turned to the folk for their major characters and a low-life milieu for their principal setting. Langston Hughes has preserved the flavor of this development: "But then there are the lowdown folks, and they are the majority—may the Lord be praised! The people who have their nip of gin on Saturday nights and are not too important to themselves or the community. Their religion soars to a shout. Work maybe a little today, rest a little tomorrow. Play awhile. Sing awhile. O, let's dance!"[1]

In the second place, whatever is culturally distinctive has been exaggerated to the point of caricature by ignorant and prejudiced whites. Cultural dualism therefore involves characterizations which run dangerously close to the stereotype. The Harlem School faced this issue squarely, by insisting on their artistic prerogatives. It was up to a mature audience, in their view, to distinguish between a dialect farce by Octavus Roy Cohen and a dialect interpretation by a serious writer, designed to achieve a greater literary realism. The Harlem School had simply outgrown what Alain Locke has called "the pathetic over-compensations of a group inferiority complex." Their bold defiance of the stereotype was a refreshing change from the lifeless, "exemplary" characterization of the prewar novel.

Thirdly, the corollary of a distinctive culture is a distinctive language. Beginning with the Harlem School, the linguistic texture of the Negro novel has been greatly influenced by the rhythms and inflections of Negro speech, and especially by jive, the colorful argot of the urban Negro. The certain mark of the Harlem School, for example, are the terms "ofay" (white man) and "dickty" (high-toned Negro). In the early Negro novel a "professor" was a school teacher (inflated achievement); in the Harlem School novel a "professor" is strictly the third party to a rickety piano and a precarious glass of beer. Even in the 1920's jive had developed to a point where one novelist felt compelled to add a "Glossary of Contemporary Harlemese" to his work, in order to make himself intelligible to a mixed audience.

Finally, the Harlem School was more interested in interpreting Negro culture than in pleading the cause of racial justice. Having affirmed the existence of a distinctive Negro culture, they chose to write novels of Negro life rather than novels dealing with relations between the races. Racial tension, though present, is a muted note in the Renaissance novel. Renaissance Harlem is a place of love and laughter, not of struggle and oppression. By insisting that the novel is an art form and not primarily an instrument of racial protest the Harlem School broke cleanly with a long tradition of overt propaganda and moral appeal. This conscious abandonment of "protest" literature freed the Negro novelist from a false conception of racial loyalty which has constantly threatened to strangle his art.

In the last analysis it was a distinctly "racial" atmosphere which gave the Harlem School its revolutionary character. It was not so much that these writers formed a literary coterie in Harlem, nor even that Harlem was a favorite setting for their novels, but rather that a Harlemesque *quality* permeated their work. In the best instances this quality was more than an exotic veneer; it expressed a unique and partially non-Western way of life. The Harlem School, in a word, discovered the advantages of straddling two worlds. . . .

17. Blacks in the Roosevelt Era

The heady days of the New Negro and the Harlem Renaissance were brought to an end by the Great Depression. Always the last to be hired and the first fired, blacks were hit earliest and most severely by the nation's economic collapse. By the mid-1930's, the proportion of blacks on relief was double that of whites, and in some southern cities as many as 80 per cent of the black population required public assistance. Moreover, in many areas the distribution of relief was marked by discrimination. Many private agencies excluded blacks altogether from their soup kitchens, and some communities gave unemployed black families less assistance than whites or distributed relief money in proportion to the black-white ratio in the entire population even though blacks had a much higher percentage out of work than whites.

It is not surprising, therefore, that blacks looked with hope to the federal relief and recovery programs inaugurated by Franklin Roosevelt in the New Deal. Most blacks in the election of 1932 continued their traditional loyalty to the Republican party, but in the next few years they became devoted adherents of the New Deal. The Roosevelt administration, August Meier and Elliott Rudwick have written, "marked a real turning point in the trends of American race relations," for it was the first time in the twentieth century that federal officials showed genuine concern for the plight of blacks. Of course there was more to this interest than mere humanitarian commitment, for the black vote in the key industrial states of the North had begun to assume a crucial role in politics. Blacks were glad to see the government appoint a "black cabinet"—a group of talented advisers including Robert Vann, appointed Special Assistant to the Attorney General; William H. Hastie, who served in the Interior Department and later became a judge and then governor of the Virgin Islands; and Robert C. Weaver, who worked in several agencies, beginning in the Interior Department. Many of these blacks began their service as advisers to Clark Foreman, a white southerner who headed an interdepartmental committee which investigated the impact of various New Deal programs on the black population.

Many of the agencies and programs established by the New Deal materially bettered the conditions of blacks in the depression years. Because they constituted so large a percentage of the unemployed, blacks received more federal relief, in proportion to their numbers in the entire population, than whites. Thousands of young blacks worked in National Youth Administration and Civilian Conservation Corps centers, although in most states CCC camps were segregated. The Public Works Administration and Federal Public Housing Authority built or financed new homes, hospitals, and schools for blacks as well as whites, and usually, although not always, employed blacks as construction workers. And the National Labor Relations Board and Agricultural Adjustment Administration allowed southern blacks, who were disfranchised in political elections, to vote in union elections and agricultural referenda. On the other hand, the crop-reduction program of the AAA forced many black sharecroppers off the land and into urban ghettos, and under the National Recovery Administration blacks often had to accept lower wages than whites for equivalent work. In general, local customs and the prejudices of administrators meant that blacks were often discriminated against in the application of New Deal programs.

In the essay below, Leslie H. Fishel examines in greater

detail the impact of the New Deal upon black Americans, and the black reaction to Franklin Roosevelt. He neglects, however, some of the movements in which ghetto blacks were involved in these years. The ghetto found a new group of heroes in the 1930's, including the boxer Joe Louis, whose victories over white fighters gave blacks a much-needed source of racial pride; and Haile Selassie, emperor of the African state of Ethiopia, which fought valiantly but unsuccessfully against Italian invasion. One of the most striking phenomena of the Depression years was the rise of Father Divine, the self-proclaimed black god, who offered Harlemites precisely what they needed in the Depression years: free food, cheap lodging, and hope. How Father Divine financed the "heavens" where his followers lived is only one of the questions which remain unanswered about this remarkable man, but his appeal combined religious nationalism with the demand for an end to all racial discrimination. Another shadowy figure, Eugene Brown, who called himself Sufi Abdul Hamid, led a boycott campaign against white Harlem merchants who refused to hire blacks. "Don't Buy Where You Can't Work" was his slogan, and the resentment against merchants which the movement aroused was one cause of the 1935 Harlem riot, which resulted in the death of three blacks and millions of dollars' worth of property damage. The increasing concern of blacks with economic issues during the Depression was symbolized by W. E. B. Du Bois' break with the NAACP in 1934, over Du Bois' new program for the creation of a separate black economy on a cooperative basis. Segregation, Du Bois now declared, would be with blacks for a long time, and rather than waging essentially fruitless legal battles against it, blacks should "make segregation a matter of careful thought and intelligent planning" through the organization of black unions, businesses, and cooperatives. In a sense, Du Bois had adopted the views of his old rival, Booker T. Washington, in stressing self-help and economic development over political action, but his program is best viewed as a new attempt to solve the continuing paradox of black life in America: how to cope with existing segregation and discrimination while at the same time not abandoning the hope of eventual equality and integration.

Fishel's article also touches on the experiences of blacks during the Second World War and the Truman administration. The expansion of industrial production in the 1940's led to a new acceleration of migration to northern cities, and an increased absorption of black workers into the industrial labor force. As a result of A. Philip Randolph's threat to mobilize a mass march on Washington in June, 1941, President Roosevelt issued his famous Executive Order 8802, which banned racial discrimination in the defense industries. As they have in all the wars of this country, blacks fought with valor in World War II, despite the segregation not only of military units but of many armed-forces posts and facilities. The efforts of black soldiers to resist discriminatory treatment led to racial clashes at several army bases and fighting between white civilians and black soldiers in a number of southern towns and cities. And the racial tensions aroused by the influx of black workers into the defense industries were one cause of riots in New York, Los Angeles, and, most serious of all, Detroit, where the outbreak of 1943 killed thirty-four persons and was only suppressed when the President ordered six thousand soldiers into the city. The nation was, however, able to avoid the bloody postwar violence which had followed World War I, and during the Truman years the interest which Roosevelt had shown in black Americans was continued. Among the landmarks of the Truman administration were the integration of the armed forces, the adoption of a strong civil-rights plank by the Democratic convention of 1948, resulting in the walkout of several southern delegations, and the personal commitment of the President to such goals as fair employment and full civil rights.

The Negro in the New Deal Era

LESLIE H. FISHEL, JR.

The rhythm and the tone of the New Deal was set by the man in the White House, since Franklin D. Roosevelt was the spokesman and the master of his administration. His first public statement, the inaugural address of March 4, 1933, pierced the depression-fostered gloom and stabbed deftly and surely at the nation's physical and psychological ills. In stark contrast to his predecessor, Roosevelt recognized the prevailing despair, "the dark realities of the moment," and committed himself and his administration to a brighter future. He lashed out in Biblical terms against the profiteers and the selfish among the monied classes and laid down an emphasis which would characterize his administration more than he then realized: "The measure of the restoration lies in the extent to which we apply social values more noble than mere monetary profit." Identifying himself with the unemployed and underprivileged—"our greatest primary task is to put people to work"—he compared the depression to a war emergency and he warned that he was prepared to mobilize the resources of the federal government to fight it.[1]

Like so many of FDR's speeches, including his informal radio fireside chats, the written version of this one paled on paper. His voice exuded warmth and a personal inflection which brought him close to his listeners. His own physical affliction and the way he bore it earned him deserved admiration and gave encouragement to those who had afflictions of their own, even a darker skin. John Gunther testified to Roosevelt's attraction for people as "concrete

"The Negro and the New Deal" originally published in *Wisconsin Magazine of History*. From *The Negro American: A Documentary History* by Leslie H. Fishel, Jr. and Benjamin Quarles. Copyright © 1967 by Scott, Foresman & Co. Reprinted by permission of Scott, Foresman & Co.

and intimate. . . . He set up goals in human terms that the average man could grasp for."[2] The general public responded to his magnetism; one of his secretaries selected a list of salutations which were used on letters addressed to him, and they ran the gamut from "Dear humanitarian friend of the people" to "My Pal!" and "Dear Buddy."[3] Almost all of his callers remarked on his personal charm and persuasiveness.

These characteristics of FDR the man, taken with his consummate ability to personalize his understanding of human exploitation and underprivilege, made him the most attractive President, for Negro citizens, since the Civil War. Robert Vann, publisher of the Negro weekly Pittsburgh *Courier,* who was brought into the 1932 campaign by some of Roosevelt's lieutenants, advised his race to "go home and turn Lincoln's picture to the wall. The debt has been paid in full."[4] Yet, like Lincoln's, Roosevelt's actual commitments to the American Negro were slim. He was more a symbol than an activist in his own right. His compassion, though real, was tempered by his own background, by the enormity of the decisions which came up to him, and by political considerations. An enthusiastic politician, he used political weights and measures on a political scale to judge the evidence, and the Negro was often found wanting. When Walter White, the executive secretary of the NAACP, obtained an audience through the good graces of Mrs. Eleanor Roosevelt to plead for the President's public support of the antilynching bill, FDR demurred because he needed Southern votes in Congress on other matters.

Nevertheless, the FDR image eventually became a favorable one; his picture hung in living rooms and infant sons carried his name. At first, though, Negroes waited to be shown. Their publications granted him the benefit of doubt when he spoke about justice and equality, in the hope that he was talking, too, to Negroes. He called lynching murder, remarked W. E. B. Du Bois, and "these things give us hope."[5] His acknowledgment, through his Secretary of Labor, of the National Urban League's survey of economic conditions among Negroes was, in the words of an *Opportunity* editorial, "an evidence of his deep interest in the Negroes' welfare."[6] By midway through his first term, FDR had captured the admiration and affection of the Negro people and, with that, their votes. During the campaign of 1936, Negroes were outspoken in their support of the Democratic national ticket. Sixteen thousand Harlem residents traveled to Madison Square Garden in September of that year to attend a political rally, and sixty other cities held similar and simultaneous rallies. The New Yorkers mixed a rich fare of music and entertainment with leading New Dealers talking politics, but it was an African Methodist Episcopal Bishop, the Reverend C. Ransome, who symbolized the affair and its meaning by reading a "New Emancipation Proclamation." The vote in November was anticlimactic; the second Roosevelt had weaned the Negro away from the Republican party.

Roosevelt did not publicly associate himself with Negro projects or Negro leaders before 1935, but his programs and some of his associates were more aggressive. Early in 1933, he approved of a suggestion that someone in his administration assume the responsibility for fair treatment of the Negroes, and he asked Harold Ickes to make the appointment. A young white Georgian, Clark Foreman, came to Washington at Ickes' request to handle the task, and brought in as his assistant an even younger Negro of great promise, Robert C. Weaver. Foreman successfully made his way through the burgeoning maze of new agencies which were springing up and did a respectable job of calling to the attention of agency heads and their assistants an awareness of the special problems of Negroes. Along with Ickes, Daniel Roper, the Secretary of Commerce; Harry Hopkins, FDR's relief administrator; and Aubrey Williams, a Hopkins deputy, were sympathetic to committing the New Deal to work more generously with and for Negroes.

From the first, the various New Deal agencies carried the major burden of this emphasis, since they translated words into bread and butter, shelter and schooling. For the Negro, the most significant were the Federal Employment Relief Administration (FERA), the National Recovery Administration (NRA), the Works Progress Administration, later called the Work Projects Administration (WPA), the Agricultural Adjustment Administration (AAA), the Tennessee Valley Authority (TVA), the National Youth Administration (NYA), the Civilian Conservation Corps (CCC), and the public housing efforts of several agencies.

There were others in the alphabetical jungle which assisted Negroes, as whites, in more specialized ways, such as the Federal Writers' Project and the Office of Education studies. The very number of agencies added credence to the emergent fact that, for the first time, the federal government had engaged and was grappling with some of the fundamental barriers to race progress.

It was one thing to engage and grapple with a problem at the federal level, and another thing to implement it at lower levels. Most of the New Deal agency programs ran afoul of local laws and customs and most of them capitulated on very practical grounds. As a consequence, Negroes vigorously attacked the inequities, even while they appreciated the limited benefits. FERA, the first New Deal agency to work directly to alleviate the plight of the destitute, tried by locally administered dole and work-projects to pump more money into circulation. Until the end of 1935, when it was abolished, it administered most of the direct relief and work relief programs which the New Dealers initiated, distributing about four billion dollars. Its progress was dogged by racial discrimination, since the design of projects and allocation of funds remained in local hands. Jacksonville, Florida, Negro families on relief outnumbered white families three to one, but the money was divided according to proportions of the total city population. Thus 15,000 Negro families received 45 per cent of the funds and 5,000 white families got 55 per cent. Along the Mississippi River, from Natchez to New Orleans, Negroes were passed over for skilled jobs and frequently received less than the stipulated minimum wage. When the state of Georgia squeezed out of the FERA administrator the right to fix hourly wages for Negroes below thirty cents an hour, *Opportunity* mournfully questioned, "Does this presage the end of that heralded concern for the Forgotten Man?"[7]

If the relief program raised questions of discrimination, the NRA brought howls of indignation. In the words of a Negro labor specialist, the NRA administrator, General Hugh A. Johnson, was "a complete failure" for not properly recognizing the Negro.[8] The industrial codes established under NRA deferred to geographic wage and employment consideration so that the Negro worker generally earned less money for equal time and was frozen out of skilled jobs. A young Negro lawyer, John P. Davis, organized the

Joint Committee on National Recovery in the fall of 1933 to persuade federal authorities to rectify these policies. "It has filed briefs, made appearances at public hearings," he wrote, and "buttonholed administrative officers relative to the elimination of unfair clauses in the codes," but to little avail.[9] In self-defense, NRA officials explained the difficulty in bucking local customs, pointing out also that the NRA was responsible only for industrial workers. Agricultural laborers, domestic servants, and the service trades were not included, and most of the unskilled workers were exempted by statute from wage and hour minimums. "It is not fair," wrote an NRA administrator in a Negro journal, "to blame the NRA for not curing all these ills, if such they be, within a year."[10] Until the Supreme Court decreed its demise in the spring of 1935, the NRA was a favored whipping boy for Negroes, as well as for others. "The Blue Eagle," a Virginia newspaper observed, "may be [for Negroes] a predatory bird instead of a feathered messenger of happiness."[11]

The TVA and the AAA came under fire in the early years of the New Deal for similar reasons. Negro critics raged at the all-white model towns, such as Norris, Tennessee, which were established in conjunction with TVA. Homes for white workers on the project were substantial, while Negro workers lived in substandard temporary barracks. Skilled jobs went first to whites and most labor crews were segregated. TVA, it appeared to two observers in 1934, "aims to maintain the *status quo*."[12] A year later, the situation seemed little better. In one sample two-week period, Negroes were 11 per cent of the working force, receiving only 9.5 per cent of the payroll. Under AAA, Negro tenant farmers and sharecroppers, as the most dispensable laborers, suffered first from the crop-reduction policy and found themselves without employment. Concerned about the evolving discriminatory pattern, the NAACP in 1934 devoted a major share of its energy to trying to prevent white landlords from illegally depriving their Negro tenants of crop-reduction bonuses.

Two New Deal programs for young people operated with a minimum of discrimination: the CCC and the NYA. The CCC established segregated camps in the South and in some parts of the North; the great bulk of the integrated camps were in New England. By 1935, its peak year, CCC had over a half million boys in camp. In general, Negroes stayed in CCC camps longer than whites, were not moved up to administrative posts in camps as readily as whites, and were restricted to less than 10 per cent of the total enrollment. Since the proportion of young Negro men in need was substantively higher than this, the quota system was actually inequitable. The NYA, which Mary McLeod Bethune served as administrator of Negro affairs, was shaped to help young men and women in school and with schooling. It grew out of the university and college student relief program established under FERA, and by the end of its first six months, in late 1935, had distributed more than forty million dollars. Conforming to existing state and regional patterns, the NYA still managed to help a critical age group among Negroes.

The debit side of the New Deal's efforts to assist Negroes fell far short of its material and psychological credits. Never before had Negro leaders participated in government affairs as freely and as frequently. The Department of Commerce had E. K. Jones, on leave from the National Urban League; the NYA had Mrs. Bethune; Interior had William H. Hastie and Weaver; the Social Security Board had Ira DeA. Reid; Labor had Lawrence W. Oxley; the Office of Education had Ambrose Caliver, to mention a few. Never before had there been so great a stress on improving the education of Negroes. Many relief programs included elementary education and training classes as part of the regimen. Negro colleges and universities received funds for buildings. The Office of Education, along with other agencies, began an important study of the status of Negro education.

Professional opportunities opened up in government, although not at the rate at which Negroes were graduating from college. For the first time, Negroes were employed as architects, lawyers, engineers, economists, statisticians, interviewers, office managers, case aids, and librarians. Nonprofessional white-collar jobs, which had rarely been within reach of the race, now became available to trained stenographers, clerks, and secretaries. While many of these jobs centered around programs for Negroes within the government, such as Negro slum clearance projects, Negro NYA offices, and the like, they broke the dam which had hitherto kept Negroes out of these kinds of positions.

Harold Ickes, a former president of the Chicago chapter of the

NAACP, was the first New Dealer to be recognized as a tried friend. He quickly ended discrimination in his department and set the example by placing professionally-trained Negroes in responsible positions. He first drew FDR's attention to Hastie, as a candidate for the federal judge vacancy in the Virgin Islands, and Roosevelt made the appointment in 1937. Ickes appeared at predominantly Negro functions and in 1936, on the occasion of an address at Howard University, even went so far as to wear a University of Alabama hood with his cap and gown because "it seemed to have the best color effect. . . ."[13] While Ickes could not breach established segregation patterns in housing, one-eighth of the federal housing projects planned before the end of 1935 were in mixed neighborhoods. Approximately one-half of them were in Negro slum areas and, thanks to the negotiating skill of Ickes' assistant, Robert C. Weaver, the contracts for a substantial portion of these called for the employment of both skilled and unskilled Negro workers.

Eleanor Roosevelt, the New Deal's conscience, made it her business to reaffirm by word and deed her faith in the equality of opportunity for all. She included Negro and mixed organizations on her itineraries, welcomed mixed groups of adults and children to the White House, and spoke up for the race at critical times. In 1936, as part of a long memo on political strategy in the presidential campaign, she urged party leaders to ask respected Negroes like Mrs. Bethune to participate among Negro groups. The penalty for her unflagging advocacy of the Negro's cause was abuse or occasionally embarrassing questions. As the European war spread after 1939, she confronted questions about the Negro's loyalty. "Rarely," she told a group of New Jersey college women in 1940, "do you come across a case where a Negro has failed to measure up to the standard of loyalty and devotion to his country."[14]

Eleanor Roosevelt was more than a symbol of the New Deal's conscience; she was a vehicle for approaching and influencing the President. She performed this service for Walter White when the antilynching bill was before Congress. When the DAR refused to allow Marian Anderson to sing in Constitution Hall, Mrs. Roosevelt was the intermediary who secured permission to use the Lincoln Memorial for the concert. It was useful for the President to have his wife serve in these varying capacities, absorbing some of the criticism, supplying him with information he could get from no other source, and sparking his conscience, when that was needed. This relieved the President from having to punctuate his speeches and press conferences with references to the Negro. Before 1935, these were almost nonexistent; after 1935, they increased in frequence and directness, but Roosevelt did not directly commit himself, as his wife did, until his famous Executive Order 8802 of June, 1941, established a Fair Employment Practice Committee to supervise all defense-contract industries.

In many ways, 1935 seemed to be a pivotal year for the President's public statements to and about the Negro. His annual message to Congress in January asserted that "in spite of our efforts and in spite of our talk, we have not weeded out the over-privileged and we have not effectively lifted up the underprivileged." Uplift and underprivilege were two words which Negroes understood, two words which footnoted their history; yet Roosevelt did not mention the Negro specifically. Shortly after that, he told WPA state administrators that "we cannot discriminate in any of the work we are conducting either because of race or religion or politics," and although he went on to speak of political pressures, the word "race" was there for Negroes to see. In two other public statements later in the year, FDR paid lip service to the accomplishments of the race and by 1936, an election year, he proclaimed his policy that "among American citizens there should be no forgotten men and no forgotten races."[15] The transformation was more one of degree than of conviction; Roosevelt was beginning to speak to the Negro, however rarely, rather than to lump him without identification into massive generalizations. But his eye was ever on the balance of political forces and he never voluntarily came out foursquare for the Negro.

In perspective, Roosevelt's circumspection on some domestic issues was less significant than his New Deal legislative program. Labor unions received substantial encouragement from Section 7a of NRA and from the Wagner Act, although the White House maintained an equivocal position toward both labor and management. The jump in union memberships and the rise of the Committee on Industrial Organization, first within the AF of L and later as the independent Congress of Industrial Organizations (CIO), gained impetus from the newly established right to strike and the newly created federal board to mediate labor disputes. A strengthened labor movement confronted, as one of its problems, the question of Negro members. Older unions such as the United Mine Workers and the International Ladies Garment Workers Union welcomed Negroes without distinction. When the CIO broke from the AF of L, its nucleus of unions including the new and somewhat fragile organizations in the automobile, rubber, and steel industries accepted Negroes on an equal basis, except in those localities where race friction was high. The United Textile Workers attempted to do the same, but the existence of textile plants in southern states made this task more onerous. It was not enough for a union to resolve, as the CIO did, to accept members without regard to race, creed, or color, or even, as the UAW and the organizing committees of the steelworkers did, to offer Negro workers a chance to join up. Negroes still hung back, alternately tempted and frightened by management's offers and threats. The wave of the future was with the industrial unions, and *Opportunity's* declaration to Negro steelworkers that it would be "the apotheosis of stupidity" for them to stay out of the union battling for recognizance in 1937, was prophetic.[16] The success of the Brotherhood of Sleeping Car Porters, under the leadership of A. Philip Randolph, in gaining recognition as the bargaining agent with the Pullman Company after a twelve-year struggle, marked the beginning of the race's influence in national labor circles and on national labor policy. After his union was recognized, Randolph prodded the AF of L to grant it an international charter, making it an equal with other member unions, and he never eased up his fight to liberalize the AF of L's racial policies. Even though he was not persuasive enough to break down these craft and railway-union prejudices, Randolph emerged before World War II as a dominant voice in Negro circles and a power to be reckoned with in American unionism.

Of the many voices which spoke out for and against the race, none was more deceptive than that of the Communists. Before 1935, their ideology committed their followers to support a separate state for Negroes, the so-called Black Republic, and insisted that they work independent of all other groups toward this end. When the NAACP unsuccessfully defended the Scottsboro boys— nine young Negroes accused of rape on an Alabama freight train in 1931—the Communists abusively blamed the NAACP for the failure. With shrill bravado, they muscled the NAACP out of the picture and took over the defense. They were unsuccessful in court, but they publicized the case all over the world as an example of capitalistic exploitation and milked the American public for uncounted (and unaccountable) thousands of dollars. In 1935, the Communist ideology swung over to a united-front tactic, and they abandoned their attacks on existing non-Communist organizations and held out the carrot of co-operation. Their purpose was to mix with these organizations and either subvert them directly or gain control behind the scenes. The National Urban League and the NAACP quickly recognized the move for what it was and co-operated at a chilly distance. The League had to dissolve some of its workers' Councils, established in northern cities, because the Communists took them over. The NAACP agreed to work with Communist support on the Scottsboro case, but continued to warn against close co-operation.

Failing to engage the two dominant Negro organizations, the Communists jumped at the chance to work with these and other Negro groups through the newly formed National Negro Congress. The brainchild of New Deal critic John P. Davis, it was organized under the co-sponsorship of almost forty Negro organizations and met in Chicago in 1936 with close to 900 delegates. The Communists stayed in the background—Davis was sympathetic—and the resolutions were non-Stalinist, but Davis was elected executive secretary and maintained close touch with Communist leaders. The 1937 Congress met in Philadelphia with even larger crowds. But soon after that the more conservative organizations and individuals withdrew their sponsorship and the Congress, handicapped by lack of funds, began to crumble. Some local councils established by the Congress were active in Western cities, but after 1937 the Congress as a national group dwindled into impotence and in 1940 became an openly controlled Communist organization. This take-over followed the Stalin-Hitler pact and signalized the 180-degree pivot which American Communists were forced to execute, exploding the united front movement. Organizations like the NAACP which had worked with Communists at a distance suddenly found themselves subject to vituperative and irrational attack, but the vast majority of Negroes merely continued to ignore Communism as a method of achieving their goals.

With the exception of the church, the major Negro organizations felt the sting of mass apathy. "We recognize our lack of skill at mass appeal," NAACP's Roy Wilkins admitted in 1941.[17] The national office of NAACP attracted men and women of an intellectual bent whose convictions on race matters had not changed with the seasons, since the organization was still dedicated to the abolition of segregation and discrimination. But the spark which had sent John Shillady, Walter White, and James Weldon Johnson into race-hatred areas, North and South, burned low. On the national level, the NAACP fought its battles in court, in Congress, and in the press, but not in communities where racism flourished. At local levels, it depended upon its branches, many of which were woefully weak in finances and leadership, to seek out and rectify racial problems of every description. Its base was too narrow for its superstructure, and its bones creaked from inaction at the community level; yet it thrived because it learned to speak the language of influence in political circles and because it chose wisely the cases of discrimination and segregation which it pursued through the courts. Indeed, the road to the 1954 desegregation decisions was charted, bulldozed, paved, and landscaped by the NAACP.

The National Urban League was tested during the Depression and not found wanting. Its leadership was similar to that of the NAACP, except that to the extent that its goals were more specific, framed in terms of employment, family welfare, health, and education, it was accused of being more timid, dominated by white liberals, and hostile to trade unionism. Its chief executive, E. K. Jones, replied to these criticisms in a private memo in 1941. The League, he said, was not a Negro but "truly an interracial movement. . . . Any movement of this character which advocates understanding through conference and discussion must necessarily refrain from advocating mass action of one race calculated to force the other group to make concessions." Gunnar Myrdal, the Swedish sociologist whose monumental study of the Negro in America was published during World War II, found that the League worked actively with unions and held "the lead as a pro-union force among the Negro people."[18] Urban League branches were beginning to receive local support from Community Funds, which gave them greater strength and a source for independent leadership. Taken together, these two Negro organizations, in spite of their lack of popular support, moved together in harmony along parallel paths to the great good of the race.

The Negro's church maintained its grip on the masses during these years as it had for centuries, but its hold was loosening. Strong in numbers and appeal, the church had inherent weaknesses which gradually reduced its potency in modern America. It was not one church but many, from the strong African Methodist Episcopal (AME) and African Methodist Episcopal Zion (AMEZ) to the independent colored branches of the Baptist denomination. To these were added smaller denominations and sects and store-front evangelical churches which dissipated the religious energies of the race. The differences were more personal than ideological; in fact, except for the split between the liberal and the fundamentalist churches—a split matched in white denominations—there was no basic theological difference. The churches' hierarchies stood in the way of closer co-operation. The Negro church was all-Negro and proudly so, a self-perpetuating, segregated institution which made no effort to reach across race barriers, individually or institutionally. In the North, this would have been troublesome for white churches, whose precepts were in advance of practice. Negro preachers generally stayed in Negro pulpits. In the South this would have been almost impossible. The Northern Negro church bred isolation; the Southern Negro church fostered accommodation. Fettered by a strain of fundamentalism and emotionalism, and weakened by the diffusion of denominations, the Negro church had little appeal for the younger generation. In the 1930's and 1940's it struggled without success to find a vehicle for its latent power, but its leadership had lost touch with the material and moral issues of the day. It failed to see its obligation as a participant in the fight for equal rights. "We are the policemen of the Negroes," a Southern colored preacher observed in 1941. "If we did not keep down their ambitions and divert them into religion, there would be upheaval in the South."[19] For the second third of the twentieth century, this message was anachronistic.

It would be simplistic to suggest as have some recent novelists, such as James Baldwin in *Go Tell It on the Mountain,* that the church's withdrawal for fear of upheaval led directly to upheaval, but there is a trace of truth in it. When Harlem rioted in 1935, *The Crisis* explained that only the patience of the Negro had delayed it that long. Patience was not enough to counter the "sneers, impertinence, and personal opinions of smart-aleck investigators, supervisors and personnel directors."[20] Unemployment, rent gouging, and the belief that Harlem had not received its share of relief money snapped the uneasy calm; the riot erupted with a frenzied attack on whites and the purposeful looting of food and clothing stores. The prompt on-the-scene appearance of New York City's popular mayor, Fiorello H. La Guardia, helped restore rationality. When the United States entered World War II, Harlem still seethed from overcrowding, white insolence, and price gouging, and again rioting broke out, followed by riots in other cities, most notably Detroit. The hands of the clock had swung half circle and the Negro had learned from the white how to use violence and lawlessness when order and the law were not sufficient.

Toward the end of the 1930's the federal government turned more and more of its attention to the European conflict, the economy flourished as the industrial bastion of the embattled Allies, and the Negro had committed himself to the New Deal and to President Roosevelt. Polls in 1940 showed that Negro voters overwhelmingly supported Roosevelt for a third term, and the polls were right. The reason for this support was not difficult to surmise. Outside of what the Democratic Administration had tried to do directly and indirectly, the decade itself was marked with identifiable milestones of progress. In athletics, Jesse Owens was an Olympic champion, and Negro football players starred on many of the major college teams. Professional baseball still resisted, but its time was not far off. In interracial activities, conferences on a variety of subjects began to meet with overbearing regularity and, though self-consciously interracial, the pattern developed almost

irrevocably. College students and adults met to talk about education, religion, economic matters, and, of course, civil rights. Even
in the South, the indomitable Mrs. Bethune organized an interracial conference at the college she founded, and the white University of Florida tentatively sent delegates. In the deep South,
interracial conferences were held on a segregated basis; Eleanor
Roosevelt told of attending one in Birmingham and inadvertently
sitting in the colored section. "At once the police appeared to
remind us of the rules and regulations on segregation. . . .
Rather than give in I asked that chairs be placed for us with the
speakers facing the whole group."[21] White Southerners began to
speak up for the Negro. They were still a small minority, but the
mere fact that a white state supervisor of schools in Georgia would
admit to the inequalities of segregated schools, or a white North
Carolina legislator would question a decreased appropriation for a
Negro college, was a sign of change. The rise of Huey Long in
Louisiana brought a different attitude, one of ignoring race differences without changing race relationships. The all-white Mississippi Education Association established a committee in 1938 to
recommend ways in which students might study Negro life, and
several Northern newspapers in 1940 editorially acknowledged the
importance of Negro History Week. The tide had turned, and
Negroes credited the turning to the New Deal.

The sudden shock of the surprise attack which drew the United
States into World War II served more to expose sore spots than to
blanket them in loyalty. In the First World War, the protests
against unequal treatment were slow to develop and not widely
heard, but the Second World War was different. Even before Pearl
Harbor, clamors arose from the South warning that the Negro was
not going to "come out of this war on top of the heap as he did in
the last one."[22] However distorted the comparison, the attitude
was clear, and it influenced the government's decision to extend
pre-Pearl Harbor patterns into the war period.

The Negro soldier remained separate in the armed services, and
not always welcome. Judge William H. Hastie resigned as civilian
aide to the Secretary of War in protest against the dissembling
tactics of the Army Air Corps to keep the Negro on the ground.

The Crisis, returning to a World War I cry, criticized the appointment of Southern white officers for Negro troops and the explanation that they could handle them better. When FDR queried Walter White about the carelessness of the Negro press and the consistency of its attack on the war effort, White replied that better treatment for Negroes in the armed services and the invitation of Negro editors to presidential press conferences and top briefings would clear up the problem.

White became an important man in the war effort and was finally sent overseas as a war correspondent in early 1944. He toured every major front in Europe and the Pacific and his reports did not make soothing reading. Wherever he went, he later wrote, "there was a minority of bigots who were more determined to force their bigotry on others than they were to win the war." This was particularly true of officers, both Northern and Southern. Separation, he found, bred this spirit, especially when key officers were "prejudiced or weak, or both." When Negroes and whites actually fought together, as they did during the Battle of the Bulge in December of 1944, attitudes changed, according to polls among white officers and men. "After the first day," a white South Carolinian admitted, "when we saw how they fought, I changed my mind."[23] The top combat brass, such as General Dwight Eisenhower and Admiral Chester Nimitz, were willing to co-operate, but they were hemmed in by Washington orders and junior officer reluctance.

At home, the intense feelings bared by war boiled up with wearying constancy. In the spring of 1941, A. Philip Randolph organized the March on Washington movement which threatened to march if the White House did not declare for fair employment practices in defense industries. President Roosevelt issued his famous Executive Order 8802 in June, establishing the FEPC and the principle of government concern with employment discrimination. Randolph continued the movement during the war, but it lapsed as the older organizations themselves became more militant.

The prosperity of war industry and the proscriptive Southern mores once again attracted thousands of Negroes to Northern cities. The consequent overcrowding and war tension heated racism to the boiling point, as the riots in New York, Detroit, and Los

Angeles demonstrated. For the Negro, racism was the same wherever it appeared. In Roy Wilkins' words, "it sounds pretty foolish
to be *against* park benches marked 'Jude' in Berlin, but to be *for*
park benches marked 'Colored' in Tallahassee, Florida."[24] Negroes could not understand why whites drew distinctions between
the Nazi ideology of Aryan supremacy and the American ideology
of white supremacy. Even back in 1933, *The Crisis* expressed its
"unholy glee" at Hitler's attack on the Jews: "Now that the
damned include the owner of the [New York] *Times,* moral
indignation is perking up."[25] The paradox which Wilkins illustrated could only be resolved by a change of face on the part of
white America.

The war itself, by drawing thousands of men and women into a
collaborative effort with whites, made such a change possible.
Negroes served in the armed services in all ratings and at all ranks,
though segregated. War industries hired skilled Negro men and
women at supervisory and managerial levels. Government used
colored workers in great numbers and in more sensitive positions
than ever before. The Negro's political power was organized in an
unprecedented manner during the wartime presidential election.
The younger generation of Negro men and women who had grown
up in prosperity and matured in depression were awakened to the
infinite possibilities of an assimilated society, and from them came
the trained leadership to plan the campaign.

The death of Roosevelt and the end of the war in 1945 termi-
nated an era. The office of the Presidency now symbolized a
concern for justice and equality for all Americans, including
Negroes. The White House had taken a stand in favor of the
principle of equal rights, although the practice had lagged. The
new President, Harry S Truman, a man of lesser parts, was to take
the next practical step and declare in specifics his belief in the
equality of men of whatever race under the law. Where Roosevelt
concealed the particular in the general principle, Truman spoke out
without check. Where Roosevelt used the excuse of war to delay
integration, Truman used the excuse of peace to accelerate it.
Where Roosevelt used the federal government to increase economic opportunities for all, Truman used the federal government

to increase economic opportunities for Negroes. While the Truman Fair Deal never approximated the energy and the excitement of the Roosevelt New Deal, it was the former which capitalized on the Negro's readiness to take an equal place in American democracy.

Three major strands marked the period between the end of the war and the Supreme Court's 1954 desegregation decision. One related to the improving economic condition of the Negro, a second to the reports of three Presidential committees, and the third to the increasingly significant role of the United States Supreme Court in racial matters. The Negro's improving economic condition stemmed from a variety of causes. In microcosm, the successful introduction of Jackie Robinson into baseball's National League in 1947 is exemplary, since his breakthrough eventually opened the gates in almost every professional sport. In like manner, the appointment of Ira DeA. Reid to the faculty of New York University was a breakthrough in higher education of lesser quantity but equal quality. Other major universities and colleges eventually followed suit. The forceful policy of the CIO, led by the United Auto Workers, brought the AF of L into line. The Negro, Walter Reuther warned in late 1945, "should not allow his painful experiences with many of the old craft unions of the American Federation of Labor to embitter him against all labor unions." Both the Negro and the AF of L took the hint.[26] Some craft unions still held out, generally by subterfuge, but the weight of the major unions and their two national federations swung unequivocally to the side of equal opportunity without regard to race.

Dark spots in the improving picture still plagued the nation. Housing was a special need and a particular irritant, since the restrictive covenant, even after the Supreme Court ruled in 1948 that it had no legal standing, was sufficient to block integrated neighborhoods, North and South. The Negro young people were restive under segregated conditions and their still limited economic opportunities. When Thurgood Marshall warned them in 1946 against a widespread disobedience movement on the grounds that it "would result in wholesale slaughter with no good achieved" and alienate public sympathy of "the cautious and the timid," his counsel only helped to delay student nonviolent protests for a decade.[27] In those federal programs where local agencies exercised jurisdiction, the Negro was frequently abused, and President Harry S Truman, early in 1947, asked his Civil Rights Committee to add this to its already full agenda.

In establishing the President's Committee on Civil Rights in December, 1946, Truman had already spoken in general terms about the preservation of civil liberties. It was, he stated, "a duty of every Government—state, Federal and local." But he pointed out that when state or local governments failed in their responsibilities, the obligation fell back on to the federal establishment. The committee was instructed to review what Truman called "these weak and inadequate statutes" and recommend new legislative or other methods to protect the civil rights of American citizens.[28] The committee, a group of representative men and women under the chairmanship of industrialist Charles E. Wilson, published its *Report* the following year, the first intensive study of its kind by a government-appointed committee. It was a sweeping endorsement of federal activity in the civil rights area and a severe indictment of the many discriminatory practices found in state and local governments.

The *Report* had immediate and far-reaching repercussions. The President's Executive Order 9980 established a fair employment procedure within the government structure. Executive Order 9981 was even more significant since it, in effect, abolished discrimination in the armed services. The committee established by this order to study the situation and make recommendations published its report, *Freedom to Serve,* in 1950, by which time all three of the service branches had abolished the quota system of enlistment and segregation in any form, including separate units and limited opportunities. The Navy was first in its implementation, having started even before the President's order, and although the Army dragged its feet, the committee was satisfied that the order and its execution were effective. A year later, a third Executive Order, 10308, established a President's Committee to insure compliance by government contractors with contractual regulations prohibiting discrimination because of race, creed, color, or national origin. The committee's report was filed early in 1953.

The political reverberations to these dramatic steps by President Truman echoed in the halls of Congress and almost split the

Democratic party asunder. In 1948, the Dixiecrats walked out of the Democratic convention in protest to the strong civil rights plank which the young junior Senator from Minnesota, Hubert Humphrey, had pushed through. Truman's election victory that year, in the face of the walkout and the left-wing Progressive party, was convincing evidence that civil rights had attracted voter support. In Congress, this message from the electorate went unheeded; Southern Democrats and conservative Republicans, whose constituencies sent different messages to them, blocked all efforts to write civil rights into statute.

Outside of politics, the nation moved slowly but certainly away from segregated positions. Professional associations in southern states began, somewhat tentatively, to invite Negroes to membership—lawyers, social workers, nurses, and librarians. The state medical association in Florida stood alone in admitting colored doctors, while other dentists and teachers in the South remained aloof. The American Friends Service Committee began a four-year program in 1951 to eliminate segregation in Washington, D.C., and in Dallas, Texas, a year earlier, the theological seminary of Southern Methodist University opened its doors to Negro students. In the North, several states adopted open-occupancy laws for public housing, and in key cities like New York, Philadelphia, Detroit, and Washington, Negroes moved into upper- and middle-class neighborhoods without difficulty.

These were straws in the wind rather than set patterns. A full quota of segregation in education and housing, employment, and places of public accommodation still existed. But as the walls began to develop cracks, the role of the Supreme Court emerged as the most significant factor in the equation. Before the milestone decision of 1954, the Supreme Court had charted a course which led, almost inevitably, to that end.

Before World War II, the Supreme Court rendered decisions in three areas involving Negro rights. One was an outgrowth of a group effort by Negroes in Washington, D.C., to persuade a store which catered to Negroes to hire them. The Court determined that this was a labor dispute within the meaning of the Norris-La Guardia Act and that the New Negro Alliance was entitled to picket and pass out literature to accomplish its aim (New Negro

Alliance *v.* Grocery Co., 1938). Southern efforts to exclude Negroes from jury service were undermined by the Court's decision in Smith *v.* Texas (1940) which, in the words of Justice Hugo Black, himself a Southerner, asserted that "for racial discrimination to result in the exclusion from jury service of otherwise qualified groups . . . violates our Constitution and the laws enacted under it. . . ."[29] And in the field of education, where the NAACP had begun to place its major legal redress emphasis, the Court found for the petitioner, Lloyd Gaines, in Missouri *ex rel.* Gaines *v.* Canada (1938). Gaines had been refused admission to the University of Missouri Law School because he was a Negro. "The basic consideration," the Court said, "is not as to what sort of opportunities other States provide, or whether they are as good as those in Missouri, but as to what opportunities Missouri itself furnishes to white students and denies to negroes solely upon the ground of color."[30]

The Court did not go beyond the limits of "separate but equal" facilities, but insisted, at the least, that equal facilities exist. Missouri hastened to appropriate a half million dollars for a Negro law school and invited Lloyd Gaines to use a two-room basement establishment in the interim. Before the NAACP could contest this dubious implementation by the state of Missouri, Gaines disappeared and the case was abandoned.

During and after the war, the Court continued to chip away at the encrustations of law which prevented Negroes from full participation as citizens. Its decisions in a series of cases involving the railroad brotherhoods, jury selection, the white primary, and the restrictive covenant generally favored the Negro. In 1948 and again in 1953, the Court made it patently clear that restrictive covenants were not enforceable, in any way, in any court of the land, federal or state. The states of Texas, Mississippi, and Georgia were instructed by the Court in separate decisions between 1947 and 1954 that "the Constitution requires only a fair jury selected without regard to race," and that the various devices used by these states and some of their local subdivisions denied minority groups the equal protection of the laws.[31] In 1944, the Court overruled a 1935 decision and insisted that primaries were sufficiently related to official state actions, even if they were declared to be private, to be regulated by the Fifteenth Amendment. Nine years later, the Court asserted that a private county association of long standing which served as a pre-primary selector of nominees was subject to the same constitutional provision.

Negroes in general and the NAACP in particular could take some satisfaction in knowing that the Court was slowly opening basic rights, but in the area of education the progress was even more marked. The NAACP invested heavily of its time and funds in widening educational opportunities by court action. The University of Maryland in 1935 had capitulated at the graduate-school level without taking the case to the Supreme Court. Three years later Missouri was instructed to educate a Negro law student, but its subterfuge worked so well that it tried it again in 1942 by establishing a two-room graduate school in journalism for one qualified Negro graduate student. The University of Oklahoma followed suit when the Supreme Court allowed Missouri's effort to stand, but the end was in sight. In 1950 Texas was told by the Court that its Negro law school had to be equal to that of the white University of Texas Law School, and the doors of the latter were duly opened to Negroes. In a parallel case, Oklahoma was rebuked for permitting a Negro student to be segregated within its state university, and the practice ceased. With a Supreme Court which read the Constitution as a document protecting the rights of all citizens and with the opening of universities at the graduate level, the time was ripe for an all-inclusive appeal for educational opportunities.

The twenty years between the inauguration of Franklin D. Roosevelt and the eve of the Supreme Court desegregation decision were the most revolutionary two decades in the history of the American Negro up to that time. In part, the elemental movements had little to do with race matters; depression, war, prosperity—these were not issues of black and white. Yet they determined a basic posture change: that whites and Negroes would work closely together on matters of national and international importance which had nothing to do with race. Perhaps the most startling development to emerge from these decades was that prominent Negroes began to assume responsibilities in government, business, labor, athletics, education, and the social services which had no connection with race. Negroes, finally, were working in critical jobs because they were needed, and not simply because they were Negroes. Ralph Bunche of the United Nations, Jackie Robinson of the Brooklyn Dodgers, Ira DeA. Reid of Haverford College, to name just a sampling, were men who were doing their jobs—and who happened to be Negroes.

While this was the wedge, slowly to be driven into the grain of American society, pressures which mounted throughout these two decades supplied the hammer to drive it home. Some of these pressures were cumulative, like the development of substantial numbers of highly skilled and highly educated Negroes, and the steady flow of Negroes from farm to city, from South to North. Other pressures were selective, like the magnetism of FDR and the dogged determination of Harry S Truman. There were economic forces, like the dawning awareness by retailers of the Negro market and the sudden realization by most unions that integration meant greater strength. Then, too, there were such forces as the quiet efforts of Southern liberals to make integration in higher education successful.

The Negro himself was a pressure on the wedge. Still smarting as a second-class citizen, more ready than ever to step up to equal citizenship, he used every resource available. Some were peaceful and passive, like the continuing desire for education and the calculated use of votes. Some were peaceful and active, like the push to break down labor union and employment barriers and the play to get more national publicity. Some were outside the law and violent. These efforts were not concerted and not always effective, but the total impact was pervasive. American society could no longer sit back, consoled by the thought that the Negro was not yet prepared. By the end of these two decades, he was ready, and in the decade to come, the young men and women of his race would make this clear.

18. The NAACP and the Fight Against Segregation

Despite the fact that it has come to be regarded as conservative by many young black militants, for most of this century the National Association for the Advancement of Colored People has been in the vanguard of the struggle for full civil rights and the end of racial discrimination in America. The NAACP was founded as a result of the Springfield race riot of 1908. William E. Walling, a writer who investigated the riot, was so shocked by what he discovered that in an article in the *Independent* he issued a call for a revival of "the spirit of the abolitionists" and the granting of full social and civil rights to black citizens. A group of prominent New York whites, including social worker Mary White Ovington, and William Lloyd Garrison's grandson, Oswald Garrison Villard, editor of the New York *Evening Post,* were so impressed with Walling's plea that they issued a call for a meeting in Springfield on the one-hundreth anniversary of Lincoln's birth, in 1909. Out of this meeting and subsequent gatherings in 1910 and 1911, the NAACP was created, with the announced goals of the abolition of segregation, the enforcement of the fourteenth and fifteenth amendments, and equal education for black and white children. The first group of NAACP officials were whites, with the notable exception of W. E. B. Du Bois, who became Director of Publications and Research and editor of the NAACP's magazine,

The Crisis, and who brought most of the black intellectuals from the Niagara movement into the new organization. Under Du Bois' editorship, *The Crisis* rapidly expanded in circulation and influence. It laid heavy stress on the achievements of blacks in such areas as education, medicine, and literature, carried articles on black history and culture, and exposed discrimination and racism throughout the country.

From the very beginning the NAACP adopted the program which has continued to characterize the organization's activities. It laid heavy stress on two means of combatting discrimination: legal battles in the courts, and education and persuasion of the nation at large. Some of its most important legal victories were won when the NAACP was still in its infancy. In 1915, the Supreme Court ruled unconstitutional Oklahoma's grandfather clause, a particularly blatant means of disfranchising black voters, and two years later a Louisville ordinance requiring residential segregation was similarly invalidated. At the same time the NAACP sought to attack white racial stereotypes by protesting D. W. Griffith's film *Birth of a Nation,* which condemned blacks during Reconstruction for ruining southern government and lusting after white women, and glorified the Ku Klux Klan and the "redeemers" of the South. During the 1920's the organization's major effort was its attempt to publicize and put an end to lynchings. Although the Dyer antilynching bill was defeated in Congress by a southern filibuster, the NAACP did succeed in awakening politicians and the public to the full extent of the evil, and was in part responsible for the decline in the number of lynchings after 1920. The antilynching campaign was organized by James Weldon Johnson, the black writer who served as NAACP Executive Secretary during the twenties. Not only did Johnson's aggressive leadership help swell the NAACP's membership rolls, but his appointment marked the beginning of a trend toward black officials replacing whites within the organization.

In 1930, the NAACP made the decision to launch a "large-scale, widespread, dramatic campaign to give the Southern Negro his constitutional rights, his political and civil equality . . . and to give the Negroes equal rights in the public schools, in the voting booths, on the railroads and on juries in every state where they are at present denied them." The new program was spearheaded by Thurgood Marshall, a brilliant black graduate of Howard University's Law School, who in 1968 became the first black Justice of the Supreme Court. At first, the NAACP concentrated on the most flagrant forms of legal oppression—forced confessions, the exclusion of blacks from southern juries, and the all-white Democratic primary, the most effective means of disfranchising southern black voters. In these areas, the organization won a series of legal victories in the 1930's and 1940's. Marshall then turned to an attack upon public-school segregation. As early as 1938 the Supreme Court ordered the University of Missouri Law School to admit a qualified black applicant, on the ground that there was no law school for blacks in the state, and to make the student seek education in another state would be unwarranted discrimination. The reasoning of the decision, however, was firmly in line with the "separate but equal" doctrine laid down in *Plessy v. Ferguson* forty years earlier, because Missouri could presumably avoid such integration in the future by establishing a law school for blacks.

During the 1940's the Supreme Court demonstrated a growing impatience with state-sponsored racial segregation. In 1941 it ordered Pullman facilities on interstate trains desegregated, in 1948 it ruled that a racial covenant in a housing contract could not be enforced in a state court, and two years later it outlawed segregated dining facilities on interstate trains. The first indication that it might be willing to apply the same principles to schools came with the Sweatt case in 1950. Sweatt, a black Texan, demanded admission to the University of Texas law school despite the fact that the state had recently built a school for blacks. Ten years earlier, the Court might have accepted this segregated facility, but it now ruled that in view of the faculty, library, other facilities, and prestige of the University of Texas law school, the black school could not possibly be equal. The decision encouraged Marshall to launch a series of cases testing the entire edifice of school segregation.

In his argument in December, 1952, Marshall insisted that segregation violated the equal-protection clause of the fourteenth amendment, and also brought to the attention of the Court sociological studies conducted by Kenneth and Mamie Clark of New York, which demonstrated that segregation had a harmful effect on the educational and psychological development of the black child. The Court waited a full year and a half before rendering its verdict, but on May 17, 1954, Chief Justice Earl Warren read the unanimous decision: "We conclude that in the field of public education the doctrine of 'separate but equal' has no place. Separate educational facilities are inherently unequal."

The two selections which follow are examinations of the NAACP and its role in winning the historic verdict of 1954. The first, from Gunnar Myrdal's *An American Dilemma,* examines the successes and failings of the organization from the vantage point of the mid-1940's. Myrdal, a sociologist at the University of Stockholm, was asked by the Carnegie Corporation in 1938 to oversee a comprehensive investigation of black life in the United States. Under his direction a team of black and white historians, economists, political scientists, and psychologists prepared massive reports, on which Myrdal relied in writing his work. In 1,024 pages of text and 526 of introduction and footnotes, *An American Dilemma* traced the history of blacks in the United States and examined racism, economic discrimination, the political role of blacks, inequities in the administration of justice, black protest organizations, and many other subjects. By drawing attention to the contradiction between America's democratic ideals and its treatment of black citizens, and marshaling overwhelming evidence of the systematic oppression of blacks in American society, Myrdal's work made a significant contribution to the rise of egalitarian racial views in the 1940's and 50's. Though hardly uncritical of the NAACP, Myrdal approves of the organization's basic approach; his views should be contrasted with the critique by Ralph Bunche, which is quoted at some length in the footnotes.

In the second selection, Anthony Lewis, a prize-winning reporter for the *New York Times,* traces the legal background of the decision in 1954, beginning with the civil-rights legislation of Reconstruction days. Lewis makes the point that the death of Chief Justice Vinson in 1953 and the installation of Earl Warren while the school cases were under consideration, had an important bearing on the unanimity which enhanced the impact of the 1954 decision. Yet even a unanimous Supreme Court did not convince the white South to abandon school segregation without resistance. In 1955 the Supreme Court set down its famous maxim that desegregation must proceed "with all deliberate speed," but southern states reacted with delaying tactics, ranging from outright interposition and "massive resistance" to legal subterfuges such as "freedom of choice" plans. As late as 1964 eight southern states had less than 2 per cent of their black children in school with whites. Not until 1969, when fewer than one quarter of the South's black pupils attended integrated public schools, did the Supreme Court abandon the "all deliberate speed" maxim, and call for "immediate" integration, an edict whose effects remain to be seen. But, despite this failure of implementation, the 1954 decision is usually regarded as the beginning of the era of the "Civil Rights Revolution."

The National Association for the Advancement of Colored People

GUNNAR MYRDAL

The National Association for the Advancement of Colored People is without question the most important agency for the Negroes in their struggle against caste. At several points in our inquiry, we have seen how it functions. It is an interracial movement. As a matter of fact, it was started on white people's initiative. In the summer of 1908 there had occurred a severe race riot in Springfield, Illinois, the home of Abraham Lincoln. Scores of Negroes had been killed or wounded and many had been driven out of the city. Wide publicity was given the affair in the press and one writer, William English Walling, threw a challenge to the nation: there was a need for a revival of the spirit of the Abolitionists to win liberty and justice for the Negro in America. The appeal was answered by Mary White Ovington. In January, 1909, Miss Ovington met with Mr. Walling and Dr. Henry Moskowitz in New York, and the plans were laid for the organization that was to become the N.A.A.C.P. Of these three, Miss Ovington is still active on the board of the N.A.A.C.P.[1]

Oswald Garrison Villard was asked to draft a call for a conference on February 12, 1909, the one hundredth anniversary of Abraham Lincoln's birth. Signed by many prominent white and Negro liberals, the document pointed in ringing phrases to the injustices inflicted upon the Negro against the letter and the spirit of the Constitution, and called upon

FROM Gunnar Myrdal, *American Dilemma.* Copyright 1944, © 1962 by Harper & Row, Publishers, Inc. Reprinted by permission of Harper & Row, Publishers, Inc.

. . . all believers in democracy to join in a national conference for the discussion of present evils, the voicing of protests, and the renewal of the struggle for civil and political liberty.[2]

At this first conference a committee of forty was formed to carry on the work. Mass meetings were held, pamphlets distributed, and memberships solicited. The following year, at a second conference, a merger was consummated of the forces of the Negro liberals of the Niagara Movement and of the white liberals of Abolitionist traditions. Out of these two groups the National Association for the Advancement of Colored People was formed. Moorfield Storey of Boston was elected the first president. He and all other officers of the new organization were white, except Du Bois, who was to become the salaried Director of Publicity and Research. The platform adopted was practically identical with that of the Niagara Movement. It was at the time considered extremely radical.[3] "Thus," comments Bunche, "the N.A.A.C.P., propelled by dominant white hands, embarked upon the civil liberties course that the Negro-inspired Niagara Movement had futilely tried to navigate."[4] From the beginning Du Bois gave the tone to the new organization's activity. By 1914 there were thirteen Negro members on the Board of Directors, most of whom were veterans of the Niagara Movement. In 1910 the publication of the organization's journal, *The Crisis,* began and it soon became popular.

The long-run objective of the organization has always been to win full equality for the Negro as an American citizen. The specific objectives can best be presented by the following citation from its program as announced in 1940:

1. Anti-lynching legislation.
2. Legislation to end peonage and debt slavery among the share-croppers and tenant farmers of the South.
3. Enfranchisement of the Negro in the South.
4. Abolition of injustices in legal procedure, particularly criminal procedure, based solely upon color or race.
5. Equitable distribution of funds for public education.
6. Abolition of segregation, discrimination, insult, and humiliation based on race or color.
7. Equality of opportunity to work in all fields with equal pay for equal work.

8. Abolition of discrimination against Negroes in the right to collective bargaining through membership in organized labor unions.[5]

The N.A.A.C.P. works through the National Office in New York City and through branches or local associations in cities everywhere in the country.[6] The National Office determines the policy of the organization and supervises the work of the branches.[7] The National Office, including *The Crisis,* employs 13 salaried executive officers and 17 other paid employees. All are Negroes. The president of the Association has always been a white man; at present he is Arthur B. Spingarn, who succeeded his brother, the late Joel E. Spingarn. The Board of Directors has members of both races; at present it is composed of 30 Negroes and 17 whites. There are 13 vice-presidents, 4 of whom are Negroes.[8] The main executive officer and the responsible head of the Association is the secretary. This office is now held by Walter White. Few branch officers are white, although some whites serve on executive committees of branches. It is estimated that about 10 per cent of the total membership of the Association is white. The Association is interracial only at the top, but practically all Negro at the base.

The war crisis is giving increasing importance to the Association and during the last few years there has been a remarkable increase in the number of local branches and in membership rolls. Currently there are 481 branches of the Association and, in addition, 77 youth councils[9] and 22 college chapters. The total membership of the Association is approximately 85,000. *The Crisis* has a circulation of about 17,500 copies. Since 1940 the Association has published a monthly paper, the *N.A.A.C.P. Bulletin,* which goes to all members. The National Office operates on a budget of around $85,000. Much the larger part of the budget is derived from membership fees, but a smaller part is raised by contributions from individuals and from a few foundations, most often given for specific purposes.[10]

The branches—and consequently the National Association— have nowhere been able to build up a real mass following among Negroes. The membership is still largely confined to the upper classes. It should be remembered, though, that lack of mass participation is not peculiar to the N.A.A.C.P. or even to the

Negro world but is a characteristic of American public life as a whole. Few similar organizations have reached the organizational stability and the membership size of the N.A.A.C.P. It should also be stressed that, while the lack of mass following is a weakness, the high intellectual quality of the membership of the N.A.A.C.P. is an asset. Few organizations in the entire country compare with the N.A.A.C.P. in respect to the education and mental alertness of the persons attracted to it. In a study of 5,512 Negro college graduates from all areas and of all ages, Charles S. Johnson found that 25 per cent of them were members of the N.A.A.C.P.[11] No other organization for Negroes approached this percentage. The quality of the membership is reflected in the National Office. The national leaders of Negroes have generally been intellectuals,[12] and the N.A.A.C.P. represents the highest manifestation of this general tendency. In most branches Negro professionals and businessmen constitute almost exclusively the officers, boards and executive committees.

More fundamentally, however, this structure of the Association is a weakness. The Association should have a much larger popular support in order to be able to fight with greatest success. The national leaders of the movement, and also most of the local branch officers I have come in contact with, are aware of the fact that the Association, if it wants to grow, must gain more members in the lower and middle classes of the Negro people. In the present war crisis the Association is making great strides forward, and it is reported that Negro workers are increasingly coming to join the Association.[13] There is also in recent years a visible tendency to try to get workers, and, particularly, trade union officials, on the boards of the branches. It is not improbable that as a result of the rigors and exigencies of the War, the N.A.A.C.P. will come out as an organization much stronger in membership and with much more of a following among the masses.

The N.A.A.C.P. Branches

The activity of the Association depends largely upon the effective organization of its branches. They provide it with membership, the larger part of its financial support, and information from and contacts with its field of work. The branches are the lifeline of the Association, and the National Office is constantly struggling to maintain them in vigor and to found new branches, especially in recent years.[14]

It is a heavy task the Association demands from the branches. We quote from a summary made by Bunche from the instructions given by the National Office:

The branches are to assume responsibility for the general welfare of the Negro population of the particular locality. In carrying out the broad program enunciated by the National Office, they are local vigilante groups covering all of the ramifications of Negro life in a prejudice ridden *milieu*. The branches are to check on "biased and discriminatory legislation, biased and discriminatory administration of the law, and injustice in the courts." They are to combat attempts at racial discrimination in civil rights, parks, museums, theaters, conveyances and other public places, and in charitable and public agencies. They are expected to bring test cases on the rights of Negro citizens before the courts, where great injustice is done because of race or color prejudice. Instances of police brutality against Negroes are to be fought, and Northern branches are admonished to be on the alert for cases of extradition involving Negroes who have sought refuge in the North against Southern injustice. Branches are to seek to secure new laws and ordinances to protect the welfare of Negro citizens and to prevent race discrimination. . . . The branches are expected to assume responsibility for stimulating school attendance of Negro children, and encouraging Negro youth to attend high school and college, and also to see to it "that careful technical training in some branch of modern industry is furnished all colored children." The branches must oppose all forms of educational discrimination, and demand equal educational accommodations and facilities for Negro youth; direct educational segregation, and the subtle zoning of educational districts so as to segregate Negro children indirectly, should be fought, and the branches should cooperate in the current fight to equalize teachers' salaries in Southern schools, and to eliminate the Negro-white differentials in educational appropriations. Similarly the branches are to look after the health needs of the Negro communities; tax supported hospitals excluding Negro patients should be attacked, and efforts put forth to place Negro nurses and internes in municipal hospitals. The branches are to strive for wider employment opportunities and better wages for Negroes; discrimination in Civil Service employments should be opposed. The branches should cooperate with all community efforts touching the welfare of Negro citizens, and should combat unfavorable treatment of the Negro in the local press. They should cultivate cordial relations between the races in the community. Negroes should be encouraged to qualify for voting and to vote; all possible influence should be brought to bear toward the adoption and enforcement of civil rights laws; discriminatory practices in the administration of relief and on government work projects should be exposed and protested; and better housing for Negroes should be striven for.[15]

As suggested in this statement, the National Office advises its branches on tactics as well as aims. The branches are advised "that injury to one Negro on racial grounds affects the status of the whole group, and hence, the health and happiness of our American civilization."[16] The present War, with the many problems it raises or aggravates for Negroes, has, of course, increased the demands upon the branches.

When these things are considered: the immensity of the tasks set for the branches; the high demands made upon the time, interest, intelligence, and tact of the branch officers; the fact that those officers are not salaried but work on a voluntary basis in their free time; the inherent difficulties of minority tactics and, particularly, the power situation in the South; the fact that few white people outside the national center of the organization are prepared to give assistance or even sympathy to the work; while poverty, ignorance, and defeatism are widespread among the Negro masses—when all these adverse factors are considered, it should not be a surprise that hardly any branch even approaches the realization of the ideals envisaged for its active working.[17] If we consider the handicaps under which the branches work, we should classify them, before the War, as a few energetic branches, some dormant branches, and the majority of branches somewhere between.[18] As is natural, branches in the South had small membership rolls and showed little activity. They often seemed to run through a sort of irregular vitality cycle.

(1) The normal condition is local inactivity but with maintenance of a basic membership roll and more or less regular meetings, where the stress is usually given to the general goals of the Association more than to the specific problems of the locality. There are always

social and educational entertainments. Belonging to the Association and paying dues is, in the upper classes, considered a minimum duty of a "race man" and a sign of community spirit and social respectability. "In the main," states a president of a local association in the Upper South, "We are concerned with collecting the dollar to aid the national group financially—you see we have so many organizations here to take up people's time."[19]

Another head of a branch in the Deep South, whose policy is one of caution because he fears greater repression by local whites, explains it this way: "Our task is to supply the material and the money; the folks up North have got to stick their necks out for us."[20]

(2) Now and then, ordinarily not for a period of many years, the local association flares up to importance in the community on account of a particularly self-sacrificing and energetic leader or group of leaders. Some actions are taken: In the North, these may be anything within the scope of the organization's aims. In the South they are usually restricted to the following things: a drive to get Negroes to register and vote; the organization of Negro voters to defeat a bond issue when Negro interests are flagrantly neglected; a representation to the authorities for more adequate schools or hospital facilities, for improved housing conditions, parks, and playgrounds, for the hiring of Negro policemen or firemen to serve in Negro districts, for the equalization of salaries of Negro teachers, against occasional police brutality; the instigation of a law suit to save a victim from the injustice of the region. No Southern branch could ever have the resources—or the boldness—to raise more than one or two such issues at a time. By its activity it receives publicity, and a membership drive will temporarily raise the enrollment considerably.

(3) After some time the activity falls again, either because the leaders move away or get disillusioned, or because of developing factionalism and internal strife and jealousy. Sometimes the cause is that influential white people in the community scare the leaders, or at least some of them, by telling them that they have to slow down. In either case the branch returns to its normal condition of relative ineffectiveness with maintenance and watchfulness. In extreme cases the branch can be totally destroyed.

In many Southern communities conservative or dependent upper and middle class Negroes shared the common white opinion in the

region that the N.A.A.C.P. is a "foreign" or "radical" organization, that its policy is "tactless" and "tends to stir up undue hostility between the races." They stayed away from it entirely or made
a compromise by paying dues but never attending meetings and by
generally advising the organization to abstain from taking any
action. I often heard the complaint that teachers are timid about
identifying themselves with the Association for fear of jeopardizing
their jobs, and that preachers are reluctant to join since their
churches are often mortgaged by white people. In other communities, teachers and preachers were important in the local associations, but they did not usually urge action. Most other upper class
Negroes also are dependent on the whites and have to proceed
carefully. One prominent Negro leader in a city in the Deep South,
which has a bad history of intimidation of Negroes, commented to
us upon a recent unsuccessful effort to get a branch started again:

They went about it wrong. The best way to get an organization like
that started here is to go talk to the white man first.[21]

This attitude should not be criticized in levity but must be understood against the background of the Southern caste situation.

Another difficulty of the typical N.A.A.C.P. branch is the
competition for interest, time, and money from churches, lodges
and social clubs of all sorts. Particularly as the N.A.A.C.P. cannot
promise much in immediate returns for the individual, this competition is serious. Other competition comes from independent
local civic organizations, often with the same local program.[22]
There are hundreds of such organizations, often several in one
city. The explanation of this is partly the same as of the great
number of splits in sects and churches. The local organizations
sometimes thrive upon the spread of suspicion and even hostility
against the N.A.A.C.P. as "foreign," "outside" or "meddling by a
clique of New Yorkers." But more often the motives for the split
are even more superficial and petty. Undoubtedly, it would mean a
great increase in strength for the N.A.A.C.P.—and an equally
great asset for the Negroes' organizational activity as a whole—if
these organizations could be integrated as branches of the Association.

Sometimes, however, there are more objective reasons for or-

ganizational duplication. . . . [In] a city in the Lower South
. . . a League for Civic Improvement was maintained to do the
pussy-footing with which the N.A.A.C.P. could not be compromised. In a city in the Upper South there is a powerful Committee
on Negro Affairs with a membership of around a thousand, carrying on most of the Negro politics in the community. The
N.A.A.C.P. branch has only about a hundred members. According
to the president, the main function of the branch now seems to be
one of patient waiting—it will step into the breach if the Committee fails or if the backing of the National Office is needed.[23] The
leaders of the Committee on Negro Affairs, on the other hand,
point out that the N.A.A.C.P. "helps us because the white man
will do things for us to keep the N.A.A.C.P. out." A prominent
Negro leader in one of the largest cities of the Deep South, who,
himself, regards the N.A.A.C.P. as "radical," explains:

> The South doesn't like the N.A.A.C.P. and regards it as an alien
> force; but though whites won't give to the radical group what it de-
> mands, the conservative group can come behind and capitalize on the
> situation created by the "radicals." Therefore, both radical and con-
> servative Negro groups are necessary—the radicals do the blocking
> and tackling and the conservatives "carry the ball."[24]

If all the difficulties under which a Negro protest movement has
to work in the South are remembered, it is rather remarkable, in
the final analysis, that the N.A.A.C.P. has been able to keep up
and slowly build out its network of branches in the region, and that
several of the Southern branches have been so relatively active. A
strength of the organization is that, even if the formal membership
is small, the great majority of Negroes in all classes in the South,
as well as in the North, back its program.

The N.A.A.C.P. branches in the Northern cities usually have
larger membership rolls than those in Southern cities, not only
because there are many more Negroes in the average Northern
Negro community, but also because most of the specific difficulties
under which the Southern branches labor are absent. They are free
to carry out campaigns and to take cases into court. The Negro
vote gives them a backing for their demands. Considering the
much more favorable conditions under which the Northern

branches work, it should be no surprise that they are generally stronger and more active than Southern branches. The surprising thing is that they are not stronger and more active than they actually are.

The N.A.A.C.P. National Office

The major part of the work carried on by the Association is performed by its National Office, which strikes the observer as unusually effective in its work. Owing to the National Office, the Association exerts—locally and nationally—an influence out of proportion to its small membership. The 33-year life span of the Association and the constant publicity it has received over the years give it prestige, stability, and respect, which the national officers know how to capitalize upon.

Generally, the National Office acts as a "watchdog" over Negro rights. When anything important develops on the national or on some local scene which is adverse to Negro interest, the Association promptly intervenes. A usual measure is that its secretary directs a telegram or letter to the responsible officials, which is made public through the press service of the Association. Of special importance is its watch on national legislation. The National Office tries to get hearings before Congressional committees and other investigating bodies and places on record its information and its demands on behalf of the Negroes. In the same way the Association fights for remedial legislation and for the adoption of changes in administrative practice. It is prepared to associate itself with other white or Negro organizations in cases touching Negro rights and interests.

Systematic lobbying, primarily in Washington, but also in state capitals, is kept up. Much of this work falls upon the shoulders of the secretary, Walter White. The Association tries to get on public record the opinions in crucial problems of federal administrators, congressmen, governors, other state officials, and important personalities in organizations and in business.

It loses no opportunity to place each and every elected or appointed official on record regarding specific cases affecting Negroes, such as lynching, riots, civil service discrimination, segregation, the right to vote, public works, unemployment relief, slander of the Negro race, etc. Where an official is derelict in his duty or openly prejudiced against Negroes, the National Office rallies the Branches to political action against him. In this way it has defeated for re-election many politicians guilty of race bias.[25]

The Association has successfully fought the appointment or election to public office of persons known to be prejudiced against Negroes.[26]

The Association puts its trust in publicity. A large part of the activity of the National Office is in the nature of educational propaganda. It not only publishes *The Crisis* and the *N.A.A.C.P. Bulletin,* but also a great many pamphlets, brochures and books on various aspects of the Negro problem. The officers of the National Office strive to present their case to the white public also through articles in outstanding national periodicals. The National Office provides data for research work on the Negro problem and for political work even when it is carried on outside the Association. From its staff or from a circle of active sympathizers, it furnishes speakers for important meetings. The officers of the Association travel widely on lecture tours all over the country. Most of the officers have traveled and lectured abroad, displaying the American Negro case to a world audience. Du Bois represented the Association as a lobbyist at the Versailles Peace Conference "in order to interpret to the Peace delegates the interests of the Negro peoples of the world."[27] The National Office has its own press service, which is used by the Negro press and, occasionally, also by liberal white magazines and newspapers. In its publicity the National Office has a militant and challenging tone but is ordinarily—as far as the present author has been able to check during the course of this study—scrupulously correct in statements of fact.

In a broader sense, all the work of the Association is centered around creating favorable publicity for the Negro people and winning a hearing for their grievances from the general American public. Publicity is, therefore, an important aspect of all its moves. It succeeds rather well in reaching the alert strata of the Negro people—mainly through Negro newspapers—but it attempts also to reach the white public. There it is less successful, but more successful than any other agency. Its unceasing efforts are based upon the typical American democratic trust in the righteousness of the common man:

> . . . we must win the American public to want this right for us. They are a just people and if we could by education get them to see how silly and needlessly cruel it is to deny a person food and shelter, they would help enforce the law.[28]

In its lobbying the National Office pretends with grace to represent the Negro people and is not afraid of making threats by referring to the Negro vote. When we consider the weakness of its local branches and the general rivalry and apathy in the Negro communities, this appears to be largely bluffing, and it is often successful bluffing. This is said not in criticism but in sincere admiration.[29]

From the very beginning, the Association has laid stress on its legal redress work, and this has always been a most important and, certainly, the most spectacular part of its activity.[30] The Association takes its stand on the legal equality of all the citizens of the country stipulated in the Constitution,[31] and in most of the laws of the several states of the South and the North. It brings selected cases of discrimination and segregation to the test of law suits.

In hundreds of cases, the lawyers of the N.A.A.C.P. have been instrumental in saving Negroes from unequal treatment by the courts, sometimes getting them acquitted when they were sentenced or in danger of being sentenced on flimsy evidence; sometimes getting death penalties or other severe penalties reduced.[32] The frequently successful fights to prevent the extradition of Negroes from Northern to Southern communities, when the likelihood of obtaining a fair trial for the Negroes sought could be shown to be questionable, has proved time and again an especially effective means of focusing national attention upon the low standards of legal culture in the South.[33] In numerous cases the exclusion of Negroes from grand and petit juries has been challenged, and the Association shares in establishing precedents by which the principle is now firmly established that the exclusion of Negroes from jury service is a denial of the equal protection of the laws guaranteed by the Fourteenth Amendment to the Constitution.[34] Police brutality, third degree methods in forcing confessions, and peonage have been fought.

The Association has likewise been continuously active in defending the Negroes' right to vote. In 1915 it succeeded in having
the "grandfather clauses" of Southern state constitutions declared
unconstitutional. It has fought several other cases connected with
the white primary and other means of disfranchising Negroes. As
we know, it has not succeeded in hindering the wholesale disfranchisement of the Southern Negro population. But it has put a
stop to Southern legislatures enacting the most bluntly discriminatory provisions against the suffrage of Negroes and has thus
achieved a strategic situation where the white South increasingly
bases disfranchisement upon extra-legal measures. In the very year
of the foundation of the Association a movement started to
legalize residential segregation by city ordinance. Challenging the
constitutionality of this type of legislation was one of the main
efforts of the Association during its first decade. In the famous
Louisville Segregation Case, a decisive victory was won. The
Association has been constantly vigilant, though with considerable
caution, against the Jim Crow laws and, particularly, against
inferior facilities for Negroes in segregated set-ups of various sorts.
In recent years it has concentrated its attack on the barriers
against Negro students[35] and on the unequal salaries of Negro
teachers.

The fights in court must not be viewed in isolation from the
attempts to influence legislatures and administrators. Both types of
efforts are part of a grand strategy to win legal equality for the
Negro people. The Association has spared no pains in pushing any
and all Congressional action in favor of the Negro people, or in
opposing measures having an actual or potential detrimental effect.
Foremost among these efforts to influence legislation is the long
fight for a federal anti-lynching law.[36] In this it has not succeeded
as yet, but the important effect has been to keep the national
conscience awake to lynching as a public scandal. In 1922, when
the anti-lynching bill was first seriously considered in Congress, the
number of lynchings dropped spectacularly. The Association—
which has employed a "watcher" in each branch of Congress and
now has a bureau in Washington—has been able to stop much
discriminatory legislation, including bills against intermarriage,
Jim Crow bills, and residential segregation bills for the District of
Columbia.[37] It has fought for increased federal aid to education,

for an equal distribution of federal funds for education; against discriminatory provisions in the Wages and Hours Act; against discrimination in C.W.A., P.W.A., W.P.A. projects; against administrational discrimination in the T.V.A., local relief, and public utilities; and for many other things.[38]

The Strategy of the N.A.A.C.P.

Both for strategic and for financial reasons the Association cannot afford to be a legal aid society for Negroes. The cases pursued are selected because of their general importance. The N.A.A.C.P. does not, therefore, substitute for institutions to enforce the laws and to aid poor people which we suggested were needed. This need is becoming less and less met by the Association, as it has shifted its emphasis from legal defense to legal offense.[39]

The author has found that some conservative Negroes and most conservative and liberal whites in the South accuse the N.A.A.C.P. of being "reckless" in striking in all directions against the caste order of the region without any thought whatever as to what can possibly be attained. When, with this criticism in mind, I have studied the actions of the N.A.A.C.P. over the decades, I have, on the contrary, come to the conclusion that the Association is working according to a quite clearly conceived tactical plan, which is only more far-seeing than is customary in America, particularly in the South. The Association has wisely avoided launching a wholesale legal campaign against the Southern segregation system, as this would have provoked a general reaction. It has selected its points of attack with care and has pushed the front with caution; sometimes it has preferred only to preserve a favorable defense position. On the other hand, when the N.A.A.C.P. is striking—for instance, for a federal anti-lynching law or for improved educational facilities for Negroes as in the Gaines Case—the effect is not, as it is often asserted, an intensified reaction in the South, but, on the contrary, a definite movement towards adjustment with the national norms.

In this sense, the tactics of the N.A.A.C.P. are "opportunistic"—though within the framework of a long-range policy to reach full equality for Negroes. The Association has often accepted segregation, and in fact, has sometimes had to promote further segregation, while it has been pressing for increased opportunity and equality within the segregated system. The principle of opportunism, but also the integration of opportunism into the long-range aims, is a conscious tactic:

In cases where race discrimination is too strongly entrenched to be attacked at present, it [the branch] should secure at least equal rights and accommodations for colored citizens.[40]

and it is:

. . . convinced of the futility of any program to produce separate but equal educational opportunities for education for one-tenth of America's population, so they work for the day when the same and not equal opportunities are open to all. But on the way to the goal, the campaign to get those opportunities for all in states having laws requiring separate systems of education must be waged. Equal buildings, equal equipment in the buildings, equal salaries, equal length of school term, equal transportation facilities, equal per capita expenditure—all these are steps toward our goal.[41]

The N.A.A.C.P. has also been accused of being "radical." This criticism has been excellently evaluated by Bunche:

The leadership and membership of the N.A.A.C.P., both Negro and white, is not recruited from the ranks of radicals. The program and tactics of the organization remain well within the bounds of respectability. It has, of course, been branded as radical by those who resent its militant demands for Negro equality and rights. But never, in the history of the organization, has there been aught but acceptance of the fundaments of the "American way" of life; the only demands for change have been directed toward Negro status. Its membership and its hold upon the black masses have never been strong enough to permit it to utter serious threats, nor to invoke mass pressure. Thus its tactics have had to conform to the dictates of expediency and opportunism; good strategy and the need for cultivating the prestige of the organization and the decree that demands shall be made and cases fought only when circumstances are of such favorable nature as to afford good chance of victory.[42]

Critique of the N.A.A.C.P.

The N.A.A.C.P. has been criticized by the most diverse groups for its concentration on publicity, suffrage and civil liberties. To the Northern sociologist with *laissez-faire* (do nothing) leanings, the N.A.A.C.P. and all the other organizations represent a superficial and inconsequential quack-doctoring of symptoms instead of a scientific treatment of causes. The "fundamental causes" are conflicts of "interests" which are not supposed to be touched by propaganda or law suits.[43] To the Southern liberal of a more contemplative temper, the struggle of the N.A.A.C.P. is a Don Quixotian battle against the unshakable "folkways and mores" of his unhappy region.[44] To the younger school of more or less Marxian-influenced Negro intellectuals, the N.A.A.C.P.'s policy is in the main only an evasion of the central problem, which is the economic one.[45] Different as these critical judgments are in motivation, they all express the fundamental defeatism in regard to the upholding of law and order which has become so widespread among American intellectuals of all colors and political creeds.

This pessimism is exaggerated and, consequently, the criticism against the N.A.A.C.P. is largely unjustified. In our inquiry we started out by stressing the faltering systems of law and order in America. The low legal culture, particularly in the South, was thereafter given great importance in nearly every specific aspect of our study. But we have also observed the definite trend toward a more equitable administration of the law in the South, and we have found that this trend is not unrelated to efforts of the type here discussed. With specific reference to the N.A.A.C.P., the present writer is inclined to agree with James Weldon Johnson who was once secretary of the organization:

> There is a school that holds that these legal victories are empty. They are not. At the very least, they provide the ground upon which we may make a stand for our rights.[46]

Very rightly Johnson points to the legal status of the Negro when the N.A.A.C.P. began to fight its battle, and the danger in the trend then under way, as the only basis for evaluating the organization:

When the N.A.A.C.P. was founded, the great danger facing us was that we should lose the vestiges of our rights by default. The organization checked that danger. It acted as a watchman on the wall, sounding the alarms that called us to defense. Its work would be of value if only for the reason that without it our status would be worse than it is.[47]

Another Negro writer, Bertram W. Doyle, though of the "accommodation" school, testifies to the same effect:

The significance of the agitation for rights and equality, as exemplified in, say, Mr. Du Bois, formerly a guiding spirit in the National Association for the Advancement of Colored People, was that under his scheme the races were not to be allowed to come to terms, and race relations were not again to be fixed in custom and formulated in codes before the Negro had fully experienced his freedom. Resistance to compromise has, then, helped to keep the racial situation in a state of flux and has tended to serve notice on the white man that weaker peoples expect him to live up to the principle established in his laws—those laws to which he proclaims loyalty.[48]

Thus, an evaluation of the N.A.A.C.P. requires us to examine the cases won by it and to note the effects of these victories. In the field of residential segregation, while the N.A.A.C.P. has not succeeded in getting the courts to outlaw private restrictive covenants, it has succeeded in having all laws to enforce residential segregation declared unconstitutional. This has meant that the Negroes are not completely ghettoized, and that they can expand in a city, though with much difficulty. More important, the legal fight still goes on, and it is not improbable that the Supreme Court will soon come to reverse its stand on the constitutionality of even the private restrictive covenants. Similarly, in regard to suffrage: it is true that the Southern states have so far succeeded in evading the Supreme Court decisions on the unconstitutionality of the white primary by having the primaries arranged as private party affairs. But the fight is continuing, and even this barricade may fall as the "grandfather clauses" fell earlier. Perhaps the poll tax stipulations also will be declared unconstitutional if Congress does not make them illegal first. Likewise, though the decision in the Gaines Case will probably not open the Southern universities to Negroes in the near future, it is already forcing the Southern states to take action to improve the education situation for Negroes. Generally speaking, the fight against injustice and discrimination in the South and the keeping of national attention on the matter are social forces working for change which it seems unrealistic not to take into account.

The young Negro intellectuals who are critical of the N.A.A.C.P. have, however, a more positive point in mind.[49] On second thought they will usually concede the importance of the legal fight and also agree that it has crystallized the Negro protest.[50] But they insist that the N.A.A.C.P. has not attacked the fundamental economic problems.[51] They want the N.A.A.C.P. to come out with a radical economic program. They understand that this would alienate from the organizations many of their white and Negro supporters,[52] but apparently they do not care about this or about the loss in effectiveness of the present activity which would be a consequence.

This criticism is not new. Early in the history of the Association, the Socialists clamored against the narrow racial program of the N.A.A.C.P. They wanted it to attack the economic system, to embrace the economic and political philosophy of socialism. In later years, the Communist party has likewise been insisting that any Negro organization which does not devote itself to the revolutionary cause is futile. As an aftermath of this discussion, the young Negro intellectuals today—who are not Communists and often not even Socialists—deprecate the N.A.A.C.P. as "bourgeois" and "middle class."

To this criticism the N.A.A.C.P. answers that it considers its work in the civil liberties sphere important enough not to be lightheartedly jeopardized by radical adventures in other directions. It has machinery set up for this work, and three decades' experience has gone into perfecting it. This is a form of capital working for the Negro people which should not be squandered. It has "good-will" and a public "respectability" which might appear only as an object of ridicule to the radical intellectual but which, in the daily fight of the organization, is an asset. For a Negro protest or betterment organization to adopt a revolutionary progam would be suicidal for the organization and damaging to the Negro cause.[53]

To the outside observer the reasons are strongly on the side of the N.A.A.C.P. against its critics. The American Constitution and the entire legal system of the land give the Negro a strategic strength in his fight against caste which it would be senseless not to utilize to the utmost. As it is possible to get the support of the Northern liberals—and of an increasing number of the Southern liberals, too—in the Negroes' fight for justice, this should be taken advantage of. A more or less radical economic program would not only jeopardize this support, but from a technical viewpoint, it is also impracticable to over-burden an agency with such divergent tasks.

Leaving aside their assumption that the economic factors are "basic," the critics are, of course, right in urging that there be organized efforts to tackle the Negroes' difficulties in breadwinning and, particularly, in gaining entrance into the labor unions. The question is, however, whether or not this is the proper task for the N.A.A.C.P. To an extent it is, undoubtedly, and the Association has, during the New Deal, become increasingly active in fighting discrimination in public welfare policy and in the labor market. Outside such questions of discriminatory legislation and administration as the Association is particularly competent to handle, it leaves most of these problems to the Urban League, and the two organizations even have a gentleman's agreement of long standing to observe such a division of responsibility. The Urban League has, however, even stronger reasons for not embarking upon broad and fundamental economic reform programs, as we shall see shortly.

There is thus, unquestionably, room for more concerted action on the side of the Negro people. Particularly there is need of an agency attempting to integrate Negro labor into the trade union movement. But the realization of this need should not be turned into criticism of the existing agencies serving other functions. Instead, the critics should go ahead and form the organizations they see the need of—soliciting advice and aid in their work from the experienced and established organizations. These critics—like most people who discuss the Negro protest and betterment organizations—assume without question that there should be just one unified Negro movement. We shall take up this important problem of Negro strategy later. Our conclusion will be that a suppressed minority group like the Negro people is best served by *several organizations* dividing the field and maximizing the support that can be gained from different groups of whites.

In this light should also be judged the criticism against the N.A.A.C.P. that it has "not become an important factor in the national political scene."[54] In our discussion of the Negro in politics, we have observed the need for organizing, locally and nationally, a collective bargaining agency for the Negro people to deal with the political parties. But again there is a question whether the N.A.A.C.P. can undertake to carry out this task to a greater degree than it already does—which involves taking a stand in local and national political conflicts and supporting one party or the other—without losing in effectiveness in its primary function of fighting for legal equality for the Negro. Again it is a question of whether this task should not be given to another agency.

An indisputable weakness of the N.A.A.C.P. is its lack of mass support.[55] This is, as we pointed out, admitted by the leaders of the Association.[56] When passing judgment on this problem of tactics, it should, in fairness, be recalled that we are actually asking why a severely disadvantaged group has not accomplished something which only rarely and imperfectly has been done among the whites in America. It should be borne in mind that the easiest means of rallying the American Negroes into a mass movement are such that they would destroy the organization. The Garvey movement demonstrated that the Negro masses can best be stirred into unity by an irrational and intensively racial, emotional appeal, the very thing which both the Association and its critics rightly shun. It is also questionable whether—as some of the critics of the Association hold—a greater stress on economic reform by itself has any more appeal than the fight against lynching and injustice. Poor and uneducated people all over the world are not particularly interested in economic revolution or even economic reform but must be educated to have such an interest.

When all this is said, it nevertheless stands out as a most pressing need for the organization to broaden its membership basis and to strengthen the activity of its branches.[57] There are, however, no easy panaceas available. It is the author's judgment that important steps are: (1) to have more working class members on the local boards; (2) to intensify propaganda in the schools and among the youth; (3) to stress adult education by organizing "study circles" and forums; (4) to get out more pamphlets and books on living issues and more printed directions for both individual studies and for adult education. More important, however, is the actual fighting done for the Negro. At present the war crisis is helping the Association win increasing support from the Negro people. Also in the somewhat longer perspective, the future seems promising for the Association. As the Negro masses are becoming educated and more articulate, and as the Negro protest is rising, this courageous organization with its experienced and cautious tactics will be able to count on increasing support.

The School Segregation Cases

ANTHONY LEWIS and the *New York Times*

> *We boast of the freedom enjoyed by our people above all other peoples. But it is difficult to reconcile that boast with a state of the law which, practically, puts the brand of servitude and degradation upon a large class of our fellow citizens.*
> —JUSTICE HARLAN, dissenting in
> *Plessy v. Ferguson,* 1896

The official southern myth sees the School Segregation decision of 1954 as a sudden and unjustified break with history, a misuse of the judicial power, a departure from the Constitution itself. The myth rests on several assumptions: that our constitutional history placed hallowed sanction on the custom of providing separate-but-equal facilities for Negroes; that the South, in faithful observance of that rule, created substantial equality for the Negro in schools and other public facilities; and that the Supreme Court relied on sociology, not law, in overruling the segregation doctrine.

But the assumptions are false, and the myth is no more than a myth. The separate-but-equal doctrine does not go back to some distant constitutional fount; it was read into the Constitution by judges at a fairly recent date, in what historians would call a political act. Through most of its history the doctrine drew only lip service from the South; there was separation but no equality whatsoever. The Supreme Court's abandonment of the rule was anything but sudden, the step being taken with the greatest care and only after many previous decisions had pointed in that direction. Nor was it unusual for the Court to overrule what it regarded as its own mistake, in the light of experience, and return to the true spirit of the Constitution.

History has to be explored at least briefly in any meaningful discussion of the 1954 decision. For it was no isolated event but the climax of a lengthy historical process—the rise and fall of racial segregation imposed by law. It is a rich history, combining strands of war and politics and economics and the special role of judges in this country.

Many of the forces that still move race relations in the United States were loosed in the Civil War. Not that the racial issue was the dominant cause of the war; most historians have concluded otherwise. But by the end of the war the Union was altogether committed to the abolition of slavery and the uplifting of the Negro from his degraded status. The Thirteenth Amendment, prohibiting slavery, was adopted in 1865, immediately after the war. The southern states responded by enacting the Black Codes, which restricted the rights of the newly freed Negroes and effectively made them serfs. Some of these laws, for example, forbade Negroes to own land outside towns or do any work but farming without a special license. Congress, dominated by the so-called Radical Republicans, set about to overcome the southern schemes for keeping the Negro submerged. Some of the Radicals doubtless had motives of revenge or plunder, but others were moved by sincere egalitarianism. Whatever the motive, the post–Civil War Congresses assuredly did march under the banner of Negro rights.

In 1866 Congress passed the first Civil Rights Act. Specifically designed to wipe out the disabilities imposed by the Black Codes, it provided that Negroes should have the same right as white men "to make and enforce contracts, to sue, be parties and give evidence, to inherit, purchase, lease, sell, hold and convey real and personal property, . . . and shall be subject to like punishment, pains and penalties, and to none other, any law, statute, ordinance, regulation or custom to the contrary notwithstanding."

President Andrew Johnson vetoed the bill, saying that it attempted to legislate in areas where Congress had no power—matters of "internal policy and economy" that the Constitution reserved for the state governments. Congress passed the act over the President's veto, but doubts remained about its constitutionality. To provide a broad constitutional basis for federal action insuring individual rights in any aspect of life, Congress proposed the Fourteenth Amendment later in 1866. It was ratified in 1868.

The Fourteenth Amendment began by declaring that all persons born or naturalized in the United States were citizens. This overruled the Supreme Court's decision in 1857 in the Dred Scott case, holding that Negroes could not be citizens. Then came the spacious language that has been the subject of so many lawsuits and so many political debates:

"No State shall make or enforce any law which shall abridge the privileges or immunities of citizens of the United States; nor shall any State deprive any person of life, liberty, or property, without due process of law; nor deny to any person within its jurisdiction the equal protection of the laws."

The one thing tolerably clear, as a matter of history, is that the primary, original purpose of the amendment was to protect the newly freed slaves. A contemporaneous Supreme Court so held. In 1873 a butchers' monopoly granted by the Louisiana legislature was attacked as a violation of the Fourteenth Amendment. In the Slaughterhouse cases, decided in 1873, a five-to-four majority of the Supreme Court held that the amendment did not extend to such an economic restriction unrelated to race. Justice Samuel F. Miller, for the majority, said the amendment's "pervading purpose" had been to secure the rights of the Negro and protect him "from the oppressions of those who had formerly exercised unlimited dominion over him." The dissenters did not disagree about this purpose of the amendment but thought "the mischief to be remedied was not merely slavery and its incidents and consequences."

The classic exposition of the Fourteenth Amendment by judges who had lived through its birth came in 1880. West Virginia law excluded Negroes from serving on juries. The Supreme Court, with only two dissents, held the law unconstitutional. Justice William Strong, for the majority, said the Fourteenth Amendment had been "designed to assure to the colored race the enjoyment of all the civil rights that under the law are enjoyed by white persons." Quoting the language of the amendment, he went on:

"What is this but declaring that the law in the States shall be the same for the black as for the white; that all persons, whether colored or white, shall stand equal before the laws of the States, and, in regard to the colored race, for whose protection the amendment was primarily designed, that no discrimination shall be made against them by law because of their color? . . . The very fact that colored people are singled out and expressly denied by a statute all right to participate in the administration of the law, as jurors, because of their color, though they are citizens, and may be in other respects fully qualified, is practically a brand upon them, affixed by law, an assertion of their inferiority, and a stimulant to that race prejudice which is an impediment to securing to individuals of the race that equal justice which the law aims to secure to all others."

But that was the end of an era. By that time northern politicians had lost interest in the cause of justice for the Negro. The Republican party was dedicated not to human egalitarianism but to laissez-faire economics and the growth of industrial empires that dominated the last part of the nineteenth century. The disputed Hayes-Tilden election of 1876 marked the political watershed. The award of the Presidency to Hayes was a bargain that historians have summarized as giving the Republicans control of the national government and economy while letting the whites of the South do as they would with the Negro.

The South began taking advantage of the bargain in the late 1880's. Jim Crow statutes segregating Negroes in railroads and streetcars were enacted by the southern legislatures. A poll tax was levied and restrictive qualifications adopted to keep Negroes from voting; the white primary completed the process of disenfranchisement. Ironically, poor whites and Populism hastened the subjugation of the Negro. Recent research has uncovered a body of upperclass southern opinion at the end of the century that wanted to absorb the Negro into society.

As the political situation changed, so did the Supreme Court's interpretation of the Fourteenth Amendment. The justices, like the country's business and political leaders, became more interested in economics than in race relations. The protection of economic rights that the Court had refused to see in the amendment in the Slaughterhouse cases was now found. The Court redefined the "persons" protected by the language of the amendment to include corporations and found various state regulations of business invalid.

As for the meaning of the Fourteenth Amendment to Negroes, that was redefined in *Plessy v. Ferguson* in 1896. Louisiana had enacted a Jim Crow transportation law in 1890. When Homer Adolph Plessy, who was one-eighth Negro, entered a railroad car reserved for whites, he was arrested. He challenged the constitutionality of the statute. The Supreme Court, by a vote of seven to one, found it valid.

"The underlying fallacy" of Plessy's argument, wrote Justice Henry B. Brown for the majority, was its "assumption that the enforced separation of the two races stamps the colored race with a badge of inferiority. If this be so, it is not by reason of anything found in the act but solely because the colored race chooses to put that construction upon it."

Justice Brown did not cite any legal authorities for that proposition. Nor could he, for it was nothing but a psychological or sociological thesis, doubtless widely accepted in his day but not universally even then. There is nothing wrong with the Supreme Court's interpreting language as broad as "equal protection of the laws" in light of the best contemporary understanding of human behavior. Indeed, there is nothing else the Court can do. But it is somewhat ironic to realize the purely sociological basis of *Plessy v. Ferguson,* a decision so admired by the same southerners who used "sociology" as a term of derision against the Court when it overruled Plessy in 1954.

The dissenter in *Plessy,* Justice John Marshall Harlan, did not accept the majority's premise. "The destinies of the two races in this country are indissolubly linked together," he wrote, "and the interests of both require that the common government of all shall not permit the seeds of race hate to be planted under the sanction of law. What can more certainly arouse race hate, what more certainly create and perpetuate a feeling of distrust between these races, than state enactments which in fact proceed on the ground that colored citizens are so inferior and degraded that they cannot be allowed to sit in public coaches occupied by white citizens? That, as all will admit, is the real meaning of such legislation as was enacted in Louisiana. . . . The thin disguise of 'equal' accommodations for passengers in railroad coaches will not mislead anyone, or atone for the wrong this day done."

Certainly the spirit of Justice Harlan's dissent was much closer to what the Court had said sixteen years earlier, in *Strauder v. West Virginia,* about laws affixing upon Negroes "a brand . . . , an assertion of their inferiority, and a stimulant to that race prejudice. . . ." The Supreme Court in 1896 had simply turned its back on the aspirations of that earlier day. It had introduced the new thesis that the Constitution's demand for equal protection of the laws could be met by legislation treating whites and Negroes as separate classes of people.

Plessy v. Ferguson was necessarily prophecy in good part. Justice Brown said: "A statute which implies merely a legal distinction between the white and colored races . . . has no tendency to destroy the legal equality of the two races." Justice Harlan, in contrast, predicted that the *Plessy* doctrine of separate but equal would "stimulate aggressions, more or less brutal and irritating, upon the admitted rights of colored citizens."

As a prophet Justice Harlan prevailed. *Plessy v. Ferguson* did help to stimulate the proliferation of segregation laws in every corner of life, from cradle to grave—literally, for Negroes were barred from both white hospitals and white cemeteries. Nor was there any real pretense at equality in the decades following the *Plessy* decision. In 1915 South Carolina spent $23.76 on the average white child in public school, $2.91 on the average Negro child. As late as 1931 six southeastern states (Alabama, Arkansas, Florida, Georgia, North and South Carolina) spent less than a third as much per Negro public-school pupil as per white child. Ten years later spending for the Negro had risen only to forty-four per cent of the white figure. At the time of the 1954 decision the South as a whole was spending $165 a year for the average white pupil, $115 for the Negro.

Other public facilities, such as hospitals, were just as inferior for the Negro as schools. Nor was this physical inequality the only result of the climate fostered by segregation. Negroes were purged wholesale from the voting rolls. They were rigorously excluded from almost all except menial jobs. Their very lives were at the hazard of terror and mass injustice; and by the turn of the century more than one hundred Negroes were being lynched every year.

Through the early decades of this century it became clearer and clearer to any detached observer that segregation was part of a deliberate pattern to degrade Negroes and deprive them of the rights they had been given after the Civil War. The Supreme Court was not blind to this change in the informed understanding of society. Slowly but with growing inevitability it eroded the foundations of *Plessy v. Ferguson.*

In 1917 the Court held unconstitutional a Louisville ordinance forbidding Negroes and whites to move into houses on city blocks occupied mostly by the other race. The opinion said: "It is urged that this proposed segregation will promote the public peace by preventing race conflicts. Desirable as this is, and important as is the preservation of the public peace, this aim cannot be accomplished by laws or ordinances which deny rights created or protected by the Federal Constitution."

In 1927 the Court held that state laws barring Negroes from voting in primary elections violated the Fourteenth Amendment. Justice Oliver Wendell Holmes said: "States may do a good deal of classifying that it is difficult to believe rational, but there are limits, and it is too clear for extended argument that color cannot be made the basis of a statutory classification affecting the right [to vote]."

Then, beginning in 1938, there came a series of cases in the field of higher education. The first held that Missouri could not meet the test of separate but equal by offering to pay the tuition of a Negro applicant for the Missouri Law School at an out-of-state school. Chief Justice Charles Evans Hughes said the state had to provide equal facilities itself. The decision drew a dissent—the last in any major Supreme Court decision on racial segregation. Justice James C. McReynolds wrote:

"For a long time Missouri has acted upon the view that the best interest of her people demands separation of whites and Negroes in schools. Under the opinion just announced, I presume she may abandon her law school and thereby disadvantage her white citizens without impairing petitioner's opportunities for legal instruction; or she may break down the settled practice concerning separate schools and thereby, as indicated by experience, damnify both races."

Professor Paul A. Freund of the Harvard Law School has made a perceptive comment on the McReynolds dissent. "It is of course dangerous," he said, "to accept a dissenting opinion as an objective guide to the meaning of a decision. But in this instance Mr. Justice McReynolds saw which way the winds of doctrine were blowing, and he did not like what he saw. What he saw was a steady, unmistakable progression on the part of the Court in applying the guarantee of equal protection of the laws to a series of issues: the right to serve on juries, the right to vote in primaries, the right to choose a place of residence without a legal color bar, the right to be considered for admission to a state professional school without discrimination because of race. The Court was recognizing the developing consciousness of the country that equal protection of the laws was to be given a full and not a qualified meaning."

In 1950 the Court held that a new law school set up by the State of Texas for Negroes did not provide equal protection of the laws because, as Chief Justice Fred M. Vinson put it, "the University of Texas Law School [for whites] possesses to a far greater degree those qualities which are incapable of objective measurement but which make for greatness in a law school. Such qualities, to name but a few, include reputation of the faculty, experience of the administration, position and influence of the alumni, standing in the community, traditions and prestige. It is difficult to believe that one who had a free choice between these law schools would consider the question close."

When such intangible factors were placed in the scale, how could any separate school ever be termed "equal"? In the *New*

York Times the day after the Texas Law School decision Arthur Krock said the separate-but-equal doctrine was now "a mass of tatters."

It was in that context that the Supreme Court came to the great issue of public-school segregation—the context of a legal history showing a developing momentum against the separate-but-equal rule. But it was not an easy next step. For here, unlike voting or juries or graduate education, there was involved the compulsory association of children day after day and year after year, and it was just such association that southern whites most feared.

Moreover, the Court was dealing with a practice that covered a large part of the country. Seventeen southern and border states and the District of Columbia, with forty per cent of the country's public-school enrollment, required segregation in the schools (The states were Alabama, Arkansas, Delaware, Florida, Georgia, Kentucky, Louisiana, Maryland, Mississippi, Missouri, North Carolina, Oklahoma, South Carolina, Tennessee, Texas, Virginia and West Virginia.) There were some segregated schools also in three other states whose statutes permitted the practice: Arizona, Kansas and New Mexico.

The Supreme Court, fully aware of the delicacy of the issue, handled it with exceptional care and deliberation. It should also be pointed out, as Professor Freund reminds us, that the Court did not go out looking for the school-segregation issue. It was brought there by Negro individuals and civil-rights groups desperate to improve Negro educational opportunities. Originally in fact, in the 1930's, the N.A.A.C.P. had proposed lawsuits to attack only the inequality of Negro school facilities and teachers' salaries; but the victories in the graduate-school cases inevitably led to a direct assault on the institution of segregation.

The first school case came to the Supreme Court in 1951, from Clarendon County, South Carolina. A three-judge federal district court had upheld the constitutionality of segregated schools by a vote of two-to-one, but ordered prompt action to correct the admitted inequality of the Negro schools. (The dissenter, Judge J. Waties Waring of South Carolina, was virtually driven out of the state by ostracism for his courage.) On January 28, 1952, the Supreme Court acted to avoid an early constitutional decision in the case. It sent the matter back to the lower court to get its views on a report filed by the school board concerning the program to equalize facilities. Justices Hugo L. Black and William O. Douglas dissented, saying the report was "irrelevant to the constitutional questions" and urging that those questions be argued at once.

In the fall of 1952 the South Carolina case was back, along now with others from Kansas, Delaware, Virginia and the District of Columbia. Because the Kansas case was listed first, it gave its name to the historic litigation: *Oliver Brown et al. v. Board of Education of Topeka, Kansas.*

The cause of the Negro plaintiffs now received a most significant boost. The Federal Government, in the last days of the Truman Administration, filed a brief as a friend of the Court attacking the constitutionality of segregation. It was prepared by Philip Elman, a career Justice Department lawyer of unusual scholarship and imagination, who had been a law clerk to Justice Felix Frankfurter of the Supreme Court.

The brief argued that the separate-but-equal doctrine was, when laid down in 1896, "an unwarranted departure, based upon dubious assumptions of fact combined with a disregard of the basic purposes of the Fourteenth Amendment, from the fundamental principle that all Americans, whatever their race or color, stand equal and alike before the law." Nor did the age of the precedent "give it immunity from re-examination and rejection," the brief went on. The Court had overruled its own decisions dozens of times. In 1944 it had said: "When convinced of former error, this Court has never felt constrained to follow precedent. In constitutional questions, where correction depends upon amendment and not upon legislative action, this Court throughout its history has freely exercised its power to re-examine the basis of its constitutional decisions."

The conclusion was that the Court should, if it reached the ultimate question, overrule the separate-but-equal doctrine. "Compulsory racial segregation is itself an unconstitutional discrimination." But this was not the only significance of the brief. Perhaps even more vital was a suggestion advanced as to the procedure for carrying out any decision against school segregation. The government said the Court would not have to order all segregation ended everywhere at once. Instead, the Court should send the cases back to the district courts so that those local tribunals could work with local authorities to devise plans for desegregation. The brief said the Court might even want to issue no final decrees with its decision but order a further argument on the question of implementation. In short, the government put forward a moderate approach that recognized, as it said, "the practical difficulties" in ending a custom with such deep roots.

What made that suggestion so significant was that the practical difficulties were just what concerned some of the members of the Supreme Court. The deliberations of the justices have not been disclosed. But it is known that some deeply feared the reaction that might be aroused by an order for immediate, total desegregation. If that had been the only course open, they might well not have voted to declare segregation unconstitutional. They might, as one alternative, have said that the magnitude of the issue made it appropriate for resolution not by the Court but by Congress, which is empowered by Section Five of the Fourteenth Amendment to enforce its terms. In this regard the position of Justice Frankfurter is believed to have been critical. For while he was personally a dedicated opponent of racial discrimination, he had often expressed concern about the effect on the Court as an institution if it tried to go too far too fast in constitutional decisions.

The Court heard the cases and then, at the end of the term in June, 1953, put them over for reargument in the term beginning the following October. The Court posed a series of broad questions now, asking counsel to deal with them in their briefs and argument. First there was a historical inquiry: Had the men who framed and ratified the Fourteenth Amendment understood that it would prohibit segregation in public schools? Then, interestingly, the Court asked about the relative powers of Congress and the judiciary in interpreting the amendment: Had its framers contemplated that future Congresses might abolish segregation? Was it "within the judicial power, in light of [changed] conditions, to construe the amendment as abolishing such segregation of its own force?" The Court also took up the suggestion in the Justice Department's brief and asked whether, if it held segregation unconstitutional, it could properly allow "gradual adjustment" and whether the proper way to carry that out was to remand the cases to the district courts.

The government answered those questions in a lengthy new brief the following November. There was political as well as legal import in the brief, for a new Administration had taken office since the first Government presentation. President Eisenhower himself took a hand in determining the position. In charge at the Justice Department were Attorney General Herbert Brownell, Jr., and Assistant Attorney General J. Lee Rankin. Mr. Elman again did the major part of the drafting.

The brief examined in great detail the legislative history of the Fourteenth Amendment as proposed by Congress and ratified in the state legislatures. While there were some references to school segregation, the Government said, they were "too few and scattered to justify any definite conclusion as to the existence of a general understanding . . . as to the effect which the amendment would have on school segregation." But "the primary and pervasive purpose of the Fourteenth Amendment" was "to secure for Negroes full and complete equality before the law and to abolish all legal distinctions based on race or color."

And the fact was that the amendment had been framed in the broadest, most general language. It did not mention schools, a point often raised by southerners as if it had some relevance. But neither did it mention voting or housing or juries or corporations, all areas in which the Supreme Court had repeatedly—and with general assent—held that the amendment barred discriminatory state action. And of course the amendment did not contain the words "separate but equal." The framers might have written a detailed code of what was and was not permissible in race relations. But they wisely had not; they had followed the example of those who wrote the original Constitution in using expansive phrases that would be given contemporary meaning by each generation. As Justice Holmes said of another constitutional provision: "When we are dealing with words that also are a constituent act, like the Constitution of the United States, we must realize that they have called into life a being the development of which could not have been foreseen completely by the most gifted of its begetters. . . . The case before us must be considered in the light of our whole experience and not merely in that of what was said a hundred years ago."

The demand of the Fourteenth Amendment was for "equal protection of the laws." There was no talisman in the history of the amendment that defined those words for all times. The separate-but-equal doctrine had itself been a fresh interpretation, a departure in 1896 from the spirit of earlier decisions. It was in the great tradition of the Constitution, the Government said, to read the words now in light of conditions now. A provision such as the equal-protection clause expresses "broad principles of government, the essence of which is their vitality and adaptability to the progressive changes and needs of the nation."

Nor did the Government's brief see anything in the suggestion that Congress rather than the Court should deal with the issue. The Supreme Court had applied the Fourteenth Amendment in hundreds of cases without reference to Congress—in the racial field most recently in the graduate-school cases. What was posed now was "a question not of legislative policy but of constitutional power—and it is a question which under our system of government must ultimately be determined by this Court."

When the brief was filed, it puzzled some observers in one respect. It did not directly urge the Court, as the previous Administration's brief had, to hold racial segregation in the public schools unconstitutional. Instead the 188-page document was confined to what was termed "an objective non-adversary discussion" of the questions posed by the Court the previous June. The brief concluded, for instance, with a conditional statement: "If the Court holds that laws providing for separate schools are unconstitutional, it should remand the instant cases to the lower courts with directions to carry out the Court's decision as the particular circumstances permit."

Just how the brief emerged in this form is disputed. Some who participated in the drafting say that it contained a direct call for a finding of unconstitutionality when the draft was submitted to Attorney General Brownell, and that it was softened by either Brownell or President Eisenhower. But Brownell states that the draft "did not include any such conclusion . . . when it reached my desk and, so far as I know, never did include it. Mr. Rankin

. . . and I agreed at all times that since the brief was filed in direct response to questions asked of the department by the Court, it should answer those questions solely." The truth is probably that Rankin and Brownell would personally have liked to include a direct statement on the unconstitutionality of segregation but did not believe President Eisenhower would approve it. The Attorney General did advise the President that Rankin, if asked by a member of the Supreme Court during the oral argument what the Justice Department's position was, would say that segregation should be struck down. The President evidently made no objection, and the question was asked and answered as planned. In any event the thrust of the new brief, for all its lack of a firm conclusion, was plainly against segregation. It told the justices that they had the power and the duty to give the Fourteenth Amendment a contemporary interpretation. And it said that the import of decisions up through the graduate-school cases was to make it "unreasonable and unconstitutional . . . for a state to establish or enforce legal distinctions based on race or color."

When the cases were reargued, in December, 1953, fate had made a most important change in the Supreme Court. Chief Justice Vinson had died during the summer, and President Eisenhower had appointed in his place the Governor of California, Earl Warren. Only when some future historians have access to the judicial papers of that period will it be possible to state accurately the impact of the new Chief Justice on the School cases. But enough has been said or hinted to make it clear that the change of membership on the Court made a real difference in the way *Brown v. Board of Education* looks to history. Chief Justice Vinson's inclination was to carry on the approach of the Texas Law School case, further tightening up the standard of equality within the separate-but-equal doctrine. In short, he thought it was not the time to challenge segregation per se; the most he was likely to have done was to say that the Negro pupils here did not have real equality. The indications were that he might have carried one or more of his colleagues with him, and there is also reason to believe that at least two members of the Court were inclined to put the whole issue to Congress. There was certainly no unanimity of desire on the Court to face up to the ultimate question—whether segregation itself denied the equal protection of the laws. In all likelihood, as things stood during the Vinson period, the Brown case would have produced a collection of differing opinions.

Unanimity was the most striking aspect of the actual decision when it came down on May 17, 1954. Chief Justice Warren delivered the opinion; there was no dissent, not even a separate concurrence.

The opinion found the history of the Fourteenth Amendment "inconclusive" in relation to school segregation, as the Justice Department had argued. In any case, history could not give an adequate answer because public education was just beginning in the 1860's. "We cannot turn the clock back to 1868 when the amendment was adopted, or even to 1896 when *Plessy v. Ferguson* was written. We must consider public education in the light of its full development and its present place in American life. . . . Today, education is perhaps the most important function of state and local governments. . . . In these days, it is doubtful that any child may reasonably be expected to succeed in life if he is denied the opportunity of an education. Such an opportunity, where the state has undertaken to provide it, is a right which must be made available to all on equal terms. We come then to the question presented: Does segregation of children in public schools solely on the basis of race, even though the physical facilities and other 'tangible' factors may be equal, deprive the children of the minority group of equal educational opportunities? We believe that it does."

The Chief Justice noted the Texas Law School case and its emphasis on intangible differences in schools. "Such considerations," he said, "apply with added force to children in grade and high schools. To separate them from others of similar age and qualifications solely because of their race generates a feeling of inferiority as to their status in the community that may affect their hearts and minds in a way unlikely ever to be undone. . . . Whatever may have been the extent of psychological knowledge at the time of *Plessy v. Ferguson,* this finding is amply supported by modern authority." Here the opinion, in a footnote that has been much criticized, cited the writings of various social scientists, including Myrdal.

"We conclude," the Chief Justice said, "that in the field of public education the doctrine of 'separate but equal' has no place. Separate educational facilities are inherently unequal."

The Court ordered still further argument the next term on problems of implementing its decision. Simon E. Sobeloff, who had now become Solicitor General, submitted a brief for the Federal Government suggesting—as the Justice Department had earlier indicated—that the cases be remanded to the trial courts to work out local problems. President Eisenhower personally inserted a passage in the brief. Where it said that the Court had outlawed "a social institution which has existed for a long time in many areas throughout the country," he added "—an institution, it may be noted, which during its existence not only has had the sanction of decisions of this Court but has been fervently supported by great numbers of people as justifiable on legal and moral grounds. The Court's holding in the present cases that segregation is a denial of constitutional rights involved an express recognition of the importance of psychological and emotional factors; the impact of segregation upon children, the Court found, can so affect their entire lives as to preclude their full enjoyment of constitutional rights. In similar fashion, psychological and emotional factors are involved —and must be met with understanding and good will—in the alterations that must now take place in order to bring about compliance with the Court's decision."

On May 31, 1955, after what was surely one of the most exhaustive considerations it had ever given to any issue, the Supreme Court finally disposed of *Brown v. Board of Education.* Chief Justice Warren's opinion on implementation generally followed the line suggested by the Justice Department but was even more gradualist in one respect: The Court did not, as proposed by the department, direct the lower courts to make local school authorities present desegregation plans within a specified time. It said only that the lower courts must require "a prompt and reasonable start toward full compliance." The process of desegregation, the opinion concluded, must proceed "with all deliberate speed"—a phrase first used in the Supreme Court in 1911, by Justice Holmes, and often invoked in recent years by Holmes's great admirer, Justice Frankfurter.

One item especially in Chief Justice Warren's 1954 opinion was seized upon by southerners as proof that the decision did not rest upon "law." This was the footnote citing social scientists as "modern authority" for the statement that segregation generated feelings of inferiority. But the footnote was at worst pretentious superfluity. It took no reference to social scientists to know that state-enforced separation of human beings on account of their race was a calculated device to exalt one group and debase another. Justice Brown had simply been proved wrong in his sociological hypothesis, in *Plessy v. Ferguson*, that there was nothing invidious about segregation unless the Negro chose "to put that construction upon it." After Adolf Hitler the world knew, and the Supreme Court would have been blind not to see, that it was invidious to separate out one group in society, whether Negroes or Jews or some other. Justice Harlan had been right when he said that segregation "puts the brand of servitude and degradation" on the Negro. The Court had moved toward his dissenting view in *Plessy v. Ferguson:* "Our Constitution is color-blind, and neither knows nor tolerates classes among citizens." Segregation was not the equal protection of the laws.

19. The Freedom Movement and the Rise of Nationalism

The decade following the Supreme Court decision of 1954 witnessed the rise of a movement for civil rights unprecedented in scope and intensity. Through television, radio, and the newspapers, the entire world became familiar with such new leaders as Martin Luther King, Jr., Bayard Rustin, and James Forman, and an alphabet-soup array of old and new organizational titles: NAACP, CORE, SCLC, SNCC and many others. Racial violence in Little Rock, Birmingham, and scores of other cities helped galvanize public sentiment in the United States in favor of desegregation, and proved a considerable source of international embarrassment for the nation. For the first time in American history, the nation appeared to be gaining an awareness of the full dimensions of the "American Dilemma."

The black leader who best articulated the aspirations of the civil-rights movement, and came to be regarded as the movement's symbolic leader, was the Reverend Martin Luther King, Jr. King did not originate the doctrine of nonviolent resistance with which his name has become associated. The doctrine had a long history in this country and overseas, and, in the realm of Civil Rights, had already been adopted by the Congress of Racial Equality, founded in 1942. But, under King's leadership, the principles of noncooperation with unjust laws, and nonviolent responses to physical assaults, became the guiding principles of a mass movement. King emphasized that the tactic of nonviolent direct action was "not a method for cowards," for it required immense courage and moral strength to apply in practice the Christian principles of loving one's enemies and turning the other cheek in response to violence, and to accept imprisonment, abuse and physical assault without retaliation. But King recognized that such tactics would arouse the moral conscience of the nation, and would also succeed in mobilizing masses of southern blacks steeped in the doctrines of Christianity.

King rose to national prominence during the Montgomery bus boycott of 1956. A black woman, Mrs. Rosa Parks, had been arrested for refusing to give up her seat to a white passenger, and in response the black community refused to patronize the city bus system until it was desegregated. But it was not until the 1960's that King's methods became the tools of a nationwide movement. The real turning point in the civil-rights movement was the decision of four black students in Greensboro, North Carolina, to refuse to leave a lunch counter at which they had been denied service. Sit-ins, as such demonstrations came to be called, spread like wildfire across the country, and succeeded in integrating hundreds of shops, restaurants, parks, and other facilities. In most cases, the demonstrators purposely violated the law by either trespassing or entering segregated facilities, and many were either arrested or assaulted by whites. But with dignity and purpose they adhered to the philosophy of nonresistance. In 1961, the sit-in technique was extended to interstate transportation, when black and white Freedom Riders journeyed into the South, testing compliance with a ruling of the Interstate Commerce Commission requiring desegregation of buses, railways, and terminal facilities, and met a violent response from southern whites.

The pace of civil-rights activities continued to quicken in 1962 and reached a climax of sorts during 1963. In the spring of that year, King led a series of massive demon-

strations in Birmingham, Alabama, protesting the segregation and discrimination which pervaded every aspect of
life in that city. Significantly, King now devoted more
attention than in the past to the desperate economic
situation of the city's black community, and demanded
increased employment for blacks as well as an end to
segregation. The unrestrained violence with which the
police broke up the demonstrations led to a wave of
sympathy among northern whites for the civil-rights cause,
and moved President Kennedy to identify himself fully
with the black movement. The federal government had
played an increasing role in attacking school segregation,
beginning with President Eisenhower's use of troops to
enforce court-ordered desegregation in Little Rock in
1957. But in his nationwide speech of June, 1963, Kennedy for the first time stated his conviction that the nation
faced a severe moral crisis, and he proposed a sweeping
civil-rights bill to outlaw segregation in all public accommodations, end discrimination in federally-assisted programs of all kinds, and empower the Justice Department
to initiate suits for school desegregation. Then in August
came what many persons today regard as the high point
and climax of the nonviolent civil-rights movement, the
March on Washington. A quarter of a million Americans,
most of them black but with many white allies, peacefully
assembled to demand "jobs and freedom," the passage of
the civil-rights act, and an end to racial discrimination in
all phases of American life. Peaceful demonstrations
would continue for some time, and the federal government
would enact Kennedy's bill soon after his death, and in
1965 a strong voting rights act, but increasingly the
movement turned to more militant tactics and demands.

   In the essay which follows, Vincent Harding, the Director of the Martin Luther King Institute in Atlanta, describes some of the reasons for the transformation of the
black movement. He begins by placing contemporary
black radicalism in historical perspective, and then discusses the philosophy of King and of other black leaders.

Harding points out that, even at the height of the non-violent phase of the movement, there were voices in the black community insisting on the right of armed self-defense, and questioning the goal of integration. The most prominent of these spokesmen was Malcolm X, first a minister in the Nation of Islam, the anti-white separatist black religious group, and later leader of a secular black nationalist organization. As assaults on civil-rights workers continued and as economic issues less susceptible to non-violent techniques moved to the fore, increasing numbers of blacks came to echo Malcolm's dictum that freedom and equality should be fought for "by any means necessary."

Black Radicalism: The Road from Montgomery

VINCENT HARDING

> *O Americans! Americans!! I call God—I call angels—I call men, to witness that your DESTRUCTION is at hand, and will be speedily consummated unless you REPENT.*
> —DAVID WALKER, *Appeal,* 1829

> *Is white America really sorry for her crimes against the black people? Does white America have the capacity to repent —and to atone? . . . What atonement would the God of Justice demand for the robbery of the black people's labor, their lives, their true identities, their culture, their history— and even their human dignity?*
> —MALCOLM X, *Autobiography,* 1965

> *America, you'd better repent and straighten up or we'll burn you down.*
> —H. RAP BROWN, 1967

The living annals of oppressed and troubled peoples abound in wry, unanswerable comments; it is said among black people here that when Lenin was told there were black conservatives in America, he raised his eyebrows and exclaimed: "Oh! And what precisely do they have to conserve?"[1] In an age when instantaneous global communications were only beginning to be exploited, this was a natural question for an outsider to ask, and especially for a stranger who dealt in revolution. At a time when lynchings and emasculations of Negroes were public celebrations,

FROM "Black Radicalism: The Road from Montgomery," by Vincent Harding. Originally published in *Dissent: Explorations in the History of American Radicalism,* edited by Alfred F. Young, copyright © 1968 by Northern Illinois University Press. Reprinted by permission of the publisher.

when urban riots meant that white mobs were raging for the lives of defenseless Negroes, who could fault such a question from afar? For anyone who was close to the black communities of the United States, however, there was an answer: They had their *lives* to conserve.

Throughout most of their strange black pilgrimage in this often threatening land, the struggle to stay alive—to conserve their lives and the lives of their children—has been the dominant concern of Afro-Americans. The bravado cry of "Liberty or Death!" has sprung from their lips no more readily than from the lips of other men. Their shaping of revolutionary institutions has not been a significant activity. Neither radical words nor deeds have surged easily from black people in America. They have, instead, survived within the realities of Claude McKay's poignant lines:

> . . . I was born, far from my native clime,
> Under the white man's menace, out of time.[2]

For most of those who live as an indelibly marked minority in the heart of such a menace, conservatism—at least in public— comes as naturally as breathing. (And, like breathing, it often seems a necessary condition for staying alive.) Indeed, even the special black breed that has courageously dared to raise voices of protest in the midst of such a hostile situation has had to come to terms with their distance from "home," and their darkly obvious status as the outnumbered ones. So for those who have been at once black, angry, and wise, protest has never moved easily over into radicalism. Even when protest has made this leap, most of its actions and energies have been defensive. Black radicalism, therefore, has been focused largely on the means for realizing "the American promise" rather than on shaping new, dissenting goals.

One facet of the dilemma was described a decade ago by one of the most famous black radicals, Paul Robeson. In his autobiographical statement, *Here I Stand,* Robeson delineated what he called "a certain protective tactic of Negro life in America." Speaking from bitter experience, this politically sensitive artist said:

Even while demonstrating that he is really an equal . . . the Negro must never appear to be challenging white superiority. Climb up if you can—but don't act "uppity." Always show that you are *grateful.*

(Even if what you have gained has been wrested from unwilling powers, be sure to be grateful lest "they" take it all away.) Above all, *do nothing to give them cause to fear you*, for then the oppressing hand, which might at times ease up a little, will surely become a fist to knock you down again![3]

Robeson's conclusions are confirmed by Lerone Bennett, another perceptive recorder of the black experience, in *The Negro Mood.* "The history of the Negro in America . . . has been a quest for a revolt that was not a revolt . . . a revolt . . . that did not seem to the white power structure to be an open revolt."[4]

If in one sense these analyses are being outstripped by the pace of current events in the nation's black communities, they nonetheless describe much that has happened up to now (and the death of Martin Luther King appeared to many persons as additional proof of their validity). Such insights, moreover, suggest a set of guidelines for understanding the nature of black radicalism in America.

At what point does black radicalism begin? Perhaps it begins when black men lose or repress their fear of the descending white fist and carry Negro protest to one of its logical conclusions, regardless of the consequences. Perhaps it begins when sensitive, restive souls lose faith in "the myth of Negro progress" within the American system.[5] Perhaps we may speak of black radicalism when men are pressed by our society to seek alternatives (even though chimerical and "unrealistic") to the American way of life for Afro-Americans. Even now, black radicalism is more a reaction than a calculated strategy, more an agonized thrust than a body of thought; and this is one of its weaknesses.

Inchoate though they may be, as one sorts out the elements of the Afro-American experience with radicalism, several themes can be identified. First of all, it becomes clear that the classic, primarily European terms of "left" and "right" or "communist" and "capitalist" usually provide insufficient contexts for a discussion of American black radicalism. Even the sometimes helpful separation into social, political, economic, and racial radicalism at last becomes a tiresome burden in probing the subject. This radicalism, which grows out of a situation as emotionally weighted and psychologically distorted as the black-white encounter in America, cannot adequately be described in terms that are largely intellectual and theoretical. For such "irrational" reasons (among others), those classic "radicals," the Communists, found American black revolutionaries a very difficult brood to cultivate.

Another thematic reality is that in every generation there has been a group of black radicals (marked with the blood that always accompanies new births and violent deaths) that has moved far beyond the acceptable or customary lines of protest and revolt. Sometimes this has been simply a personal groping with the menace; sometimes it has been organized. At various times the emphasis of the radical approach has been on armed self-defense; and occasionally it has urged armed uprisings against the status quo. In each generation the "radical edge" has reached a different point in the overall experience, but it has always been present—marked by despair, alienation, fierce anger, and sometimes even by hope.

A third continuity is found in the constantly recurring, religiously oriented themes of apocalyptic messianism and atonement. Basically this has implied the conviction that there could be no ultimate deliverance for blacks (or whites) without a black-led rebellious movement, which would involve levels of anguish and blood-letting surpassing those of the Civil War. From the first attempts to capture their slave ships to the current talk of "taking over the ghettos," the black radical impulse has been informed by a vision of blood, a vision often understood as being of divine origin.

Usually, however, the goal of black radicalism has appeared to be the simplistic, "moderate" goal of assimilation into American society; but many radicals have realized there is nothing simple or moderate about such an aim. They knew that the American nation would have to be drastically transformed before it would fully open itself to the native-yet-alien presence in its midst. This was what a black leader of the Communist Party meant when she said, in the 1930's, "It is impossible to take one step in the direction of winning for the Negro people their elementary rights that is not revolutionary."[6] Nevertheless, other radicals eventually became convinced that such a transformation is impossible. Thus black nationalism and black zionism also have sought to chart a course in the endless search. Their path, of course, has not been towards assimilation.

Against such a background it becomes clear that the transformation of black radicals from the singing, integration-directed marchers of Montgomery, Alabama, in 1955 into the avowed guerrilla fighters and alienated rebels of the late 1960's was in keeping with historical precedents.[7]

I

In 1955 Martin Luther King and the black community in Montgomery faced a situation that contained much that was new as well as much that was brutally old. Social, political, and economic injustices to Negro citizens were evident on every hand; the South was considered the major bastion of enforced second-class citizenship; and segregation in public facilities seemed the most blatant example of racial humiliation. But there was something new as well. The previous spring the Bandung Conference in Southeast Asia had reminded the world how much World War II had done to intensify the struggles of formerly colonized people in wrenching themselves free of Western domination. In New York City the United Nations was an expanding forum for the views of the formerly silent peoples of the earth. The United States was deeply engaged in ideological—and occasionally military—struggles with powers that were quick to exploit this nation's poor record as a protector of its own oppressed. Younger, better-educated black people and their families were moving from rural to urban areas and were determined to play a new role in American society.

In this context, and under the prodding of the National Association for the Advancement of Colored People, the Supreme Court in 1954 had declared that racial segregation in public schools was unconstitutional. Concern about school segregation focused on the South, for it was recognized that the decision, if firmly enforced, also could signal the end of many other institutionalized forms of segregation. Some blacks who saw this possibility now moved forward with a conviction that, for the first time, the nation's highest tribunal was on their side. At the same moment, the Court's decision was a call to fierce resistance for many white persons.[8]

It was at this point that Martin Luther King entered the scene.

The decision of a gentle black lady to retain her disputed seat on a segregated bus, then the decision of Montgomery's Negro community that her subsequent arrest be protested—these and other events helped press the twenty-six-year-old Baptist minister into the radical path.[9] Neither his somewhat sheltered middle-class Atlanta background nor his rather conventional education had prepared him for such a mission, but he accepted it. Martin Luther King's brand of radicalism can be traced to a number of sources: the lives and the teachings of Christ and Gandhi, the thinking of Thoreau, the aborted hopes of James Farmer and A. Philip Randolph,[10] the tough strategy talks of Bayard Rustin, and the exigencies of the situation. From these and other sources King shaped his old-new hope, catalyzed by his own creative impulses.

Love was the answer. Not sentimentality, but the tough and resolute love that refused bitterness and hatred but stood firmly against every shred of injustice. Few brands of black radicalism had ever required so much. Men were not only urged to stand and face the menace, they were called upon to be true to themselves and to reject the very weapons that had destroyed them for so long. They were called upon to transform American life by substituting moral and spiritual courage for its traditional dependence upon violence and coercion. This new (and untried) weapon could easily be distributed to—eventually—the overwhelming majority of ordinary black people. To the confused and often fearful white faces behind the menacing fists Dr. King addressed these words:

We will match your capacity to inflict suffering with our capacity to endure suffering. We will meet your physical force with soul force. We will not hate you, but we cannot . . . obey your unjust laws. Do to us what you will and we will still love you. Bomb our homes and threaten our children; send your hooded perpetrators of violence into our communities and drag us out on some wayside road, beating us and leaving us half dead, and we will still love you. But we will soon wear you down by our capacity to suffer. And in winning our freedom we will so appeal to your heart and conscience that we will win you in the process.[11]

After the victory against segregation in public buses in Montgomery (which many persons explained away in legal terms), King sought to institutionalize his vision in the Southern Christian

Leadership Conference. King and the SCLC still harbored David
Walker's messianic hope that black people would lead the way to a
redeemed America, but they would not use Walker's method. The
new radical hope (is it not always radical to think of redemption
for America?) was expressed in an SCLC document:

Creatively used, the philosophy of nonviolence can restore the broken
community in America. SCLC is convinced that nonviolence is the
most potent force available to an oppressed people in their struggle for
freedom and dignity.[12]

In uniting the broken community King and the SCLC sought to
build what they called "the beloved community," in which black
and white Americans of every social and economic level would
recognize their bonds of human unity.

The power of nonviolence, however, was temporarily vitiated in
the attempt to apply the tactic to its immense task. SCLC could
not maintain the dynamic level of Montgomery in the new challenges it faced. Perhaps this was partly because SCLC was made
up not of black radicals but for the most part of Negro Baptist
ministers, but, whatever the reasons, it was not until 1960 that the
vision King projected was snatched up by an even younger generation of southern Negro students; and the sit-in movement was
born. Black southern students had not been noted for their radicalism, but this generation had grown up as witnesses of the
successful struggles of other non-white peoples for freedom. Although they had seen white resistance to legal desegregation
solidify in their own section, they had less to lose than Baptist
ministers.

Beginning in Greensboro, North Carolina, they went beyond the
marches and sermons of Montgomery; they walked through the
"white only" doors, stood and sat where blacks had never dared go
before, and confronted the protectors of the status quo with their
insistent black presence. In all of this the students were aided by
television and other mass media, which carried their crusading
image to other students and persons all over the world.

As the movement spread across the southland and even into the
Deep South, and to many places in the North, it was clear that this
public defiance of all the institutions of the fist was a most radical

move for that place and hour. There had been scattered precedents, but never a campaign that involved thousands of persons in hundreds of cities. In a revolutionary generation, however, the radical actions of the preceding year may appear moderate or even acceptable the next year, especially in America, where the domesticating of radical impulses seems to take place with ease and rapidity. In some ways this was what happened to the nonviolent (actually un-violent) attempts to desegregate public facilities in the South.[13]

II

As the sit-ins, freedom rides, and other demonstrations moved across the South, white resistance stiffened, and some black radicals were not convinced that nonviolence was their most effective weapon. They saw little evidence of the pliable "hearts and consciences" to which King had addressed his appeal; rather, they saw mobs, heard bombs, felt the impact of heavy clubs. Thereupon they chose Denmark Vesey, David Walker, and Nat Turner as the fathers of their black radicalism. Indeed, it was in North Carolina, the state in which the mass sit-in movement was born, that the newest call to armed Negro self-defense was sounded.

In 1959 Robert F. Williams, a Marine Corps veteran, drew attention to himself and to his branch of the NAACP in Monroe, North Carolina. Williams had changed the usual middle-class makeup of the association's branches by forming a group from laborers and other persons whose thoughts and inclinations were closer to his own. He had already begun to talk of Negroes' arming themselves when, in 1959, a white man was acquitted of charges of physical assault and attempted rape of a black woman, despite the testimony of a number of Negro witnesses.

This . . . shows [Williams said] that the Negro in the South cannot expect justice in the courts. He must convict his attackers on the spot. He must meet violence with violence, lynching with lynching.

The NAACP's national office immediately disassociated itself from Williams' statement and attempted to remove him from his position. Eventually, however, the local and state officials took care of this matter; they hounded the burly, outspoken black radical from the city and the state. But Williams was not silenced. In 1962, when nonviolence was still in its ascendancy, he maintained that

any struggle for liberation should be a flexible struggle. We must use non-violence as a means as long as this is feasible, but the day will come when conditions become so pronounced that non-violence will be suicidal. . . . The day is surely coming when we will see more violence on the same American scene. The day is surely coming when some of the same Negroes who have denounced our using weapons for self-defense will be arming themselves.[14]

Events made Williams a prophet; but the question that continues to rise from such thinking is whether the call to armed self-defense is a conservative or a radical move. It can be argued that Williams—and others like him—simply become part of the violent pattern of American life and promise no more than its continuation. Can a nation that is built on violence be constructively transformed by violence? On the other hand one faces the perennial, inherent ambiguity in black radicalism: in the minds of some persons nothing could have been more radical, even in the 1960's, than the decision of Negroes to arm themselves. Williams' group, in arming itself, determined to defy both the southern mob and the southern police, who seemed ready to expose them to the mob's fury. On one such occasion a "very old . . . white man . . . started screaming and crying like a baby, [while saying:]

'God damn, God damn, what is this God damn country coming to that niggers have got guns, the niggers are armed and the police can't even arrest them.' "[15]

Whatever the accuracy of definitions of black radicalism from the lips of very old southern white men, Williams soon would follow a familiar black radical path as he moved from Cuba to Moscow to Peking. Later, his call for armed self-defense would be accepted by a black revolutionary liberation struggle in America, and by 1968 he would be elected Provisional President of a separatist black nation in American exile.[16]

Behind the most militant words and deepest commitments to black radicalism of all who have spoken of black revolution in

America, whatever the variety, has been a battery of unresolved but realistic questions. How does an easily identifiable minority carry out such a revolution? Where does it find allies in a hostile and threatened nation? Against whom will the revolution be directed, and what are its goals? These were the questions of the early sixties, when nonviolence was counterposed against armed and militant self-defense.

After 1954 it was generally assumed that the enemy was the system of segregation in the South and that the major allies were the federal government, the liberals of the North, and the conscience of the nation. But step by step this assumption was transformed. More and more black persons began to ask whether segregation properly could be isolated in the South merely because it was supported by law only in that region. Others wondered how a "federal government" could be separate from the pervasive prejudice and discrimination black men had always found in the nation as a whole. Was the United States Congress really more liberal than the homeowners, real estate dealers, and corporations it represented? Was it not obvious that, when serious attempts were made to direct action into the North, there was a noticeable cooling of ardor among erstwhile allies, especially when issues of compensatory hiring, suburban housing, and integrated education were raised?[17]

Moreover, as the nation became more deeply enmeshed in Vietnam, who was willing to approve the scores-of-billions-of-dollars price tag for the rehabilitation of the black communities? And what kind of radicalism was needed to force a complacent nation to confront the need to rehabilitate the black community? What kind of a "revolution" depended on federal troops to protect and advance it? These were some of the vexing questions of the post-Montgomery decade. In Birmingham, Alabama, in the spring of 1963, SCLC activists attempted tentative answers to some of those questions.[18] More black people than ever before were called into the streets to face the prospect of jail. Larger numbers of children and young people were involved in SCLC-directed civil disobedience. At the same time, King's group raised its sights beyond the integration of public facilities: jobs for black people became part of the broader demands. But broader demands meant the willingness to launch in Birmingham a long siege of direct action, and SCLC did not seem prepared for such a trial. Besides, more and more young people of the city became involved in the protest, and their susceptibility to violent radicalism was not easy to control. Therefore the city's business leaders (forever concerned with images), the federal administration, and parts of the SCLC leadership seemed ready to bring the Birmingham campaign to a halt sooner than the results might have indicated. Thus the expanded agenda did not bring the predicted results, but some observers thought they saw the direction nonviolent action must take if it was to remain on the constantly moving forward edge of black radicalism.

One of the insights that emerged from the Birmingham demonstrations was the need for even larger attempts at civil disobedience, aimed at Washington, D.C., and utilizing the pent-up energies of thousands of black young people. A civil rights bill had finally been introduced in Congress, in response to Birmingham, but some SCLC staff members and others were determined to push the nation even beyond such legalities. It was proposed that A. Philip Randolph's old idea for a march on Washington be revived and that thousands of black people be brought to the capital for a massive act of nonviolent civil disobedience. The objective was to paralyze the life of the nation's capital until Congress and the country were willing to move much more meaningfully toward equality. But because of opposition within the civil rights establishment—from financial benefactors and from the highest level of the federal government—this massive nonviolent "attack" on the nation's capital became the "polite" March on Washington.[19]

America had domesticated another radical movement. The militant speeches were censored, the taverns were closed for the day. Radicalism that sought to reach the heart of the black condition in America also sought to remain on good terms with the President and the Attorney General. It had been easily seduced, but the lesson was not lost on some of the younger militants. The words that had been censored from one of the speeches had questioned whether the federal government was truly an ally of the black movement, and some of these perceptive young people soon answered this question in the negative.[20] Other radicals continued to urge that the nonviolent movement engage in massive civil disobedience or lose its relevance to the condition of black America.

At a SCLC convention soon after the Washington march, Wyatt Tee Walker, the conference's executive director, said:

The question is, whether we want to continue local guerrilla battles against discrimination and segregation or go to all-out war . . . has the moment come in the development of the non-violent revolution that we are forced . . . on some appointed day . . . literally [to] immobilize the nation until she acts on our pleas for justice and morality? . . . Is the day far-off that major transportation centers would be deluged with mass acts of civil disobedience; airports, train stations, bus terminals, the traffic of large cities, interstate commerce, would be halted by the bodies of witnesses non-violently insisting on "Freedom Now"? I suppose a nationwide work stoppage might attract enough attention to persuade someone to do something to get this monkey of segregation and discrimination off our backs, once, now and forever. Will it take one or all of these?[21]

Because Walker was known to be given to flights of rhetoric, it was difficult to ascertain how serious he was, but he seemed to sense the new mood. The nonviolent movement would die if it did not become more radical—to a degree that would shock most civil rights leaders and more radical than its chief financial backers would approve. Part of the familiar frustration was symbolized by Walker's vague reference to the need "to persuade someone to do something": *Who* should they try to persuade, with even the most radical action, and *what* should they be persuaded to do? Walker's organization did not support him, nor was there support for a proposed large cadre of nonviolent demonstrators who would commit themselves for at least a year of continuous action before they returned to their homes, jobs, or school. In the North, attempts at school boycotts, traffic disruption, and other forms of civil disobedience met with indifferent success. None of the major organizations was ready to move in the direction of large-scale civil disobedience. With court-enforced desegregation depriving the black movement of easily articulated goals for the struggle, momentum could not be built. Meanwhile, however, another kind of black momentum built fiercely.

III

In the summer of 1967 the transportation, commerce, commuting, and other schedules of more than one American city were totally disrupted by "witnessing" blacks, but not in the way that Walker had considered four years earlier. The young people who were to have been the core of the rejected nonviolent campaigns stormed angrily through the cities, witnessing with bricks, Molotov cocktails, and rifles. Much of their violence was a reaction to the callousness of American society at large, but it was certainly aggravated by the lack of meaningful alternatives, the result of the nonviolent movement's failure to move with the urgency the situation demanded.

What had happened between Walker's speech in 1963 and the immobilization of the cities by fear and fire in 1967? What turns black minds upon the path of alienation and armed violence? One of the crucial events was the bombing in Birmingham, less than a month after the March on Washington. The exhausted civil rights movement was mesmerized before the spectacle of the death of four black children in Birmingham, the result of a bomb that had been planted in the Sixteenth Street Baptist Church. Negro radicals saw this atrocity as a typical white American response to increasingly cautious, impotent, religiously oriented nonviolence. One of the younger black radicals wrote:

What was needed that Sunday [of the bombing] was ol' John Brown to come riding into Birmingham as he had ridden into Lawrence, Kansas, burning every building that stood and killing every man, woman and child that ran from his onslaught. Killing, killing, killing, turning men into fountains of blood . . . until Heaven itself drew back before the frothing red ocean.

But the Liberal and his Negro sycophants would've cried, Vengeance accomplishes nothing. You are only acting like your oppressor and such an act makes you no better than him. John Brown, his hands and wrists slick with blood, would've said, oh so softly and so quietly, Mere Vengeance is folly. Purgation is necessary.[22]

Atonement by blood is a persistent motif in the minds of black radicals.

Other youths were utterly embittered by the refusal of "liberal" northern political leaders even to admit that psychological violence and destruction was wreaked daily upon the lives of black ghetto-dwellers. Nothing was getting better for the submerged black people despite all the talk of "Negro progress" and "going too fast." Their schools were progressively miseducating more black children. Their houses were still decaying. Their incomes relative to whites' were decreasing. No one—radical or otherwise—seemed to be creating meaningful programs to deal with the immense problems, to challenge the widening alienation.

Equally significant, perhaps, was the growing perception that political leaders did not intend to take chances with their white constituencies by enforcing the civil rights legislation that had been enacted in 1964. When tough choices had to be made, they still seemed to favor the whites. In this "reconstruction," as in the first, the key to basic change for Negroes seemed to be in the hands of the white North, which in the mid-1960's appeared no more committed to full equality and restitution for black men than it had been a century before. Perhaps now, as then, politicians and people intuitively recognized that the social, economic, and political changes that were necessary for the rehabilitation of black America would constitute a revolution. What majority has ever presented a minority with a legislated revolution?

Therefore, as he had predicted, Robert Williams—in Cuba—spoke for more and more black persons when he said: "What is integration when the law says yes, but the police and howling mobs say no? Our only logical and successful answer is to meet organized and massive violence with massive and organized violence. Our people must prepare to wage an urban guerrilla war of self-defense."[23] In Williams' opinion, racism had become so intrinsic a part of the nation's life that it could be exorcised only with "shock treatment." Only in this way, he said, could America be saved.

Other conclusions also were drawn from Williams' premise. By 1963 America's attention had been called to Elijah Muhammad's Nation of Islam, largely through the work of the group's outstanding spokesman, Malcolm X. The Nation, which claimed a tie to the Islamic peoples of the world, had its organizational roots in the broken black hopes of the 1930's. Focusing on the black lower classes and teaching a version of religious black nationalism, the group successfully attempted to rehabilitate some of society's most alienated black rejects, and Malcolm X was one of these. He had heard the teachings of the "messenger," Elijah Muhammad, while serving a term in prison for his activities as "Detroit Red," a pimp and a narcotics pusher.[24]

Speaking for his group, Minister Malcolm said: "We don't think that it is possible for the American white man in sincerity to take the action necessary to correct the unjust conditions that 20 million black people here are made to suffer morning, noon, and night." From such a premise there followed a logical conclusion, one also derived from a long history of black radicalism. Malcolm continued,

Because we don't have any hope or confidence or faith in the American white man's ability to bring about a change in the injustices that exist, instead of asking or seeking to integrate into the American society we want to face the facts of the problem the way they are, and separate ourselves. . . .

. . . This doesn't mean that we are anti-white or anti-American, or anti-anything. We feel, that if integration all these years hasn't solved the problem yet, then we want to try something new, something different and something that is in accord with the conditions as they actually exist.[25]

Elijah Muhammad's people were moved by what was surely to come, by Malcolm's conviction that "we are living at the end of time," when "the earth will become all . . . Islam," and when those who reject the Prophet's teachings will be destroyed by Allah. They were separatists, therefore, because "we don't want to be wiped out with the American white man." What other conclusions were logical for those who had lost all faith in American whites but had gained a faith in a just and all-conquering God? Except for "Allah," of course, the script had been written in America many times over since 1800.[26]

By 1964 this remarkable young radical had rejected Elijah Muhammad's version of the old script, apparently having decided against separatism, and therefore he was faced with the dilemma Frederick Douglass and others had faced before him. In a speech before an integrated group in New York that same year, Malcolm X demonstrated his ambivalence. First he predicted that

1964 will see the Negro revolt evolve and merge into the world-wide black revolution that has been taking place on this earth since 1945. The so-called revolt will become a real black revolution. . . . Revolutions are never . . . based upon . . . begging a corrupt society or a corrupt system to accept us into it. Revolutions overturn systems. And there is no system on this earth which has proved itself more corrupt, more criminal, than this system that in 1964 still colonizes 22 million . . . Afro-Americans.

But instead of describing the terrors of the coming revolution, he seemed to backtrack: "America is the only country in history in a position to bring about a revolution without violence and bloodshed by granting the suffrage to all black people." Like Douglass, however, he had to admit: "But America is not morally equipped to do so."[27] Malcolm seemed to be caught in a painful ambivalence similar to that which had dogged the earlier radicals.

In an anguished display of mixed emotions and convictions, Malcolm nevertheless predicted that blacks' use of the franchise would "sweep all of the racists and the segregationists out of office." This, in his opinion, would "wipe out the Southern segregationism that now controls America's foreign policy, as well as America's domestic policy." More and more frequently Malcolm X proclaimed that, for the Negroes, it had to be "either ballots or bullets," either a revolution of votes or guerrilla warfare. How he expected to gain the franchise in a totally corrupt system was never made clear. (This, of course, is one of the basic dilemmas for all black leaders who have tried to help their people through a reformist ballot method. Who will vote with this minority, with those who are at once powerless and most in need of the help that can come only from a transformed society? Who will vote with them when giving that help may mean the loss of a significant share of power? In light of this conundrum, what shall black radicals do if they are determined to remain loyal to the way of life that has been blessed as most truly democratic by the rest of the society?)

Struggling with the problems of tactics and strategy, Malcolm X formed his own group, the Organization of Afro-American Unity.

Avowedly black nationalist, he saw no other position for those who would work for, with, and in the black ghettos. As he traveled in various parts of the world his religious commitment deepened and was transformed. He also became more convinced of the classic black nationalist vision of the need for internationalizing the struggle of American Negroes, and with this in mind he began to seek aid from African leaders in bringing the plight of Afro-Americans before the United Nations. "Our African . . . Asian . . . [and] Latin-American brothers can throw their weight on our side, and . . . 800 million Chinamen are . . . waiting to throw their weight on our side."[28] A troubled spirit, Malcolm moved through the ghettos and college campuses trying to construct a way where so many other brilliant black radicals before him had failed.

On self-defense he was positive and clear. Black men must exercise their right, he said, especially "in areas where the government has proven itself either unwilling or unable to defend the lives and the property of Negroes." On other issues he moved from guerrilla warfare to the ballot, but he never seemed to believe that the vote could be gained without the shedding of much blood, and perhaps not even then. On economic issues he took the predictable path of espousing socialism, partly because "almost every one of the countries that has gotten independence has devised some kind of socialistic system." Besides, he said, "you can't operate a capitalistic system unless you are vulturistic; you have to have someone else's blood to suck to be a capitalist. You show me a capitalist, I'll show you a bloodsucker."[29]

Up to the time of his death, however, Malcolm had had no vision of the path to final liberation. Near the end of his life, and before a predominantly black audience, he succumbed to the natural temptation to oversimplify the problem and its solution. In late 1964 he said: "What we need in this country is the same type of Mau Mau here that they had over there in Kenya. . . . If they were over here, they'd get this problem straightened up just like that."[30] But such loose words were testimony more to the desperation he felt before a host of enemies and an unfeeling nation than to the real level of his searching. His seeking was profound, burdened by all the agony that radical black integrity must carry, and it was complicated by his new vision of Islam and its commitment to an all-inclusive brotherhood of many-colored men. How could this be achieved in a country whose seeds of racism were embedded so deep? Perhaps all that one can, tentatively, say of him was compressed into the lines of Robert Hayden:

> He fell upon his face before
> Allah the raceless in whose blazing Oneness all
> Were one. He rose renewed, renamed, became
> much more than there was time for him to be.[31]

First among the black rebels to be cut down in the classic American style—by gunfire at a public meeting—Malcolm X had become a martyr and a saint even before his last breath escaped his body. He had helped bring modernity and a new respectability to black nationalism among the younger militants of his day. Even before he died the integrity of his life and his obvious identification with the masses among whom he had hustled and been reborn had deeply impressed the angry young men. Just before and just after his death a new flowering of militant black nationalist organizations testified to his impact on the ghettos.

IV

If one group inherited the time that had been denied Malcolm it was the Student Nonviolent Coordinating Committee, which earlier had served as the shock troops of the nonviolent movement. Organized in 1960, soon after the sit-in movement began, and committed to radical nonviolent direct action, these high school and college-age young people invaded the worst hard-core racist sections of the Deep South: southwest Georgia, black belt Alabama, and Mississippi's rural areas. They had paid more of the dues of the movement than any other group. In 1962 and 1963 SNCC leaders had agreed (for complicated and fascinating reasons) to switch from conventional direct action to voter-registration campaigns. Although such campaigns would be considered a defiant form of action in many of the most resistant parts of the South, by the 1960's they could certainly not be called radical action. Nevertheless the SNCC corps seemed to founder, physically and psychologically, and became increasingly impatient with southern resistance and increasingly disillusioned by temporizing and northern evasion. They had been influenced, moreover, by Malcolm X, a man who was "up tight" and "knew what was happening." Then, in 1964, several developments drove SNCC into a more radical nationalist direction.[32]

After having decided to organize a new black-led nonsegregated Democratic party in Mississippi, SNCC and other groups sponsored the "Mississippi Summer."[33] During these months hundreds of white persons, especially college students, moved into the state to help with various kinds of community organization and voter-registration tasks among black people (few were willing to try their skills on Mississippi whites). Forthrightly, SNCC admitted that the white newcomers had been invited as hostages to a white world that did not seem to care as much about black deaths as it did about white deaths. But the young white crowd brought something more than their willing bodies. Often, despite great personal bravery and compassion, they were insensitive to the kind of development that had to take place in the black persons with whom they worked. Too often they tended to take over tasks, conversations, meetings, and publicity that should have been handled by Negroes. Sexual competition and jealousy was another divisive issue. Many of the less articulate but no less sensitive Mississippi Negroes who worked in the summer project grew restive and resentful; and by the time the summer was over it was clear that all this would force SNCC to examine its much-publicized interraciality more closely. Could black people really grow and develop under the tutelage of white allies? "Black Power" became one of the basic responses to this basic question.

The summer of 1964 also saw the failure of the Mississippi Freedom Democratic Party to win official recognition and the state's delegate votes at the Democratic National Convention. The maneuvering and attempts at political compromise that met this challenge only strengthened the conviction of young radicals that allies were not to be found in any of the traditional sources that the civil rights movement had heretofore taken for granted. Of even more significance was the increased disillusionment with the black civil rights establishment that resulted from the Atlantic City experience.[34]

Finally, 1964 was the summer in which the black ghettos exploded, after which black leaders everywhere were forced to ask what effect their programs thus far had had in the ghettos. Among the radicals, only Malcolm X seemed to have even a tenuous claim to leadership in a dissenting, explosive world. His "thing" had been blackness; and other radicals now saw that this also would have to be their "thing" if they were to learn to speak with and for the Negro masses. SNCC heard the message.

In 1965 the impulse to a new version of black radicalism was intensified when Malcolm X was cut down by bullets. Almost none of the black radicals believed the story that the Muslims were responsible. Why, they asked, had the French government refused Malcolm permission to visit that country just before his death? What did the French know of Malcolm's enemies? Had the CIA somehow been involved? It seemed to them that America had destroyed another black man who had refused to cower before the fist and who had threatened to bring its shame fully before the world. The alienation deepened; this was not a nation that listened to moral appeals, they said. In the month after Malcolm's death the last major attempt at tactical nonviolence in the South reached a cruel climax in Selma, Alabama, one of the areas in which SNCC had conducted a voter-registration campaign. State troopers, "performing" on foot and horseback before television cameras, waded into marchers and scattered broken bodies and broken hopes before them. Understandably, many persons asked if a march in support of the right to vote was worth all of that.[35]

The summer of 1965 was the summer of Watts, of burning, of a hostile, fearful response from a nation that for many generations had prepared the tinder and matches. The event was followed by the usual investigation, the usual recommendations, and the usual inaction. Meanwhile, urban school segregation went on unchecked in the North. In South Vietnam, another American war for the right of self-determination of other men was absorbing more energies, more money, and the best of the black "rejects."

So the score was in for the new breed of black radicals, grouped organizationally in SNCC and CORE but spread throughout the ghettos of America. It seemed to them that nonviolence and integration were not only failures but probably a betrayal: "The only thing nonviolence proved was how savage whites were."[36] Other radicals claimed that integration meant only a constant drain of the best-trained black brains into a white-oriented world, leaving the ghettos as exploited, colonized infernos. Holding such convictions, the younger radicals turned ever more sharply from the path of Martin Luther King, not only because they could not believe in his weapon but because they no longer believed in his dream of integration. King's eloquent vision seemed irrelevant to the conditions of the black masses, who, like Malcolm X, began to assail the dream of middle-class integration as the substitute for the nightmare all around them. Like other radicals before them, they questioned the ultimate value of a way of life that permitted so much suffering and injustice in the most affluent nation in the world. They turned their backs on the respectable and secure ideology of assimilation to such a society, and they trumpeted their refusal to take up arms to fight such a society's overseas wars.

Like Malcolm X, their hero, these radicals are often tossed on uncertain waves of ideology. Sometimes they search for new weapons, new programs, new issues that might lead to black freedom; at other times they are given to despair, and occasionally to blind rage. Sometimes, in sheer frustration, they break down and weep. Almost always, they look only to the black communities.

Much of the feeling of this new generation of Afro-American rebels was gathered up by Julius Lester, a gifted writer:

America has had chance after chance to show that it really meant that "all men are endowed with certain inalienable rights." America has had precious chances in this decade to make it come true. Now it is over. The days of singing freedom songs and the days of combating bullets and billy clubs with Love. "We Shall Overcome" (and we have overcome our blindness) sounds old, out-dated and can enter the pantheon of the greats along with the IWW songs and the union songs. As one SNCC veteran put it after the Mississippi March, "Man, the people are too busy getting ready to fight to bother with singing anymore." And as for Love? That's always been better done in bed than on the picket lines and marches. Love is fragile gentle and seeks a like response. They used to sing "I Love Everybody" as they ducked bricks and bottles. Now they sing

> "Too much love,
> Too much love,

> Nothing kills a nigger like
> Too much love."

They know, because they still get headaches from the beatings they took while love, love, loving. They know, because they died on those highways and in those jail cells, died from trying to change the hearts of men who had none. They know, the ones who have bleeding ulcers when they're twenty-three and the ones who have to have the eye operations. They know that nothing kills a nigger like too much love.[37]

Perhaps because the hopes had been so immense, rarely had a movement of black radicalism turned so fully from its former dreams.

At one time [Lester wrote], black people desperately wanted to be American, to communicate with whites, to live in the Beloved Community. Now that is irrelevant. They know that it can't be until whites want it to be and it is obvious now that the whites don't want it.

As Lester saw it, while some black radicals would now like all whites who so deeply disappointed them to be destroyed, he was personally convinced that "the white man is simply to be ignored, because the time has come for the black man to control the things which affect his life." According to this view the black man must no longer live his life in reaction to whites. And, Lester continues:

Now he will live it only within the framework of his own blackness and his blackness links him with the Indians of Peru, the miner in Bolivia, the African and the freedom fighters of Vietnam. What they fight for is what the American black man fights for—the right to govern his own life. If the white man interprets that to mean hatred, it is only a reflection of his own fears and anxieties and black people leave him to deal with it. There is too much to do to waste time and energy hating white people.[38]

20. The Urban Ghetto Today

Among the developments which influenced the growing acceptance of the use of violence within the black movement were the uprisings which have shaken the nation's black ghettos since 1964. Although there were outbreaks of violence and looting in a few cities, including New York's Harlem, in 1964, the uprising which riveted the attention of the nation and the world on the ghetto and its grievances was the Watts outbreak of 1965. Triggered by an incident involving the arrest of a motorist, the riot in Watts, the black section of Los Angeles, raged for five days and was only suppressed by the use of the National Guard. It is estimated that as many as ten thousand blacks took part in some way, looting stores, burning buildings, and attacking police and firemen. Watts gave the nation a fearful new slogan—"Burn, baby, burn"—and, by the time the rioting subsided, thirty-four persons, mostly blacks, were dead, almost four thousand were under arrest, and property damage was estimated at $50 million.

Watts was the most serious racial outbreak of the twentieth century, but it was soon surpassed by even more violent uprisings. In 1966, over twenty cities experienced racial outbreaks of some kind, and in the summer of 1967 racial violence became so widespread that for a time it appeared the nation was heading for an all-out racial civil war. The most serious uprisings took place in Newark and Detroit. Entire city blocks in Detroit went up in flames, and by the time the riot was over forty-three persons were dead, over five thousand had been arrested and estimates of property damage ranged into the hundreds of millions of dollars.

Following the rioting of 1967, President Johnson appointed a commission headed by Governor Otto Kerner of Illinois to conduct a comprehensive investigation of the riots and their causes. In 1968 the Kerner Commission released its report, one of the most significant public documents ever written in this country. It minced no words in portraying a nation torn asunder by racial antagonisms: "Our nation is moving towards two societies, one black, one white—separate and unequal." It sharply criticized police practices both before and during the rioting, particularly the conduct of both police and National Guard troops in Detroit, where indiscriminate shooting by law-enforcement forces led to many unnecessary deaths. And it was equally clear in placing the ultimate blame for the uprisings: "White racism is essentially responsible for the explosive mixture which has been accumulating in our cities since the end of World War II." Black leaders hailed the report as a possible first step toward racial conciliation, and endorsed the Commission's proposals for massive federal spending to wipe out slum conditions, economic discrimination, and poverty. But, unable to commit the necessary funds because of the Vietnam War, Johnson all but ignored the report, and no action was taken on its recommendations. In the spring of 1968, another series of outbreaks swept the country following the assassination of Martin Luther King, and early the next year the Commission issued a follow-up report, concluding that conditions had continued to deteriorate and that the trend toward two societies was accelerating.

One of the more significant of the Kerner Commission's findings concerned the participation of the ghetto dwellers in the racial outbreaks. Many Americans had comforted

themselves with the theory that the riots had been insti-
gated by a few conspiratorial agitators, and that only the
criminal element in the ghettos—the "riffraff"—had participated. But, in the section reproduced below, the Commission concluded that a significant number of ghetto
dwellers participated in the disturbances, and that there
was no important difference between rioters and non-
rioters in education or arrest record. The typical rioter
was a young male, likely to be unemployed or working in
a menial job, but who combined a sense of racial pride
with anti-white sentiments. In fact, the most striking thing
about the Commission's conclusions is that the rioter was
an average young black of the ghetto. His grievances
against American society included brutal and degrading
police practices, unemployment, inadequate housing and
inferior education.

In the second section below, the black sociologist St.
Clair Drake discusses the "folkways" of the ghetto, the
status symbols, means of enjoyment, and other aspects of
the life styles of the different classes within the urban
black community. Yet the dominant feature of ghetto life
which emerges from his survey is the "victimization" of
the ghetto by the outside society. All the institutions of the
ghetto, its schools, businesses, hospitals, etc., are inferior
to those of the larger society and incapable of meeting the
needs of the black community. Education takes place in
overcrowded, dilapidated schools, and the majority of
black children in urban ghettos never graduate from high
schools with academic diplomas. Studies in New York
City have shown that the I.Q. of the black child actually
decreases after he enters the school system. Inadequate
education makes it impossible for blacks to compete for
high-paying jobs in an industrial society, and is one cause
of the fact that unemployment rates are so much higher in
black communities than in white. In 1967, during a period
of national prosperity, the overall unemployment rate for
blacks was 8 per cent, more than double that for whites.
And in the central ghetto the figures are much higher—it
is estimated that in some sections of Watts at the time of

the uprising there unemployment ran as high as 25 per cent. Today, in the richest nation in the world, over two-fifths of non-white families have incomes below the poverty line, while the figure for whites is about one-eighth.

The job ceiling which came into existence when blacks entered the industrial labor force during and after World War I continues to exist today, the result of inadequate education and discrimination by both employers and unions. Blacks still find it extremely difficult to rise out of menial and unskilled jobs into higher-paying skilled positions. In 1966 only 9 per cent of black workers were in professional or managerial work, while over a quarter of white workers were in these positions. By contrast, over one-third of black males were in jobs described by the Kerner Commission as "service workers and non-farm laborers," compared with only 12 per cent of whites. It is true that there are today more blacks than ever before in skilled jobs above the ceiling, but since whites have risen into these positions even faster than blacks, the income gap between the two races has continued to widen. In 1964, whites earned an average of $3,000 more than blacks, a figure double that for 1947.

Both the Kerner Commission Report and Drake's essay foresee increasing ghettoization of the black community in the years ahead. Even black families which rise into the middle class find it difficult to escape from the ghetto. As the black urban population has increased over the past decades, whites have increasingly fled the central city for the suburbs, but housing discrimination and low incomes combine to make it extremely difficult for blacks to follow them. This has been one of the major differences between the experience of the black ghetto and the ghettos of such immigrant groups as Italians, Irish, and Jews. The immigrant ghettos, whose social and economic condition was as desperate as that of blacks today, slowly dissolved as second and third generations assimilated into American culture, and moved into better neighborhoods. But because of white resistance to black neighbors, the black ghetto has remained intact and has expanded. The index of residential segregation—the percentage of an ethnic group living in an area populated predominantly by that group—has remained constant for blacks, while it has steadily declined for white immigrants. A study of Chicago, for example, reveals that the index for blacks today is as high as 85 per cent, while Puerto Ricans, the latest migrants to the city, have a significantly lower index. Puerto Ricans have a lower median income than blacks, but their lighter color seems to make them more acceptable to whites as neighbors.

It is impossible to understand the racial violence of the 1960's or the rising militancy and frustration of black leaders without always bearing in mind conditions of life in the ghetto—not merely low incomes and inadequate education, but rat-infested housing, high rates of crime and juvenile delinquency, and low life expectancy and high infant mortality rates. The responsibility for these immense social problems was placed by the Kerner Commission squarely on white society: "What white Americans have never fully understood—but what the Negro can never forget—is that white society is deeply implicated in the ghetto. White institutions created it, white institutions maintain it, and white society condones it."

Riot Participation

THE NATIONAL ADVISORY COMMISSION ON CIVIL DISORDERS

It is sometimes assumed that the rioters were criminal types, overactive social deviants, or riffraff—recent migrants, members of an uneducated underclass—alienated from responsible

FROM U. S. Government Report of the National Advisory Commission on Civil Disorders.

Negroes, and without broad social or political concerns. It is often implied that there was no effort within the Negro community to attempt to reduce the violence.

Determining who participated in a civil disorder is difficult. We have obtained data on participation from four different sources.[1]

Eyewitness accounts, from more than 1,200 interviews in our staff reconnaissance survey of 20 cities;

Interview surveys based on probability samples of riot area residents in the two major riot cities—Detroit and Newark—designed to elicit anonymous self-identification of participants as rioters, counter-rioters or non-involved;

Arrest records from 22 cities;

A special study of arrestees in Detroit.

Only partial information is available on the total numbers of participants. In the Detroit survey, approximately 11 percent of the sampled residents over the age of 15 in the two disturbance areas admittedly participated in rioting; another 20 to 25 percent admitted to having been bystanders but claimed that they had not participated; approximately 16 percent claimed they had engaged in counter-riot activity; and the largest proportion (48 to 53 percent) claimed they were at home or elsewhere and did not participate. However, a large proportion of the Negro community apparently believed that more was gained than lost through rioting, according to the Newark and Detroit surveys.[2]

Greater precision is possible in describing the characteristics of those who participated. We have combined the data from the four sources to construct a profile of the typical rioter and to compare him with the counter-rioter and the noninvolved.

The Profile of a Rioter

The typical rioter in the summer of 1967 was a Negro, unmarried male between the ages of 15 and 24 in many ways very different from the stereotypes. He was not a migrant. He was born in the state and was a life-long resident of the city in which the riot took place. Economically his position was about the same as his Negro neighbors who did not actively participate in the riot.

Although he had not, usually, graduated from high school, he was somewhat better educated than the average inner-city Negro, having at least attended high school for a time.

Nevertheless, he was more likely to be working in a menial or low status job as an unskilled laborer. If he was employed, he was not working full time and his employment was frequently interrupted by periods of unemployment.

He feels strongly that he deserves a better job and that he is barred from achieving it, not because of lack of training, ability, or ambition, but because of discrimination by employers.

He rejects the white bigot's stereotype of the Negro as ignorant and shiftless. He takes great pride in his race and believes that in some respects Negroes are superior to whites. He is extremely hostile to whites, but his hostility is more apt to be a product of social and economic class than of race; he is almost equally hostile toward middle-class Negroes.

He is substantially better informed about politics than Negroes who were not involved in the riots. He is more likely to be actively engaged in civil rights efforts, but is extremely distrustful of the political system and of political leaders.

The Profile of the Counter-Rioter

The typical counter-rioter, who risked injury and arrest to walk the streets urging rioters to "cool it," was an active supporter of existing social institutions. He was, for example, far more likely than either the rioter or the noninvolved to feel that this country is worth defending in a major war. His actions and his attitudes reflected his substantially greater stake in the social system; he was considerably better educated and more affluent than either the rioter or the noninvolved. He was somewhat more likely than the rioter, but less likely than the noninvolved, to have been a migrant. In all other respects he was identical to the noninvolved.[3]

Characteristics of Participants

Race—Eighty-three percent of the arrestees were Negroes; 15 percent were whites.[4] Our interviews in 20 cities indicate that almost all rioters were Negroes.

Age—The survey data from Detroit, the arrest records, and our interviews in 20 cities, all indicate that the rioters were late teenagers or young adults.[5] In the Detroit survey, 61.3 percent of the self-reported rioters were between the ages of 15 and 24, and 86.3 percent were between 15 and 35. The arrest data indicate that 52.5 percent of the arrestees were between 15 and 24, and 80.8 percent were between 15 and 35.

Of the noninvolved, by contrast, only 22.6 percent in the Detroit survey were between 15 and 24, and 38.3 percent were between 15 and 35.

Sex—In the Detroit survey 61.4 percent of the self-reporteed rioters were male. Arrestees, however, were almost all male—89.3 percent.[6] Our interviews in 20 cities indicate that the majority of rioters were male. The large difference in proportion between the Detroit survey data and the arrest figures probably reflects either selectivity in the arrest process or less dramatic, less provocative riot behavior by women.

Family Structure—Three sources of available information—the Newark survey, the Detroit arrest study, and arrest records from four cities—indicate a tendency for rioters to be single. The Newark survey indicates that rioters were single—56.2 percent—more often than the noninvolved—49.6 percent.

The Newark survey also indicates that rioters were more likely to have been divorced or separated—14.2 percent—than the noninvolved—6.4 percent. However, the arrest records from four cities indicate that only a very small percentage of the arrestees fall in this category.[7]

In regard to the structure of the family in which he was raised, the self-reported rioter, according to the Newark survey, was not significantly different from many of his Negro neighbors who did not actively participate in the riot. Twenty-five and five tenths percent of the self-reported rioters and 23.0 percent of the noninvolved were brought up in homes without a male head of household.[8]

Region of Upbringing—Both survey data[9] and arrest records[10] demonstrate unequivocally that those brought up in the region in which the riot occurred are much more likely to have participated in the riots. The percentage of rioters brought up in the North is almost identical for the Detroit survey—74.4 percent—and the Newark survey—74.0 percent. By contrast, of the noninvolved, 36.0 percent in Detroit and 52.4 percent in Newark were brought up in the North.[11]

Data available from five cities on the birthplace of arrestees indicate that 63 percent of the arrestees were born in the region in which the disorder occurred. Although birthplace is not necessarily identical with place of upbringing, the data are sufficiently similar to provide strong support for the conclusion.

Of the self-reported counter-rioters, however, 47.5 percent were born in the North, according to the Detroit survey, a figure which places them between self-reported rioters and the noninvolved. It appears from the data on Northern riots that a significant consequence of growing up in the South was a tendency toward noninvolvement in a riot situation, while involvement in a riot, either in support of or against existing social institutions, was more common among those born in the North.

Residence—Rioters are not only more likely than the noninvolved to have been born in the North, but they are also more likely to have been long-term residents of the city in which the disturbance took place.[12] The Detroit survey data indicate that 59.4 percent of the rioters, but only 34.6 percent of the noninvolved, were born in Detroit. The comparable figures in the Newark survey are 53.5 percent and 22.5 percent.

Outsiders who temporarily entered the city during the riot might have left before the surveys were conducted and therefore may be underestimated in the survey data. However, the arrest data,[13] which is contemporaneous with the riot, suggest that few outsiders were involved: 90 percent of those arrested resided in the riot city. Seven percent lived in the same state. Only 1 percent was from outside the state. Our interviews in 20 cities also corroborate these conclusions.

Income—In the Detroit and Newark survey data, income level alone does not seem to correlate with self-reported riot participation.[14] The figures from the two cities are not directly comparable since respondents were asked for individual income in Detroit, and family income in Newark. More Detroit rioters (38.6 percent) had annual incomes under $5,000 per year than the noninvolved (30.3 percent), but even this small difference disappears when the factor of age is taken into account.

In the Newark data, in which the age distributions of the rioters and the noninvolved are more similar, there is almost no difference between the rioters, 32.6 percent of whom had annual incomes under $5,000, and the noninvolved, 29.4 percent of whom had annual incomes under $5,000.

The similarity in income distribution should not, however, lead to the conclusion that more affluent Negroes are as likely to riot as poor Negroes. Both surveys were conducted in disturbance areas in which incomes are considerably lower than in the city as a whole and the surrounding metropolitan area.[15] Nevertheless, the data show that rioters are not necessarily the poorest of the poor.

While income does not distinguish rioters from those who were not involved, it does distinguish counter-rioters from rioters and the noninvolved. Less than 9 percent of both those who rioted and those not involved earn more than $10,000 annually. Yet almost 20 percent of the counter-rioters earned this amount or more. In fact, there were no *male* self-reported counter-rioters in the Detroit survey who earned less than $5,000 annually. In the Newark sample there were seven respondents who owned their own homes; none of them participated in the riot. While extreme poverty does not necessarily move a man to riot, relative affluence seems at least to inhibit him from attacking the existing social order and may motivate him to take considerable risks to protect it.

Education—Level of schooling is strongly related to participation. Those with some high school education were more likely to riot than those who had only finished grade school.[16] In the Detroit survey 93 percent of the self-reported rioters had gone beyond grade school, compared with 72.1 percent of the noninvolved. In the Newark survey the comparable figures are 98.1 percent and 85.7 percent. The majority of self-reported rioters are not, however, high school graduates.

The counter-rioters were clearly the best educated of the three groups. Approximately twice as many counter-rioters had attended college as had the noninvolved, and half again as many counter-rioters had attended college as had rioters. Considered along with the information on income, this suggests that counter-rioters are probably well on their way into the middle class.

Education and income are the only factors which distinguish the counter-rioter from the noninvolved. Apparently, high levels of education and income not only prevent rioting but are more likely to lead to active, responsible opposition to rioting.

Employment—The Detroit and Newark surveys, the arrest records from four cities, and the Detroit arrest study all indicate that there are no substantial differences in unemployment between the rioters and the noninvolved.[17]

Unemployment levels among both groups were extremely high. In the Detroit survey, 29.6 percent of the self-reported rioters were unemployed; in the Newark survey, 29.7 percent; in the four-city arrest data, 33.2 percent; and in the Detroit arrest study, 21.8 percent. The unemployment rates for the noninvolved in the Detroit and Newark surveys were 31.5 and 19.0 percent.

Self-reported rioters were more likely to be only intermittently employed, however, than the noninvolved. Respondents in Newark were asked whether they had been unemployed for as long as a month or more during the last year.[18] Sixty-one percent of the self-reported rioters, but only 43.4 percent of the noninvolved, answered, "Yes."

Despite generally higher levels of education, rioters are more likely than the noninvolved to be employed in unskilled jobs.[19] In the Newark survey, 50.0 percent of the self-reported rioters, but only 39.6 percent of the noninvolved, had unskilled jobs.

Attitudes About Employment—The Newark survey data indicate that self-reported rioters were more likely to feel dissatisfied with their present jobs than were the noninvolved.[20]

Only 29.3 percent of the rioters, compared with 44.4 percent of the noninvolved, thought their present jobs to be appropriate for them in responsibility and pay. Of the self-reported rioters, 67.6 percent, compared with 56.1 percent of the noninvolved, felt that it was impossible to obtain the kind of job they wanted.[21] Of the self-reported rioters, 69 percent, as compared with 50.0 percent of the noninvolved, felt that racial discrimination was the major obstacle to their finding better employment.[22] Despite this feeling, surprising numbers of rioters (76.9 percent) responded that "getting what you want out of life is a matter of ability, not being in the right place at the right time."[23]

Racial Attitudes—The Detroit and Newark surveys indicate that rioters have strong feelings of racial pride, if not racial superiority.[24] In the Detroit survey, 48.6 percent of the self-reported rioters said that they felt Negroes were more dependable than whites. Only 22.4 percent of the noninvolved stated this. In Newark, the comparable figures were 45.0 and 27.8 percent. The Newark survey data indicate that rioters want to be called "black" rather than "Negro" or "colored" and are somewhat more likely than the noninvolved to feel that all Negroes should study African history and languages.[25]

To what extent this racial pride antedated the riot and to what extent it was produced by the riot is impossible to determine from the survey data. Certainly the riot experience seems to have been associated with increased pride in the minds of many of the participants. This was vividly illustrated by the statement of a Detroit rioter:

Interviewer: You said you were feeling good when you followed the crowd?

Respondent: I was feeling proud, man, at the fact that I was a Negro. I felt like I was a first class citizen. I didn't feel ashamed of my race because of what they did.

Similar feelings were expressed by an 18-year-old Detroit girl who reported that she had been a looter:

Interviewer: What is the Negro then if he's not American?

Respondent: A Negro, he's considered a slave to the white folks. But half of them know that they're slaves and feel that they can't do nothing about it because they're just going along with it. But most of them they seem to get it in their heads now how the white folks treat them and how they've been treating them and how they've been slaves for the white folks. . . .

Along with increased racial pride there appears to be intense hostility toward whites.[26] Self-reported rioters in both the Detroit and Newark surveys were more likely to feel that civil rights groups with white and Negro leaders would do better without the whites. In Detroit, 36.1 percent of the self-reported rioters thought that this statement was true, while only 21.1 percent of the non-involved thought so. In the Newark survey, 51.4 percent of the self-reported rioters agreed; 33.1 percent of the noninvolved shared this opinion.

Self-reported rioters in Newark were also more likely to agree with the statement, "Sometimes I hate white people." Of the self-reported rioters, 72.4 percent agreed; of the noninvolved, 50.0 percent agreed.

The intensity of the self-reported rioters' racial feelings may suggest that the recent riots represented traditional interracial hostilities. Two sources of data suggest that this interpretation is probably incorrect.

First, the Newark survey data indicate that rioters were almost as hostile to middle-class Negroes as they were to whites.[27] Seventy-one and four-tenths percent of the self-reported rioters, but only 59.5 percent of the noninvolved, agreed with the statement, "Negroes who make a lot of money like to think they are better than other Negroes." Perhaps even more significant, particularly in light of the rioters' strong feelings of racial pride, is that 50.5 percent of the self-reported rioters agreed that "Negroes who make a lot of money are just as bad as white people." Only 35.2 percent of the noninvolved shared this opinion.

Second, the arrest data show that the great majority of those arrested during the disorders were generally charged with a crime relating to looting or curfew violations.[28] Only 2.4 percent of the arrests were for assault and 0.1 percent were for homicide, but 31.3 percent of the arrests were for breaking and entering—crimes directed against white property rather than against individual whites.

Political Attitudes and Involvement—Respondents in the Newark survey were asked about relatively simple items of political information, such as the race of prominent local and national political figures. In general, the self-reported rioters were much better informed than the noninvolved.[29] For example, self-reported rioters were more likely to know that one of the 1966 Newark mayoral candidates was a Negro. Of the rioters, 77.1 percent—but only 61.6 percent of the noninvolved—identified him correctly. The overall scores on a series of similar questions also reflect the self-reported rioters' higher levels of information.

Self-reported rioters were also more likely to be involved in activities associated with Negro rights.[30] At the most basic level of political participation, they were more likely than the noninvolved to talk frequently about Negro rights. In the Newark survey, 53.8 percent of the self-reported rioters, but only 34.9 percent of the noninvolved, said that they talked about Negro rights nearly every day.

The self-reported rioters also were more likely to have attended a meeting or participated in civil rights activity. Of the rioters, 39.3 percent—but only 25.7 percent of the noninvolved—reported that they had engaged in such activity.

In the Newark survey, respondents were asked how much they thought they could trust the local government.[31] Only 4.8 percent of the self-reported rioters, compared with 13.7 percent of the noninvolved, said that they felt they could trust it most of the time; 44.2 percent of the self-reported rioters and 33.9 percent of the noninvolved reported that they could almost never trust the government.

In the Detroit survey, self-reported rioters were much more likely to attribute the riot to anger about politicians and police than were the noninvolved.[32] Of the self-reported rioters, 43.2 percent—but only 19.6 percent of the noninvolved—said anger at politicians had a great deal to do with causing the riot. Of the self-reported rioters, 70.5 percent, compared with 48.8 percent of the noninvolved, believed that anger at the police had a great deal to do with causing the riot.

Perhaps the most revealing and disturbing measure of the rioters' anger at the social and political system was their response to a question asking whether they thought "the country was worth fighting for in the event of a major world war."[33] Of the self-reported rioters, 39.4 percent in Detroit and 52.8 percent in Newark shared the view that it was not. By contrast, 15.5 percent of the noninvolved in Detroit and 27.8 percent of the noninvolved in Newark shared this sentiment. Almost none of the self-reported counter-rioters in Detroit—3.3 percent—agreed with the self-reported rioters.

Some comments of interviewees are worthy of note:

Not worth fighting for—if Negroes had an equal chance it would be worth fighting for.

Not worth fighting for—I am not a true citizen so why should I?

Not worth fighting for—because my husband came back from Vietnam and nothing had changed.

. . . .

Grievances

To measure the present attitudes of people in the riot cities as precisely as possible, we are sponsoring two attitude surveys among Negroes and whites in 15 cities and four suburban areas, including four of the 20 cities studied for this chapter. These surveys are to be reported later.

In the interim we have attempted to draw some tentative conclusions based upon our own investigations and the more than 1200 interviews which we conducted relatively soon after the disorders.[34]

In almost all the cities surveyed, we found the same major grievance topics among Negro communities—although they varied in importance from city to city. The deepest grievances can be ranked into the following three levels of relative intensity:

First Level of Intensity

1. Police practices
2. Unemployment and underemployment
3. Inadequate housing

Second Level of Intensity

4. Inadequate education[35]
5. Poor recreation facilities and programs[36]
6. Ineffectiveness of the political structure and grievance mechanisms

Third Level of Intensity

7. Disrespectful white attitudes
8. Discriminatory administration of justice
9. Inadequacy of federal programs
10. Inadequacy of municipal services[37]
11. Discriminatory consumer and credit practices[38]
12. Inadequate welfare programs

Our conclusions for the 20 cities have been generally confirmed by a special interview survey in Detroit sponsored by the Detroit Urban League.[39]

Police practices were, in some form, a significant grievance in virtually all cities and were often one of the most serious complaints.[40] Included in this category were complaints about physical or verbal abuse of Negro citizens by police officers, the lack of adequate channels for complaints against police, discriminatory police employment and promotion practices, a general lack of respect for Negroes by police officers, and the failure of police departments to provide adequate protection for Negroes.

Unemployment and underemployment were found to be grievances in all 20 cities and also frequently appeared to be one of the most serious complaints.[41] These were expressed in terms of joblessness or inadequate jobs and discriminatory practices by labor unions, local and state governments, state employment services and private employment agencies.

Housing grievances were found in almost all of the cities studied and appeared to be one of the most serious complaints in a majority of them.[42] These included inadequate enforcement of building and safety codes, discrimination in sales and rentals, and overcrowding.

The educational system was a source of grievance in almost all the 20 cities and appeared to be one of the most serious complaints in half of them.[43] These grievances centered on the prevalence of *de facto* segregation, the poor quality of instruction and facilities, deficiencies in the curriculum in the public schools (particularly because no Negro history was taught), inadequate representation of Negroes on school boards, and the absence or inadequacy of vocational training.

Grievances concerning *municipal recreation programs* were found in a large majority of the 20 cities and appeared to be one of the most serious complaints in almost half.[44] Inadequate recreational facilities in the ghetto and the lack of organized programs were common complaints.

The *political structure* was a source of grievance in almost all of the cities and was one of the most serious complaints in several.[45] There were significant grievances concerning the lack of adequate representation of Negroes in the political structure, the failure of local political structures to respond to legitimate complaints and the absence or obscurity of official grievance channels.

Hostile or racist attitudes of whites toward Negroes appeared to be one of the most serious complaints in several cities.[46]

In three-quarters of the cities there were significant grievances growing out of beliefs that the *courts* administer justice on a double, discriminatory standard, and that a presumption of guilt attaches whenever a policeman testifies against a Negro.[47]

Significant grievances concerning *federal programs* were expressed in a large majority of the 20 cities, but appeared to be one of the most serious complaints in only one.[48] Criticism of the federal anti-poverty programs focused on insufficient participation by the poor, lack of continuity, and inadequate funding. Other significant grievances involved urban renewal, insufficient community participation in planning and decision-making, and inadequate employment programs.

Services provided by municipal governments—sanitation and garbage removal, health and hospital facilities, and paving and lighting of streets—were sources of complaint in approximately half of the cities, but appeared to be one of the most serious grievances in only one.[49]

Grievances concerning *unfair commercial practices* affecting Negro consumers were found in approximately half of the cities, but appeared to be one of the most serious complaints in only two.[50] Beliefs were expressed that Negroes are sold inferior quality goods (particularly meats and produce) at higher prices and are subjected to excessive interest rates and fraudulent commercial practices.

Grievances relating to the *welfare system* were expressed in more than half of the 20 cities, but were not among the most serious complaints in any of the cities. There were complaints related to the inadequacy of welfare payments, "unfair regulations," such as the "man in the house" rule, which governs welfare eligibility, and the sometimes hostile and contemptuous attitude of welfare workers. The Commission's recommendations for reform of the welfare system are based on the necessity of attacking the cycle of poverty and dependency in the ghetto.

Chart I. Pervasiveness of Grievances

Grievances Found and Number of Cities Where Mentioned as Significant

1. EMPLOYMENT AND UNDEREMPLOYMENT (found in at least one of the following forms in 20 cities)

Unemployment and underemployment (General lack of full-time jobs)	19
Union discrimination	13
Discrimination in hiring by local and state government	9
Discrimination in placement by state employment service	6
Discrimination in placement by private employment agencies	3

2. POLICE PRACTICES (found in at least one of the following forms in 19 cities)

Physical abuse	15
Verbal abuse	15
Nonexistent or inadequate channels for the redress of grievances against police	13
Discrimination in employment and promotion of Negroes	13
General lack of respect for Negroes, i.e., using derogatory language short of threats	11
Abuse of Negroes in police custody	10
Failure to answer ghetto calls promptly where Negro is victim of unlawful act	8

3. INADEQUATE HOUSING (found in at least one of the following forms in 18 cities)

Poor housing code enforcement	13
Discrimination in sales and rentals	12
Overcrowding	12

4. INADEQUATE EDUCATION (found in at least one of the following forms in 17 cities)

De facto segregation	15
Poor quality of instruction and facilities	12
Inadequacy of curriculum (e.g., no Negro history)	10
Inadequate Negro representation on school board	10
Poor vocational education or none at all	9

5. POLITICAL STRUCTURE AND GRIEVANCE MECHANISM (found in at least one of the following forms in 16 cities)

Lack of adequate Negro representation	15
Lack of response to legitimate grievances of Negroes	13
Grievance mechanism nonexistent or inadequately publicized	11

6. INADEQUATE PROGRAMS (found in at least one of the following forms in 16 cities)

Poverty program (OEO) (e.g., insufficient participation of the poor
in project planning; lack of continuity in programs; inadequate
funding; and unfulfilled promises)   12

Urban renewal (HUD) (e.g., too little community participation in
planning and decision-making; programs are not urban renewal
but "Negro removal")   9

Employment training (Labor-HEW) (e.g., persons are trained for
jobs that are not available in the Community)   7

7. DISCRIMINATORY ADMINISTRATION OF JUSTICE (found in
at least one of the following forms in 15 cities)

Discriminatory treatment in the courts   15

Lower courts act as arm of police department rather than as an
objective arbiter in truly adversary proceedings   10

Presumption of guilt when policeman testifies against Negro   8

8. POOR RECREATION FACILITIES AND PROGRAMS (found
in at least one of the following forms in 15 cities)

Inadequate facilities (parks, playgrounds, athletic fields, gymnasiums
and pools)   15

Lack of organized programs   10

9. RACIST AND OTHER DISRESPECTFUL WHITE ATTITUDES
(found in at least one of the following forms in 15 cities)

Racism and lack of respect for dignity of Negroes   15

General animosity toward Negroes   10

. . . .

Conclusion

One of the first witnesses to be invited to appear before this
Commission was Dr. Kenneth B. Clark, a distinguished and perceptive scholar. Referring to the reports of earlier riot commissions, he said:

I read that report . . . of the 1919 riot in Chicago, and it is as if I
were reading the report of the investigating committee on the Harlem
riot of '35, the report of the investigating committee on the Harlem
riot of '43, the report of the McCone Commission on the Watts riot.

I must again in candor say to you members of this Commission—it
is a kind of Alice in Wonderland—with the same moving picture re-

shown over and over again, the same analysis, the same recommendations, and the same inaction.

These words come to our minds as we conclude this Report.

We have provided an honest beginning. We have learned much. But we have uncovered no startling truths, no unique insights, no simple solutions. The destruction and the bitterness of racial disorder, the harsh polemics of black revolt and white repression have been seen and heard before in this country.

It is time now to end the destruction and the violence, not only in the streets of the ghetto but in the lives of people.

The Social and Economic Status of the Negro in the United States

St. Clair Drake

Caste, Class, and "Victimization"

During the 1930's, W. Lloyd Warner and Allison Davis developed and popularized a conceptual scheme for analyzing race relations in the Southern region of the United States which viewed Negro-white relations as organized by a color-caste system that shaped economic and political relations as well as family and kinship structures, and which was reinforced by the legal system. Within each of the two castes (superordinate white and subordinate Negro), social classes existed, status being based upon possession of money, education, and family background as reflected in distinctive styles of behavior. "Exploitation" in the Marxist sense was present within this caste-class system, but also much more; for an entire socio-cultural system, not just the economic order, func-

FROM St. Clair Drake, "The Social and Economic Condition of Negroes." Copyright © 1965 by Daedalus. Reprinted by permission of *Daedalus,* Journal of the American Academy of Arts and Sciences, Boston, Mass. volume 94, number 4.

tioned to distribute power and prestige unevenly between whites and Negroes and to punish any individuals who questioned the system by word or behavior.[1]

Students of the situation in the North rarely conceptualized race relations in terms of caste, but tended rather to view specific communities as areas in which *ethnic* groups were involved in continuous competition and conflict, resulting in a hierarchy persisting through time, with now one, and again another, ethnic group at the bottom as previous newcomers moved "up." Each ethnic group developed a social class structure within it, but as individuals acquired better jobs, more education, and some sophistication, they and their families often detached themselves from immigrant colonies (usually located in slum areas) and sometimes from all ethnic institutions as well. They tended to become a part of the middle class. The Negroes who migrated North in large numbers during World War I were the latest arrivals in this fluid and highly competitive situation, but their high visibility became a crucial factor limiting their upward mobility. Upwardly mobile Negroes could not "disappear" into the middle class of the larger society as did European ethnics.[2]

Thus, on the eve of World War II, students of race relations in the United States generally described the status of Negroes as one in which they played subordinate roles in a caste system in the South and an ethnic-class system in the North. The actions of persons toward those of another race were explained not in terms of some vaguely defined emotions connected with "prejudice," but rather in terms of the behavior they felt was expected of them by others in various positions within the social structure, and as attempts to protect and maximize whatever power and prestige accrued to them at their locus in the system. John Dollard, a psychologist, in his *Caste and Class in a Southern Town,* added an additional dimension. He analyzes the situation in terms of the "gains" and "losses"—sexual, psychological, economic, and political—which both Negroes and whites sustained at different levels in the Southern caste-class system.[3]

The caste-class analysis still provides a useful frame of reference for studying the behavior of individuals and groups located at various positions in the social structure. It can also serve as a starting point for viewing the *processes* of race relations in terms of their consequences. Of the racial and ethnic groups in America only Negroes have been subjected to caste-deprivations; and the ethnic-class system has operated to their disadvantage as compared with European immigrants. In other words, Negroes in America have been subject to "victimization" in the sense that a system of social relations operates in such a way as to deprive them of a chance to share in the more desirable material and non-material products of a society which is dependent, in part, upon their labor and loyalty. They are "victimized," also, because they do not have the same degree of access which others have to the attributes needed for rising in the general class system—money, education, "contacts," and "know-how."

The concept of "victimization" implies, too, that some people are used as means to other people's ends—without their consent—and that the social system is so structured that it can be deliberately manipulated to the disadvantage of some groups by the clever, the vicious, and the cynical, as well as by the powerful. The callous and indifferent unconsciously and unintentionally reinforce the system by their inaction or inertia. The "victims," their autonomy curtailed and their self-esteem weakened by the operation of the caste-class system, are confronted with "identity problems." Their social condition is essentially one of "powerlessness."

Individual "victims" may or may not accept the rationalizations given for the denial to them of power and prestige. They may or may not be aware of and concerned about their position in the system, but, when they do become concerned, victimization takes on important social psychological dimensions. Individuals then suffer feelings of "relative deprivation" which give rise to reactions ranging from despair, apathy, and withdrawal to covert and overt aggression. An effective analysis of the position of the Negro in these terms (although the word "victimization" is never used) may be found in Thomas F. Pettigrew's *A Profile of the Negro American* (1964).

Concepts developed by Max Weber are useful for assessing the degree of victimization existing within the American caste-class system.[4] Individuals and groups can be compared by examining what he refers to as "life chances," that is, the extent to which people have access to economic and political power. *Direct victimization* might be defined as the operation of sanctions which deny access to power, which limit the franchise, sustain job discrimination, permit unequal pay for similar work, or provide inferior training or no training at all. *Indirect victimization* is revealed in the consequences which flow from a social structure which decreases *"life chances,"* such as high morbidity and mortality rates, low longevity rates, a high incidence of psychopathology, or the persistence of personality traits and attitudes which impose disadvantages in competition or excite derogatory and invidious comparisons with other groups. Max Weber also compared individuals and groups in terms of differences in *"life styles,"* those ways of behaving which vary in the amount of esteem, honor, and prestige attached to them. Differences in "life chances" may make it impossible to acquire the money or education (or may limit the contacts) necessary for adopting and maintaining prestigious life styles. The key to understanding many aspects of race relations may be found in the fact that, in American society, the protection of their familiar and cherished life styles is a dominating concern of the white middle classes, who, because many Negroes have life styles differing from their own, have tried to segregate them into all Negro neighborhoods, voluntary associations, and churches.[5] (Marxist sociologists tend to overemphasize protection of economic interests as a dynamic factor in American race relations, important though it is.)

The "Ghettoization" of Negro Life

Pressure upon Negroes to live within all-Negro neighborhoods has resulted in those massive concentrations of Negro population in Northern metropolitan areas which bitter critics call "concentration camps" or "plantations" and which some social scientists refer to as "Black Ghettos."[6] Small town replicas exist everywhere throughout the nation, for the roots of residential segregation lie deep in American history. In older Southern towns slave quarters were transformed into Negro residential areas after Emancipation —a few blocks here, a whole neighborhood there, often adjacent to white homes. In newer Southern towns and cities a less secure upwardly mobile white population usually demanded a greater degree of segregation from ex-slaves and their descendants. Prior to World War I, the residential patterns did not vary greatly between North and South, but the great northward migration of Negroes between 1914 and 1920 expanded the small Negro neighborhoods into massive Black Belts. Middle-class white neighbors used "restrictive-covenants" as their main device for slowing down and "containing" the expansion of Negro neighborhoods. Thus, with continued in-migration and restricted access to housing in "white neighborhoods," the overcrowded Black Ghetto emerged with its substandard structures, poor public services, and high crime and juvenile delinquency rates.

Scholars know from careful research, and increasingly wider circles are becoming aware of the fact, that Negroes do not depress property values, but that middle-class white attitudes toward Negroes do.[7] As long as Negroes, as a group, are a symbol of lower social status, proximity to them will be considered undesirable and such social attitudes will be reflected in the market place. The problem is complicated by the fact that a very high proportion of Negro Americans actually does have lower-class attributes and behavior patterns. The upward mobility of white Americans, as well as their comfort and personal safety, is facilitated by spatial segregation. (Older cities in the South have been an exception.) The white middle class could protect its values by acting solely in terms of class, letting middle-class Negro families scatter into white neighborhoods irrespective of race. Instead, the white middle class in American cities protects its own neighborhoods from behavior patterns it disapproves of and from chronic social disorganization by "ghettoizing" the Negro. Real-estate operators, black and white, have exploited the fears of the white middle class from the beginning of the northern migration by "block busting," that is, by buying property for less than its normal market value and reselling it at a higher price to Negroes barred from the open market or by charging them higher rentals. Eventually the profit-potential in residential segregation was maximized by the institutions which controlled mortgage money and refused to finance property for Negro residence outside of the Black Belts except under conditions approved by them.

In 1948, the Supreme Court declared racial restrictive covenants unenforceable in the courts, but this action tended to
accelerate rather than reverse the process of ghettoization, for
many whites proceeded to sell to Negroes at inflated prices and
then moved to the suburbs, or they retained their properties,
moved away, and raised the rents. The Court's decision was based
partly upon a reevaluation of the concept of civil rights and partly
upon a recognition of the fact that serious economic injustice was
a by-product of residential segregation, a situation summed up by
Thomas Pettigrew:

While some housing gains occurred in the 1950's, the quality of Negro
housing remains vastly inferior relative to that of whites. For example,
in Chicago in 1960, Negroes paid as much for housing as whites, despite their lower incomes. . . . This situation exists because of essentially two separate housing markets; and the residential segregation
that creates these dual markets has increased steadily over past decades
until it has reached universally high levels in cities throughout the
United States, despite significant advances in the socio-economic status
of Negroes. . . .[8]

The trend has not yet been reversed despite F.H.A. administrative
regulations and Supreme Court decisions.

The spatial isolation of Negroes from whites created Negro
"communities." Within these Negro neighborhoods, church and
school became the basic integrative institutions, and Negro entrepreneurs developed a variety of service enterprises—barbershops
and beauty parlors, funeral homes and restaurants, pool parlors,
taverns, and hotels—all selling to what came to be called "The
Negro Market." Successful banking and insurance businesses also
grew up within some Negro communities. A Negro "subculture"
gradually emerged, national in scope, with distinctive variations
upon the general American culture in the fields of literature, art,
music, and dance, as well as in religious ritual and church polity.

The spatial isolation of Negroes from whites in "Black Belts"
also increased consciousness of their separate subordinate position,
for no whites were available to them as neighbors, schoolmates, or
friends, but were present only in such roles as school teachers,
policemen, and social workers, flat janitors and real-estate agents,
merchants and bill collectors, skilled laborers involved in mainte-

nance, and even a few white dentists and doctors with offices in the Black Belt. Such a situation inevitably generated anti-white sentiments (often with anti-Semitic overtones), and the pent-up feelings have occasionally erupted in anti-white riots. Normally, however, this intense racial consciousness finds expression in non-violent forms of social protest and is utilized by Negro leaders to sanction and reinforce Negro institutions and their own personal welfare. It has also lent powerful support to the segments of municipal political machines existing within Negro neighborhoods. As long as ghettos remain, race consciousness will be strong.

Residential segregation created the demographic and ecological basis for "balance of power" politics, since the possibility of a Negro bloc vote had to be recognized by both political parties. Northern Black Belt voters are not only occasionally the decisive factor in municipal elections, but have also sent a half-dozen Negroes to Congress. Indeed, it is ironic that one of the most effective weapons against segregation and discrimination in the South has been the political power generated in Negro precincts and wards of Northern Black Ghettos, thus reinforcing the direct action tactics of the civil rights movement. In the South, too, with the passage of the Civil Rights Act of 1964 and subsequent legislation, the political strength of newly enfranchised voters lies in their spatial concentration. There is some evidence that fear of this strength may operate as a factor in Northern cities to support "open occupancy," desegregation being considered preferable to Negro dominance.[9]

While the development of machine politics has brought some gains to Negro communities, it has also resulted in various forms of indirect victimization. Local Negro leaders often co-operate with the city-wide machine in the protection of "the rackets"—policy, dope, and prostitution—and sacrifice group welfare to personal gain for self and party. They have not hesitated, in some places, even to drag their heels in the fight for residential desegregation rather than risk wiping out the base of their power. Being saddled with a "bought leadership" is one of the greatest burdens Black Ghettos have had to bear. Economic victimization is widespread, too. In the "affluent society" of the sixties, consumption-oriented and given to the "hard sell," Negroes like other Americans are under social pressure to spend beyond their means. Given the lack of sophistication of many recent migrants and the very low median income of those with less than a high-school education, it is not surprising that loan sharks and dubious credit merchants (of all races) make the Black Ghetto a prime target. Negroes pay a high price for "protection" of the white middle-class way of life, since those who aspire to leave the ghetto are trapped, and those who are content to stay develop a limited and restricted view of the world in which they live.

Folkways and Classways Within the Black Ghetto

Black Ghettos in America are, on the whole, "run down" in appearance and overcrowded, and their inhabitants bear the physical and psychological scars of those whose "life chances" are not equal to those of other Americans. Like the European immigrants before them, they inherited the worst housing in the city. Within the past decade, the white "flight to the suburbs" has released relatively new and well-kept property on the margins of some of the old Black Belts. Here, "gilded ghettos" have grown up, indistinguishable from any other middle-class neighborhoods except by the color of the residents' skin.[10] The power mower in the yard, the steak grill on the rear lawn, a well stocked library and equally well stocked bar in the rumpus room—these mark the homes of well-to-do Negroes living in the more desirable portions of the Black Belt. Many of them would flee to suburbia, too, if housing were available to Negroes there.

But the character of the Black Ghetto is not set by the newer "gilded," not-yet-rundown portions of it, but by the older sections where unemployment rates are high and the masses of people work with their hands—where the median level of education is just above graduation from grade school and many of the people are likely to be recent migrants from rural areas.[11]

The "ghettoization" of the Negro has resulted in the emergence of a ghetto subculture with a distinctive ethos, most pronounced, perhaps, in Harlem, but recognizable in all Negro neighborhoods. For the average Negro who walks the streets of any American Black Ghetto, the smell of barbecued ribs, fried shrimps, and chicken emanating from numerous restaurants gives olfactory reinforcement to a feeling of "at-homeness." The beat of "gut music" spilling into the street from ubiquitous tavern juke boxes and the sound of tambourines and rich harmony behind the crude folk art on the windows of store-front churches give auditory confirmation to the universal belief that "We Negroes have 'soul.' " The bedlam of an occasional brawl, the shouted obscenities of street corner "foul mouths," and the whine of police sirens break the monotony of waiting for the number that never "falls," the horses that neither win, place, nor show, and the "good job" that never materializes. The insouciant swagger of teen-age drop-outs (the "cats") masks the hurt of their aimless existence and contrasts sharply with the ragged clothing and dejected demeanor of "skid-row" types who have long since stopped trying to keep up appearances and who escape it all by becoming "winos." The spontaneous vigor of the children who crowd streets and playgrounds (with Cassius Clay, Ernie Banks, the Harlem Globe Trotters, and black stars of stage, screen, and television as their role models) and the cheerful rushing about of adults, free from the occupational pressures of the "white world" in which they work, create an atmosphere of warmth and superficial intimacy which obscures the unpleasant facts of life in the overcrowded rooms behind the doors, the lack of adequate maintenance standards, and the too prevalent vermin and rats.

This is a world whose urban "folkways" the upwardly mobile Negro middle class deplores as a "drag" on "The Race," which the upper classes wince at as an embarrassment, and which race leaders point to as proof that Negroes have been victimized. But for the masses of the ghetto dwellers this is a warm and familiar milieu, preferable to the sanitary coldness of middle-class neighborhoods and a counterpart of the communities of the foreign-born, each of which has its own distinctive subcultural flavor. The arguments in the barbershop, the gossip in the beauty parlors, the "jiving" of bar girls and waitresses, the click of poolroom balls, the stomping of feet in the dance halls, the shouting in the churches are all *theirs*— and the white men who run the pawnshops, supermarts, drug stores, and grocery stores, the policemen on horseback, the teachers in blackboard jungles—all these are aliens, conceptualized collectively as "The Man," intruders on the Black Man's "turf." When an occasional riot breaks out, "The Man" and his property become targets of aggression upon which pent-up frustrations are vented. When someone during the Harlem riots of 1964 begged the street crowds to go home, the cry came back, "Baby, we *are* home!"

But the inhabitants of the Black Ghetto are not a homogeneous mass. Although, in Marxian terms, nearly all of them are "proletarians," with nothing to sell but their labor, variations in "life style" differentiate them into social classes based more upon differences in education and basic values (crystallized, in part, around occupational differences) than in meaningful differences in income. The American caste-class system has served, over the years, to concentrate the Negro population in the low-income sector of the economy. In 1961, six out of every ten Negro families had an income of less than $4000.00 per year. This situation among whites was just the reverse: six out of every ten white families had *over* $4000.00 a year at their disposal. (In the South, eight out of ten Negro families were below the $4000.00 level.) This is the income gap. Discrimination in employment creates a job ceiling, most Negroes being in blue-collar jobs.

With 60 per cent of America's Negro families earning less than $4000.00 a year, social strata emerge between the upper and lower boundaries of "no earned income" and $4000.00. Some families live a "middle-class style of life," placing heavy emphasis upon decorous public behavior and general respectability, insisting that their children "get an education" and "make something out of themselves." They prize family stability, and an unwed mother is something much more serious than "just a girl who had an accident"; pre-marital and extra-marital sexual relations, if indulged in at all, must be discreet. Social life is organized around churches and a welter of voluntary associations of all types, and, for women, "the cult of clothes" is so important that fashion shows are a popular fund raising activity even in churches. For both men and women, owning a home and going into business are highly desired goals, the former often being a realistic one, the latter a mere fantasy.

Within the same income range, and not always at the lower

margin of it, other families live a "lower-class life-style," being part of the "organized" lower class, while at the lowest income levels an "unorganized" lower class exists whose members tend always to become *dis*organized—functioning in an anomic situation where gambling, excessive drinking, the use of narcotics, and sexual promiscuity are prevalent forms of behavior, and violent interpersonal relations reflect an ethos of suspicion and resentment which suffuses this deviant subculture. It is within this milieu that criminal and semi-criminal activities burgeon.

The "organized" lower class is oriented primarily around churches whose preachers, often semi-literate, exhort them to "be in the 'world' but not of it." Conventional middle-class morality and Pauline Puritanism are preached, although a general attitude of "the spirit is willing but the flesh is weak" prevails except among a minority fully committed to the Pentecostal sects. They boast, "We *live* the life"—a way of life that has been portrayed with great insight by James Baldwin in *Go Tell It on the Mountain* and *The Fire Next Time.*

Young people with talent find wide scope for expressing it in choirs, quartets, and sextets which travel from church to church (often bearing colorful names like The Four Heavenly Trumpets or the Six Singing Stars of Zion) and sometimes travel from city to city. Such groups channel their aggressions in widely advertised "Battles of Song" and develop their talent in church pageants such as "Heaven Bound" or "Queen Esther" and fund-raising events where winners are crowned King and Queen. These activities provide fun as well as a testing ground for talent. Some lucky young church people eventually find their fortune in the secular world as did singers Sam Cooke and Nat King Cole, while others remain in the church world as nationally known gospel singers or famous evangelists.

Adults as well as young people find satisfaction and prestige in serving as ushers and deacons, "mothers," and deaconesses, Sunday-school teachers and choir leaders. National conventions of Negro denominations and national societies of ushers and gospel singers not only develop a continent-wide nexus of associations within the organized lower class, but also throw the more ambitious and capable individuals into meaningful contact with middle-class church members who operate as role models for those talented persons who seek to move upward. That prestige and sometimes money come so easily in these circles may be a factor militating against a pattern of delaying gratifications and seeking mobility into professional and semi-professional pursuits through higher education.

Lower-class families and institutions are constantly on the move, for in recent years the Negro lower class has suffered from projects to redevelop the inner city. By historic accident, the decision to check the expansion of physical deterioration in metropolitan areas came at a time when Negroes were the main inhabitants of substandard housing. (If urban redevelopment had been necessary sixty years ago immigrants, not Negroes, would have suffered.) In protest against large-scale demolition of areas where they live, Negroes have coined a slogan, "Slum clearance is Negro clearance." They resent the price in terms of the inconvenience thrust upon them in order to redevelop American cities,[12] and the evidence shows that, in some cities, there is no net gain in improved housing after relocation.

At the opposite pole from the Negro lower class in both life styles and life chances is the small Negro upper class whose solid core is a group in the professions, along with well-to-do businessmen who have had some higher education, but including, also, a scattering of individuals who have had college training but do not have a job commensurate with their education. These men and their spouses and children form a cohesive upper-class stratum in most Negro communities. Within this group are individuals who maintain some type of contact—though seldom any social relations—with members of the local white power élite; but whether or not they participate in occupational associations with their white peers depends upon the region of the country in which they live. (It is from this group that Negro "Exhibit A's" are recruited when white liberals are carrying on campaigns to "increase interracial understanding.") They must always think of themselves as symbols of racial advancement as well as individuals, and they often provide the basic leadership at local levels for organizations such as the N.A.A.C.P. and the Urban League. They must lend sympathetic support to the more militant civil rights organizations, too, by financial contributions, if not action.[13]

The life styles of the Negro upper class are similar to those of the white upper *middle* class, but it is only in rare instances that Negroes have been incorporated into the clique and associational life of this group or have intermarried into it. (Their participation in activities of the white upper class occurs more often than with those whites who have similar life styles because of Negro upper-class participation as members of various civic boards and inter-racial associations to which wealthy white people contribute.) Living "well" with highly developed skills, having enough money to travel, Negroes at this social level do not experience victimization in the same fashion as do the members of the lower class. Their victimization flows primarily from the fact that the social system keeps them "half in and half out," preventing the free and easy contact with their occupational peers which they need; and it often keeps them from making the kind of significant intellectual and social contributions to the national welfare that they might make if they were white. (They are also forced to experience various types of nervous strain and dissipation of energy over petty annoyances and deprivations which only the sensitive and the cultivated feel. Most barbershops, for instance, are not yet de-segregated, and taxi drivers, even in the North, sometimes refuse Negro passengers.)

The Negro upper class has created a social world of its own in which a universe of discourse and uniformity of behavior and outlook are maintained by the interaction on national and local levels of members of Negro Greek-letter fraternities and sororities, college and alumni associations, professional associations, and civic and social clubs. It is probable that if all caste barriers were dropped, a large proportion of the Negro upper class would wel-come complete social integration, and that these all-Negro institu-tions would be left in the hands of the Negro middle class, as the most capable and sophisticated Negroes moved into the orbit of the general society. Their sense of pride and dignity does not even allow them to imagine such a fate, and they pursue their social activities and play their roles as "race leaders" with little feeling of inferiority or deprivation, but always with a tragic sense of the irony of it all.

The Negro middle class covers a very wide income range, and whatever cohesion it has comes from the network of churches and social clubs to which many of its members devote a great deal of time and money. What sociologists call the Negro middle class is merely a collection of people who have similar life styles and aspirations, whose basic goals are "living well," being "respectable," and not being crude. Middle-class Negroes, by and large, are not concerned about mobility into the Negro upper class or integration with whites. They want their "rights" and "good jobs," as well as enough money to get those goods and services which make life comfortable. They want to expand continuously their level of consumption. But they also desire "decent" schools for their children, and here the degree of victimization experienced by Negroes is most clear and the ambivalence toward policies of change most sharp. Ghetto schools are, on the whole, inferior. In fact, some of the most convincing evidence that residential segregation perpetuates inequality can be found by comparing data on school districts in Northern urban areas where *de facto* school segregation exists. (Table 1 presents such data for Chicago in 1962.)

Awareness of the poor quality of education grew as the protest movement against *de facto* school segregation in the North gathered momentum. But while the fight was going on, doubt about the desirability of forcing the issue was always present within some sections of the broad Negro middle class. Those in opposition asked, "Are we not saying that our teachers can't teach our own children as well as whites can, or that our children can't

TABLE 1.   Comparison of White, Integrated and Negro Schools in Chicago: 1962

Indices of Comparison	Type of School		
	White	Integrated	Negro
Total appropriation per pupil	$342.00	$320.00	$269.00
Annual teachers' salary per pupil	256.00	231.00	220.00
Per cent uncertified teachers	12.00	23.00	49.00
No. of pupils per classroom	30.95	34.95	46.80
Library resource books per pupil	5.00	3.50	2.50
Expenditures per pupil other than teachers' salaries.	86.00	90.00	49.00

Adapted from a table in the U.S. Commission on Civil Rights report, *Public Schools, Negro and White* (Washington, D.C., 1962), pp. 241–248.

learn unless they're around whites? Aren't we insulting ourselves?" Those who want to stress Negro history and achievement and to use the schools to build race pride also express doubts about the value of mixed schools. In fact, the desirability of race consciousness and racial solidarity seems to be taken for granted in this stratum, and sometimes there is an expression of contempt for the behavior of whites of their own and lower income levels. In the present period one even occasionally hears a remark such as "Who'd want to be integrated with *those* awful white people?"

Marxist critics would dismiss the whole configuration of Negro folkways and classways as a subculture which reinforces "false consciousness," which prevents Negroes from facing the full extent of their victimization, which keeps them from ever focusing upon what they could be because they are so busy enjoying what they are—or rationalizing their subordination and exclusion. Gunnar Myrdal, in *An American Dilemma,* goes so far as to refer to the Negro community as a "pathological" growth within American society.[14] Some novelists and poets, on the other hand, romanticize it, and some Black Nationalists glorify it. A sober analysis of the civil rights movement would suggest, however, that the striking fact about all levels of the Negro community is the absence of "false consciousness," and the presence of a keen awareness of the extent of their victimization, as well as knowledge of the forces which maintain it. Not lack of knowledge but a sense of powerlessness is the key to the Negro reaction to the caste-class system.

Few Negroes believe that Black Ghettos will disappear within the next two decades despite much talk about "open occupancy" and "freedom of residence." There is an increasing tendency among Negroes to discuss what the quality of life could be within Negro communities as they grow larger and larger. At one extreme this interest slides over into Black Nationalist reactions such as the statement by a Chicago Negro leader who said, "Let all of the white people flee to the suburbs. We'll show them that the Black Man can run the second largest city in America better than the white man. Let them go. If any of them want to come back and integrate with *us* we'll accept them."

It is probable that the Black Belts of America will increase in size rather than decrease during the next decade, for no city seems likely to commit itself to "open occupancy" (although a committee in New York has been discussing a ten-year plan for dismantling Harlem).[15] And even if a race-free market were to appear Negroes would remain segregated unless drastic changes took place in the job ceiling and income gap. Controlled integration will probably continue, with a few upper- and upper-middle-class Negroes trickling into the suburbs and into carefully regulated mixed neighborhoods and mixed buildings within the city limits.[16] The basic problem of the next decade will be how to change Black Ghettos into relatively stable and attractive "colored communities." Here the social implications of low incomes become decisive.

Social Implications of the Job Ceiling and the Income Gap

Nowhere is direct victimization of Negroes more apparent than with respect to the job ceiling and the income gap; but indirect victimization which is a consequence of direct victimization is often less obvious. For instance, it has been mentioned that family incomes for Negroes are lower than for whites; but family income figures are inadequate tools for careful sociological analysis unless we know which, and how many, members of a family labor to earn a given income. In 1960, half of the white families were being supported by a husband only, while just a few more than a third of the Negro families could depend solely upon the earnings of one male breadwinner. In six out of ten nonwhite families where both a husband and wife were present, two or more persons worked; yet less than half of the white families had both husband and wife working. But even in those families which commanded an income of over $7,000.00 a year, twice as many nonwhite wives had to help earn it as white.[17] One not unimportant consequence is that a smaller proportion of Negro than white wives at this income level can play roles of unpaid volunteers in civic and social work, a fact which should be remembered by those who criticize Negroes in these income brackets for not doing more to "elevate their own people."

One of the most important effects of the income gap and the job ceiling has been the shaping of social class systems within Negro communities which differ markedly in their profiles from those of the surrounding white society. Negro class structure is "pyramidal," with a large lower class, a somewhat smaller middle class, and a tiny upper class (made up of people whose income and occupations would make them only middle class in the white society). White class profiles tend to be "diamond shaped," with small lower and upper classes and a large middle class. Unpromising "life chances" are reflected in inferior "life styles," and Black Ghettos are on the whole "rougher" and exhibit a higher degree of social disorganization than do white communities.

The job ceiling and the income gap do not create classways—for these reflect educational levels and cultural values, as well as the economic situation—but job ceiling and income gap do set the limits for realization of class values. It is a fact of American life (whether one approves of it or not) that as long as Negroes are predominantly lower-class they will, as a group, have low esteem. Yet, Negroes are victimized in the sense that the job ceiling and the income gap make it more difficult for them than for whites to maintain middle-class standards equivalent to those obtaining among whites. A given life style demands a minimum level of income, but it is evident that Negroes are victimized in the sense that their effort as reflected in the acquisition of an education does not bring equal rewards in terms of purchasing power, for they have less to spend than their white counterparts at any given educational level. Nonwhite family heads in 1960 had a smaller median income than whites for every educational level. (See Table 2.)[18]

TABLE 2.   White and Nonwhite Median Family Income by Educational Level, 1960: U.S.A.

Amount of Education in Yrs. of School Completed	White	Nonwhite
ELEMENTARY SCHOOL		
Less than 8 years	$3,656	$2,294
8 years	4,911	3,338
HIGH SCHOOL		
1–3 years	5,882	3,449
4 years	6,370	4,559
COLLEGE		
1–3 years	7,344	5,525
4 or more years	9,315	7,875

In a sense, getting an education "pays off" for Negroes as for all other Americans; but while some individuals "get ahead" of other Negroes, education has not yet raised their earning power to the level of whites with equivalent training. In fact, the average income for a nonwhite family with a male head who had finished high school was less than that of a white male head who had finished only the eighth grade. Since any aspects of the caste-class system which make it more difficult for Negroes than for whites to achieve middle-class norms of family behavior retard the process of eventual "integration," the income differential and the necessity for more members of the family to work operate in this negative fashion. Even more serious in determining deviations from general middle-class family norms is the manner in which both income distribution and the occupational structure function to reinforce the number of families without fathers and to lower the prestige of Negro males *vis-à-vis* their mates, prospective mates, and children. Thus a pattern of male insecurity which originated under slavery persists into the present. In fact, the struggle of Negro men, viewed as a group, to attain economic parity with Negro women has, up to the present, been a losing fight. Norval Glenn, in an exhaustive study of this problem,[19] has concluded that "Among full-time workers, non-white females were, in 1959, less disadvantaged relative to whites than were non-white males." Women were obtaining employment at a relatively faster rate than men and sustained a more rapid proportionate increase in income between 1939 and 1959. According to Glenn, there was an actual reversal in the income growth pattern of Negro males and females during a twenty-year period, and he notes that if their respective rates remain the same it will take twice as long for Negro males to catch up with white males as for Negro women to catch up with white women (93 years to achieve occupational equality and 219 to achieve equality of income). This is a case of *relative* deprivation, of course, but is significant nevertheless. An impressive body of evidence indicates that rather serious personality distortions result from the female dominance so prevalent in the Negro subculture, since the general norms of the larger society stress the opposite pattern as more desirable.

The interplay between caste evaluations and economic and

ecological factors has tended not only to concentrate a low-income Negro population within ghettos, but has also concentrated a significant proportion of them in vast public housing projects—sometimes "high rise." In the 1930's public housing projects were often exciting experiments in interracial living, but there has been a tendency in many cities for them to become ghettos within ghettos. Within housing projects as well as out, a small hard core of mothers without husbands and a larger group of youth without jobs are developing a pattern which social psychologist Frederick Strodtbeck has called "the poverty-dependency syndrome." Here and there an integrated program of professional family services has proved its usefulness, but, in general, family case-work becomes a mere "holding operation."

Only the future will tell whether a large-scale "Poverty Program" coordinated through federally sponsored agencies will break the interlocking vicious circles which now victimize urban Negro populations. The dominant pattern in the American economic system has never been one of racial segregation. In fact, the racial division of labor has always involved considerable close personal contact, while demanding that Negroes play subordinate occupational roles carrying the lesser rewards in terms of economic power and social prestige. Doctrines of racial inferiority originated as dogmas to defend the use of African slave labor and were later used by white workers to defend their own privileged position against Negro competition. Trade union restrictionism reinforces employer preference in maintaining a job ceiling. Often, even when an employer decided it was profitable to use Negro labor, white workers used intimidation or violence against both white employer and black employee.

Access to new roles in the economic structure has occurred during periods of a great shortage of labor, as in the North during both world wars. Negroes entered at the bottom of the hierarchy, but were "last hired and first fired." Yet the job ceiling *was* raised, and, beginning with the organization of industrial unions in the 1930's and reaching a climax in the civil rights movement of the 1960's, ideological factors have reinforced economic interest in breaking the job ceiling. Now, for the first time in American history the full weight of top leadership in labor, industry, and government has been thrown in the direction of "fair employment practices," and public opinion is tolerating an all-out drive against job discrimination (partly because the economy is still expanding). Yet so drastic are the effects of the past victimization of the Negro that any decisive alteration in the caste-class structure without more drastic measures seems remote. Thomas Pettigrew, after an analysis of recent changes, concludes:

At the creeping 1950–1960 rate of change, non-whites in the United States would not attain equal proportional representation among clerical workers until 1992, among skilled workers until 2005, among professionals until 2017, among sales workers until 2114, and among business managers and proprietors until 2730![20]

21. Black Power and Beyond

Among the grievances and resentments of the black
ghetto, none is more pervasive than its feeling of powerlessness. The ghetto's sense of being controlled from the
outside was captured by Langston Hughes, when he remi-
nisced shortly before his death about his first days in
Harlem. "I soon learned," Hughes wrote, "that it was
seemingly impossible for black Harlem to live without
white downtown. My youthful illusion that Harlem was a
world unto itself did not last very long. It was not even an
area that ran itself. Almost all the stores were owned by
whites, and many at that time did not even (in the middle
of Harlem) employ Negro clerks."

The pervasive sense of powerlessness was only height-
ened when the achievements of the civil-rights movement
in desegregation and voting rights failed to produce any
significant changes in the conditions of life of the masses
of urban blacks. And it was partially as a response to this
situation that a new outlook, symbolized by the slogan
"Black Power," emerged in the later 1960's. The phrase
"Black Power" first came to national attention during the
June, 1966, march through Mississippi. This had begun as
a one-man venture by James Meredith, but expanded into
a mass demonstration after Meredith was shot and
wounded by a white sniper. Many black leaders, including
Martin Luther King, Jr., took part in the march, but the

spotlight was taken by a new figure, Stokely Carmichael, the young chairman of the Student Nonviolent Coordinating Committee (SNCC). "Black Power" was Carmichael's slogan, and it was quickly seized by the national press and given extensive national publicity.

In the eyes of the mass media, and of millions of whites, Black Power means simply that blacks are willing to use violent means to achieve their objectives. And it was true that King's brand of nonviolence was increasingly going out of style with younger, more radical blacks, some of whom went so far as to advocate "urban guerrilla warfare" to overthrow white domination of black communities. But "Black Power" meant far more than a new willingness to take extreme measures, and in the article below, "What We Want," Carmichael explained his position to an audience of white liberal and radical intellectuals. For Carmichael, Black Power meant that blacks should organize themselves into an effective political and social force, to gain control of the communities in which they lived. He condemned political alliances with whites, insisting that blacks should rely on all-black organizations to define their goals, and he rejected the goal of integration into American society. To the most frequent question from sympathetic whites—what would be the role of whites in a black power movement?—Carmichael replied that they should work in their own communities to mobilize support for the black movement. He added that while he was abandoning integration as an immediate goal it could still be a long-range objective. "The concept of Black Power," he wrote in a book co-authored by the political scientist Charles Hamilton, "rests on a fundamental premise: Before a group can enter the open society, it must first close ranks. By this we mean that group solidarity is necessary before a group can operate effectively from a bargaining position of strength in a pluralistic society." But at the same time, Carmichael made clear that blacks did not wish merely to become part of American society, for they rejected that society's basic values.

Much as he differed with integrationists like King and even Du Bois, Carmichael agreed with them that blacks could help to bring about fundamental changes in American society, by insisting on the virtues of brotherhood and humanity in the face of American materialism and racism.

The most common expressions of the Black Power outlook in the past few years have been the new emphasis on racial pride and identity by almost all black leaders, including King, (who otherwise rejected the idea of black power), and the struggle for community control of the institutions of the ghetto. In many cities, blacks have demanded the right to control their own schools, police, hospitals, and other public facilities, and have attempted to organize a black political force to support candidates who favor such demands. Although such predictions are notoriously risky, it seems likely that in the years ahead the black movement will continue to focus on these demands, attempting to improve the immediate conditions of life within the black ghetto, rather than pursuing the traditional integrationist goals which now seem both illusory and superficial.

Yet there are many problems with the doctrine of Black Power, some of which are outlined in the second essay below, the concluding chapter of Harold Cruse's provocative study *The Crisis of the Negro Intellectual.* Cruse's work took a caustic attitude toward most of the leading black figures of the twentieth century, and few came away without battle scars. In his section on Black Power, Cruse complains that the slogan is so confused and muddy that its leading proponents disagree with one another as to what it means. While it is true that this is often the fate of widely-used slogans, Cruse is certainly correct in saying that Black Power seems to have lost much of its meaning. Some black spokesmen speak of "black capitalism"—the demand for black-owned shops and businesses in the ghetto—as a species of Black Power, while others demand complete racial separation as the logical conclusion of the Black Power philosophy, and have even revived the old dream of a separate black state in this country, or emigration to Africa. What is most striking, Cruse believes, is that Black Power seems to combine extremely radical rhetoric—promises of racial warfare and massive black uprisings—with essentially reformist demands. Even the Black Panther party, the revolutionary socialist organization now under attack by police in cities across the country, works for reformist goals like better housing and jobs for ghetto residents. And in politics, Cruse charges, Black Power has so far meant running black candidates for office, relying on black votes to elect them. This tactic has succeeded in cities like Gary and Cleveland, where the unified vote of the ghetto, with the addition of some white support, elected black mayors, but, as Cruse observes, there are many white politicians who endorse the reforms proposed by these black candidates.

What does Cruse demand in place of Black Power? He calls for "a social theory based on the living ingredients of Afro-American history." Black Power, Cruse argues, is an expression of black nationalism, which, along with its opposite pole of integration, has competed for support from the black community throughout American history. What is needed, Cruse seems to say, is a synthesis of these two trends, a combination of the integrationist demand for civil rights and an end to discrimination with the nationalist insistence upon group solidarity and self-help. Du Bois, he believes, came closest of all black leaders to synthesizing these divergent trends; and the success or failure of the black movement in the 1970's may well depend on whether there emerges from the black community a leader with the depth of racial pride, human dignity, and social awareness which characterized Du Bois.

What We Want

STOKELY CARMICHAEL

One of the tragedies of the struggle against racism is that up to now there has been no national organization which could speak to the growing militancy of young black people in the urban ghetto. There has been only a civil rights movement, whose tone of voice was adapted to an audience of liberal whites. It served as a sort of buffer zone between them and angry young blacks. None of its so-called leaders could go into a rioting community and be listened to. In a sense, I blame ourselves—together with the mass media—for what has happened in Watts, Harlem, Chicago, Cleveland, Omaha. Each time the people in those cities saw Martin Luther King get slapped, they became angry; when they saw four little black girls bombed to death, they were angrier; and when nothing happened, they were steaming. We had nothing to offer that they could see, except to go out and be beaten again. We helped to build their frustration.

For too many years, black Americans marched and had their heads broken and got shot. They were saying to the country, "Look, you guys are supposed to be nice guys and we are only going to do what we are supposed to do—why do you beat us up, why don't you give us what we ask, why don't you straighten yourselves out?" After years of this, we are at almost the same point—because we demonstrated from a position of weakness. We cannot be expected any longer to march and have our heads broken in order to say to whites: come on, you're nice guys. For you are not nice guys. We have found you out.

An organization which claims to speak for the needs of a

FROM Stokely Carmichael, "What We Want," *New York Review of Books*, 1966. Copyright © 1966 by New York Review of Books. Reprinted by permission of SNCC, Atlanta, Ga. and Stokely Carmichael.

community—as does the Student Nonviolent Coordinating Committee—must speak in the tone of that community, not as somebody else's buffer zone. This is the significance of black power as a slogan. For once, black people are going to use the words they want to use—not just the words whites want to hear. And they will do this no matter how often the press tries to stop the use of the slogan by equating it with racism or separatism.

An organization which claims to be working for the needs of a community—as SNCC does—must work to provide that community with a position of strength from which to make its voice heard. This is the significance of black power beyond the slogan.

Black power can be clearly defined for those who do not attach the fears of white America to their questions about it. We should begin with the basic fact that black Americans have two problems: they are poor and they are black. All other problems arise from this two-sided reality: lack of education, the so-called apathy of black men. Any program to end racism must address itself to that double reality.

Almost from its beginning, SNCC sought to address itself to both conditions with a program aimed at winning political power for impoverished Southern blacks. We had to begin with politics because black Americans are a propertyless people in a country where property is valued above all. We had to work for power, because this country does not function by morality, love, and nonviolence, but by power. Thus we determined to win political power, with the idea of moving on from there into activity that would have economic effects. With power, the masses could *make or participate in making* the decisions which govern their destinies, and thus create basic change in their day-to-day lives.

But if political power seemed to be the key to self-determination, it was also obvious that the key had been thrown down a deep well many years earlier. Disenfranchisement, maintained by racist terror, makes it impossible to talk about organizing for political power in 1960. The right to vote had to be won, and SNCC workers devoted their energies to this from 1961 to 1965. They set up voter registration drives in the Deep South. They created pressure for the vote by holding mock elections in Mississippi in 1963 and by helping to establish the Mississippi Freedom

Democratic Party (MFDP) in 1964. That struggle was eased, though not won, with the passage of the 1965 Voting Rights Act. SNCC workers could then address themselves to the question: "Who can we vote for, to have our needs met—how do we make our vote meaningful?"

SNCC had already gone to Atlantic City for recognition of the Mississippi Freedom Democratic Party by the Democratic convention and been rejected; it had gone with the MFDP to Washington for recognition by Congress and been rejected. In Arkansas, SNCC helped thirty Negroes to run for School Board elections; all but one were defeated, and there was evidence of fraud and intimidation sufficient to cause their defeat. In Atlanta, Julian Bond ran for the state legislature and was elected—twice—and unseated—twice. In several states, black farmers ran in elections for agricultural committees which make crucial decisions concerning land use, loans, etc. Although they won places on a number of committees, they never gained the majorities needed to control them.

All of the efforts were attempts to win black power. Then, in Alabama, the opportunity came to see how blacks could be organized on an independent party basis. An unusual Alabama law provides that any group of citizens can nominate candidates for county office and, if they win 20 per cent of the vote, may be recognized as a county political party. The same then applies on a state level. SNCC went to organize in several counties such as Lowndes, where black people—who form 80 per cent of the population and have an average annual income of $943—felt they could accomplish nothing within the framework of the Alabama Democratic Party because of its racism and because the qualifying fee for this year's elections was raised from $50 to $500 in order to prevent most Negroes from becoming candidates. On May 3, five new county "freedom organizations" convened and nominated candidates for the offices of sheriff, tax assessor, members of the school boards. These men and women are up for election in November—if they live until then. Their ballot symbol is the black panther: a bold, beautiful animal, representing the strength and dignity of black demands today. A man needs a black panther on his side when he and his family must endure—as hundreds of Alabamians have endured—loss of job, eviction, starvation, and sometimes death, for political activity. He may also need a gun and SNCC reaffirms the right of black men everywhere to defend themselves when threatened or attacked. As for initiating the use of violence, we hope that such programs as ours will make that unnecessary; but it is not for us to tell black communities whether they can or cannot use any particular form of action to resolve their problems. Responsibility for the use of violence by black men, whether in self defense or initiated by them, lies with the white community.

This is the specific historical experience from which SNCC's call for "black power" emerged on the Mississippi march last July. But the concept of "black power" is not a recent or isolated phenomenon: It has grown out of the ferment of agitation and activity by different people and organizations in many black communities over the years. Our last year of work in Alabama added a new concrete possibility. In Lowndes County, for example, black power will mean that if a Negro is elected sheriff, he can end police brutality. If a black man is elected tax assessor, he can collect and channel funds for the building of better roads and schools serving black people—thus advancing the move from political power into the economic arena. In such areas as Lowndes, where black men have a majority, they will attempt to use it to exercise control. This is what they seek: control. Where Negroes lack a majority, black power means proper representation and sharing of control. It means the creation of power bases from which black people can work to change statewide or nationwide patterns of oppression through pressure from strength—instead of weakness. Politically, black power means what it has always meant to SNCC: the coming-together of black people to elect representatives and *to force those representatives to speak to their needs*. It does not mean merely putting black faces into office. A man or woman who is black and from the slums cannot be automatically expected to speak to the needs of black people. Most of the black politicians we see around the country today are not what SNCC means by black power. The power must be that of a community, and emanate from there.

SNCC today is working in both North and South on programs of voter registration and independent political organizing. In some places, such as Alabama, Los Angeles, New York, Philadelphia, and New Jersey, independent organizing under the black panther symbol is in progress. The creation of a national "black panther party" must come about; it will take time to build, and it is much too early to predict its success. We have no infallible master plan and we make no claim to exclusive knowledge of how to end racism; different groups will work in their own different ways. SNCC cannot spell out the full logistics of self-determination but it can address itself to the problem by helping black communities define their needs, realize their strength, and go into action along a variety of lines which they must choose for themselves. Without knowing all the answers, it can address itself to the basic problem of poverty; to the fact that in Lowndes County, 86 white families own 90 per cent of the land. What are black people in that county going to do for jobs, where are they going to get money? There must be reallocation of land, of money.

Ultimately, the economic foundations of this country must be shaken if black people are to control their lives. The colonies of the United States—and this includes the black ghettos within its borders, north and south—must be liberated. For a century, this nation has been like an octopus of exploitation, its tentacles stretching from Mississippi and Harlem to South America, the Middle East, southern Africa, and Vietnam; the form of exploitation varies from area to area but the essential result has been the same—a powerful few have been maintained and enriched at the expense of the poor and voiceless colored masses. This pattern must be broken. As its grip loosens here and there around the world, the hopes of black Americans become more realistic. For racism to die, a totally different America must be born.

This is what the white society does not wish to face; this is why that society prefers to talk about integration. But integration speaks not at all to the problem of poverty, only to the problem of blackness. Integration today means the man who "makes it," leaving his black brothers behind in the ghetto as fast as his new sports car will take him. It has no relevance to the Harlem wino or to the cottonpicker making three dollars a day. As a lady I know in Alabama once said, "the food that Ralph Bunche eats doesn't fill my stomach."

Integration, moreover, speaks to the problem of blackness in a despicable way. As a goal, it has been based on complete acceptance of the fact that *in order to have* a decent house or education, blacks must move into a white neighborhood or send their children to a white school. This reinforces, among both black and white, the idea that "white" is automatically better and "black" is by definition inferior. This is why integration is a subterfuge for the maintenance of white supremacy. It allows the nation to focus on a handful of Southern children who get into white schools, at great price, and to ignore the 94 per cent who are left behind in unimproved all-black schools. Such situations will not change until black people have power—to control their own school boards, in this case. Then Negroes become equal in a way that means something, and integration ceases to be a one-way street. Then integration doesn't mean draining skills and energies from the ghetto into white neighborhoods; then it can mean white people moving from Beverly Hills into Watts, white people joining the Lowndes County Freedom Organization. Then integration becomes relevant.

Last April, before the furor over black power, Christopher Jencks wrote in a *New Republic* article on white Mississippi's manipulation of the antipoverty program:

The war on poverty has been predicated on the notion that there is such a thing as *a community* which can be defined geographically and mobilized for a collective effort to help the poor. This theory has no relationship to reality in the Deep South. In every Mississippi county there are *two* communities. Despite all the pious platitudes of the moderates on both sides, these two communities habitually see their interests in terms of conflict rather than cooperation. Only when the Negro community can muster enough political, economic and professional strength to compete on somewhat equal terms, will Negroes believe in the possibility of true cooperation and whites accept its necessity. En route to integration, the Negro community needs to develop greater independence—a chance to run its own affairs and not cave in whenever "the man" barks. . . . Or so it seems to me, and to most of the knowledgeable people with whom I talked in Mississippi. To OEO, this judgment may sound like black nationalism . . .

Mr. Jencks, a white reporter, perceived the reason why America's antipoverty program has been a sick farce in both North and South. In the South, it is clearly racism which prevents the poor from running their own programs; in the North, it more often seems to be politicking and bureaucracy. But the results are not so different: In the North, non-whites make up 42 per cent of all families in metropolitan "poverty areas" and only 6 per cent of families in areas classified as not poor. SNCC has been working with local residents in Arkansas, Alabama, and Mississippi to achieve control by the poor of the program and its funds; it has also been working with groups in the North, and the struggle is no less difficult. Behind it all is a federal government which cares far more about winning the war on the Vietnamese than the war on poverty; which has put the poverty program in the hands of self-serving politicians and bureaucrats rather than the poor themselves; which is unwilling to curb the misuse of white power but quick to condemn black power.

To most whites, black power seems to mean that the Mau Mau are coming to the suburbs at night. The Mau Mau are coming, and whites must stop them. Articles appear about plots to "get Whitey," creating an atmosphere in which "law and order must be maintained." Once again, responsibility is shifted from the oppressor to the oppressed. Other whites chide, "Don't forget—you're only 10 per cent of the population; if you get too smart, we'll wipe you out." If they are liberals, they complain, "what about me?—don't you want my help any more?" These are people supposedly concerned about black Americans, but today they think first of themselves, of their feelings of rejection. Or they admonish, "you can't get anywhere without coalitions," when there is in fact no group at present with whom to form a coalition in which blacks will not be absorbed and betrayed. Or they accuse us of "polarizing the races" by our calls for black unity, when the true responsibility for polarization lies with whites who will not accept their responsibility as the majority power for making the democratic process work.

White America will not face the problem of color, the reality of it. The well-intended say: "We're all human, everybody is really decent, we must forget color." But color cannot be "forgotten" until its weight is recognized and dealt with. White America will not acknowledge that the ways in which this country sees itself are contradicted by being black—and always have been. Whereas most of the people who settled this country came here for freedom or for economic opportunity, blacks were brought here to be slaves. When the Lowndes County Freedom Organization chose the black panther as its symbol, it was christened by the press "the Black Panther Party"—but the Alabama Democratic Party, whose symbol is a rooster, has never been called the White Cock Party. No one ever talked about "white power" because power in this country *is* white. All this adds up to more than merely identifying a group phenomenon by some catchy name or adjective. The furor over that black panther reveals the problems that white America has with color and sex; the furor over "black power" reveals how deep racism runs and the great fear which is attached to it.

Whites will not see that I, for example, as a person oppressed because of my blackness, have common cause with other blacks who are oppressed because of blackness. This is not to say that there are no white people who see things as I do, but that it is black people I must speak to first. It must be the oppressed to whom SNCC addresses itself primarily, not to friends from the oppressing group.

From birth, black people are told a set of lies about themselves. We are told that we are lazy—yet I drive through the Delta area of Mississippi and watch black people picking cotton in the hot sun for fourteen hours. We are told, "If you work hard, you'll succeed"—but if that were true, black people would own this country. We are oppressed because we are black—not because we are ignorant, not because we are lazy, not because we're stupid (and got good rhythm), but because we're black.

I remember that when I was a boy I used to go to see Tarzan movies on Saturday. White Tarzan used to beat up the black natives. I would sit there yelling, "Kill the beasts, kill the savages, kill 'em!" I was saying: Kill *me*. It was as if a Jewish boy watched Nazis taking Jews off to concentration camps and cheered them on. Today, I want the chief to beat hell out of Tarzan and send him back to Europe. But it takes time to become free of the lies and their shaming effect on black minds. It takes time to reject the most important lie: that black people inherently can't do the same things white people can do, unless white people help them.

The need for psychological equality is the reason why SNCC today believes that blacks must organize in the black community. Only black people can convey the revolutionary idea that black people are able to do things themselves. Only they can help create in the community an aroused and continuing black consciousness that will provide the basis for political strength. In the past, white allies have furthered white supremacy without the whites involved realizing it—or wanting it, I think. Black people must do things for themselves; they must get poverty money they will control and spend themselves, they must conduct tutorial programs themselves so that black children can identify with black people. This is one reason Africa has such importance: The reality of black men ruling their own natives gives blacks elsewhere a sense of possibility, of power, which they do not now have.

This does not mean we don't welcome help, or friends. But we want the right to decide whether anyone is, in fact, our friend. In the past, black Americans have been almost the only people whom everybody and his momma could jump up and call their friends. We have been tokens, symbols, objects—as I was in high school to many young whites, who liked having "a Negro friend." We want to decide who is our friend, and we will not accept someone who comes to us and says: "If you do X, Y, and Z, then I'll help you." We will not be told whom we should choose as allies. We will not be isolated from any group or nation except by our own choice. We cannot have the oppressors telling the oppressed how to rid themselves of the oppressor.

I have said that most liberal whites react to "black power" with the question, What about me?, rather than saying: Tell me what you want me to do and I'll see if I can do it. There are answers to the right question. One of the most disturbing things about almost all white supporters of the movement has been that they are afraid to go into their own communities—which is where the racism exists—and work to get rid of it. They want to run from Berkeley to tell us what to do in Mississippi; let them look instead at Berkeley. They admonish blacks to be nonviolent; let them preach nonviolence in the white community. They come to teach me Negro history; let them go to the suburbs and open up freedom schools for whites. Let them work to stop America's racist foreign policy; let them press this government to cease supporting the economy of South Africa.

There is a vital job to be done among poor whites. We hope to see, eventually, a coalition between poor blacks and poor whites. That is the only coalition which seems acceptable to us, and we see such a coalition as the major internal instrument of change in American society. SNCC has tried several times to organize poor whites; we are trying again now, with an initial training program in Tennessee. It is purely academic today to talk about bringing poor blacks and whites together, but the job of creating a poor-white power bloc must be attempted. The main responsibility for it falls upon whites. Black and white can work together in the white community where possible; it is not possible, however, to go into a poor Southern town and talk about integration. Poor whites everywhere are becoming more hostile—not less—partly because they see the nation's attention focused on black poverty and nobody coming to them. Too many young middle-class Americans, like some sort of Pepsi generation, have wanted to come alive through the black community; they've wanted to be where the action is—and the action has been in the black community.

Black people do not want to "take over" this country. They don't want to "get whitey"; they just want to get him off their backs, as the saying goes. It was for example the exploitation by Jewish landlords and merchants which first created black resentment toward Jews—not Judaism. The white man is irrelevant to blacks, except as an oppressive force. Blacks want to be in his place, yes, but not in order to terrorize and lynch and starve him. They want to be in his place because that is where a decent life can be had.

But our vision is not merely of a society in which all black men have enough to buy the good things of life. When we urge that black money go into black pockets, we mean the communal pocket. We want to see money go back into the community and used to benefit it. We want to see the cooperative concept applied in business and banking. We want to see black ghetto residents demand that an exploiting store keeper sell them, at minimal cost, a building or a shop that they will own and improve cooperatively;

they can back their demand with a rent strike, or a boycott, and a community so unified behind them that no one else will move into the building or buy at the store. The society we seek to build among black people, then, is not a capitalist one. It is a society in which the spirit of community and humanistic love prevail. The word love is suspect; black expectations of what it might produce have been betrayed too often. But those were expectations of a response from the white community, which failed us. The love we seek to encourage is within the black community, the only American community where men call each other "brother" when they meet. We can build a community of love only where we have the ability and power to do so: among blacks.

As for white America, perhaps it can stop crying out against "black supremacy," "black nationalism," "racism in reverse," and begin facing reality. The reality is that this nation, from top to bottom, is racist; that racism is not primarily a problem of "human relations" but of an exploitation maintained—either actively or through silence—by the society as a whole. Camus and Sartre have asked, can a man condemn himself? Can whites, particularly liberal whites, condemn themselves? Can they stop blaming us, and blame their own system? Are they capable of the shame which might become a revolutionary emotion?

We have found that they usually cannot condemn themselves, and so we have done it. But the rebuilding of this society, if at all possible, is basically the responsibility of whites—not blacks. We won't fight to save the present society, in Vietnam or anywhere else. We are just going to work, in the way *we* see fit, and on goals *we* define, not for civil rights but for all our human rights.

Postscript on Black Power—the Dialogue
Between Shadow and Substance

HAROLD CRUSE

The old proverb, "Necessity is the mother of invention," was given a unique civil rights configuration when the slogan of Black Power was popularized during the summer of 1966. The necessity lay in the fact that the SNCC-CORE united front, in its direct-action-protest phase, had bogged down. Like an army that had outdistanced its supply units, it had finally been stopped by the enemy counter-attack—the backlash.

The slogan Black Power was conjured up and used in the manner of a rallying victory cry. In effect it covers up a defeat without having to explain either the basic reasons for it or the flaws in the original strategy; it suggests the dimensions of a future victory in the attainment of goals while, at the same time, dispelling the fears of more defeats in the pursuit of such goals. Yet, each and every goal was already implicit in the direct-action movements even before the slogan was projected. Black Power, then, was raised when social reality forced so-called revolutionaries to put action aside and start thinking. A movement that up to then had placed its highest premiums on practical activism now turned over a new leaf and began to get theoretical about the real *substance* of its civil rights objectives. The old slogans about "justice," "liberation," "Freedom Now," etc., were now mere shadow terms. If direct-action-protest had been defeated by certain structural barriers of society, the new slogan became a commitment to deal with the real substance of those barriers that block the attainment of civil rights. Thus fears, opposition, and startled cries of alarm were immediately raised. A new threat fell across the land like an ominous shadow, even though the exact concept of Black Power has not yet been clearly defined. At this writing, as a concept it remains as vague as the former abstractions—Justice and Liberation. Although the Black Power concept is a more specific and provocative abstraction than Freedom, it is open to just as many diverse and conflicting interpretations. While it tries to give more clarity to what forms Freedom will assume in America as the end-product of a new program, the Black Power dialogue does not close the conceptual gap between shadow and substance, any more than it plots a course for the program dynamic. Whatever Black Power is supposed to mean to its adherents and its foes, its implications cannot be clearly understood unless one examines the slogan's aims and origin. Who originated the slogan? Are its aims revolutionary or reformist?

It was originated by a leading member of the radical wing of the black bourgeoisie, Adam Clayton Powell: He first mentioned it at a Chicago rally in May, 1965, and elaborated upon it in his Howard University Commencement speech of May 29, 1966. It was picked up and popularized by a leading member of the radical wing of the civil rights movement, Stokely Carmichael, from the lower-middle-class students' front. Carmichael was then joined by certain nationalist elements from integration-minded CORE, the radical wing of the civil rights movement in the North. Thus, the slogan of Black Power appeared to signal a concerted shift from SNCC-CORE radical-protest integrationism—not to nationalist separatism—but to some intermediate position between separatism and racial integration.

Since all of these diverse protest elements, separatists, nationalists, and direct actionists, had made up the sum total of what was called the Black Revolution, formal logic would conclude that this tumultuous shift to Black Power denoted a turn to a more revolutionary posture than formerly held by SNCC and CORE when their direct-action battering rams were at full strength North and South. But a closer examination of every analysis by each Black Power exponent from SNCC and CORE reveals that while the slogan cast a revolutionary *sounding* theme and a threat of more intense revolt across the land, the *substance* was, in fact, a methodological retreat to black social reforms. In pragmatic America the slogans catch the imagination while the implicit substances are glossed over and ignored. The Negro thinks and acts like the American he is; thus the leaders of the Black Revolution who seized so readily upon Black Power had never made the distinction between social revolution and social evolution, or social reform. . . .

There can be no such thing in America as a *purely* economic, or political or civil rights revolution. There *can* be economic or political or civil rights reforms, but these are all *evolutionary* social changes that are part and parcel of the very gradualism of the NAACP. Never mind the fact that Roy Wilkins and his "class-brothers" are frightened by Black Power—that proves nothing. What a Wilkins is really saying is—"Please don't start throwing around power you don't really have, or power which you *might* have but you obviously don't know how to use. All you are doing is scaring people (like me) and provoking other people to mobilize white power for a showdown which you are not ready for." What these gentlemen want most avidly are a number of civil rights, legal, economic, social, and educational reforms in America. But the radical direct-action civil righters (plus the nationalists) vociferously claim that this is inadequate. They say: "Those bourgeois NAACP Uncle Toms can't reform this white man's society. Man, you got to resort to revolutionary tactics if you want to shake up these white folks!" But what were these so-called revolutionary tactics? The Black Revolution included everything in the pot: sit-ins, freedom rides, demonstrations and marches of all kinds, ghetto uprisings, stall-ins, voter registration, self-defense, boycotts, black (third) party attempts, etc. These were the elements of the revolution particularly in the South. But today when the main bulk of the direct actionists of SNCC and others have quit the South, what have they left behind? Scattered groups devoted to voter registration and economic programs for self-help. CORE has left a "cooperative marketing program for farm produce" in Louisiana. There were a few local election victories here and there, but the political reform movement of the Mississippi Freedom Democrat Party has closed its doors in LeFlore County. This is not to say that the achievements of the direct actionists are not valuable bases upon which other things can be structured, but they are still *reformist and gradualistic ideas with which not a single NAACP-er nor King passive resister could argue.* The question arises: Why was it necessary for all those idealistic and intrepid direct actionists to submit themselves to such a terrible physical and psychological battering in the South to establish a few struggling groups for local reforms in politics and economics, attempting in vain to breach the jimcrow barriers, which are, in effect, "separate" movements? It was because these young radicals did not understand, at the outset, the divergent natures of reforms and revolutionary movements for social change. They confused the methods without understanding them, thus imputing revolutionary interpretations to merely reformist methods. Hence, when direct-action methods failed against hardening barriers, they had to fall back on what few political and economic reform gains they had won. From this point on, the direct actionists advanced to the slogan of Black Power, as if to convince themselves that they were taking a revolutionary step forward, to wit: instead of radical integrationism the theme became *economic and political control by blacks in the black ghettoes and in geographical areas of black majority in the South.* But is this a step forward or backward . . . or perhaps a one-step-backward-two-steps-forward sort of gambit? Whatever it is, it is essentially another variation of the old Communist leftwing doctrine of "self-determination in the black belt areas of Negro majority"—but with certain innovations. The old Communist Party doctrine did not include the Northern ghettos in this scheme as the Black Power exponents do. Moreover, the Communists did not envision any separatist black party movements as part of "self-determination," nor include any separatist economic reforms for self-help (such as cooperative consumers and producers movements). For the Communists then, and forever more, trade unionism was of paramount importance. The Northern CORE found itself in the 1960's, for instance, still forced to battle for integration in certain unions such as the building and construction trades. But when the subterranean nationalists inside the organization came to the fore in 1966 in answer to Carmichael's Black Power call, they demanded that Negroes reject integration as their major aim. Negroes were called on to band themselves into a racially-oriented mass movement, using political power and economic boycotts to win complete economic and political control of Northern ghettos and Southern counties in which they are in the majority. Except for time, place, circumstances, plus a few innovative, ideological twists, there is very little that is new in all of this.

In essence Black Power represents nothing more than a strategic retreat for a purpose. It proposes to change, not the white world outside, but the black world inside, by reforming it into something else politically and economically. In its own way and for other purposes the Nation of Islam has already achieved this in a limited way, substituting religion for politics.

Malcolm X quit the Nation of Islam because this type of Black Power lacked a dynamic, was static and aloof to the broad struggle. He proposed to create another movement (the Organization for Afro-American Unity, OAAU) and link up with all the direct actionists and even passive resisters, believing that one must be involved in all forms of struggle wherever they are on all fronts. But after Malcolm's passing, the most dynamic of all the direct actionists gave up their dynamism and took a position almost in the lap of the Nation of Islam. They merely substituted politics for a parochial religion to go along with economics, but they added a more secular religion of Black Power invented by a Baptist minister-politician. As the fates would have it, all of this took place at a time when Powell, in whom more black political power was invested than in anyone else at the moment, was under fire from a Congressional white backlash in Washington, D.C.

On the face of it, Black Power adds up to some profound questions: Does this strategic retreat from integrationism mean that the civil righters are settling for gradual evolutionary reforms within the black communities? Can these economic and political reforms be achieved without effect on, and interaction with, the white world? Will the achievement of certain levels of Black Power enable the exponents to deal more effectively with the white world than the dynamics of direct-action integrationism? What manner of social dynamic is to be added to Black Power to make up for the dynamic that was discarded along with direct action? The real answer at this stage is that the Black Power slogan has no other dynamic than what is implied in its emotional necessity. Taken by themselves, all purely economic and political reorganizations of any type in America can be only reformist movements, whether in black ghettoes or the white world. In order to be revolutionary in method to effect social change, such as transforming ghettoes, other dynamic elements must be added to the economic and political combination. The Black Power exponents have not understood these elements. Yet there is a unique inner dialectic at work in all this that must be examined.

For this purpose the Black Power exponents themselves have laid out their thinking for all to see. We can discount the frenetic avowals of black consciousness that made *New York Times* headlines and television panels, that frightened the bourgeois "Toms," white resisters, and lost "friends." It was but a new way of singing the same nationalist theme heard before from other quarters. But the CORE Black Power exponents came out in midwinter with a new publication called *Rights & Reviews* (Winter 1966–67), subtitled the "Black Power Issue," in which the substance of the slogan was discussed at some length. Here it was revealed that behind the brave verbalizations of Black Power, lay a muddled intellectual world of vague ideas and conceptual confusion. Sixteen articles by an interracial lineup of nationalists, Black Power integrationists, white leftwingers, Jews, Africans and others, spelled out the implicit Black Power retreat to the more leveled progression of an evolutionary black reformation. One cannot argue against this tactic since it is premature to state categorically where it will lead; but one should not, in this instance, refrain from calling reformism what it is. After all, the social realist must be aware that the New Deal heritage of the 1930's still hangs heavy over the land, and the American social dynamic has the built-in persuasion to bend all so-called revolutionary inclinations into the reformist groove. This is what Anti-Poverty is all about; it is why the Anti-Poverty program is able to buy off all the ghetto rebels with consummate ease. At a recent Anti-Poverty meeting in Harlem where an Independent Citizens' Committee[1] was challenging the efficiency and propriety of HARYOU-ACT's dominant role in

Anti-Poverty politics, certain CORE leaders were present—and silent. It remains to be seen just how Black Power will handle Anti-Poverty issues within CORE.

But in the maiden issue of *Rights & Reviews* on Black Power, Roy Inniss opened up with "Black Power—Phase 1: Psychological Warfare," in which he said:

> There is an impelling need to emphasize the socio-psychological aspect of Black Power. We can cry "Black Power" until doomsday, but until black children stop saying, "You're blacker than me and so is your mama"; until grown black men stop using black as a curse word; until *Ebony* stops asking such asinine questions as: "Are Negro women getting prettier?" and stops carrying bleaching cream advertisements; until black people stop saying such things as: "She's dark, but pretty"; in short, until black people accept values meaningful to themselves, there can be no completely effective organizing for the development of Black Power.[2]

Mr. Inniss, a West Indian nationalist (once removed), was not merely being rhetorical about the much maligned values of "blackness." He himself is black and Africanesque. In fact, his sensitivity to this question was shown much earlier, in a *New York Times* article where he discussed his fears of "genetic destruction" through enforced "integration." Yet, if one is to discuss the color question among Negroes one cannot be as superficial as Mr. Inniss and leave it there. Granted, the Negro in America has been conditioned in many ways to a disrespect of blackness, but this is not as universal as Inniss makes out. On the other hand, if Inniss truly believes that there can be no "effective organizing . . ." (even for Black Power) until Negroes stop derogating "blackness," then he will never see "Black Power," whatever he means by it. Ideas about skin-color and the social values attached thereto are like ideas about all things social. Take the notion, for example, that holds slavery as a human institution to be a good thing. Had the slaves waited for the slavemasters to *change* their views on slavery before fighting for freedom, they would never be free. For even *after* the slaves won their freedom there would still be ex-slavemasters and ex-slaves who thought that slavery was a good thing. By the same token, even after the hoped-for ascent to Black Power, there will still be Negroes who will wish they were white inasmuch as Black Power will demand more responsibility than some blacks care to assume. However, the conceptual flaws noted here in Mr. Inniss' thinking on social dynamics are typical of the social thinking of all black revolutionaries. Either they are activists without ideas or they fail to connect their ideas to the appropriate kind of social actions. If a person has a low opinion of himself and is unhappy because he lives in a filthy, dilapidated, rat-infested house, you cannot tell him to apply positive thinking—and "Be happy!" Happiness will begin to blossom only when he finds a way to get out of his physical trap into improved surroundings. In other words, what are the social dynamics of the program implicit in a Black Power kind of happiness?

It was noted that this Black Power magazine issue went to great lengths to play up the ideas, the imagery and the symbolism of the African Personality. All of the artwork, with exception of an amusing Jules Feiffer cartoon, relied on African tribal symbolism. One of the articles, written by a Black Nationalist-Africanist, Yosef Ben-Jochannan, asked—"What is Black Power?" He said:

It is that power which black peoples had in Africa before the invasion and domination of Africa by the Europeans under the guise of "taking Christianity to the heathen Africans." . . . It is that power which caused Africans to build their many civilizations of high culture and institutions of science, law, medicine, philosophy, religion, etc., while Europeans were still asleep in their ignorance of the universe around and about them.[3]

Here, along with the historical romance of the African past, was an echo of Back-to-Africa Garveyism. For Ben-Jochannan, Black Power means that Negroes in America must take their "rightful place within the African community." "Why all the sudden fuss and fury against the call for Black Power?" he asks. Why the fear?—"Fear by those who allegedly lead those of us who remain on the colonial plantations throughout the Harlems of the United States of America." There is an element of truth in Ben-Jochannan's message, but also much propagandist rhetoric, and it is the rhetoric that one must watch out for. It is from a school of Harlem thought that condemns *any* effort on the part of the American Negro to seek racial equality within the American system.

Thus, within the CORE Black Power outlook reappears the old dichotomy between Du Bois–NAACPism and West Indian nationalist-Garveyism, for one must remember that CORE, the first direct-action group following World War II, merely extended the NAACP philosophy on another level. Even the present transition of the CORE philosophy to Black Power reformism is not complete, for witness the interracial lineup of the magazine content. The Black Power concept is due for a possible split between African Black Power and Afro-American Black Power, two related but different propositions in terms of emphasis. The clue to all this lies in the fact that neither in Ben-Jochannan's article, nor elsewhere in the issue, is the status of the West Indies (or the West Indian) discussed. Recall that when Black Power was first projected, the white press plus Inniss, Carmichael, and Lynch, played up the alleged Caribbean influence behind the slogan. Yet, although Ben-Jochannan discusses White Power vs. Black Power all over the world wherever it involves "the undying and unquenching energy of African peoples everywhere . . . ," he makes no reference to either the black West Indies or the British Commonwealth. The implicit, typically Garveyite, assumption here is that the black West Indies already has Black Power (poor but proud), and that the Caribbean islands, unlike the "Harlems of the United States . . ." are not what Ben-Jochannan calls "colonial plantations." For the West Indian nationalists in the United States, the Caribbean "image" must be preserved and the exact nature of the "political independence" achieved is not to be examined too closely especially since the success of Black Power (at home and abroad) is predicated on both *political and economic independence.*

However, let us see what an African representative says about Black Power in the same publication. Chief S. O. Adebo is Nigeria's Permanent Representative to the United Nations. Writing on "The Black Revolution—An African View,"[4] he discusses the "parallel movements" for freedom and independence of Africans and people of African descent in the United States:

Where the blacks constitute the majority of the country's population, as in Africa, the movement has taken the form of a struggle to take over the exercise of the governing power; where, as in the United

States, the blacks are a minority, the struggle has been one for participation on level terms with everybody else. . . .

So far even the NAACP and King would concur, but Chief Adebo added "but, fundamentally, the objective is the same, an objective which can be described as securing a square deal for the black man in this world."

On the implementation of this objective, every faction from the NAACP to the Nation of Islam—clear across the spectrum, including the Black Power exponents themselves—are divided. But, as Chief Adebo said, "The wind of change has of course caused a lot of transformation on the African continent" and in the United States. "But you will no doubt agree with me that here, as in Africa, the task still to be done is more than that which is already accomplished. For both of our communities it is a long, long way to Tipperary."

"We must coordinate and work together," Adebo advised. "In order to do this, an essential prerequisite is that we should strive to remove the misunderstanding created between the African and the American Negro by centuries of lack of intelligent communication between our communities." And he concluded:

The African must recognize the American Negro as his brother, and American Negroes must acknowledge Africa as their ancestral home, and Africans as their kith and kin. This mutual understanding already exists within the top echelons both in Africa and in the United States. But this is not enough; it must go right down to the grass roots.

Again, curiously, the African said nothing, even in passing, about the West Indies, the natural home of Garveyism abroad. And, exactly who are those "top echelon" leaders in Africa and America who have this "mutual understanding" of which Adebo speaks? Such American Negro top echelon leaders would also, presumably, support Black Power. But which top leaders besides Powell support Black Power? They are not found in the NAACP, the Urban League, or in King's top echelon (the very leadership, in fact, that Ben-Jochannan sees as fearing Black Power). No, there is much confusion here both in the outlook of Africans such as Adebo and in the Afro-American Black Power exponents over the African Revolution, the alleged Black Revolution, and their parallels. There is too much romanticizing about Africa going on in certain nationalist circles; too much rhetoric and too much Garveyite Back-to-Africa lip service by certain black redemptionists in America who haven't the least intention of going to Africa unless there is the guarantee of a good job or a money-making scheme in the offing, or the possibility of a "top echelon" marriage into the African diplomatic corps.

Africans such as Chief Adebo are just as much in the dark about the inner dynamic demands of the American Black Revolution as the Black Power exponents are about the dynamic substances of their new slogan. As a result, the readiness of most Black Nationalist trends, to lean heavily on the African past and the African image, is nothing but a convenient cover-up for an inability to come to terms with the complex demands of the American reality. A Roy Inniss, for example, will have one believe that no one in the black world but the American Negro has a complex about being black. In a black African country, inasmuch as nearly everyone is black, there is no basis for any psychological conditioning of inferiority complexes. However, pick up any popular African magazine such as *Spears* from Nigeria, *Parade* from Rhodesia, *Post* from South Africa, and also *Drum* of Ghana and Nigeria, and Lo and behold! There are skin-bleaching advertisements galore, also hair-straightening creams and black women in long-haired wigs—just like Harlem. Said one full-page, Madison Avenue-ish spread in *Drum:* "Amazing ARTA made my skin— Lighter, Smoother, Clearer . . . Because it is Pure White." "This is how I look now that I use pure white Arta." But, . . . "this was how I looked before. . . ." (She was *dark,* but pretty!)

Roy Inniss thinks *Ebony's* query "Are Negro Women Getting Prettier" rather asinine. But if he looks, he will observe that the African male in the United States has a female-beauty standard that parallels not only the prevailing standards of American Negro males and *Ebony* magazine, but also the standards of the varicolored spectrum of the United Nations. On this question there is very little misunderstanding between the two ancestral progeny. The problem is deeper: The American Negro is wedded to America and does not want to return to his ancestral Africa except in fancy, perhaps. The African *has* Africa, but a severe psychic problem has cropped up among Africans sent to the United States on various assignments: Many of them have very little contact with American Negroes, feel alienated within themselves, *but do not want to return to Africa.* Alienated or no, they have become passionately attached to the ways of the cosmopolitan West, the high standard of living, the creature comforts of the affluent society. These sons of Africa do not care to share the enforced status of the American Negro (who can blame them?), but they exist from day to day, from year to year, in levels and areas of American society where for years our American Negro integrationist leadership sought to be accepted on a peer basis of merit and educational qualifications. Despite his blackness, the African is handed this status almost *gratis,* without a "civil rights" struggle. This is what he wants, and he likes it, and regrets to have to give it up. Compared to the American Negro, he is *persona grata.* Ironically, however, for the Black Nationalists and the Black Power exponents in Harlem, any American Negro from the black elite functioning in these privileged areas of metropolitan interracial life has sold out his birthright to the white power structure.

Despite the historical affinities, the African and the Afro-American dilemmas differ—each has its own qualities, peculiarities, and imperatives. And the Black Power controversy illuminates all too well the deep confusions about these imperatives. What *is* the program for Black Power? *That* is the fundamental, unanswered question. In *Rights & Reviews,* Julian Bond, formerly of SNCC, wrote: "Black Power must be seen as a natural extension of the work of the civil rights movement for the past few years. From the courtroom to the streets in favor of integrated public facilities; from the streets onto backwoods roads in quest of the right to vote; from the ballot box to the meat of politics, the organization of voters into self-interest units." This is the dialectic of reformism! But Bond advised that "conflict and struggle are necessary for social change."[5]

However, another writer said: "Forget Black Power. There is more to it than that, and our life might perhaps become the truth of the moment we seek without the need of slogans. In times past people were content to *experience* their lives, but today one is not really living unless one has a program."[6]

Floyd McKissick, CORE's top man, wrote: "The doctrine of Black Power is this new thrust which seeks to achieve economic power and to develop political movements that would make changes that are vast and significant."[7] *But economic power for whom?* For workers? Black capitalists? Black farmers? Black middleclass? Black racketeers? Welfare clients? The crucial economic issue in the ghettos today is Anti-Poverty *but Anti-Poverty is not only a black issue*. How would CORE Black Power deal with this question? Or, on the question of political movements—around what particular issues would these political movements be developed? So far, the mentality of the Black Power theorists is so narrow that they see politics on merely one plane—running some black candidate for office—a hackneyed reformist tactic. No one can beat the Democrats and Republicans in the field of reform politics, especially black reform. Black radicals do not understand the art of creative politics, which is to make the superabundance of people's grievances political. But this is not all that is awry in Black Power ideology.

When one starts with the skin-color premise of a Roy Inniss on the Afro-American problem, one is, unfortunately, feeding a strong tendency within the Black Nationalist movement towards black-skin chauvinism—a policy which cannot work politically in the United States. It has never worked in the West Indies either; it can work only in Africa, it seems. But, in the United States, the American Negro group is too large and mixed with too many racial strains for the ideology of black-skin supremacy to function within the group. It can lead to the reasoning that "I'm blacker than you, and so is my mama, so I'm purer than you and your mama. Therefore, I am also more nationalistic than you, and more politically trustworthy than you and your mama, in the interests of Black Power." But inside America this is a pure fiction. The blacker skin does not always denote the deeper racial pride. In fact, some of the darkest Negroes are the most "white-minded." In America, the Negro group is more an *ethnic* than a racial group—meaning a group of mixed African, Indian, and white strains. Of course, the American–West Indian fusion of Black African-nationalists prefer their converts to be truly "black" both in pigmentation and ideology, and look rather doubtfully at others.

There have been several trends who have tried to exclude Negroes with non-Negroid features and straight hair, overlooking the fact that Marcus Garvey's second wife, just such a female type, wrote of Garvey: "My hair let down, thrilled him. It was long and naturally wavy, he asked me never to cut it. The first time he saw it down, curiously he felt some strands and said, 'why it is soft,' as I tossed my head, he exclaimed, 'Oh, but it so live.' "[8] There is little doubt that Mrs. Garvey, a racial hybrid, was just as much of a Black Nationalist as the great redemptionist. And in our time, the two leading exponents of Black Power and Black Nationalism have been racial hybrids—Adam Clayton Powell and Malcolm X. The color problem among American Negroes is more complex than Roy Inniss admits.

Yet this problem among Negroes is of less signal importance today than the glaring fact that the Black Power theorists have learned very little from Afro-American history, which is of more immediate political significance than how many black Africans sat on the thrones of ancient Egypt. The trouble with the Black Nationalist Africanists is that most of their intellectual capacities are used up glorifying the most attractive aspects of Africa's pre-slavery past, while most of the African elite today have ceased being revolutionaries (if they ever were). In fact, most American Negroes who have been to Africa and back have almost as low an opinion of the African elite in Africa as some of the Africans have of the American Negroes' lack of cohesion. Hence, it would serve a very good purpose here in America for Negroes to cease romanticizing Africa and pre-feudal tribalism.

The radical wing of the Negro movement in America sorely needs a social theory based on the living ingredients of Afro-American history. Without such a theory all talk of Black Power is meaningless. One of the keys to the confusion over the meaning of the slogan is the ambivalence in CORE's publication over the choice of historical leadership symbols and the interpretation given to the implications of these leadership trends. For example, the strong tendency of the Black Power theorists to associate only the names of Denmark Vesey, Harriet Tubman, Nat Turner, Marcus Garvey, Elijah Muhammad and Malcolm X with the social, political and ideological implications of Black Power is being absolutely false to history. Even the addition of Frederick Douglass to this historical leadership gallery is insufficient. For one thing, Douglass was no nationalist, and no pre-Civil War data is complete without the name of Martin R. Delany, the real prototype of Afro-American Nationalism.

But of more relevance to the present-day Negro movement as a whole are the twentieth-century leaders and their trends—Washington, Du Bois, and Garvey. *These are the big three for our century.* Anyone who does not understand this cannot talk seriously about Black Power or any other slogan. But the Black Power theorists are romantics who do not understand this. Of course, spokesmen like Roy Inniss, Ben-Jochannan, etc., will find it difficult to accept this. In their conceptual scheme of things they would accept Marcus Garvey and reject Washington and Du Bois. But this is predicated not on any profound theoretical or scientific examination of historical facts but on passion, emotionalism, and prejudice. They accept Garvey without Washington because they have not examined the reasons Washington was Garvey's only American hero. Similarly, they accept Douglass without Du Bois, although it was Du Bois who upheld Douglass and carried his abolitionist-protest-civil rights trend into the twentieth century. Although in terms of economics, Elijah Muhammad carried out Booker T. Washington's philosophy of economic self-sufficiency and self-help more thoroughly than any other movement, the Black Power theorists accept the Nation of Islam, yet reject Booker T-ism. They fail to see the fallacy of such reasoning because they have no understanding of economics as a science or the different schools of economic theory and how to apply them to the Negro movement. With such an innocence about economics, politics becomes child's play once the direct-action dynamic is taken away. Unschooled in the deep politics of the Negro movement since World War One, the leaders of CORE and SNCC are unaware that even the few economic cooperatives they initiated in the South are forty years too late. How can people like this expect to cope with the economic policies of Anti-Poverty today?

In terms of economics, the Negro's heritage today is New Deal capitalism and Anti-Poverty, broadly speaking. His only "race" economics of any importance are those of Elijah Muhammad.

Garvey's economic ideology which was tied to the African scene is useless today, since there is no Back-to-Africa momentum. The only leader of the big three who left behind, in writing, an economic program for the United States was W. E. B. Du Bois, yet nationalist prejudice against him prevents Negro leaders from acknowledging this. Moreover, it was Du Bois' brand of Pan-Africanism that won out in Africa, not Garvey's, *because Garvey was not a socialist but a thoroughgoing capitalist.* In terms of economics, neither Africa nor the West Indies has achieved the kind of independence and autonomy Garvey wanted. However, the unreality of Garvey's program in the 1920's meant he would have had even less chance of expunging neo-colonialism from Africa than the leaders of the African Revolution have had today. The result has been that Garveyism has failed to muster up any aid or political and economic assistance from Negroes in the Western hemisphere. The real foreign aid must come from both capitalist and socialist governments. The politics of certain African leaders are sufficiently ambivalent that they avidly seek this capitalistic and socialistic aid with one hand (for their version of Black Power), while with the other they either point the finger of criticism at the American Negro or else mouth vague platitudes about black cooperation. They simply do not understand the Afro-American's complex problem and its imperatives.

The Black Power enthusiasts practice the same dubious verbal skin-game in another way. They cannot cope with the realities of the economics of their own foreign aid, *i.e.,* Anti-Poverty, yet they talk boldly about economic independence as the basis of real power. How can such people talk seriously of cooperating with Africa when they cannot help themselves with a definitive economic program for Black Power in America? The "reluctant African" in the United States has adequate reasons for his stand-offishness. He has deep personal problems of identity to cope with, in the midst of a situation that has trapped the American Negro both physically and intellectually. The worst effect of his American conditioning is not his color-complex about blackness, but that it renders him unable to look at his own history and influence in America objectively and understand it scientifically. He is so bedazzled by the personalities of his chosen leadership symbols that he cannot peer behind the façade and examine what were the political, economic, class, and cultural trends that influenced the actions of those chosen leaders.

Another important issue the Black Power theorists evade is the class problem among Negroes. When one talks bravely about developing political and economic black power one had best start clarifying which class is going to wield this power. Better yet— which class among Negroes has the most power now? And which class will benefit from Black Power when it arrives? Here is another clue to the essential reformism inherent in the Black Power slogan: The theorists, although they snipe at the black bourgeoisie, are themselves prey to bourgeois aspirations—major or minor. This is by no means a bad thing in itself. To better one's material (if not spiritual) condition in America necessarily means adopting either the petty or the garish trappings of middle-class existence. However, the Black Power theorists are thrown into a reformist muddle involving class aspirations and economic power for the simple reason that they have no recognizable basis for economic power. To be brutally frank, some do not even know what economic theory is, while others do not want to be bothered with it. Despite their vaunted anti-Americanism, they are more American than they think. Congenitally pragmatic to the core, they are anti-theoretical. Thus, the white power structure does their economic theory and practice for them. New Deal economics, in force for thirty-four years, decides how Anti-Poverty funds are allotted to black ghettos, but people in ghettos have no say in how much funds or how often they are to be allotted. Is *this* economic Black Power? If not, ask any Black Power theorist what kind of politics can change this arrangement. Or better—ask any Black Power theorist whether economics determine politics, or vice versa? Ask any Black Power theorist why Anti-Poverty funds pay out so much money in middle-class salaries? Is this good or bad—for Black Power economics? You will get no clear answers.

However, from one familiar source we get some very clear convictions on the question of which class attributes and Black-Power economics go together. Discussing Black Power in the *Negro Digest* of November, 1966, . . . John O. Killens had this to say:

It seems to me there need be no strong schism at this moment between the advocates of black power and the "black bourgeoisie." . . . If one of the principle [sic] tenets of Black Consciousness is economic power, the starting place is with the black middle class. May their tribe increase. Black Power advocates are no present danger to them.[9]

When Black Power was simply Black Nationalism unqualified, Killens was by no means so certain that no middle-class Negroes were endangered. But since Black Nationalism is obviously here to stay, let us reform it nearer to the heart's desire. If John O. Killens had been told during the early 1950's that the black middle class on *Freedom* newspaper, with Robeson leading, had reformed leftwing Communism into leftwing integrationism (which is not Black Power) in the interests of the black middle class, Killens would have replied something like this—"Oh no, Robeson's *Freedom* appeals to the black working class, may their tribe increase. But this is no present danger to the black middle class." In fact, it was not. But today it should be clear to all Black Power advocates that these two "tribes"—workingclass and bourgeois—cannot both increase. Somebody has to give in, or give up, or simply "give" somewhere. Moreover, when a John O. Killens declares "all power to the black bourgeoisie" instead of the black proletariat, he admonishes: "Black Power is not an advocate of violence. It advocates non-violence, but in depth. It keeps everybody non-violent. It stays the hand of the practitioners of violence."[10] Of course, it was not long ago that Mr. Killens was upholding "violence" when "necessary.". . .

The last outstanding leader was Malcolm X, but did his followers really understand the man's positive side, or his limitations, or why he acted as he did? Did they see any Afro-American historical trends repeating themselves in Malcolm X's career? Unfortunately, they did not. The editors of CORE's magazine leaned heavily on quotations from Frederick Douglass' speeches and writings. But, historically, Douglass' Abolitionism and Reconstructionism are nineteenth-century achievements that became overshadowed by American twentieth-century developments. Besides, Frederick Douglass is also the chief hero of the NAACP integrationists, hence, the Black Power fellows are in strange company, sharing "heroes." Yet Malcolm X was no hero to the NAACP

worshippers at Douglass' shrine, so how, then, do divergent integrationist and nationalist trends wind up honoring the same hero?
Because neither integrationists nor nationalists truly understand
the crucial impact of the integrationist vs. nationalist conflict
within the contours of American Negro history.

The Black Power exponents who uphold Malcolm X, yet cannot
come to terms with either Washington or Du Bois as historical
leaders, understand neither the break between Du Bois and Washington, nor the break between Malcolm X and Elijah Muhammad.
These two breaches are historically related and stem from the
same root in Afro-American history, albeit under different circumstances. Malcolm X broke with the Nation of Islam because of
Muhammad's refusal to participate in the broad struggle for
human rights, as Malcolm X explained it. But W. E. B. Du Bois,
the turn-of-the-century radical, broke with Booker T. Washington's leadership school for the same reasons (as a reading of *The
Souls of Black Folk* will show). Du Bois said that Washington
shied away from participating in the struggle for the Negro's
manhood rights. Malcolm X's break was that of a radical nationalist with the conservative nationalism of Elijah Muhammad, the
latter inherited from Booker T. Washington, by way of Garvey
who had "radicalized" Washington's economic philosophy.

The only way to understand this process is not to be led astray
by mere slogans, but to see the fundamentals at work: the underlying conflict between integrationist and nationalist tendencies historically projected in the contrasted outlooks of Douglass and
Delany. No matter how nationalistic Malcolm X remained after
his break, he was forced by circumstances to swing closer to the
civil rights–integrationist forces in order to participate more fully
in the broad struggle.[11] That was why certain of Malcolm X's
former followers could charge him with "selling out" by seeking an
alliance with the direct-action-integrationist forces.

American Negro history is basically a history of the conflict
between integrationist and nationalist forces in politics, economics,
and culture, no matter what leaders are involved and what slogans
are used. After Malcolm X's death, the Black Power slogan was
actually a swing back to the conservative nationalism from which
Malcolm X had just departed. The pendulum swings back and

forth, but the men who swing with it always fail to synthesize composite trends. W. E. B. Du Bois came the closest of all the big three to understanding this problem, when he wrote in *Dusk of Dawn:* "There faces the American Negro therefore an intricate and subtle problem of combining into one object two difficult sets of facts."[12]

The "two difficult sets of facts" Du Bois refers to are integrationism (civil rights, racial equality, freedom) versus nationalism (separatism, accommodationist self-segregation, economic nationalism, group solidarity and self-help). This was truly the first theoretical formulation of the historic conflict between tendencies, but Du Bois never developed his basic theoretical premise. He failed to go beyond this first principle into a greater synthesis of all the historical ingredients of Afro-Americana, which he knew better than all the Washingtons and the Garveys combined. Like Karl Marx, W. E. B. Du Bois was one of history's great researchers—a sifter, interpreter and recorder of historical and contemporary knowledge; but unlike Marx, he could not reinterpret his data into new conceptions of social reality. Still, he came close, albeit late in life.

It was historically unfortunate that the American Negro created no social theorists to back up his long line of activist leaders, charismatic deliverers, black redemptionists, and moral suasionists. With a few perceptive and original thinkers, the Negro movement conceivably could long ago have aided in reversing the backsliding of the United States toward the moral negation of its great promise as a new nation of nations. Instead the American Negro has, unwittingly, been forced to share in many of the corrupted values of the society—not enough, to be sure, to cancel out completely his inherent potential for social change. However, the intellectual horizons of the black intelligentsia have been so narrowed in scope and banalized by the American corrosion that Negro creativity has been diminishing since the 1920's. An examination of the pronouncements of the Black Power theorists reveals that they have not advanced one whit in their thinking, beyond the 1919 writers of A. Philip Randolph's *Messenger* magazine. They have, in fact, retrogressed. There is not a single Negro publication in existence today that matches the depth of the old *Messenger.*

CORE's new Black Power publication talks of developing "political and economic power" as if speaking for the first time. But back in the 1920's, when Randolph's writers were chastising Du Bois and boasting of how they were "correctly" giving precedence to economics and politics over culture and art, they knew what they were talking about and said it with infinitely more expertise than today's Black Power exponents. In fact, the Black Power theorists do not even know how to deal with culture and art, as the CORE publication reveals. This is shocking to contemplate.

Black Power slogans reveal the depth of unpreparedness and the lack of knowledge that go along with the eagerness of the new black generation of spokesmen. The farther the Negro gets from his historical antecedents in time, the more tenuous become his conceptual ties, the emptier his social conceptions, the more superficial his visions. His one great and present hope is to know and understand his Afro-American history in the United States more profoundly. Failing that, and failing to create a new synthesis and a social theory of action, he will suffer the historical fate described by the philosopher who warned that "Those who cannot remember the past are condemned to repeat it."

A Selected Bibliography
of Black History

The standard black history text is John Hope Franklin, *From Slavery to Freedom* (3rd. ed., 1967). Other surveys include Lerone Bennett, *Before the Mayflower* (1962), Saunders Redding, *They Came in Chains* (1950), and August Meier and Elliott M. Rudwick, *From Plantation to Ghetto* (1966), an excellent interpretive study. Eugene D. Genovese, "The Legacy of Slavery and the Roots of Black Nationalism," *Studies on the Left* (1966), is a provocative essay, which should be read in conjunction with the criticisms by Herbert Aptheker, Frank Kofsky, and C. Vann Woodward, included in the same issue. Ralph Bardolph, *The Negro Vanguard* (1959) contains biographical information about the leading black figures in American history, and Lerone Bennett, *Pioneers in Protest* (1968) is a series of portraits of prominent blacks. Thomas F. Gossett, *Race: The History of an Idea in America* (1963) is a good survey of American racial attitudes. See also the comparative approach in Pierre L. van den Berghe, *Race and Racism* (1967). Vincent Harding, *Black Radicalism in America* (forthcoming) examines black militancy in American history, and Hanes Walton, Jr., provides a good survey of *Black Political Parties* (1970).

There are a number of collections of essays and readings in black history: Melvin Drimmer, ed., *Black History* (1969); August Meier and Elliott M. Rudwick, eds., *The Making of Black America* (1969); Dwight Hoover, ed., *Understanding Negro History* (1968); Allen Weinstein and Frank O. Gatell, eds., *The Segregation Era, 1863–1954* (1970); William G. Shade and Roy Herrenkohl, eds., *Seven on Black* (1969); and Talcott Parsons and Kenneth Clark, eds., *The Negro American* (1966). The most exhaustive collection of primary sources is the *Encyclopaedia Britannica's* three-volume collection, *The Negro in American History* (1969), but also useful are Herbert Aptheker, ed., *A Documentary History of the Negro People in the United States* (1951), which is particularly good for the nineteenth century; Gilbert Osofsky, ed., *The Burden of Race* (1967); William L. Katz, ed., *Eyewitness: The Negro in American History* (1967); Leslie H. Fishel and Benjamin

557

Quarles, eds., *The Negro American: A Documentary History* (1967); Jay David, ed., *Growing Up Black* (1969), a collection of excerpts from autobiographies; Joanne Grant, ed., *Black Protest* (1968) and John H. Bracey, Jr., August Meier, and Elliott M. Rudwick, eds., *Black Nationalism in America* (1970). Documentary collections which cover more limited time spans include Howard Brotz, ed., *Negro Social and Political Thought 1850–1920* (1966), a particularly useful work with an excellent introductory essay; Francis Broderick and August Meier, eds., *Negro Protest Thought in the Twentieth Century* (1965), another very useful collection; Carter G. Woodson, ed., *The Mind of the Negro as Reflected by Letters Written During the Crisis, 1800–1860* (1926); John Hope Franklin and Isidore Starr, eds., *The Negro in Twentieth Century America* (1967); Richard Resh, ed., *Black America: Confrontation and Accommodation in the Twentieth Century* (1969); Carter G. Woodson, ed., *Negro Orators and Their Orations* (1925); Albert P. Blaustein and Robert L. Zangrando, eds., *Civil Rights and the American Negro* (1968); and Louis Ruchames, ed., *Racial Thought in America, from the Puritans to Abraham Lincoln* (1969).

For bibliographical information see the old but still useful work by Monroe N. Work, *A Bibliography of the Negro in Africa and America* (1928); Elizabeth Miller, *The Negro in America: A Bibliography* (1966); John P. Davis, ed., *The American Negro Reference Book* (1950); and the bibliographies in the texts by Franklin and Meier and Rudwick, cited above. Two interesting articles on historians' approaches to black history are Robert Starobin, "The Negro: A Central Theme in American History," *Journal of Contemporary History* (1968), and I. A. Newby, "Historians and Negroes," *Journal of Negro History* (1969). On the study of black history, see the collection edited by Armsted L. Robinson, *et al., Black Studies in the University* (1969); C. Vann Woodward, "Clio with Soul," *Journal of American History* (1969); and the February, 1970 issue of *The Black Scholar*.

African Background

Roland Oliver and J. D. Fage, *A Short History of Africa* (2nd ed., 1966) is a good introduction to African history. Other useful surveys include Basil Davidson, *A History of West Africa* (1965), and J. D. Fage, *An Introduction to the History of West Africa* (2nd ed., 1962). See also Philip Curtin's pamphlet, published by the American Historical Association, *African History* (1964). Two useful collections of documents are Basil Davidson, ed., *The African Past* (1964), and Roland Oliver and Caroline Oliver, eds., *Africa in the Days of Exploration* (1965). Daniel F. McCall, *Africa in Time-Perspective* (1969), is a good introduction to the use of oral tradition and other kinds of unwritten evidence.

The best introduction to the kingdoms of the Sudan can be found in Basil Davidson's *The Lost Cities of Africa* (1959). E. W. Bovill, *The Golden Trade of the Moors* (2nd ed., 1968) is an excellent study of the Sudanic states and their economic relations with North Africa, and J. S. Trimingham, *History of Islam in West Africa* (1959) is also extremely good. See also the lectures by the Ghanaian historian Adu Bohaen, *Topics in West African History* (1966). Works on other African states include Melville Herskovits, *Dahomey* (1938); Georges Ballinder, *Daily Life in the Kingdom of the Kongo* (1968); R. S. Rattray, *Ashanti* (1923); Jacob Eghaevba, *A History of Benin* (3rd ed., 1960); Jan Vansina, *Kingdoms of the Savanna* (1966); and K. O. Dike, *Trade and Politics in the Niger Delta, 1830–1885* (1956). E. G. Parrinder, *African Traditional Religions* (1954) is the best survey of its subject. Two good collections of readings on many aspects of African history are Roland Oliver, ed., *The Middle Age of African History* (1967), and Robert Collins, ed., *Problems in African History* (1968).

On the controversial subject of African survivals in the New World, particularly the United States, the starting point is Melville Herskovits, *The Myth of the Negro Past* (1941). Herskovits' sharpest critic, E. Franklin Frazier, explained his position in *The Negro in the United States* (1957). See also *Africa from the Point of View of American Scholars*, a special issue of the magazine *Présence Africaine* (1958); Romeo B. Garrett, "African Survivals in American Culture," *Journal of Negro History* (1966); and Norman Whitten and John Szewd, "Negroes in the New World," *Trans-Action* (1968).

The Slave Trade

Two good histories of the Atlantic slave trade are Daniel Mannix and Malcolm Cowley, *Black Cargoes* (1962), and Basil Davidson, *The African Slave Trade* (1961), while James Pope-Hennessy, *Sins of the Fathers* (1968) focuses on the slavetraders. Philip Curtin gives the most recent estimate of the numbers involved in the trade in *The Atlantic Slave Trade: A Census* (1969), and his "Epidemiology and the Slave Trade," *Political Science Quarterly* (1968), discusses the importance of disease in the development of the New World's labor systems. On slavery in Africa before the coming of the Europeans, see chapter three in Eugene D. Genovese's *The Political Economy of Slavery* (1965), Herskovits' treatment in *Dahomey*, and the article by A. Norman Klein in *Slavery in the New World* (1969), eds. Eugene D. Genovese and Laura Foner. The impact of the trade on Africa is considered in two articles by Walter Rodney: "African Slavery and Other Forms of Social Oppression on the Upper Guinea Coast in the Context of the Atlantic Slave-Trade," *Journal of African History* (1966), and "The Impact of the Slave Trade on West Africa," in Oliver, ed., *The Middle Age of African History*, and in J. D. Fage, "Slavery and the Slave Trade in the Context of West African History," *Journal of African History* (1969). See also Karl Polanyi, *Dahomey and the Slave Trade* (1966); Darold D. Wax, "Negro Resistance to the Early Slave Trade," *Journal of Negro History* (1966); W. E. B. Du Bois' classic, *The Suppression of the African Slave Trade to the United States* (1896); and K. G. Davies, *The Royal African Company* (1957). Elizabeth Donnan, ed., *Documents Illustrative of the History of the Slave Trade to America* (1930–35) is an exhaustive four-volume collection, and Philip Curtin, ed., *Africa Remembered* (1968) presents writings and reminiscences by Africans directly involved in the slave trade.

David Brion Davis discusses the persistence of slavery in medieval Europe in *The Problem of Slavery in Western Culture* (1966). For the planting of slavery in the New World, see Caio Prado, Jr., *The Colonial Background of Modern Brazil* (1967), and *Plantation Systems of the New World* (1959), a publication of the Pan-American Union. The role of slavery and the slave trade in the first British Empire is examined in Lawrence Gipson's magisterial twelve-volume study of *The British Empire Before the American Revolution,* especially volume II (1936). On the abolition of the slave trade by Great Britain, Eric Williams' controversial interpretation in *Capitalism and Slavery* (1944) is criticized in *The Transatlantic Slave Trade* (1965), a report of a historical conference, published by the University of Edinburgh's Centre of African Studies. Blacks came to the New World in other capacities than as slaves; for their role in exploration and discovery, see Rayford Logan, "Estevanicio, Negro Discoverer of the Southwest," *Phylon* (1940), and Richard R. Wright, "Negro Companions of the Spanish Explorers," *Phylon* (1941).

Slavery in the Colonial United States

Louis Ruchames, "The Sources of Racial Thought in Colonial America," *Journal of Negro History* (1967), contains interesting suggestions on the origins of American racism. The controversy over the evolution of slavery in Virginia can be approached via the following articles: Oscar and Mary Handlin, "Origins of the Southern Labor System," *William and Mary Quarterly* (1950); Carl N. Degler, "Slavery and the Genesis of American Race Prejudice," *Comparative Studies in Society and History* (1959); Winthrop D. Jordan, "The Influence of the West Indies on the Origins of New England Slavery," *William and Mary Quarterly* (1961); Jordan, "Modern Tensions and the Origins of American Slavery," *Journal of Southern History* (1962); and Paul C. Palmer, "Servant into Slave: The Evolution of the Legal Status of the Negro Laborer in Colonial Virginia," *South Atlantic Quarterly* (1966). For the institution of slavery in the colonial South, see Thad W. Tate's excellent study of *The Negro in Eighteenth Century Williamsburg* (1965); Thomas J. Wertenbaker's classic, *The Planters of Colonial Virginia* (1922); and two recent articles: Eugene Sirmans, "The Legal Status of the Slave in South Carolina, 1670–1740," *Journal of Southern History* (1962), and Darold D. Wax, "Georgia and the Negro Before the American Revolution," *Georgia Historical Quarterly* (1967). Slavery in the northern colonies is dealt with in Lorenzo Greene,

The Negro in Colonial New England (1942); Robert C. Twombly and Robert H. Moore, "Black Puritan: The Negro in Seventeenth Century Massachusetts," *William and Mary Quarterly* (1967); Edward J. McManus, *A History of Negro Slavery in New York* (1966); and Edward R. Turner, "Slavery in Colonial Pennsylvania," *Pennsylvania Magazine of History and Biography* (1911). See also Darold Wax, "The Negro in Early America," *Social Studies* (1969). For the major system of unfree labor aside from slavery, see Abbott E. Smith's study of indentured servitude, *Colonists in Bondage* (1947).

Winthrop D. Jordan's prize-winning *White Over Black* (1968) discusses the rise of antislavery sentiment in the second half of the eighteenth century, and the views of the founding fathers, and carries its examination of American racial attitudes to 1812. David Brion Davis' *The Problem of Slavery in Western Culture* deals with the rise of antislavery in a somewhat different manner. The impact of the Revolution upon slavery is discussed in Bernard Bailyn, *The Ideological Origins of the American Revolution* (1967), and J. Franklin Jameson, *The American Revolution Considered as a Social Movement* (1925), while Arthur Zilversmit, *The First Emancipation* (1967) examines the abolition of slavery in the northern states. The role of blacks in the Revolutionary War is the subject of Benjamin Quarles, *The Negro in the American Revolution* (1961). For the views of the founding fathers regarding slavery and the failure of the Constitutional Convention to abolish the institution, see Staughton Lynd, *Class Conflict, Slavery, and the United States Constitution* (1967); Don B. Kates, "Abolition, Deportation, Integration: Attitudes Toward Slavery in the Early Republic," *Journal of Negro History* (1968); and Robert McColley, *Slavery and Jeffersonian Virginia* (1964). Those wishing to consult the founders' views at first hand should see Thomas Jefferson, *Notes on the State of Virginia* (1785), and Matthew T. Mellon's collection, *Early American Views of Negro Slavery* (1934).

Plantation Slavery

Allan Weinstein and Frank O. Gatell, eds., *American Negro Slavery: A Modern Reader* (1968) is an excellent collection of readings on slavery, with an exhaustive bibliography. The two best one-volume introductions to the slave system are Ulrich B. Phillips, *American Negro Slavery* (1918), and Kenneth M. Stampp, *The Peculiar Institution* (1956). Stampp's work is better in most respects, but Phillips' offers many revealing insights, and neither can be disregarded. See also Phillips' *Life and Labor in the Old South* (1929). There are good shorter introductions to slavery in Allan Nevins, *Ordeal of the Union* (1947), volume one; Clement Eaton, *The Growth of Southern Civilization* (1961); and James G. Randall and David Donald, *The Civil War and Reconstruction* (2nd ed., 1961). Two excellent studies of individual states are Charles Sydnor, *Slavery in Mississippi* (1933), and Joe Gray Taylor, *Negro Slavery in Louisiana* (1961). Specific aspects of the slave system are dealt with in Frederic Bancroft, *Slave Trading in the Old South* (1931); William K. Scarborough, *The Overseer* (1966); Richard Wade, *Slavery in the Cities* (1964); Ernest J. Clark, "Aspects of the North Carolina Slave Code, 1715–1860," *North Carolina Historical Review* (1962); and Robert Starobin, *Industrial Slavery in the Old South* (1970). John H. Moore tells the story of a remarkable slave in "Simon Gray, Riverman: A Slave Who Was Almost Free," *Mississippi Valley Historical Review* (1962). On the thorny subject of the economics of slavery and the system's profitability, see Harold D. Woodman, "The Profitability of Slavery: An Historical Perennial," *Journal of Southern History* (1963); Eugene D. Genovese, *The Political Economy of Slavery* (1965); Alfred Conrad and J. H. Meyer, *The Economics of Slavery* (1964); and Robert Fogel and Stanley Engerman's contribution to Robert Fogel, ed., *The Reinterpretation of American Economic History* (forthcoming). And for the impact of slavery upon the white southern mentality, see the classic study by W. J. Cash, *The Mind of the South* (1941).

The best introduction to slave life and culture is still the narratives and reminiscences of ex-slaves. The best of these is the autobiography of Frederick Douglass, which appeared in three different versions during his lifetime. The most complete is *The Life and Times of Frederick Douglass* (1881), but *My Bondage and My Freedom* (1855) contains some interesting views not included in the later work. The slave narratives of Solomon Northrup William Welles Brown, Austin Steward, Josiah Henson, and others have recently appeared in new editions. Harvey Wish has collected excerpts from a number of them in *Slavery in the South* (1964), and Gilbert Osofsky reprints three slave narratives in *Puttin' On Ole Massa* (1969). See also Arna Bontemps, ed., *Great Slave Narratives* (1969). Charles H. Nichols, *Many Thousands Gone* (1963) uses the slave narratives to investigate aspects of slave life in the United States. Another type of primary evidence, the reminiscences of ex-slaves, is somewhat more suspect, since most of the recollections were collected long after the slavery years. Benjamin Botkin's *Lay My Burden Down* (1945) is the most extensive collection of these reminiscences, but see also Julius Lester, ed., *To Be a Slave* (1968); John B. Cade, ed., "Out of the Mouths of Ex-Slaves," *Journal of Negro History* (1935); J. Ralph Jones, ed., "Portraits of Georgia Slaves," *Georgia Review* (1967); and E. Opheilia Settle, "Social Attitudes During the Slave Regime: Household Servants Versus Field Hands," *Publications of the American Sociological Society* (1934). Sterling Brown *et al.*, eds., *The Negro Caravan* (1941) includes many slave songs and spirituals, and for analyses of these songs, see Brown's "Negro Folk Expression; Spirituals, Seculars, Ballads, and Songs," *Phylon* (1953), and Miles M. Fisher, *Negro Slave Songs in the United States* (1953). The impact of slavery upon the black family is discussed in the opening chapters of E. Franklin Frazier, *The Negro Family in the United States* (1939), and for the controversy over the "Elkins

Thesis," see Ann J. Lane, ed., *Slavery and Personality: The Elkins Thesis and Its Critics* (forthcoming).

Resistance to Slavery

Herbert Aptheker, *American Negro Slave Revolts* (1943) is a controversial study of rebellions in the United States. For studies of specific revolts, see Kenneth Scott, "The Slave Insurrection in New York in 1712," *New-York Historical Society Quarterly* (1961); T. W. Clark, "The Negro Plot of 1741," *New York History* (1944); Ferenc M. Szasz, "The New-York Slave Revolt of 1741: A Re-examination," *New York History* (1967); and Gerald W. Mullin, "Patterns of Slave Behavior in Eighteenth Century Virginia" (unpublished doctoral dissertation, University of California, Berkeley, 1968), which contains the most recent examination of the Gabriel rebellion. John Lofton, *Insurrection in South Carolina* (1964) is a study of Vesey's rebellion, which should be read along with William Freehling's account in *Prelude to Civil War* (1966), and Richard Wade, "The Vesey Plot Reconsidered," *Journal of Southern History* (1964). William Styron's novel, *The Confessions of Nat Turner* (1967) has stirred a considerable historical controversy over the Turner insurrection. See Herbert Aptheker, *Nat Turner's Slave Rebellion* (1966), which includes the original *Confessions* dictated by Turner as he awaited execution; John Henrik Clarke, ed., *William Styron's Nat Turner: Ten Black Writers Respond* (1968); and Eugene D. Genovese's review of the Clarke book, in *New York Review of Books,* September 12, 1968, and Vincent Harding's response, November 8, 1968. A recent examination of American slave revolts is Marion D. Kilson, "Towards Freedom: An Analysis of Slave Revolts in the United States," *Phylon* (1964). For other forms of resistance, see George M. Frederickson and Christopher Lasch, "Resistance to Slavery," *Civil War History* (1967); Raymond and Alice Bauer, "Day to Day Resistance to Slavery," *Journal of Negro History* (1943); and Larry Gara's study of the underground railroad, *The Liberty Line* (1961).

Studies of slave rebellions in other parts of the western hemisphere include Charles E. Chapman, "Palmares, The Negro Numantia," *Journal of Negro History* (1918); R. K. Kent, "Palmares: An African State in Brazil," *Journal of African History* (1965); C. L. R. James, *The Black Jacobins* (1938), which tells the story of the Haitian revolution; Mary Reckford, "The Jamaica Slave Rebellion of 1831," *Past and Present* (1968); and H. Orlando Patterson, *The Sociology of Slavery* (1967), whose chapter on slave resistance in Jamaica contains important implications for the United States.

Slavery in Hemispheric Perspective

The best starting point on this controversial subject is Frank Tannenbaum's classic, *Slave and Citizen* (1946). Works which have tended to agree with Tannenbaum's interpretation include Stanley Elkins, *Slavery* (1959) and

Herbert Klein, *Slavery in the Americas* (1967). Critics include David Brion Davis, *The Problem of Slavery in Western Culture;* Marvin Harris and Charles Wagley, *Minorities in the New World* (1958); and Marvin Harris, *Patterns of Race in the Americas* (1964). Eugene D. Genovese criticizes the critics and Tannenbaum in "Materialism and Idealism in the History of Negro Slavery in the Americas," *Journal of Social History* (1968). See also Arthur Sio, "Interpretations of Slavery: The Slave Status in the Americas," *Comparative Studies in Society and History* (1965). Eugene D. Genovese, *The World the Slaveholders Made* (1969) is the latest contribution to this controversy.

Brazilian slavery has been the subject of several excellent works: Gilberto Freyre, *The Masters and the Slaves* (1946); Arthur Ramos, *The Negro in Brazil* (1939); C. R. Boxer, *The Golden Age of Brazil, 1690–1750* (1960); and Stanley J. Stein, *Vassouras: A Brazilian Coffee County, 1850–1900* (1957). For the West Indies, see Patterson's *Sociology of Slavery;* Elsa Goveia's excellent study, *Slave Society in the British Leeward Islands at the End of the Eighteenth Century* (1965); Sidney Mintz, "Labor and Sugar in Puerto Rico and in Jamaica," *Comparative Studies in Society and History* (1959); and Joseph L. Ragatz, *The Fall of the Planter Class in the British Caribbean* (1929). On Cuba, see Ramiro Guerra y Sanchez, *Sugar and Society in the Caribbean* (1964). Two provocative studies of race relations are Magnus Morner, *Race Mixture in Latin America* (1967), and Winthrop D. Jordan, "American Chiaroscuro: The Status and Definition of Mulattoes in the British Colonies," *William and Mary Quarterly* (1962). Genovese and Foner's *Slavery in the New World* contains excellent selections and a good bibliography.

The Free Negro

The status of free blacks in the ante-bellum South is a subject which sorely needs reexamination. There are, however, several good studies of individual states: John Hope Franklin, *The Free Negro in North Carolina, 1790–1860* (1943); Charles S. Sydnor, "The Free Negro in Mississippi Before the Civil War," *American Historical Review* (1927); Russell Gavin, "The Free Negro in Florida before the Civil War," *Florida Historical Quarterly* (1967); Horace Fitchett, "Origin and Growth of the Free Negro Population of Charleston, South Carolina," *Journal of Negro History* (1941); and John H. Russell, *The Free Negro in Virginia* (1913). See also Carter G. Woodson, *Free Negro Heads of Families in the United States in 1830* (1925).

Leon Litwack's *North of Slavery* (1961) is the standard source on conditions of northern free Negroes, but there are also a number of good studies of individual states and cities, including Robert Ernst, "The Economic Status of New York City Negroes, 1850–1863," *Negro History Bulletin* (1949); Lee Calligaro, "The Negro's Legal Status in Pre-Civil War New Jersey," *New Jersey History* (1967); Frank U. Quillin, *The Color Line in*

Ohio (1913); Emma Lou Thornbrough, *The Negro in Indiana Before 1900* (1957); and Richard Wade, "The Negro in Cincinnati, 1800–1830," *Journal of Negro History* (1954). There is information about the status of free blacks in Philadelphia in W. E. B. Du Bois, *The Philadelphia Negro* (1898). Gilbert Osofsky compares the pre-war ghetto with the contemporary in "The Enduring Ghetto," *Journal of American History* (1968). On political discrimination, see Charles H. Wesley, "Negro Suffrage in the Period of Constitution-Making," *Journal of Negro History* (1947).

Alexis de Tocqueville's classic study of Jacksonian America, *Democracy in America* (1835), has some interesting things to say about the treatment of blacks in the free states. The "scientific" basis of racism is examined in William Stanton, *The Leopard's Spots* (1959), and minstrelsy, one of the most striking cultural expressions of racial prejudice, is the subject of Carl Wittke, *Tambo and Bones* (1930), and Hans Nathan, *Dan Emmett and the Rise of Early Negro Minstrelsy* (1962). On the Negro church see Charles H. Wesley, *Richard Allen* (1935) and Carter G. Woodson, *History of the Negro Church* (1921); and for black education, see Woodson's *The Education of the Negro Prior to 1861* (1919), and Dorothy B. Porter, "The Organized Educational Activities of Negro Literary Societies, 1818–1846," *Journal of Negro Education* (1936).

Black Abolitionism

For general information on the abolitionist movement, see Louis Filler, *The Crusade Against Slavery* (1960), which contains an excellent bibliography, and Dwight Dumond, *Anti-Slavery* (1961). The best one-volume survey of black abolitionism is Benjamin Quarles, *Black Abolitionists* (1969), but because of the brevity of this work it is necessary to consult other studies for more detailed information about leaders and trends in the black movement against slavery. On Frederick Douglass, the best starting point is Douglass's autobiography, *The Life and Times of Frederick Douglass*. Benjamin Quarles, *Frederick Douglass* (1948) is the best of several biographies, and Philip S. Foner, *The Life and Writings of Frederick Douglass* (1950–55) is an invaluable four-volume collection. For other black abolitionists, see Herbert Aptheker, ed., *One Continual Cry* (1965), an edition of David Walker's *Appeal*, with a good introductory essay; William Brewer, "Henry Highland Garnet," *Journal of Negro History* (1928); Brewer's "John B. Russwurm," *Journal of Negro History* (1923); Dorothy Porter, "David Ruggles, An Apostle of Human Rights," *Journal of Negro History* (1943); Ray A. Billington, "James Forten, Forgotten Abolitionist," *Negro History Bulletin* (1949); and Monroe Work, "The Life of Charles B. Ray," *Journal of Negro History* (1919). Other considerations of the role of blacks in the abolitionist movement may be found in two collections of essays by Herbert Aptheker: *Essays in Negro History* (1945), and *To Be Free* (1948); Larry Gara, "The Professional Fugitive in the Abolitionist Movement," *Wisconsin Magazine of History* (1965); the collection of essays edited by Martin Duberman, *The Antislavery Vanguard* (1965); and three essays by Charles H. Wesley: "The Negro in the Organization of Abolition," *Phylon* (1941); "The Participation of Negroes in Anti-Slavery Political Parties," *Journal of Negro History* (1944); and "The Negroes of New York in the Emancipation Movement," *Journal of Negro History* (1939).

Howard H. Bell has written a number of essays on aspects of black militancy and emigrationist sentiment: "The Negro Emigration Movement, 1849–1854: A Phase of Negro Nationalism," *Phylon* (1959); "Expressions of Negro Militancy in the North, 1840–1860," *Journal of Negro History* (1960); and "Negro Nationalism: A Factor in Emigration Projects, 1858–1861," *Journal of Negro History* (1962). See also Bell's unpublished doctoral dissertation (Northwestern University, 1953), "A Survey of the Negro Convention Movement 1830–1861," and his edition of the writings of two black emigrationists of the 1850's, Martin R. Delany and Robert Campbell, *Search for a Place* (1969). Hollis R. Lynch also examines emigrationist sentiment in "Pan-Negro Nationalism in the New World Before 1862," *Boston University Papers on Africa* (1966). For white colonization activity—not at all the same as black emigrationism—see Philip J. Staudenraus, *The African Colonization Movement, 1816–1865* (1961). See also L. Mehlinger, "The Attitude of the Free Negro Toward African Colonization," *Journal of Negro History* (1916); and H. N. Sherwood, "Paul Cuffe," *Journal of Negro History* (1923).

Good introductions to the question of white abolitionists' racial attitudes are contained in William and Jane H. Pease, "Anti-Slavery Ambivalence: Immediatism, Expediency, Race," *American Quarterly* (1965); and Leon F. Litwack, "The Abolitionist Dilemma: The Antislavery Movement and the Northern Negro," *New England Quarterly* (1961). Benjamin Quarles, "The Breach Between Garrison and Douglass," *Journal of Negro History* (1938), and William and Jane H. Pease, "Boston Garrisonians and the Problem of Frederick Douglass," *Canadian Journal of History* (1967), discuss that famous controversy, a subject ignored in Aileen Kraditor's otherwise excellent study of Garrison, *Means and Ends in American Abolitionism* (1969). Racism in the political antislavery movement is examined in Eugene H. Berwanger, *The Frontier Against Slavery* (1967). For a somewhat different approach, see my works, "Racial Attitudes of the New York Free Soilers," *New York History* (1965); "Politics and Prejudice: The Free Soil Party and the Negro, 1849–1852," *Journal of Negro History* (1965); and *Free Soil, Free Labor, Free Men* (1970).

The Civil War

There are two good surveys of the role of blacks in the Civil War: Benjamin Quarles, *The Negro in the Civil War* (1953), and Dudley Cornish, *The Sable Arm* (1956). James McPherson, ed., *The Negro's Civil War* (1965) is an excellent documentary collection. The experience of one northerner with black troops is recorded in Thomas Wentworth Higginson, *Army Life in a Black Regiment* (1870). See also the following useful articles: Herbert Aptheker, "Negro Casualties in the Civil War," *Journal of Negro History* (1947); Edgar A. Toppin, "Humbly They Served: The Black Brigade in the Defense of Cincinnati," *Journal of Negro History* (1963); and Richard H. Abbott, "Massachusetts and the Recruitment of Southern Negroes, 1863–1865," *Civil War History* (1968). For the southern side of the story, see N. W. Stephenson, "The Question of Arming the Slaves," *American Historical Review* (1913); Harvey Wish, "Slave Disloyalty Under the Confederacy," *Journal of Negro History* (1938); Charles H. Wesley, "The Employment of Negroes as Soldiers in the Confederate Army," *Journal of Negro History* (1919); and Bell I. Wiley, *Southern Negroes 1861–1865* (1953).

The development of Lincoln's emancipation policy is traced in John Hope Franklin, *The Emancipation Proclamation* (1962), and in Benjamin Quarles, *Lincoln and the Negro* (1962), while James M. McPherson, *The Struggle for Equality* (1964) discusses the pressure from abolitionists and radicals for emancipation. Lincoln's continuing desire to colonize the freedmen outside the country is the subject of Charles H. Wesley, "Lincoln's Plan for Colonizing the Emancipated Negro," *Journal of Negro History* (1919). Various aspects of the reaction to emancipation are discussed in V. Jacque Voegeli, *Free But Not Equal* (1967); Mark M. Krug, "The Republican Party and the Emancipation Proclamation," *Journal of Negro History* (1963); and Williston Lofton, "Northern Labor and the Negro in the Civil War," *Journal of Negro History* (1949). James McCague, *The Second Rebellion* (1968) is a study of the New York City draft riots of 1863. The process of emancipation in a single state is examined in C. L. Wagandt, *The Mighty Revolution: Negro Emancipation in Maryland* (1965).

Reconstruction

Although the work of revising the history of Reconstruction has gone on for several years, there is still no one-volume work which assimilates the revisionists' insights. Bernard Weisberger, "The Dark and Bloody Ground of Reconstruction Historiography," *Journal of Southern History* (1959), explains the need for historical revision, and Kenneth Stampp and Leon Litwack, eds., *Reconstruction: An Anthology of Revisionist Writings* (1969) contains selections from the best recent works on the period. The work which opened a new era of writing Reconstruction history was W. E. B. Du Bois, *Black Reconstruction* (1935), but many years earlier Du Bois had written the important essay "Reconstruction and Its Benefits," *American Historical Review* (1910). Among the useful recent one-volume surveys are Kenneth Stampp, *The Era of Reconstruction* (1965); Lerone Bennett, *Black Power USA, The Human Side of Reconstruction, 1867–77* (1967); and John Hope Franklin, *Reconstruction After the Civil War* (1961). The best of the revisionist studies of national politics are Eric McKitrick, *Andrew Johnson and Reconstruction* (1960); LaWanda and John Cox, *Politics, Principle, and Prejudice* (1963); and W. R. Brock, *An American Crisis*

(1963). Reconsiderations of radicals and carpetbaggers are contained in Hans L. Trefousse, *The Radical Republicans: Lincoln's Vanguard for Racial Justice* (1969); Richard N. Current, "Who Were the Carpetbaggers?," in *Festscrift for Frederick Artz* (1964); and Henry L. Swint, *The Northern Teacher in the South, 1862–1870* (1941). An important early aspect of Reconstruction is examined in Theodore Wilson, *The Black Codes of the South* (1965).

The role of blacks in Reconstruction still needs extensive treatment. Robert Cruden, *The Negro in Reconstruction* (1969) is a short survey of the current state of knowledge, while Henderson Donald, *The Negro Freedman* (1952) is an unsatisfactory study of an important subject. There are, however, good studies of the black role in individual states, particularly Joel Williamson, *After Slavery* (1965), and Willie Lee Rose, *Rehearsal for Reconstruction* (1964), both on South Carolina; Joe M. Richardson, *The Negro in the Reconstruction of Florida* (1966); Vernon Lane Wharton, *The Negro in Mississippi, 1865–1890* (1947); and the older but still useful works, Horace Mann Bond, "Social and Economic Forces in Alabama Reconstruction," *Journal of Negro History* (1933), and A. A. Taylor, *The Negro in the Reconstruction of Virginia* (1926). Special aspects of the black role are treated in Otis A. Singletary, *Negro Militia and Reconstruction* (1957), and Samuel Smith, *The Negro in Congress 1870–1901* (1940). Much information can be gleaned from reminiscences and biographies of some of the leading black political leaders: John M. Langston, *From the Virginia Plantation to the National Capitol* (1894); John R. Lynch, *The Facts of Reconstruction* (1913); Joseph A. Barome, ed., "The Autobiography of Hiram Revels," *Midwest Journal* (1952–53); A. E. Perkins, "Oscar James Dunn," *Phylon* (1943); Robert H. Woody, "Jonathan Jasper Wright," *Journal of Negro History* (1933); and Edward Sweat, "Francis L. Cardozo—Profile of Integrity in Reconstruction Politics," *Journal of Negro History* (1961). There is also information about the black role in Harold Hyman, ed., *New Frontiers of the American Reconstruction* (1966), and in two collections of documents: Walter C. Fleming's three-volume work, *Documentary History of Reconstruction* (1906–1907), and James P. Shenton, ed., *The Reconstruction* (1963). See also E. Merton Coulter, *Negro Legislators in Georgia During the Reconstruction Period* (1968).

On the controversial history of the Freedman's Bureau, see George Bentley, *A History of the Freedman's Bureau* (1955); Martin Abbott, *The Freedman's Bureau in South Carolina* (1967); William McFeely, *Yankee Stepfather* (1968); and two articles by LaWanda Cox: "General O. O. Howard and the 'Misrepresented Bureau,'" *Journal of Southern History* (1953), and "The Promise of Land for the Freedman," *Mississippi Valley Historical Review* (1958). Aspects of the overthrow of Reconstruction are dealt with in Otto Olsen, "The Ku Klux Klan, A Study in Reconstruction Politics and Propaganda," *North Carolina Historical Review* (1962); David Chalmers, *Hooded Americanism* (1965); Patrick W. Riddleberger, "The

Radical's Abandonment of the Negro During Reconstruction," *Journal of Negro History* (1960); and C. Vann Woodward, *Reunion and Reaction* (1951). For the northern scene as it affected blacks, see three articles by Leslie H. Fishel: "Northern Prejudice and Negro Suffrage, 1865–1870," *Journal of Negro History* (1954); "The Negro in Northern Politics 1870–1900," *Mississippi Valley Historical Review* (1955); and "Repercussions of Reconstruction: The Northern Negro 1870–1883," *Civil War History* (1968).

The New South

C. Vann Woodward, *Origins of the New South* (1951) is the leading work on the subject. The best survey of the last century of southern history is Thomas Clark and Albert Kirwan, *The South Since Appomattox* (1967), and Charles Wynes, ed., *The Negro in the South Since 1865* (1965) is a useful collection of essays. Race relations in individual states are dealt with in George B. Tindall, *South Carolina Negroes 1877–1900* (1952); Frenise Logan, *The Negro in North Carolina, 1876–1894* (1964); Clarence Barote, "Negro Proscription and Proposed Solutions in Georgia, 1880–1908," *Journal of Southern History* (1959); and Albert D. Kirwan, *Revolt of the Rednecks* (1951), a study of Mississippi politics. The northern reaction is examined in Stanley P. Hirshhorn, *Farewell to the Bloody Shirt* (1962); Vincent P. DeSantis, *Republicans Face the Southern Question* (1959); and Rayford Logan, *The Betrayal of the Negro* (1954). On the development of segregation, see C. Vann Woodward, *The Strange Career of Jim Crow* (3rd ed., 1966), and the following articles: John Hope Franklin, "The Negro Goes to School: The Genesis of Legal Segregation in Southern Schools," *South Atlantic Quarterly* (1959); Louis R. Harlan, "Desegregation in New Orleans Public Schools During Reconstruction," *American Historical Review* (1962); and Roger H. Fischer, "Racial Segregation in Ante-Bellum New Orleans," *American Historical Review* (1969). See also Jack Abramowitz, "The Negro in the Populist Movement," *Journal of Negro History* (1953). John H. Garraty, ed., *Quarrels That Have Shaped the Constitution* (1964) has chapters on the Supreme Court decisions in the Civil Rights Cases and *Plessy v. Ferguson*. The latter is also the subject of Otto Olsen's documentary collection, *The Thin Disguise* (1967).

The decline of black education in the South is examined in Horace Mann Bond, *Negro Education in Alabama* (1939); Louis R. Harlan, *Separate and Unequal* (1958); and Henry Bullock, *A History of Negro Education in the South* (1967). Some black reactions to their deteriorating status are examined in Edwin S. Redkey, "Bishop Turner's African Dream," *Journal of American History* (1967); Edwin S. Redkey, *Black Exodus* (1969); and August Meier and Elliott M. Rudwick, "The Boycott Movement Against Jim Crow Streetcars in the South, 1900–1906," *Journal of American History* (1969). A neglected aspect of black life during these years is the role of blacks in the West, both as cowboys and soldiers. See Philip Durham and Everett L. Jones, *The Negro Cowboys* (1965); William H. Leckie, *The Buffalo Soldiers* (1967); and the chapter on black troops in Jack D. Foner, *The United States Soldier Between Two Wars* (1970).

The Era of Washington and Du Bois

August Meier, *Negro Thought in America, 1880–1915* (1963) is an outstanding examination of black life and thought in these years. The most recent biography of Washington is Samuel R. Spencer, *Booker T. Washington and the Negro's Place in American Life* (1957). For a full understanding of Washington's thought, one should consult his voluminous writings, especially *The Future of the American Negro* (1899); *Up From Slavery* (1900); *The Negro in the South* (1907); and *Selected Speeches of Booker T. Washington* (1932), edited by E. Davidson Washington. See also three articles by August Meier: "Booker T. Washington and the Negro Press," *Journal of Negro History* (1953); "Booker T. Washington and the Rise of the NAACP," *Crisis* (1954); and "Toward a Reinterpretation of Booker T. Washington," *Journal of Southern History* (1957); Daniel Walden, "The Contemporary Opposition to the Political Ideas of Booker T. Washington," *Journal of Negro History* (1960); Donald J. Calesta, "Booker T. Washington: Another Look," *Journal of Negro History* (1964); and Louis R. Harlan, "Booker T. Washington and the White Man's Burden," *American Historical Review* (1966).

There are two adequate biographies of Du Bois: Francis Broderick, *W. E. B. Du Bois: Negro Leader in a Time of Crisis* (1959); and Elliott M. Rudwick, *W. E. B. Du Bois, Propagandist of the Negro Protest* (1961). Du Bois' autobiographies, *Dawn of Dusk* (1940), and *The Autobiography of W. E. B. Du Bois* (1968) are both fascinating and rewarding reading, and his *The Souls of Black Folk* (1903) is essential for an understanding of the twentieth-century black protest movement. See also the articles by Vincent Harding, "W. E. B. Du Bois and the Black Messianic Tradition," *Freedomways* (1969), and Mary L. Chaffee, "W. E. B. Du Bois' Concept of the Racial Problem in the United States," *Journal of Negro History* (1956). For the views of two other black spokesmen of these years, see T. Thomas Fortune, *Black and White: Land, Labor and Politics in the South* (1884); Kelly Miller, *Race Adjustment* (1908); and Bernard Eisenberg, "Kelly Miller: The Negro Leader as a Marginal Man," *Journal of Negro History* (1960).

The origins and early history of the NAACP are dealt with in Elliott M. Rudwick, "The Niagara Movement," *Journal of Negro History* (1957); C. Kellogg, *NAACP* (1967); Langston Hughes, *Fight for Freedom: Story of the NAACP* (1962); Robert L. Jack, *History of the NAACP* (1943); Loren Miller, *The Petitioners* (1966); and Thomas R. Cripps, "The Reaction of the Negro to the Motion Picture *Birth of a Nation,*" *Historian* (1963). Works which shed light on black conditions just after the turn of the century are Ray Stannard Baker, *Following the Color Line* (1908); Dewey W. Grantham, Jr., "The Progressive Movement and the Negro," *South Atlantic Quarterly* (1955); Kathleen Wolgemuth, "Woodrow Wilson and Federal Segregation," *Journal of Negro History* (1959); Nancy J. Weiss, "The Negro and the New Freedom: Fighting Wilsonian Segregation," *Political Science Quarterly* (1969); and I. A. Newby, *Jim Crow's Defense: Anti-Negro Thought in America, 1900–1930* (1965).

Black Labor

This is a subject which desperately needs investigation. Two older works contain a good deal of useful information, but are now dated: Charles Wesley, *Negro Labor in the United States 1850–1925* (1927); and Sterling D. Spero and Abram Harris, *The Black Worker* (1931). Two collections of essays which shed considerable light on the conditions of black labor today and the history of organized labor's attitudes toward blacks are Julius Jacobson, ed., *The Negro and the American Labor Movement* (1968); and Arthur Ross and Herbert Hill, eds., *Employment, Race, and Poverty* (1967). Works on specific problems are: Bernard Mandel, "Samuel Gompers and the Negro Workers, 1886–1914," *Journal of Negro History* (1955); Gerald Grob, "Organized Labor and the Negro Worker 1865–1900," *Labor History* (1960); Herman D. Bloch, "Labor and the Negro, 1866–1900," *Journal of Negro History* (1965); Herbert R. Northrup, "Organized Labor and Negro Workers," *Journal of Political Economy* (1943); and Herbert Hill, "Racism Within Organized Labor: 1950–1960," *Journal of Negro History* (1961). Horace R. Cayton and George S. Mitchell examine relations between the CIO and black workers in *Black Workers and the New Unions* (1939). See also two works by F. Ray Marshall: *The Negro and Organized Labor* (1965); and *The Negro Worker* (1967); B. R. Brazeal, *The Brotherhood of Sleeping-Car Porters* (1946); and John Leggett, *Race, Class, and Labor* (1968), a study of attitudes among Detroit workers.

The Rise of the Ghetto

The evolution of Harlem from a genteel white neighborhood to a black ghetto and slum is traced in Gilbert Osofsky, *Harlem: The Making of a Ghetto* (1966). See also James Weldon Johnson, *Black Manhattan* (1930); Seth Scheiner, *Negro Mecca* (1965); Claude McKay, *Harlem: Negro Metropolis* (1940); and E. Franklin Frazier, "Negro Harlem: An Ecological Study," *American Journal of Sociology* (1937). For Chicago, see Allan Spear, *Black Chicago* (1967); and St. Clair Drake and Horace Cayton, *Black Metropolis* (1940). There is no recent scholarly study of black migration, but several contemporary works are still useful: Emmett J. Scott, *Negro Migration During the War* (1920); Thomas J. Woofter, *The Negro Problem in Cities* (1928); Louise V. Kennedy, *The Negro Peasant Turns Cityward* (1930); Claude V. Kiser, *Sea Island to City* (1932);

Carter G. Woodson, *A Century of Negro Migration* (1918); and Charles S. Johnson, "How Much Is the Migration a Flight from Persecution?," *Opportunity* (1923). See also Arna Bontemps and Jack Conroy, *Anyplace But Here* (1966); and Emmett J. Scott, ed., "Letters of Negro Migrants," *Journal of Negro History* (1919).

Violent white reactions to black migration are examined in Charles Crowe, "Racial Violence and Social Reform—Origins of the Atlanta Riot of 1906," *Journal of Negro History* (1968); James L. Crouthamel, "The Springfield Race Riot of 1908," *Journal of Negro History* (1960); Elliott M. Rudwick, *Race Riot at East St. Louis* (1964); and Arthur Waskow, *From Race Riot to Sit-In* (1966). See also Kenneth T. Jackson, *The Ku Klux Klan in the City* (1967). The riots in Chicago in 1919 and Harlem in 1935 led to the establishment of investigation commissions, whose reports are extremely useful examinations of ghetto conditions and the causes of race riots: Chicago Commission on Race Relations, *The Negro in Chicago* (1922); and Mayor's Commission on Conditions in Harlem, *The Negro in Harlem* (1935).

World War I and Garveyism

Emmett J. Scott, *The American Negro in the World War* (1919), surveys the black role in World War I. Robert Kerlin, ed., *Voice of the Negro, 1919* (1920) is a collection of newspaper editorials which reflect black attitudes at the war's close. On Garvey and his movement, the best works are Edmund D. Cronon, *Black Moses* (1955), a good biography; Amy Jacques-Garvey, ed., *Philosophy and Opinions of Marcus Garvey* (1923–25), a collection of Garvey's writings and speeches; and Amy Jacques-Garvey, ed., *Garvey and Garveyism* (1963), which contains interesting recollections by Garvey's widow. In some ways, religious nationalist movements like Father Divine's in the 1930's, and the Nation of Islam, which was founded in the 1930's and is still powerful today, are successors of Garveyism. On Father Divine, see Arthur Fauset, *Black Gods of the Metropolis* (1944); Hadley Cantril, *The Psychology of Social Movements* (1941); John Hoshor, *God in a Rolls-Royce* (1936); and Sara Harris, *Father Divine: Holy Husband* (1953). There are two excellent studies of the Muslims: C. Eric Lincoln, *The Black Muslims in America* (1961); and E. U. Essien-Udom, *Black Nationalism* (1962). See also Elijah Muhammad, *Message to the Black Man in America* (1965).

The Harlem Renaissance

John A. Emanuel and Theodore Gross, eds., *Dark Symphony* (1968) is an anthology of black literature, which contains an exhaustive bibliography of primary and critical works concerning black writers from Charles W. Chesnutt to LeRoi Jones, including such major figures as Paul Lawrence

Dunbar, Claude McKay, Countee Cullen, Jean Toomer, Langston Hughes, Richard Wright, Ralph Ellison and James Baldwin. Other collections of black literature include LeRoi Jones and Larry Neal, eds., *Black Fire* (1968); John Henrik Clarke, ed., *American Negro Short Stories* (1966); Langston Hughes, ed., *The Best Short Stories by Negro Writers* (1967); Robert Hayden, ed., *Kaleidoscope* (1967); Abraham Chapman, ed., *Black Voices* (1968); and Herbert Hill, ed., *Soon, One Morning: New Writing by American Negroes, 1940–1962* (1963).

Two collections of critical essays on black literature are Herbert Hill, ed., *Anger and Beyond* (1966); and Seymour L. Gross and John E. Hardy, eds., *Images of the Negro in American Literature* (1966). Several works include studies of Renaissance writers and other black literary figures of the twentieth century: S. P. Fullinwider, *The Mind and Mood of Black America* (1969); Edward Margolies, *Native Sons* (1968); Sterling Brown, *The Negro in American Fiction* (1937); Saunders Redding, *To Make a Poet Black* (1939); Robert Bone, *The Negro Novel in America* (2nd ed., 1965); Margaret Just Butcher, *The Negro in American Culture* (1956); and Stephen Bronz, *Roots of Negro Racial Consciousness* (1964). See also M. Cook and Stephen E. Henderson, *The Militant Black Writer in Africa and the United States* (1969); Ralph Ellison, *Shadow and Act* (1964); and Loften Mitchell, *Black Drama* (1967).

On the Renaissance writers themselves, the best source collection is Alain Locke, ed., *The New Negro* (1925). See also *The New Negro Thirty Years After* (1955). Critical studies of individual writers include Blanche Ferguson, *Countee Cullen and the Negro Renaissance* (1966); Arthur P. Davis, "The Alien-and-Exile Theme in Countee Cullen's Racial Poems," *Phylon* (1953); and Wayne Cooper, "Claude McKay and the New Negro of the 1920's." Two autobiographies, James Weldon Johnson's *Along This Way* (1933) and Langston Hughes' *The Big Sea* (1940), contain interesting insights into the intellectual milieu of Renaissance Harlem. For the reaction of the black middle class, see Benjamin Brawley, "The Negro Literary Renaissance," *Southern Workman* (1927).

The 1930's and 1940's

Historians have not devoted sufficient attention to the transitional years between the rise of the ghetto and the emergence of the modern civil-rights movement; indeed a recent article by Richard M. Dalfiume on the World War II period is called "The 'Forgotten Years' of the Negro Revolution," *Journal of American History* (1968). Bernard Sternsher, ed., *The Negro in Depression and War* (1969) is a good collection of articles and documents, but on most aspects of black life during the Depression, works written at the time must suffice, including Charles S. Johnson, *The Economic Status of Negroes* (1933); Arnold Hill, *The Negro and Economic Reconstruction* (1937); and Abram Harris, *The Negro as Capitalist* (1936). On changes in the tenant-farming system in the South during the 1930's, see Charles S.

Johnson *et al.*, *The Collapse of Cotton Tenancy* (1938); and Charles S. Johnson, *Shadow of the Plantation* (1934). John Dollard, *Caste and Class in a Southern Town* (1937) is a classic study of the small-town southern mentality. On black politics, see Harold Gosnell, *Negro Politicians* (1935); and James A. Harrell, "Negro Leadership in the Election Year 1936," *Journal of Southern History* (1968). The controversial subject of blacks and the Communist party can be examined in Harold Cruse, *The Crisis of the Negro Intellectual* (1967); Dan T. Carter, *Scottsboro* (1969); and two books by Wilson Record: *The Negro and the Communist Party* (1951), and *Race and Radicalism* (1964). The two major race riots of the period are studied in James W. Ford, *Hunger and Terror in Harlem* (1935); and Norman Humphrey and Alfred M. Lee, *Detroit Race Riot* (1943). Claude McKay, *Harlem: Negro Metropolis* describes various trends in Harlem during the 1930's. See also John A. Salmond, "The CCC and the Negro," *Journal of American History* (1965); and E. Franklin Frazier, *Negro Youth at the Crossroads* (1940).

Ulysses Lee, *The Employment of Negro Troops* (1966) contains information about the role of blacks in World War II. For the March on Washington Movement, see Herbert Garfinkel, *When Negroes March* (1959). The black mood at the war's close may be gauged from Rayford Logan, ed., *What the Negro Wants* (1944). For the legal battles of the NAACP in the 1940's, see Loren Miller, *The Petitioners;* and Walter White, *A Rising Wind* (1945) and *A Man Called White* (1948). Two studies of the Fair Employment Practices Commission are Louis Ruchames, *Race, Jobs and Politics: The Story of FEPC* (1953); and Louis Kesselman, *The Social Policies of FEPC* (1953). The role of blacks in the election of 1948 was examined in Henry L. Moon, *Balance of Power: The Negro Vote* (1948). On one of the major reforms of the Truman administration, see Richard J. Stillman, II, *Integration of the Negro in the United States Armed Forces* (1968); and Richard Dalfiume, *Desegregation of the U.S. Armed Forces* (1969). For critical comments on Myrdal's *American Dilemma,* see Ralph Ellison, *Shadow and Act,* and Carl N. Degler, "The Negro in America—Where Myrdal Went Wrong," *New York Times Magazine,* December 9, 1969.

The Civil Rights Movement

Benjamin Muse, *Ten Years of Prelude* (1964) and *The American Negro Revolution* (1968) trace the freedom movement from 1954 to 1967. Lerone Bennett, *What Manner of Man?* (1964) is a biography of Martin Luther King, Jr.; see also David L. Lewis, *King: A Critical Biography* (1970), and King's writings, including *Stride Toward Freedom* (1958); *Why We Can't Wait* (1964); *Where Do We Go From Here* (1967); and *The Trumpet of Conscience* (1969); and an essay by August Meier, "On the Significance of Martin Luther King," *New Politics* (1965). The founding of the Congress on Racial Equality is described by Meier and Elliott M. Rudwick in "How CORE Began," *Social Science Quarterly*

(1969); and CORE's best-known activity of the early 1960's is the subject of James Peck, *Freedom Ride* (1962). James Farmer, CORE's leader in the early 60's, explains his views in *Freedom—When?* (1965). On the sit-in movement, see Arthur J. Waskow, *From Race Riot to Sit-in* (1966); Merrill Proudfoot, *Diary of a Sit-In* (1962); and Howard Zinn, *SNCC: The New Abolitionists* (1964). The "freedom summer" in Mississippi in 1964 is the subject of Elizabeth Sutherland, ed., *Letters from Mississippi* (1965); Len Holt, *The Summer That Didn't End* (1965); and Sally Belfrage, *Freedom Summer* (1965). See also James Silver, *Mississippi: The Closed Society* (2nd ed., 1966), and Edward A. Leonard "Nonviolence and Violence in American Racial Protests, 1945–1967," *Rocky Mountain Social Science Journal* (1969).

Among the better works on the civil-rights movement and the ideas of its black leaders are Louis Lomax, *The Negro Revolt* (1962); Charles Silverman, *Crisis in Black and White* (1964); Alan Westin, ed., *Freedom Now!* (1964); and Lerone Bennett, *The Negro Mood* (1964). The influence of Africa on American blacks, and vice versa, can be examined in Harold Isaacs, *The New World of Negro Americans* (1963); George Shepperson, "Notes on American Negro Influences on the Emergence of African Nationalism," *Journal of African History* (1960); and Immanuel Wallerstein, *Africa: The Politics of Independence* (1961). For changing attitudes toward race, see Ethel Alpenfels, *Sense and Nonsense About Race* (1957); and Ashley Montagu, *Man's Most Dangerous Myth: The Fallacy of Race* (1952). See also James Q. Wilson, *Negro Politics: The Search for Leadership* (1960); Jack Greenberg, *Race Relations and American Law* (1959); and Donald R. Matthews and James W. Prothro, *Negroes and the New Southern Politics* (1966).

The Contemporary Ghetto

Robert C. Weaver, *The Negro Ghetto* (1948) was a pioneering study which is still very useful; see also Kenneth Clark's more recent *Dark Ghetto* (1965). The economic plight of the black urban ghetto is examined in Louis A. Feinman, *et al.*, eds., *Negroes and Jobs* (1968), Thomas F. Pettigrew, *A Portrait of the Negro American* (1964); and Alphonso Pinckney, *Black Americans* (1969). The problem of housing is studied in Charles Abrams, *The Future of Housing* (1946); Karl E. Taeuber and Alma F. Taeuber, *Negroes in Cities* (1965); Stanley Lieberson, *Ethnic Patterns in American Cities* (1963); and Reginald A. Johnson, *Racial Bias and Housing* (1963). Other forms of exploitation are discussed in David Caplovitz, *The Poor Pay More* (1963); Jerome Skolnick, *Justice Without Trial* (1966); Jonathan Kozol, *Death at an Early Age* (1967); and Paul Jacobs, *Prelude to Riot: A View of Urban America from the Bottom Up* (1967). The controversy over the black family is the subject of Lee Rainwater and William Yancey, *The Moynihan Report and the Politics of Controversy* (1967).

Studies of urban riots include Robert Conot, *Rivers of Blood, Years of Darkness* (1967), on Watts; Fred Shapiro and James Sullivan, *Race Riot, New York, 1964* (1964); Tom Hayden, *Rebellion in Newark* (1967); Robert Shoggan and Tom Craig, *The Detroit Race Riot* (1964); and Ben W. Gilbert, *Ten Blocks from the White House* (1969). Among analyses of riots are Robert Fogelson, "From Resentment to Confrontation: The Police, the Negroes, and the Outbreak of the Nineteen-Sixties Riots," *Political Science Quarterly* (1968); Nathan S. Caplan and Jeffrey M. Paige, "A Study of Ghetto Rioters," *Scientific American* (1968); and *Urban Riots: Violence and Social Change* (1968), an issue of the *Proceedings of the Academy of Political Science*. A particularly horrifying incident in the Detroit riot of 1967 is the subject of John Hersey, *The Algiers Motel Incident* (1968). Louis H. Masotti and Don R. Bowen, eds., *Riots and Rebellion* (1969) is a collection of articles on urban violence.

The classic study of the psychological effect of racism and discrimination on blacks is Abram Kardiner and Lionel Ovesey, *The Mark of Oppression* (1951); see also the more recent work by William H. Grier and Price M. Cobbs, *Black Rage* (1968); and Calvin Hernton, *Sex and Racism in America* (1967). E. Franklin Frazier, *Black Bourgeoisie* (1957) is a classic study of the social attitudes of the black middle class. Ghetto "folkways" are examined in William McCord, *et al., Life Styles in the Black Ghetto* (1969); and Ulf Hannerz, *Soulside* (1969). See also Claude Brown's autobiography, *Manchild in the Promised Land* (1965). For an introduction to contemporary black music, see Charles Keil, *Urban Blues* (1966); LeRoi Jones, *Blues People* (1963); Paul Oliver, *The Meaning of the Blues* (1960); Marshall W. Stearns, *The Story of Jazz* (1956); and two books by Samuel Charters: *The Bluesmen* (1967); and *The Country Blues* (1959). A good summary of the social significance of "soul" rhetoric is Ulf Hannerz, "What Negroes Mean by Soul," *Trans-Action* (1968). The effect of ghetto life on black religion is discussed in E. Franklin Frazier, *The Negro Church in America* (1963); and Joseph R. Washington, *Black Religion* (1964).

Black Power

The writings of the Algerian revolutionary Frantz Fanon have strongly influenced American black militants. See Fanon's *The Wretched of the Earth* (1961); and his collection of essays, *Black Skins, White Masks* (1952). The best introduction to Malcolm X is his *Autobiography* (1965), a classic work of twentieth-century black America. George Breitman has collected a number of his speeches in *Malcolm X Speaks* (1965), and discusses Malcolm X's transformation in the last year of his life in *The Last Year of Malcolm X* (1967). See also Archie Epps, ed., *The Speeches of Malcolm X at Harvard* (1968). A number of Black writers discuss the impact of Malcolm X in John Henrik Clarke, ed., *Malcolm X: The Man and His Times* (1969). The views of another black militant of the early 1960's are expressed in Robert F.

Williams, *Negroes with Guns* (1962). Floyd Barbour, ed., *The Black Power Revolt* (1968) is a collection of documents with a useful bibliography. Stokely Carmichael and Charles Hamilton explain their conception of the slogan in *Black Power* (1967); and H. Rap Brown, Carmichael's successor as SNCC chairman has written *Die, Nigger, Die!* (1969). The contemporary position of CORE is expressed in Floyd McKissick's *Three-Fifths of a Man* (1969); and the views of Whitney M. Young, Jr., head of the more moderate National Urban League, can be found in his *Beyond Racism: Building an Open Society* (1969). See also Julius Lester, *Look Out Whitey, Black Power's Gonna Get Your Momma* (1968); Nathan Wright, *Black Power and Urban Unrest* (1967); Lewis M. Killian, *Impossible Revolution? Black Power and the American Dream* (1968); Chuck Stone, *Black Political Power in the United States* (1968); the symposium on black power in *Partisan Review* (Spring, 1968); and Martin Kilson's criticism of the black power outlook, "Black Power: Anatomy of a Paradox," *Harvard Journal of Negro Affairs* (1968). A. James Gregor suggests some of the reasons for the rising tide of black nationalism in "Black Nationalism: A Preliminary Analysis of Negro Radicalism," *Science and Society* (1963). The views of black America's most recent expatriate leader are expressed in Eldridge Cleaver, *Soul on Ice* (1968); *Eldridge Cleaver* (1969); and *Post-Prison Writings and Speeches* (1969). Harold Cruse's *Rebellion or Revolution* (1968) is a provocative collection of essays. For a good introduction to the contemporary black mood, see C. Eric Lincoln, ed., *Is Anybody Listening to Black America?* (1968), and Gary T. Marx, *Protest and Prejudice* (1969 ed.); and for a well-argued critique of various aspects of today's black movement, see Robert Allen, *Black Awakening in Capitalist America* (1969).

Notes

The African Heritage

1. J. A. Tillinghast, *The Negro in Africa and America* (New York, 1902).

2. J. Dowd, *The Negro Races* (New York, 1907–14).

3. W. D. Weatherford, *The Negro from Africa to America* (New York, 1924).

4. *The Negro in Africa and America,* p. 28.

5. Collected during field work in Eastern Nigeria, 1938–1939.

6. "Land and Labour in a Cross River Village, Southern Nigeria," *Geographical Journal,* 90:24–51, 1937.

7. *Op. cit.,* p. 29.

8. *Ibid.,* p. 31.

9. *Ibid.,* p. 33.

10. *Ibid.,* pp. 31 f.

11. *Ibid.,* p. 72.

12. *Ibid.,* p. 80.

13. *Ibid.,* p. 86.

14. J. M. Mecklin, *Democracy and Race Friction* (New York, 1914), pp. 82 f. A footnote reference after the first sentence of the quotation was an article by Reinsch, "The Negro Race and European Civilization," *American Journal of Sociology,* 11:155, 1905. Reinsch's paper, one of the most extreme examples of the position being considered here, is not cited because, except for Mecklin, references to it are practically never encountered.

15. *The American Race Problem* (New York, 1927) (1st ed.), pp. 197 ff.

16. " 'Secret Societies,' Religious Cult-Groups, and Kinship Units among

the West African Yoruba," unpublished doctor's thesis, Northwestern University, 1939.

17. R. S. Rattray, *Ashanti* (Oxford, 1923), pp. 90 f.

18. *Nights with Uncle Remus* (Boston, 1911); *Uncle Remus Returns* (Boston, 1918); *Uncle Remus, His Songs and Sayings* (New York, 1929).

19. By M. J. Herskovits, principally in Dahomey and among the Ashanti.

20. *Religion and Art in Ashanti* (Oxford, 1927), *passim*.

The Development of the Negro Slave Trade

1. *Calendar of State Papers, Colonial Series,* V, 167. Renatus Enys to Secretary Bennet, Nov. 1, 1663.

2. C. Whitworth (ed.) *The Political and Commercial Works of Charles Davenant* (London, 1781), V, 146.

3. G. F. Zook, *The Company of Royal Adventurers trading into Africa* (Lancaster, 1919), 9, 16.

4. M. Postlethwayt, *Great Britain's Commercial Interest Explained and Improved* (London, 1759), II, 148–149, 236; Postlethwayt, *The African Trade, the Great Pillar and Support of the British Plantation Trade in North America* (London, 1745), 38–39; Postlethwayt, *The National and Private Advantages of the African Trade Considered* (London, 1746), 113, 122.

5. J. Gee, *The Trade and Navigation of Great Britain Considered* (Glasgow, 1750), 25–26.

6. Whitworth, *op. cit.,* II, 37–40.

7. *Ibid.,* V, 140–141. The whole essay, "Reflections upon the Constitution and Management of the African Trade," will repay reading.

8. E. Donnan (ed.), *Documents Illustrative of the History of the Slave Trade to America* (Washington, D.C., 1930–1935), II, 129–130.

9. *Ibid.,* I, 265. In 1681 these debts were estimated at £271,000. E. D. Collins, *Studies in the Colonial Policy of England, 1672–1680* (Annual Report of the American Historical Association, 1900), 185.

10. J. Latimer, *Annals of Bristol in the Eighteenth Century* (Bristol, 1893), 271.

11. C. S. S. Higham, *The Development of the Leeward Islands under the Restoration, 1660–1688* (Cambridge, 1921), 158.

12. Latimer, *op. cit.,* 272.

13. Anonymous, *Some Matters of Fact relating to the present state of the African Trade* (London, 1720), 3.

14. Pitman, *The Development of the British West Indies, 1700–1763* (New Haven, 1917), 67.

15. *Ibid.*, 69–70, 79.
16. Postlethwayt, *Great Britain's Commercial Interest . . .*, II, 479–480. See also pp. 149–151, 154–155.
17. H. H. S. Aimes, *A History of Slavery in Cuba, 1511 to 1868* (New York, 1907), 33, 269.
18. W. E. H. Lecky, *A History of England in the Eighteenth Century* (London, 1892–1920), II, 244.
19. *Report of the Lords of the Committee of Privy Council appointed for the consideration of all matters relating to Trade and Foreign Plantations, 1788.* Part VI, Evidence of Messrs. Baillie, King, Camden and Hubbert. The following figures, taken from the same report (Part IV, No. 4 and No. 15, Supplement No. 6, and Papers received since the date of the report), give some indication of the extent of the re-export trade:

Colony	Years	Imports	Re-Exports
Jamaica	1784–1787	37,841	14,477
St. Kitts	1778–1788	2,784	1,769
Dominica	1784–1788	27,553	15,781
Grenada	1784–1792	44,712	31,210

According to Dundas, the total British West Indian importation for 1791 amounted to 74,000, the re-exports to 34,000. *Cobbett's Parliamentary History of England* (referred to hereafter as *Parl. Hist.*), XXIX, 1206. April 23, 1792.

20. B. Edwards, *The History, Civil and Commercial, of the British Colonies in the West Indies* (London, 1801), I, 299.
21. J. Ramsay, A Manuscript entirely in his own hand mainly concerned with his activities towards the Abolition of the Slave Trade, 1787 (Rhodes House Library, Oxford), f. 23(v). "Memorial on the Supplying of the Navy with Seamen."
22. W. Enfield, *An Essay towards the history of Liverpool* (London, 1774), 67.
23. Donnan, *op. cit.*, II, 630. Liverpool's progress is seen from the following table:

Year	Liverpool	London	Bristol
1720	21	60	39
1753	64	13	27
1771	107	58	23

Between 1756 and 1786 Bristol sent 588 ships to Africa, Liverpool 1,858; between 1795 and 1804 Liverpool sent 1,099 vessels to Africa,

London 155, Bristol 29. (The figures for 1720 come from *Some Matters of Fact* . . . , 3; the others from C. M. MacInnes, *Bristol, A Gateway of Empire* (Bristol, 1939), 191.)

24. *Cobbett's Parliamentary Debates* (Referred to hereafter as *Parl. Deb.*), IX, 127. George Hibbert, March 16, 1807.

25. Correspondence between Robert Bostock, master mariner and merchant, and others, giving particulars of the slave trading of Liverpool ships in the West Indies, 1789–1792 (MS. Vol., Liverpool Public Library). Bostock to Capt. James Fryer, July 17, 1790.

26. MacInnes, *op. cit.*, 202.

27. T. Clarkson, *History of the Rise, Progress, and Accomplishment of the Abolition of the African Slave Trade by the British Parliament* (London, 1839), 197.

28. Donnan, *op. cit.*, I, 132. The Guinea Company to Francis Soane, Dec. 9, 1651.

29. Journals of Liverpool Slave Ships ("Bloom" and others); with correspondence and prices of slaves sold (MS. Vol., Liverpool Public Library). Bostock to Knowles, June 19, 1788.

30. E. Martin (ed.), *Journal of a Slave Dealer. "A View of some Remarkable Axcedents in the Life of Nics. Owen on the Coast of Africa and America from the year 1746 to the year 1757"* (London, 1930), 77–78, 97–98.

31. Latimer, *op. cit.*, 144–145.

32. A. P. Wadsworth and J. de L. Mann, *The Cotton Trade and Industrial Lancashire* (Manchester, 1931), 228–229.

33. Donnan, *op. cit.*, II, 625–627.

34. *Ibid.*, 631.

35. Latimer, *op. cit.*, 476; Wadsworth and Mann, *op. cit.*, 225.

36. Donnan, *op. cit.*, II, 627.

37. J. Wallace, *A General and Descriptive History of the Ancient and Present State of the Town of Liverpool . . . together with a Circumstantial Account of the True Causes of its Extensive African Trade* (Liverpool, 1795), 229–230. For instances of subdivision see also Wadsworth and Mann, *op. cit.*, 224–225.

38. Edwards, *op. cit.*, II, 72, 74, 87–89; J. Atkins, *A Voyage to Guinea, Brasil, and the West-Indies* (London, 1735), 179. For an authoritative modern discussion, see M. J. Herskovits, *The Myth of the Negro Past* (New York, 1941), 34–50.

39. Correspondence between Robert Bostock . . . Bostock to Fryer, Jan., 1790; Bostock to Flint, Nov. 11, 1790.

40. W. Sypher, *Guinea's Captive Kings, British Anti-Slavery Literature of the XVIIIth Century* (Chapel Hill, 1942), 170. The slaves were in-

spected as carefully as cattle in the Smithfield market, the chief qualities emphasized being height, sound teeth, pliant limbs, and lack of venereal disease. Atkins, *op. cit.,* 180.

41. E. F. Gay, "Letters from a Sugar Plantation in Nevis, 1723–1732," *Journal of Economic and Business History* (Nov., 1928), 164.

42. Donnan, *op. cit.,* II, 626.

43. Correspondence between Robert Bostock . . . , Bostock to Cleveland, Aug. 10, 1789.

44. T. Clarkson, *Essay on the Impolicy of the African Slave Trade* (London, 1788), 29.

45. W. Roscoe, *A General View of the African Slave Trade demonstrating its Injustice and Impolicy* (London, 1788), 23–24.

46. A. Mackenzie-Grieve, *The Last Years of the English Slave Trade* (London, 1941), 178.

47. C. M. Andrews, *The Colonial Period of American History* (New Haven, 1934–1938), IV, 61.

48. C. M. Andrews, "Anglo-French Commercial Rivalry, 1700–1750," *American Historical Review* (April, 1915), 546.

49. Donnan, *op. cit.,* II, 45.

50. *H. of C. Sess. Pap., Accounts and Papers, 1795–1796.* A. & P. 42, Series No. 100, Document 848, 1–21.

51. Add. MSS. 12433 (British Museum), ff. 13, 19. Edward Law, May 14, 1792.

52. P. Cunningham (ed.), *The Letters of Horace Walpole* (London, 1891), II, 197. To Sir H. Mann, Feb. 25, 1750.

53. *Parl. Hist.,* XVII, 507–508. May 5, 1772.

54. R. Terry, *Some Old Papers relating to the Newport Slave Trade* (Bulletin of the Newport Historical Society, July, 1927), 10.

55. *Calendar of State Papers, Colonial Series,* X, 611. Evidence of Barbados planters before the Lords of Trade and Plantations, Oct. 8, 1680. For a vigorous dissent from the view that the slaves had no means of communication except in the language of their masters, see Herskovits, *op. cit.,* 79–81.

56. *Calendar of State Papers,* XIV, 448. Governor Russell, March 23, 1695.

57. The governor of Barbados opposed the building of churches on the ground that permission to the Negroes thus to assemble would turn their minds to plots and insurrections. C.O. 28 92 (Public Record Office), Nov. 4, 1823. The planters justified their attitude by the plea that the missionaries instilled dangerous notions into the heads of the slaves which were subversive of plantation discipline.

58. Lecky, *op. cit.*, II, 249.

59. Sypher, *op. cit.*, 14.

60. V. T. Harlow, *Christopher Codrington* (Oxford, 1928), 211, 215.

61. Sypher, *op. cit.*, 65.

62. Latimer, *op. cit.*, 100.

63. *Ibid.*, 478.

64. S. H. Swinny, *The Humanitarianism of the Eighteenth Century and its results,* in F. S. Marvin (ed.), *Western Races and the World* (Oxford, 1922), 130–131.

65. L. Strachey, *Eminent Victorians* (Phoenix ed., London, 1929), 3.

66. Mackenzie-Grieve, *op. cit.*, 162.

67. G. R. Wynne, *The Church in Greater Britain* (London, 1911), 120.

68. *H. of C. Sess. Pap.*, 1837–8, Vol. 48. The exact figure was £12,729.4.4 (pp. 19, 22).

69. Zook, *op. cit.*, 18.

70. Swinny, *op. cit.*, 140.

71. G. Williams, *History of the Liverpool Privateers, with an Account of the Liverpool Slave Trade* (Liverpool, 1897), 473–474.

72. Latimer, *op. cit.*, 147.

73. M. Steen, *The Sun is My Undoing* (New York, 1941), 50.

74. M. D. George, *London Life in the Eighteenth Century* (London, 1925), 137–138.

75. Anonymous, *Recollections of Old Liverpool, by a Nonagenarian* (Liverpool, 1863), 10.

76. Ramsay, MS. Vol., f. 65. "An Address on the Proposed Bill for the Abolition of the Slave Trade."

77. G. Williams, *op. cit.*, 586.

78. *Hansard, Third Series*, CIX, 1102. Hutt, March 19, 1850.

79. H. W. Preston, *Rhode Island and the Sea* (Providence, 1932), 70, 73. The author was Director of the State Bureau of Information.

80. Latimer, *op. cit.*, 142.

81. J. W. D. Powell, *Bristol Privateers and Ships of War* (London, 1930), 167.

82. H. R. F. Bourne, *English Merchants, Memoirs in Illustration of the Progress of British Commerce* (London, 1866), II, 63; J. B. Botsford, *English Society in the Eighteenth Century as Influenced from Oversea* (New York, 1924), 122; Enfield, *op. cit.*, 48–49. For Blundell's slave trading, see Donnan, *op. cit.*, II, 492.

83. For Cunliffe, see Bourne, *op. cit.*, II, 57; Botsford, *op. cit.*, 122; Enfield, *op. cit.*, 43, 49; Donnan, *op. cit.*, II, 492, 497.

84. Donnan, *op. cit.*, II, 631; J. Hughes, *Liverpool Banks and Bankers, 1760–1817* (Liverpool, 1906), 174.

85. L. H. Grindon, *Manchester Banks and Bankers* (Manchester, 1878), 55, 79–80, 187–188; Bourne, *op. cit.*, II, 64, 78; Botsford, *op. cit.*, 122; Donnan, *op. cit.*, II, 492.

86. Donnan, *op. cit.*, I, 169–172.

87. *Ibid.*, II, 468.

88. Latimer, *op. cit.*, 476–477.

89. For examples, see Wadsworth and Mann, *op. cit.*, 216 n; Hughes, *op. cit.*, 109, 139, 172, 174, 176; Donnan, *op. cit.*, II, 492 n.

90. L. B. Namier, "Antony Bacon, an Eighteenth Century Merchant," *Journal of Economic and Business History* (Nov., 1929), 21.

91. Donnan, *op. cit.*, II, 642–644, 656–657 n.

92. *Parl. Deb.*, IX, 170. March 23, 1807.

93. *Ibid.*, VII, 230. May 16, 1806.

94. Wilberforce, *Life of Wilberforce*, III, 170. Wilberforce to John Newton, June, 1804.

95. C.O. 137/91. Petition of Committee of Jamaica House of Assembly on the Sugar and Slave Trade, Dec. 5, 1792.

96. Adam Smith, *The Wealth of Nations* (Cannan edition, New York, 1937), 415–416, 590–591.

97. W. Wood, *A Survey of Trade* (London, 1718), Part III, 193.

98. J. F. Rees, "The Phases of British Commercial Policy in the Eighteenth Century," *Economica* (June, 1925), 143.

99. Gee, *op. cit.*, 111.

100. Postlethwayt, *The African Trade, the Great Pillar . . .*, 4, 6.

101. *Cambridge History of the British Empire*, I, 565.

102. Whitworth, *op. cit.*, II, 20.

103. J. Bennett, *Two Letters and Several Calculations on the Sugar Colonies and Trade* (London, 1738), 55.

104. Wood, *op. cit.*, 156.

105. Sir D. Thomas, *An Historical Account of the Rise and Growth of the West India Colonies, and of the Great Advantages they are to England, in respect to Trade* (London, 1690). The essay is printed in the Harleian Miscellany, II, 347.

106. Pitman, *The Settlement . . . of British West India Plantations . . .*, 271.

107. *Report of the Committee of Privy Council, 1788*, Part IV, No. 18, Appendix.

108. J. H. Rose, *William Pitt and the Great War* (London, 1911), 370.

109. Adam Smith, *op. cit.*, 366.

110. Whitworth, *op. cit.*, II, 18.

111. Sir C. Whitworth, *State of the Trade of Great Britian in its imports and exports, progressively from the year 1697–1773* (London, 1776), Part II, pp. 1–2, 47–50, 53–72, 75–76, 78, 82–91. . . .

112. Bennett, *op. cit.*, 50, 54.

113. L. F. Stock (ed.), *Proceedings and Debates in the British Parliament Respecting North America* (Washington, D.C., 1924–1941), IV, 329. Sir John Barnard, March 28, 1737.

114. Postlethwayt, *The African Trade, the Great Pillar* . . . , 13–14.

115. E. D. Ellis, *An Introduction to the History of Sugar as a Commodity* (Philadelphia, 1905), 82.

First Impressions

1. Kenneth G. Davies, *The Royal African Company* (London, 1957), 38–46; John W. Blake, trans. and ed., *Europeans in West Africa, 1450–1560; Documents to Illustrate the Nature and Scope of Portuguese Enterprise in West Africa, the Abortive Attempt of Castilians to Create an Empire There, and the Early English Voyages to Barbary and Guinea* (*Works Issued by the Hakluyt Society*, 2d Ser., 87 [1942]), II, 254–60.

2. "The voyage made by M. John Hawkins . . . to the coast of Guinea and the Indies of Nova Hispania . . . 1564," in Richard Hakluyt, *The Principal Navigations, Voyages, Traffiques and Discoveries of the English Nation* . . . , 12 vols., 1598 ed. (Glasgow, 1903–05), X, 15. See Katherine Beverly Oakes, Social Theory in the Early Literature of Voyage and Exploration in Africa (unpubl. Ph.D. diss., University of California, Berkeley, 1944), 120–23.

3. "The First Voyage of Robert Baker to Guinie . . . 1562," in Richard Hakluyt, *The Principall Navigations, Voiages and Discoveries of the English Nation* . . . (London, 1589), 132. The entire poem was omitted in the 1598 edition.

4. "The Voyage of M. George Fenner . . . Written by Walter Wren" (1566), Hakluyt, *Principal Navigations*, VI, 270. All ensuing references are to this reprinted 1598 edition unless otherwise indicated.

5. Warner Grenelle Rice, Turk, Moor and Persian in English Literature from 1550–1660, with Particular Reference to the Drama (unpubl. Ph.D. diss., Harvard University, 1926), 401–2n; Robert R. Cawley, *The Voyagers and Elizabethan Drama* (Boston, 1938), 31; Samuel C. Chew, *The Crescent and the Rose: Islam and England during the Renaissance* (N.Y., 1937), 521–24; Wylie Sypher, *Guinea's Captive Kings: British Anti-Slavery Literature of the XVIIIth Century* (Chapel Hill, 1942), 26.

6. An early instance is in "The Second Voyage to Guinea . . ." (1554), in Hakluyt, *Principal Navigations*, VI, 167–68. See the associations made by Leo Africanus, *The History and Description of Africa and of the Notable Things Therein Contained . . .*, trans. John Pory [*ca.* 1600], ed. Robert Brown, 3 vols. (London, 1896), I, 130.

7. Hakluyt, *Principal Navigations*, VI, 176, 200, 217–18. Just how little Europeans knew about Africa prior to the Portuguese explorations is evident in T. Simar, "La géographie de l'Afrique central dans l'antiquité et au moyen âge," *La Revue Congolaise*, 3 (1912), 1–23, 81–102, 145–69, 225–52, 288–310, 440–41.

8. Francisco López de Gómara, in Peter Martyr (D'Anghera), *The Decades of the Newe Worlde . . .*, trans. Richard Eden (London, 1555), in Edward Arber, ed., *The First Three English Books on America . . .* (Birmingham, Eng., 1885), 338.

9. Thomas Percy, *Reliques of Ancient English Poetry . . .*, ed. Robert A. Willmott (London, 1857), 27 (Sir Cauline, pt. 2, stanza 1).

10. Numerous examples in Middle English, Shakespeare, the Bible, and Milton are given by P. J. Heather, "Colour Symbolism," *Folk Lore,* 59 (1948), 169–70, 175–78, 182-83; 60 (1949), 208–16, 266–76. See also Harold R. Isaacs, "Blackness and Whiteness," *Encounter,* 21 (1963), 8–21; Caroline F. E. Spurgeon, *Shakespeare's Imagery and What It Tells Us* (Boston, 1958), 64, 66–69, 158; Arrah B. Evarts, "Color Symbolism," *Psychoanalytic Review,* 6 (1919), 129–34; Don Cameron Allen, "Symbolic Color in the Literature of the English Renaissance," *Philological Quarterly,* 15 (1936), 81–92; and for a different perspective, Francis B. Gummere, "On the Symbolic Use of the Colors Black and White in Germanic Tradition," *Haverford College Studies,* 1 (1889), 112–62.

11. Walter Clyde Curry, *The Middle English Ideal of Personal Beauty; As Found in the Metrical Romances, Chronicles, and Legends of the XIII, XIV, and XV Centuries* (Baltimore, 1916), 3, 80–98.

12. Elkin Calhoun Wilson, *England's Eliza* (Cambridge, Mass., 1939), 337; Charles Carroll Camden, *The Elizabethan Woman* (Houston, N.Y., and London, 1952), chap. 7; Cawley, *Voyagers and Elizabethan Drama,* 85; Elizabeth Jenkins, *Elizabeth the Great* (London, 1958), 62, 100, 159, 296; Gamaliel Bradford, *Elizabethan Women,* ed. Harold O. White (Boston, 1936), 82, 212; Violet A. Wilson, *Queen Elizabeth's Maids of Honour and Ladies of the Privy Chamber* (N.Y., n.d.), 4–5. Hugh Plat, *Delightes for Ladies, Written Originally by Sir Hugh Plat, First Printed in 1602, London, England,* ed. Violet and Hal W. Trovillion (Herrin, Ill., 1939), 87–94, 99, 102–3, contains advice on cosmetics.

13. [George Puttenham?], *Partheniades* (1579), quoted in Wilson, *England's Eliza,* 242.

14. *Twelfth Night,* I, v, 259–60, W. J. Craig, ed., *The Complete Works of Shakespeare* [London, N.Y., Toronto, 1943]. For other expressions of

this ideal, *A Midsummer-Night's Dream.* I, i, 128–29; III, i, 98–99; III, ii, 137–44.

15. *Love in Its Ecstacy,* quoted in Cawley, *Voyagers and Elizabethan Drama,* 86n; "A Letter written from Goa . . . by one Thomas Stevens . . . 1579," Hakluyt, *Principal Navigations,* VI, 384. Curry, *Middle English Ideal of Personal Beauty,* 64–66, 113–14, indirectly makes abundantly clear how very far Negro women were from matching prevalent English ideals for beautiful noses, lips, and breasts.

16. Sonnet CXXX; see also nos. CXXVII, CXXXI, CXXXII. Shakespeare's "Dark Lady" is discussed by George B. Harrison, *Shakespeare under Elizabeth* (N.Y., 1933), 64–67, 310.

17. Harrison, *Shakespeare,* 310–11, quoting Weever, *Epigrams* (1599), Third Week, Epig. 12, *In Byrrham.*

18. Aphra Behn, *Oroonoko; Or, the Royal Slave,* Montague Summers, ed., *The Works of Aphra Behn,* V (London, 1915), 145.

19. In the Middle Ages a man's "complexion" was conceived as revealing his temperament because it showed his particular blend of humors, each of which was associated with certain colors: Lynn Thorndike, "De Complexionibus," *Isis,* 49 (1958), 398–408. Yet Englishmen seem not to have made efforts to link the Negro's skin color specifically to his bile or dominant humor and hence to his temperament.

20. P[eter] H[eylyn], *Microcosmus, or a Little Description of the Great World. A Treatise Historicall, Geographicall, Politicall, Theologicall* (Oxford, 1621), 379; Peter Heylyn, ΜΙΚΡΟΚΟΣΜΟΣ. *A Little Description of the Great World,* 3d ed. (Oxford, 1627), 735; *The Golden Coast, or a Description of Guinney . . . Together with a Relation of Such Persons, As Got Wonderful Estates by Their Trade Thither* (London, 1665), 3; Thomas Phillips, *A Journal of a Voyage Made in the Hannibal of London, Ann. 1693, 1694, from England to Cape Monseradoe, in Africa; and Thence Along the Coast of Guiney to Whidaw, the Island of St. Thomas, and So Forward to Barbadoes. With a Cursory Account of the Country, the People, Their Manners, Forts, Trade, etc.,* in John and Awsham Churchill, comps., *A Collection of Voyages and Travels, Some Now First Printed from Original Manuscripts. Others Translated Out of Foreign Languages, and Now First Published in English . . . ,* 6 vols. (London, 1704–32), VI, 219; Thomas Browne, "Of the Blackness of Negroes," Charles Sayle, ed., *The Works of Sir Thomas Browne,* 3 vols. (London, 1904–07), II, 383–84; *Newport* [R. I.] *Mercury,* Jan. 11, 1768. See Karl Pearson, E. Nettleship, and C. H. Usher, *A Monograph on Albinism in Man* (Department of Applied Mathematics [or Statistics], University College, University of London, *Drapers' Company Research Memoirs,* Biometric Ser., 6, 8, 9 [6 vols.] [London, 1911–13]), I, 48.

21. Peter Martyr (D'Anghera), *De Orbe Novo: The Eight Decades of Peter*

Martyr D'Anghera, trans. Francis A. MacNutt, 2 vols. (N.Y. and London, 1912), II, 39; Morgan Godwyn, *The Negro's and Indians Advocate* . . . (London, 1680), 21; *The Works of Michael Drayton, Esq.,* 4 vols. (London, 1753), III, 1177; W. Gifford, ed., *The Works of Ben Jonson,* 9 vols. (London, 1816), VII, 11; Cawley, *Voyagers and Elizabethan Drama,* 32n. Cf. Katherine George, "The Civilized West Looks at Primitive Africa; 1400–1800. A Study in Ethnocentrism," *Isis,* 49 (1958), 62–72.

22. Francis Moore, *Travels into the Inland Parts of Africa: Containing a Description of the Several Nations for the Space of Six Hundred Miles up the River Gambia* . . . (London, 1738), 131.

23. Nathaniel Uring, *A History of the Voyages and Travels of Capt. Nathaniel Uring* . . . (London, 1726), 40–41. Also Behn, *Oroonoko,* 136; John Barbot, *A Description of the Coasts of North and South-Guinea; and of Ethiopia Inferior, Vulgarly Angola* . . . , in Churchill, comps., *Voyages,* V, 100; William Snelgrave, *A New Account of Some Parts of Guinea, and the Slave-Trade* . . . (London, 1734), 40–41; Moore, *Travels into the Inland Parts,* 29–30, 214.

24. Phillips, *Journal,* in Churchill, comps., *Voyages,* VI, 219.

25. Sypher, *Guinea's Captive Kings,* 51.

Unthinking Decision

1. There is an eloquent revivification by William Bradford, *Of Plymouth Plantation, 1620–1647,* ed. Samuel Eliot Morison (N.Y., 1952), 61–63.

2. Susan M. Kingsbury, ed., *Records of the Virginia Company of London,* 4 vols. (Washington, D.C., 1906–35), III, 216–19, 231–32.

3. Cotton Mather, *A Pillar of Gratitude* . . . (Boston, 1700), 32–33.

4. From his own "Discourse on Western Planting" (1584), in E. G. R. Taylor, ed., *The Original Writings and Correspondence of the Two Richard Hakluyts* (*Works Issued by the Hakluyt Soc.,* 2d Ser., 76–77 [1935]), II, 314–15. See Perry Miller, "Religion and Society in the Early Literature of Virginia," in his *Errand into the Wilderness* (Cambridge, Mass., 1956), 99–140.

5. William Waller Hening, ed., *The Statutes at Large Being a Collection of All the Laws of Virginia,* 13 vols. (Richmond, N.Y., and Phila., 1809–23), I, 257, 435, 439–42, II, 113–14, 240, 388, III, 447–62; *Archives of Maryland,* 69 vols. (Baltimore, 1883–   ), I, 53, 80, 352–53, 409–10, 428, 443–44, 453–54, 464, 469, II, 147–48, 335–36, 527.

6. Kingsbury, ed., *Recs. Virginia Company,* III, 672–73, 704–7.

7. Edward Arber, ed., *Travels and Works of Captain John Smith* . . . , 2 vols. (Edinburgh, 1910), II, 541.

8. *A Perfect Description of Virginia* . . . (London, 1649), reprinted in Peter Force, ed., *Tracts* . . . , 4 vols. (N.Y., 1947), II, no. 8.

9. Henry R. McIlwaine, ed., *Minutes of the Council and General Court of Colonial Virginia, 1622–1632, 1670–1676* (Richmond, 1924), 196. Lists and musters of 1624 and 1625 are in John C. Hotten, ed., *The Original Lists of Persons of Quality* . . . (N.Y., 1880), 169–265.

10. Philip A. Bruce, *Economic History of Virginia in the Seventeenth Century* . . . , 2 vols. (N.Y., 1896), II, 73.

11. Further details are in Winthrop D. Jordan, "Modern Tensions and the Origins of American Slavery," *Journal of Southern History,* 28 (1962), 18–30.

12. Susie M. Ames, *Studies of the Virginia Eastern Shore in the Seventeenth Century* (Richmond, 1940), 99; John H. Russell, *The Free Negro in Virginia, 1619–1865* (Baltimore, 1913), 23–39; and his "Colored Freemen As Slave Owners in Virginia," *Journal of Negro History,* 1 (1916), 234–37.

13. *Archives Md.,* I, 41, 80, also 409, 453–54.

14. "Decisions of the General Court," *Virginia Magazine of History and Biography,* 5 (1898), 236–37.

15. For these four cases, Northampton County Deeds, Wills, etc., no. 4 (1651–54), 28 (misnumbered 29), 124, Virginia State Library, Richmond; *Archives Md.,* XLI, 261–62; York County Records, no. 2 (transscribed Wills and Deeds, 1645–49), 256–57, Va. State Lib.

16. Lancaster County Loose Papers, Box of Wills, 1650–1719, Folder 1656–1659, Va. State Lib.

17. Northampton County Orders, Deeds, Wills, etc., no. 2 (1640–45), 224; York County Deeds, Orders, Wills, etc. (1657–62), 108–9; in 1645 two Negro women and a boy sold for 5,500 lbs. of tobacco, York County Records, no. 2, 63; all Va. State Lib.

18. York County Records, no. 2, 390, Va. State Lib.

19. Nora Miller Turman and Mark C. Lewis, eds., "Inventory of the Estate of Argoll Yeardley of Northampton County, Virginia, in 1655," *Va. Mag. of Hist. and Biog.,* 70 (1962), 410–19.

20. Hening, ed., *Statutes Va.,* I, 144, 242, 292, 454; *Archives Md.,* I, 342, II, 136, 399, 538–39, XIII, 538–39.

21. John Hammond, *Leah and Rachel, or, the Two Fruitfull Sisters Virginia, and Mary-land: Their Present Condition, Impartially Stated and Related* . . . (London, 1656), 9.

22. Hening, ed., *Statutes Va.,* II, 267.

23. *Ibid.,* I, 226; for the same act in more detail, "Acts of General Assembly, Jan. 6, 1639–40," *Wm. and Mary Qtly.,* 2d Ser., 4 (1924), 147. In Bermuda, always closely connected with Virginia, the first prohibition

of weapons to Negroes came in 1623, only seven years after the first Negro landed. The 1623 law was the first law anywhere in English specifically dealing with Negroes. After stressing the insolence of Negroes secretly carrying "cudgells and other weapons and working tools, very dangerous and not meete to be suffered to be carried by such vassalls," it prohibited (in addition to arms) Negroes going abroad at night, trespassing on other people's lands, and trading in tobacco without permission of their masters. Unfortunately the evidence concerning lifetime service for Negroes is much less definite in the scanty Bermuda sources than in those for Maryland and Virginia; the first known incident suggestive of the practice might reasonably be placed anywhere from 1631 to 1656. Later evidence shows Bermuda's slavery and proportion of Negroes similar to Virginia's, and it seems unlikely that the two colonies' early experience was radically different. Henry C. Wilkinson, *The Adventurers of Bermuda; A History of the Island from Its Discovery until the Dissolution of the Somers Island Company in 1684* (London, 1933), 114; J. H. Lefroy, comp., *Memorials of the Discovery and Early Settlement of the Bermudas or Somers Islands, 1515–1685* . . . , 2 vols. (London, 1877–79), I, 308–9, 505, 526–27, 633, 645, II, 34–35, 70. But Negroes were to be armed at times of alarm (*ibid.*, II, 242, 366, 380 [1666–73]): Bermuda was exposed to foreign attack.

24. Hening, ed., *Statutes Va.*, I, 146. (The term "negro woman" was in very common use.) *Archives Md.*, X, 114–15.

25. Hening, ed., *Statutes Va.*, I, 552; McIlwaine, ed., *Minutes Council Va.*, 477.

26. Bruce, *Economic History of Va.*, II, 110.

27. "The History of Bacon's and Ingram's Rebellion, 1676," in Charles M. Andrews, ed., *Narratives of the Insurrections, 1675–1690* (N.Y., 1915), 96. Cf. the will of John Fenwick (1683), *Documents Relating to the Colonial, Revolutionary and Post-Revolutionary History of the State of New Jersey* . . . [New Jersey Archives], 1st Ser. (Newark, etc., 1880–1949), XXIII, 162.

28. Hening, ed., *Statutes Va.*, II, 170, III, 86–87; *Archives Md.*, I, 533–34, VII, 204; Lefroy, comp., *Memorials Bermudas*, II, 190 (a resolution, not a statute). Some evidence suggests miscegenation was not taken as seriously in 17th-century Bermuda as on the mainland: *ibid.*, I, 550, II, 30, 103, 141, 161, 228, 314.

29. *Archives Md.*, I, 464.

30. *Ibid.*, XLI, 476–78, XLIX, 123–24. Compare the contemporary difficulties of a Negro servant: William P. Palmer *et al.*, eds., *Calendar of Virginia State Papers* . . . , 11 vols. (Richmond, 1875–93), I, 9–10.

31. Hening, ed., *Statutes Va.*, I, 539, II, 26; *Archives Md.*, I, 449, 489, 526, 533–34. The "any negroes who are incapable" suggests explicit recogni-

tion that some were free, but in several sources the law as re-enacted the next year included a comma between "negroes" and "who," as did the Maryland act of 1663. See *The Lawes of Virginia Now in Force: Collected out of the Assembly Records* . . . (London, 1662), 59.

32. Hening, ed., *Statutes Va.*, II, 170, 270, 283, 490–91, III, 137–40, 447–48; *Archives Md.*, VII, 203–5, XIII, 546–49, XXII, 551–52.

33. Especially Hening, ed., *Statutes Va.*, II, 270–71, 481–82, 493, III, 86, 102–3; *Archives Md.*, XIII, 451–53, XIX, 167, 193, XXII, 546–48, XXVI, 254–56.

34. Hening, ed., *Statutes Va.*, II, 270; compare law for servants, I, 538, II, 118.

35. *Ibid.*, II, 299.

36. Robert Beverley, *The History and Present State of Virginia,* ed. Louis B. Wright (Chapel Hill, 1947), 271–72.

37. For illustration, Hening, ed., *Statutes Va.*, II, 288, 479–80 (Negro *children* taxed from age 12, white *boys* from 14), III, 102–3; *Archives Md.*, VII, 76 (county courts required to register births, marriages, burials of all "Except Negroes Indians and Molottos").

38. Hening, ed., *Statutes Va.*, III, 447–62.

Slavery and Personality

1. The historian Samuel Eliot Morison was taken to task a few years ago by students of Queens College, Long Island, for his use of the name "Sambo" (in Volume I of his and H. S. Commager's text, *The Growth of the American Republic*) and for referring to the pre–Civil War Negroes as "a race with exasperating habits" and to the typical slave as "childlike, improvident, humorous, prevaricating, and superstitious." As a result, the use of the text at Queens was discontinued. See *Time,* February 26, 1951, pp. 48–49.

The following is from the "Concluding Summary" of one of the series of studies begun in the late 1930's under the inspiration of Gunnar Myrdal: "The description of the stereotypes held concerning the American Negro indicates the widespread tendency to look upon the Negro as inferior, and to ascribe to him qualities of intellect and personality which mark him off with some definiteness from the surrounding white American population . . . [;] not all these alleged characteristics of the Negro are uncomplimentary, but even those which may be regarded as favorable have the flavor of inferiority about them. When the Negro is praised, he is praised for his childlike qualities of happiness and good nature or for his artistic and musical gifts. . . . Negro writers do express much more frequently, as one would expect, the belief that whites and Negroes have essentially equal potentialities, and that it is only the accidents of training and economic opportunity which have produced temporary differences; even among Negro writers, however, some have accepted the prevailing stereotype." Otto Klineberg (ed.), *Characteristics of the American Negro* (New York: Harper, 1944). Instead of proposing an actual program of inquiry, the intentions of this line of thought appear to be primarily moral and its objectives to be of a normative sort: desistance from the use of stereotypes.

2. See Elkins, *Slavery*, Part IV, pp. 190–91.

3. Kenneth Stampp, "The Historian and Southern Negro Slavery," *American Historical Review*, LVII (April, 1952), 617.

4. There is such a word as "Zambo" in Latin America, but its meaning has no relation to our "Sambo." "A Zambo or Sambo (Spanish, *Zambo,* 'bandy-legged') is a cross between a *Negro* and an Amerindian (sometimes this name is given to the cross between a pure Negro and a mulatto, which the French called 'griffe')." Sir Harry Johnston, *The Negro in the New World* (London: Methuen, 1910), p. 3. I am not implying that racial stigma of some kind did not exist in South America (see Elkins, *Slavery*, pp. 77–78, n. 113); indeed anthropological research has shown that the Latin-Americans were, and are, a good deal more conscious of "race" than such writers as Gilberto Freyre have been willing to admit. Even in Brazil, derogatory Negro stereotypes are common, and are apparently of long standing. On this point see Charles Wagley, *Race and Class in Rural Brazil* (Paris: UNESCO, 1952). On the other hand, it would be very difficult to find evidence in the literature of Brazil, or anywhere else in Latin America, of responsible men seriously maintaining that the Negro slave was constitutionally incapable of freedom. The views of a man like James H. Hammond, or for that matter the views of any average Southerner during the ante-bellum period, would have had little meaning in nineteenth-century Latin America. One is even inclined to think that these Latin-American stereotypes would compare more closely with the stereotypes of eastern and southern European immigrants that were held by certain classes in this country early in the twentieth century. See, e.g., Madison Grant's *Passing of the Great Race* (New York: Scribner, 1916). There are stereotypes and stereotypes: it would be quite safe to say that our "Sambo" far exceeds in tenacity and pervasiveness anything comparable in Latin America.

5. It is, however, one thing to say that no longer are there any responsible men of science to be found advancing the racial argument, and quite another to assert that the argument is closed. In an odd sense we still find any number of statements indicating that the *other* side of the controversy is still being carried on, long after the bones of the enemy lie bleaching on the sands. For example, in the preface to a recent study on the American Negro by two distinguished psychologists, the authors define their "scientific position" by announcing that their book was "con-

ceived and written on the premise that group characteristics are adaptive in nature and therefore not inborn, but acquired" and that "anyone who wishes to quote from [its] conclusions . . . to uphold any other thesis risks doing injustice to the material in the book, to the intentions of the authors, and to the Negro people." They then quote a kind of manifesto, signed by a group of prominent psychologists and social scientists, attesting that "as social scientists we know of no evidence that any ethnic group is inherently inferior." This is followed by a portion of the 1950 UNESCO "Statement on Race" which declares that "biological studies lend support to the ethic of universal brotherhood." From Abram Kardiner and Lionel Ovesey, *The Mark of Oppression: A Psychosocial Study of the American Negro* (New York: Norton, 1951), pp. v–vi. While these are sentiments which may (and must) be pronounced on any number of occasions among men of good will (the President regularly conceives it his duty to do this), their *scientific* content (which is the level at which they are here being offered) has long since ceased to be a matter of controversy.

6. The line between "accommodation" (as conscious hypocrisy) and behavior inextricable from basic personality, though the line certainly exists, is anything but a clear and simple matter of choice. There is reason to think that the one grades into the other, and vice versa, with considerable subtlety. In this connection, the most satisfactory theoretical mediating term between deliberate role-playing and "natural" role-playing might be found in role-psychology. See Elkins, *Slavery*, pp. 131–33.

7. Although the majority of Southern slaveholders were not planters, the majority of slaves were owned by a planter minority. "Considerably more than half of them lived on plantation units of more than twenty slaves, and one-fourth lived on units of more than fifty. That the majority of slaves belonged to members of the planter class, and not to those who operated small farms with a single slave family, is a fact of crucial importance concerning the nature of bondage in the ante-bellum South." Stampp, *Peculiar Institution*, p. 31.

8. Bruno Bettelheim, "Individual and Mass Behavior in Extreme Situations," *Journal of Abnormal Psychology,* XXXVIII (October, 1943), 424.

9. A description of such a trip may be found in Olga Lengyel, *Five Chimneys: The Story of Auschwitz* (Chicago, 1947), pp. 7–10. See also Eugen Kogon, *The Theory and Practice of Hell* (New York: Farrar, Straus, 1946), p. 67.

10. Elie Cohen, *Human Behavior in the Concentration Camp* (New York: Norton, 1953), pp. 118–22; Kogon, *Theory and Practice,* pp. 66–76; Lengyel, *Five Chimneys,* pp. 12–22.

11. One aspect of this registration ceremony involved a sham "inspection" of the body, whose effect on the women prisoners in particular was apparently very profound. See Lengyel, *Five Chimneys*, p. 19; Ella Lingens-Reiner, *Prisoners of Fear* (London: Victor Gollancz, 1948), p. 26. This may be compared with Degrandpré's description of a similar "inspection" on the African slave coast in the 1780's; see his *Voyage*, II, 55–56. "Apart from the fact that for every newcomer his transformation into a 'prisoner' meant a degradation," writes an ex-prisoner of Auschwitz and Mauthausen, "there was also the *loss of his name*. That this was no trifling circumstance should be apparent from the great importance which, according to Freud, a man attaches to his name. This is, in Freud's view, sufficiently proven by 'the fact that savages regard a name as an essential part of a man's personality. . . .' Anyhow, whether one agrees with Freud or not, the loss of one's name is not without significance, for the name is a personal attribute. Because he no longer had a name, but had become a number, the prisoner belonged to the huge army of the nameless who peopled the concentration camp." Cohen, *Human Behavior*, pp. 145–46.

12. *Ibid.*, pp. 134–35, 140–43.

13. These punishments are discussed most vividly in Kogon, *Theory and Practice*, pp. 102–8, 207–11.

14. Bettelheim, "Individual and Mass Behavior," p. 445.

15. The effects of never being alone are noted in Cohen, *Human Behavior*, pp. 130–31, and David Rousset, *The Other Kingdom* (New York: Reynal & Hitchcock, 1947), p. 133.

16. "When the author [Bettelheim] expressed to some of the old prisoners his astonishment that they seemed not interested in discussing their future life outside the camp, they frequently admitted that they could no longer visualize themselves living outside the camp, making free decisions, taking care of themselves and their families." Bettelheim, "Individual and Mass Behavior," p. 439.

17. M. Rousset tells of how, on one of the death marches, a prisoner came to him bringing a French compatriot and begging his protection for the wretched man. "He told me that he was a lawyer from Toulouse, and it was only with the greatest difficulty that I kept from laughing aloud. For this social designation, *lawyer*, no longer fitted the poor wretch in the slightest. The incongruity of the thought was irresistibly comic. And it was the same with all of us." Rousset, *Other Kingdom*, p. 77.

18. Kogon, *Theory and Practice*, p. 274; Cohen, *Human Behavior*, p. 155; Hilde O. Bluhm, "How Did They Survive?" *American Journal of Psychotherapy*, II (January, 1948), 5.

19. Kogon, *Theory and Practice*, p. 277.

20. Bettelheim, "Individual and Mass Behavior," p. 438.

21. Cohen, *Human Behavior*, p. 169.

22. This should in no sense be considered as a calculating, "rational" alertness, but rather as something quite primitive. "Of myself," writes Dr. Cohen, "I know that I was not continuously occupied by the reflection: I am going to win through. The actions which contributed to my survival were performed instinctively rather than consciously. . . . Like animals warned by their instinct that danger is imminent, we would act instinctively at critical moments. These instinctive acts must, I think, be considered as manifestations of the life instinct. If the life instinct is not strong enough, the instinct will desert the individual, and instead of rising to the emergency, the individual will succumb, whereas a stronger life instinct would have seen him through." *Human Behavior*, p. 163.

23. Those who had in fact succumbed to this apathy—who had given up the struggle, and for whom death would be a mere matter of time—were known as "Moslems."

24. Bettelheim, "Individual and Mass Behavior," p. 141.

25. Says Dr. Cohen, "I am not asserting that sex was never discussed; it was, though not often. Frankl also states 'that in contrast to mass existence in other military communities . . . here (in the concentration camp) there is *no smut talk*.'" *Human Behavior*, p. 141.

26. "With reference to this phenomenon Miss Bluhm has pointed out that it is not at all unusual that people in extraordinary circumstances, for example soldiers in wartime, 'are able to give up their habitual standards of cleanliness without deeper disturbance; yet only up to certain limits.' The rules of anal cleanliness, she adds, are not disregarded. 'Their neglect means return to instinctual behavior of childhood.'" *Ibid.*, p. 175.

27. Bettelheim, "Individual and Mass Behavior," p. 445.

28. *Ibid.*, p. 421.

29. Quoted in Cohen, *Human Behavior*, p. 176.

30. *Ibid.*

31. *Ibid.*, p. 174.

32. Bettelheim, "Individual and Mass Behavior," pp. 445–46. This same phenomenon is noted by Curt Bondy: "They tell great stories about what they have been before and what they have performed." "Problems of Internment Camps," *Journal of Abnormal and Social Psychology*, XXXVIII (October, 1943), 453–75.

33. Cohen, *Human Behavior*, p. 177. Italics in original.

34. Bettelheim, "Individual and Mass Behavior," p. 447.

35. *Ibid.*, pp. 448–50. "Once, for instance, a guard on inspecting the prisoners' apparel found that the shoes of some of them were dirty on the

inside. He ordered all prisoners to wash their shoes inside and out with water and soap. The heavy shoes treated this way became hard as stone. The order was never repeated, and many prisoners did not execute it when given. Nevertheless there were some old prisoners who not only continued to wash the inside of their shoes every day but cursed all others who did not do so as negligent and dirty. These prisoners firmly believed that the rules set down by the Gestapo were desirable standards of human behavior, at least in the camp situation." *Ibid.,* p. 450.

36. *Ibid.* See also Cohen, *Human Behavior,* pp. 189–93, for a discussion of anti-Semitism among the Jews.

37. Cohen, *Human Behavior,* pp. 176–77.

38. *Ibid.,* p. 179. On this and other points I must also acknowledge my indebtedness to Mr. Ies Spetter, a former Dutch journalist now living in this country, who was imprisoned for a time at Auschwitz during World War II. Mr. Spetter permitted me to see an unpublished paper, "Some Thoughts on Victims and Criminals in the German Concentration Camps," which he wrote in 1954 at the New School for Social Research; and this, together with a number of conversations I had with him, added much to my understanding of concentration-camp psychology.

39. Kogon, *Theory and Practice,* p. 284.

40. *The Other Kingdom,* p. 137.

41. "In the preference camp Bergen Belsen, only four cases of attempted suicide were witnessed by Tas, three of which were saved with great effort, while in the Stammlager Auschwitz only one successful attempt came to my knowledge. This does not mean that there were not more, but their number was certainly small. Kaas, on the other hand, witnessed several attempted suicides in Buchenwald. He has remembered three that were successful (two by hanging, one by rushing into the electric fence). He also knows of prisoners who were known to be depressive cases, and who were shot down when during the night they had deliberately gone out of bounds. As compared with the large number of prisoners, the number of suicides, however, was very small." Cohen, *Human Behavior,* p. 158.

42. Kogon, *Theory and Practice,* pp. 166–67. This occurred during fearful tortures at the quarry, where the Jews knew they were about to be killed anyway.

43. A. Hottinger, *Hungerkrankheit, Hungerödem, Hungertuberkulose,* p. 32, quoted in Cohen, *Human Behavior,* p. 197. "After the liberation many writers were struck by the callousness of the one time prisoners, and particularly by their apathy when relating their experiences, even the most horrible." *Ibid.,* p. 144.

44. The experience of American prisoners taken by the Chinese during the Korean War seems to indicate that profound changes in behavior and

values, if not in basic personality itself, can be effected without the use of physical torture or extreme deprivation. The Chinese were able to get large numbers of Americans to act as informers and to co-operate in numerous ways in the effort to indoctrinate all the prisoners with Communist propaganda. The technique contained two key elements. One was that all formal and informal authority structures within the group were systematically destroyed; this was done by isolating officers, non-commissioned officers, and any enlisted men who gave indications of leadership capacities. The other element involved the continual emphasizing of the captors' power and influence by judicious manipulation of petty rewards and punishments and by subtle hints of the greater rewards and more severe punishments (repatriation or non-repatriation) that rested with the pleasure of those in authority. See Edgar H. Schein, "Some Observations on Chinese Methods of Handling Prisoners of War," *Public Opinion Quarterly,* XX (Spring, 1956), 321–27.

45. In a system as tightly closed as the plantation or the concentration camp, the slave's or prisoner's position of absolute dependency virtually compels him to see the authority-figure as somehow really "good." Indeed, all the evil in his life may flow from this man—but then so also must everything of any value. Here is the seat of the only "good" he knows, and to maintain his psychic balance he must persuade himself that the good is in some way dominant. A threat to this illusion is thus in a real sense a threat to his very existence. It is a common experience among social workers dealing with neglected and maltreated children to have a child desperately insist on his love for a cruel and brutal parent and beg that he be allowed to remain with that parent. The most dramatic feature of this situation is the cruelty which it involves, but the mechanism which inspires the devotion is not the cruelty of the parent but rather the abnormal dependency of the child. A classic example of this mechanism in operation may be seen in the case of Varvara Petrovna, mother of Ivan Turgenev. Mme Turgenev "ruled over her serfs with a rod of iron." She demanded utter obedience and total submission. The slightest infraction of her rules brought the most severe punishment: "A maid who did not offer her a cup of tea in the proper manner was sent off to some remote village and perhaps separated from her family forever; gardeners who failed to prevent the plucking of a tulip in one of the flower beds before the house were ordered to be flogged; a servant whom she suspected of a mutinous disposition was sent off to Siberia." Her family and her most devoted servants were treated in much the same manner. "Indeed," wrote Varvara Zhitova, the adopted daughter of Mme Turgenev, "those who loved her and were most devoted to her suffered most of all." Yet in spite of her brutality she was adored by the very people she tyrannized. David Magarshack describes how once when thrashing her eldest son she nearly fainted with sadistic excitement, whereupon "little Nicholas, forgetting his punishment, bawled at the top of his voice: 'Water! Water

for mummy!'" Mme Zhitova, who knew Mme Turgenev's cruelty intimately and was herself the constant victim of her tyranny, wrote: "In spite of this, I loved her passionately, and when I was, though rarely, separated from her, I felt lonely and unhappy." Even Mme Turgenev's maid Agatha, whose children were sent to another village when still infants so that Agatha might devote all her time to her mistress, could say years later, "Yes, she caused me much grief. I suffered much from her, but all the same I loved her! She was a real lady!" V. Zhitova, *The Turgenev Family*, trans. A. S. Mills (London: Havill Press, 1954), p. 25; David Magarshack, *Turgenev: A Life* (New York: Grove, 1954), pp. 14, 16, 22.

46. Bruno Bettelheim tells us of the fantastic efforts of the old prisoners to believe in the benevolence of the officers of the SS. "They insisted that these officers [hid] behind their rough surface a feeling of justice and propriety; he, or they, were supposed to be genuinely interested in the prisoners and even trying, in a small way, to help them. Since nothing of these supposed feelings and efforts ever became apparent, it was explained that he hid them so effectively because otherwise he would not be able to help the prisoners. The eagerness of these prisoners to find reasons for their claims was pitiful. A whole legend was woven around the fact that of two officers inspecting a barrack one had cleaned his shoes from mud before entering. He probably did it automatically, but it was interpreted as a rebuff of the other officer and a clear demonstration of how he felt about the concentration camp." Bettelheim, "Individual and Mass Behavior," p. 451.

47. Professor Stampp, in a chapter called "To Make Them Stand in Fear," describes the planter's resources for dealing with a recalcitrant slave. *Peculiar Institution*, pp. 141–91.

48. Edward A. Pollard, *Black Diamonds Gathered in the Darkey Homes of the South* (New York: Pudney & Russel, 1859), p. 58.

49. *Ibid.*, p. viii.

50. John Pendleton Kennedy, *Swallow Barn* (Philadelphia: Carey & Lea, 1832).

51. John Dollard, *Caste and Class in a Southern Town* (2d ed.; New York: Harper, 1949), p. 255. The lore of "accommodation," taken just in itself, is very rich and is, needless to say, morally very complex. It suggests a delicate psychological balance. On the one hand, as the Dollard citation above implies, accommodation is fraught with dangers for the personalities of those who engage in it. On the other hand, as Bruno Bettelheim has reminded me, this involves a principle that goes well beyond American Negro society and is to be found deeply imbedded in European traditions: the principle of how the powerless can manipulate the powerful through aggressive stupidity, literal-mindedness, servile fawning, and irresponsibility. In this sense the immovably stupid "Good

Soldier Schweik" and the fawning Negro in Richard Wright's *Black Boy* who allowed the white man to kick him for a quarter partake of the same tradition. Each has a technique whereby he can in a real sense exploit his powerful superiors, feel contempt for them, and suffer in the process no great damage to his own pride. Jewish lore, as is well known, teems with this sort of thing. There was much of it also in the traditional relationships between peasants and nobles in central Europe.

Still, all this required the existence of some sort of alternative forces for moral and psychological orientation. The problem of the Negro in slavery times involved the virtual absence of such forces. It was with the end of slavery, presumably, that they would first begin to present themselves in generally usable form—a man's neighbors, the Loyal Leagues, white politicians, and so on. It would be in these circumstances that the essentially intermediate technique of accommodation could be used as a protective device beneath which a more independent personality might develop.

52. Even Negro officeholders during Reconstruction, according to Francis B. Simkins, "were known to observe carefully the etiquette of the Southern caste system." "New Viewpoints of Southern Reconstruction," *Journal of Southern History,* V (February, 1939), 52.

Through the Prism of Folklore: The Black Ethos in Slavery

1. Historians who have provided stereotypical treatments of slave thought and personality are Ulrich B. Phillips, *American Negro Slavery* (New York, 1918); Samuel Eliot Morison, and Henry Steele Commager, *The Growth of the American Republic* (New York, 1950); and Stanley Elkins, *Slavery: A Problem in American Institutional and Intellectual Life* (Chicago, 1959).

2. See Herbert Aptheker, *American Negro Slave Revolts;* Kenneth M. Stampp, *The Peculiar Institution* (New York, 1956); Richard Wade, *Slavery in the Cities* (New York, 1964); and Alice and Raymond Bauer, "Day to Day Resistance to Slavery," *Journal of Negro History,* XXVII, No. 4, October, 1942.

3. I am here concerned with the Stanley Elkins version of "Sambo," that is, the inference that the overwhelming majority of slaves, as a result of their struggle to survive under the brutal system of American slavery, became so callous and indifferent to their status that they gave survival primacy over all other considerations. See Chapters III through VI of *Slavery* for a discussion of the process by which blacks allegedly were reduced to the "good humor of everlasting childhood." (p. 132).

4. I am indebted to Guy Johnson of the University of North Carolina for suggesting the use of the term "ethos" in this piece, and for helpful commentary on the original paper, which was read before the Associa-

tion for the Study of Negro Life and History at Greensboro, North Carolina, on October 13, 1967.

5. Professor Brown made this remark in a paper delivered before The Amistad Society in Chicago, Spring, 1964. Distinguished poet, literary critic, folklorist, and teacher, Brown has long contended that an awareness of Negro folklore is essential to an understanding of slave personality and thought.

6. I subscribe to Alan Lomax's observation that folk songs "can be taken as the signposts of persistent patterns of community feeling and can throw light into many dark corners of our past and our present." His view that Afro-American music, despite its regional peculiarities, "expresses the same feelings and speaks the same basic language everywhere" is also accepted as a working principle in this paper. For an extended treatment of these points of view, see Alan Lomax, *Folk Songs of North America* (New York, 1960), Introduction, p. xx.

7. Frederick Douglass, *Narrative of the Life of Frederick Douglass* (Cambridge, Massachusetts: The Belknap Press, 1960), p. 38. Originally published in 1845.

8. John Hope Franklin (ed.), *Souls of Black Folk* in *Three Negro Classics* (New York, 1965), p. 380. Originally published in 1903.

9. Douglass, *Narrative*, p. 38. Douglass' view adumbrated John and Alan Lomax' theory that the songs of the folk singer are deeply rooted "in his life and have functioned there as enzymes to assist in the digestion of hardship, solitude, violence (and) hunger." John A. and Alan Lomax, *Our Singing Country* (New York: The Macmillan Co. 1941), Preface, p. xiii.

10. Sterling Brown, "Negro Folk Expression," *Phylon,* October, 1953, p. 47.

11. *Ibid.,* p. 48.

12. *Ibid.,* p. 407.

13. *Ibid.,* p. 48.

14. Addressing himself to the slave's posture toward God, and the attitudes toward the gods which the slave's African ancestors had, Lomax has written: "The West African lives with his gods on terms of intimacy. He appeals to them, reviles them, tricks them, laughs at their follies. In this spirit the Negro slaves humanized the stern religion of his masters by adopting the figures of the Bible as his intimates." Lomax, *Folk Songs of North America,* p. 463.

15. Quoted from Lomax, *Folk Songs of North America,* p. 475.

16. Quoted from Brown, Sterling A., Davis, Arthur P., and Lee, Ulysses, *The Negro Caravan* (New York: The Dryden Press, 1941), p. 436.

17. Vincent Harding, *Black Radicalism in America.* An unpublished work which Dr. Harding recently completed.

18. See Harold Courlander, *Negro Folk Music, U.S.A.* (New York: Columbia University Press, 1963), pp. 42, 43. If a great many slaves did not consider Harriet Tubman the "Moses" of her people, it is unlikely that most failed to grasp the relationship between themselves and the Israelites, Egypt and the South, and Pharaoh and slavemasters in such lines as: "Didn't my Lord deliver Daniel / And why not every man"; "Oh Mary don't you weep, don't you moan / Pharaoh's army got drowned / Oh Mary don't you weep"; and "Go down Moses / Way down in Egyptland / Tell old Pharaoh / To let my people go."

19. Quoted from Lomax, *Folk Songs of North America*, p. 471.

20. *Ibid.*, p. 476.

21. Frederick Douglass, *The Life and Times of Frederick Douglass* (New York: Collier Books, 1962), p. 146.

22. Brown, "Folk Expression," p. 51.

23. Brown *et. al.*, *Caravan*, p. 447.

24. Lomax, *Folk Songs of North America*, p. 514.

25. *Ibid.*, p. 515.

26. *Ibid.*, p. 527.

27. Courlander, *Negro Folk Music*, p. 117.

28. *Ibid.*, p. 89.

29. Brown, "Folk Expression," p. 54. Steel-driving John Henry is obviously in the tradition of the axe-wielding blacks of the ante-bellum period. The ballad of John Henry helped spawn John Henry work songs:

> Dis ole hammer—hunh
> Ring like silver—hunh (3)
> Shine like gold, baby—hunh
> Shine like gold—hunh
>
> Dis ole hammer—hunh
> Kilt John Henry—hunh (3)
> Twont kill me baby, hunh
> Twon't kill me. (Quoted from Brown, "Folk Expression," p. 57.)

30. Frances Anne Kemble, *Journal of a Residence on a Georgia Plantation, 1838–1839* (New York: Alfred Knopf), pp. 260–61. Miss Kemble heard slaves use the epithet "nigger": "And I assure you no contemptuous intonation ever equalled the prepotenza (arrogance) of the despotic insolence of this address of these poor wretches to each other." Kemble, *Journal*, p. 281. Here she is on solid ground, but the slaves also used the word with glowing affection, as seen in the "Run, Nigger, Run" secular. At other times they leaned toward self-laceration but refused to go the whole route: "My name's Ran, I wuks in de sand, I'd rather be a nigger dan a po' white man." Brown, "Folk Expression," p. 51. Some blacks also

sang, "It takes a long, lean, black-skinned gal, to make a preacher lay his Bible down." Newman I. White, *American Negro Folk Songs* (Cambridge, 1928), p. 411.

31. Elkins, who believes Southern white lore on slavery should be taken seriously, does not subject it to serious scrutiny. For a penetrating—and devastating—analysis of "the richest layers of Southern lore" which, according to Elkins, resulted from "an exquisitely rounded collective creativity," see Sterling A. Brown, "A Century of Negro Portraiture in American Literature," *The Massachusetts Review* (Winter, 1966).

32. Quoted from Archie Epps, "A Negro Separatist Movement," *The Harvard Review,* IV, No. 1 (Summer-Fall, 1956), 75.

33. Quoted in William Styron, "This Quiet Dust," *Harper's,* April, 1965, p. 135.

34. For excerpts from David Walker's *Appeal* and Henry H. Garnet's *Call to Rebellion,* see Herbert Aptheker (ed.), *A Documentary History of the Negro People in the United States.* 2 vols. (New York: Citadel Press, 1965). Originally published in 1951.

35. Thomas Wentworth Higginson, *Army Life in a Black Regiment* (New York: Collier, 1962), p. 199.

36. *Ibid.*

37. W. E. B. Du Bois, *Black Reconstruction* (Philadelphia: Albert Saifer), p. 122. Originally published in 1935 by Harcourt, Brace and Company.

38. Brown, "Folk Expression," p. 49.

39. Du Bois, *Reconstruction,* p. 124.

40. Quoted in Brown *et al., Caravan,* pp. 440–41. One of the most tragic scenes of the Civil War period occurred when a group of Sea Island freedmen, told by a brigadier-general that they would not receive land from the government, sang, "Nobody knows the trouble I've seen." Du Bois, *Souls,* p. 381.

41. Du Bois, *Reconstruction,* p. 124.

42. If some slavemasters encouraged slaves to steal or simply winked at thefts, then slaves who obliged them were most assuredly *not acting against their own interests,* whatever the motivation of the masters. Had more fruitful options been available to them, then and only then could we say that slaves were playing into the hands of their masters. Whatever the masters thought of slaves who stole from them—and there is little reason to doubt that most slaves considered it almost obligatory to steal from white people—the slaves, it is reasonable to assume, were aware of the unparalleled looting in which masters themselves were engaged. To speak therefore of slaves undermining their sense of self-respect as a result of stealing from whites—and this argument has been advanced by Eugene Genovese—is wide of the mark. Indeed, it appears more likely that those who engaged in stealing were, in the context of an oppressor-

oppressed situation, on the way to realizing a larger measure of self-respect. Moreover, Genovese, in charging that certain forms of "day to day" resistance, in the absence of general conditions of rebellion, "amounted to individual and essentially nihilistic thrashing about," fails to recognize that that which was possible, that which conditions permitted, was pursued by slaves in preference to the path which led to passivity or annihilation. Those engaging in "day to day" resistance were moving along meaningful rather than nihilistic lines, for their activities were designed to frustrate the demands of the authority-system. For a very suggestive discussion of the dependency complex engendered by slavery and highly provocative views on the significance of "day to day" resistance among slaves, see Eugene Genovese, "The Legacy of Slavery and the Roots of Black Nationalism," *Studies on the Left,* VI, No. 6 (Nov.-Dec. 1966), especially p. 8.

43. Higginson, *Black Regiment,* p. 212. Alan Lomax reminds us that the slaves sang "in leader-chorus style, with a more relaxed throat than the whites, and in deeper-pitched, mellower voices, which blended richly." "A strong, surging beat underlay most of their American creations . . . words and tunes were intimately and playfully united, and 'sense' was often subordinated to the demands of rhythm and melody." Lomax, *Folk Songs of North America,* Introduction, p. xx.

44. Lomax, *Folk Songs,* p. 460.

45. Commenting on the group nature of much of slave singing, Alan Lomax points out that the majority of the bondsmen "came from West Africa, where music-making was largely a group activity, the creation of a many-voiced, dancing throng. . . . Community songs of labour and worship (in America) and dance songs far outnumbered narrative pieces, and the emotion of the songs was, on the whole, joyfully erotic, deeply tragic, allusive, playful, or ironic rather than nostalgic, withdrawn, factual, or aggressively comic—as among white folk singers." Lomax, *Folk Songs,* pp. xix and xx of Introduction. For treatments of the more technical aspects of Afro-American music, see Courlander, *Negro Folk Music,* especially Chapter II; and Richard A. Waterman, "African Influences on the Music of the Americas," in *Acculturation in the Americas,* edited by Sol Tax.

46. Arna Bontemps and Langston Hughes (ed.), *The Book of Negro Folklore* (New York: Dodd, Mead & Company, 1965), Introduction, p. viii. Of course if one regards each humorous thrust of the bondsmen as so much comic nonsense, then there is no basis for understanding, to use Sterling Brown's phrase, the slave's "laughter out of hell." Without understanding what humor meant to slaves themselves, one is not likely to rise above the superficiality of a Stephen Foster or a Joel Chandler Harris. But once an effort has been made to see the world from the slave's point of view, then perhaps one can understand Ralph Ellison's

reference to Afro-Americans, in their folklore, "backing away from the chaos of experience and from ourselves," in order to "depict the humor as well as the horror of our living." Ralph Ellison, "A Very Stern Discipline," *Harper's* (March, 1967), p. 80.

47. For additional discussions of folk tales, see Zora Neale Hurston, *Mules and Men* (Philadelphia: J. B. Lippincott, 1935); Richard Dorson, *American Negro Folktales* (Greenwich, Connecticut: Fawcett, 1967); and B. A. Botkin, *Lay My Burden Down* (Chicago: University of Chicago Press, 1945).

48. Bontemps and Hughes, *Negro Folklore*, Introduction, p. ix.

49. The fact that slaveowners sometimes took pleasure in being outwitted by slaves in no way diminishes the importance of the trickster tales, for what is essential here is how these tales affected the slave's attitude toward himself, not whether his thinking or behavior would impress a society which considered black people little better than animals. Du Bois' words in this regard should never be forgotten: "Everything Negroes did was wrong. If they fought for freedom, they were beasts; if they did not fight, they were born slaves. If they cowered on the plantation, they loved slavery; if they ran away, they were lazy loafers. If they sang, they were silly; if they scowled, they were impudent. . . . And they were funny, funny—ridiculous baboons, aping men." Du Bois, *Reconstruction*, p. 125.

50. Ralph Ellison offers illuminating insight into the group experience of the slave: "Any people who could endure all of that brutalization and keep together, who could undergo such dismemberment and resuscitate itself, and endure until it could take the initiative in achieving its own freedom is obviously more than the sum of its brutalization. Seen in this perspective, theirs has been one of the great human experiences and one of the great triumphs of the human spirit in modern times, in fact, in the history of the world." Ellison, "A Very Stern Discipline," p. 84.

51. Elkins sets forth this argument in *Slavery*, p. 84.

52. *Ibid.*, p. 93.

53. Gilberto Freyre, *The Masters and the Slaves* (New York: Alfred A. Knopf, 1956). Originally published by Jose Olympio, Rio de Janeiro, Brazil.

54. F. S. C. Northrop, *The Meeting of East and West* (New York: The Macmillan Co., 1952), pp. 159–60.

55. Du Bois, *Souls of Black Folk*, p. 378. Kenneth M. Stampp in his *The Peculiar Institution* (New York: Alfred A. Knopf, 1956), employs to a limited extent some of the materials of slave folklore. Willie Lee Rose, in *Rehearsal for Reconstruction* (New York: The Bobbs-Merrill Company, 1964), makes brief but highly informed use of folk material.

A Troublesome Property

1. Guion C. Johnson, *Ante-Bellum North Carolina* (Chapel Hill, 1937), p. 496; W. P. Harrison, *The Gospel Among the Slaves* (Nashville, 1893), p. 103.

2. James W. Bell to William S. Pettigrew, May 3, 1853, Pettigrew Family Papers.

3. Frederick Law Olmsted, *A Journey in the Back Country* (New York, 1860), pp. 154–55; Edwin A. Davis (ed.), *Plantation Life in the Florida Parishes of Louisiana, 1836–1846. As Reflected in the Diary of Bennet H. Barrow* (New York, 1943), p. 164.

4. E. B. R. to James B. Bailey, March 24, 1856, James B. Bailey Papers; Lewis C. Gray, *History of Agriculture in the Southern United States to 1860* (Washington, 1933), I, p. 519.

5. Frederick Douglass, *My Bondage and My Freedom* (New York, 1855), p. 81.

6. *Farmers' Register,* V (1837), p. 32.

7. William S. Pettigrew to [James C. Johnston], October 3, 1850, Pettigrew Family Papers.

8. William C. Adams, Ms. Diary, entries for July 18, 20, 1857.

9. Frederick Law Olmsted, *A Journey in the Seaboard Slave States* (New York, 1856), pp. 387–88; Edward S. Abdy, *Journal of a Residence and Tour in the United States* (London, 1835), II, p. 214; William Chambers, *Things as They Are in America* (London, 1854), pp. 269–70.

10. [Joseph H. Ingraham], *The South-West By A Yankee* (New York, 1835), II, p. 286; Hammond Diary, entries for October 23, 24, 1834; Olmsted, *Seaboard,* pp. 434–36.

11. Douglass, *My Bondage,* pp. 261–62; Helen T. Catterall (ed.), *Judicial Cases Concerning American Slavery and the Negro* (Washington, 1926–37), II, pp. 73–74, 210–11.

12. *De Bow's Review,* VII (1849), p. 220; XVII (1854), p. 422; XXV (1858), p. 51.

13. Joseph C. Robert, *The Story of Tobacco in America* (New York, 1949), p. 89.

14. *De Bow's Review,* XI (1851), pp. 333–34.

15. Hammond Diary, entry for June 7, 1839; Lewis Thompson to Thomas Thompson, December 31, 1858, Lewis Thompson Papers.

16. Olmsted, *A Journey Through Texas* (New York, 1857), p. 120; *id., Seaboard,* pp. 44–45, 91, 480–82.

17. *American Farmer,* 4th Ser., I (1846), p. 295.

18. Olmsted, *Seaboard,* pp. 186–90; *id., Back Country,* pp. 77–79.

19. Frances Anne Kemble, *Journal of a Residence on a Georgian Plantation in 1838–1839* (New York, 1863), pp. 135–36, 235.

20. Olmsted, *Seaboard,* pp. 188–90.

21. James S. Buckingham, *The Slave States of America* (London, 1842), I, pp. 135, 402; Clement Claiborne Clay to Clement Comer Clay, April 19, 1846, Clement C. Clay Papers; Susan Dabney Smedes, *Memorials of a Southern Planter* (Baltimore, 1887), p. 80.

22. *Southern Cultivator,* VII (1849), p. 140; XII (1854), p. 206.

23. John W. Brown Diary, entry for January 24, 1854.

24. Hammond Diary, entry for December 13, 1831.

25. See, for example, Catterall (ed.), *Judicial Cases,* II, pp. 129, 421, 438.

26. *Southern Cultivator,* XVIII (1860), p. 151.

27. Willie [Empie] to James Sheppard, October 27, 1859, Sheppard Papers; Manigault Plantation Records.

28. Doctrine Davenport to Ebenezer Pettigrew, February 21, May 16, December 31, 1836, Pettigrew Papers.

29. Ulrich B. Phillips and James D. Glunt (eds.), *Florida Plantation Records from the Papers of George Noble Jones* (St. Louis, 1927), pp. 107–18.

30. *Southern Cultivator,* XVIII (1860), p. 131.

31. Phillips and Glunt (eds.), *Florida Plantation Records,* p. 150; John Berkeley Grimball Ms. Diary, entries for October 12, 17, 20, November 2, 3, 1832.

32. James Pickens to Samuel Pickens, June 15, 1827 (typescript), Israel Pickens and Family Papers.

33. Raymond A. and Alice H. Bauer, "Day to Day Resistance to Slavery," *Journal of Negro History,* XXVII (1942), pp. 388–419.

34. *De Bow's Review,* XI (1851), pp. 331–33.

35. Olmsted, *Back Country,* p. 476; Newstead Plantation Diary, entry for June 7, 1860; Davis (ed.), *Diary of Bennet H. Barrow,* p. 165.

36. Baltimore *Sun,* September 25, 1856; New Orleans *Picayune,* March 17, 1846.

37. Baltimore *Sun,* August 1, 1840; Olmsted, *Seaboard,* pp. 190–91.

38. Richmond *Enquirer,* August 1, 1837; Mobile *Commercial Register,* November 20, 1837; John Walker Diary, entry for December 16, 1848.

39. James B. Sellers, *Slavery in Alabama* (University, Alabama, 1950), pp. 13–14.

40. Huntsville *Southern Advocate,* December 11, 1829; Tallahassee *Floridian and Journal,* May 20, 1854; Charleston *Courier,* April 10, 1847; March 10, 1856.

41. Balie Peyton to Samuel Smith Downey, January 6, March 7, 1831, Samuel Smith Downey Papers; John C. Pickens to Samuel Pickens, June 28, 1827, Pickens Papers.

42. Olmsted, *Seaboard,* pp. 100–101, 434–36; Phillips and Glunt (eds.), *Florida Plantation Records,* p. 95; Ulrich B. Phillips, *American Negro Slavery* (New York, 1918), p. 303; John Spencer Bassett, *The Southern Plantation Overseer As Revealed in His Letters* (Northampton, Mass., 1925), p. 18; Marston Diary, entry for May 19, 1828.

43. Phillips and Glunt (eds.), *Florida Plantation Records,* p. 57.

44. Olmsted, *Back Country,* p. 79; Memphis *Daily Appeal,* July 23, 1859; New Orleans *Picayune,* October 5, 1847; Stephen Duncan to Thomas Butler, September 20, 1851, Butler Family Papers.

45. Elisha Cain to Alexander Telfair, October 10, 1829, Telfair Plantation Records.

46. Milledgeville *Southern Recorder,* February 16, 1836.

47. Gavin Diary, entry for July 4, 1857; Vicksburg *Weekly Sentinel,* August 9, 1849.

48. Wilmington (N.C.) *Journal,* September 5, 1851; July 5, 1855; Tallahassee *Floridian,* March 13, 1847; Richmond *Enquirer,* September 4, 1832.

49. Rachel O'Connor to Mary C. Weeks, April 9, 1833, David Weeks and Family Collection.

50. Davis (ed.), *Diary of Bennet H. Barrow,* pp. 226–27; Solomon Northup, *Twelve Years a Slave* (Buffalo, 1853), pp. 236–49.

51. Mrs. Andrew McCollam Ms. Diary, entry for April 20, 1847; Hammond Diary, entries for July 1, 18, 19, 1832; Stephen Duncan to Thomas Butler, July 1, 1823, Butler Family Papers.

52. Catterall (ed.), *Judicial Cases,* II, p. 434; Howell M. Henry, *The Police Control of the Slaves in South Carolina* (Emory, Va., 1914), p. 121; Davis (ed.), *Diary of Bennet H. Barrow,* pp. 341–43.

53. Pensacola *Gazette,* November 3, 1838.

54. Milledgeville *Southern Recorder,* July 18, 1843; Raleigh *North Carolina Standard,* November 7, 1855.

Peter Still Versus the Peculiar Institution

1. In the category of Pickard's book, the slave narrative, see, for example, Solomon Northrup, *Twelve Years as a Slave* (Auburn and Buffalo, 1854); J. W. Loguen, *The Reverend J. W. Loguen as a Slave and as a Freeman* (Syracuse, 1859); Josiah Henson, *Father Henson's Story of His Own Life* (1849 and 1858).

2. Julia E. R. Marvin to Dr. Lord, Oct. 11, 1854, in the Peter Still Papers, Rutgers University Library. The Still Papers, concerning Still's activities

from 1850–1861, were a gift to the Rutgers Library from Philip D. Sang, Lake Forest, Illinois.

3. Kenneth M. Stampp, *The Peculiar Institution: Slavery in the Ante-Bellum South* (New York, 1956), p. 72.

4. Sections of *The Kidnapped and the Ransomed* pertaining to Joseph Friedman have been reprinted with an introduction and editorial notes by Maxwell Whiteman in *The American Jewish Archives,* IX (Apr., 1957), 3–31.

5. By completing his own purchase, Still became the fortunate member of a minority group. As Stampp notes: "Only a small number of bondsmen ever had the chance to show their desire for freedom by embracing an opportunity to gain legal emancipation. The handful who were permitted to buy themselves . . . left little doubt about how much they valued liberty." *The Peculiar Institution,* p. 97.

6. The danger of encountering professional slave hunters was especially great at this time, shortly after the passage of the Fugitive Slave Act of 1850.

7. William Still was active in helping to coordinate the work of the underground railroad. His well-known book, *The Underground Railroad* (Philadelphia, 1886), includes many accounts based on his experiences and the records of the Philadelphia Anti-Slavery Society.

8. William Still, *The Underground Railroad,* pp. 27–34.

9. *Ibid.,* pp. 34–35.

10. William Still to B. McKiernan, Aug. 16, 1851, *Journal of Negro History,* XI (1926), 107–109.

11. William Still, *The Underground Railroad,* p. 36.

12. Samuel J. May, *Some Recollections of Our Anti-Slavery Conflict* (Boston, 1869); *Memoirs of Samuel Joseph May* (Boston, 1873).

13. William Still to Peter Still, May 10, 1852, Peter Still Papers; Kate E. R. Pickard, *Peter Still: The Kidnapped and the Ransomed* (Syracuse, 1856), p. 319.

14. William Still to Peter Still, Dec. 18, 1852, Peter Still Papers.

15. Kate E. R. Pickard to Peter Still, Mar. 21, 1853, *ibid.*

16. J. Miller McKim, a leading Pennsylvania abolitionist, was also active in freedmen relief work in the 1860's. James M. McPherson, *The Struggle for Equality: Abolitionists and the Negro in the Civil War and Reconstruction* (Princeton, 1964), pp. 4, 76, 127.

17. Pickard, *Peter Still,* pp. 321–322.

18. Undated ms.; Pickard, *Peter Still,* p. 322.

19. The Concklin narrative was written by William Henry Furness, a Pennsylvania abolitionist. Elizabeth M. Geffen, "William Henry Furness, Philadelphia Anti-Slavery Preacher," *The Pennsylvania Magazine of*

History and Biography, LXXXII (1958), 259–292. Samuel J. May to Peter Still, Aug. 9, 1853, Peter Still Papers.

20. Letter from Horace Greeley, May 10, 1854, *ibid.* Pickard, *Peter Still*, p. 332.

21. *Ibid.*, p. 323.

22. *Ibid.*, p. 332; Louis Filler, *The Crusade Against Slavery: 1830–1860* (New York, 1960), pp. 261–262.

23. Ms. in Peter Still's "Memo Book," a record of funds collected in New England, Peter Still Papers.

24. Morris L. Hollowell to Peter Still, Sept. 19, 1854, *ibid.*

25. Letter from Morris L. Hollowell, Sept. 19, 1854, *ibid.*

26. William Still to Peter Still, Nov. 9, 1853, *ibid.*

27. Kate E. R. Pickard to Peter Still, June 24, 1855, *ibid.*

28. Kate E. R. Pickard to Peter Still, Aug. 26, 1855, *ibid.*

29. Kate E. R. Pickard to Peter Still, June 24, 1855, *ibid.*

30. The fabricated story about kidnapping in Maryland sounded plausible, as this state was overrun by kidnappers in the early 1800's. Dwight Lowell Dumond, *Antislavery: The Crusade for Freedom in America* (New York, 1966), p. 46.

31. An edition of *The Kidnapped and the Ransomed* was published by the Negro Publication Society of America, Inc., in 1941.

32. James Still, *Early Recollections and Life of Dr. James Still* (Philadelphia, 1877), pp. 153–156.

The Economics of Repression

1. Charles C. Andrews, *History of the New-York African Free-Schools* (New York, 1830), p. 132.

2. Jacques P. Brissot de Warville, *New Travels in the United States of America* (Dublin, 1792), pp. 282–83; Duke de la Rochefoucault Liancourt, *Travels through the United States of North America* (2 vols.; London, 1799), I, 531–32, II, 166–67; *Mass. Hist. Soc. Colls.*, Ser. 5, III, 400.

3. Minutes of the Committee for Improving the Condition of Free Blacks, Pennsylvania Abolition Society, 1790–1803, Historical Society of Pennsylvania, pp. 112, 220.

4. Brissot de Warville, *New Travels in the United States*, pp. 282–83.

5. Charles H. Wesley, *Negro Labor in the United States, 1850–1925* (New York, 1927), pp. 30–32, 37–39, 42–50; *Proceedings of the Colored National Convention . . . Philadelphia, October 16th, 17th and 18th, 1855* (Salem, N.J., 1856), pp. 19–24; *Stimpson's Boston Directory* (Boston, 1840), pp. 445–51; *Register of the Trades of the Colored*

People in the City of Philadelphia and Districts (Philadelphia, 1838), pp. 3–8; *Statistics of the Colored People of Philadelphia* (Philadelphia, 1856), pp. 13–15; *Douglass' Monthly,* March, 1859; Robert Ernst, "The Economic Status of New York City Negroes, 1850–1863," *Negro History Bulletin,* XII (March, 1949), 139–41, 142 n., 143 n.

6. *Pennsylvania Constitutional Debates of 1837–38,* IX, 364.

7. A New York Merchant, *The Negro Labor Question* (New York, 1858), pp. 5–6, 21–22.

8. *African Repository,* IV (1828), 118.

9. *Pennsylvania Constitutional Debates of 1837–38,* V, 457 Senate Document, 20 Cong., 1 sess., No. 178 (April 28, 1828), p. 14.

10. *New England Magazine,* II (1832), 17.

11. Abdy, *Journal of a Residence and Tour,* III, 185.

12. Frederick Douglass, *Life and Times* (Hartford, 1884), pp. 259–63; Philip S. Foner (ed.), *The Life and Writings of Frederick Douglass* (4 vols.; New York, 1950–55), I, 24, II, 234.

13. *North Star,* January 21, 28, 1848.

14. John Fowler, *Journal of a Tour in the State of New York* (London, 1831), p. 218; Kenneth and Anna M. Roberts (eds.), *Moreau de St. Mery's American Journey* (New York, 1947), pp. 302–3; James Stirling, *Letters from the Slave States* (London, 1857), p. 55; *Minutes and Proceedings of the Fourth Annual Convention for the Improvement of the Free People of Colour in the United States* (New York, 1834), p. 27; *North Star,* April 10, 1851; *Frederick Douglass' Paper,* May 18, 1855; Carl D. Arfwedson, *The United States and Canada in 1832, 1833, and 1834* (2 vols.; London, 1834), I, 239.

15. Charles Mackay, *Life and Liberty in America* (2 vols.; London, 1859), II, 45–46.

16. Samuel D. Hastings to Lewis Tappan, August 19, 1842, Tappan Papers, Library of Congress; *The Liberator,* September 20, 1834.

17. *Colored American,* September 16, 1837; Abdy, *Journal of a Residence and Tour,* III, 318 n.

18. *Frederick Douglass' Paper,* June 26, 1851; *The [12th] Annual Report of the American and Foreign Anti-Slavery Society* (New York, 1852), p. 21; Wesley, *Negro Labor in the United States,* pp. 57, 73–74.

19. Ernst, "The Economic Status of New York City Negroes," p. 132; Ohio Anti-Slavery Society, *Condition of the People of Color,* p. 8.

20. *Frederick Douglass' Paper,* February 2, 16, 1855; Wesley, *Negro Labor in the United States,* pp. 79–80; Albon P. Man, Jr., "Labor Competition and the New York Draft Riots of 1863," *Journal of Negro History,* XXXVI (1951), 393–94. See also Abdy, *Journal of a Residence and Tour,* I, 116.

21. Abdy, *Journal of a Residence and Tour*, III, 246–47; *The Liberator*, February 15, 1834; *California Constitutional Debates of 1849*, pp. 49, 138, 144, 148, 333.

22. *Minutes of the Eighteenth Session of the American Convention for Promoting the Abolition of Slavery, and Improving the Condition of the African Race* (Philadelphia, 1824), p. 13; Carter G. Woodson (ed.), *The Mind of the Negro as Reflected in Letters Written During the Crisis, 1800–1860* (Washington, 1926), p. 225.

23. Francis J. Grund, *The Americans in Their Moral, Social, and Political Relations* (2 vols.; London, 1837), II, 314, 321–22.

24. Oscar Handlin, *Boston's Immigrants, 1790–1865* (Cambridge, 1941), p. 100; Mary C. Crawford, *Romantic Days in Old Boston* (Boston, 1922), pp. 93–94; John Daniels, *In Freedom's Birthplace: A Study of the Boston Negroes* (Boston and New York, 1914), p. 17; Richard Wade, "The Negro in Cincinnati, 1800–1830," *Journal of Negro History*, XXXIX (1954), p. 44; Robert Ernst, *Immigrant Life in New York City, 1825–1863* (New York, 1949), pp. 40–41; Robert Collyer, *Lights and Shadows of American Life* (Boston, 1836), pp. 6–7; *A Statistical Inquiry into the Condition of the People of Colour, of the City and Districts of Philadelphia* (Philadelphia, 1849), pp. 31–41.

25. [William T. Thompson], *Major Jones's Sketches of Travel* (Philadelphia, 1848), pp. 103–4. See also [William Bobo], *Glimpses of New-York City* (Charleston, 1852), pp. 94–97, 126–30.

26. Ernst, *Immigrant Life in New York City*, p. 238.

27. *Statistical Inquiry into the Condition of the People of Colour, of the City and Districts of Philadelphia*, pp. 34–36.

28. William Bentley, *Diary* (4 vols.; Salem, 1905–14), II, 34; *The Liberator*, February 15, 1834; *Indiana Constitutional Debates of 1850*, I, 446.

29. Abdy, *Journal of a Residence and Tour*, I, 169; Handlin, *Boston's Immigrants*, p. 102.

30. Wade, "Negro in Cincinnati," p. 45.

31. Martin Delany, *The Condition, Elevation, Emigration, and Destiny of the Colored People of the United States* (Philadelphia, 1852), pp. 92–137; Abram L. Harris, *The Negro Capitalist* (Philadelphia, 1936), pp. 5–23; William C. Nell, *The Colored Patriots of the American Revolution* (Boston, 1855), pp. 327–28; Ernst, "The Economic Status of New York City Negroes," p. 142; *The Liberator*, January 27, 1854, July 2, 1858; C. J. Furness, "Walt Whitman Looks at Boston," *New England Quarterly*, I (1928), p. 356.

32. *Colored American*, June 5, 26, July 10, 1841.

33. Henry B. Fearon, *Sketches of America* (London, 1818), pp. 58–60. See also Issac Candler, *A Summary View of America* (London, 1824), p. 284.

34. *Ohio Colored Convention of 1852*, p. 6.

35. *Statistical Inquiry into the Condition of the People of Colour, of the City and Districts of Philadelphia*, p. 31.

36. Joseph W. Wilson, *Sketches of the Higher Classes of Colored Society in Philadelphia* (Philadelphia, 1841), pp. 47–48.

37. Alexander Mackay, *The Western World; or, Travels in the United States in 1846–47* (3 vols.; London, 1850), I, 132–33.

38. John Cummings, *Negro Population in the United States, 1790–1915* (Washington, D.C., 1918), p. 210.

39. M. H. Freeman, "The Educational Wants of the Free Colored People," *Anglo-African Magazine*, I (April, 1859), 116–19.

40. Wilson, *Sketches of the Higher Classes*, pp. 95–97.

41. *Ibid.*, pp. 54, 56, 60.

42. John Howison, *Sketches of Upper Canada . . . and Some Recollections of the United States of America* (Edinburgh, 1821), pp. 312–13; Arfwedson, *United States and Canada*, I, 27; Francis Lieber, *Letters to a Gentleman in Germany* (Philadelphia, 1834), p. 68; John M. Duncan, *Travels through Part of the United States and Canada in 1818 and 1819* (2 vols.; New York, 1823), I, 60; Edward D. Seeber (ed.), *Edouard de Montule Travels in America, 1816–1817* (Bloomington, Ind., 1951), p. 181; Edward Marryat, *A Diary in America* (3 vols.; London, 1839), I, 294.

43. Pennsylvania Anti-Slavery Society, *Address to the Coloured People of the State of Pennsylvania* (Philadelphia, 1837), p. 6; Henry Highland Garnet, *The Past and the Present Condition, and the Destiny, of the Colored Race* (Troy, N.Y., 1848), p. 19.

The Church and the Negro

1. See, for example, *Colored American*, edited by the Reverend Samuel Cornish, January 28, February 4, 11, 1837.

2. Robert A. Warner, *New Haven Negroes, A Social History* (New Haven, 1940), pp. 92–94; Robert A. Warner, "Amos Gerry Beman—1812–1874: A Memoir on a Forgotten Leader," *Journal of Negro History*, XXII (1937), 200–221.

3. Richard Allen, *Life, Experience, and Gospel Labors* (Philadelphia, 1887), pp. 14–15; William Douglass, *Annals of the First African Church in the USA, now styled the African Episcopal Church of St. Thomas, Philadelphia* (Philadelphia, 1862), p. 11; Charles H. Wesley, *Richard Allen* (Washington, D.C., 1935), pp. 52–53.

4. Wesley, *Richard Allen*, pp. 59–68; W. E. Du Bois, *The Philadelphia Negro* (Philadelphia, 1899), pp. 19–20; L. H. Butterfield (ed.), *Letters of Benjamin Rush* (2 vols.; Princeton, 1951), I, 608.

5. Butterfield (ed.), *Letters of Benjamin Rush*, I, 600, 602, 608, 620–21, 624, II, 636, 639; George W. Corner (ed.), *The Autobiography of Ben-*

jamin Rush (Princeton, 1948), pp. 202–3, 228–29; Wesley, *Richard Allen*, pp. 69–71.

6. Wesley, *Richard Allen*, pp. 71–73, 90–91; Du Bois, *The Philadelphia Negro*, pp. 21–22; *Colored American*, October 14, 1837.

7. Wesley, *Richard Allen*, pp. 86–91, 134–41, 150–57; Carter G. Woodson, *The History of the Negro Church* (2d ed.; Washington, D.C., 1945), pp. 65–66, 87.

8. Woodson, *History of the Negro Church*, pp. 73–78, 81–84.

9. William R. Staples, *Annals of the Town of Providence* (Providence, 1843), p. 490.

The Emancipation of the Negro Abolitionist

1. James Forten to William Lloyd Garrison, March 21, 1831, Garrison Papers, Boston Public Library.

2. Martin R. Delany, *The Condition, Elevation, Emigration, and Destiny of the Colored People of the United States* (Philadelphia, 1852), p. 27.

3. Garrison to Samuel Joseph May, February 14, 1831, Garrison Papers.

4. Theodore Weld to Gerrit Smith, October 23 [1839], in Gilbert H. Barnes and Dwight L. Dumond, eds., *Letters of Theodore Dwight Weld, Angelina Grimké Weld and Sarah Grimké, 1822–1844* (2 vols., New York, 1934), II, 811; John A. Collins to Garrison, January 18, 1842, quoted in Philip S. Foner, *The Life and Writings of Frederick Douglass* (4 vols., New York, 1950–55), I, 46.

5. See Leon F. Litwack, *North of Slavery: The Negro in the Free States, 1790–1860* (Chicago, 1961), pp. 216–22.

6. Sarah Forten to Angelina Grimké, April 15, 1837, in Barnes and Dumond, eds., *Weld-Grimké Letters*, I, 380.

7. *Address of the Rev. Theodore S. Wright before the Convention of the New York State Antislavery Society, . . . held at Utica, Sept. 20, 1837,* in Carter G. Woodson, ed., *Negro Orators and Their Orations* (Washington, D.C., 1925), p. 91.

8. William G. Allen to Garrison, June 20, 1853, in *The Liberator*, July 22, 1853.

9. *Colored American*, November 4, 1837.

10. *Ibid.*, July 28, 1838.

11. *The* [12th] *Annual Report of the American and Foreign Anti-Slavery Society, presented at New York, May 11, 1852* (New York, 1852), pp. 29–30.

12. Charles L. Reason, "The Colored People's 'Industrial College,'" in Julia Griffiths, ed., *Autographs for Freedom* (Second Series, Auburn, Rochester, 1854), pp. 12–15.

13. *Frederick Douglass' Paper*, May 18, 1855.

14. *Ibid.*, March 4, 1853.

15. Delany, *The Condition, Elevation, Emigration, and Destiny of the Colored People,* p. 28.

16. *Colored American,* October 5, 1839.

17. *Ibid.*, August 26, September 2, 9, 1837; March 15, 1838.

18. *Ibid.*, October 7, 1837.

19. *Ibid.*, October 5, 1839.

20. New York *National Anti-Slavery Standard,* July 2, 1840.

21. Reprinted in Woodson, ed., *Negro Orators and Their Orations,* pp. 150–57.

22. Henry Highland Garnet to Mrs. Maria W. Chapman, November 17, 1843, in Carter G. Woodson, ed., *The Mind of the Negro as Reflected in Letters Written During the Crisis, 1800–1860* (Washington, D.C., 1926), p. 194.

23. *Minutes and Address of the State Convention of the Colored Citizens of Ohio, convened at Columbus, January 10th, 11th, 12th, and 13th, 1849* (Oberlin, 1849), p. 18.

24. Frederick Douglass, *Life and Times of Frederick Douglass* (Boston, 1892), p. 322; see also Foner, *Life and Writings of Frederick Douglass,* II, 52–53, 149–50, 152–53, 155–57.

25. Foner, *ibid.*, pp. 350, 425.

26. Douglass, *Life and Times,* p. 269.

27. *Ibid.*, pp. 269–70.

28. Frederick Douglass to Maria W. Chapman, March 29, 1846, in Foner, *Life and Writings of Frederick Douglass,* I, 144.

29. Douglass, *Life and Times,* pp. 282–83. See also Douglass to Chapman, September 10, 1843, in Foner, *Life and Writings of Frederick Douglass,* I, 110–12.

30. *The North Star,* December 3, 1847.

31. Douglass to Gerrit Smith, August 18, 1853, in Foner, *Life and Writings of Frederick Douglass,* II, 270.

32. *Address of the Rev. Theodore S. Wright . . . Sept. 20, 1837,* in Woodson, ed., *Negro Orators and Their Orations,* pp. 90–91.

33. *Colored American,* May 18, 1839.

34. *Douglass' Monthly,* November 1860.

35. *Frederick Douglass' Paper,* April 5, 1856.

36. *The Liberator,* July 13, 1860.

37. *Douglass' Monthly,* October 1860.

38. See, for example, the speeches of Dr. John S. Rock and Robert Purvis, as reported in *The Liberator,* May 22, 1857; March 16, May 18, 1860, and H. Ford Douglass, in Herbert Aptheker, ed., *A Documentary His-*

tory of the Negro People in the United States (New York, 1951), pp. 366–68; *Proceedings of a Convention of the Colored Men of Ohio, held in the City of Cincinnati, on the 23d, 24th, 25th and 26th Days of November, 1858* (Cincinnati, 1858), pp. 6–7; *Proceedings of the Second Annual Convention of the Colored Citizens of the State of California* (San Francisco, 1856), pp. 14, 19.

39. *Frederick Douglass' Paper,* June 2, 1854.

40. *The Liberator,* March 16, 1860.

41. Delany, *The Condition, Elevation, Emigration, and Destiny of the Colored People,* p. 155; Delany to Garrison, May 14, 1852, in Woodson, ed., *Mind of the Negro,* p. 293.

42. *Proceedings of the National Emigration Convention of Colored People; held at Cleveland, Ohio, . . . the 24th, 25th, and 26th of August, 1854* (Pittsburgh, 1854), pp. 5, 40.

43. "A Word to Our People," *The Anglo-African Magazine,* I (1859), pp. 293–98.

44. "Apology," *ibid.,* p. 1.

45. *Frederick Douglass' Paper,* May 18, 1855.

The General Strike

1. *Public Opinion Before and After the Civil War,* p. 4.

2. George W. Williams, *History of the Negro Race in America from 1619 to 1880* (New York, 1883), II, p. 244.

3. Ellis P. Oberholtzer, *Abraham Lincoln* (Philadelphia, 1904), p. 263.

4. *Results of Emancipation in the United States of America* by a Committee of the American Freedman's Union Commission in 1867, p. 6.

5. *Journal of Negro History,* X, p. 134.

6. John Eaton, *Grant, Lincoln and the Freedmen* (New York, 1907), p. 2.

7. *Results of Emancipation in the United States of America* by a Committee of the American Freedman's Union Commission in 1867, p. 21.

8. Junius H. Browne, *Four Years in Secessia* (Chicago, 1865), p. 368.

9. Samuel A. Ashe and Lyon G. Tyler, *Secession, Insurrection of the Negroes, and Northern Incendiarism* (Richmond, 1933), p. 12.

10. Eaton, *Grant, Lincoln and the Freedmen,* pp. 2, 3, 19, 22, 134.

11. Eaton, *Grant, Lincoln and the Freedmen,* p. 22.

12. Eaton, *Grant, Lincoln and the Freedmen,* p. 166.

The Negro and Politics, 1870–1875

1. Mississippi *Weekly Pilot,* August 12, 1870; John R. Lynch, *Some Historical Errors of James Ford Rhodes* (Boston and New York, 1922), p. 91.

2. M. G. Abney, "Reconstruction in Pontotoc County," *Publications of the Mississippi Historical Society* (hereafter cited as *P.M.H.S.*), XI, 234, 235.

3. J. S. McNeily, "War and Reconstruction in Mississippi," *Publications of the Mississippi Historical Society, Centenary Series* (hereafter cited or *P.M.H.S.C.S.*), II, 420; J. L. Power, "The Black and Tan Convention," *P.M.H.S*, III, 79; Ruth Watkins, "Reconstruction in Marshall County," *P.M.H.S.*, XII, 163.

4. Adelbert Ames to J. W. Garner, January 17, 1900, J. W. Garner Papers, Mississippi State Archives.

5. *Senate Reports,* no. 527, 44th Congress, 1st session, "Documentary Evidence," p. 62.

6. Charles Nordhoff, *The Cotton States in the Spring and Summer of 1875* (New York, 1876), p. 77.

7. M. G. Abney, *op. cit.,* XI, 234.

8. Hinds County *Gazette,* May 2, 1877, July 7, 1883; C. Nordhoff, *op. cit.,* p. 77.

9. A. K. McClure, *The South: Its Industrial, Financial, and Political Condition* (Philadelphia, 1886), pp. 113, 115–116.

10. Hiram R. Revels, "Autobiography," Carter G. Woodson Papers, Library of Congress; Samuel D. Smith, *The Negro in Congress 1870–1901* (Chapel Hill, 1943), pp. 12–14; W. J. Simmons, *Men of Mark* (Cleveland, 1887), pp. 948–949; Benjamin Brawley, *Negro Builders and Heroes* (Chapel Hill, 1937), p. 125; *Dictionary of American Biography,* XV, 513.

11. H. R. Revels, *op. cit.;* S. D. Smith, *op. cit.,* pp. 19, 23.

12. Hinds County *Gazette,* October 2, 1872.

13. H. R. Revels, *op. cit.;* S. D. Smith, *op. cit.,* pp. 23–25; A. A. Taylor, "Negro Congressmen a Generation After," *Journal of Negro History,* VII (1922), 131–132.

14. B. Brawley, *op. cit.,* p. 127.

15. S. D. Smith, *op. cit.,* pp. 25–27; B. Brawley, *op. cit.,* pp. 127–128; Robert R. Moton, *What the Negro Thinks* (New York, 1929), p. 160.

16. Franklin A. Montgomery, *Reminiscences of a Mississippian in Peace and War* (Cincinnati, 1901), p, 279.

17. S. D. Smith, *op. cit.,* pp. 27–41.

18. *Ibid.,* p. 41; Jackson, *Weekly Clarion,* January 27, 1881.

19. Raymond *Gazette,* May 19, 1883.

20. S. D. Smith, *op. cit.,* pp. 85–86; W. J. Simmons, *Men of Mark,* pp. 1042–1043; A. A. Taylor, *op. cit.,* VII, 127.

21. Jackson *Clarion,* April 24, 1873; John R. Lynch, *The Facts of Reconstruction* (New York, 1913), p. 66.

22. Samuel D. Smith, *op. cit.,* p. 86.

23. F. A. Montgomery, *op. cit.,* p. 292.

24. S. D. Smith, *op. cit.,* pp. 109–111; Jackson *Clarion,* March 17, 1881.

25. S. D. Smith, *op. cit.,* pp. 111–112; J. R. Lynch, *op. cit.,* pp. 235–238, 278; U.S. Army *Register,* 1914, p. 565.

26. Personal letter from John R. Lynch, Chicago, January 3, 1939.

27. Mississippi *Weekly Pilot,* September 25, 1875; R. Watkins, *op. cit.,* XII, 173.

28. B. Brawley, *op. cit.,* p. 128.

29. Hinds County *Gazette,* August 9, 1882.

30. R. Watkins, *op. cit.,* XII, 173.

31. J. R. Lynch, *op. cit.,* pp. 74–75.

32. Mississippi *House Journal,* 1878, p. 9.

33. Forrest Cooper, "Reconstruction in Scott County," *P.M.H.S.,* XIII, 164; Ruth Watkins, *op. cit.,* XII, 172; Julia C. Brown, "Reconstruction in Yalobusha and Grenada Counties," *P.M.H.S.,* XII, 242, 260; E. F. Puckett, "Reconstruction in Monroe County," *P.M.H.S.,* XI, 130; C. H. Brough, "The Clinton Riot," *P.M.H.S.,* VI, 62; Fred Z. Browne, "Reconstruction in Oktibbeha County," *P.M.H.S.,* XIII, 278; J. S. McNeily, "The Enforcement Act of 1871 and the Ku-Klux Klan in Mississippi," *P.M.H.S.,* IX, 131; Elizabeth Caldwell, "Reconstruction in Yazoo County," unpublished master's thesis, University of North Carolina, 1931, pp. 35–36; A. T. Morgan, *Yazoo* (Washington, 1884), pp. 495–496; Hinds County *Gazette,* December 15, 1875; Mississippi *Weekly Pilot,* November 19, 1870; *Senate Reports,* no. 527, 44th Congress, 1st session, pp. 119, 437–438.

34. Hattie Magee, "Reconstruction in Lawrence and Jeff Davis Counties," *P.M.H.S.,* XI, 190, 192; J. Kendel, *op. cit.,* XIII, 237, 238; Hinds County *Gazette,* July 10, 1868.

35. Hinds County *Gazette,* July 10, 1868.

36. E. F. Puckett, *op. cit.,* XI, 128.

37. *Senate Reports,* no. 527, 44th Congress, 1st session, pp. 1707–1708.

38. R. Watkins, *op. cit.,* XII, 185.

39. H. Magee, *op. cit.,* XI, 186.

40. John W. Kyle, "Reconstruction in Panola County," *P.M.H.S.,* XIII, 51, 72; Jackson *Daily Times,* November 1, March 3, 1876.

41. Fred Z. Browne, *op. cit.,* XIII, 286–287.

42. Jackson *Daily Times,* August 26, October 31, 1876.

43. J. C. Brown, *op. cit.,* XII, 234; J. W. Kyle, *op. cit.,* XIII, 74.

44. J. C. Brown, *op. cit.,* XII, 234.

45. Fred M. Witty, "Reconstruction in Carroll and Montgomery Counties," *P.M.H.S.*, X, 120.

46. Mississippi *Weekly Pilot,* October 1, 1870; Hinds County *Gazette,* October 5, November 2, 1870; J. S. McNeily, "War and Reconstruction in Mississippi," *P.M.H.S.C.S.*, II, 393.

47. Hinds County *Gazette,* September 6, 1871.

48. Jackson *Clarion-Ledger,* November 27, 1890.

49. Hiram Revels' statement in his "Autobiography" that John R. Lynch served as mayor of Natchez seems to be an error.

50. John R. Lynch, *The Facts of Reconstruction,* p. 92.

51. Goodspeed Publishing Company, *Biographical and Historical Memoirs of Mississippi* (Chicago, 1891), II, 174.

52. Edward King, *The Great South* (Hartford, 1875), p. 293; Natchez *Tri-Weekly Democrat and Courier,* August 13, 1873.

53. J. W. Garner, *Reconstruction in Mississippi* (New York, 1901), pp. 329–330.

54. *Report on the Condition of Affairs in the Late Insurrectionary States,* "Mississippi," I, 479.

55. Jackson *Clarion-Ledger,* December 26, 1889.

56. *Senate Miscellaneous Documents,* no. 166, 50th Congress, 1st session, p. 276.

57. J. C. Brown, *op. cit.,* XII, 217, 269; Lee Richardson and Thomas D. Godman, *In and Around Vicksburg* (Vicksburg, 1890), p. 97.

58. J. C. Brown, *op. cit.,* XIII, 270; Forrest Cooper, *op. cit.,* XIII, 164; Hattie Magee, *op. cit.,* XI, 199.

59. H. Magee, *op. cit.,* XI, 175.

60. J. W. Garner, *op. cit.,* p. 309.

61. *Senate Reports,* no. 527, 44th Congress, 1st session, pp. 1704, 876, 616; J. W. Garner, *op. cit.,* p. 310. Illiteracy was fairly common among the officials of the hill counties before the war. E. C. Coleman, "Reconstruction in Attala County," *P.M.H.S.*, X, 149–150.

62. John R. Lynch, *op. cit.,* p. 93.

63. *Ibid.,* p. 17.

64. Irby C. Nichols, "Reconstruction in De Soto County," *P.M.H.S.*, XI, 307; *Senate Reports,* no. 527, 44th Congress, 1st session, p. 1446.

65. J. W. Garner, *op. cit.,* p. 306.

66. I. C. Nichols, *op. cit.,* p. 307.

67. *Senate Miscellaneous Documents,* no. 45, 44th Congress, 2d session, pp. 156–157.

68. Jackson *Weekly Clarion,* July 21, 1881.

69. Charles Nordhoff, *The Cotton States,* p. 79.

70. *Senate Reports,* no. 527, 44th Congress, 1st session, "Documentary Evidence," p. 85.

71. Hinds County *Gazette,* December 29, February 24, 1875, April 5, 1876, July 31, 1878, July 14, 1880, August 3, 1881; Jackson *Weekly Clarion,* July 14, 1881.

72. Natchez *Daily Courier,* November 8, 1866; John R. Lynch, *Some Historical Errors of James Ford Rhodes,* pp. 17–18.

73. Mississippi *Weekly Pilot,* January 1, 23, 1875; J. W. Garner, *op. cit.,* p. 313.

74. Vicksburg *Times and Republican,* February 2, 1873.

75. W. H. Braden, "Reconstruction in Lee County," *P.M.H.S.,* X, 136.

76. Mississippi *Weekly Pilot,* October 23, 1875.

77. J. H. Jones, "Reconstruction in Wilkinson County," *P.M.H.S.,* VIII, 164.

78. F. M. Witty, *op. cit.,* X, 119, 120, 122; E. C. Coleman, *op. cit.,* X, 150, 155, 156, 161; W. H. Braden, *op. cit.,* 136; R. Watkins, *op. cit.,* XII, 183, 208; H. Magee, *op. cit.,* XI, 181.

79. C. Nordhoff, *op. cit.,* p. 76; Hinds County *Gazette,* July 31, 1872.

80. J. W. Garner, *op. cit.,* p. 293; Mississippi *Weekly Pilot,* March 6, 1875.

81. C. Nordhoff, *op. cit.,* pp. 76, 81–82; Hinds County *Gazette,* April 21, 1875; Mississippi *Weekly Pilot,* August 21, 1875; Vicksburg *Herald,* August 17, 1875; Hinds County *Gazette,* June 19, 1878, February 3, 1883.

82. J. S. McNeily, "War and Reconstruction in Mississippi," *P.M.H.S.C.S.,* II, 381; John R. Lynch, *The Facts of Reconstruction,* pp. 44–45.

83. J. W. Garner Papers, Mississippi State Archives, Alexander Warner to J. W. Garner, May 4, 1900; J. W. Garner, *op. cit.,* p. 295; *Senate Reports,* no. 527, 44th Congress, 1st session, p. 795.

84. J. W. Garner, *op. cit.,* p. 281; Dunbar Rowland, *History of Mississippi, the Heart of the South* (Chicago, 1929), II, 176; J. S. McNeily, *op. cit.,* II, 426.

85. Mississippi *House Journal,* 1870, pp. 56–57.

86. Hinds County *Gazette,* November 1, 1867, July 5, August 9, 30, 1871.

87. *Appleton's Cyclopedia,* 1873, p. 514.

88. Mississippi *Senate Journal,* 1874, pp. 24–25.

89. Edward King, *The Great South,* pp. 314–315.

90. Mississippi *Session Laws,* 1875.

91. Mississippi *Senate Journal,* 1872, *Appendix,* p. 125.

92. Mississippi Auditor of Public Accounts, *Report,* 1876.

93. J. W. Garner, *op. cit.,* pp. 322–323.

94. Hinds County *Gazette,* March 22, 1890; J. Dunbar Rowland, *History of Mississippi,* II, 242–245; J. D. Rowland, *Encyclopedia of Mississippi History* (Madison, 1907), II, 743–744.

Mudsills and Bottom Rails

1. *Tenth Census, 1880,* V, *Cotton Production,* "Mississippi," 154–55; Tennessee," 104–105, "Louisiana," 83–84; VI, *Cotton Production,* "Georgia," 172–73.

2. Quoted in Glenn W. Rainey, "The Negro and the Independent Movement in Georgia" (Manuscript in possession of author), Chap. I.

3. Robert P. Brooks, *The Agrarian Revolution in Georgia 1865–1912,* University of Wisconsin *Bulletin* No. 639 (Madison, 1914), 44, 122.

4. United States Census Bureau, *Negro Population in the United States, 1790–1915* (Washington, 1918), 571–72.

5. *Tenth Census, 1880,* V, *Cotton Production,* 60–66; VI, *Cotton Production,* 154–55.

6. Montgomery *Advertiser,* August 12, 1881.

7. *Tenth Census, 1880,* V, *Cotton Production,* "Arkansas," 104–105; "Louisiana," 83–84; "Mississippi," 154–55; "Tennessee," 104–105; "Texas," 160–61; VI, *Cotton Production,* "Alabama," 154–55; "Florida," 70–71; "Georgia," 172–73; "South Carolina," 60–66.

8. Philip A. Bruce, *The Plantation Negro as a Freeman* (New York, 1889), 200–201.

9. The exception was the "Exodus" of 1879. This has been treated in E. Merton Coulter, *The South During Reconstruction 1865–1877* (Baton Rouge, 1947), 100–101. On Negro migration, see Vernon Lane Wharton, *The Negro in Mississippi 1865–1890* (Chapel Hill, 1947), 106–24.

10. *Tenth Census, 1880,* VI, *Cotton Production,* "Alabama," 64.

11. A. W. S. Anderson, in *Proceedings of the Third Semi-Annual Session of the Alabama State Agricultural Society* (Montgomery, 1888), 93–95.

12. Quoted in Wharton, *Negro in Mississippi,* 121.

13. Walter G. Cooper, *The Piedmont Region* . . . (Atlanta, 1895), 77.

14. Diary of J. L. M. Curry, January 13, 1877, in Curry Papers.

15. Wharton, *Negro in Mississippi,* 232. The evolution of "caste as a method of social control" is admirably worked out by this author.

16. Belton O'Neall Townsend, "South Carolina Society," in *Atlantic Monthly,* XXXIX (1877), 676. Commenting in 1879 on the "perfect equality" of races in Southern tramcars, a member of Parliament wrote: "I was, I confess, surprised to see how completely this is the case; even an English Radical is a little taken aback at first." Sir George Campbell, *White and Black* . . . (New York, 1879), 195.

17. George Washington Cable, *The Silent South* (New York, 1928), 85–86. Cable was quoting the Charleston *News and Courier* with regard to South Carolina. The observation on Virginia custom is his own.

18. Richmond *Dispatch,* October 13, 1886.

19. Editorial, *Southland* (Salisbury, N.C.), I (1890), 166–67.

20. The Tennessee legislature passed an act in 1875 abrogating the common law and releasing common carriers and other public servants from serving anyone they chose not to serve. A Federal circuit court declared this unconstitutional in 1880. An act of 1881 required separate first-class accommodations for Negroes, but left the two races unsegregated in second-class coaches. Stanley J. Folmsbee, "The Origin of the First 'Jim Crow' Law," in *Journal of Southern History,* XV (1949), 235–47.

21. Franklin Johnson, *Development of State Legislation Concerning the Free Negro* (New York, 1919), 15, 54, 62–207; Gilbert T. Stephenson, *Race Distinctions in American Law* (New York, 1910), 216–17.

22. *Report of the United States Commissioner of Labor, 1886, Convict Labor* (Washington, 1887), especially pp. 72–79. For a dispassionate account by a warden, see J. C. Powell, *The American Siberia; or, Fourteen Years' Experience in a Southern Convict Camp* (London, 1891), *passim;* Wharton, *Negro in Mississippi,* 237–40.

23. *Biennial Report of the Inspectors of the Alabama Penitentiary from September 30, 1880 to September 30, 1882* (Montgomery, 1882), *passim.*

24. Jackson *Clarion,* July 13, 1887.

25. Little Rock *Daily Gazette,* March 24, 27, 1888; Powell, *American Siberia,* 22.

26. Georgia *House Journal,* 1879, Pt. I, 386–91.

27. Fletcher M. Green, "Some Aspects of the Southern Convict Lease System in the Southern States," in Fletcher M. Green (ed.), *Essays in Southern History Presented to Joseph Gregoire de Roulhac Hamilton . . .* (Chapel Hill, 1949), 122.

28. Georgia *House Journal,* 1879, Pt. I, 386–91.

29. Robert McKee to Boyd, February 3, 1882, in McKee Papers.

30. Boyd to McKee, February 26, 1883; also Morgan to McKee, March 15, 1882; McKee to Thomas R. Roulhac, February 25, 1883, *ibid.*

The Mississippi Plan as the American Way

1. A symposium, "Ought the Negro to be Disfranchised," in *North American Review,* CXXVIII (1879), 231–32, 241–42. "He will never be disfranchised," wrote Bishop Atticus G. Haygood in *Our Brother in Black: His Freedom and His Future* (Nashville, 1881), 81.

2. Mobile *Register,* quoted in Jackson *Clarion-Ledger,* June 23, 1892.

3. . . . Virginia, Alabama, and Georgia passed new election codes after 1892 which put new restrictions on the voters.

4. Southern press, quoted in Ralph C. McDanel, *The Virginia Constitutional Convention of 1901–1902,* in Johns Hopkins University *Studies in Historical and Political Science,* XLVI (Baltimore, 1928), pp. 9–10; in William A. Mabry, "Louisiana Politics and the 'Grandfather Clause,'" in *North Carolina Historical Review* (Raleigh), XIII (1936), 292; and in Malcolm G. McMillan, "A History of the Alabama Constitution of 1901" (M.A. thesis, University of Alabama, 1940), 58.

5. 170 U.S. 213 (1898).

6. John Hope, "Negro Suffrage in the States whose Constitutions Have Not Been Specifically Revised," in *American Negro Academy Occasional Papers,* No. 11 (Washington, 1905), 53.

7. Charles B. Spahr, *America's Working People* (New York, 1900), 104.

8. Another Negro the same year published a book in which he concluded that "Our failure [as voters] . . . was humiliating and complete all along the line" and that "white leadership is preferable." Jerome R. Riley, *The Philosophy of Negro Suffrage* (Hartford, 1895), 19, 34.

9. *Nation,* LXVI (1898), 398–99.

10. *Report of the Hawaiian Commission,* in *Senate Documents,* 55 Cong., 3 Sess., No. 16, pp. 149–50.

11. Boston *Evening Transcript,* January 14, 1899.

12. Anonymous, "Reconstruction and Disfranchisement," in *Atlantic Monthly,* LXXXVIII (1901), 435.

13. John W. Burgess, *Reconstruction and the Constitution, 1866–1876* (New York, 1902), 298.

14. William A. Dunning, *Essays on the Civil War and Reconstruction and Related Topics* (New York, 1898), 250–51.

15. Emmett O'Neal, in *Official Proceedings of the Constitutional Convention of the State of Alabama, May 21st, 1901 to September 3d, 1901 . . .* (Wetumpka, Ala., 1941), III, 2783. See also, Alfred P. Thom, quoting Dunning and *Atlantic Monthly,* in *Report of the Proceedings and Debates of the Constitutional Convention, State of Virginia . . . June 12, 1901, to June 26, 1902* (Richmond, 1906), II, 2966–67; George H. Rountree, quoted in Raleigh *News and Observer,* February 18, 1899.

16. S. S. Calhoon, "Causes and Events that Led to the Calling of the Constitutional Convention of 1890," in *Mississippi Historical Society Publications* (Oxford), VI (1902), 109.

17. Chester H. Rowell, *Digest of Contested Election Cases . . .* (Washington, 1901).

18. *Proceedings of the Constitutional Convention of . . . Alabama,* 1901, III, 2788–89.

19. New Orleans *Times-Democrat,* January 11, 1898. The same paper of May 8, 1892, referred to Louisiana as "the head center of ballot box stuffing."

20. Quoted in Richmond *Virginia Sun,* June 14, 1893.

21. Delegate Albert P. Gillespie, in *Proceedings and Debates of the Constitutional Convention . . . of Virginia,* 1901–1902, II, 3014.

22. Delegate William A. Handley, in *Proceedings of the Constitutional Convention of . . . Alabama,* 1901, III, 2276–77.

23. Jackson *Clarion-Ledger,* January 26, 1898.

24. Okolona (Miss.) *Chickasaw Messenger,* quoted *ibid.,* March 14, 1889. Using total population as a basis for representation, the white man of the Black Belt often exceeded two and three times the power of his brother in the white counties. Thus eleven Black-Belt counties with a white population of 56,659 were entitled to 144 votes in the Democratic party conventions of Alabama, while eleven white counties with a white population of 61,376 were entitled to only 44 votes. Albert B. Moore, *History of Alabama* (University, Ala., 1934), 582 n.

25. D. C. O'Flaherty, in *Proceedings and Debates of the Constitutional Convention . . . of Virginia,* 1901–1902, I, 140.

26. Robert J. Love, in *Proceedings of the Constitutional Convention of . . . Alabama,* 1901, III, 2826.

27. *Ibid.,* 260; McMillan, "History of the Alabama Constitution," 93–94.

28. J. S. McNeilly, "History of the Measures Submitted to the Committee on Elective Franchise, Apportionment, and Elections in the Constitutional Convention of 1890," in *Mississippi Historical Society Publications,* VI (1902), 134–35; Vicksburg *Commercial Herald,* quoted in New Orleans *Times-Democrat,* December 18, 1895.

29. See especially, Allen C. Braxton of Staunton, in *Proceedings and Debates of the Constitutional Convention . . . of Virginia,* 1901–1902, II, 2451; other delegates, *ibid.,* 2996, 3007.

30. *Proceedings of the Constitutional Convention of . . . Alabama,* 1901, I, 71.

31. J. A. P. Campbell to editor, Jackson *Clarion-Ledger,* April 3, 1890.

32. *Proceedings of the Constitutional Convention of . . . Alabama,* 1901, III, 2789.

33. *Proceedings and Debates of the Constitutional Convention . . . of Virginia,* 1901–1902, II, 2864.

34. Edgar Gardner Murphy, *Problems of the Present South* (New York, 1904), 193 n.

35. New Orleans *Times-Democrat,* January 18, 1898.

36. New Orleans *Daily Picayune,* March 23, 1898.

37. Quoted in Asheville *Gazette,* July 3, 1900.

38. John B. Knox, "Reduction of Representation in the South," in *Outlook,* LXXIX (1905), 171.

39. Possession of taxable property was an alternative qualification in South Carolina, Louisiana, Alabama, and Georgia.

40. David D. Wallace, *The South Carolina Constitution of 1895* (Columbia, 1927), 34.

41. Jackson *Clarion-Ledger,* September 18, 1890. See similar appeal of E. H. Bristow, in letter to editor, *ibid.,* August 14, 1890.

42. Quoted in Jackson *Clarion-Ledger,* September 18, 1890.

43. *Proceedings of the Constitutional Convention of . . . Alabama,* 1901, III, 3137.

44. Newman H. Freeman, *ibid.,* III, 2809–10.

45. John S. Bassett to Herbert B. Adams, February 18, 1899, in W. Stull Holt (ed.), *Historical Scholarship in the United States, 1876–1901: As Revealed in the Correspondence of Herbert B. Adams,* in Johns Hopkins University *Studies in Historical and Political Science,* LVI, No. 4 (Baltimore, 1938), 265.

46. J. F. Rippy (ed.), *F. M. Simmons, Statesman of the New South: Memoirs and Addresses* (Durham, 1936), 24–26.

47. Quoted in Richmond *Times,* November 5, 1898.

48. Raleigh *News and Observer,* February 18, 1899.

49. *Ibid.,* April 19, 1900.

Negro Class Structure and Ideology in the Age of Booker T. Washington

1. The research on which this article was based was greatly facilitated by grants from the American Council of Learned Societies (Advanced Graduate Fellowship, 1952) and from the Morgan State College Faculty Research Committee (1957–1959).

2. E. Franklin Frazier, *Black Bourgeoisie* (Chicago, 1957), Chapter VII; Abram L. Harris, *The Negro as Capitalist* (Philadelphia, 1936); Ralph J. Bunche, "Extended Memorandum on the Programs, Ideologies, Tactics and Achievements of Negro Betterment and Interracial Organizations" (unpublished manuscript prepared for the Carnegie-Myrdal Study of the Negro in America), II, 314.

3. On the role of Negro business and businessmen in the late nineteenth century, see W. E. B. Du Bois, *The Philadelphia Negro* (Philadelphia, 1899), pp. 115–31; Jeffrey R. Brackett, *The Colored People of Maryland Since the War* (Baltimore, 1890), pp. 28–29, 37–39; Du Bois (ed.), *The Negro in Business* (Atlanta University Publications, No. 4, 1899),

passim; St. Clair Drake and Horace Cayton, *Black Metropolis* (New York, 1945), pp. 433–34; *Christian Educator,* V (July, 1894), 167–68; *Proceedings of the National Negro Business League,* 1900 (no imprint); Robert A. Warner, *New Haven Negroes: A Social History* (New Haven, 1940), p. 233; Du Bois, "The Negroes of Farmville, Virginia: A Social Study," *Bulletin of the Department of Labor,* No. 14 (1898), pp. 17–19; Du Bois, "The Negro in the Black Belt: Some Social Sketches," *Bulletin of the Department of Labor,* No. 22 (1899), pp. 403, 407–08, 412, 413, 415; Harris, *op. cit.,* Chaps. III–VIII.

4. Harris, *loc. cit.;* Joseph Pierce, *Negro Business and Business Education* (New York, 1947), Chapter I; Drake and Cayton, *op. cit.,* pp. 434–37; Du Bois (ed.), *Some Efforts of Negroes for Their Own Social Betterment* (Atlanta University Publications, No. 3, 1898), pp. 18–27; Du Bois, *Economic Co-Operation Among Negro Americans* (Atlanta University Publications, No. 12, 1907); Mary White Ovington, *Half a Man* (New York, 1911), Chapter V; George Edmund Haynes, *The Negro at Work in New York City* (New York, 1912), Part II; R. R. Wright, Jr., "The Negro in Philadelphia," Part I, *A.M.E. Church Review,* XXIV (July, 1907), 137–39; *The Negro in Pennsylvania* (Philadelphia, [1909 ?]), pp. 30–33; Booker T. Washington, "Durham, North Carolina: A City of Negro Enterprise," *Independent,* LXX (1911), 542–50; E. Franklin Frazier, "Durham: Capital of the Black Middle Class," in Alain Locke (ed.), *The New Negro* (New York, 1925), pp. 333–40; Ray Stannard Baker, *Following the Color Line* (New York, 1908), pp. 39–44; Warner, *op. cit.,* pp. 233–36; Du Bois, "The Economic Revolution in the South," in Washington and Du Bois, *The Negro in the South* (New York, 1907), pp. 95–101; Annual *Reports* of the National Negro Business League (title and imprint vary), 1900 *et seq.;* Ira De A. Reid, "The Negro in the American Economic System" (unpublished memorandum for the Carnegie-Myrdal Study of the Negro in America, 1940), 3 vols.; E. Franklin Frazier, *Negro Youth at the Crossways* (Washington, 1940), *passim;* Du Bois, *Philadelphia Negro, loc. cit.;* John Daniels, *In Freedom's Birthplace* (Boston, 1914), pp. 362–73.

5. *Annual Report of the Sixteenth Annual Session of the National Negro Business League* (Nashville, 1915), p. 9.

6. The generalizations in the preceding paragraph and the accounts of the following cities (except Boston and Chicago) are based chiefly upon interview materials gathered between 1957 and 1959, supplemented by whatever printed and manuscript sources were available. On Atlanta see August Meier and David Lewis, "History of the Negro Upper Class in Atlanta, Georgia, 1890–1958," *Journal of Negro Education,* XXVIII (Spring, 1959), 130–39. It will be noted that the reconstruction of the history of the Negro class structure differs from that given by Frazier in *Black Bourgeoisie.* See also August Meier, "Some Observations on the Negro Middle Class," *Crisis,* LXIV (October, 1957), 463–64.

7. Andrew F. Hilyer, "Some Facts Relating to the Rich Negroes of Washington" (manuscript in Hilyer Papers, Howard University, Washington, D.C.).

8. Wright, *Negro in Pennsylvania,* pp. 178–79; Wright, "Negroes in Philadelphia," Part I, 29–31, and Part II, *A.M.E. Church Review,* XXIV (October, 1907), 143; Du Bois, *Philadelphia Negro,* pp. 317–19.

9. Drake and Cayton, *op. cit.,* pp. 433–34, 543. On Morris and Williams, interview with Charles S. Johnson, October 19, 1953.

10. Daniels, *op. cit.,* pp. 174–83.

11. For details on the ideologies of these individuals see August Meier, "Negro Thought in the Age of Booker T. Washington: A Study in Racial Ideologies, ca. 1880–1915," (unpublished doctoral dissertation, Columbia University, 1957), *passim.*

12. Baker, *op. cit.,* pp. 218–19.

The Paradox of W. E. B. Du Bois

1. All works cited are by Du Bois unless otherwise stated. The Du Bois Papers have been closed to scholars for some years. All references to letters to and from Du Bois and all references to manuscript materials by Du Bois are to the notes on these materials made by Francis L. Broderick and placed on file at the Schomburg Collection of the New York Public Library.

2. "Strivings of the Negro People," *Atlantic Monthly,* LXXX (Aug., 1897), 194; *Dusk of Dawn* (New York, 1940), 2.

3. "Strivings of the Negro People," 194–95; "Public Rhetoricals," Fisk University, MS [1885–88]; *Dusk of Dawn,* 23–24, 101, 36; "A Vacation Unique," MS, 1889; "What Will the Negro Do?" MS, 1889.

4. New York *Globe,* e.g., Sept. 8, 1883; Fisk *Herald,* V (Dec., 1887), 8 and V (March, 1888), 8–9; "Political Serfdom," MS, 1887; "An Open Letter to the Southern People," MS, 1888 [?]; "What Will the Negro Do?"; "Harvard and the South," MS, 1891; "The Afro-Americans," MS [1894–96]; *Age,* June 13, 1891.

5. *Dusk of Dawn,* 85. Unfortunately the files of the *Age* are not available for the early 1890's.

6. "Harvard and the South"; "The Afro-American"; "The True Meaning of a University," MS, 1894.

7. *Some Efforts of American Negroes For Their Own Social Betterment* (Atlanta University Publications, No. 3, 1898), 43.

8. *The Philadelphia Negro* (Philadelphia, 1899), 325, 388–91, chap. xvii, and *passim.*

9. "Careers Open to College-Bred Negroes," in Du Bois and H. H. Proctor, *Two Addresses* (Nashville, 1898), 7, 12; "The Meaning of Business,"

MS, 1898; quotation at end of paragraph is from resolutions of the Fourth Atlanta University Conference, *The Negro in Business* (AUP No. 4, 1899), 50.

10. Du Bois and others, *Memorial to the Legislature of Georgia Upon the Hardwick Bill,* Pamphlet, 1899, Du Bois Papers; "The Suffrage Fight in Georgia," *Independent,* LX (Nov. 30, 1899), 3226–28.

11. *The Conservation of Races* (American Negro Academy, Occasional Papers No. 2, 1897), 7, 9–13. Nor was Du Bois averse to a considerable number of American Negroes migrating to Africa, uniting for the uplift and economic development of the continent. See "Possibility of Emigration to Congo Free State," Memorial to Paul Hegeman, Belgian Consul-General to the United States [1895–97].

12. "A Rational System of Negro Education," MS [1897–1900]; Du Bois, ed., *The College-Bred Negro* (AUP No. 5, 1900), 29.

13. "The Relations of the Negroes to the Whites of the South" (Annals of the American Academy of Political and Social Science, XVIII, July, 1901), 121–33; "The Case for the Negro," MS, 1901.

14. "The Talented Tenth," in BTW and others, *The Negro Problem* (New York, 1903), 60–61; *The Negro Artisan* (AUP No. 7, 1902), 81; "Of the Training of Black Men," *Atlantic Monthly,* XC (Sept., 1902), 291; "The Talented Tenth," 45, 33–34.

15. Samuel R. Spencer, Jr., *Booker T. Washington and the Negro's Place in American Life* (Boston, 1955), 146, 148–49.

16. "The Evolution of Negro Leadership," *The Dial,* XXXI (July, 1901), 54 (an article which anticipated in several significant respects Du Bois' discussion in "Of Booker T. Washington and Others"); Boston *Guardian,* July 27, 1902.

17. Miller, *Race Adjustment* (3d ed.; New York, 1909), 14; *Guardian,* Jan. 10, 1903; *Dusk of Dawn,* 70–77.

18. Spencer, *Booker T. Washington,* 157; on Pullman Car matter see Meier, *Negro Thought in America,* Chap. VII; Du Bois to Clement Morgan, Oct. 19, 1903, and Du Bois to George Foster Peabody, Dec. 28, 1903.

19. *Dusk of Dawn,* 82–83, 86, 95. On embarrassment Du Bois' stand caused Atlanta University, see Horace Bumstead to Du Bois, Dec. 5, 1903 and Jan. 26, 1905.

20. E.g., *Crisis,* VII (Feb., 1914), 189–90; I (Dec., 1910), 27.

21. *Crisis,* II (June, 1911), 63–64; "The Forward Movement," MS, 1910.

22. *Crisis,* XVI (Nov., 1917), 11; *Horizon,* II (Oct., 1907), 16; *Crisis,* I (Feb., 1911), 20–21; *Horizon,* II (Oct., 1907), 7–8.

23. *Negro American Artisan* (AUP No. 17, 1913), 128–29; E. H. Clement to Du Bois [Dec. ? 1907], Dec. 18, 1907, and Du Bois to Clement, Dec. 10 and 30, 1907; *Economic Co-operation among Negro Americans*

(AUP No. 12, 1907), 12; *Crisis*, XV (Nov., 1917), 9; *Crisis*, V (Jan., 1913), 184–86.

24. "The Marrying of Black Folk," *Independent*, LXIX (Oct. 13, 1910), 812–13.

25. *Philadelphia Negro*, 359; "Relations of Negroes to the Whites of the South," 121–22; *The Souls of Black Folk* (Chicago, 1903), 50; *Horizon*, III (March, 1908), 5–6; *Crisis*, II (Aug., 1911), 157–58; "The Negro in Literature and Art," in *The Negro's Progress in Fifty Years* (Annals of the American Academy of Political and Social Science, XXXIX [Sept., 1913]), 233–37.

26. Circular of African Development Company, March 1, 1902; Melville J. Herskovits, *Myth of the Negro Past* (New York, 1941); *The Negro Church* (AUP No. 6, 1903), 5–6; *The Negro American Artisan*, 24; *The Negro American Family* (AUP No. 13, 1908), 10–17; *Economic Co-operation Among Negro Americans*, 12–14; *The Negro* (New York, 1915), chap. ii, 241–42; Sergi, *The Mediterranean Race* (London, 1901).

27. *The Negro Artisan*, 25; Du Bois to I. M. Rubinow, Nov. 17, 1904; *Horizon*, I (Feb., 1907), 7–8; "A Field for Socialists," MS [1907–9]; "The Economic Revolution in the South," in BTW and Du Bois, *The Negro in the South* (Philadelphia, 1907), 116; Du Bois to Mr. Owens, April 17, 1908; Elliott Rudwick to author, July 17, 1954; *The Negro*, 238–41. Note also his Marxist economic interpretation in his first novel, *The Quest of the Silver Fleece*, 1911.

28. *Crisis*, XVI (1918), 216–17.

29. Elliott Rudwick to author, Nov. 14, 1955.

The Negro and the United Mine Workers of America

1. The author is indebted to the State University of New York at Buffalo for making available research funds to gather the materials for this essay. Critical comments by Professor C. Vann Woodward of Yale University resulted in significant changes in the tone of the concluding section of this essay. I remain indebted to him for the frankness of his comments—and his wisdom. The Center for Advanced Study in the Behavioral Sciences, Stanford, California, made it possible for me to read portions of this essay at the annual meetings of the Association for the Study of Negro Life and History in Baltimore, Maryland, in October 1966.

2. Robert V. Bruce, *1877: Year of Violence* (Indianapolis, 1959), 292–94; Andrew Roy, *A History of the Coal Miners of the United States* (Columbus, 1906), 353.

3. "Testimony of John Mitchell, April 11, 1899," *Report of the Industrial Commission*, VII (Washington, D.C., 1901), 51–53.

4. *Ibid.*, 31–32, 51–53.

5. "Testimony of W. C. Pearce," *ibid.*, 101.

6. *Ibid.*, 30–58, 101, 136, 149.

7. See the tables and other statistical materials in Sterling D. Spero and Abram L. Harris, *The Black Worker: The Negro and the Labor Movement* (New York, 1931), 209, 215; and in Herbert R. Northrup, "The Negro and the United Mine Workers of America," *Southern Economic Journal* (April, 1943), 314.

8. *Report of the Immigration Commission. Immigrants in Industries,* VI and VII (Washington, D.C., 1911), *passim; Report of the Industrial Commission,* XV (Washington, D.C., 1901), 405–7 and *passim;* Frank Julian Warne, *The Coal Mine Workers: A Study in Labor Organization* (New York, 1905), *passim,* and *The Slav Invasion and the Mine Workers: A Study in Immigration* (Philadelphia, 1904), *passim.* The Industrial Commission made interesting but as yet unexplored observations about the impact of ethnic diversity on American trade union organization. "This problem of mixed nationalities," it concluded, results in at least one novelty in the method of organization of American labor unions compared with those of other countries, namely, branch organization based on race." The Commission found that this pattern tended to disappear as "the races assimilate or the needs of the industry dictate." In the UMW, it found disappearance of this form of organization by 1900. Whether or not this "principle" affected unions that organized Negroes into separate locals before 1900 has not yet been studied fully. But the Commission found, for example, that in 1886 the Chicago hod carriers first formed an ineffective "mixed" union of all nationalities. In 1896 it set up a "council" that included representatives from four locals: A German-speaking local with a few Negro members, a Bohemian local, a Polish local, and an English-speaking local that included Italians and Swedes along with 250 to 300 Negroes. (*Report of the Industrial Commission, op. cit.*, 313, 426–28.)

9. Brief biographical sketches of Davis are found in the *United Mine Workers' Journal,* April 23, 1896 and January 25, 1900 (hereafter cited as *UMWJ*).

10. Richard L. Davis to the editor, *UMWJ,* Feb. 28, 1895 (hereafter cited as RLD).

11. RLD to the editor, *UMWJ,* April 30, 1896.

12. RLD to the editor, *ibid.,* Feb. 11, 1897.

13. RLD to the editor, *ibid.,* Sept. 10, 1896.

14. "Editorial Note," *ibid.,* Sept. 10, 1896.

15. RLD to the editor, *ibid.,* Dec. 17, 1896.

16. RLD to the editor, *ibid.,* May 19, 1898. "Old Dog," a Congo, Ohio, Negro miner, took up Davis' complaint. "He can't get work in the mines,

and he says he can't get work to do as an organizer." Old Dog called
Davis "a staunch union man" and reminded *Journal* readers that Davis
had "done more" than any single person to bring Ohio Negroes into the
union. "I think he should be provided for in some way," he went on.
"You do not often meet up with colored men like Dick. . . . He has a
family to keep and I think we owe him something. He nor [*sic*] his children can not live on wind, and further, if he was a white man he would
not be where he is—mark that—but being a negro he does not get the
recognition he should have . . . such treatment will not tend to advance
the interest of our union, but will retard its progress and cause colored
men to look with suspicion upon it. . . . Give us an equal show. Dick
deserves better usage. . . . He feels sorely disappointed. . . . For my
part, I think if we would do right he could either go in mines to work or
we should see to it that he was started up in a small business or given
field work. I want President [Michael] Ratchford to show all colored
men that he values a man irrespective of his color and he can best do
this by giving Dick a helping hand. I hope you will excuse my bad writing and language and also method of speaking, but I believe in calling
a spade a spade. I am sure we are not being treated just as we should."
("Old Dog" to the editor, *ibid.,* May 12, 1898.) In 1909, William
Scaife, British-born, an Illinois miner and then retired editor of the
United Mine Workers' Journal, remembered the troubled last years of
Davis. Scaife gave no details but noted: "R. L. Davis, by his devotion
to the miners' union, deserved better treatment than that accorded him
in the last few years of his life." He scorned those who criticized Davis
as a "has been" and "a barnacle," calling them "some of the mushroom
growth of latter-day leaders" who were "unmanly and unremindful
of the past." Davis had worked for the union when it "took sand, pluck,
and grit to do it." Scaife lamented: "I sometimes think the poet of nature
was hitting the right head with a ten-pound hammer when he said,
'Man's inhumanity to man makes countless thousand mourn.' . . . Our
ignorance has often led us to injure, abuse and crucify our best friends."
(Old Timer [William Scaife], "Forty Years a Miner and Men I Have
Known," *United Mine Workers' Journal,* Nov. 19, 1909.)

17. RLD to the editor, *ibid.,* Dec. 8, 1898.

18. *Ibid.,* Jan. 25, 1900.

19. *Ibid.,* Jan. 25, 1900.

20. Twenty-eight men stood for the office; six were elected; Davis ran seventh
and got 173 votes.

21. *Ibid.,* RLD to the editor, Feb. 21, 1895 and April 23, 1896, and RLD to
the editor, Feb. 28, 1895.

22. *Ibid.,* April 23, 1896.

23. Although renominated in 1898, he failed to win a third term. For unknown reasons, his popularity among convention delegates fell dramati-

cally, and he got only ninety-four votes. In 1897 Davis got 124 votes and the candidate ahead of him netted 156 votes (*ibid.,* Jan. 21, 1897). Details on the 1898 election appear in *ibid.,* Dec. 22, 1897 and Jan. 20, 1898.

24. *Ibid.,* April 23, 1896.

25. RLD to the editor, *ibid.,* April 30, 1896.

26. See, e.g., Chris Evans, *History of the United Mine Workers of America* II (Indianapolis, 1918), 464–69, 492–95.

27. RLD to the editor, *UMWJ,* Sept. 9, 1897.

28. RLD to the editor, *ibid.,* June 9, 1892.

29. RLD to the editor, *ibid.,* May 24, 1894.

30. RLD to the editor, *ibid.,* March 24, 1892.

31. RLD to the editor, *ibid.,* June 30, 1892.

32. Spero and Harris, *op. cit.,* 215; and Robert D. Ward and William W. Rogers, *Labor Revolt in Alabama. The Great Strike of 1894* (University of Alabama, 1965), *passim.* This recent study contains much useful information about Alabama coal mining and relations between employers and Negro and white miners before 1895. Although it is marred by superficial analysis, it nevertheless deserves attention.

33. Davis wrote three letters from Alabama and another from Rendville about his Alabama experiences, and they appear in *UMWJ,* Dec. 16 and 23, 1897 and Jan. 6 and Feb. 10, 1898.

34. RLD to the editor, *ibid.,* May 24, 1894. Davis took pleasure in 1892 in his successes among East European miners. That year he and another organizer went among these recent immigrants, and he reported of one meeting: "Another feature of the meeting was the large number of foreigners present and what I mean by that is the Polanders, Hungarians, Bohemians, Slavs, etc. One thing that I would like to say about these people is that they were very attentive to the business of the meeting and especially when one of their own number was speaking. I will just here make this plainer. The checkweighman at this mine is a Polander, but can speak the English language quite fluently. After Vice President Miller and myself got through speaking, this gentleman got up and interpreted it to the Polanders, Huns and Slavs in a very able manner. It was quite interesting to notice how they would flock around him while he was talking. . . . Although the meeting was an out-door one, one could almost hear a pin fall while he was talking. After he was through a motion was made that they would join in a body; the vote was taken by the raising of the hands and the motion was unanimously carried, with loud cheers from the foreign-speaking element. At this juncture a secretary was elected from each nationality to take their names as members of the organization. . . . Of the officers chosen, among them were one Hungarian, one negro, one Polander, one Slav and one white, so

you can readily see that these people mean business and have started about it in the right way. . . ." RLD to the editor, *ibid.*, March 3, 1892.

35. RLD to the editor, *ibid.*, March 14, 1894.

36. See, e.g., RLD to the editor, *ibid.*, Nov. 22, 1894 and March 3, 10, and 24, 1898.

37. RLD to the editor, *ibid.*, June 23, 1898.

38. RLD to the editor, *ibid.*, March 24, 1898. A year earlier Davis had urged the celebration of yet another holiday: "You forget the day I love most, and that is emancipation day. By all means let us celebrate the day when the shackles were cut loose and 4,000,000 of black men were liberated from the galling yoke of chattel slavery." (RLD to the editor, *ibid.*, March 11, 1897.

39. The works of Evans, Roy, and Warne, previously cited, are entirely unsatisfactory accounts of the early UMW history. Additional information can be found in Norman Ware, *The Labor Movement in the United States, 1860–1895* (New York, 1929), 214–22; Philip Taft, *The A.F. of L. in the Time of Gompers* (New York, 1957), 137–40; and McAlister Coleman, *Men and Coal* (New York, 1943), *passim*. There remains a serious need for a full, scholarly history of the UMW.

40. Woodward, *op. cit.*, 321–49.

41. This figure is quoted widely in the standard sources. See, for examples, Spero and Harris, *op. cit.*, 76–78; and Ira DeA. Reid, *Negro Membership in American Labor Unions* (New York, 1930), 101–3. It seems originally to come from W. E. B. Du Bois, ed., *The Negro Artisan* (Atlanta, 1902), 158. Du Bois wrote that "the figures as to Negro membership [in 1900] are reported to us by the unions." Efforts by this writer to secure independent sources that verify this important fact have not been successful.

42. *Report of the Industrial Commission*, XVII, *op. cit.*, 184–85; John Mitchell to Samuel Gompers, April 12, 1900, as cited in Philip Foner, *History of the Labor Movement in the United States*, II (New York, 1955), 345. See also Ware, *op. cit.*, 214–22.

43. Taft, *op. cit.*, 233.

44. For a reasonable explanation of the absence of Negro anthracite miners, see Spero and Harris, *op. cit.*, 207.

45. Woodward, *op. cit.*, 362–65; Spero and Harris, *op. cit.*, 352–57; Northrup, *op. cit.*, 319–21; Roy, *op. cit.*, 430–32.

46. *Locomotive Firemen's Magazine*, XXV (Oct. 1898), 378–79.

47. *Proceedings of the Twentieth Annual Convention of the American Federation of Labor . . . 1900*, 22–23. See also Gompers' testimony before the Industrial Commission in 1899 (*Report of the Industrial Commission*, VII, *op. cit.*, 647–49) and his early recognition that exclusion of

Negroes would encourage strikebreaking in Taft, *op. cit.,* 308–12, and Bernard Mandel, *Samuel Gompers* (Yellow Springs, Ohio, 1963), 142–45.

48. "Trade Union Attitude Toward Colored Workers," *American Federationist* VIII (April 1901), 118–19. See also Logan, *op. cit.,* 149–50.

49. Quoted by Ray Marshall, *The Negro and Organized Labor* (New York, 1965), 19.

50. O. H. Underwood to the editor, *UMWJ,* July 20, 1899.

51. Quoted in Woodward, *op. cit.,* 364.

52. W. H. Councill, "Negro Labor and Labor Organizations," *The Tradesman* (Chattanooga), Jan. 1900, reprinted in the *Locomotive Firemen's Magazine* XXVIII (March 1900), 197–98. A vivid sketch of Councill is found in August Meier, *Negro Thought in America, 1880–1915* (Ann Arbor, 1963), 209–10. Councill's paper appeared in *The Tradesman,* a leading Southern commercial publication, as a part of a symposium on "the South and its future." Other contributors included the secretary of Huntsville Chamber of Commerce and Southern Industrial Convention, N. F. Thompson, and a former Georgia governor who found in the Negro "one of the South's best undeveloped resources . . . if properly trained." He urged Northern capital to come into the South whose "labor" made that section "a stranger to riots, strikes and ugly uprisings among the people . . ." Thompson argued for legislation that would "make it a crime to inaugurate a strike that in any way affected the general public." (*The Tradesman, loc. cit.,* 195–97.) That same year, Thompson, who had also spent five years in Johnstown, Pennsylvania, and been secretary of the Birmingham, Alabama, Commercial Club, at another time, warned the Industrial Commission that Birmingham Negroes "are being taken into the unions practically on the same basis as all others." Thompson complained of "a deficiency of collective education among the masses" and that "the educational influence of the labor organizations" had gone unchallenged in the South for twenty-five years." He even favored the use of violence against outspoken union activists (*Report of the Industrial Commission,* VII, *op. cit.,* 755–59). John P. Coffin, Vice-President of the Southern Industrial Council, urged that Negroes be used as "a reserve force in case of strikes." "I believe," he told the Commission, "that in the negro labor of the South lies the panacea for the wrongs frequently committed by organized labor, and a reserve force from which can be supplied any needed number of workers when the time shall come that they will be needed." Before they would "submit to unjust domination by unions," Coffin predicted, the "Southern people" would "negroize their industries." An amazed Commission investigator pressed Coffin on this point and only the Mad Hatter could untangle what followed:

"*Q:* That would bring negro domination in industry then, would it not?

A: It will bring negro domination of the labor market if labor is unjust. *Q.:* And the white man will dominate the social and political conditions of the South, and the negro will dominate the labor market of the South? . . . If they dominated white labor, white labor would be suppressed? *A.:* No; they would never dominate white labor. He [*sic*] will take their places, but domination will rest with the whites. There is no fear of negro domination in the South.

Q.: I do not mean domination over the employer, but domination over the white labor. They would be eliminated, would they not? *A.:* No; the employer would dominate the labor, not the negro. The negro will never dominate the Anglo-Saxon. He may take his place in work under certain conditions; but the Anglo-Saxon was not created to be dominated. . . . *Q:* Is it not really, then, to be held up as a menace over the white labor to make them understand that they must not make unjust demands, but that they must submit to the employer in all things? *A.:* . . . I believe in white labor as far as possible; but I also believe in justice." (*Ibid.,* 790–91.)

53. Quoted in Woodward, *op. cit.,* 361.

54. Meier, *op. cit., passim.*

55. St. Louis *Advance,* n. d., reprinted in *The Carpenter,* XXIII (April 1903), 6–7. See also the letter of a Texas trade unionist, probably white, who wrote to Du Bois: "The Negro question is the one drawback to the success of the labor movement today [1900–1], especially is this true in the South. The Negro has always been the stumbling block in the way of success in many cases; this, however, is not the fault of the Negro, but until the white men realize that it is with the organization and assistance of the Negro, that they can and must win, the labor movement will not be as successful as we hope for." He went on: "They are laborers, in a larger percentage, than their white brothers; they are the ones used to whip the white men into line when striking for their rights or demanding recognition from their employers, whereas, if they were organized, no inducement could be made to cause them to falter in their duty to mankind" (unidentified letter from Texas, quoted in Du Bois, *op. cit.,* 178).

56. In 1909, William Scaife recorded his memories of the early UMW years. Scaife devoted an entire article to Richard Davis and called him "a heroic fighter." Scaife scorned those who neglected the pioneering efforts of the Ohio Negro miner and reminded his readers of his "unflagging zeal . . . against trials and tribulations that would have daunted and discouraged the best of them." "If he was black," Scaife said of Davis, "he had a heart as white as any man, and a devotion to union principles that was second to no man in the movement. His color he could not help, and I don't know that it matters a great deal anyhow." Scaife found in men like Davis reason not to "erect in the miners' organization

a 'color standard,' but one of manhood." "We need more colored men like Dick Davis," he concluded, "and we white men want to treat them right for the common good of all of us." (Old Timer [William Scaife], "Forty Years a Miner and Men I Have Known," *United Mine Workers' Journal,* Nov. 19, 1909.)

From the South to the South Side

1. Gunnar Myrdal, *An American Dilemma* (New York: Harper & Brothers, 1944), p. 193; see also Thomas J. Woofter, Jr., *Negro Migration* (New York: W. D. Gray, 1920), pp. 14–15; and Louise V. Kennedy, *The Negro Peasant Turns Cityward* (New York: Columbia University Press, 1930), pp. 42–52.

2. U.S. Bureau of Immigration, *Annual Report of the Commissioner-General of Immigration, 1922,* p. 108. It has often been maintained that the labor supply was further diminished by the emigration of European aliens returning to their native lands to fight in the war. Official reports, however, show a steady decrease in the number of emigrant aliens departing each year from 1914 to 1917. *Annual Report, 1922,* pp. 106–7.

3. Charles Wesley, *Negro Labor in the United States, 1850–1925* (New York: Vanguard Press, 1927), pp. 290–91; Kennedy, *The Negro Peasant Turns Cityward,* pp. 42–44.

4. U.S. Department of Labor, *Negro Migration in 1916–17* (Washington: Government Printing Office, 1919), pp. 17–18, 58–60, 78–79; Emmett J. Scott, *Negro Migration During the War* (New York: Oxford University Press, 1920), pp. 13–15.

5. U.S. Department of Labor, *Negro Migration in 1916–17,* p. 71.

6. The role of the labor agents has often been exaggerated, due to widely publicized southern attempts to proscribe their activities. But they were undoubtedly important in the initial stages of the migration. See Scott, *Negro Migration During the War,* pp. 36, 55; Charles S. Johnson, "The New Negro in a New World," *The New Negro,* ed. Alain Locke (New York: Albert & Charles Boni, 1925), pp. 280–81; U.S. Department of Labor, *Negro Migration in 1916–17,* pp. 66, 85; and *Chicago Defender,* August 19, 1916.

7. *Defender,* August 12, 1916; *Crisis* (New York), 13 (January, 1917): 123; Scott, *Negro Migration During the War,* pp. 36–37, 73–74; U.S. Department of Labor, *Negro Migration in 1916–17,* pp. 62–63.

8. "Letters of Negro Migrants of 1916–18," collected under the direction of Emmett J. Scott, *Journal of Negro History* (Washington), 4 (October, 1919): 457.

9. *Ibid.,* 4: 464.

10. Scott, *Negro Migration During the War,* p. 36; *New York Times,* October 7, 1917.

11. *Defender,* October 7, 1916.

12. *Ibid.,* May 28, 1917.

13. *Ibid.,* February 24, 1917.

14. *Ibid.,* March 24, 1917.

15. *Ibid.,* May 28, 1917.

16. *Ibid.,* April 30, 1917.

17. For a selection of such advertisements, see Scott, *Negro Migration During the War,* pp. 17–18.

18. "Letters of Negro Migrants," 4: 327.

19. *Defender,* September 15, 1917.

20. Scott, *Negro Migration During the War,* p. 30.

21. Johnson, "The New Negro in a New World," p. 280.

22. "Letters of Negro Migrants," 4: 454–55.

23. Scott, *Negro Migration During the War,* pp. 28–29.

24. *Ibid.,* pp. 44–45.

25. U.S. Department of Labor, *Negro Migration in 1916–17,* p. 33.

26. Ray Stannard Baker, "The Negro Goes North," *World's Work* (New York), 34 (July, 1917): 319.

27. U.S. Department of Labor, *Negro Migration in 1916–17,* p. 95.

28. E. Franklin Frazier, *The Negro in the United States,* rev. ed. (New York: Macmillan Company, 1957), p. 527.

The Struggle for Homes and Jobs

1. The description of the migrants' arrival is based on an interview with Chester Wilkins, who worked for many years as a Red Cap and, eventually, Chief Usher at the Illinois Central Station, Chicago, March 28, 1963.

2. Chicago Commission on Race Relations, *The Negro in Chicago: A Study of Race Relations and a Race Riot* (Chicago: University of Chicago Press, 1922), pp. 93, 186; Junius B. Wood, *The Negro in Chicago* (Chicago: *Chicago Daily News,* 1916), *passim.*

3. Chicago Commission on Race Relations, *The Negro in Chicago,* pp. 152–53, 191–92; Alice Q. Rood, "Social Conditions Among the Negroes on Federal Street Between Forty-fifth and Fifty-third Streets," unpublished master's thesis, University of Chicago, 1924, pp. 15–16, 41–45.

4. Alzada P. Comstock, "Chicago Housing Conditions: VI: The Problem of the Negro," *American Journal of Sociology* (Chicago), 18 (September, 1912): 241–57.

5. Rood, "Social Conditions Among the Negroes," p. 25. Rood and Comstock each surveyed segments of Federal Street that were, at the time of their studies, the heart of the Negro slum. Rood used Comstock's

schedule cards and attempted to apply the same criteria in evaluating the adequacy of the houses.

6. Chicago Commission on Race Relations, *The Negro in Chicago*, pp. 187–91.

7. *Ibid.*, pp. 188, 192.

8. Rood, "Social Conditions Among the Negroes," pp. 27–28.

9. Chicago Commission on Race Relations, *The Negro in Chicago*, p. 157.

10. Comstock, "Chicago Housing Conditions," 18: 244–45; Chicago Commission on Race Relations, *The Negro in Chicago*, p. 158. These two surveys are not directly comparable. But it is probable that the high proportion of lodgers was maintained throughout the migration era.

11. "Letters of Negro Migrants of 1916–18," collected under the direction of Emmett J. Scott, *Journal of Negro History* (Washington), 4 (October, 1919): 457.

12. Chicago Commission on Race Relations, *The Negro in Chicago*, p. 164.

13. *Ibid.*, p. 165.

14. Interview with Grace Garnett, Negro landlady, transcript in "The Negro in Illinois," a file of reports and interviews compiled by the Illinois Writers Project of the Works Progress Administration (George Cleveland Hall Branch of the Chicago Public Library), cited hereafter as Illinois Writers Project Files.

15. The housing conflict and the violence it engendered are fully treated in chapter 11 [of *Black Chicago* by Allan H. Spear].

16. See the instructions to the census workers on the use of this term in U.S. Bureau of the Census, *Fourteenth Census, 1920*, 4: 30.

17. In addition to the census reports, see Chicago Commission on Race Relations, *The Negro in Chicago*, pp. 391–92.

18. Forrester B. Washington, "Reconstruction and the Colored Woman," *Life and Labor* (Chicago), 8 (January, 1919): 4–5.

19. Chicago Commission on Race Relations, *The Negro in Chicago*, pp. 380–83, 391–92.

20. *Ibid.*, p. 167.

21. *Ibid.*, pp. 166–68.

22. Quoted by Wood, *The Negro in Chicago*, p. 7.

23. Chicago Commission on Race Relations, *The Negro in Chicago*, p. 373.

24. Wood, *The Negro in Chicago*, p. 7.

25. *Ibid.*, pp. 7–8; Chicago Urban League, *Annual Report, 1919;* Chicago Commission on Race Relations, *The Negro in Chicago*, pp. 366–67.

26. Chicago Commission on Race Relations, *The Negro in Chicago*, pp. 367, 370.

27. *Ibid.*, p. 365.

28. *Ibid.,* p. 371.

29. *Ibid.,* p. 387.

30. Alma Herbst, *The Negro in the Slaughtering and Meat Packing Industry in Chicago* (New York: Houghton, Mifflin & Company, 1932), pp. xxi–xxiii; Chicago Commission on Race Relations, *The Negro in Chicago,* p. 390.

31. *Chicago Tribune,* April 12, 1919.

32. Washington, "Reconstruction and the Colored Woman," 8: 4.

Migration and Negro Community Life

1. Chicago Commission on Race Relations, *The Negro in Chicago: A Study of Race Relations and a Race Riot* (Chicago: University of Chicago Press, 1922), p. 145.

2. For a general description of Holiness churches in Chicago, see the report on churches in the Illinois Writers Project Files. On the relationship of the migration to the development of these churches, see Benjamin E. Mays and Joseph W. Nicholson, *The Negro's Church* (New York: Institute of Social and Religious Research, 1933), pp. 98–99.

3. Herbert W. Smith, "Three Negro Preachers in Chicago: A Study in Religious Leadership," unpublished master's thesis, University of Chicago Divinity School, 1935, pp. 17–19; report on churches in Illinois Writers Project Files.

4. Report on churches in Illinois Writers Project Files. In 1920, sixty-seven of the eighty-six Negro Baptist churches in Chicago met in storefronts. Chicago Commission on Race Relations, *The Negro in Chicago,* p. 145.

5. Robert L. Sutherland, "An Analysis of Negro Churches in Chicago," unpublished doctoral dissertation, University of Chicago, 1930, pp. 41–43; report on churches in Illinois Writers Project Files.

6. Report on churches in Illinois Writers Project Files.

7. Mays and Nicholson, *The Negro's Church,* pp. 178–79; Miles Mark Fisher, "History of Olivet Baptist Church of Chicago," unpublished master's thesis, University of Chicago, 1922, pp. 84–97; *Defender,* September 4, 1920.

8. Levi J. Coppin, *Unwritten History* (Philadelphia: A. M. E. Book Concern, 1919), pp. 341–43.

9. Junius B. Wood, *The Negro in Chicago* (Chicago: *Chicago Daily News,* 1916), p. 19; Chicago Commission on Race Relations, *The Negro in Chicago,* p. 145.

10. Reports on Pilgrim, Progressive, Provident, Liberty, and Monumental Baptist Churches in Illinois Writers Project Files.

11. George W. Mundelein, *Two Crowded Years* (Chicago: Extension Press, 1918), pp. 291–300.

12. Interview with Dr. Arthur G. Falls, prominent Negro Catholic layman, March 19, 1963; *Defender,* November 17, 1917.

Garvey and Garveyism

1. Edmund D. Cronon, *Black Moses: The Story of Marcus Garvey and the Universal Negro Improvement Association* (Madison: The University of Wisconsin Press), 1955.
2. Quoted in Amy Jacques-Garvey, *Garvey and Garveyism* (12 Mona Road, Kingston 6, Jamaica), p. 4.
3. Cronon, *op. cit.,* p. 118.
4. *Ibid.*
5. Quoted in *Garvey and Garveyism,* p. 128. After Garvey had dismissed his first lawyer, he retained Mr. Kohn for private consultation during the trial before Judge Mack.
6. *Blackism* (Lagos), 1965, p. 13.
7. *Ghana, Autobiography of Kwame Nkrumah* (New York: Thomas Nelson & Sons, 1957), p. 45.
8. *Black Manhattan* (New York: Knopf, 1930), p. 256.
9. *Dusk of Dawn* (New York, Harcourt, Brace, 1940), p. 277.
10. *Daily Comet,* 23 November, 1948.

The Background of the Negro Renaissance

1. "The Negro's Contribution to American Culture," *Journal of Negro Education,* 8 (1939), 521–29.
2. Gunnar Myrdal, *An American Dilemma* (New York, 1944), pp. 191–96.
3. *The Yogi and the Commissar* (New York, 1945), pp. 61–76.
4. *A Long Way from Home* (New York, Lee Furman, 1937), p. 69.
5. The *parents* of the Renaissance novelists were 55 per cent professionals and 45 per cent white collar (compare 13 per cent and 20 per cent in the early period).
6. *The Big Sea* (New York and London, Knopf, 1940), p. 39.
7. The Writers' Guild, New York; Black Opals, Philadelphia; The Saturday Evening Quill Club, Boston; The Ink-Slingers, Los Angeles; Book and Bench, Topeka, Kansas, etc.
8. Most of this material is presently housed in the James Weldon Johnson Collection of Negro Arts and Letters at Yale University.
9. See *Along This Way* (New York, Viking Press, 1933), pp. 381–82.
10. See Hugh Gloster, "The Van Vechten Vogue," *Negro Voices in American Fiction,* pp. 157–73.
11. "Racial Self-Expression," *Ebony and Topaz* (1927), pp. 119–21 (special supplement to *Opportunity*).

12. The numerical strength of the Garvey movement has been estimated at one to four million.
13. *Plum Bun* (1928), p. 218.

The Harlem School

1. "The Negro Artist and the Racial Mountain," *Nation, 122* (1926), 692–94.

The Negro in the New Deal Era

1. Franklin D. Roosevelt (ed.), *The Public Papers of Franklin D. Roosevelt* (New York, 1938), II: 11, 12, 13.
2. John Gunther, *Roosevelt in Retrospect: A Profile in History* (New York, 1950), 37.
3. Lela Stiles to FDR, April 25, 1940, in Elliott Roosevelt (ed.), *FDR: His Personal Letters* (New York, 1950), II: 1018–1019.
4. Quoted in Arthur M. Schlesinger, Jr., *The Politics of Upheaval: The Age of Roosevelt* (Boston, 1960), III: 430.
5. *The Crisis,* XLI: 20 (January, 1934).
6. *Opportunity,* XI: 167 (June, 1933).
7. *Ibid.,* XII: 360 (December, 1934).
8. T. Arnold Hill in the *New York Times,* June 25, 1937, p. 7.
9. John P. Davis, "What Price National Recovery?," in *The Crisis,* XL: 272 (December, 1933).
10. Gustav Peck, "The Negro Worker and the NRA," in *ibid.,* XLI: 262 (September, 1934).
11. Quoted in the *New York Times,* August 19, 1933, p. 10.
12. Charles H. Houston and John P. Davis, "TVA: Lily-White Construction," in *The Crisis,* XLI: 291 (October, 1934).
13. Harold L. Ickes, *The First Thousand Days, 1933–1936: The Secret Diary of Harold L. Ickes* (New York, 1953), I: 541.
14. *New York Times,* December 29, 1940, p. 12.
15. Roosevelt, *Public Papers,* IV: 16, 262; V: 538.
16. *Opportunity,* XV: 133 (May, 1937).
17. Quoted in Gunnar Myrdal, *An American Dilemma* (New York, 1944), II: 836n.
18. *Ibid.,* II: 840, 841.
19. *Ibid.,* II: 876n.
20. *The Crisis,* XLII: 145 (May, 1935).
21. Eleanor Roosevelt, *This I Believe* (New York, 1949), 173–174.

22. Washington *Post,* February 26, 1941, quoted by Rayford Logan (ed.), *What the Negro Wants* (New York, 1944), 8.

23. Walter White, *A Man Called White* (New York, 1948), 246, 248, 250.

24. Roy Wilkins, "The Negro Wants Full Equality," in Logan, *What the Negro Wants,* 130.

25. *The Crisis,* XL: 197 (September, 1933).

26. Walter P. Reuther, "The Negro Worker's Future," in *Opportunity,* XXIII: 203 (Fall, 1945).

27. *New York Times,* November 23, 1946, p. 17.

28. *To Secure These Rights, The Report of the President's Committee on Civil Rights* (New York, 1947), vii.

29. 311 U.S. 130 (1940).

30. 305 U.S. 349 (1938).

31. The quotation is from the majority opinion of Justice Stanley Reed in Cassell *v.* Texas, 339 U.S. 286 (1950).

The National Association for the Advancement of Colored People

1. Mary White Ovington, *How the National Association for the Advancement of Colored People Began* (1914), cited by Ralph Bunche, "The Programs, Ideologies, Tactics, and Achievements of Negro Betterment and Interracial Organizations," unpublished manuscript prepared for this study [1940], Vol. 1, p. 24. The following account of the N.A.A.C.P. has drawn heavily from Bunche's memorandum, compared with critical comments and information given by Walter White, the Secretary of the N.A.A.C.P., and Roy Wilkins, the Assistant Secretary of the N.A.A.C.P. and Editor of *The Crisis.* See also Paul E. Baker, *Negro-White Adjustment* (1934), pp. 43 ff.

2. Cited in Bunche, *op. cit.,* Vol. 1, p. 27.

3. James Weldon Johnson, *Black Manhattan* (1930), pp. 140 ff.

4. *Op. cit.,* Vol. 1, p. 29.

5. *The Acid Test of Democracy,* Leaflet (1940); cited in *ibid.,* p. 44.

6. In the following states and regions the branches have formed conferences which hold periodic state or regional conventions: Virginia, Oklahoma, Pennsylvania, New Jersey, South Carolina, Ohio, Illinois, Iowa, Maryland, Michigan, New York, Texas; and Southern, Northwest and New England regions. (Information from Roy Wilkins, memorandum [August 11, 1942].)

7. A branch is ". . . a constituent and subordinate unit of the Association, subject to the general authority and jurisdiction of the Board of Directors of the Association. Its objects shall be to promote the economic, political, civic and social betterment of colored people and their harmoni-

ous cooperation with other peoples." (Quoted in Bunche, *op. cit.,* Vol. 1, p. 36.

8. Information from Roy Wilkins, memorandum (August 11, 1942).

9. The local Youth Councils are an intrinsic part of the structure of the Association. "This is an attempt by the Association to canalize . . . the current tendencies of restless youth to organize and to attract young Negroes to the organization. . . . The Youth Councils devote themselves to the broad program of the Association, with special attention to the problems of youth and employ similar tactics." (Bunche, *op. cit.,* Vol. 1, p. 42.)

10. Information from Roy Wilkins, memorandum (August 11, 1942).
    Concerning the last point, Wilkins comments: "Offhand, I do not believe we receive contributions from more than five foundations, and the largest gift from any of them is less than 1/80 of our total budget."

11. *The Negro College Graduate* (1938), p. 349.

12. Greene found that only 10 out of 367 Negro "leaders" were not college or professional school graduates. His complete figures are as follows:

Academic Preparation of Negro Leaders as Determined by the Number of Degrees they Received "In Course"

Degree	Number
Bachelor's	127
Master's	104
Doctoral	33
Professional	87
No degree indicated	10
No report	6

(Harry W. Greene, *Negro Leaders* [1936], p. 12.)
    Some of the persons in Greene's sample were selected because they were outstanding in academic fields. Still, the high educational level of nearly everyone on Greene's list is nothing less than phenomenal and is probably not paralleled among white leaders.

13. The Detroit branch has secured 12,000 new members in a recent membership campaign and other branches have doubled, and in some cases, trebled their membership. (Letter from Walter White [July 29, 1942].) A great proportion of the members in some branches as in Norfolk, Virginia, and Mobile, Alabama, are workers. (Roy Wilkins in memorandum [August 11, 1942].)

14. One of the officers of the National Office is Branch Director, one is Field Secretary, one Branch Coordinator, and one, Youth Director. The National Secretary and the other national officers frequently visit the branches.

15. Bunche, *op. cit.,* Vol. 1, pp. 45–47.

16. *Program Book for N.A.A.C.P. Branches* (1939), p. 1. Quoted in *ibid.*, p. 45.

A main tactic, for the branches as well as for the National Office, is legal redress. The great majority of the cases handled by the Association originate in the branches. The branches are advised to carry the financial and legal responsibility for local cases themselves as far as possible. When they cannot be so handled, the branches appeal to the National Office and its Legal Committee for assistance. If the National Office enters a case, it works in collaboration with the branches. (See *ibid.*, p. 38.) It is held that neither the National Office nor the branches should function, or could function, as a legal aid society:

"It [the Association] only handles cases where it seems great injustice has been or is about to be done because of race or color prejudice, or cases where its entry will clearly establish a precedent affecting the rights of colored people in general." (E. Frederic Morrow, *An Outline of Branch Functions;* cited in *ibid.*, p. 39.)

Thus, even if the individual sufferings cannot be disregarded as a motive for action, the main consideration must be its importance as a test case. Bunche summarizes:

"In the selection of the issues on which fights are to be waged, the branches are told to select 'live issues,' in which discriminations are glaring, 'where the correction of the injustices will benefit a large number of Negroes,' and where there is a chance to win. Publicizing the fight is regarded as an important element in the struggle, and the branches are advised never to 'start on a big campaign without telling the folks that count . . . what it is the branch is about to do,' and enlisting their support. The aid of the other organizations, such as interracial, civic, religious, and labor union groups, is also to be solicited in the campaigns, in efforts to bring maximum pressure to bear on officials, and to mold a favorable public opinion." (*Ibid.*, pp. 49–59.)

Publicity should be a vital part of the work of the branches, they are told. They are advised to build up a "contact list" of prominent people of both races, "who could assist in sending telegrams and letters of protest to officials when impending legislation is detrimental to the best interest of the group, or letters and telegrams urging enactment of impending legislation that will protect or enhance the best interests of colored people." (E. Frederic Morrow, *An Outline of Branch Functions,* p. 1; cited in *ibid.*, pp. 49–50.)

17. The Association has been unable, for financial reasons, to carry out its old plan to employ regional secretaries to supervise and stimulate the activity of the branches. (Information from Roy Wilkins in memorandum [March 12, 1941].)

18. An account of the observations made of N.A.A.C.P. branches by interviewers for this study is given in Bunche, *op. cit.*, Vol. 1, pp. 108 ff. See also White's and Wilkins' critiques. The present writer himself visited, in

the years 1938–1940, a great many N.A.A.C.P. branches in all parts of the country.

19. Bunche, *op. cit.*, Vol. 1, p. 117.

20. *Ibid.*, Vol. 1, p. 118.

21. *Ibid.*, Vol. 1, pp. 128–129.

22. For a survey of the independent local organizations, see *ibid.*, Vol. 4, pp. 587–667.

23. *Ibid.*, Vol. 1, pp. 116–117; compare *ibid.*, Vol. 4, pp. 598 ff.

24. Interview (November, 1939); quoted in *ibid.*, Vol. 1, p. 130.

25. *N.A.A.C.P. Press Service*, Series No. 22; cited in *ibid.*, Vol. 1, p. 40. (See also *ibid.*, Vol. 1, p. 100.)

26. *Ibid.*, Vol. 1, pp. 100 ff.

27. *Ibid.*, Vol. 1, p. 105.

28. *Program Book for N.A.A.C.P. Branches*, p. 6; cited in *ibid.*, Vol. 1, p. 50.

29. Roy Wilkins comments on this point: ". . . the issues on which the N.A.A.C.P. uses the threat of reprisal by voters are carefully selected out of our long experience with items we know colored voters will resent at the polls, regardless of party affiliations or other distracting factors. But it must be remembered that we labor under no illusions so far as marshalling a complete bloc of Negro voters as such against any particular candidate or proposal. We know that party affiliation comes first with many colored people, just as it does with other racial groups. They are loyal, Democratic workers, for instance, first of all. We know that job-holding, or the hope of winning jobs will influence the vote more than consideration for racial ideals. We know that some communities will vote for segregated Negro schools on the excuse that only through those schools can they get jobs for their daughters as teachers. In other words, there is no such thing as a purely Negro vote. Nevertheless, on some broad questions, grievously aggravated in some community or by some politician, it is possible to swing a goodly section of the Negro vote in the way it should go, despite other factors operating." (Memorandum [August 11, 1942].)

30. For a summary of N.A.A.C.P.'s achievements in the legal field, see *ibid.*, Vol. 1, pp. 55 ff.; and the critical memoranda by Walter White and Roy Wilkins.

31. There is an interesting story from the First World War told by James Weldon Johnson. Du Bois, who was then editor of *The Crisis*, had been to the front in France and had a good deal to say about the treatment of the Negro soldier:

"The utterances of Dr. Du Bois in *The Crisis*, the organ of the association, brought a visit to the office from agents of the Department of Justice; in reply to the query: 'Just what is this organization fighting for?' Dr. Du Bois said: 'We are fighting for the enforcement of the Constitution of the United States.' This was an ultimate condensation of the program of the association." (*Black Manhattan*, p. 247.)

32. See Bunche, *op. cit.*, Vol. 1, pp. 69 ff.
33. *Ibid.*, Vol. 1, pp. 63 ff.
34. *Ibid.*, Vol. 1, pp. 78 ff.
35. *Ibid.*, Vol. 1, pp. 98 ff.
36. See *ibid.*, Vol. 1, pp. 79 ff.
37. See *ibid.*, Vol. 1, pp. 83 ff.
38. *Ibid.*, Vol. 1, pp. 83–100.
39. ". . . instead of waiting until cases arose out of fundamental legal and cultural patterns which were viciously anti-Negro, we began as far as our means would permit to attack the fundamental evils." (Letter from Walter White [March 15, 1941].)

This change is usually not seen or understood by the few social scientists, Negro or white, who have given some attention to the Association. Guy B. Johnson, for example, writes:

"While the organization has carried on a great deal of educational work along the line of stimulating race consciousness and race pride and has taken the offensive in a few legislative ventures, it has for the most part found itself carrying on a defensive legalistic program. That is, it has largely been concerned with specific cases involving disfranchisement, segregation, discriminatory legislation, injustice in the courts, lynching, peonage, etc." ("Negro Racial Movements and Leadership in the United States," in the *American Journal of Sociology* [July, 1937], p. 66.)

40. E. Frederic Morrow, *An Outline of Branch Functions*, p. 1; cited by Bunche, *op. cit.*, Vol. 1, p. 46.
41. *Program Book for N.A.A.C.P. Branches*, p. 6; cited in *ibid.*, Vol. 1, p. 50.
42. Bunche, *op. cit.*, Vol. 1, p. 51.
43. ". . . the possible influence of reform organizations as well as of individual reformers in the field of race relations is definitely limited to the correction of particular instances of injustice—especially those which are so outrageous as to exceed the limits of popular prejudiced approval —and to campaigns of public enlightenment concerning the basic community of interests among all people in the United States.

"This is our reason for omitting discussion of the hundreds of organizations and movements for the improvement of race relations and the securing of justice for minorities in our country. What have such organizations as the National Urban League, the National Association for the Advancement of Colored People, the Association for the Study of Negro Life and History, the Commission on Interracial Cooperation accomplished to justify their existence? The answer is: Much in the way of fighting particular instances of atrocious injustice, a little in the way of the dissemination of interracial facts, and nothing so far as any general change in racial attitudes is concerned. Shortly after the World War, lynchings of Negroes declined rapidly, and a good share of the credit for this decline was claimed by the Commission on Interracial Cooperation. Seven Negroes were reported to have been lynched in 1929, counting only those who were killed by mobs and not those who were otherwise mistreated, and twenty in 1930. If the Commission was responsible for declines in lynchings, is its negligence also responsible for this increase? Actually, of course, lynchings fluctuate in practical independence of the efforts of such organizations, which have no means of attacking the fundamental causes of lynching. All praise should go to the efforts of the interracial pioneers who are sacrificing much for their ideals and who have fought valiantly for the adjustment of interracial relations. Nothing, however, is to be gained by carrying our confidence in them to the extent of believing that they may do more than battle the symptoms of race prejudice, as a fever may be reduced by the application of ice, affording some relief to the patient but not curing the disease." (Donald Young, *American Minority Peoples* [1932], pp. 589-590; compare *ibid., passim.*)

Young's proof against the claims of the Commission on Interracial Cooperation of a good share in the credit for the decline in lynching is not entirely convincing. No one denies that other factors than the fight of the organizations have influence on the yearly *fluctuations*—and even the trend—of lynchings. But this does not exclude the fact that the organizations also have an influence, primarily on the *trend,* but also on the fluctuations. (See footnote ᵃ on p. 423 [of Myrdal, *An American Dilemma*].)

44. "Now, while this legalistic approach has been successful in the sense that it has sometimes served as a goal to the South and that it has won numerous important legal cases—some of the United States Supreme Court decisions involving new precedents—it is doubtful whether it has brought the Negro any nearer his goal. The N.A.A.C.P. has been, from the standpoint of the southern white man, in the same class with abolitionists and carpetbaggers, an outside agency which has tried to impose its ideas upon him. Sociologically the weakness of the movement is inevitable and incurable; it attempts to undo the folkways and mores of the southern caste system by attacking the results and symptoms of the system. Paradoxically, if it leaves the attitudes and folkways of the white man out of its picture, it is doomed to fail; and if it takes those attitudes and folkways into account, it is either forced back to the gradualistic and conciliatory position of Booker Washington or forced forward into revolutionary tactics. One wonders then, whether its chief function, *aside from its value in actually obtaining racial rights* [n.b.], has not been to serve as a catharsis for those discontented, impatient souls who, while they see no hope of normal participation in American life, feel that they must

never give in and admit that they are beaten down spiritually." (Guy B. Johnson, "Negro Racial Movements and Leadership in the United States," *op. cit.;* p. 67 [italics ours].) The obtaining of "racial rights" is, of course, the main purpose of the N.A.A.C.P.

45. ". . . it can scarcely be claimed that these victories [won by resort to court] have materially altered any of the fundamental conditions determining the relations between the races in the country." (Bunche, *op. cit.,* Vol. 1, p. 141; compare *ibid.,* Vol. 1, pp. 143–144; see also Chapter 38, Section 5, of Myrdal, *An American Dilemma.*)

46. *Negro Americans, What Now?* (1934), p. 39.

47. *Ibid.,* p. 38.

48. Bertram W. Doyle, *The Etiquette of Race Relations in the South* (1937), p. 162.

49. We shall exemplify this widespread criticism of the N.A.A.C.P., as well as the other Negro betterment organizations, by statements made by Bunche in the work which has been basic to the description and analysis presented in this chapter. Even if we differ from Bunche on fundamental points, we want to stress that we have chosen to use his presentation as an object for criticism, not because it is weak, but, on the contrary, because it is the most clearly argued and ablest presentation of a view which we cannot share.

50. "The N.A.A.C.P. unquestionably deserves full credit for setting a new pattern of thought among Negroes with respect to their problems. The vigor with which the Association, from the date of its inception, fought for the rights of Negroes before the courts opened the eyes of the Negro to an entirely new vista." (Bunche, *op. cit.,* Vol. 1, p. 141.)

51. ". . . it [the N.A.A.C.P.] has ignored the fundamental conditions giving rise to the race problem. It has understood well enough that the Negro suffers from race prejudice, but has failed to concern itself with the root causes of race prejudice." (*Ibid.,* Vol. 1, p. 142; compare *ibid.,* Vol. 1, pp. 145, *passim.*)

". . . the South must be subjected to a new agrarian and industrial revolution before any significant changes in the fundamental relationship —political, economic or racial—will occur. This is what the N.A.A.C.P. apparently lacks the understanding and courage to face." (*Ibid.,* Vol. 1, p. 147.)

52. "The interracial make-up of the N.A.A.C.P. is also an undoubted source of organizational weakness. There can be no doubt that the Negro leaders in the organization have always kept a weather eye on the reactions of their prominent and influential white sponsors to any innovation in the program of the organization. These white sympathizers are, in the main, either cautious liberals or mawkish, missionary-minded sentimentalists on the race question. Their interest in the Negro problem is motivated either by a sense of 'fair play' and a desire to see the ideals of the Consti-

tution lived up to, or an 'I love your people' attitude. Both attitudes are far from touching the realities of the problem. But the evident concern for the opinions of the white supporters of the organization, especially on the part of the National Office, has been a powerful factor in keeping the Association thoroughly 'respectable' and has certainly been an influence in the very evident desire of the Association to keep its skirts free of the grimy bitterness and strife encountered in the economic arena. This has also been a responsibility of the Negro members of the Board, who, by and large, have never been distinguished for the advanced nature of their social thinking. At best they have been cautious, racially minded liberals, and not infrequently, forthright reactionaries. In general they have suffered from an intellectual myopia toward all but narrowly racial problems. The liberal, white or black, northern or southern, recoils from the shock of class conflict. Yet the twitchings of liberalism within him seek release; lacking the courage and conviction to face the harsher realities, he seeks to find release and solace in counterfeit substitutes, in political and social *ersatz*. He recognizes and revolts against injustices, but seeks to correct them with palliatives rather than solutions; for the solutions are harsh and forbidding, and are not conducive to optimism and spiritual uplift.

"The N.A.A.C.P. is an interracial organization, and, though to lesser degree than the less militant interracial groups, still leans heavily upon interracial good-will and understanding. Such reliance is a basic weakness in any organization designed to work on behalf of an economically and politically oppressed group, and where 'good-will' and inter-group 'understanding' are only will-o'-the-wisps which confuse the problem and mislead thinking on it." (Bunche, *op. cit.*, Vol. 1, pp. 147–148.)

53. "I feel very strongly that critics of the Association are not being reasonable where they maintain, in the light of the known American public opinion, and the known shackled condition of the Negro in the country, that an organization for his improvement should embark upon a political and economic revolutionary program.

"These organizations, if you will, must be somewhat opportunistic in their operation. The identification of the Negro's cause prominently and predominantly with a political and economic revolutionary program would be suicidal. The dangers inherent in such a procedure are but demonstrated by the fact that no racial group in America has adopted such a program.

"Indeed, it may be questioned whether the white masses have accepted such a philosophy as the way out of their obvious difficulties. Only an infinitesimal minority of persons in this country subscribes openly to and works actively in such a program. To ask the Negro, the most vulnerable, the poorest, the one most at mercy of the majority, to embark upon this is asking more than is practicable or sensible." (Roy Wilkins, in memorandum of March 12, 1941.)

"The white masses of America are not radical, to say nothing of the black masses. They are radical only with respect to the status of the Negro; on all other matters they are as conservative as the average American." (Roy Wilkins in memorandum of August 11, 1942.)

54. "It has not been able to become a solid political factor . . . through taking a strong hand for or against a particular party, because of the conflicting political interests of its membership. Thus, its politics is 'Negro' politics; its political interests are measured solely in terms of the attitude of a candidate or a party toward measures directly concerned with Negro welfare." (Bunche, *op. cit.*, Vol. 1, p. 54.)

55. ". . . the N.A.A.C.P. does not have a mass basis. It has never assumed the proportions of a crusade, nor has it ever, in any single instance, attracted the masses of people to its banner. It is not impressed upon the mass consciousness, and it is a bald truth that the average Negro in the street has never heard of the Association nor of any of its leaders. It has shown a pitiful lack of knowledge of mass technique and of how to pitch an appeal so as to reach the ears of the masses. Were it able to stir the people, it could establish itself on a sound and independent financial basis; it could develop a feeling of solidarity among Negroes; and it could then employ an expanded paid professional leadership which would make possible the execution of an effective national program." (Bunche, *op. cit.*, Vol. 1, p. 151; compare *ibid*, Vol. 1, pp. 142 ff.)

56. "There are weaknesses in our branch structure and we have not yet found the formula for selling to the public the nature, the extent, the details, and the significance of the Association's program. Some have suggested that we might follow the example of Marcus Garvey and others in the utilization of fancy titles and robes. The Association, however, has felt that reverting to some of these methods of attracting the masses would do more harm in the long run to the organization, than good." (Walter White, in letter, March 15, 1941.)

"I believe that we recognize our lack of skill at mass appeal, and I believe we are on the way to doing something about it." (Roy Wilkins, in memorandum, March 12, 1941.)

57. Winning a greater membership is also important in order to give the Association a solid financial basis. On the other hand, a main impediment to the organization in attempting to recruit a larger membership is its lack of financial resources.

It is, of course, a vital necessity to the Association to keep independent as far as possible from outside support in order to maintain freedom of action. It is a public secret that one of the foundations working in the Negro field, that had earlier contributed to the Association, has tried to convince the N.A.A.C.P. that it should merge, first with the Urban League and, at a later occasion, with both the Urban League and the Commission on Interracial Cooperation. The N.A.A.C.P. refused as it was not greatly dependent on support from foundations and Community

Chests and felt that a merger would hamstring the program of the Association and infringe upon its freedom to challenge the interracial *status quo*. As a result, it lost its earlier support from the foundation.

Black Radicalism: The Road From Montgomery

1. It has not been possible to trace this comment to its source; perhaps it is only part of the black mythology.
2. "Outcast," in *Selected Poems* (New York, 1953), p. 41.
3. *Here I Stand* (New York, 1958), p. 28 (emphasis in original). In my history of the development of black radicalism since 1800, *Black Radicalism in America* (Indianapolis, forthcoming), I deal with Robeson at some length. One of the most interesting evaluations of his role in the Negro protest movement is Harold Cruse's *The Crisis of the Negro Intellectual* (New York, 1967), pp. 285–301.
4. Lerone Bennett, Jr., *The Negro Mood* (Chicago, 1964), p. 10.
5. *Idem, Confrontation: Black and White* (Baltimore, 1966), p. 169: "The Myth of Negro Progress . . . is the only thing that stands between the Negro and revolt."
6. Louise Thompson, "Southern Terror," *Crisis*, 41 (November, 1934): 328.
7. For a brief and perhaps more philosophically oriented examination of the path from Montgomery to the ghetto explosions, see my "Where Have All the Lovers Gone?" in Alan D. Austin, ed., *The Revolutionary Imperative* (Nashville, 1966), pp. 110–27.
8. Few works deal adequately with the historical developments of the 1945–55 preparatory period, but two lively and valuable accounts are Bennett's *Confrontation*, pp. 169–91, and Langston Hughes' *Fight for Freedom* (New York, 1962), pp. 90–139.
9. The story of Montgomery is covered adequately (but not critically) in Martin Luther King, Jr., *Stride toward Freedom* (New York, 1958), and Lerone Bennett, *What Manner of Man?* (Chicago, 1965), pp. 55–105.
10. Some of the earlier ideas of Farmer and Randolph on nonviolent direct action are recorded in Bennett's *Confrontation* (pp. 145–54) and James Farmer's "Memorandum to A. J. Muste" in Francis L. Broderick and August Meier, eds., *Negro Protest Thought in the Twentieth Century* (Indianapolis, 1965), pp. 210–21.
11. King, *Stride toward Freedom,* pp. 177–78.
12. In "This Is SCLC," in Broderick and Meier, eds., *Negro Protest Thought,* pp. 269–70.
13. A general treatment of the student movement up to 1963 is Howard Zinn's *SNCC, The New Abolitionists* (Boston, 1964).

14. Robert F. Williams, *Negroes with Guns* (New York, 1962), p. 63. Harold Cruse's *Crisis of the Negro Intellectual* (esp. pp. 347–419) raises important questions about the meaning of Williams' call for armed self-defense and about the current popularity of the urban guerrilla-warfare concept among black radicals.

15. Williams, *Negroes with Guns,* p. 46.

16. See *idem,* "U.S.A.: The Potential of a Minority Revolution," in Broderick and Meier, eds., *Negro Protest Thought,* pp. 321–33 (published originally in *The Crusader Monthly Newsletter,* vol. 5 [May–June, 1964]).

17. It is not possible to give proper attention to concurrent developments in the black communities of the North in this essay, but they will be discussed in the aforementioned work on *Black Radicalism.*

18. Much of the material that follows is based on my own participation in the events in Birmingham. See also Bennett's treatment in *Confrontation,* pp. 235–44, and *The Negro Mood,* pp. 3–23. (Randolph's March on Washington Movement developed in the 1940's.)

19. This section is based on my recollections of conversations I heard in Birmingham and elsewhere at that time.

20. This is based on my conversation during the fall of 1963 with John Lewis, whose speech was censored. The unabridged version of the speech is available in Staughton Lynd, ed., *Nonviolence in America* (Indianapolis, 1966), pp. 482–85. See also Julius Lester, "The Angry Children of Malcolm X," *Sing Out* (November, 1966), p. 22, for his knowledgeable account of the circumstances of the March on Washington. It was from the speakers' platform in Washington that the nation first heard of the death of W. E. B. Du Bois in Ghana, announced by Roy Wilkins.

21. In Bennett, *Confrontation,* p. 244. The Poor People's Campaign of 1968 was meant to realize much of Walker's hope for massive civil disobedience.

22. Lester, "The Angry Children of Malcolm X," pp. 24–25.

23. Williams, "U.S.A.," in Broderick and Meier, eds., *Negro Protest Thought,* p. 330.

24. The most fascinating account of Malcolm X's conversion to the Nation of Islam cause is in his *Autobiography* (New York, 1966), pp. 151–210. The first edition of the *Autobiography* was published in 1965.

25. In Malcolm X and James Farmer, "Separation or Integration: A Debate," in Broderick and Meier, eds., *Negro Protest Thought,* p. 363 (published originally in *Dialogue Magazine,* vol. 2 (May, 1962).

26. *Ibid.,* p. 365. Unfortunately, it is not possible for this essay to develop the ironic theme of the "Americanness"—and therefore innate conservatism—of the Nation of Islam.

27. In George Breitman, ed., *Malcolm X Speaks* (New York, 1965), pp. 49–50, 56–57.

28. *Ibid.*, p. 35. Of course Malcolm X knew that mainland China was not a member of the United Nations. Rather he was being pointedly precise when he referred to that country as "waiting" to throw its weight on the side of the black cause.

29. *Ibid.*, pp. 43, 128–29.

30. *Ibid.*, pp. 141–42.

31. Quoted in Dudley Randall and Margaret G. Burroughs, eds., *For Malcolm X* (Detroit, 1967), p. 16. Hayden's lines are part of a longer poem, "El-Hajj Malik El-Shabazz."

32. For the background of SNCC's participation in the Voter Education Project, see Pat Watters and Reese Cleghorn, *Climbing Jacob's Ladder* (New York, 1967), pp. 41–74.

33. Again, much of the material that follows is based on my experience in Mississippi and my relationships with many persons who were involved in the 1964 experiment. For an independently formulated corroboration of my views, see Alvin F. Poussaint, "How the 'White Problem' Spawned 'Black Power,'" *Ebony,* August, 1967, pp. 88–94.

34. This paragraph is based partly on my conversations with SNCC staff members who helped formulate the strategy for the MFDP challenge and who were present in Atlantic City (especially Charlie Cobb, James Forman, and Robert Moses). See also Len Holt, *The Summer That Didn't End* (New York, 1965), pp. 149–183.

35. The Selma episode is treated in Bennett, *Confrontation*, p. 252.

36. In Clyde Halisi and James Mtume, eds., *The Quotable Karenga* (Los Angeles, 1967), p. 13.

37. Lester, "The Angry Children of Malcolm X," p. 25.

38. *Ibid.*

Riot Participation

1. All four sources are subject to limitations, and we have therefore used each as a reliability check on the others. Eyewitness accounts are subject to retrospective distortion. Data on arrestees also involve built-in biases. The fact of arrest alone, without subsequent trial and conviction, does not constitute evidence of the crime charged, and there has not been sufficient time for many of the 1967 riot arrestees to be brought to trial. Many of the most active rioters may have escaped arrest, while many of the uninvolved, or even counter-rioters, may have been arrested in the confusion. Finally, questions about riot activity in interview surveys may elicit overstatements of participation by some interviewees and understatements by others.

We are conducting a continuing study of arrest records in a number of cities which experienced disorders in 1967 and in some earlier years as well. So far we have studied the records of 13,788 persons arrested during disturbances in 22 cities in 1967. The unpublished study of arrestees in Detroit, which was sponsored by the Department of Labor, Manpower Administration, involved interviews with 496 arrestees.

The Detroit and Newark surveys furnish the most comprehensive information on mass participation.

The Detroit survey data represent a reanalysis by Dr. Nathan S. Caplan and Jeffery M. Paige, Institute for Social Research, University of Michigan, of data collected during the two weeks following the disorder, in a study sponsored by the Detroit Urban League. The Newark study was conducted for the Commission by Dr. Caplan and Mr. Paige, approximately six months after the disorder. . . .

2. In Detroit, 11.2 percent (44) of the 393 respondents identified themselves as rioters, 15.8 percent (62) as counter-rioters, and the majority, 73 percent (287), as noninvolved. Bystanders included approximately 5 percent who admitted to having gone into the riot area but claimed not to have participated; and another 15 to 20 percent who claimed to have watched from the front steps or sidewalk in front of their homes. For purposes of analysis all of the 393 respondents other than the self-reported rioters and counter-rioters were treated as the "noninvolved." In the Newark survey, where the sample was restricted to Negro males between the ages of 15 and 35, 45.4 percent identified themselves as rioters, and 54.6 percent as noninvolved. About 5 percent of the respondents identified themselves as counter-rioters, but were included as noninvolved because the number of persons was so small. The proportion of respondents who admitted active participation does not necessarily indicate the levels of support for rioting among inner-city Negroes. In Detroit, 23.3 percent of those interviewed felt that more was to be gained than lost through rioting. In Newark 47.0 percent agreed that more was to be gained and 77.1 percent said that they were generally sympathetic to the rioters.

3. In the more detailed discussion which follows, only those characteristics of the counter-rioter which differed from those of the noninvolved are highlighted.

4. Of 13,012 arrestees in 22 cities (Atlanta, Bridgeton, Cincinnati, Dayton, Detroit, Elizabeth, Englewood, Grand Rapids, Houston, Jackson, Jersey City, Milwaukee, Nashville, New Brunswick, New Haven, Newark, Paterson, Phoenix, Plainfield, Rockford, Tampa and Tucson; six major, nine serious and seven minor) 10,792 (82.9 percent) were Negroes, 1967 (15.1 percent) were whites, 78 (.6 percent) were Puerto Ricans and 37 (.3 percent) were of other races. The ethnic origin of 138 arrestees (1.1 percent) was unknown.

A study of 348 arrestees in Grand Rapids (serious) divided the disorder in that city into two time segments of 4 hours and 36 hours. During the first 4 hours of the disorder, 95 percent were Negroes. The proportion of Negro arrestees declined to 66 percent during the remaining 48 hours of the disorder. See "Anatomy of a Riot," United Community Services, Research Department, Grand Rapids and Kent County, Michigan, 1967.

5.

Age Distribution

	Detroit Survey		Arrest Records 16 Cities
Age	**R (44)	**NI (287)	**A (10,771)
15–24	61.3%	22.6%	52.5%
25–35	25.0	15.7	28.3
36–50	11.4	32.4	15.6
over 50	2.3	29.3	3.6
	100.0%	100.0%	100.0%

p< .001***

The Grand Rapids data indicate that during the first 4 hours of the disorder 82 percent of the arrestees were under 25 years of age. During the remaining 48 hours, the proportion of arrestees under 25 years of age declined to 58 percent. See "Anatomy of a Riot," op. cit. . . .

**R —Rioters
NI —Noninvolved
A —Arrestees

***The symbol "p" represents the probability that a difference this great is a product of chance. The symbol ">" means greater than. The symbol "<" means less than.

6.

Sex Distribution

	Detroit Survey		Arrest Records 21 Cities
Sex	R (44)	NI (287)	A (11,415)
Male	61.4%	43.9%	89.3%
Female	38.6	56.1	10.7
	100.0%	100.0%	100.0%

p< .025

The Grand Rapids data indicate that during the first 4 hours of the disorders, 45 of the 46 persons arrested (98 percent) were males. During the remaining 48 hours of the disorder female arrestees increased, comprising 10 percent of a total of 274 adults. . . .

7.

Marital Status	Newark Survey		Detroit Arrest Study	Arrest Records 4 Cities
Marital Status	R(105)	NI(125)	A(496)	A(487)
Married	28.6%	44.0%	38.9%	19.3%
Single	56.2	49.6	47.8	73.9
Divorced/ Separated	14.2	6.4	11.3	0.2
Widowed	1.0	0.0	1.2	0.0
Undetermined	0.0	0.0	.8	6.6
	100.0%	100.0%	100.0%	100.0%

p< .10

8.

Family Structure in Newark Survey

Adult Male Present in Family of Upbringing	R(106)	NI(126)
Yes	74.5%	77.0%
No	25.5	23.0
	100.0%	100.0%

p< .50

9.

Region of Upbringing	Detroit Survey			Newark Survey	
Region	R(39)	NI(275)	CR(61)**	R(104)	NI(124)
South	25.6%	64.0%	52.5%	26.0%	47.6%
North	74.4	36.0	47.5	74.0	52.4
	100.0%	100.0%	100.0%	100.0%	100.0%

R-NI	p< .001
CR-NI	p< .025
R-CR	p< .05

**CR-Counter-Rioters

10. Of 266 arrestees in five cities (Atlanta, New Brunswick, Plainfield, Tampa and Tucson; two major, one serious and two minor), 106 (40 percent) were born in the state in which the disorder occurred, 98 (37 percent) were born in the South (but not in the state in which the disorder occurred in the cases of Atlanta and Tampa; one major and one serious) and 23 (8 percent) were born elsewhere. The state of birth of 39 persons (15 percent) was undetermined. . . .

11. The discrepancy between the percentages of the noninvolved brought up in the North in Newark and Detroit (two major) is not significant since the Detroit sample includes more older people than the Newark sample.

This difference does not affect the validity of the figures for youthful rioters.

12.

	Place of Birth			
	Detroit Survey		Newark Survey	
Born in Riot City	R(43)	NI(285)	R(127)	NI(106)
Yes	59.4%	34.6%	53.5%	22.5%
No	40.6	65.4	46.5	77.5
	100.0%	100.0%	100.0%	100.0%
	p< .001		p< .001	

13. Of 3,395 arrestees in 15 cities . . . 3,054 (90 percent) resided in the city in which the disorder occurred, 228 (7 percent) resided in the state in which the disorder occurred, and 48 (1 percent) resided elsewhere. The residence of 65 persons (2 percent) was undetermined.

14.

	Income Level				
	Detroit Survey			Newark Survey	
Annual Income*	R(44)	NI(287)	CR(62)	R(104)	NI(126)
Less than 2,000	13.6%	12.9%	4.8%**	4.7%	3.2%
2,000–5,000	25.0	17.4	16.2**	27.9	26.2
5,000–7,500	13.6	20.6	22.6	27.9	30.1
7,500–10,000	18.2	13.9	17.7	14.4	11.1
10,000–12,500	2.3	3.8	14.5	1.0	4.0
12,500–15,000	0.0	1.7	1.6	1.0	1.6
More than 15,000	2.3	0.3	3.2	0.0	3.2
No answer	25.0	29.4	19.4	23.1	20.6
	100.0%	100.0%	100.0%	100.0%	100.0%
				p< .50	

R–NI   p< .50
CR–NI p< .005
R–CR   p< .25

*Annual income for Detroit based on individual income, for Newark on family income.

**All self-reported counter-rioters with incomes under $5,000 were female.

15. See the section on "The Pattern of Disadvantage" in Part IV of chapter 2, Kerner Commission Report.

16.

	Educational Level				
	Detroit Survey			Newark Survey	
Education	R(43)	NI(272)	CR(59)	R(106)	NI(126)
Less than grades 1–6	2.3%	7.7%	1.7%	0.0%	3.2%
Grade school	4.7	20.2	18.6	1.9	11.1
Some high school	53.5	33.8	22.0	63.2	46.8
Graduated high school	23.3	26.1	32.2	29.2	31.0
Some college	14.0	10.3	22.1	5.7	6.3
Graduated college	0.0	1.5	0.0	0.0	1.6
Graduate work	2.2	0.4	3.4	0.0	0.0
	100.0%	100.0%	100.0%	100.0%	100.0%

$p < .06$

$R–NI \quad p < .05$
$CR–NI \quad p < .025$
$R–CR \quad p < .05$

17.

	Employment Status			
	Detroit Survey*		Newark Survey**	
Currently Employed	R(27)	NI(127)	R(84)	NI(105)
Yes	70.4%	68.5%	70.3%	81.0%
No	29.6	31.5	29.7	19.0
	100.0%	100.0%	100.0%	100.0%
	$p > .75$		$p < .50$	

	Detroit Arrest Study	Newark Arrest Records 4 cities
Currently Employed	A (496)	A (310)
Yes	78.2%	66.8%
No	21.8	33.2
	100.0%	100.0%

*Males only
**Excludes students

18.

Underemployment in Newark Survey		
Have you been unemployed as long as a month during the last year?	R(104)	NI(124)
Yes	61.0%	43.4%
No	39.0	56.6
	100.0%	100.0%

$p < .05$

19.   *Occupation Level in Newark Survey*

Level	R(125)	NI(126)
Unskilled	50.0%	39.6%
Semiskilled or better	50.0	60.4
	100.0%	100.0%

p< .06

20.   *Job Aspiration in Newark Survey*

*Do you feel your job
is appropriate con-
sidering the education
you have?*

	R(82)	NI(99)
Present job is about right	29.3%	44.4%
Should have job with more income and responsibility	70.7	55.6
	100.0%	100.0%

p< .05

21.   *Perceived Job Opportunity in Newark Survey*

Perceived opportunity	R(105)	NI(126)
Is possible to obtain desired job	32.4%	43.9%
Is not possible to obtain desired job	67.6	56.1
	100.0%	100.0%

p< .06

22.   *Perceived Obstacles to Employment in Newark Survey*

Obstacle	R(71)	NI(68)
Lack of Training	18.3%	41.2%
Lack of Experience	12.7	8.8
Discrimination	69.0	50.0
	100.0%	100.0%

p< .025

23.   *Ability and Success in Detroit Survey*

*Is getting what you
want out of life a
matter of ability or
being in the right place?*

	R(39)	NI(251)	CR(54)
Ability	76.9%	76.1%	88.9%
Right Place	23.1	23.9	11.1
	100.0%	100.0%	100.0%

R–NI   p< .90
CR–NI   p< .05
R–CR   p< .25

24.

	Racial Consciousness			
	Detroit Survey		Newark Survey	
Who do you think are more dependable?	R(37)	NI(247)	R(91)	NI(108)
Negroes	48.6%	22.4%	45.0%	27.8%
Whites	21.7	27.6	35.2	49.1
About the same	29.7	50.0	19.8	23.1
	100.0%	100.0%	100.0%	100.0%
	p< .001		p< .05	

	Detroit Survey		Newark Survey	
Who do you think are nicer?	R(41)	NI(262)	R(96)	NI(110)
Negroes	61.0%	36.3%	78.1%	57.3%
Whites	4.9	5.0	21.9	37.3
About the same	34.1	58.7	0.0	5.4
	100.0%	100.0%	100.0%	100.0%
	p< .001		p< .025	

25.

	Black Conscious in Newark Survey	
Self-description	R(105)	NI(126)
Black	52.4%	33.3%
Negro	28.6	34.9
Colored	10.4	17.5
No difference	8.6	14.3
	100.0%	100.0%
	p< .025	

	Newark Survey	
All Negroes should study African History and Language	R(125)	NI(104)
Agree	79.8%	68.8%
Disagree	20.2	31.2
	100.0%	100.0%
	p< .06	

26.

Anti-White Attitudes

Civil rights groups which have white and Negro leaders would do better without whites	Detroit Survey		Newark Survey	
	R(36)	NI(245)	R(105)	NI(124)
True	36.1%	21.1%	51.4%	33.1%
False	63.9	78.9	48.6	66.9
	100.0%	100.0%	100.0%	100.0%
	p< .1		p< .005	

Newark Survey

Sometimes I Hate White People	R(105)	NI(126)
Agree	72.4%	50.0%
Disagree	27.6	50.0
	100.0%	100.0%
	p< .001	

27.   *Hostility Toward Middle-Class Negroes in Newark Survey*

Negroes who make a lot of money like to think they are better than other Negroes	R(105)	NI(126)
Agree	71.4%	59.5%
Disagree	28.6	40.5
	100.0%	100.0%
	p< .06	

Negroes who make a lot of money are just as bad as whites	R(105)	NI(122)
Agree	50.5%	35.2%
Disagree	49.5	64.8
	100.0%	100.0%
	p< .05	

28. Half the arrestees were charged with one or more of three offenses: breaking and entering, trespassing, or curfew violation.

Of 13,112 offenses charged against 12,457 persons in 19 cities . . . 4,108 (31 percent) were charges of breaking and entering or trespassing and 2,506 (19 percent) were charges of curfew violation. The breakdown of charges by categories was:

Charges*	Number	Percent
Breaking and entering or trespassing	4,108	31.3%
Curfew violation	2,506	19.1
Burglary, larceny, robbery or theft	2,000	15.3

Disorderly conduct, disturbing the peace or rioting	807	6.2
Resisting arrest, drunk or traffic violations	550	4.2
Weapons charges	526	4.0
Assault	317	2.4
Vagrancy, loitering, unlawful assembly, suspicious conduct	129	1.0
Narcotics charges	67	.5
Arson	56	.4
Juvenile delinquency	25	.2
Homicide	17	.1
Other charges	1,156	8.8
Unknown	848	6.5
	13,112	100.0%

*These arrest statistics should be interpreted with caution. Felony, misdemeanor and ordinance violation charges are combined. Later dispositions may change this distribution.

29.　　　　　　*Political Information in Newark Survey*

Identification of Political *Figures—Kenneth Gibson*	R(105)	NI(125)
Negro	77.1%	61.6%
White	1.0	5.6
Don't know	21.9	32.8
	100.0%	100.0%

$p < .025$

Political Information Test	R(106)	NI(127)
High Score	68.9%	51.2%
Low Score	31.1	48.8
	100.0%	100.0%

$p < .025$

30.   *Political Involvement in Newark Survey*

Frequency of Negro
Rights Discussion   R(106)   NI(126)

	R(106)	NI(126)
Nearly everyday	53.8%	34.9%
Once a week	12.3	7.9
From time to time	31.1	52.4
Never	0.0	0.0
Don't know	2.8	4.8
	100.0%	100.0%

p< .025

Attend meeting or par-
ticipation in civil rights group   R(89)   NI(113)

	R(89)	NI(113)
Yes	39.3%	25.7%
No	60.7	74.3
	100.0%	100.0%

p< .05

31.   *Trust of the Government in Newark Survey*

How much do you think
you can trust the Newark
Government to do what is right?   R(105)   NI(127)

	R(105)	NI(127)
Just about always	2.9%	1.6%
Most of the time	4.8	13.7
Some of the time	48.1	50.8
Almost never	44.2	33.9
	100.0%	100.0%

p< .1

32.   *Political Grievances in Detroit Survey*

How much did anger with
politicians have to do with
causing riot?

	R(44)	NI(286)
Great deal	43.2%	19.6%
Something	31.8	39.1
Nothing	18.2	24.5
Don't know	6.8	16.8
	100.0%	100.0%

$p < .05$

How much did anger with
police have to do with
causing riot?

	R(44)	NI(287)
Great deal	70.5%	48.8%
Something	20.5	30.3
Nothing	2.2	14.3
Don't know	6.8	6.6
	100.0%	100.0%

$p < .05$

33.   *Perception of Country as Not Worth Fighting For*

Country worth fight-ing for in major world war	Detroit Survey			Newark Survey	
	R(38)	NI(264)	CR(56)	R(106)	NI(126)
Worth fighting	55.3%	75.0%	86.9%	33.0%	50.8%
Not worth fighting	39.4	15.5	3.3	52.8	27.8
Don't know	5.3	9.5	9.8	14.2	21.4
	100.0%	100.0%	100.0%	100.0%	100.0%

R–NI $p < .005$
CR–NI $p < .05$ $p < .001$
R–CR $p < .001$

Totals   48,319 $14,964,647 $10,556,737 $10,106,206 $35,627,590

34. Using this material we sought to identify and assign weights to the four
types of grievances which appeared to have the greatest significance to
the Negro community in each city. We made judgments with regard
to the severity of particular grievances and assigned a rank to the four
most serious. These judgments were based on the frequency with which
a particular grievance was mentioned, the relative intensity with which it
was discussed, references to incidents exemplifying the grievance, and
estimates of severity obtained from the interviewees themselves. Each
priority ranking was weighted by points (4 points for the first priority, 3
for second, 2 for third and 1 for fourth). The points for each grievance
for all cities were added to create an inter-city ranking. Whenever two
grievances were judged to be equally serious for a particular city, the
points for the two rankings involved were divided equally (e.g., in case

two were judged equally suitable for the first priority, the total points for first and second were divided and each received 3½ points).

35. Education and recreation were ranked equally; municipal services and consumer and credit practices were also ranked equally.

36. *Ibid.*

37. *Ibid.*

38. *Ibid.*

39. In this survey 437 Negroes from the Detroit disturbance area were asked which of 23 grievances had a "great deal," "something" or "nothing" to do with the riot. The grievances which received the most responses of "a great deal" were: (1) police brutality, (2) overcrowded living conditions, (3) poor housing, (4) lack of jobs, (5) poverty, and (6) anger with business people. Interviewees who identified themselves as participants in the riot were singled out for special analysis and chose the same six causes but in a slightly different order. Overcrowded living conditions was first instead of police brutality.

40. We found significant grievances concerning police practices in each of 19 cities. Grievances concerning police practices were ranked first in eight cities, second in four cities, third in none, and fourth in two cities. Although such grievances were present in five other cities, they were not ranked in the first four orders of intensity.

41. Grievances in the employment area were ranked first in three cities, second in seven cities, third in four cities, and fourth in three cities. In only three cities was such a grievance present but not ranked among the highest four levels of intensity.

42. Grievances in the housing area were found in 18 cities and were ranked first in five cities, second in two cities, third in five cities, and fourth in two cities. In four cities where housing was a grievance, it was not ranked in the first four levels of intensity.

43. Educational grievances were found in 17 cities and were ranked first in two cities, second in two cities, third in two cities, and fourth in three cities. In eight cities where such a grievance was present, it was not ranked in the first four levels of priority.

44. Grievances relating to recreation were found in 15 cities and were ranked first in three cities, second in one city, third in four cities, and fourth in none. In seven cities where such a grievance was present, it was not ranked in the first four levels of priority.

45. Grievances relating to the political structure were found in 16 cities and were ranked first in two cities, second in one city, third in one city, and fourth in one city. In 11 cities where such a grievance was present, it was not ranked in the first four levels of priority.

46. Grievances relating to white attitudes were found in 15 cities and were ranked first in no city, second in one city, third in one city, and fourth

in two cities. In 11 cities where such a grievance was present, it was not ranked in the first four levels of priority.

47. Grievances relating to the administration of justice were found in 15 cities and were ranked first in no city, second in none, third in two cities, and fourth in one city. In 12 cities where such a grievance was present, it was not ranked in the first four levels of priority.

48. Grievances relating to federal programs were found in 16 cities and were ranked first in no city, second in one city, third in none, and fourth in none. In 15 cities where such a grievance was present, it was not ranked in the first four levels of priority.

49. Grievances relating to municipal services were found in 11 cities and were ranked first in no city, second in none, third in one city, and fourth in none. In 10 cities where such a grievance was present, it was not ranked in the first four levels of priority.

50. Grievances relating to unfair commercial practices were found in 11 cities and were ranked first in no city, second in none, third in none and fourth in two cities. In nine cities where such a grievance was present, it was not ranked in the first four levels of priority.

The Social and Economic Status of the Negro in the United States

1. The first systematic formulation of a caste-class hypothesis to explain American race relations appeared in an article by W. Lloyd Warner and Allison Davis, "A Comparative Study of American Caste," one of several contributions to a volume edited by Edgar Thompson, *Race Relations and The Race Problem* (Raleigh, N.C., 1939). The field research upon which much of the article was based was published later as Allison Davis, Burleigh Gardner, and Mary Gardner, *Deep South* (Chicago, 1941). For a Marxist criticism of the caste-class interpretation of American race relations see Oliver Cromwell Cox, *Caste, Class and Race* (New York, 1948).

2. Analysis of inter-ethnic mobility in terms of conflict, accommodation, and assimilation characterized the work of "The Chicago School" of Sociology during the 1920's and early 1930's. For more sophisticated analysis, note W. L. Warner and Leo Srole, *The Social Systems of American Ethnic Groups* (New Haven, Conn., 1946), in which studies of comparative mobility rates of various ethnic groups are made. Nathan Glazer and Patrick D. Moynihan, in *Beyond The Melting Pot* (Cambridge, Mass., 1963), have recently suggested that ethnic solidarities are much more enduring than earlier sociologists had expected them to be.

3. John Dollard, in association with Allison Davis, has added other dimensions to his analysis in *Children of Bondage* (Washington, D.C., 1940).

4. For a discussion of these concepts see Hans Gerth and C. Wright Mills, *From Max Weber: Essays in Sociology* (New York, 1946), chapter on "Caste, Class and Party."

5. The distinguished psychotherapist, Bruno Bettelheim, of the Orthogenic School of the University of Chicago, in a provocative and perceptive article in *The Nation*, October 19, 1963 ("Class, Color and Prejudice"), contends that protection of social class values is a more important variable than race prejudice in structuring relations between Negroes and whites in the North of the U.S.A.

6. St. Clair Drake and Horace R. Cayton, in *Black Metropolis* (New York, 1962), use the term "Black Ghetto" to refer to the involuntary and exploitative aspect of the all-Negro community and "Bronzeville" to symbolize the more pleasant aspects of the segregated community. Robert C. Weaver, another Negro scholar, called his first book *The Negro Ghetto* (New York, 1948). The term is widely used by contemporary Negro leaders with pejorative implications. See also Kenneth Clark, *Dark Ghetto* (New York, 1965).

7. The most careful study of the effect of Negro entry into all-white neighborhoods is to be found in a book published by the University of California Press in 1961 which reports upon the results of research in Detroit, Chicago, Kansas City, Oakland, San Francisco, Philadelphia, and Portland, Oregon—Luigi Laurenti's *Property Values and Race* (Berkeley, Calif., 1961).

8. Thomas F. Pettigrew, *A Profile of the Negro American* (Princeton, N.J., 1964), p. 190. His wife, Dr. Ann Pettigrew, M.D., collaborated with him on the chapter dealing with health.

9. Though based upon only one community in Chicago, *The Politics of Urban Renewal* by Peter Rossi and Robert A. Dentler (Glencoe, Ill., 1961) analyzes basic processes to be found in all Northern cities.

10. Professor Everett C. Hughes makes some original and highly pertinent remarks about new Negro middle-class communities in his introduction to the 1962 edition of Drake and Cayton's *Black Metropolis*.

11. Pettigrew, *op. cit.*, pp. 180–181.

12. The issue of the extent to which Negroes have been victimized by urban redevelopment is discussed briefly by Robert C. Weaver in *The Urban Complex: Human Values in Urban Life* (New York, 1964). See also Martin Anderson, *The Federal Bulldozer: A Critical Analysis of Urban Renewal: 1949–1962* (Cambridge, Mass., 1964).

13. Drake and Cayton, *op. cit.*, Chap. 23, "Advancing the Race."

14. See section on "The Negro Community as a Pathological Form of an American Community," Chap. 43 of Gunnar Myrdal, *An American Dilemma* (New York, 1944), p. 927.

15. A report appeared on the front page of *The New York Times*, April 5, 1965, stating that a commission was at work trying to elaborate plans for "integrating" Harlem by 1975. Columbia University was said to be co-operating in the research aspects of the project.

16. A successful experiment in "controlled integration" has been described by Julia Abrahamson in *A Neighborhood Finds Itself* (New York, 1959).

17. Jacob Schiffman, "Marital and Family Characteristics of Workers, March, 1962," in *Monthly Labor Review*, U.S. Department of Labor, Bureau of Labor Statistics, Special Labor Force Report No. 26, January 1963.

18. *Ibid.*

19. Norval D. Glenn, "Some Changes in the Relative Status of American Nonwhites: 1940–1960," *Phylon*, Vol. 24, No. 2 (Summer 1963).

20. Pettigrew, *op. cit.*, p. 188.

Postscript on Black Power—the Dialogue Between Shadow and Substance

1. This Independent Citizens Committee of Harlem has its roots in a rank-and-file oppositional move against the undemocratic control of HAR-YOU-ACT over the dispensation of Anti-Poverty funds. Active within the ICC are individuals from the Harlem Neighborhoods Association (HANA), a pioneer middleclass civic organization established in 1958. HANA grew out of the Central Harlem Coordinating Council established in 1938 for the purpose of encouraging and supporting "resident involvement and self-determination in community affairs." Harlem community politics is such that HANA was actually the creator of HARYOU and a number of other autonomous social welfare groups. The executive director of HANA, James Soler, is active in the ICC.

2. *Rights & Reviews*, Winter 1966–67, p. 5.

3. *Ibid.*, p. 28.

4. *Ibid.*, p. 32.

5. *Ibid.*, p. 6.

6. *Ibid.*, Lorenzo Thomas, "Spontaneous History and the Ethics of a Revolution," p. 9.

7. *Ibid.*, p. 7.

8. Amy Jacques-Garvey, *Garvey and Garveyism* (Kingston, 1963), p. 186.

9. *Negro Digest*, November, 1966, p. 34.

10. *Ibid.*

11. Malcolm X's plan to take the Negro issue to the United Nations as a Human Rights question in 1964 had been first attempted in 1947 by

W. E. B. Du Bois in collaboration with the NAACP. See "Appeal to
the World," A Statement on the Denial of Human Rights to Minorities
in the Cace of Citizens of Negro Descent in the United States and an
Appeal to the United Nations for Redress (NAACP, pamphlet, 1947).

12. W. E. B. Du Bois, *Dusk of Dawn* (New York, 1940), p. 199.

Index

DATE DUE

FEB 1 '72			
MAR 31 72			
APR 11 '72			
APR 27 '72			
AP 2 '79			
NO 13 '79			
DE 5 '80			
DE 15 '80			
NOV 9			
GAYLORD			PRINTED IN U.S.A.